News Reporting and Writing

Eighth Edition

Melvin Mencher

Columbia University

Mc
Graw
Hill

Boston   Burr Ridge, IL   Dubuque, IA   Madison, WI   New York   San Francisco   St. Louis
Bangkok   Bogotá   Caracas   Lisbon   London   Madrid
Mexico City   Milan   New Delhi   Seoul   Singapore   Sydney   Taipei   Toronto

McGraw-Hill Higher Education

A Division of The **McGraw-Hill** *Companies*

NEWS REPORTING AND WRITING

Copyright © 2000 by Melvin Mencher. All rights reserved. Previous editions © 1997, 1994, 1991, 1987, 1984, 1981, and 1977. Printed in the United States of America. Except as permitted under the United States Copyright Act of 1976, no part of this publication may be reproduced or distributed in any form or by any means, or stored in a data base or retrieval system, without the prior written permission of the publisher.

This book is printed on acid-free paper.

1 2 3 4 5 6 7 8 9 0 QPF/QPF 9 0 4 3 2 1 0 9

ISBN 0-07-230011-6

Editorial director: *Phillip A. Butcher*
Associate sponsoring editor: *Valerie Raymond/Kailin Maureen Fenn*
Marketing manager: *Kelly May*
Project manager: *Pat Frederickson*
Senior production supervisor: *Heather D. Burbridge*
Designer: *Jennifer McQueen Hollingsworth*
Photo research coordinator: *Sharon Miller*
Supplement coordinator: *Mark Sienicki*
Compositor: *Shepherd Incorporated*
Typeface: *10.5/12 Times Roman*
Printer: *Quebecor Printing Book Group/Fairfield*

Library of Congress Cataloging–in–Publication Data
Mencher, Melvin
  News reporting and writing / Melvin Mencher.: 8th ed.
    p. cm.
  ISBN 0-07-230011-6
  Includes bibliography references (p.) and index.
  1. Reporters and reporting. 2. Journalism—Authorship.
I. Title.
PN4781.M4 2000
0.70.4'3 dc—21   99-25513

http://www.mhhe.com

Contents

PART SIX

Laws, Taste and Taboos, Codes and Ethics   647

Preface

News Reporting and Writing, Eighth Edition, proposes to teach the beginner how to become a practicing journalist. Learning to report accurately and to write precisely and vigorously are no simple tasks. The young man or woman who would join the ranks of journalists must learn and then put into practice principles and concepts that have been developed over the years by practitioners who understand first, that truth is elusive and second, that its pursuit and capture on paper require mastery of a demanding discipline.

To explain and illustrate these principles, we will spend a lot of time with truth seekers—another way to describe good journalists—as they go about their work. We will accompany a young reporter as he conducts his first interview, and we will watch an experienced reporter cover a racial confrontation. We will overhear another reporter's thinking as she works out the lead to her story about a city council meeting. We will peer over the shoulder of a reporter massaging a database to find filthy restaurants that continue to serve food despite failing inspections.

We will sit in the press box with reporters covering high school football and major league baseball games. We will join a police reporter as she makes her rounds and races to a triple murder.

We will watch a reporter labor over his story until "little beads of blood form on his forehead," as Red Smith described the agony of the journalist's search for the words that accurately portray the event. And we will share in the reporter's joy when the story is finished and is given a byline and placed on the front page or makes the evening network newscast.

In other words, we will be concerned with the processes of reporting and writing—how reporters gather information from sources and from their observations, how they verify the material, and how they put it together in stories.

The journalists we will be watching work for small newspapers in Iowa, South Dakota and Oregon, and they are on the staffs of metropolitan dailies in Chicago and Los Angeles. They serve online news services and online newspapers. One reporter writes for a network television station in New York; another covers local events for a television station in San Francisco. We will see how general assignment reporters and the men and women assigned to cover politics, sports, business, the police, city hall, education and other beats do their jobs.

Covering a Rotary Club luncheon speech or the president's State of the Union address, the journalist follows the same basic processes. The general assignment reporter in a town of 25,000 and the AP's White House correspondent share a way of thinking, a set of techniques and an approach to journalism.

The Morality of Journalism

We will see that these journalists also share an ethic that directs and gives meaning to their work. The literary critic Northrop Frye could have been describing journalistic morality: "The persistence of keeping the mind in a state of disciplined sanity, the courage of facing results that may deny or contradict everything that one had hoped to achieve—these are obviously moral qualities, if the phrase means anything at all."

James O. Freedman, the president of Dartmouth, might have been speaking of journalism when he described his experience as a law clerk to Thurgood Marshall: "In that year, I learned from a great advocate that law must be practiced not only with craft and passion but also with a tenacious commitment to ideals."

Mary McGrory, the Washington columnist, described an aspect of the journalist's approach to his or her work in comments she made after interviewing 45 journalists who had applied for Nieman Fellowships at Harvard. She said she found these journalists to have a "great deal of commitment and compassion." Most had a trait in common, she said: "They knew a great deal about what they were doing. They did not think it enough."

In our journey to look at the work of journalists, we will pause to listen to Donna Ferrato. As she became increasingly alarmed at the growing abuse of women and children, she found that some material had been written on the topic but there was almost no photographic documentation. She was determined to show domestic abuse, although editors told her that "domestic violence wasn't important," she says.

"The more I saw, the more I knew that I had to get their stories out so that people would care about them," Ferrato says.

She took photographs of the victims, and, slowly, gradually, editors used them. And people cared. Her work helped place domestic abuse on the public agenda. As a result of her photojournalism, an enlightened public insisted on stricter laws and their enforcement.

The journalists I know—my former colleagues and students, from whom I have shamelessly taken time and borrowed ideas—would shrink at being described as moralists. Yet they consider their work to have a large moral component. Most of them worry about the abuse of power.

Although adversary journalism is often criticized and sometimes ignored, it is as old as the Republic. In our third century as a nation, we must remember that today's journalists are descended from a press described by the historian Robert A. Ruthland as "obstreperous newspapers (that) signalled the rise of a new kind of journalism in America that would not truckle long to any officialdom."

The journalist knows that democracy is healthiest when the public is informed about the activities of captains of industry and chieftains in public office.

> **Power of Knowing.** "Knowledge will govern ignorance, and a people who mean to be their own governors must arm themselves with the power knowledge gives. A popular government without popular information or the means of acquiring it is but a prologue to a farce or a tragedy or perhaps both."
> *James Madison*

Only with adequate information can people check those in power. Repression and ignorance are the consequences of unbridled power. Walt Whitman, journalist and poet, described the fragility of democracy and its source of strength this way: "There is no week nor day nor hour when tyranny may not enter upon this country, if the people lose their supreme confidence in themselves—and lose their roughness and spirit of defiance."

Confident, rough and defiant. An apt description of the journalist—but also characteristics that have aroused public animosity. In its role as watchdog for the public, the press has been attacked by those it has relentlessly scrutinized.

Entertainment vs. Information

Journalists know that the path of the truth teller is not always smooth, that people are sometimes disturbed by what they do not want to hear. Journalists also know that many in their audience prefer entertainment to information.

Over the past 25 years, the number of daily newspapers has declined from 1,748 to 1,585. Readership has dropped among those ages 21 to 35, the young men and women considered society's big spenders, thus attractive to advertisers, the lifeblood of the mass media.

The consequence has been alarm and retreat. Journalists are urged to look to what have been regarded as the peripheral areas of journalism: graphics, short features, color, layout and design.

As this eighth edition moves into classrooms and newsrooms, students and practitioners are being counseled to provide "reader-friendly news"—stories about food, fitness, investing, dieting. Celebrity stories abound. News magazine shows—sexy blends of fiction and fact—are big on television. Christopher Lasch, a cultural historian, says, "Much of the press, in its eagerness to inform the public, has become a conduit for the equivalent of junk mail."

Despite the fear-driven urge to seek the lowest common denominator, newspapers and television programs that offer their readers and viewers telling insights into contemporary society remain in sound financial condition. We will visit the newsrooms of these newspapers and drop in on Ted Koppel's "Nightline," whose executive producer tells us, "People turn on 'Nightline' to find out if there's something they need to know. . . . They aren't interested in being entertained. 'Nightline' has its largest audiences when there is real news," says Tom Bettag.

"At a time when television has gone more and more down the tabloid road, 'Nightline' has differentiated itself by refusing to take that route." The result: "It is a big commercial success for ABC," Bettag says.

The newspapers and stations and magazines that do not skimp on hiring a full and competent local staff, that do not flinch from taking on powerful adversaries—whether in a corporate boardroom or city hall—are healthy despite the uncertainties of the economy.

This eighth edition is offered to students with a commitment to and a belief in the traditional role of the press as the means of enabling people to improve their lot and to govern themselves intelligently through robust debate on relevant issues. It takes seriously the comment in the Book of Proverbs: "The instruments of both life and death are contained within the power of the tongue."

Public Service Journalism

The kind of journalism that animates this textbook can be described as public service journalism. It has a long and glorious history that was expressed well by Charles Dickens in his crusading newspaper *Household Words.* Week after week, Dickens poured into his newspaper his indignation at the indecencies visited on the young, the poor and the powerless.

Dickens' biographer, Edgar Johnson, described the novelist-journalist-editor as practicing an "uncompromising humanitarian radicalism." Dickens visited orphanages, saw for himself the conditions of homeless women. He urged schooling for the young born into poverty.

Dickens said his ambition as an editor was that his newspaper "be admitted into many homes with confidence and affection," and it was. Johnson says the result of Dickens' crusades was a "huge and steadily growing audience ranging in both directions from the middle and upper middle classes."

Through the power of the computer, today's journalists are practicing public service journalism everywhere. They are revealing campaign finance abuses and the lax law enforcement of polluters and health care profiteers.

One of the premises of this book is that journalists do not write writing; they write reporting. The vitality of democracy depends on a press that is able to grasp the complexities of modern society and communicate them intelligibly to the public, on a press that puts important issues on the public agenda.

Consequently, I have resisted advice to delete some of the more difficult subject areas and replace them with more writing tips, and I have declined suggestions that I jazz up the appearance of this edition. *News Reporting and Writing* will have to stand on the merits—or the inadequacies—of its content as a guide to serious journalism.

Journalism's Tradition

Journalism has always had its down periods, and there has been no shortage of nostrums offered for a quick cure. Its survival, however, has rested on the bedrock of its tradition. Albert Camus, the French journalist and author, was sustained by that sense of his calling during the Nazi occupation of France when he wrote from the underground. Accepting the Nobel Prize for literature in 1957, Camus said, "Whatever our personal frailties may be, the nobility of our calling will always be rooted in two commitments difficult to observe: refusal to lie about what we know and resistance to oppression."

In much of what the journalist does, there is an awareness of the relevance of his or her work to human needs and purposes, for the reporter knows that news represents reality to most people. The reporter is interested in ideas but avoids the sin of making the concrete abstract.

Journalism "is something more than a craft, something other than an industry, something between an art and a ministry," says Wickham Steed, an editor of *The Times* of London. "Journalists proper are unofficial public servants whose purpose is to serve the community."

My model for this amalgam of artist, sentry, public servant and town crier is Ralph M. Blagden, who taught a generation of journalists their duty and introduced them to the power and splendor of their native language. Ralph's classrooms were the newsrooms of newspapers from New Hampshire to California, where he worked as reporter and editor.

Ralph was my competitor as a state capitol correspondent, and never was there such a mismatch. As a beginning reporter, I reported what people said and did and stopped there. Ralph generously took the youngster in tow and showed him that a good reporter never settles for the surface of the news, that the compelling commandment of the journalist is to dig out the truth. He refused to make reporting divisible: All good reporting is investigative reporting, he insisted.

Long before investigative reporting became the fashion, Ralph was digging out documents and records to disclose truths. His journalism was in the tradition of Joseph Pulitzer and that publisher's crusading editor, O.K. Bovard. Those of us who were fortunate to work with Ralph feel ourselves to be members of a journalistic family whose roots are embedded in a noble tradition.

Benjamin C. Bradlee of *The Washington Post* says of Blagden:

> Ralph taught me to be dissatisfied with answers and to be exhaustive in questions. He taught me to stand up against powers that be. He taught me to spot bullies and resist them. He taught me about patience and round-the-clock work. He taught me about ideas and freedom and rights—all of this with his own mixture of wit and sarcasm and articulate grace. He could also throw a stone farther than I could, which annoys me to this day.

Bradlee, who directed the *Post*'s coverage of the Watergate story that earned his newspaper a Pulitzer Prize for meritorious public service, recalls his first story for Blagden when he was a young reporter.

"It had to do with the post-war housing mess, and he made me rewrite it 16 times. I've never done that to a reporter, but I suspect I should have. He had a great dollop of righteous indignation, which I learned to admire enormously.

"And of course he wrote with style and punch and clarity."

I recall the first story I covered with Ralph. He had heard that patients in a state hospital for the mentally ill were being mistreated. Some had mysteriously died. We interviewed doctors, nurses, attendants and former patients, and we walked through the wards and corridors of the institution. I learned that secondhand accounts are just a starting point, that direct observation and other techniques of verification are essential, and when we wrote the story I learned the power of the simple declarative sentence. I also learned that journalists can be useful members of society, for after the story appeared and both of us had moved on, the state built a modern hospital to replace that aging snake pit.

Additional Supplements for Students

Workbook for News Reporting and Writing (Mencher): The *Workbook* is used in conjunction with the textbook. It includes writing exercises and reporting assignmnets on such currenct topics as student binge drinking, educational reform and college admission policies. The eighth editon has a new set of exercises, "Web Work."
ISBN: 0-07-230012-4

Reporter's Checklist and Notebook (Mencher): This handy guide to handling beats and covering stories also includes "Useful Math for Reporters."
ISBN: 0-697-29404-8

Brush Up: A Quick Guide to Basic Writing and Math Skills CD-ROM (Mencher and Wendy P. Shilton): A self-teaching interactive CD-ROM designed to help students with their writing and math. The CD-ROM is packaged free with the textbook.
ISBN: 0-07-233653-6

Package Options

News Reporting and Writing, 8/e + Workbook + Brush Up CD-ROM.
ISBN: 0-07-399715-3

News Reporting and Writing, 8/e + Reporter's Checklist and Notebook + Brush Up CD-ROM.
ISBN: 0-07-399716-1

News Reporting and Writing, 8/e + Workbook + Reporter's Checklist and Notebook + Brush Up CD-ROM.
ISBN: 0-07-233653-6

(The *Instructor's Manual* is provided with the *Workbook.*)

Acknowledgments

New Reporting and Writing was written in the belief that journalism is a moral enterprise and that this gives meaning to its practice. The morality of journalism can be taught, as it was by Ralph L. Crosman, Zell Mabee and A. Gayle Waldrop at the University of Colorado. Theirs was a journalism of commitment, compassion and conscience. Those of us who studied with them are forever in their debt.

I am also indebted to my former newsroom colleagues and to my students. They all have contributed to this book, some indirectly, like George Baldwin, my first city editor at *The Albuquerque Tribune,* and some directly, like Berkley Hudson, one of my former students, whose work is included here. I learned from the young woman who stormed out of my classroom when I said I would not assign her to a certain story because I worried about her safety, and I learned from the copy editor many years ago who had worn down a pencil putting black lines through my copy. "Just show us what the guy did," he told me. "Let the reader draw the conclusions."

For this eighth edition, Sheila Thalhimer prepared the index and the following colleagues made useful suggestions: Andy O. Alali, California State University at Bakersfield; Joan Deppa, Syracuse University; Kim E. Karloff, California State University at Northridge; Bill Kovarik, Radford University; Jay Perkins, Louisiana State University; William C. Porter, Brigham Young University.

The following list acknowledges some of those who shared in the preparation of *News Reporting and Writing.* Only I bear responsibility for the contents.

Marjorie Arnold
The Fresno (Calif.) *Bee*

Jeff Barbanel
The New York Times

Brian Barrett
Office of the New York County
District Attorney

Frank Barrows
The Charlotte (N.C.) *Observer*

Barbara Belford
Columbia University

Tom Bettag
"Nightline"

Joan Bieder
Columbia University

Mervin Block
Broadcast writing coach

Art Carey
Bucks County (Pa.) *Courier Times* and
The Philadelphia Inquirer

Marcia Chambers
The New York Times

Susan Clark
Associated Press

Kenneth Conboy
Coordinator of the New York City
Criminal Justice System

Claude Cookman
The Miami Herald

Jere Downs
The Philadelphia Inquirer

Robert A. Dubill
Executive Director,
Gannett News Service

Jack Dvorak
Indiana University

Julie Ellis
Freelance writer,
Photo researcher

Fred Endres
Kent State University

Heidi Evans
Daily News, New York City

Ellen Fleysher
WCBS-TV, New York City

Joseph Galloway
UPI

Mary Ann Giordano
Daily News, New York City

Joel M. Gora
American Civil Liberties Union

Sara Grimes
University of Massachusetts, Amherst

Susan Hands
The Charlotte Observer

Donna Hanover
WTVN-TV, Columbus, Ohio

Jena Heath
The News & Observer, Raleigh, N.C.

Michael Hiltzik
Courier-Express, Buffalo, N.Y., and
Los Angeles Times

Louis E. Ingelhart
Ball State University

Thomas H. Jones
Chicago Sun-Times

Melissa Jordan
Associated Press

E.W. Kenworthy
The New York Times

Jeff Klinkenberg
St. Petersburg Times

Eric Lawlor
The Houston Chronicle

Lynn Ludlow
San Francisco Examiner

Jack Marsh
Argus Leader, Sioux Falls, S.D.

Tony Mauro
Gannett News Service

John McCormally
The Hawk Eye, Burlington, Iowa

Frank McCulloch
The Sacramento Bee

Bill Mertens
The Hawk Eye, Burlington, Iowa

Alan Miller
University of Maine at Orono

John D. Mitchell
Syracuse University

Ellen Perlman
City & State

Merrill Perlman
The New York Times

L.D. Pinkham
University of Massachusetts at
Amherst

Lew Powell
The Charlotte Observer

Ron Rapoport
*Los Angeles Times, Chicago Sun-
Times* and Los Angeles *Daily News*

Elizabeth Rhodes
The Charlotte (N.C.) *Observer* and
Seattle Times

Ronald Robinson
Augustana College, Sioux Falls, S.D.

Sam Roe
The Blade, Toledo, Ohio

Mort Saltzman
The Sacramento Bee

Sydney Schanberg
The New York Times

John Schultz
Columbia University

Wendy Shilton
University of Southern Maine,
Portland

Allan M. Siegal
The New York Times

Eleanor Singer
Public Opinion Quarterly

Jeff C. South
Virginia Commonwealth University

Herbert Strentz
Drake University

Diana K. Sugg
The Sacramento Bee

Lena H. Sun
The Washington Post

Mike Sweet
The Hawk Eye, Burlington, Iowa

Jeffrey A. Tannenbaum
The Wall Street Journal

Bob Thayer
The Providence Journal

Jim Toland
San Francisco Chronicle

Carolyn Tuft
Belleville (Ill.) *News-Democrat*

Mary Voboril
The Miami Herald

Howard Weinberg
Executive producer, "Bill Moyers'
Journal"

Elizabeth Weise
USA Today

Jan Wong
The Globe and Mail, Toronto

Emerald Yeh
KRON-TV, San Francisco

Phoebe Zerwick
Winston-Salem Journal

The affiliations of the contributors are given as of the time of their assistance.

A Personal Word

Some of you may be thinking of the future, the kind of journalism you will want to be doing and the best place to launch your careers. Fortunately for you, the field is wide open. Journalism is a gateway to a variety of opportunities.

You may choose the path to a newspaper, magazine or broadcast career. Or you may have a particular interest that leads you to one of the several thousand special publications, the so-called business newspapers, magazines and newsletters.

Or you may choose to travel on the Cyberspace Highway and report and write for the online media. By the beginning of the new century, 1,000 newspapers are expected to be online, and there are opportunities in online news services as well. One indication of the growing reach of online journalism is its recognition by the Pulitzer Prize Board, which decided to include online newspapers for its Public Service gold medal beginning with the 1999 award.

Starting Out

Years ago, a reporter who had worked on several newspapers around the country advised a journalism student: "Find a small newspaper or station where you can keep learning, where you will be assigned to everything—schools, local politics, the courthouse, police, the city council and the Kiwanis Club."

Such advice is still given, and it's still sound. Why a small newspaper or station? Let Eugene Roberts, former managing editor of *The New York Times,* answer the question. Roberts, who had his pick of job applicants, says he had a prejudice "in favor of the reporter who cut his professional teeth doing everything under the sun on a small newspaper.

"If you're on a paper of, say, less than 20,000 circulation, during the run of the year you're probably going to cover every conceivable type of story—trials and floods and politics and crime and breaking news and nonbreaking news and features."

Not every small newspaper or station is worth your time. Some are understaffed and do little more than slap at the news. But there are many good ones, and it isn't difficult to find out which they are.

These are the newspapers and stations that win awards for their reporting. The Du Pont-Columbia and George Foster Peabody Awards honor broadcast journalists, the Pulitzer Prizes and the Associated Press Managing Editors awards are for newspaper journalists. Many honors exist for both print and broadcast journalists, such as the George Polk Awards and the Sigma Delta Chi Awards of the Society of Professional Journalists.

Reading through professional publications such as *Broadcasting* and *Editor & Publisher,* you will come across pieces about the good work being done by smaller staffs. Ever hear of *The Winter Haven News Chief,* circulation 15,000? Probably not. This small central Florida daily newspaper was the subject of a long article in *Editor & Publisher.* The *News Chief* revealed that inadequate background checks were made of Florida teachers and, as a result, more than 35 convicted child molesters, rapists, drug sellers and other criminals were teaching children. After the stories appeared, a state law was adopted requiring more extensive background checks of applicants. Newspapers over the country followed the lead of the small Florida daily.

In *News Reporting and Writing* we will be looking at the work of many good newspapers, stations and other media enterprises. You may want to jot down their names for future use.

There are plenty of newspapers like the *News Chief* that beginners can look into. It is not difficult to find newspapers and stations that take pride in public service journalism.

Such newspapers and stations are the first step on the ladder. The next jump is to a medium-size newspaper or station, and then, if you are interested in metropolitan journalism or foreign correspondence, the big stations and newspapers.

Prize Winners

Some newspapers regularly figure in lists of the country's best newspapers. At the head of the list, invariably, is *The New York Times,* the nation's newspaper of record. It has a large Washington and foreign staff, and its national correspondents span the continent. Right behind are *The Washington Post* and *Los Angeles Times,* both likely to do more investigative reporting than *The New York Times. The Wall Street Journal* is considered the best written newspaper of all. Much more than a daily chronicle of business, the *Journal* offers excellent Washington coverage and has an enterprising staff of digging reporters. *The Miami Herald* is considered to offer the best coverage of Latin America. It is one of the crown jewels in a string of excellent newspapers operated by the Knight-Ridder newspaper chain.

The Philadelphia Inquirer, another Knight-Ridder newspaper, has stressed investigative journalism and has won many Pulitzer Prizes. *The Boston Globe, Newsday, Chicago Tribune, The Milwaukee Journal, The Courier-Journal* (Louisville, Ky.) and *St. Petersburg Times* are also among the nation's best.

Here are the call letters of some of the radio and television stations that have won prizes for outstanding reporting over the past few years:

WBAP, Arlington Tex. KVUE-TV, Austin, Tex. WJZ-TV, Baltimore. WBRZ-TV, Baton Rouge, La. WGBH-TV, WCVB-TV, WBUR, Boston. KGAN-TV, Cedar Rapids, Iowa. WBBM-TV, WMAQ-TV, WTTW-TV, Chicago. WVXU-FM, Cincinnati. WFFA-TV, KRLD-AM, Dallas. KBDI, Denver.

KTVS-TV, Detroit. KSEE-TV, Fresno, Calif. KPRC-TV, KTRH-AM, Houston. WJXT-TV, Jacksonville, Fla. KAIT-TV, Jonesboro, Ark. KNX-AM, KNXT-TV, Los Angeles. WHAS, Louisville. WPLG-TV, Miami.

WCCO-TV, WTCN, Minneapolis. WSMV-TV, Nashville. WWL-AM, WWL-TV, New Orleans. WMTV-TV, Omaha. KWY, KWY-TV, WCAU-TV, Philadelphia. WRAL-TV, Raleigh. KXTV, Sacramento. KSBW-TV, Salinas, Calif. KSL-TV, Salt Lake City. KCST-TV, San Diego. KGO-AM, KGO-TV, KRON-TV, KPIX-TX, San Francisco. KCTS-TV, KING-TV, Seattle. KMOX, KMOV, St. Louis. KGUN-TV, Tucson. KOTV, KTUL-TV, Tulsa. WDVM-TV. WRC-TV, WJLA, Washington, D.C. KWWL-TV, Waterloo, Iowa.

A number of online publications and services have been cited for excellent work, among them Channel 4000 (wcco.com) in Minneapolis, Salon magazine in San Francisco (salonmagazine.com) and NEWS.COM (news.com) also in San Francisco.

Opportunities

Race and gender are no longer barriers to media jobs. Most newspapers are committed to finding and hiring men and women of all races. In fact, women make up half the new hires, and one of five beginners is a member of a minority group.

In the not-too distant past, women were confined to the so-called society section, and a black or Hispanic in the newsroom was a rarity. Some years ago, Nan Robertson applied for a transfer from *The New York Times* local staff to its Washington bureau. During her visit to Washington, Russell Baker turned to the bureau chief, James Reston, and asked, "Do I encourage her or discourage her, Scotty?" Reston replied, "Discourage her." Robertson threatened to quit the paper, and the managing editor persuaded Reston to give Robertson a chance.

Much has changed. Today, more than a third of all journalists are female; the majority of reporters on small newspapers are female.

Minority journalists now constitute 11 percent of newsroom workers. About one-fourth of new hires are black, Hispanic, Native American or Asian American.

Beginners

A study of newspapers with circulations under 25,000 showed that 90 percent hire graduates of journalism programs with no professional experience. The survey by Michael Shelly of Illinois State University found the editors looked for graduates with experience in desktop publishing and the computer, an internship experience and an academic grounding in history, political science, economics and English. Shelly says he found, "Most editors want plenty of hands-on experience and a good knowledge of language and of government."

Salaries

Beginning salaries vary with location and with the medium. Large-city media pay more than small-city newspapers and stations. Online media offer the highest annual salaries because of low overhead. Here are the salary ranges:

Newspapers	$21,000–27,500
Magazines	$19,000–25,000
Television	$16,000–22,000
Radio	$16,000–20,000
Online	$27,000–33,000.

Part Opener Photos

Part One

Reporters are at the scene, notepads, cameras and tape recorders at the ready.

Photo by Kurt Steidle, *Pottsville* (Pa.) *Republican*

Part Two

The story of the killer tornado's aftermath calls for accuracy, clarity, human interest.

Photo by Val Hoeppner, *Argus Leader*

Part Three

The story of the crime, the fire, the accident sparkles when human interest is included.

Photo by Jim Gehrz, *Milwaukee Journal Sentinel.*

Part Four

Men overboard—get their names, addresses, cause of the capsizing, injuries.

Photo by Gregg Lovett

Part Five

There's always a story behind the result and the score.

Photo by Bob Zellar, *The Billings* (Mont.) *Gazette.*

Part Six

A question of taste and ethics: Do we run these graphic photos?

Photos by Stewart Bowman, *The Louisville Times*

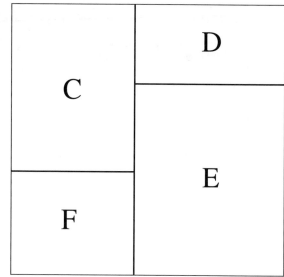

Cover Photos: Anguish, Suspense, Desperation and Renewal

The photographs on the front and back covers of the eighth edition of *News Reporting and Writing* illustrate and illuminate the scope and variety of journalism.

(A) Jacqueline Arzt of the Associated Press took this photograph of a girl looking out into an uncertain future in war-torn Bosnia where Serb and Muslim forces battled.

(B) The Jackson, Miss., SWAT team is just about to storm into an apartment where a man had barricaded himself with his child as a hostage. John Severson of *The Clarion-Ledger* in Jackson took this shot just as the lead member of the team tossed a chair off the balcony.

(C) Firefighters Mike Sande and Randy Johnson of Grand Forks, N.D., finally locate a hydrant in the floodwaters rushing through the downtown area, only to find no pressure. Later, while treated for hypothermia, Sande said, "At the time I was thinking, we could lose the whole downtown easily. There isn't anything we can do. We have to sit and watch our town burn down." The photo is by Bill Alkofer of the *St. Paul Pioneer Press.*

(D) Families in Jarrell, Tex., where a tornado took 27 lives, center their emotional rebuilding on their children, many of whom lost friends in the disaster. Ted S. Warren of the *Austin American-Statesman* took this photograph of youngsters playing on a trampoline, trying to forget.

(E) More than 50 years in the making, the huge memorial to the Oglala Sioux Indian warrior Crazy Horse takes shape in the Black Hills of South Dakota. When finished, it will be the largest sculpted figure on earth. AP photo by Charles Bennett.

(F) In Somalia, where life expectancy is 44 years and only one in four people can read and write, schools are trying to teach the young. Jean-Marc Bouju of the AP took this photograph of girls in northern Somalia attentively following their teacher's instructions.

1 On the Job

Reporters are at the scene of news events.

Preview

Watching reporters at work, we see that they are:

- Hard working
- Enterprising
- Curious
- Dependable despite pressure
- Knowledgeable
- Compassionate
- Courageous

Reporters are tenacious in their search for facts that will give their readers and viewers information about events. They work quickly and efficiently against deadlines. They have a passion for accuracy and a determination to dig out all aspects of the story.

a0662   11:41 AM
BC — APNewsAlert, 0021<
Shooting at Jonesboro, Ark., middle school; school office reports one dead, at least 13 hurt.

A killer tornado strikes a small South Dakota community, virtually wiping it out.

Freeport Parent–Teacher Association discusses raising teacher salaries $2,000 a year.

The State Board of Education decides to ask the Planned Parenthood Federation to help it develop a program to educate high school students about AIDS.

A candidate for the city council says he opposes a proposed city park and recreation bond issue.

Residents of Winston-Salem, N.C., are disturbed by a series of events: The mayor-elect joins the Council of Conservative Citizens in a pledge to the Confederate battle flag; the board of aldermen splits along racial lines on police use of pepper spray; the Ku Klux Klan holds a rally downtown.

Few people witness these events. But everyone will be able to see them or read or hear about them tonight or tomorrow morning because a reporter is covering the story. The reporter is the link between the event and the viewer, reader or listener. The public can follow the Jonesboro shooting and the South Dakota tornado through the work of journalists. People will see the PTA discussion through the reporter's eyes, hear the city council candidate's opposition to the bond issue through the reporter's ears.

People will be able to track events as they develop. Alarmed by the events that "stripped away the veneer of civility that concealed long-held racial tensions in Winston-Salem," the city's daily newspaper embarked on a massive reporting project, "Dividing Lines, Race Relations in Forsyth County."

Even when people witness events, they want to savor the experience again and to have details they may have missed. The news story also provides interpretations and explanations. Readers want to know how the proposed salary scale for teachers will affect the property tax, whether the mayor opposes the bond issue, whether the AIDS program will involve distribution of condoms in the schools.

The Agreement

A tacit agreement exists between the reporter and the public:

1. **The reporter** will do his or her best to give the public a complete and accurate account of the event. After the first reports of the shooting in Jonesboro, the AP notified editors:

An AP reporter and photographer are heading to the scene of the school shootings in Jonesboro, Ark.

Within 15 minutes of moving its NewsAlert, the AP had this story on its wires:

JONESBORO, Ark. (AP)— Two youths wearing camouflage opened fire on middle school students Tuesday as they assembled outside during a fire alarm. At least one person was killed and other injured.

When reporters at the *Argus Leader* in Sioux Falls, S.D., heard about the storm moving toward southeastern South Dakota, they headed for the newsroom, though it was their day off.

2. **The public** presumes that the reporter's account is honestly and accurately reported and written. Although pollsters tell us that people are wary of the news they see and read, the reality is that people act on the information they obtain from their newspapers and broadcast stations:

The mother of three children in Little Rock schools who is disturbed by the Jonesboro shootings asks her state senator to press for stringent gun-control laws.

The last paragraph of the story on the Freeport Parent-Teacher Association meeting states that parents are invited to a dinner meeting

Thursday at the local high school where teacher salaries will be discussed. A Freeport couple decides to attend.

A local parents' organization drafts a petition that opposes AIDS education in the high schools.

A mother of three small children, angered by the candidate's position on the park and recreation program, calls friends and tells them to vote against him.

Disturbed by reading in the *Winston-Salem Journal* or a deepening racial gulf, Carol Eickmeyer spends several hundred dollars to have 500 bumper stickers printed that read: **"Hate? Not in MY town."**

Several interracial supper clubs are formed.

Continuous Coverage

Reporters stay with their assignments until they feel they have answered questions the public might have.

Freeport reporters continued their coverage of the proposed teacher-salary increase that the PTA approved. They watched the local school board discuss the issue, and one reporter wrote a story comparing local teacher salaries with those of teachers in other cities in the state. She found local teachers were among the lowest paid.

Local reporters also looked into the State Board of Education proposal for AIDS education in the high schools. How representative of local sentiment was the organization actively opposing the proposal? The city editor asked a reporter to find out.

Reporters for the *Argus Leader* spent a week in Spencer to tell the full story of the tragedy. Let's watch a couple of them go about their work. Then we will go out to Arkansas and look over the shoulder of Kelly P. Kissel, the news editor of the AP Little Rock bureau just as he sends newswoman Jenny Price to Jonesboro following state police reports of a shooting at the Westside Middle School.

First to Sioux Falls.

A Tornado Hits Spencer

The skies are darkening over southeastern South Dakota and they are growing more ominous by the minute. In the *Argus Leader* newsroom in Sioux Falls, the small Saturday night staff is alerted to the possibility of worsening weather. Assistant City Editor Rosemary McCoy calls reporter Rob Swenson at home to tell him he may have to go back to the newsroom to help with coverage. Swenson decides to return.

David Kranz, another reporter, has Saturday off but decides to go in when he hears of the gathering storm. "We have a limited staff on weekends," he says, "so I offered to help." He shows up at 9 p.m., just as a weather bureau warning of a tornado rushing toward Sioux Falls sends people into basements from 9 to 9: 30 p.m., not the place to be with a 10:10 p.m. deadline for the first edition.

As the Sioux Falls alert is ended the newsroom hears that the tornado has hit the small town of Spencer, 50 miles west of Sioux Falls. The tornado struck the town with its full fury.

McCoy sends Swenson and a photographer to Spencer. "Our mission was to get there quickly and call back with observations in time for the Sunday edition," Swenson says. "The deadline was a major factor the moment we left the parking lot."

Blocked   But Swenson could not drive into town. "We were stopped at a roadblock by law officers," he says. They parked about a quarter of a mile outside town. "The town was dark except for a slow-moving parade of flashing lights from ambulances, fire trucks and other emergency vehicles, which stretched from where we stood to the center of town." Officers would not talk, so Swenson interviewed "terrified Spencer residents who had been out of town when the tornado struck. They were waiting at the roadblock to return to what was left of their homes."

When it was clear Swenson would not be able to contribute much more to the Sunday paper, he was sent to Salem, a nearby town to which Spencer residents had been evacuated, for interviews for the Monday paper.

In the Newsroom

Knowing that Swenson and photographer Ken Klotzbach were unable to get into Spencer, Kranz started to work the phones. He had good contacts, having been the editor of *The Daily Republic* in Mitchell, which serves the Spencer area. "I was fairly familiar with the town," Kranz says, "but I only knew a handful of people. I began calling them, suspecting the lines might be down, and got no answer. I then worked the phones in the area, thinking some rural Spencer people may have been in the town to check on things. No answer anywhere."

Enterprise   "At that point, I shifted my attention to law enforcement types. I called the wives of two law enforcement or emergency people that I knew would be there. First, I called the Minnehaha County Emergency Management director's wife. I asked for his cell phone number."

He continued to call and hit paydirt by finding the Davison County sheriff's cell phone number.

"The sheriff saved our day. He stood in the middle of the debris and described the situation to me. He pointed out areas familiar to me. He then handed the phone to the U.S. Marshal who gave us a vivid description of the way Spencer was and what he was now seeing.

"As deadline neared, the sheriff told us he knew there were fatalities. He saw one for sure, but expected there were others."

Governor's Comments   Kranz continued to call the sheriff and with 10 minutes before the deadline for the last Sunday edition, he asked the sheriff if the governor, Bill Janklow, were anywhere near.

"He told me he was standing five feet away. I asked him to hand the governor the phone and I asked the governor how many people were dead. He put the number at four. Without the source Kranz had, the local TV station could only confirm one death.

"The governor told me what he would have to do in the next few days and he gave me a plea for citizens not to visit Spencer the next day. He asked that they stay home and pray, that being there would only make the situation worse."

With the minute hand sweeping toward deadline, Kranz made one more call, this one to a woman in an area outside Spencer. Again, he was lucky. She had driven into Spencer to check on her mother. Her observations of the devastation in the town added a "real people" voice to the story, Kranz says.

Continued Coverage Within minutes of putting the Sunday paper to bed, the staff began planning further coverage of the disaster. Jill Callison, the religion writer, was to cover church services. Six other reporters also would go to Spencer. In the Sioux Falls newsroom, several reporters would write obituaries and gather information on how people could help the town.

The full dimension of the disaster was reflected in the headline in Monday's newspaper:

'The town is gone'

Under this banner headline were two stories. One was about the tornado's effects. Written by Kranz and Swenson, it begins:

SPENCER — Shocked survivors wandered their ripped-apart community Sunday searching for tornado-scattered belongings and mourning six neighbors who died.

The whole community reeled from the devastation that Saturday's vicious storm left behind.

"It's just like a bomb hit us," Tom Simmons said. "Just like a bomb hit."

Most of the homes had been reduced to rubble.

"This whole town is gone," said Gov. Bill Janklow.

The other story began:

Here are ways people may help victims of the spencer Tornado:

Red Cross

Donations made to the American Red Cross may be earmarked to help with disaster relief for Spencer. . . .

The story went on to describe how people could donate food, collected at local markets, and send blankets and clothing to the victims.

Ken Klotzbach, *Argus Leader*

The Morning After

Summing Up

Managing Editor Peter Ellis says, "We covered every angle of this story we could think of. We told about the heroes, the 8,000 volunteers who showed up to help, the governor who camped out there for a week, the prisoners who were happy to help, the minister who was spared while his wife died a few feet away from him.

"The main lesson from Spencer, I think, is that nothing beats good reporting, and lead reporter Dave Kranz is one of the best. He is always working his beat, including keeping up with former sources from years ago. It was because of this that we were able to get the sensational coverage, especially on the first day, that we did."

School Shooting

Next to the AP bureau in Little Rock. It is getting on to noon and Kelly Kissel, the bureau's news editor, is about to have his chicken lunch when he hears that the state police have been asked to set up a perimeter outside Westside

Middle School. There has been a shooting at the school in Jonesboro. A person has been killed. This is a major story, and Kissell needs a reporter on the scene. He shoves his lunch aside, tells reporter Jenny Price to take off for Jonesboro.

He wants her to call him every half hour on the cell phone. During her first calls, Kissel, who knows northeastern Arkansas from having spent summers at his grandparents' farm there, gives Price shortcuts: Take a left a mile past the grain elevator, another left, then right just past the railroad tracks. But even with these instructions, it will take Price two hours to reach Jonesboro and Kissel must put something on the AP wire quickly.

Early Stories

Kissel calls state police, local reporters in Jonesboro, the school superintendent's office. It isn't until he has the superintendent's secretary on the line that he has something good enough for the wire. He writes these three paragraphs:

> BC — School Shooting, 0089
> URGENT
> Shooting at Arkansas school; more than a dozen injured
> JONESBORO, Ark. (AP) — Two men wearing camouflage opened fire on middle school students Tuesday as they assembled outside during a fire alarm. At least one person was killed.
> Connie Tolbert, secretary to the school district superintendent, said eight to 13 people, mostly students, were injured. Other reports put the number of injured at up to 16.
> Jonesboro is a city of 46,000 about 130 miles northeast of Little Rock.

This is a big story, and Kissel calls the AP general desk in New York to discuss coverage. He is given the green light to send another reporter, Peggy Harris, to the scene. Over the next week, seven AP staff members will be rotated in and out of Jonesboro.

As Price is making her way to Jonesboro, Kissel and other staffers gather more information to try to flesh out the story.

Escalating Deaths   Bulletins, more NewsAlerts, new leads follow in rapid order through the day. At 12:07, a NewsAlert reports a second death. At 12:11, the second lead has 15 injured. In a few minutes a third lead corrected the 15 to 13. Then, at 12:31, the AP reports two suspects, ages 11 and 13, have been taken into custody. Then a story with background about other school shootings and the figure of 13 injured is reduced to 12. At 13:03 (1:03 p.m.), a NewsAlert reports a third death. At 13:37, a NewsAlert about a fourth death.

Now, with Price on the scene, it is time to collect these pieces of information and move a definitive story. It will be followed during the six and a half hours by 10 Writethrus, complete stories, each with new information. Kissel's comments are alongside Price's wrapup story:

By JENNY PRICE=
Associated Press Writer
With AP Photos<

JONESBORO, Ark. (AP) — Two boys in camouflage lay in wait in the woods behind a school, then opened fire with rifles on students and teachers when they came out during a false fire alarm Tuesday. Four girls were killed and 11 other people were wounded, including two teachers.

The boys — ages 11 and 13 — were caught trying to run away shortly after the midday ambush at the Westside Middle School, police said. Police were looking for a third boy who allegedly pulled the fire alarm.

Broadcast reports said more than a dozen shots were fired. Students said they thought they were firecrackers at first, but when they saw that people had been hit, they started screaming and running back inside the school. Youngsters cried as they waited for emergency workers.

"We had children lying everywhere. They had all been shot," said paramedic Charles Jones.

Sheriff Dale Haas cried as recounted the shootings.

The school has about 250 students in sixth and seventh grades. Jonesboro is a city of 46,000 about 130 miles northeast of Little Rock.

The two boys, wearing camouflage shirts, pants and hats, were caught near the school. Officer Terry McNatt said they offered no resistance and said little. Two rifles and other weapons were recovered. The boys were being held at the county jail.

Authorities wouldn't say whether they were students at the school.

Karen Pate, a parent volunteer, was in the school gym when the fire alarm went off just after sixth-graders had finished lunch and returned to their classrooms. She fled outside and "saw girls falling to the ground."

"I helped one teacher who had been shot in the abdomen get out of there where she could lay down and we could start medical attention," Mrs. Pate said. "Another student had got shot in the leg. As soon as she got hit, she couldn't walk and she fell into the doorway."

Mrs. Pate and her sixth-grade daughter were not hurt.

President Clinton, on a visit to Kampala, Uganda, said in a statement that he and the first lady were "deeply shocked and heartbroken."

"We don't know now and we may never fully understand what could have driven two youths to deliberately shoot into a crowd," he said. "Our thoughts and prayers are with the victims, their families and the entire Jonesboro community."

It was at least the third fatal shooting rampage in a school in the past five months.

On Dec. 1, a boy opened fire on a student prayer circle at a high school in West Paducah, Ky., killing three students and wounding five. A 14-year-old student, described as small and emotionally immature, was arrested.

Jenny was the first AP reporter on the scene, and her byline went on the story. Early versions had no byline. She wasn't there.

Police's original theory was that a third person had to be involved because the shooting started so quickly. Late in the evening, they rolled back after witnesses said they saw one of the boys near the alarm.

The first four grafs paint an almost complete picture:
• Boys in camouflage.
• Woods behind the school.
• Screaming and running back into the school.
• "Children lying everywhere."

With the "camouflage" and "woods" references, it wasn't necessary to call it a "rural school district." That would have wasted words.

Two months earlier, a 16-year-old outcast in Pearl, Miss., was accused of killing his mother, then going to school and shooting nine students. Two of them died, including the boy's ex-girlfriend. Authorities later charged six friends with conspiracy, saying the suspects were part of a group that dabbled in satanism.

On Dec. 15, a sniper in the woods wounded two students outside a school in the southwestern Arkansas town of Stamps. A 14-year-old boy was arrested after a manhunt.

Added Detail

As AP reporters on the scene called Kissel, he put the new material into Writethrus. Here are excerpts from some of them, with Kissel's comments:

1st Ld — Writethru

Authorities said as many as 27 shots were fired. Youngsters ran screaming back inside the school as their classmates fell bleeding, then cried as they waited for emergency workers.

• Previously, we had "more than a dozen shots." Keep pressing for more exact information. Now we have a specific number, 27.

Said paramedic Charles Jones: "We had children lying everywhere. They had all been shot."

Sheriff Dale Haas cried as he recounted the shootings.

Two of the dead girls were 12 and another was 11, state police spokesman Bill Sadler said. He did not know the age of the fourth victim.

• An important image—Haas crying—of how horrible this was to the community. Most sheriffs think they have seen it all.

The two boys, wearing camouflage shirts, pants and hats, were caught near the school with handguns and rifles. Officer Terry McNatt said they offered no resistance and said little. The boys, both students at the school, were being held at the county jail.

Investigators said the boys were running in the direction of a white van found about a half-mile away from the school with more guns and ammunition in it. It wasn't immediately certain if the vehicle was related to the shootings.

• The result of more pressing inquiry—The boys were students at the school, and we find out they were running toward a van with more ammunition.

President Clinton, on a visit to Kampala, Uganda, said in a statement that he and the first lady were "deeply shocked and heartbroken." . . .

Gov. Mike Huckabee said he was angry, as a parent, that such a tragedy could happen at a public school. . . .

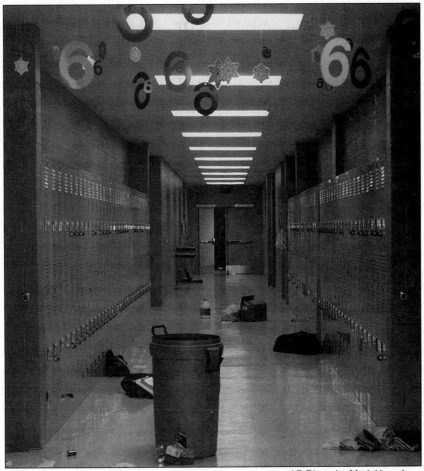

AP Photo by Mark Humphrey

False Alarm

Backpacks and cleaning supplies were dropped in the hallway of the Westside Middle School when students left as the fire alarm sounded. As the students and their teachers walked out, the two boys hidden in a wooded area opened fire.

Arkansas law does not prohibit minors from possessing shotguns or rifles, but it does bar people younger than 21 from possessing handguns. Other laws prohibit anyone from possessing a gun on public property or with criminal intent.

It was at least the third fatal shooting rampage in a school in the past five months. . . .

• **The reporter on the scene can't do all the legwork. Here, the AP White House staff, the Arkansas capitol correspondent and other writers in the bureau gather important information.**

The Associated Press. The AP is the oldest and largest news-gathering organization in the world and supplies more than 1,700 newspapers and 6,000 television and radio stations in the U.S. with national and international news. It is a not-for-profit news cooperative, owned by its thousands of members.

AP's news originates in its vast network of 237 bureaus around the world in which 3,500 staff members produce an average of 20 million words and 1,000 photos a day. Most stories begin on state or regional news wires. If a story is seen to have more than regional interest, it is sent to AP's New York headquarters where the story is edited and placed on the major DataStream report.

Members of the AP also contribute news stories to the AP via their local bureaus.

The wire service supplies photographs and graphics to members, and the AP Network News is a full-service radio network.

AP also distributes news online via The WIRE, http://wire.ap.org, which is a 24-hour news service of headlines, story summaries that link to full stories, audio news summaries from the radio news feed, photos and a search capability.

2nd Ld — Writethru

All the victims were female.

• Bad information from the school and the police. The hospital got it right for us for the next version of the story. (A boy had been treated and released.)

Arkansas law does not prohibit minors from possessing shotguns or rifles, but it does bar people younger than 21 from possessing handguns. Other laws prohibit anyone from possessing a gun on public property or with criminal intent.

• An interesting bit of information.

4th Ld — Writethru

Authorities identified the dead girls as Natalie Brooks, Paige Ann Herring, Stephanie Johnson, all 12, and Brittheny R. Varner, who was 11.

• A change in the story to include the names of the victims.

5th Ld — Writethru

Police did not offer a motive, but a classmate said one of the suspects had recently broken up with his girlfriend.

"He told me after seventh period (Monday) that he was never going to see me again and I wouldn't be able to see him again because he was going to run away," said Jennifer Nightingale. She did not say if any of the victims was the former girlfriend.

• As the city calmed down, witnesses agreed to talk, often with scores of microphones around. As police remained mum about motives, this student was among the first to step forward. (These became the third and fourth paragraphs of the story.)

Ten of the wounded were female, including the two teachers, who required surgery and were listed in critical condition. They were identified as Sara Thetford, who teaches social studies, and Shannon Wright, a language teacher.

• Adding the names of the teachers. By this point, we had learned that Mrs. Wright was not expected to make it. We staked out the hospital with one writer (Price), while a second writer (Harris) stayed at the police command post for official information from the clearinghouse. (Mrs. Wright died, and this was reported in the 6th Lead, which moved on the wire five minutes later.

7th Ld — Writethru

The wounded students were between 11 to 13 years old. State police said a 12th person was wounded, but was not treated at the hospital. They did not have any more details.

• Police started saying that a 12th person had been wounded, but eventually this was found to be the result of a "double" body count.

Police later determined that it must have been one of the teachers who was counted on the ground at the school and again at the hospital.

This shows why it's important to get the names of the dead and wounded—so there's no duplication.

8th Ld — Writethru

English teacher Shannon Wright, 32, died Tuesday night after surgery for wounds to her chest and abdomen, Craighead County coroner Toby Emerson said.

"She loved kids," her husband, Mitchell, said after her death.

• **Jenny bumped into Mr. Wright at the hospital shortly after he had been told of his wife's death. It's not much, but what can one really expect? He did an interview later with Jenny.**

9th Ld — Writethru

The two boys, wearing camouflage shirts, pants and hats, were caught near the school with handguns and rifles. Officer Terry McNatt said they offered no resistance and said little. The boys, who were not identified and were students at the school, were being held at the county jail. They were scheduled for court appearances at the jail Wednesday morning.

• **No one was officially identifying the suspects yet. The court later opened the proceedings, citing the notoriety of the case.**

10th Ld — Writethru

The pair — cousins aged 11 and 13 — were caught trying to run away shortly after the midday ambush at the Westside Middle School, police said. One of the boys was seen near the fire alarm, a witness said.

• **Police pull back from the theory that a third boy had to be involved after witnesses said they saw one of the suspects in the school shortly before the shooting. (This became the second paragraph of the Writethru. The students had filed out of the school after the fire alarm was sounded, providing targets for the two boys.)**

Amber Vanoven, 11, said she saw Mrs. Wright step in front of sixth-grader Emma Pittman.

"This guy was aiming at her (Pittman)," Amber told the Jonesboro Sun newspaper. "He was fixing to shoot her, and Mrs. Wright moved out in front of her. She got shot. . . . She did. I sat and watched her."

"I saw my best friend, Natalie Brooks, get killed — shot in the head twice," she said.

Amber also said she saw the 11-year-old suspect standing near a fire alarm and then watched him run out of the building as an electric buzzer hummed.

• **Great cooperation from the local newspaper, also backing up the belief that the younger boy set off the alarm.**

Here is how the 10th lead appeared as it moved on the wires at 11:22 p.m. Central time. You might want to compare it with Kissel's NewsAlert sent 12 hours earlier.

By JENNY PRICE=
Associated Press Writer
JONESBORO, Ark. (AP) — Two boys in camouflage lay in wait in the woods behind their school, then opened fire with rifles on classmates and teachers when they came out during a false fire alarm Tuesday. Four girls and a teacher were killed and 11 people were wounded.

Questions, Answers

Why all the leads and Writethrus? Why the drive to get names, details, quotations, to verify every detail, to find the specific number of shots fired?

Well, this is the way journalists work. In this case, the story is being covered by a wire service, which has clients all over the world at newspapers and broadcast stations with different deadlines. Each wants to go on the air or into print with the latest information, the latest accurate and complete information. Readers, viewers, listeners want to know.

A newspaper in Virginia may have a first edition that closes at 6 p.m., whereas the first edition of a California newspaper closes three hours later. The Virginia newspaper has to use the early Writethru, but the California newspaper can wait. The same decisions affect broadcast stations. On a breaking news story like this horrendous shooting, the AP must keep a stream of information moving, packaged in a complete story ready for use.

So much for the mechanics of the Associated Press. What about the reporting: Was a third boy involved? . . . How many shots were fired? . . . What were the names of the dead and injured? . . . Can we locate any eyewitnesses? The reason the reporters searched for accurate details, specifics and drama takes us to the heart of journalism.

The task of the journalist is to tell us what happened. Journalism is history in a hurry, someone said. It is the journalist's responsibility to make this record as accurate and as complete as humanly possible. The public depends on us.

We'll be looking at a newspaper reporter new on the job, an experienced TV reporter, a veteran police reporter, a reporter using a database for his story and the specialists who work for business magazines, a fast-growing field that has attracted many journalism graduates. Different as their workplaces may be, they all share a way of going about their work, a commitment to accuracy and fairness and the conviction that their work is important.

Everywhere. "I suppose when I go to the hereafter and stand at the Golden Gate, the first person I shall meet will be a correspondent of The Associated Press."
—Mahatma Gandhi, on meeting an AP reporter at a remote railway station in western India after his release from prison.

An Announcement and a Fire

We are in the newsroom of a midwestern newspaper with a circulation of 25,000. The telephone on the city editor's desk rings and, after listening for a moment, the city editor calls out to a young reporter. "Bob, the publicity director of the Lions Club has a story."

The caller tells the reporter his club intends to donate some equipment to a city playground next Saturday at 10 a.m. at a ceremony the governor will attend.

The reporter calls the governor's press secretary to check the governor's itinerary in case he is making other local stops. In 15 minutes, he has written a short piece, putting the governor in the lead. He again checks the date, time and location of the ceremony against his notes.

A few minutes later, he is told to cover a fire with a photographer.

An hour later, Bob returns to the newsroom.

Human Interest   "It was a small fire, about $7,500 in damages, but there's some good human interest in it," he tells the city editor.

"Don't tell me you've got three columns on a three-paragraph fire, Bob," the city editor replies. "What's it about?"

Without looking at his notes, he answers. "The story isn't the fire but the background. I found out the family bought the house a few months ago. They had just remodeled it, and this week the wife went to work to help pay for it. She leaves their 10-year-old boy home with his 12-year-old brother for a few hours every day.

"Well, the 12-year-old wanted to make some money cutting grass. He knows they're short of money. He was filling the lawn mower with gasoline in the garage when the tank tipped over against the water heater. Woosh. Lucky he wasn't hurt."

The city editor thinks a moment.

"Got any good quotes from the older boy?" he asks.

"Yes."

"Well, it sounds as though it's worth more than a couple of paragraphs. But don't make it a chapter in the book, Bob."

At his desk, Bob pauses before writing. He can start his story like most accounts of fires he has read:

A fire of accidental origin caused $7,500 in damages to a dwelling at 1315 New Hampshire St. today.

No one was injured in the blaze that started in the garage when the 12-year-old son of the owners, Mr. and Mrs. Earl Ruman . . .

Direct Lead   He has put a direct news lead on the story, which he knows his newspaper prefers for stories of this sort. But he is unhappy with this start. This is not the way he described the fire to the editor, he recalls. Then he remembers advice he was given by a reporter: "Every story demands to be told a certain way. Don't impose a form or style on it. The way you write it has to flow from the nature of the event."

The nature of his story was the youngster's good intentions gone awry. So he starts again:

> Two months ago, Mr. and Mrs. Earl Ruman moved into a three bedroom house at 1315 New Hampshire St. It was their dream house.
> After years of skimping and saving . . .

At this rate, he will write the book his editor warned him against, he thinks. Although he wants a dramatic story—one that will build to a climax—he cannot take forever to develop the point. Readers will drift away.

Feature Lead   His editor has been telling his reporters to try for feature-type leads when the event makes it possible. Perhaps this is one of those events. The youngster is the heart of the story, he reasons, and the boy must go into the lead. He tries again:

> Teddy Ruman knew his father and mother had skimped and saved to put aside enough money to buy their dream house at 1315 New Hampshire St.
> This morning, he decided to help, too. But his well-intentioned efforts turned to tragedy.
> The 12-year-old . . .

That seems to be more like it. In 40 minutes, he has the story in good shape, he thinks.

The city editor reads through the copy.

"Yes, it's a sad story," he tells his cub reporter. "It's hardly a tragedy, but it would be sadder if they didn't have insurance to cover their loss."

Bob makes for the telephone on his desk. He remembers another bit of advice: "Don't leave unanswered any questions the reader may have. Don't leave any holes in your story."

Next, to another fire, this one far more serious, that is covered by a TV reporter.

TV Covers a Fire

It is Christmas Day in the newsroom of a television station. A teletype clicks off a story about a fire in a small town in New Jersey. The AP reports that while a family was asleep, a fire broke out and flames raced through their house. Four died. Only two boys escaped.

The news editor calls to a reporter, "Elaine, take this one on."

On the way to the fire, Elaine thinks of questions to ask and the locations in which to shoot the story.

"When I go out on an assignment I am conscious of the need for pictures," she said later. "I look for things that have an immediate impact, because I have a short time to tell the story—maybe two-and-a-half minutes.

"So I look for the strongest statement in a talk, the most emotionally appealing part of the running story. When I arrive at a story, I want to be the first one to interview the eyewitness, so that the person is still experiencing the event. The emotional facts have to tell the story."

On the scene, Elaine learns from the fire chief that the surviving youngsters had run to a neighbor's house during the fire. As crews from competing stations arrive, she and her crew approach the neighbor's house through the backyard to avoid being spotted.

"When I spoke to the woman next door, I asked her what happened when the boys burst into her home. She became tense and distraught as she described one boy's face, burned and blackened by the fire," Elaine recalled.

"On a breaking story, a broadcast journalist usually asks fewer questions than the print journalist. On this story all I needed to ask the neighbor was two or three questions and let her tell the story."

On the return drive, Elaine structures the script in her mind. She has pictures of the fire scenes and interviews of the neighbor and the fire chief. She works the script around these, the most dramatic shots.

A Child's Death

It was a drive-by shooting. The victim: 2-year-old Heather Brown. The family had been to church and stopped on the way home at McDonald's for ice cream. At home, Heather was fidgety and wouldn't go to sleep, so her father took her into the living room and began to rock her to sleep on the couch.

Suddenly, 60 high-caliber slugs tore into the house. One struck Heather in the head and she died in her father's arms.

For Diane Sugg of *The Sacramento Bee* the story was not so much the shooting death but the story of a lovable little girl. She found that story by driving out to the Valley Christian Church and waiting for its pastor, A. D. Olivan. He was close to Heather's parents and had spoken to them since the shooting.

Sugg had telephoned the minister but he didn't want to talk, so she drove to the church and waited. One hour. Two. After three hours, he arrived and Sugg persuaded him to talk to her about the child who used to run around the church singing to herself and hugging everyone she saw. There was something special about Heather, and everyone knew it.

"I would never have gotten Heather's story if I hadn't waited in a dark parking lot for three hours, hoping the family's pastor would come back to the church," Sugg says. "He did, and he could see I was sincere."

Las Vegas Crime

It's a short hop from Sacramento to Carson City, Nev., where Brendan Riley of the AP has been working on a story about crime in Las Vegas, the fastest-growing city in the United States. Riley is especially interested in the effectiveness of the Las Vegas Metro Police Department in solving crimes.

An Ethic. "Making a living is nothing; the great difficulty is making a point, making a difference—with words."
—*Elizabeth Hardwick*

By digging into the FBI database on crime, www.fbi.gov/ucr/crimeus/crimeus.htm, Riley has found a good story: Las Vegas police solve only a fifth of the violent crimes committed in the city. This is the worst rate in the country.

Riley runs the data by the police and asks for comments. The response he gets sends him scurrying back to his figures. The police say their data shows Las Vegas has problems solving crimes, but it definitely isn't the lowest-ranking city in the country in this category. Miami, San Francisco and several others are worse, they tell him. In fact, a department spokesman says, Las Vegas is seventh or eighth worst.

Riley checks his data and compares it with the material the Las Vegas police have made available to him.

He spots the reason for the difference. "Either accidentally or deliberately, Metro failed to count one of the lesser crime categories," Riley says. "That has the effect of skewing the numbers so Las Vegas doesn't look so bad." Riley stands by his numbers. But he will need comments from the police about the reasons for the low ranking.

He will also need comments from an outside authority, someone at the University of Nevada who is an expert on criminal justice. And he wants human interest. After all, a numbers story is not the most interesting reading.

Human Interest   The logical person to try to reach is a crime victim, someone involved in an unsolved crime. Riley locates Joyce McKay in Fresno, Calif. Her son and his girlfriend were shot to death in Las Vegas. Riley puts this human interest as high in the story as he can. He quotes McKay: "There's no closure. It's an ugly thing and an ugly feeling to be left with."

Expert's Comment   For an interpretation of the figures from outside the police department, Riley turns to Grant Stitt, chairman of the Criminal Justice Department at the University of Nevada, Reno, who is quoted as saying, "To a certain extent, it shows what the police are up against. You can have a very effective police force, but also have a community full of criminals. The police may be as effective as possible, but that's all they can do."

Riley quotes the police as saying the force has 1.54 officers per 1,000 Las Vegas residents, well below the national average. Add tourists to the population figure, and the ratio of officers to residents is even lower. Also, Riley quotes Stitt as saying, the voters refused to approve a bond issue that would have expanded the jail. "We live in a democratic society," Stitt says, "and the police are an agency of government. We pay for government, and we get what we pay for." With this quotation, Riley ends his story.

The Computer Revolution

The computer has become as much a reporting tool as the telephone and the tape recorder. As journalism enters the new century, new reporting practices have taken hold and changed the journalist into what Stephen Miller of *The New*

York Times calls "the multi-media reporter." This new-style journalist uses all the available tools in reporting—online databases, e-mail, spreadsheets, websites, Windows and the other newer tools along with the traditional ones.

We saw how Riley dug into FBI data for his story. The available material is endless. Reporters have used data from the Census Bureau, www.census.gov/, to compare their city's growth with others in the state, and they have used information on air quality from the Environmental Protection Agency, www.epa.gov/ to see whether pollution is up or down.

Some Projects

Cities, states and the federal government are putting their records into databases, which makes the information fingertip accessible. Mike Trautmann of the *Argus Leader* cross matched the computerized list of private lawyers doing state work with another computerized list of contributors to gubernatorial and legislative races.

In Austin, Stuart Eskenazi and Jeff South analyzed Texas public safety records and found more than 118,000 motorists were driving without insurance, and that a fourth of all accidents involved uninsured drivers.

A frequent use of city databases is the determination of how much city-worker overtime is costing. Trautmann found $1 million was paid out by Sioux Falls, and in Austin South and Mike Todd discovered dozens received more than $15,000 a year each in overtime payments.

Polluters *The Plain Dealer* in Cleveland checked records of the Nuclear Regulatory Commission to find that sewage plants were routinely accepting radioactive waste from hospitals, universities and other sources. In California, the McClatchy Newspapers analyzed pesticide reports to learn that a health threat existed in the populated area of the Central Valley.

A reporter for *The Times-Picayune* in New Orleans who was working on the decline of the world's fisheries navigated among the Internet e-mail discussion groups. He read the messages scientists were sending each other and gathered useful material. Then he identified himself and asked for help with his reporting project. "It was amazing," he said. "Not only were they eager to help, but they bent over backwards to get things to us."

Contributors "The power of the database is that you can make connections that were difficult before," Miller says. One of the most frequently used databases during political campaigns is the one maintained by the Federal Election Commission, www.tray.com/fecinfo. The commission lists the names of donors, their occupations and employers, zip codes, how much money they donated and to whom. Reporters use the information to see what influence money seeks to buy from officials.

"It's tough to find a story that doesn't have numbers in it," says Miller, and "the spreadsheet is the key to digging into these stories."

City Guides

The computer, via the Internet, has made it possible for news organizations to put information on the screen for use at home and office. Many newspapers have online versions with links to the longer stories. One of the newer news services is the localized city guide. America Online operates Digital City, which provides links to local newspapers. Yahoo! Metros integrates news stories into its local guides. Knight-Ridder uses editorial content from its 28 local newspapers for Real Cities. Writers for the seven city guides summarize news stories from the traditional media for the guides.

Business Magazines

We all know about the general business publications—*Fortune, Forbes, Business Week, The Wall Street Journal.* But there is another group of publications less well known, the specialized business publications that focus on specific subjects. One such publication, *Electronic Business,* spent eight months gathering information on how Russia stole U.S. electronic science and technology.

An *Automotive Industries* reporter looked into Japanese automobile factories for an article comparing them with U.S. factories. He found that Japan's "secret weapon" is more efficient use of resources.

More than 4,000 business publications serve a wide variety of trades, professions and industries.

The Nature of News

News is multifaceted. A lot of it consists of reports of happenings. We've seen a newspaper cover a tornado, the AP report a school shooting, reporters cover fires and a child's shooting. We could call this breaking news coverage. It is part of the journalist's job of record keeping. The governor gives a talk and a reporter is there to record it. Two cars collide at Vermont and Madison and the newspaper and local radio station describe the accident and the injuries.

Then there is the news that we can classify as entertainment: Profiles of TV stars, news about the latest Spice Girls hit, an interview with the lead in the local theater's presentation next week of the musical "Pajama Game." Entertainment news makes up an increasingly large portion of the news people are offered.

Beneath these surface events is a stratum of material that some reporters mine. This reporter-initiated coverage goes by several descriptions—depth reporting, interpretative reporting, investigative reporting. We saw the result of this enterprise reporting in the description of the use of the computer to dig into databases.

Investigative Reporting

A few weeks after Cammy Wilson took a reporting job with the *Minneapolis Tribune,* her city editor gave her a feature assignment: Spend a day with a woman in a wheelchair to see how disabled people get around in the city. Wilson accompanied the woman as she went about her chores, shopped and had lunch. At the end of the day, the woman remarked to Wilson, "Isn't it awful how much we have to pay to be taken to the doctor?" "How much?" Wilson asked. "Forty to fifty dollars," she replied.

Wilson sensed a story of greater impact than the feature she was assigned to write. Wilson asked the woman if she had a receipt for a trip to the doctor. The woman did.

Overbilling   By the time she finished her reporting, Wilson had a major scandal laid out: The transportation of the disabled was a multimillion-dollar operation in which people were being billed $40 to $120 for a round-trip to a medical facility. Companies were billing at an individual rate even when they took groups from a nursing home or a senior citizen center to a clinic.

Her stories interested the Health, Education and Welfare Department in Washington D.C., and, because Medicaid money was involved, HEW investigated. The Minnesota legislature held hearings and enacted several laws to regulate the transportation firms.

Exploitation   A couple of weeks later, Wilson was house hunting. In one house, she noticed that every item was for sale. From worn-out washcloths to underwear, everything had a price tag. "Has the owner died?" she asked the realtor. "No," he said, "the owner is in a nursing home." "Why is he selling?" "He's not selling. The conservator is," the realtor replied.

Once again, Wilson had a story. She learned that the owner, Ludvig Hagen, 86, suffered a fall and was taken to a nursing home to recover. While there, the church that he had named in his will marked the house and all of Hagen's possessions for sale. Wilson began her story this way:

> "4415 17th Ave. S."
> "4415 17th Ave. S."
> The old man in his wheelchair repeated the address, tears beginning to well.
> "I don't have to sell my house. It's paid for."
> But his house is for sale. It and all his possessions are part of an estate valued at $140,000. . . .

As a result of the story, the county attorney launched an investigation.

Wilson then looked at probate, the handling of wills and estates by the courts. She learned that the county probate court had appointed a management firm to handle the estates of various people and that the firm had sold their homes for well under the market price to the same buyer, who within six months resold the houses for 50 to 100 percent more than the purchase price.

A Tip and an Exposé

"The message on my answering machine was straightforward: 'I have a story that may be of interest to you.'

"Although reporters often get calls like this, many of which lead nowhere, I was intrigued, given the source, someone I had interviewed from time to time during the three years I covered the health, hospital and AIDS beat for the New York *Daily News* . . . someone who had never called me before . . . someone who sounded troubled."

Heidi Evans returned the call. The caller told her that the city health department had quietly stopped giving Pap smear tests to thousands of low-income women who depended on its clinics for free gynecological care.

"Since many of the clients of these clinics fit the profile of women most at risk of developing cervical cancer—sexually active women who have had several partners and little access to medical care—I knew I had the start of an important story," she said.

She dug into the records, interviewed people and found an even bigger story—the health department had endangered the lives of many women.

Here is how Evans began her story:

More than 2,000 Pap smears languished in a city health department laboratory for as long as a year, leaving hundreds of women at high risk of developing cervical cancer without knowing it.

A TV Documentary

The U.S. is sports obsessed, and the media respond to the obsession with large sports staffs and acres of newsprint and hours of TV and radio time. The name of the game is winning, Howard Weinberg, a TV producer and director, learned, and this led him to develop a documentary for Bill Moyers about the price paid for the drive to win on the field.

His documentary begins:

America is a society obsessed with winning.
Many American universities have made a business of winning.

And then:

BILL MOYERS, Host: (voice-over) The name of the game is winning, to be number one, to sell the university's image and gain the money to do it all again, especially by getting on television. It's mass entertainment and America's colleges are providing more of it than ever before. The top 100 big-time sports universities, the ones you see on TV, now take in total revenues of more than a billion dollars a year.

The Qualities of a Reporter

Different as these journalists may appear at first glance, they share certain characteristics, and there are many similarities in the way they handle their assignments.

One characteristic we notice is the reporter's attitude. He or she is curious. The reporter wants to know what is happening—firsthand. This curiosity is not born of nosiness. Journalists learn early that seeing and hearing for themselves is better than secondhand accounts. The firsthand account rings with authenticity.

Persistence

The journalist knows how important persistence is in getting to the truth. "Let me tell you the secret that has led me to my goal," said Louis Pasteur, the French chemist whose studies of bacteria led to the pasteurization process. "My only strength lies in tenacity."

Persistence allowed Lisa Newman to tell the story of how a Chicago police officer was transferred as punishment for giving the daughter of the police superintendent a traffic ticket. Newman heard about the incident from an officer, but when she talked to the officer who issued the ticket he refused to confirm her tip.

Newman, a reporter for *The Daily Calumet and Pointer,* gradually lessened the police officer's resistance, and he finally gave her the details. She also learned that the ticket was dismissed in traffic court.

With the information, Newman wrote several stories that led to an investigation.

Asking Questions   Persistence also means asking question after question until the issue is clarified, the situation made understandable for the reader or viewer. The columnist Dave Barry says, "I was a pretty good writer and I thought that was all that mattered. But journalism isn't about writing. You learned that what it's really about is asking hard questions, being persistent."

Confronting Editors   Sometimes, a reporter has to move beyond persistence. "You must be a little pushy, a little bit abrasive, a little bit obnoxious," says Bill Kovach, former executive editor of the Atlanta *Journal and Constitution* and now Curator of the Nieman Foundation at Harvard. He is talking about the behavior that may be necessary "to get important subjects into the newspaper. You have to be up-front, confronting editors face-to-face."

Night Owl. The juror was the lone holdout in a major trial, but finally gave in and allowed the Oakland Raiders to move to Los Angeles. All the reporters in both cities wanted to interview the juror, but he wasn't talking. Andy Furillo, then with the *Herald Examiner,* followed the juror home and camped on the curb in front of the juror's house. He stayed the night, and next morning the juror, obviously impressed by Furillo's persistence, invited him in and gave him the interview.

Knowledge

Stanley Walker, one of the great city editors, was once asked, "What makes a good reporter?"

"The answer is easy," he replied, with a show of a smile around his eyes. "He knows everything. He is aware not only of what goes on in the world today, but his brain is a repository of the accumulated wisdom of the ages." Walker, who helped make *The New York Herald Tribune* into a writer's newspaper, continued: "He hates lies and meanness and sham, but keeps his temper. He is loyal to his paper and to what he looks upon as his profession; whether it is a profession, or merely a craft, he resents attempts to debase it."

Enterprise

Number One. David Mazzarella, editor of *USA Today,* has for his staff what he calls the Ten Commandments. The first one is "Enterprise," which Mazzarella defines as, "Break stories. Investigate. Spot the trends."

News conferences, interviews and ball games present few problems. But for every easily accessible situation there is a tougher assignment, a less accessible source. The lore of journalism includes tales of enterprising reporters such as the one about the Chicago reporter who was blocked from a crime scene. He noticed doctors being waved into the building. He sprinted down the street to a pawn shop, pointed to a small suitcase, handed over a few dollars and raced back. Holding the case in his most professional manner, the reporter was allowed to pass.

Finding the Casualties   When Chinese troops shot down hundreds of students demonstrating in Tiananmen Square for democratic reforms, reporters were prevented from entering the area. Officials denied that any of the young men and women were killed. Jan Wong realized she could learn about casualties by going to local hospitals. She found the front doors were barred to outsiders.

"But no one guards the back door," and she went in. "Dozens of corpses, mostly unrefrigerated, decompose on the fifth day after Chinese troops slaughtered unarmed demonstrators near Tiananmen Square," she wrote for her newspaper, *The Globe and Mail* of Toronto.

A week later, the authorities decided Wong was finding out too much. As she was walking down a street, a car with no license plate cut her off, secret servicemen grabbed her and tried to shove her in the car.

Naming the Coach   In the days of intense competition between the United Press International and the Associated Press, reporters knew that a beat would result in a major play in newspapers and on stations. Sources did not want to show preference, so they would hold news conferences which allowed all the media an even shot. The trick was to break down the wall of silence before the scheduled conference, and the UPI did just that when a new football coach was to be announced at Rice University.

The Houston UPI bureau called around the country to the candidates who had been mentioned as candidates. No luck. The only one left was the assistant coach at Rice, and a call went out to his home. The maid answered. No, the coach wasn't in. Nor his wife.

"Is she going to go to the news conference this afternoon?" the UPI reporter asked.

"Yes, sir. She wouldn't miss that for the world," the maid answered.

In seconds, the bureau put out a story about the assistant coach's new job.

You might say that was risky. But would the assistant coach's wife be going to a news conference to hear someone else named coach?

Sending a Bulletin   Sometimes, getting the news out is a problem. During the Truman–Dewey presidential campaign when the candidates toured the country by train, there were long stretches without a stop, which meant the reporters could not get out to phone in their stories.

Merriman Smith, the United Press White House reporter, was aboard the Dewey train during a stop in St. Louis when the candidate was pelted with eggs, a far better story than the routine political talks Dewey had been giving.

But the train quickly pulled out of the station and there was no scheduled stop for four hours. The reporters complained, to no avail. (Remember, this was long ago, 1948, and there were no cellular phones then.) They would miss all the afternoon newspapers.

Smith didn't join in the complaining. He sat down and with paper and pencil began to jot down bulletins, which he rolled up and wrapped in $5 bills with a "Note to finder." The note instructed the finder to call the UPI collect and read the bulletin.

Every time the train passed a station, Smith would toss out one of his packets. Then he would return to the rest of the reporters and join in on the grousing.

Smith's packets did the trick. The United Press had a four-hour beat.

Courage

Some might say that journalists are courageous in pursuit of the news, although many reporters would shrug off this description. It was obviously courageous for Ellen Whitford of *The Norfolk Virginian-Pilot* to go into an abortion clinic and allow herself to be examined and prepared for an abortion. Whitford wanted to prove what she had learned secondhand, that abortions were being performed on women who were not pregnant.

Reporters and photographers have died covering wars and disasters. Mark Kellogg, an AP correspondent, fell while riding with Custer and the 7th Cavalry at Little Big Horn in 1876. Ernie Pyle, the legendary war corespondent, was shot by a sniper in the closing days of World War II.

Every journalist is familiar with harassment. A reporter needs a dash of courage and confidence to refuse the official version and to ask questions that seem to challenge an official's probity. Reporters question authority, and those in command dislike being questioned.

The reporter needs courage to face facts, especially those that contradict his or her beliefs.

Of course, information gatherers, as reporters are sometimes described, have other qualities. We can detect some of these by watching some information gatherers at work.

At "Nightline"

Let's drop in on Tom Bettag, the executive producer of "Nightline." It's 10 a.m. in Washington, D.C., and Bettag is making a conference call to the ABC News bureau chiefs around the world. The program won't air until 11:35 p.m., more than 13 hours later, but Bettag has been thinking about the news for that day from the moment he awoke.

In Moscow, Russia's president has been taken to the hospital with a serious heart condition. In Burma, Aung San Suu Kyi, the champion of the country's democratic movement, who had been under house arrest for six years, was suddenly released. Bettag asks his correspondents what these developments mean.

He takes a breather from the task of laying out the day's news agenda. "Our job is to illuminate the major issues of our time," he tells a visitor. He makes no apologies for the seriousness of the "Nightline" program. "People turn on 'Nightline' to find out if there's something they need to know, if there's something people are going to be talking about in the morning.

"They aren't interested in being entertained. 'Nightline' has its largest audience when there is real news." The program's high ratings attest to the public's appetite for serious news.

A Metro Daily

We are on West 33rd Street in New York City in the newsroom of the *Daily News* and the phone rings. An assistant city editor takes the call and turns to the city editor.

"This fellow says the governor's daughter is going to get a marriage license at 2:30. Maybe we ought to get a picture," he suggests.

The city editor is not enthusiastic.

"We had her announcement a few weeks ago," he says. But he decides they may as well take it. Nothing better may turn up for inside pages. (Nothing does, and the picture will run on page 3.)

A courthouse reporter calls about a suit he thinks will make a good story. A 21-year-old woman on welfare has won $925,000 from a car-rental company. The reporter is given the go-ahead and is told to slug the story "Suit." (The slug is important, for this is the story's identifying mark.) Usually, the desk will tell a reporter how long the piece should run, but the city editor knows that his courthouse man, an experienced reporter, will hold it to 450 to 500 words.

"Slay"

Early in the day, the city desk has made up a schedule of stories the local staff would work on. (See the next page.) One of these, a murder, had broken the day before in the *New York Post*. The *Post* story began:

A 22-year-old American Airlines employee was slain by one of three holdup men in her Bronx apartment early today while her husband, bound hand and foot, lay helplessly in another room.

A *News* reporter in the Bronx is told to dig into the story, which is slugged "Slay." The reporter learns that the victim was a flight attendant, which gives the slaying what journalists describe as "class." The death of someone with a glamorous or out-of-the-ordinary job is assumed to perk up reader interest.

The *News* picks up a few other facts the *Post* did not have. The police report that the gunmen had asked for $25,000 and that the woman was slain with a shot from a pistol that was placed against her head. The rewriteman double-checks the names, and he learns that the victim's name was Gwendolyn Clarke, not Gwendolin Clark. Also, she was 27, not 22.

Mulligan's Theory   The rewriteman, Arthur Mulligan, asks if there are any pictures of the victim. There is nothing available yet, he is told.

"I have a theory on this one," he says. A copy editor looks up. "Take it easy," she tells Mulligan. "Remember your theory on the Rainslayer?" (After three holdup victims were murdered during nighttime rainstorms several months before, Mulligan had theorized the killer was the "Roving Rainstorm Robber," who preyed on people when their heads were bent under umbrellas. Nope.)

CAREY–Names Joes Hynes and Morris Abrams as special
nursing home prosecutor and Moreland Commissioner,
respectively.

PROFILES–of Hynes and Abrams.

NURSE–Nearly half of the 175 nursing homes in city could face
cutoff of federal funds, according to list made available to
us.

BERGMAN–files libel suit against Times, Stein et al for
$1 million.

SLAY–Robbers invade home, slay wife, bind hubby and escape
with car.

SUIT–Good reader on young woman, blinded and severely hurt
in car crash in France, living off welfare's $154 Month,
wins $925,000.

JOBS–On deadline, city submits proposal for $46.7M in fed job
funds.

UN–Ralph Bunche Institute report finds incompetence,
cronyism and nepotism in the folks who work for our
world body.

ABORT–Morgy OK's abortion for woman in her 28th week,
2 weeks late.

AUDIT–Levitt report says city isn't even close to coping with
fraud in the welfare department, citing huge jump in
fraudulent checks.

CIVIL–Service News column.

BRIEFS–Etc.

Mulligan says, "My theory is that it was narcotics. Must be. Who has $25,000 sitting around the house? The guy has no job and drives a new Lincoln Continental. She'd just come in from a run, too."

It makes sense, the city editor agrees, and calls his Manhattan police headquarters man to check out the narcotics possibility.

It is 3:40 p.m. and "Slay" has not yet taken shape. The reporters have not called in. At the news conference, the city editor had suggested that "Slay" might be page 1 material, and the managing editor gave the story the green light. (Murders are given good play in the *News*. The day before, a knifeslaying in New Jersey was displayed on page one of the *News*. The New York Times—the *News'* morning competition—played the story on page 39.)

It is now 4 p.m.—an hour before the copy should be off the city desk— and the activity in the newsroom picks up. Reporters are writing faster, copy is moving to the various desks in greater volume, and the tension increases. Copy should be in the hands of the news editor by 5 p.m., but on big stories the paper can hold until 6 p.m. for the first edition.

Drug Connection   At 4:30 p.m., the police reporter in Manhattan headquarters calls in with additional information on "Slay." He reports that the narcotics bureau is looking into the possibility that drugs were involved. Mulligan has enough information to go to work on the story.

Ten minutes later, the picture editor relays information from the police radio, which has been crackling with calls all day. "The police think they've spotted a suspect in that bank holdup where the cop was killed," he says. "They're stopping the subways around 42nd Street and Eighth Avenue."

This could be a good story—a chase for a cop killer through the New York subway system during the rush hour. But the desk takes the information calmly. Rather than send someone out, an editor calls the Manhattan police reporter—a busy man today—and asks him to pinpoint the search area. He had already started to do so.

At 4:58, Mulligan finished 500 words of "Slay." The city editor changes a couple of words, deletes others. It now reads:

> Bronx homicide police were puzzled yesterday by circumstances surrounding the murder of a 27-year-old American Airlines flight attendant who was shot in the head by one of three men who burst in on her and her husband shortly after midnight in the couple's apartment.

After describing the demands of the men and the details of the slaying, giving the address of the victim and explaining how the men got away, the story refers to "speculation by the police that the shooting involved narcotics. . . ."

At 5:01, the police radio carries the information that a man has been picked up in the subway for questioning. Later, he is released. No one is ruffled by the collapse of the story about the search for a cop killer in the darkened subway tunnels.

At 5:07, more of "Slay" is on the desk. At 5:15, the Manhattan police reporter calls Mulligan and says that the police think there may be a link between the murder of the flight attendant and the slaying of two men whose bodies were discovered in the Bronx. One of the victims was stuffed into a steamer trunk and the other was put into a wooden box. An insert is written for "Slay," and a short piece that had been written about the bodies and slugged "Trunk," is killed.

Folo Story   The next day, a general assignment reporter, Daniel O'Grady, is assigned to check out the narcotics angle. Police confirm Mulligan's theory about narcotics, and the lead in Sunday's newspaper reads:

> A gangland war for control of the lucrative narcotics trade in Harlem and the Bronx reportedly has left six dead in the last two months, including an American Airlines flight attendant who, police believe, may have smuggled drugs from the Caribbean for one faction of the mob.

John Carl D'Annabile, *Times Union*

**Downed,
But Still Feisty**

Stella Jabonaski makes her point emphatically to reporter Cailin Brown, who covers the Christmas fund drive for the *Times Union.* The drive is devoted to aiding the elderly needy in the Albany, N.Y., area. During the holiday season, Brown profiles 25 men and women for front-page stories of courage and perseverance despite debilitating physical conditions and too often forgetful families. Brown's stories have led to a steady increase in donations to the Christmas fund.

Christmas Fund

When Cailin Brown took over the Christmas Fund stories for the *Times Union* in Albany, N.Y., the newspaper had been running brief pieces taken from material submitted by local social service agencies. Fictitious names were used for the people briefly profiled. The reporters handling the Fund drive never interviewed those whose stories they told.

Brown decided to change everything. She believed that the "same tenets of journalism" that work for other stories should be applied to the fund-raising drive.

"After countless meetings and some heated disagreements, the newspaper, social service workers and I came to terms on my plan," she says. She would interview the elderly the newspaper profiled and the paper would run their photographs. The pictures, Brown says, "made sense to me because newspaper readers are drawn to illustrated stories."

The stories, which appear on page 1 of the *Times Union,* are tales of courage and despair, devotion and loneliness. Brown, a general assignment reporter during the year, says that the people she interviews "are usually forgotten by their families, something unthinkable to our readers.

"I have covered my share of crime, both violent and white collar. I have written the story of a vibrant 3-year-old waiting for the death knell of leukemia. Yet never in 13 years as a reporter have I been so moved by the human condition as I have been listening to these people talk about getting old."

A Press Release That Needs Backgrounding

In the newsroom of a daily newspaper in Maryland, the editor calls the education reporter over to his desk. "Dick, here's something pretty important. Overnight took these notes from a fellow who said he is the publicity chairman of an organization called the Black Parents Association. See if the outfit amounts to anything and, if it does, let's have some comments. Write it down the middle. It's a touchy issue."

The notes read as follows:

The association has just sent a complaint to the state board of education. We are disturbed by the use of certain books our children are being given in the city's schools and school libraries.

Some of this reading gives the children—black or white—a stereotyped view of minority people. At a time when we are in danger of becoming two societies, every effort must be made to understand each other. Some of the books our children are being asked to read do not accomplish this. They portray black people as ignorant, lacking in culture, childlike, sexually loose, etc.

We are asking that certain books be removed from the library and the classroom—Huck Finn, Manchild in the Promised Land and Down These Mean Streets. We intend to add to the list.

"The picture of Jim in the Twain book is that of the stereotyped black man of slave days," says James Alberts, association president. "Impressionable children are led to think of black people as senseless, head-scratching, comic figures. We object to that portrayal of Nigger Jim."

Alberts said that in 1957 the Finn book was banned from elementary and junior high schools in New York City by the city board at the request of the NAACP. Later, he said, black students at Brandeis University picketed a school near the university that used the book. In recent years, some cities have removed the book from reading lists. In Waukegan, Ill., it was removed on the ground that it was offensive to blacks. Dr. John H. Wallace, an educator on the Chicago School Board, calls it "the most grotesque example of racist trash ever written."

"If it is to be read, it should be read at home under the direction of their parents," Alberts said.

The group met in Freedom Hall of the Mt. Zion Baptist Church tonight.

Background Check

Dick checks his newspaper's morgue (library) to see if there are any stories about the association. He finds that the association was formed in 1955, one year after the U.S. Supreme Court ruling on school desegregation, and has been active in local school affairs.

He telephones the president of the association to ask if any particular incident provoked the action. The president tells him a parent brought up the issue at a meeting last month. Dick asks for the name of the parent, but the president has forgotten it.

For reaction from the schools, he looks up the telephone numbers of the city school superintendent, some high school principals and the head of the board of education. He calls for their comments. If he has time, he thinks he will try to go over to a high school. It would be appropriate to interview black students, he decides. But that may have to wait for a folo (follow-up story).

He rereads the release. Many readers will know *Huckleberry Finn,* but what about the other books? He will have to find out something about them.

Balance He remembers that, when he took a course in American literature, one of his textbooks described *Huckleberry Finn* as the greatest of all American novels. Maybe he will work that in to give the story some balance. He read the book for the course and remembers Jim as a man of dignity. But his reactions certainly are not those a black high school student might have, he concedes. Yes, he will have to talk to students and to their parents as well. He also will have to guard against putting his opinions into the story.

Dick looks under *Twain* in the encyclopedia and, to his surprise, he finds that the book is properly titled, *The Adventures of Huckleberry Finn.* He had better check the other titles.

Censored Books. "Cumulative findings since 1982 show that the most frequently attacked books are American classics. The top three targets since we began our monitoring have been John Steinbeck's *Of Mice and Men,* J.D. Salinger's *The Catcher in the Rye* and Mark Twain's *The Adventures of Huckleberry Finn.*"
—People for the American Way, a constitutional liberties group.

Censored Writers

Dick admits to himself he does not like what the association is doing. It is too close to censorship, he thinks. After all, Mark Twain is a great writer. And people are always objecting that some authors are dangerous reading for the young—Hemingway, Salinger, Vonnegut, Steinbeck. But Mark Twain?

Can a great writer be prejudiced? There's a running debate about Shakespeare's *The Merchant of Venice* and Dickens' *Oliver Twist.* He recalls reading a wire story from a city in Canada about some parents asking that *The Merchant of Venice* be restricted to high school seniors on the ground that younger students are vulnerable to the anti-Semitic stereotypes in the play.

He also recalls reading that, when Twain was a young reporter in San Francisco, he wrote an account of an attack by a gang of young whites on a Chinese man. Several policemen stood by and watched, Twain had written. Twain's story, a straightforward account of the incident, never ran in the newspaper. Even so, it's possible Twain could have been a racist by today's definition.

Dick has a vague recollection of reading a story about Twain helping a black student at Yale. Better look into that, too. He will need time to check out all these recollections, he decides. He will not trust his memory.

Also, he will need to look into the whole issue of book censorship, which has been in the news for some time. He knows that battles are being waged across the country over appropriate material for the school curriculum. He will have to use a database for a lot of background material.

Database Check

Dick decides to consult the online information service his newspaper uses, Lexis®-Nexis®, to find material about Twain and about book censorship. A colleague in the newsroom has told Dick that she recalls reading about Twain's black butler as the inspiration for the character of Jim, the runaway slave in *Huckleberry Finn*.

He locates a 1994 story datelined Hartford that describes Twain's relationship with George Griffin, Twain's butler for 18 years. The home in which Twain and Griffin lived in Hartford has been made into a museum, the Mark Twain Memorial. Museum officials say Griffin, who Twain said came "one day to wash the windows and stayed for 18 years," became Twain's close friend, confidant, adviser on legal and literary matters and playmate for Twain's children.

Twain wrote of Griffin as "shrewd, wise, polite, always good-natured, cheerful to gaiety, honest, religious, a cautious truth-speaker, devoted friend to the family," the story relates. The story also contains the reaction Twain and Griffin experienced when they walked into the Century Building in New York:

> A white man and a negro walking together was a new spectacle to them. The glance embarrassed George but not me, for the companionship was proper; in some ways, he was my equal, in some others my superior; and besides deep down in my interior I know that the difference between any two of those poor, transient things called beings was but microscopic, trivial, a mere difference between worms.

Dick also notes that the story includes a comment about *Huckleberry Finn* by the actor Hal Holbrook, who has portrayed Twain on stage for more than 30 years. Holbrook says that many people misread *Huckleberry Finn* as racist, but that it actually satirizes prejudice.

Book Censorship

In Dick's search, dozens of articles come up on the screen. As he scans the summaries, he sees that his story is national as well as local. Many communities are facing demands by parents and religious groups to remove books from libraries and school reading lists.

He tells his editor that making a full check will take time. No great rush, his editor tells him. "Just make sure to get all sides." They agree he will write a story for the next day's newspaper on the association's complaint and then do an extensive takeout as soon as he can gather background and conduct interviews, possibly for this Sunday's paper.

He sets to work on the story before him. He wants to include as much background as possible in this first piece rather than simply rewrite the organization's press release.

Mark Twain's Generosity

Dick locates a *New York Times* story about the discovery of a letter that Twain wrote in 1865 to the dean of Yale Law School. In it, Twain offered to provide financial help to one of the school's first black students.

"I do not believe I would very cheerfully help a white student who would ask benevolence of a stranger," Twain wrote, "but I do not feel so bad about the other color. We have ground the manhood out of them, & the shame is ours, not theirs; & we should pay for it." Twain subsidized the student until he graduated in 1867.

Another story quotes the American Library Association's finding that more than a thousand attempts had been made to ban or restrict book usage in public schools in the 1980s. School book censors were even more active in the 1990s. Dick reads a story that reports that in the past year there were 475 incidents in 44 states in which attacks were made on schools and libraries because of the materials in their classrooms, on their reading lists and on their shelves.

The censors, he learns, were successful 41 percent of the time in removing or restricting the materials they challenged.

Book Banning Unconstitutional

He finds a U.S. Supreme Court decision in a Long Island, N.Y., book banning. The Court upheld an appeal against book banning. Dick calls up the story from the database. The school board of the Island Trees Union Free School District had removed nine books from the shelves of junior and senior high schools on the grounds they were "anti-American, anti-Christian, anti-Semitic and just plain filthy." *Down These Mean Streets* was one of the banned books.

Writing the Story

He has an hour before his first deadline and decides he had better start writing:

> A local school group, the Black Parents Association, has asked the city school system to remove three books from high school libraries because they allegedly present a stereotyped view of blacks.

Too long, he thinks. Dull. Maybe he should try a more dramatic lead:

> Huckleberry Finn should be banned from high school libraries, a local black parents organization urged today.

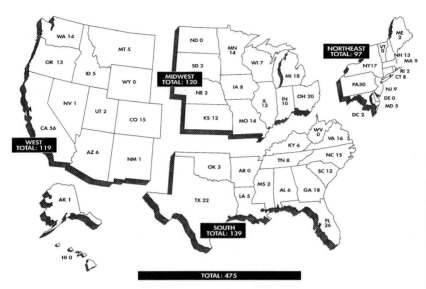

ATTACKS ON THE FREEDOM TO LEARN

REGIONAL AND STATE BREAKDOWN

WA 14 · MT 5 · ND 0 · MN 14 · NORTHEAST TOTAL: 97 · ME 2 · VT 0 · NH 13 · MA 9 · NY 17 · RI 2 · CT 8 · OR 13 · ID 5 · WY 0 · SD 2 · WI 7 · MI 18 · MIDWEST TOTAL: 120 · IA 8 · NE 2 · IL 13 · IN 10 · OH 20 · PA 30 · NJ 9 · DE 0 · MD 5 · NV 1 · UT 2 · CO 15 · KS 12 · MO 14 · DC 2 · CA 56 · WEST TOTAL: 119 · AZ 6 · NM 1 · WV 0 · VA 16 · KY 6 · NC 15 · OK 3 · AR 0 · TN 8 · SC 12 · MS 2 · AL 6 · GA 18 · AK 1 · TX 22 · LA 5 · SOUTH TOTAL: 139 · FL 26 · HI 0

TOTAL: 475

Censorship Attempts

Among the information Dick gathers is this map released by People for the American Way, an organization that checks on censorship. The "attacks" include censorship of school books, library books and art works. The organization ranks California, Pennsylvania, Florida, Texas and Ohio, in that order, as having the most frequent attempts at censorship. Dick notes the organization's website, www.pfaw.org. He decides he will check further to see what the organization has on record about his state.

Too sensational for this kind of story, he decides, and discards this lead. Another couple of tries, and he hits on something he likes:

A local black parents organization has charged that the city school system uses books that debase blacks and other minorities.

The organization, the Black Parents Association, asked that the State Board of Education order three books removed from Freeport School libraries and classrooms. The group charged that the books present a "stereotyped view of minority people."

The books are "The Adventures of Huckleberry Finn" by Mark Twain, "Manchild in the Promised Land" by Claude Brown and "Down These Mean Streets" by Piri Thomas.

The association, which took the action at a meeting last night in the Mt. Zion Baptist Church, said it intends to add other books to the three it named.

Dick realizes he will need to put the reaction of educators up high in his story and that he must quote extensively from the association statement so that readers have the full flavor of the group's anger.

"Too bad," he says to himself, "we didn't have a reporter there." Then he would have something to work with—the sense of outrage, rebuttals. He puts aside the luxury of speculation and settles down to more writing.

Interviewing Students

After he has written his story, Dick decides to drive to a luncheonette near the high school where students hang out. He sits at the counter and orders a pizza and a soft drink. Around him, students are talking about a basketball game. Gradually, Dick eases into the conversation. He remarks that the team will have its work cut out for it next week. The students agree.

In a short time, he is chatting easily with three boys. He slowly turns the conversation from sports to school work and asks them about the books they read for English classes. He asks if any one has been assigned *Huckleberry Finn.* One student says he has read the book on his own.

Dick decides that this is the time to identify himself. He asks the student for his reaction to the book and then tells him about the association's action. One of the boys calls over some other students in a booth nearby, and soon several students, both black and white, are chatting with Dick. He lets them talk. He does not take out his notebook. He wants them to speak freely. He trusts his memory for this part of the discussion.

One student says, "Maybe there are some bad things in those books. But maybe censorship is worse." The others agree. Dick takes out his pad.

"That's interesting," he says. "Mind if I jot that down here?"

They go on talking, and Dick quickly writes down what he has stored in his memory as he tries to keep up with the running conversation.

He asks some students for their names. He would like to use them in his piece, he says. He knows that readers distrust the vague attribution to "a student."

Back in the newsroom, Dick tells his editor about his chat with the students. The editor suggests Dick use the material as the basis for his Sunday interpretative piece. He and Dick discuss other people to interview.

"Maybe you'd better talk to some of the people over at the university," the editor suggests. "They can tell us about efforts to condemn or censor important works."

Other Stories

We will be looking at other reporters as they cover stories for their newspapers, magazines and broadcast stations. We will follow Carolyn Tuft of *The Belleville* (Mo.) *News-Democrat* as she reveals the existence of a special police squad whose job it was to harass black motorists to keep them out of the city's affluent west end.

We will go along with Sam Roe of *The Blade* in Toledo as he gathers material for his series on single-parent families. One out of every two babies born in Toledo, he learns, is born to a single mother.

By watching a TV newswriter put together his evening newscast, we will learn something about the art of rewriting the AP news wire for broadcast.

We will see how journalists do their twofold job of describing events—covering breaking news—and developing their own stories, which we call enterprising.

Developing Story Ideas

As you familiarize yourself with the ways in which journalists work, and as you develop an interest in the subjects that journalists cover, ideas for stories will begin to flow. In fact, your only problem will be how to find time to handle all the ideas you come up with along with covering breaking news events.

A Useful Tactic

One tactic some journalists use to develop story ideas is to remember that an event has a cause and a consequence. By going back to causes and ahead to consequences, we produce interesting and newsworthy ideas.

Cause: Take one of the stories we looked at in this chapter, the garage fire. The youngsters filled the lawn mower with gasoline in a closed area. Usually, such machines have warnings about filling their fuel tanks. Did the mower? Do other such home-use machines? Or, more generally, how about making a survey of home accidents, fires and other mishaps for the last six months or year? The home is said to be the most dangerous place for humans, not the highways or sports fields. Now that we've started thinking about this, what's the most dangerous *room* in the home? Bathroom? Kitchen? Or adjoining rooms—garage, workroom?

Consequence: Look at the Christmas fire that took four lives. It suggests that smoke alarms could have saved those four. Are smoke alarms a good idea to require for all households? Is anyone thinking of introducing such an ordinance for the city? Interview the chief of the fire department, city council members, insurance firms.

We might list under *consequence* the journalist's conscience. That is, journalists make news out of situations and events they find intolerable, that need the spotlight of public attention so that remedies can be put in place. We've seen Heidi Evans and Cammy Wilson make journalism out of situations they considered abusive, immoral. Major changes in society have resulted from the focus of media attention on such subjects as domestic abuse, sexual harassment, the treatment of gays and lesbians, racism and environmental degradation.

Read, Look and Listen

Journalists develop story ideas by being alert to what interests people as well as by consulting their consciences. Go where people congregate—a lunch counter, the laundromat, a hotel lobby. Listen in. Read the popular magazines . . . and the not so popular.

An article in a sociology journal says that more and more young women, girls really, are taking diet pills. This conclusion is from a study made by several college sociologists. It has the makings of a good local story. The enterprising reporter will talk to physicians, school counselors, parents and, of course, the young women themselves.

Advertisements are a good source of story ideas. What's the latest fashion in men's shoes and youth apparel? Has the price of a foodstuff suddenly gone up? Is there some new electronic game that has captured the youth market?

There is no end to the ideas available to the alert and the inquisitive, which takes us back to our description of the journalist. Fully functioning journalists know how to handle breaking news stories and the assignments their editors make. They also are fountains of story ideas that will interest and entertain their readers and viewers.

Summing Up

Journalists live in a world of confusion and complexity. Nevertheless, they manage through enterprise, wit, energy and intelligence to move close to the truth of the event and to shape their understanding into language and a form that can be understood by all. The task ahead of us in this book is to help you develop the journalist's craft and to find a personal credo to work by. A reporter who worked her way from small newspapers in New Mexico, Pennsylvania and New Jersey to the AP and then to *The New York Times* says her motto is "Keep cool but care." This philosophy seems to describe the reporters we will be following in the rest of this book.

Journalists make mistakes. It is important to learn from mistakes and not to be discouraged. Although mistakes can be embarrassing and humiliating, they are unavoidable. Look at the Corrections box on page two of any issue of *The New York Times,* which is staffed by some of the best journalists in the business. Day after day, two to five admissions of error are published—wrong names, wrong addresses, wrong figures. Don't live in fear of making a mistake; that will cut down your range. Do the best you can. That's all anyone can ask of you.

Further Reading

At the end of each chapter, suggested supplementary reading is listed. The listed books have been recommended by journalists and by authorities in the fields discussed in the chapter.

This list includes, for example, the autobiography of a major figure in American journalism, Lincoln Steffens. It also includes Vincent Sheean's recollections of his life as a foreign correspondent, a book that persuaded many young men and women that journalism is for them. Also listed is a biography of Edward R. Murrow, the eminent broadcast journalist, and a study of the country's most influential newspaper, *The New York Times.* One book describes the women journalists who broke through barriers at the *Times.* Finally, no journalism bibliography would be complete without the book that describes how two young reporters, Bob Woodward and Carl Bernstein, toppled a president.

Alabiso, Vincent, Kelly Smith Tunney and Chuck Zoeller, eds. *Flash! The Associated Press Covers the World.* New York: Abrams, 1998.

Bogart, Leo. *Commercial Culture: The Media System and the Public Interest.* New York: Oxford University Press, 1995.

Frankel, Max. *The Times of My Life and My Life with The Times.* New York: Random House, 1999.

Kendrick, Alexander. *Prime Time: The Life of Edward Murrow.* Boston: Little, Brown, 1969.

Kroeger, Brooke. *Nellie Bly: Daredevil, Reporter, Feminist.* New York: Times Books, 1994.

Robertson, Nan. *The Girls in the Balcony: Women, Men, and The New York Times.* New York: Random House, 1992.

Sheean, Vincent. *Personal History.* Boston: Houghton Mifflin, 1969.

Steffens, Lincoln. *The Autobiography of Lincoln Steffens.* New York: Harcourt Brace, 1931.

Talese, Gay. *The Kingdom and the Power.* New York: World Publishing, 1969.

Waldron, Ann. *Hodding Carter: The Reconstruction of a Racist.* Chapel Hill, N.C.: Algonquin Books of Chapel Hill, 1993.

Woodward, Bob, and Carl Bernstein. *All the President's Men.* New York: Simon & Schuster, 1974.

PART TWO: The Basics

2 Components of the Story

Ken Klotzbach, *Argus Leader*

Reporters look for the human dimension of the event.

Preview

News stories must be:

• **Accurate.** All information is verified before it is used.

• **Properly attributed.** The reporter identifies his or her sources of information.

• **Balanced and fair.** All sides in a controversy are presented.

• **Objective.** The news writer does not inject his or her feelings or opinions.

• **Brief and focused.** The news story gets to the point quickly and keeps to the point.

• **Well-written.** Stories are clear, direct, interesting.

Direct observation is the surest way to obtain accurate information. With secondhand and thirdhand accounts, the reporter tries to verify the material by seeking out documents and records. When only human sources are available for verification, reporters check the source's reliability.

If we were to generalize from the work of the reporters we have been watching, we might conclude that the reporter:

1. Attempts to report accurately the truth or reality of the event through:
   A. Direct observation.
   B. The use of (a) authoritative, knowledgeable and reliable human sources and (b) relevant and reliable physical sources.
2. Tries to write an interesting, timely and clearly written story. Quotations, anecdotes, examples and human interest enliven the story.

If journalism needs rules, these would be the starting points.

Underlying and directing the application of these rules or guidelines is the reporter's imperative: The story must be accurate. Whether news story or feature, conveyer of fact or entertainment, accuracy is essential.

Accuracy

The highest praise A. J. Liebling, a master reporter for newspapers and *The New Yorker* magazine, could pay a colleague was, "He is a careful reporter," by which Liebling meant that the reporter took great care to be accurate. Although the reporter often works under severe space and time limitations, he or she makes every effort to check the accuracy of information through verification and documentation.

Joseph Pulitzer, a towering figure in U.S. journalism, had a cardinal rule for his staff: "Accuracy, accuracy, accuracy." There may be arguments in newsrooms about writing style, about the best way to interview a reluctant source, but there is no debate about errors. A journalist may be tolerated if his or her writing does not sparkle, but reporters won't last the week if they are error-prone.

When the news editor of *The New York Times* spotted a line in a story that described the Canadian city of Sudbury as a "suburb of Toronto," he checked an atlas. Sudbury, he found, is 250 miles north of Toronto. The reporter blamed the source, an FBI agent, but the editor found that to be no excuse. "It should have been second nature to check," he said.

Check and Check Again

Mistakes occur when the writer fails to check an assumption or a source's assertion:

The headline writer put the famous mountain peak El Capitan in Yellowstone National Park.

In one story, *The New York Times* writer wrote of "the University of Wisconsin at Ann Arbor" and Los Alamos in "the desert sands of New Mexico."

A caption in a *Times* story about a documentary film refers to the "Ida P. Wells housing project in Chicago."

In another *Times* story, a westward train makes several stops "before arriving in Santa Fe." The writer also describes Santa Fe as being "in New Mexico's desert."

The caption in a midwestern newspaper refers to 22 women in the Washington State Senate. The picture shows 23 women.

Newsweek recommends parents let their 5-month-olds feed themselves raw carrot sticks and zweiback.

No, El Capitan isn't where the headline put it, but west in Yosemite National Park. And we all know where the University of Wisconsin is located. It's Ida **B.** Wells. No trains stop in Santa Fe, which is hardly in the desert being some 7,000 feet high, as is Los Alamos. As for *Newsweek*'s recommendation for feeding children, the magazine had to call back several hundred thousand copies of the issue. Its recommendation of carrots and zweiback could cause 5-month-olds to choke.

Costly Difference. The recipe in *Gourmet* magazine called for a dash of wintergreen oil. While the magazine was on the press, someone discovered that wintergreen *extract* was called for. Wintergreen *oil* is poisonous. Oops. The magazine printed the proper ingredients on a sticker and put it on the 750,000 copies of the magazine.

Corrections

When mistakes are made, corrections follow so that the record is accurate. Here's a correction that appeared in a newspaper whose name we will generously not mention:

CORRECTION

In last week's edition of the Michigan Chronicle, the story "Fauntroy stirs breakfast crowd," Congressman Walter Fauntroy's grandmother was misidentified. The matriarch was known to Fauntroy family members as "Big Ma," not "Big Mouth" as reported.

Language, Too

Accuracy also applies to the use of language. Words are chosen carefully to match the situation, event or individual. The writer who settles for the imprecise rather than the exact word or words lives dangerously, teetering on the brink of being misunderstood or misleading readers and listeners.

Precision   We don't say she was "unusually tall." We write she was "an inch over six feet tall." No matter how concise our broadcast news item is, we don't write that "the ship damaged the pier." We write, "the tanker (freighter, battleship, ferry) damaged the pier."

We can be foolishly precise. The reporter wrote that "93 percent of the 41 stores" sold the mercury capsules. Who would argue that the percentage isn't accurate? You would if you took 93 percent of 41. If you did you would come up with 38.13. And, pray tell, what's .13 of a store? Be exact: It was 38 of the 41 stores that sold the capsules.

Hold It   Speed, the essential ingredient of much journalism, is accuracy's enemy. Checking—whether it involves calling another source or consulting the dictionary for the proper shade of a word's meaning—takes time. That extra 2 minutes, even 30 seconds, may mean the story won't make the 6 o'clock broadcast or the first edition. But check we must, even on the biggest stories that are the most competitive.

At 3:22 a.m., a note appeared on the AP news wire: Frank Sinatra was dead. A big story, all right, for Sinatra was probably the best-known singer of the last half of the 20th century. On the AP's general desk in New York, overnight editor Dave Zelio immediately checked the report. He called the Los Angeles bureau for confirmation, and in less than two minutes this moved over the wire:

```
            A0487 (03:23:43 EDT)
            abx
            bBC — APNewsAlert
+Frank+     +Sinatra dies of heart attack, publicist says.
```

In 90 seconds, a bulletin ran, and at 3:38 a.m., a 1,200-word story was moving to newspapers and broadcast stations.

Firsthand Observation

The reporter knows that a story based on the reporter's firsthand observation is superior in accuracy and reader interest to one based on secondhand information.

As Bertrand Russell, the British philosopher, advised students:

> Make the observation yourself. Aristotle could have avoided the mistake of thinking that women have fewer teeth than men by the simple device of asking Mrs. Aristotle to keep her mouth open while he counted. Thinking you know, when in fact you don't, is a fatal mistake to which we are all prone.

During the Vietnam War, a wire service reporter wrote a graphic account of a battle from a government press release, a secondhand account. Homer Bigart, one of the great war correspondents, was working for *The New York Times* and was appalled to find the young reporter's story on page 1 of the *Times*. Bigart had been to the front and knew the release made exaggerated claims.

Bigart took the reporter to the scene. "See," he told the reporter, "it isn't there."

Peter Arnett, another much-respected war reporter, says his motto is "to write only what I saw myself."

Despite the air of certainty in the tone of news stories, a close reading reveals that many are not based on the reporter's direct observation. The reporter rarely sees the burglar breaking in, the policy being drafted, the automobile hitting the telephone pole. The reporter obtains information about these events from authoritative sources such as documents and records (police files for the burglary and the accident) and from reliable individuals (policy makers and participants and witnesses).

News Filters

When the reporter bases his or her story on direct observation, the story is a firsthand account. But when the reporter is not on the scene and information is obtained from those who were present, the reporter's story is a secondhand account. It has been filtered through the source.

Some stories are based on accounts that have been filtered twice before reaching the reporter. For example, an official agency holds a meeting at which the participants are sworn to secrecy. The reporter learns that one of those attending the meeting described it to a member of his staff, who happens to be a good source of news for the reporter. The reporter manages to obtain the staff member's account of the executive's account of what occurred.

Two Types. "In Vietnam, it was said that there were two kinds of observers, those who heard about the war from others and those with muddy boots. I preferred the latter."
—Malcolm W. Browne, *Muddy Boots and Red Socks.*

Here are examples of stories based on direct observation and on secondary sources:

By Elaine Silvestrini and Sherry Figdore

Press Staff Writers

SHREWSBURY — About 250 anti-abortion demonstrators were arrested yesterday and charged with trespassing and violating a court order after they blocked the doors to the Planned Parenthood clinic for several hours.

The protesters, who prayed and sang as they were dragged and carried to police vans and a rented bus, were part of a new national group, called Operation Rescue, which has targeted abortion clinics. The group takes its name from a Bible passage in the Book of Proverbs: "Rescue those who are being drawn away to death."

WASHINGTON (UPI) — Two U.S. aircraft carrier battle groups left Italian ports Wednesday and steamed south toward the central Mediterranean for an expected third round of flight operations off Libya, U.S. officials said.

FBI agents have established that the Watergate bugging incident stemmed from a massive campaign of political spying and sabotage conducted on behalf of President Nixon's re-election and directed by officials of the White House and the Committee for the re-election of the President.

The activities, according to information in FBI and Department of Justice files, were aimed at all the major Democratic presidential contenders and—since 1971— represented a basic strategy of the Nixon re-election effort.

During their Watergate investigation federal agents established that hundreds of thousands of dollars in Nixon campaign contributions had been set aide to pay for an extensive undercover campaign aimed at discrediting individual and Democratic presidential candidates and disrupting their campaigns. . . .

—*The Washington Post*

Covering a Riot

Reporters want to be on the scene, to let the reader see the event through their eyes, hear the sounds of conflict through their ears. When Miami's black section erupted in violence following the police shooting of an unarmed motorcyclist, Will Lester of the Associated Press went to police headquarters to obtain police reaction.

He spotted a city commissioner leaving the headquarters. She told him she was on her way to Overtown, which had been torched by rioters. "Mind if a reporter comes along?" Lester asked. No, the commissioner replied, and with police permission they left the closed-off area. They rode in an unmarked car, through barricades, past police officers on every corner. When they sped down one darkened street, Lester said, "policemen at the end of the street ducked behind closed car doors and leveled pistols at our heads." They heard gunfire as they sped on. Flames leaped from shops. Snipers' bullets whizzed by.

The commissioner talked to a group of young people. "The police are too quick to use their guns," one told her. "The Cubans take our jobs." Lester jotted it down. He noted that, as the rioters spoke, they grew angrier. A rock flew into the street near them. Police officers leveled their rifles. The crowd grew ugly, and police fired tear gas to back people away from the street.

"One of the young men standing by the street gave me a look of desperation," Lester said. "You put it in the paper. Tell them how we feel," the man told Lester. Lester said he understood, but the young man countered, "You can't understand."

But Lester wrote his story, describing what he had seen and heard, hoping that his readers would understand.

Clinton and the Intern   The most dazzling display of secondhand and thirdhand journalism occurred during the grand jury investigation of possible perjury by President Clinton in his relationship with the White House intern Monica Lewinsky. It was, said a University of Virginia professor, a "feeding frenzy" with unsourced, poorly-sourced, judgmental and opinionated pieces passing for reporting. Because grand juries operate in secrecy, there was no first-hand reporting. But reporters, anxious not to be out-reported by the competition, grabbed at anything and everything that floated by.

"The picture that emerges," said the Committee of Concerned Journalists, "is of a news culture that is increasingly involved with disseminating information rather than gathering it."

We now turn to attribution, the sourcing of stories. To the public, proper attribution increases the credibility of the news story.

Attribution

The farther the reporter is from direct observation, the more concerned he or she is about the accuracy of the report. Accurate and comprehensive direct observation is difficult enough. After the information has been filtered once or twice, only the most foolhardy journalist would stake his or her reputation on the accuracy of the report. To make clear to the reader that secondhand and third-hand accounts are not based on the reporter's direct observation of the event, the reporter attributes the information about the event to a source.

Here are the first two paragraphs from a story in *The Detroit News:*

> For six minutes, a Detroit police operator listened on the telephone as 24 bullets were fired into the bodies of an East Side couple.
>
> But, according to the police, the civilian mistook the shots for "someone hammering or building something" and dispatched the call as a routine burglary.

The lead may give the reader the impression the reporter was at the phone operator's elbow. But the second paragraph attributes the information to the police.

How the News Is Filtered

Firsthand Account
The story is based on direct observation of the event by the reporter.

Secondhand Account
The story is based on the account passed on by a participant or witness.

Thirdhand Account
The story is based on information supplied by a source who was informed by a participant.

Attribution actually refers to two concepts:

1. **Statements** are attributed to the person making them.
2. **Information** about the events not witnessed by the reporter is usually attributed to the source of the information.

Here is a story that contains both types of attribution:

Doug Carroll, *The Norfolk Daily News*

(**1**) Mayor Stanley Kretchmer said yesterday the city probably could balance its budget this year and next without laying off any workers.

(**1**) The decision, he said, "depends on a number of factors — the passage of a new tax package, the cooperation of municipal labor unions, general prosperity that keeps revenues high."

(**2**) At a meeting last week, the mayor told department heads they should consider the possibility of layoffs of about 10 percent of their work force, according to city officials who attended the meeting.

(**2**) Police and fire department personnel would be exempt from the cuts, sources reported.

Attribute?

Not really necessary here. No member of *The Norfolk Daily News* staff was on hand when this stolen car plowed into a home at 3 a.m. But the evidence speaks for itself.

Generally, we attribute what we do not observe or know to be factual. Although the reporter may take the information from a police record, the document does not necessarily attest to the truth of the information, only that some source—the police, a victim, the suspect, a witness—said that such-and-such occurred. The reporter attributes the information to this source.

Some news organizations such as the AP demand rigid adherence to the following policy: Always attribute what you do not see unless it is common knowledge.

Let us examine three stories to see how this policy is carried out. Under each story is the speculation of an experienced reporter about the reasons attribution was or was not used. (Her direct quotes follow each story.)

YMCA

(**1**) NEW YORK AP — Dr. Jesse L. Steinfeld, former Surgeon General of the U.S. Public Health Service, has been appointed chairman of the National YMCA Health and Physical Education Advisory Council.

(**2**) Steinfeld is professor of medicine at the University of California at Irvine, Calif., and chief of medical services for the Veterans Hospital in Long Beach, Calif.

(**3**) The advisory council will play an important role in the setting of future directions of the Y's nationwide programs, national board chairman Stanley Enlund said today in announcing Steinfeld's appointment to the nonsalaried post.

(**1**) There is no need for attribution of the appointment because the action is obviously on the record.

(**2**) Steinfeld's background is taken from records and needs no attribution.

(**3**) The role of the council is an opinion offered by the chairman of the board and must be attributed to him.

Hotel Fire

(1) BRANFORD, Conn. AP — The Waverly Hotel, popular earlier in the century, was destroyed by a two-alarm fire today.

(2) The roof collapsed into the heart of the building. At daylight the burned-out hotel was still smouldering.

(3) Myrtle Braxton, 73, who lived alone in the massive three-story building, was reported in fair condition at Yale-New Haven Hospital suffering from smoke inhalation.

(4) Officials said the fire was reported by Mrs. Braxton at 3:41 a.m. They said it apparently started in the kitchen area where Mrs. Braxton was living after having closed off most of the rest of the building. She was living there without central heating or electricity, officials said.

(5) A neighbor said that a large number of antiques on the third floor were destroyed. Also lost was a huge ship's wheel from a sailing ship, a centerpiece in the dining room.

(6) The bank that holds the mortgage said the land and hotel were worth $40,000 to $50,000.

(1)(2) The condition of the hotel is a physical fact about which the reporter has no doubt.

(3) The attribution is implied as coming from the hospital.

(4) "Officials," presumably fire department officials, are cited as the authority because only they could have known this. In the second sentence, the cause is attributed. (Always attribute the cause of a fire.)

(5)(6) Attribution gives the information credibility.

CBC

(1) The Citizen's Budget Commission, a private taxpayer's organization, said today that the proposed city budget of $185 million is more than the city can afford.

(2) The budget was submitted two weeks ago. Mayor Sam Parnass described it as an austerity budget.

(3) The Commission said it concluded after studying the budget that "significant cuts can be made."

(4) The $185 million spending plan is up 12 percent from the current year.

(5) When he submitted the budget, Mayor Parnass said anticipated revenues would cover the increase. The Commission is supported by the city's business community.

(1) A charge, allegation or opinion is always attributed, usually at the beginning of the lead. Here, the Commission is immediately identified as the source of the allegation.

(2) Background need not be attributed because it is part of the record.

(3) Attribution to the source of the material.

(4) Background needing no attribution.

(5) Attribute the mayor's statement. (The last sentence is the reporter's attempt to give the reader the why of the Commission's opposition—it's a taxpayer's group that likes austerity budgets because it means lower taxes. Nice touch.)

"Remember," the editor cautioned, "attribution does not guarantee the accuracy or truth of the material. All it does is place responsibility for the material with a source.

"If it turns out the information is inaccurate, the publication or station isn't responsible for the misinformation. The source is.

"If you don't identify the source, the reader or listener is going to assume that we stand behind the statements because we know they are true."

Types of Attribution

When the source of information for a story says nothing about being quoted, the reporter can presume that the information is on the record, that the source can be named.

A source may ask to go on background, usually so that the source can provide the reporter with information that will clarify an event or situation. The source cannot be named but may be described as a "city hall official" or a "state legislator" or by some other general term. To some sources, *background* means no direct quotes; others permit direct quotes. The reporter must be clear about the terms of the agreement with the source.

Sometimes, a source asks to go off the record, and it is up to the reporter to decide whether to accept information on this basis.

Some reporters refuse to accept material if there is a condition that it may not be used in any form. They may bargain with the source, asking if they can go to another source to obtain confirmation. Or they may ask if the material can be used without using the source's name.

Caution: Many editors refuse to accept copy that contains charges or accusations with no named source. They will not accept attribution to "an official in city hall," "a company spokesperson."

Background and off-the-record information pose problems for conscientious reporters because they know that backgrounders can be used to float *trial balloons*. These stories are designed by the source to test public reaction without subjecting the source to responsibility for the material. Reporters, eager to obtain news of importance and sometimes motivated by the desire for exclusives, may become the conduits for misleading or self-serving information.

When a reporter attributes assertions to a source, the reader can assess the accuracy and truth of the information on the basis of the general reliability of the source and his or her stake in the information.

The lesson for reporters is clear: Avoid commitments not to use names of sources.

Anonymous Sources

The reporter's job is to put sources on record, by name. Readers and listeners trust such a report. "When we write 'sources say,' they're convinced we're making it up," writes David Shaw, media critic of the *Los Angeles Times*.

Some publications and stations insist that all material be attributed to a named source, but others will use nonattributed information when the reporter is sure the material is reliable. In these cases, the editor usually wants to know the name of the source.

Four Types

On the Record: All statements are directly quotable and attributable, by name and title, to the person who is making the statement.

On Background: All statements are directly quotable, but they cannot be attributed by name or specific title to the person commenting. The type of attribution to be used should be spelled out in advance: "A White House official," "an Administration spokesman."

On Deep Background: Anything that is said in the interview is usable but not in direct quotation and not for attribution. The reporter writes it on his or her own.

Off the Record: Information is for the reporter's knowledge only and is not to be printed or made public in any way. The information also is not to be taken to another source in hopes of getting official confirmation.

Special care must be exercised when an anonymous source makes a charge of wrongdoing. *The New York Times* tells its staff:

> We do not want to let unidentified sources (like "law enforcement officials") use us to circulate charges against identifiable people when they provide no named complainants or other verifiable evidence.

Here is the policy of the Associated Press:

> We do not routinely accede to requests for anonymity. We want information on the record. When a news source insists that he or she not be identified by name, we say so. If we accept the condition of anonymity, we keep our word. But within the rule set by the newsmaker, we do everything possible to tell readers the source's connections, motivations and viewpoints.

Warning

Attributing secondhand and thirdhand accounts to their sources does not absolve reporters of responsibility for libelous statements in their stories. A reporter for a Florida newspaper reported that a county employee smoked marijuana, and the worker brought suit. "The reporter's own testimony indicated she had relied on second- and thirdhand accounts when writing the story," *Editor & Publisher* reported. A jury awarded the employee $70,000. (See Chapter 25 for further discussion of libel.)

Ask for Proof Journalists sometimes go astray when they rely on human sources and neglect to ask for proof of assertions the sources make. Records, documents, reports are more reliable than a source's version of them. But even a physical source can be misleading unless it is carefully examined.

A cornerstone of a journalist's allegation about Hillary Clinton's honesty in the Whitewater scenario was that she had vastly overstated the value of the Clintons' real estate holdings in a loan application.

The allegation was given widespread attention. Then a reporter who checked the document found that at the bottom of the front page was the notation: "Both sides of this document must be complete." On reading the other side, the reporter found that Mrs. Clinton had accurately stated the value.

The journalist whose original piece had criticized Mrs. Clinton defended his story by stating that his source had not provided the back of the page.

Verification

Attributing material to a source does not prove its truth. All a reporter does when attributing information is to place responsibility for it with the source named in the story. Attribution says only this: It is true that the source said this.

The reporter who cares about truth is reluctant to settle for this half step but often is prevented from moving on by deadline pressures and the difficulty of verifying material. If a reporter tried to check every piece of information, most stories would never be written. There are, of course, certain routine verifications a reporter must make:

- Names, addresses and telephone numbers are checked in the newspaper's library, the telephone directory and the city directory.
- Background information is taken from clips in the morgue.
- Dubious information is checked against records, with other sources.

This kind of verification is essential to the reporter's work. Yet error, inaccuracy and fanciful tales creep into the news daily. When Judy Garland died, her death was noted in a syndicated column:

Her end was inevitable, from the day in Chicago's Oriental Theater when George Jessel was to introduce the child singer, Frances Gumm. His tongue resisted the clumsy sound, "Frances Gumm." He suddenly thought of the message he'd just sent to Judith Anderson, who was opening in a Broadway play:

"Dear Judy, may this new play add another garland to your Broadway career."

Jessel therefore blurted the name, "Judy Garland." Then he turned to the child singer waiting in the wings and told her: "Judy Garland . . . That's you, honey."

Even a columnist should tell truths. Had this one sought to check the anecdote he might have learned the truth, that Garland was the maiden name of Judy's mother.

When the Giants and the 49ers met in a National Football League playoff, Mayor Edward Koch of New York wagered a New York deli feast—pastrami, corned beef, dill pickles with cornrye bread—against Mayor Dianne Feinstein's cracked crab and California wine. The Giants and Koch lost. *The New York Times* reported the food was shipped by the Second Avenue Deli. *The Washington Post* said the Carnegie Deli supplied the sandwiches.

Big deal. Who cares what delicatessen shipped the corned beef and pastrami? Whoa, hold the mayo. The delis care. And we care, as journalists. It's trifles such as this that make the reader shake his or her head knowingly—journalists just can't get the simplest things right.

Nonverifiable Information

The reporter can verify this statement: "The mayor submitted a $1.5 million budget to the city council today." All the reporter needs to do is examine the minutes of the meeting or the budget. But he or she cannot verify the truth of this statement: "The budget is too large (or too small)." A city councilman might have indeed stated that he would oppose the budget because it was too large, whereas the head of the Municipal League might have declared her organization's distress at the "paltry budget that endangers health and welfare projects." We can determine that the statements were made, but we cannot determine the truth of opinions and judgments.

The Techniques of Verification

Verification is not the use of another opinion to counter the view of one source with that of another on controversial issues. Journalists should offer several views on controversial matters, and they should seek out the victims of charges. But that is balance, not verification.

When a minister charged that a magazine used as educational material by a public school system in California was Communist inspired, a *Fresno Bee* reporter balanced the charge with a reply from school officials. But he also sought to verify the allegation by checking whether the publication had ever been listed as subversive. The reporter examined several publications that listed so-called subversive organizations and individuals. The magazine was not listed.

Here is how he began his story:

> Rev. August Brustat, a Lutheran minister, has charged the "Scholastic" magazine, which is used in some Fresno schools, with carrying the Communist line to students. But a librarian in Fresno County Free Library and a school official said they can find no evidence the magazine is subversive.

When President Clinton sent U.S. planes to bomb sites in Iraq, Sen. Trent Lott, the Republican leader in the Senate, said it was done in an attempt to divert attention from Clinton's impeachment. He was quoted as saying that in 1991 when President George Bush asked for authorization to use force against Iraq, "I don't believe there was a single Democrat that voted for that."

Then the reporter inserted in his story: "In fact, 86 Democrats in the House and 10 in the Senate, including Al Gore, voted for the authorization."

The reporter, David E. Rosenbaum, checked the files rather than allow an accusation to appear in print without verification.

Not all assertions can be verified, of course, and when this happens and the source has not offered proof, the news writer says so. Here is how one reporter handled such a situation:

> She said that test scores have improved "substantially," although she offered no documentation.

During wartime, journalists depend on official sources because so much happens out of range of the reporter. Sometimes, however, a reporter will try to verify a release from an official source. The result can be illuminating.

In Vietnam

When the United States announced its planes had accidentally bombed the Cambodian village of Neak Luong, the U.S. Embassy told correspondents that the damage was minimal. Sydney H. Schanberg, a *New York Times* correspondent, decided to see for himself and sought air transportation to the village. The Embassy intervened to keep him from flying there, but Schanberg managed to find a boat.

Firsthand Account   Schanberg stayed in Neak Luong a day and night, interviewing villagers and taking pictures. When local authorities learned he had been gathering material, they put him in confinement overnight. But he managed to send his story to his newspaper. Here is how Schanberg's story begins:

The destruction in this town from the accidental bombing on Monday is extensive.

Big chunks of the center of town have been demolished, including two-story concrete buildings reinforced with steel. Clusters of wood and thatch huts where soldiers lived with their families have been erased, so that the compounds where they once stood look like empty fields strewn with rubble

Schanberg quotes the air attaché at the Embassy as saying, "I saw one stick of bombs go through the town, but it was no great disaster." Schanberg then goes on to point out that there were almost 400 casualties, and he takes the reader through the village:

The atmosphere in Neak Luong, on the east bank of the Mekong River 38 miles southeast of Phnom Penh, is silent and sad—bewildered at being bombed by an ally. Everyone has lost either relatives or friends; in some cases entire large families were wiped out.

Yesterday afternoon a soldier could be seen sobbing uncontrollably on the riverbank. "All my family is dead! Take my picture, take my picture! Let the Americans see me!"

His name is Keo Chan and his wife and 10 of his children were killed. All he has left is the youngest—an 8-month-old son. The 48-year-old soldier escaped death because he was on sentry duty a few miles away when the bombs fell.

The bombs went down right in the middle of this town from north to south as it lay sleeping shortly after 4:30 a.m. Over 30 craters can be seen on a line nearly a mile long, and people reported others in jungle areas outside the town that this correspondent could not reach.

The story states that a third of the village hospital was demolished and then quotes the Air Force spokesman as saying there was a "little bit of damage to the northeast corner of the hospital" and some "structural cracks" in a wall. In his story, Schanberg is like a bulldog that refuses to let his quarry go.

Although the attaché had described a compound for Cambodian Marines that had been destroyed as consisting of "hootches," the *Times* reporter points out that the Cambodians lived with their families in these shacks.

A woman's scalp sways on a clump of tall grass. A bloody pillow here, a shred of a sarong caught on a barbed wire there. A large bloodstain on the brown earth. A pair of infant's rubber sandals among some unexploded military shells.

Purpose. "My goal, always, when I was overseas was to say to myself, 'Now, try to put the reader where you were today. Make the reader feel and smell and hear what you felt and smelled and heard.' Get the reader engaged. That's your challenge, and when you can do that, draw them into your experience. If you witness something awesome or awful, then you want the awfulness to come out. (I think that emotion belongs in stories, too.) That was my purpose every day, to bring people where I was."

—*Sydney H. Schanberg.*

The colonel is quoted as saying about the reactions of the townspeople, "They were sad, but they understand that this is war and that in war these things happen."

> "I do not understand why it happens," said Chea Salan, a 21-year-old soldier who lost relatives and army buddies. "Before, every time we saw the planes coming we were happy because we knew the planes came to help us. Now I have lost heart."

Schanberg's story demonstrates how journalistic guidelines can be used with consummate craftsmanship:

• **Verification:** Assertions are checked against the reporter's observations.
• **Dramatization:** Interviews with those involved personalize the event.
• **Conviction:** The detailed and specific observations give a reader the sense of the relationship of the report to truth.
• **Balance:** Both views, the military's and that of the victims, are presented.

Schanberg won a Pulitzer Prize and a Sigma Delta Chi Award for his coverage of Cambodia.

Fairness

One of journalism's values is to follow the facts wherever they may lead. When Walter Anderson, now the editor in chief of *Parade,* was a young reporter he interviewed a woman whom he described as the "unmarried mother of five." After the story appeared, the woman's son called to ask Anderson, "Why did you write that? Why is that anyone's business?"

On reflection two decades later, Anderson said, "The article I wrote was accurate, but I don't think it was fair. I had gotten the facts right, but I was not right."

The Essentials

• No story is fair if it omits facts of major importance or significance. So fairness includes completeness.
• No story is fair if it includes essentially irrelevant information at the expense of significant facts. So fairness includes relevance.
• No story is fair if it consciously or unconsciously misleads or even deceives the reader. So fairness includes honesty—leveling with the reader.
• No story is fair if reporters hide their biases or emotions behind such subtly pejorative words as "refused," "despite," "admit" and "massive." So fairness requires straightforwardness ahead of flashiness.
• No story is fair if innocent people are hurt.

Know Thyself. "Fairness requires that the journalist try to avoid all bias and stereotyping. And that means accepting that all of us have biases and that we must try and identify them so we can avoid them in our public job of reporting, writing and editing."

—August Gribbin

Judgment Necessary

But does fair play mean that each side in an argument is given equal attention by the journalist? When *The New York Times* published a profile of a spokeswoman for the Tobacco Institute, the reaction was immediate and angry.

One letter writer condemned the article as an example of the media's desire to present "all points of view," and the result as endowing "all ideas with equal intellectual currency." The article, the letter stated, should have offered a "framework for analysis."

Another letter writer, the chief of gastroenterology at the Veterans Affairs Medical Center in Ann Arbor, was also angered by the spokeswoman's advocacy as publicized by the *Times:*

> I would like to invite her and members of the tobacco industry to make hospital rounds with me or any other physician to meet the beneficiaries of her so-called advocacy. I suspect she might feel differently about her job after meeting patients disfigured by surgery for head and neck cancer, speechless from the loss of their larynxes or dependent on artificial ventilatory support because of chronic obstructive pulmonary disease, clinging to the last vestiges of dignity and life.

Balance

During political campaigns, editors try to balance—in some cases down to the second of air time or the inch of copy—candidate A and candidate B.

Balance is important. But some journalists contend that balance does not mean they must station themselves precisely at the midpoint of an issue. If candidate A makes an important speech today, the speech may be worth page 1 play. If, on the same day, opponent B repeats what he said yesterday or utters nonsense, the newspaper or station is under no obligation to balance something with nothing. A journalism of absolute balance can add up to zero. Balance is a moral commitment and cannot be measured by the stopwatch or the ruler.

The same common sense should be applied to matters that require fair play. Should candidate A make a serious accusation against opponent B, the reporter should seek out B for a reply. The targets of charges and accusations should always be given their say, and the reply should be placed as closely to the allegation as possible.

When *The Atlanta Journal-Constitution* revealed that a state legislator was helping his son sell computers to the state, the newspaper carried the senator's reply as well as the charge.

When charges are made for which no documentation is offered, the reporter is required to say so, as high in the story as possible. During his first presidential campaign, Ronald Reagan said there had been a federal deficit every year since World War II. After quoting Reagan, Lou Cannon, White House reporter for *The Washington Post,* added, "According to budget documents Mr. Reagan sent to Congress earlier this year, there have been eight budget surpluses during this period, five of them during Democratic administrations."

A reader complained to the *Post,* "Why is Cannon debating with the president? Why doesn't he just report what the president says?" Sam Zagoria, the newspaper's ombudsman, replied, "No story is fair if it consciously or unconsciously misleads or even deceives the reader. So fairness includes honesty—leveling with the reader." Zagoria said Cannon was right, that "the added facts were necessary for completeness."

Here is the AP's policy on balance:

> We make every reasonable effort to get comment from someone who has a stake in a story we're reporting—especially if the person is the target of an attack or allegations. . . . If someone declines comment, we say so. If we can't get comment from someone whose side of a story should be told, we spell out in our copy the steps we took to try to get that comment. . . . Whenever possible we also check our files to see what, if anything, the person has said in the past relating to the allegations. Including past comment may provide needed balance and context.

Objectivity

Lack of balance and the absence of fairness are often inadvertent. Because writing is as much an act of the unconscious as it is the conscious use of controlled and disciplined intelligence, the feelings of reporters can crop up now and then.

In describing an official the reporter dislikes, a reporter might write, "C. Harrison Gold, an ambitious young politician, said today. . . ."

Or, writing about an official the reporter admires, that reporter might write, "Gerald Silver, the dynamic young state controller, said today. . . ."

It is acceptable for a young man or woman to be "ambitious," but when the word is used to describe a politician, it can have a negative connotation. On the other hand, the "dynamic" politician conjures up an image of a young man or woman hard at work serving the public. Maybe the reporter is accurate in these perceptions. Maybe not. The reporter's job is to let the reader draw conclusions by describing what the politician says and does.

Danger exists any time a reporter departs from the recital of observed and documented material. Similes and metaphors can cause trouble because their use sometimes leads the reporter to inject his or her feelings into a piece. One reporter wrote, "Looking as though he would be more comfortable in a scarlet bowling shirt than in the business suit he wore, State Assemblyman Louis Montano faced tenants from the end of a long table." The imagery ran away from the reporter's good sense and decency. The sentence implies that the legislator was more suited to bowling than lawmaking. Montano, like others written about by the press in disparaging ways, had little rejoinder. He could write a letter to the editor. But the damage had been done.

Edward Reed

Self-Discipline

Whatever the reporter feels about a candidate for office, the account of his campaign is written objectively. The reporter lets the mayoral candidate speak, asks him questions about issues and describes his appearances at street rallies. The reporter allows the reader to make judgments.

Unfair and unbalanced journalism might be described as a failure in objectivity. When journalists talk about objectivity, they mean that the news story is free of the reporter's opinion or feelings, that it contains facts and that the account is from an impartial and independent observer. Stories are objective when they can be checked against some kind of record—the text of a speech, the minutes of a meeting, a police report, a purchase voucher, a payroll, unemployment data, or vital statistics. Stories are objective when material in them is borne out by evidence.

If readers want to weep or laugh, write angry letters to their senators or send money to the Red Cross for tornado victims, that is their business. The reporter is content to lay out the facts. Objective journalism is the reporting of the visible, what people say and do.

A Test   What do you think of these four paragraphs from a lead story on page 1 of *The Globe and Mail* written by the newspaper's Washington bureau correspondent? Do you consider this an objective report?

Defiant, charming and evasive, the Bill Clinton that Americans saw testifying under oath revealed the slippery side of the man whom they twice elected president and whose personal failings may yet oust him from the Oval Office.

For millions glued to their television sets yesterday for the broadcast of 4 hours 14 minutes of unprecedented and raw presidential testimony to a grand jury, there were no stunning new revelations, only the fullness of Mr. Clinton's artful defence.

But no amount of careful preparation could spare the President massive embarrassment as he endured detailed questioning on Aug. 17 about his "inappropriate intimate contact" with former White House intern Monica Lewinsky.

If Mr. Clinton survives as President, it will be because Americans are prepared to overlook his behaviour no matter how repulsive it was or the degree to which it disgraced their country's highest office.

Objectivity's Limitations

In the 1950s, social and political problems that had been proliferating since the end of World War II began to cause cleavages in society, and reporters found their methodology—the prevailing concept of objective reporting—inadequate in finding causes and fixing responsibility.

Journalists were concerned about the attention they had given Joseph McCarthy, the Wisconsin senator whose charges of Communist conspiracies had been given front-page play over the country. Their tortured self-analysis led them to assume collective responsibility for the senator's rise to power. They realized it was not enough to report what McCarthy had said—which was objective reporting. McCarthy had indeed made the charges, but many of the charges were later found to be false.

Journalists asked themselves whether they had a responsibility to go beyond mere transcription of what people say and do. They found they were waiting for events to develop, the authority to speak out. They did not venture into areas that are not discernible or not measurable. They did not seek the depths of the iceberg but settled for the observable tip. That kind of journalism, with little predictive capacity, is unable to fulfill journalism's role of supplying people with information on which they can make decisions.

Journalists reported the announcement of policies and programs but infrequently examined the consequences for those affected. The monitoring was left to the bureaucracy, taxpayer organizations, other special interest groups and a few columnists. Journalism failed to alert the public to the problems of poverty, racism, inequality and the domestic consequences of the Cold War. It seemed to be committed to institutions rather than to people and to have a built-in bias for established authority, presumed to be rational, disinterested and responsive.

Frustrated Journalists   Elmer Davis, a courageous radio journalist, pointed to the limitations of objective journalism during the McCarthy period. He described the frustrations of reporters who knew officials were lying but were unable to say so in their stories.

Davis said that the principle of objectivity holds that a newspaper or station will run "everything that is said on both sides of a controversial issue and let the reader make up his mind. A noble theory; but suppose that the men who talk on one side (or on both) are known to be lying to serve their own personal interest, or suppose they don't know what they are talking about. To call attention to these facts, except on the editorial page, would not, according to most newspaper practice, be objective."

Davis wondered whether readers have enough background on many subjects and he asked, "Can they distinguish fact from fiction, ignorance from knowledge, interest from impartiality?"

The newspaper is unworthy of the reader's trust, Davis continued in his book *But We Were Born Free,* "if it tells him only what somebody says is the truth, which is known to be false." The reporter has no choice, he wrote, but to put into "the one-dimensional story the other dimensions that will make it approximate the truth." The reporter's obligation is to the person who goes to the news "expecting it to give him so far as humanly possible not only the truth and nothing but the truth, but the whole truth." Then, in a paragraph that influenced many journalists, Davis wrote:

> The good newspaper, the good news broadcaster, must walk a tightrope between two great gulfs—on one side the false objectivity that takes everything at face value and lets the public be imposed on by the charlatan with the most brazen front; on the other, the "interpretive" reporting which fails to draw the line between objective and subjective, between a reasonably well-established fact and what the reporter or editor wishes were the fact. To say that is easy; to do it is hard. No wonder that too many fall back on the incontrovertible objective fact that the Honorable John P. Hoozis said, colon quote—and never mind whether he was lying or not.

Adjustments

Another broadcast journalist, Edward R. Murrow, who had moved from radio to television, pioneered in-depth reporting. He sought to make television journalism more than a bulletin board with news for the middle class. In his work in the 1950s, Murrow demonstrated passion and conviction along with curiosity and journalistic discipline.

Davis, Murrow and a few print journalists gave a broader scope to objective reporting. Journalists—with their unique nonpartisan perspective and their commitment to democratic values, accurate observation and truth—began to see how they could provide insights for the public and for policy-makers. To do so more effectively, they knew they had to change some of their traditional practices. Underlying their conviction that change was needed was their assumption that journalists are publicly useful men and women.

Providing Context   The Commission on Freedom of the Press in the late 1940s (see *A Free and Responsible Press. A General Report on Mass Communications: Newspapers, Radio, Motion Pictures, Magazines, and Books,* pp. 21–22) told journalists that they are most useful when they give "a truthful, comprehensive, and intelligent account of the day's events in a context which gives them meaning. . . . It is no longer enough to report *fact* truthfully. It is now necessary to report the *truth about the fact.*"

Journalists began finding ways to work themselves away from the constrictions that impeded truth telling. One of their responses was to look behind the breaking news story for causes and to find those with the authority to speak about possible consequences.

Viewing the urban crisis as having its roots in the problems of race and class, journalists began digging into the previously invisible worlds of blacks, the Spanish speaking, youth and women. Journalists made analyses of their own, putting their intelligence as well as their craft to work.

Journalists sought to give an added dimension to their stenographic function by examining the background of assertions and the cause of actions and by looking for the "truth of the fact." This kind of journalism, demonstrated in Schanberg's reporting from Vietnam, moves the reader, listener and viewer closer to the truth.

Facts are the stars that provide guidelines as we navigate toward the destination of truth. But they can never fully illuminate our passage. They require context, meaning. The journalist had to take on this task. At the same time, universities began to train large numbers of journalists, responding to society's need for knowledgeable practitioners.

Brevity

In our generalization about the reporter's job at the outset of this chapter, we pointed out that the news story is succinct. The tersely told story is admired by editors and by busy readers and listeners. Here is a two-paragraph story that says a great deal although it contains only four sentences:

JOHANNESBURG, South Africa, Nov. 8 — The bodies of 60 victims of an accidental dynamite explosion a mile and a half down a gold mine 100 miles southwest of Johannesburg were brought to the surface today.

Of the dead, 58 were Basuto tribesmen from Lesotho, chosen for the dangerous job of shaft-sinking, or blasting a way down to the gold-bearing reef. The two others were white supervisors. The black Africans will be buried in a communal grave tomorrow.

—*The New York Times*

The Ultimate Art. ". . . there is but one art: to omit! O if I knew how to omit, I would ask no other knowledge. A man who knew how to omit would make an *Iliad* of a daily newspaper."

—*Robert Louis Stevenson*

Too Brief. Headline writers are the brevity experts. But sometimes their tightening misdirects meaning:

Kids Make Nutritious Snacks

Squad Helps Dog Bite Victim

Eye Drops off Shelf

Stud Tires Out

Then there are the signs and notices that try to compress much in little, like these in a local church: "Don't let worry kill you—let the church help." Another: "Thursday, there will be a meeting of the Little Mothers Club. All wishing to become little mothers, please see the minister in his study."

All creative work is based on the art of omission. In architecture, the 20th century was marked by structures that follow the dictum: Less is more.

Economy of expression is the hallmark of the artist. When Beethoven was struggling with the music to his opera "Fidelio," he realized that the leisurely pace of the music did not meet the demands of the theater, and for years he pared down his work. David Hamilton, the music critic, describes Beethoven's effort as a "ruthless piece of self criticism . . . Beethoven expunged balancing phrases, trimmed decorative expansions, excised anything that did not move forward, eventually achieving the terse urgency that now marks the opera's crucial scenes."

In eliminating large sections of his music, Beethoven rejected three overtures he had written. One, "Leonore No. 3," became one of the most popular pieces in the orchestral repertory. Despite its obvious beauty and power, Beethoven found it unsuited to his opera.

Joseph G. Herzberg, an editor on several New York City newspapers, said, "Newspapering is knowing what to leave out and condensing the rest."

Too often, beat reporters and specialists write more than is necessary because they forget they are writing for general readers, not for their sources. The reporter covering new transplant technology for a newspaper cannot go into the kind of detail that a reporter for the *Journal of the American Medical Association* must in her story.

How Come? But stories can be so brief they omit essential information. The Canadian Broadcasting Corporation reported on its morning newscast that hepatitis and HIV were spreading four times as fast in Canadian prisons than five years before. Heroin and cocaine injected with dirty needles was given as the reason for the surge in diseases. Nothing was said that would answer the listener's obvious question: How are such quantities of drugs getting into the prisons?

Selectivity

The way out of the dilemma of being brief but not writing telegrams is through Herzberg's advice, which can be summed up in one word—selectivity. Brevity is a function of selectivity—knowing what to leave out. The ability to select essential facts from the welter of material that the reporter gathers comes with experience.

Selectivity also involves the use of language that makes the point succinctly. Edna Buchanan, the police reporter for *The Miami Herald,* began her account of a record-breaking week of violence in Dade County this way:

> Dade's murder rate hit new heights this week as a wave of violence left 14 people dead and five critically hurt within five days.

A couple of paragraphs compared these figures with murder figures of previous years, and then Buchanan summarized most of the deaths:

In the latest wave of violence, a teenager's throat was cut and her body dumped into a canal. A former airline stewardess was garroted and left with a pair of scissors stuck between her shoulder blades. Four innocent bystanders were shot in a barroom gun battle. An 80-year-old man surprised a burglar who battered him fatally with a hammer. An angry young woman who "felt used" beat her date to death with the dumbbells he used to keep fit. And an apparent robbery victim was shot dead as he ran away from the robbers.

Strain   A natural tension exists between the editor and the reporter over the issue of brevity. The desk, confronted with ever-decreasing space and time, wants shorter stories. The reporter, excited by the event and driven by a compulsion to tell the full story, wants more time and more space. Online journalists are even more pressed to compress their work.

Some editors contend that, if Genesis can describe the earth's creation in a thousand words, then no reporter needs any more than four pages of copy for any event of human dimension. But some events are so complex that only an extended account will do. Important stories often require scene setting and background that consume time and space. The guide for the length of stories is: Make it brief but complete.

Clarity

The executives of 40 daily newspapers in Iowa and journalism instructors at the state's three journalism schools were asked to rank characteristics considered most important for beginning reporters. Both groups put the ability to write clearly and interestingly first.

Clear prose follows comprehension. That is, the reporter must be able to understand the event before he or she can explain it clearly and succinctly. You cannot clarify what you do not understand.

Clarity is enhanced by simplicity of expression, which generally means short sentences, short words, coherence and logical story structure. We shall be looking at these in detail in Chapter 7.

Human Interest

To make certain the story is read, the journalist must recount events in ways that substitute for the drama of the personal encounter. One of the ways the journalist does this is to tell the story in human terms. Reporters personalize and dramatize the news by seeking out the people involved in the event. Human interest is an essential ingredient of news.

A change in city zoning regulations is dramatized by pointing out that now low-income families can move into an area that had been effectively sealed off to them by the previous two-acre zoning rule. A factory shutdown is personalized by talking to workers who must line up at the unemployment office instead of at a workbench.

Polluting   In a story about chemicals polluting the Hudson River and ruining the fishing industry, Barry Newman of *The Wall Street Journal* begins:

GRASSY POINT, N.Y.—In the gray-shingled shack at water's edge, four fishermen sit playing cards around an old kitchen table, ignoring the ebb tide laden with the spring run of shad. The wall is hung with foul-weather gear; rubber boots are piled in the corner. On the refrigerator door somebody has taped up a newspaper clipping about the awful chemical in the fish of the Hudson River.

"I do my fishing from the window here," an old man says, looking off to the quiet hills on the east bank, three miles across the river from this small valley town.

"No nets for me this year," another man says. "No pay," says the third. And the fourth: "A lot of trouble, this."

Localizing   In Washington, all the talk was of budget cutting, of eliminating federal spending. Members of Congress used the podium as a pulpit to expound on the morality of frugality.

Back home in Minneapolis, the *Star Tribune* decided to see just what role federal spending played in Anoka County. "This was an attempt to bring down to a personal level the debate in Washington over extremely intricate financial and policy issues," said Mike Kaszuba, suburban affairs reporter. He teamed with the newspaper's Washington bureau chief Sharon Schmickle to do the reporting and writing.

The reporters found that billions of dollars had flowed into the county since the New Deal built the Anoka high school stadium. Federal money "built the bridge that carries traffic over the Rum River into downtown. Now it pays Mary Wellman, hired last year as Anoka's only female police officer."

The series gave faces and names to people helped by federal funds—students eating school lunches, students attending the local technical college, people using the Anoka ambulance, people who need help with their heating bills, salaries for teachers who help special education students.

Responsibility

Ted Williams was one of baseball's greatest players. The Boston Red Sox outfielder won six batting titles over a span of 17 years and was one of the few to win the Triple Crown twice, leading the league in 1942 and in 1947 in batting, runs batted in and home runs. To many baseball fans, he was heroic. To some sports writers, he was, as Roger Kahn put it, "a pill."

It was possible for readers to know the real Williams because, Kahn says, when nine writers covered Red Sox games "it was impossible to conceal" the truth about Williams. "If one writer courted The Thumper by refusing to report a tantrum as news, another inevitably seized the tantrum as news. Regardless of each reporter's skill, an essential, imperfect system of checks and balances worked. If you cared enough about Williams, and I did, you could find a portrait that was honest by consensus."

But many of the Boston newspapers that covered Williams are gone, as are others in many cities. There are fewer than 30 cities with competing daily newspapers. This means that the responsibility for truth telling falls on fewer shoulders. It falls, in most U.S. cities, in fact, on a single reporter, for most local news beats are covered by only one journalist.

Responsibility is not a visible part of a news story. It is an attitude that the reporter carries to the job. It encompasses all the components we have discussed in this chapter.

Responsibility is the reporter's commitment to the story, to journalism and to the public. Responsibility demands of the reporter that the story be accurate, fair and balanced, that it be so clear anyone can understand it.

Nothing in the law requires a reporter to be responsible. In fact, journalists sometimes flinch at the word. The reason for their discomfort is that some people and some groups use the word as a club with which to beat journalists when the newspaper or station presents material they dislike.

Journalists testily reply that they can be as irresponsible as they like. That's understandable, and it is true. But beneath the surface, reporters and editors understand that journalism is a moral enterprise, that theirs is a calling practiced with honesty and diligence within the limits of verifiable truth and scant time.

"Irresponsible Journalists." "I wish I could remember how many times when I was Ambassador to Yugoslavia I was officially requested to persuade, convince, or direct *The New York Times* and *The Washington Post* to behave 'responsibly.' I doubt whether there is, in truth, any objective standard of responsible journalism. We tend to think papers are responsible when we agree with them and irresponsible when we object to their content."
—*Laurence Silberman, Judge of the District of Columbia Circuit of the U.S. Court of Appeals*

Summing Up

Editors tell their new news writers that journalism begins with the ABCs—accuracy, brevity and clarity. Of course, there is more required of the journalist, but these are excellent as starters.

Accuracy of fact and language.

Brevity in making the point succinctly.

Clarity so there is no doubt about what happened.

These can be seen as moral requirements as well as necessities of the practice of the craft. Journalists take on the responsibility of telling people about the world around them so that they can act on what they read, see and hear. But action depends on clear, understandable and accurate information. Without such information, action may be misdirected or, just as bad, never taken.

We are witnessing a steady decline in the trust the public places in journalists. This is dangerous for democracy, which functions only when an informed public is involved in the give-and-take of communal life.

Returning journalism to its status as trusted and reliable informer may begin simply with spelling names correctly, getting the address right, quoting someone accurately.

Misspelled Name

Writing

Finally, a word about writing. A news story may be accurate, properly attributed, balanced and fair, objective and brief. The reporter may be compassionate and understanding, may have carried out his or her tasks with responsibility. The story may have something interesting and exciting to say. But unless it is written with some skill, the reader or listener will not bother.

Good writing—direct and clear, simple and straightforward—is an important component of the story. Good writing avoids clichés and redundancies. It does not strain for effect. It does not call attention to itself but to the story it tells.

Further Reading

Benjamin, Burton. *Fair Play: CBS, General Westmoreland, and How a Television Documentary Went Wrong.* New York: Harper & Row, 1988.

Bensman, Joseph, and Robert Lilienfield. *Craft and Consciousness.* New York: Wiley, 1973.

Chancellor, John, and Walter R. Mears. *The News Business.* New York: Harper & Row, 1983.

Commission on Freedom of the Press. *A Free and Responsible Press.* Chicago: University of Chicago Press, 1947.

Edwards, Julia. *Women of the World: The Great Foreign Correspondents.* Boston: Houghton Mifflin, 1988.

Liebling, A. J. *The Press.* New York: Ballantine Books, 1964.

Mills, Kay. *A Place in the News: From the Women's Pages to the Front Page.* New York: Dodd, Mead, 1988.

Schiller, Dan. *Objectivity and the News: The Public and the Rise of Commercial Journalism.* Philadelphia: University of Pennsylvania Press, 1981.

Siebert, Fred S., et al. *Four Theories of the Press.* Urbana: University of Illinois Press, 1956.

3 What Is News?

Steven Campbell, *Houston Chronicle*

Impact . . . timeliness . . . proximity.

Preview

Journalists look to a set of news values to help them determine the newsworthiness of events. These values are:

- Timeliness.
- Impact, consequence or importance.
- Prominence of the people involved.
- Proximity to readers and listeners.
- Conflict.
- The unusual nature of the event.
- Currency, the sudden interest people have in an ongoing situation.

At least three-fourths of all stories fall into the categories of impact or importance and the unusual.

We have discussed several essentials of journalism—accuracy, attribution, verification, balance and fairness, objectivity, brevity, clarity, human interest and responsibility. These elements are the reporter's guides to reporting and writing the story. But what leads the reporter to the events worth reporting? Among the cascade of events the reporter encounters in a workday, which should be singled out for attention?

How does the courthouse reporter leafing through a dozen civil complaints decide which is the newsworthy document? How does the police reporter determine which of the score of arrests is noteworthy? After determining that an event or idea is worth reporting, how does the reporter decide whether to write two paragraphs or seven? How does the broadcast journalist know a story is worth 60 seconds at the start of the 6 p.m. newscast or 10 seconds toward the end? If journalism can be described as the art of selection, then what guidelines does the journalist use in practicing selectivity?

Some Answers, Past and Present

If we go back to the beginning of formal news communication, we learn that what we read, see and hear today is not much different from the material in the daily bulletins posted in the Roman forum and what was later printed in gazettes and newsbooks.

Realizing that Roman citizens needed to know about official decisions that affected them, Julius Caesar posted reports of government activities in the *Acta Diurna.* In China, the T'ang dynasty (618–906 a.d) published a gazette—handwritten or printed by woodblock—to inform court officials of its activities. The more immediate predecessor of the newspaper was the handwritten newsletter, containing political and economic information, that circulated among merchants in early 16th-century Europe.

Wars, Dragons and Business

The first printed newsbook, published in 1513 and titled *The trewe encounter,* described the Battle of Flodden Field in which James IV of Scotland was killed during his invasion of England. The Anglo-Scottish wars that followed provided printers with material for more newsbooks. The elements of our modern-day journalism were included in these accounts—names of officers in the wars and their deeds. Adventure, travel and crime were featured, along with accounts of disasters.

As one printer-pamphleteer put it, people are interested in "and most earnestly moved with strange novelties and marvelous things." These early day journalists favored stories of monsters and dragons, not unlike our own day's tales of the Abominable Snowman and the Loch Ness monster.

During the 17th century, news sheets spread to the business centers of Europe, reporting news of commerce. In this country, as historian Bernard Weisberger has pointed out, the newspaper "served as a handmaiden of commerce by emphasizing news of trade and business."

To this day, much of our news is about the actions of government and business, and our journalism continues to stress the drama of war and other calamities.

Day and Bennett

The newspaper editors of the 19th century understood the need to appeal to a large audience to stay in business, and their acumen led to definitions of news that hold to this day. The papers in the large cities were printing news for the newly literate working class. One of the first penny papers—inexpensive enough for working people—contained the ingredients of popular journalism. In 1833, the first issue of Benjamin H. Day's *New York Sun* included a summary of police court cases and stories about fires, burglaries and a suicide. Other stories contained humor and human interest.

Several years later, James Gordon Bennett—described by historians as the originator of the art, science and industry of news gathering—used the recently developed telegraph to give the readers of his *Herald* commercial and political news to go along with his reports of the everyday life of New York City, its sins and scandals. His formula of news for "the merchant and man of learning, as well as the mechanic and man of labor" guides many editors today.

The Library of Congress

Joseph Pulitzer

Pulitzer

Day and Bennett followed the tastes and appetites of their readers, but they also directed and taught their readers by publishing stories they deemed important. This blend of entertainment, information and public service was stressed by Joseph Pulitzer, who owned newspapers in St. Louis and New York. He, too, gave his readers what he thought they wanted—sensational news and features. But Pulitzer was not content with entertainment. He also used his news staff for his campaigns to curb business monopolies and to seek heavy taxes on income and inheritance. In 1883, Pulitzer charged the staff of his New York *World* with this command:

> Always fight for progress and reform, never tolerate injustice or corruption, always fight demagogues of all parties, never belong to any party, always oppose privileged classes and public plunderers, never lack sympathy with the poor, always remain devoted to the public welfare, never be satisfied with merely printing news, always be drastically independent, never be afraid to attack wrong, whether by predatory plutocracy or predatory poverty.

Hearst

Pulitzer and William Randolph Hearst were locked in a circulation war for New York readers when Cuba rebelled against its Spanish rulers. Spain was severe in repressing the insurrection and the New York newspapers seized on the story of the helpless Cubans trying to free themselves from oppression.

Hearst's *Journal* was particularly imaginative. After the United States declared war in 1898 and the troops were slow in making it to Cuba, Hearst urged them on with an inventive news story that had 5,000 troops on their way.

"Over the next week," writes Arthur Lubow in *The Reporter Who Would Be King,* "the *Journal* reported an exciting sequence of landings, bombardments and fleet battles, all admirably detailed, all entirely fictitious. The *Journal* was selling so well thanks to its apocryphal scoops that its rivals began to play the same game, often rewriting the accounts of the creative *Journal* writers."

Today's Editors

Modern mass media editors overseeing newsrooms humming with the latest electronic wonders apply many 19th-century concepts of news. They would define their news menu as a blend of information, entertainment and public service. They would also agree with the definition of news offered by Charles A. Dana, who ran the *New York Sun* from 1869 to 1897. Dana said news is "anything that interests a large part of the community and has never been brought to its attention before."

One of Dana's editors, John B. Bogart, contributed the classic definition, "When a dog bites a man, that is not news, because it happens so often. But if a man bites a dog, it's news."

Another enduring definition of news was offered by Stanley Walker, a Texan gone East to succeed as city editor of *The New York Herald Tribune* in the early 1930s. He said news was based on the three W's, "women, wampum, and wrongdoing." By this he meant that news was concerned with sex, money and crime—the topics people desired to know about. Actually, Walker's formula is as old as the contents of Caesar's *Acta Diurna* 2,000 years ago, which, along with information about public affairs, offered news of sports, crime and sensational events. And in England, while newspapers were carrying material directed at the commercial class, handbills and pamphlets were carrying sensational crime news.

By the mid-1970s, the United States had been through three crises: a war in Vietnam that wound down with guilt and defeat for many Americans; the Watergate scandals; and the failure of some political, social and economic experiments of the 1950s and 1960s that had been hailed as solutions to international conflict, racial tension and poverty.

It was not surprising, then, to see a shift in the criteria used to determine the news. Av Westin, the executive producer of the American Broadcasting Company's "Evening News" program, said Americans wanted their news to answer the following questions: Is the world safe? Are my home and family safe? If they are safe, then what has happened in the last 24 hours to make them better off? Is my pocketbook safe?

People not only wanted more pocketbook stories but escape stories as well. Reflecting the interests of their readers, editors asked for more entertainment in the form of copy about lifestyles, leisure subjects and personalities.

In the 1990s, editors devised the "reader-friendly" story. Readers, they argued, want to learn how to diet, how to raise their children, where to invest their money. The news agenda was being shaped to conform to the interests of middle-class readers and viewers. Also, editors became aware that a major segment of the female population consists of working women. Coverage followed this awareness.

Reporters follow the guidelines of their editors and publishers. Reporters also agree among themselves on what constitutes news. Thus, at any given time, news in the mass media is similar.

Summing up, two general guidelines emerge:

- News is information about a break from the normal flow of events, an interruption in the expected.
- News is information people need to make sound decisions about their lives.

How does a reporter or editor determine what events are so unusual and what information is so necessary that the public should be informed of them?

News Values

The following seven factors determine the newsworthiness of events, personalities and ideas:

1. Timeliness

Events that are immediate, recent. The daily newspaper and the hourly newscast seek to keep readers and listeners abreast of events. Thus, broadcast news is written in the present tense, and most leads on newspaper stories contain the word *today*. No matter how significant the event, how important the people involved, news value diminishes with time. André Gide, the French novelist, defined journalism as "everything that will be less interesting tomorrow than today."

The media are commercial enterprises that sell space and time on the basis of their ability to reach people quickly with a perishable commodity. The marketplace rewards a fast news carrier. Although newspapers place less emphasis on speed than do the electronic media, a newspaper that offers its readers too much rehashed news will not survive. Radio, which was being prepared for its funeral when television captured a large segment of the listening audience, staged a comeback with the all-day, all-news station.

Online journalism provides Internet surfers with a running report on everything from hourly stock market prices to traffic flows and the scores of various games. When *The Dallas Morning News* was told that Timothy McVeigh, the Oklahoma City bomber, confessed his guilt to his lawyer, the newspaper put the story on its online version rather than hold it for the print version.

Recognizing the importance of timeliness, the Associated Press and other news providers pump out a steady stream of urgents, bulletins and Writethrus on breaking stories. As we saw in Chapter 1, the AP met the public's need for the latest information with an 11-hour torrent of material beginning with:

> JONESBORO, Ark. (AP) — Two men wearing camouflage opened fire on middle school students Tuesday as they assembled outside during a fire alarm. At least one person was killed.

And then when as much information as possible had been gathered, with this 10th Lead—Writethru:

> JONESBORO, Ark. (AP) — Two boys in camouflage lay in wait in the woods behind their school, then opened fire with rifles on classmates and teachers when they came out during a false fire alarm Tuesday. Four girls and a teacher were killed and 11 people were wounded.

Timely Information Essential   There is another side to our need to know quickly. Timeliness is important in a democracy. People need to know about the activities of their officials as soon as possible so they can assess the directions in which their leaders are moving. Told where they are being led, citizens can react before actions become irreversible. In extreme cases, the public can rid itself of an inefficient or corrupt official. Officials also want quick distribution of information so that they can have feedback from the public. This

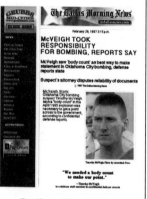

Online Exclusive

Values. "While I found that journalists, like everyone else, have values, the two that matter most in the newsroom are getting the story and getting it better and faster than their prime competitors—both among their colleagues and at rival news media."
—*Herbert J. Gans*

interaction is one of the reasons the Constitution protects the press. Without the give-and-take of ideas, democracy could not work.

Timeliness is also the consequence of advertising necessities. Because most businesses are based on the quick turnover of goods, advertisements must appear soon after goods are shipped to stores. The news that attracts readers to the advertisements must be constantly renewed.

2. Impact

Events that are likely to affect many people. Here, journalists talk about significance, importance, the kinds of information that interest people or that journalists decide people need to know to be informed. A postal workers' strike will be covered in detail because everyone is affected by the delivery of mail. A campaign for Congress will receive attention in the candidate's district because journalists consider it essential that voters know the candidates' positions before voting.

Some news that has considerable impact in one community may be unimportant in another. To residents in Milwaukee, a November cold snap has little impact because cold weather in that month is hardly an interruption in the expected. But when 40-degree weather was forecast for St. Petersburg, Fla., many of whose residents had fled northern winters, it was front-page news under a large headline.

3. Prominence

Events involving well-known people or institutions. When the president trips disembarking from an airplane, it is front-page news; when a city councilmember missteps, it is not worth a line of print. A local banker's embezzlement is more newsworthy than a clerk's thievery, even when the clerk has stolen more. When Michael Jackson sprains a thumb while working on a Walt Disney movie, it is network news. Names make news, goes the old adage, even when the event is of little consequence.

Two events that probably received the most massive media coverage of the 1990s were the result of prominence—the pursuit, arrest and trials of O.J. Simpson and the sexual affair of President Clinton with a young White House intern. Never mind that the economies of several large countries were crumbling, that the Middle East and Northern Ireland saw carnage amidst peace efforts, that nuclear proliferation arose and that ethnic warfare killed hundreds of thousands and made refugees of many more. Names made news, big and bigger news.

Prominence applies to organizations as well, and even to some physical objects. The repair of a major bridge in Akron is given coverage in that city, but when the Golden Gate Bridge shuts down that action merits national coverage.

In 1884, the American poet and journalist Eugene Field was moved by the journalism of personalities to write:

Now the Ahkoond of Swat is a vague sort of man

Who lives in a country far over the sea;

Pray tell me, good reader, if tell me you can,

What's the Ahkoond of Swat to you folks or me?

Despite Field's gentle poke, journalists continue to cater to what they perceive as the public's appetite for newsworthy names.

4. Proximity

Events that are geographically or emotionally close to the reader, viewer or listener interest them. In Chapter 1, we read about the coverage of a tornado that ripped apart the town of Spencer, S.D. The *Argus Leader,* the state's major newspaper, sent reporters and photographers 50 miles west to the small town. In 1 1/2-inch type on page 1, the newspaper headline quoted the governor:

'The town is gone'

Newspapers and stations around the country carried the news the day the tornado hit. But as disasters go, it wasn't a big story outside the state—six had died. While elsewhere attention turned to other news, the *Argus Leader* kept its staffers in Spencer and for six days running, the Spencer tornado was the number one story on page 1.

Obviously, people are interested in, and affected by, activities close at hand. A city ordinance requiring the licensing of dogs in Memphis, Tenn., would be of interest to that city's residents, of some interest to Nashville, Tenn., residents, and of no interest to dog owners in Butte, Mont.

If 42 people die in an airplane crash in the Andes and one of the passengers is a resident of Little Rock, the news story in Little Rock will emphasize the death of the local resident. This process is known as *localizing* the news.

When two tour buses collided in Wales, injuring 75 people, here is how *USA Today* began its brief:

> Teen-agers from Lancaster, Pa., Houston and St. Louis were among 75 people hurt when two tour buses returning from Ireland collided in Wales.

Emotional Closeness　People also feel close to events and individuals with whom they have emotional ties. Newspapers and stations in communities with large Catholic or Jewish populations will give considerable space and time to news from the Vatican or the Middle East.

After the space shuttle *Challenger* exploded and sent seven crew members to their deaths, the *Amsterdam News,* a weekly in New York City with a predominantly black readership, headlined on page 1 the death of the black astronaut who was aboard.

When commemorative ceremonies were planned to mark the sacrifice of four Army chaplains during World War II, *The Jewish Week* began its story this way:

> Rosalie Goode Fried does not remember her father, Rabbi Alexander David Goode — she was only 3 years old when he died in 1943.
>
> But America has never forgotten him.
>
> Goode and three Christian chaplains gave up their life jackets — and their lives — when their Army transport was sunk by a German submarine near Greenland 50 years ago.

When a proposal to bar education, health and welfare benefits to undocumented aliens was being discussed in California, reader interest closely followed ethnic lines. The proposal was clearly aimed at the large Mexican population. Given their interest, it was no surprise a poll showed that the issue was closely followed by 43 percent of Hispanics but only 24 percent of whites.

5. Conflict

Strife, antagonism, warfare have provided the basis of stories since the early peoples drew pictures on their cave walls of their confrontations with the beasts that surrounded them. People and their tribes and their countries have been at war with each other, and with themselves, since history has been kept, and the tales that resulted have been the basis of saga, drama, story and news.

Modern journalism recognizes conflict of a wider dimension than saga and myth. There is conflict in the battle of ideas and ideologies. For example: Have bilingual education and affirmative action outlived their usefulness? Should taxpayers subsidize religious schooling through vouchers? Should campuses have dormitories based on race and ethnicity? The list is endless.

Although critics of the press condemn what they consider to be an overemphasis on conflict, the advance of civilization can be seen as an adventure in conflict and turmoil. Indeed, one way to define, and to defend, journalism is that it is a forum for discussion of the conflicts that divide people and groups, and that this peaceful debate makes conflict resolution possible.

6. The Unusual

Events that deviate sharply from the expected, that depart considerably from the experiences of everyday life make news. We know that. But here we are talking about the truly different, the bizarre, strange and wondrous.

When a dog bites a man, it isn't news. But when a police dog, a tried and true member of the K-9 Corps, sinks his teeth into the arm of his police handler, that's unusual, and it's news. We've all seen big watermelons in the supermarket, but the 40-pound monster makes page 1 of the B section of the *Freeport News* when the farmer offers it to the First Baptist Church for its annual picnic.

Domestic Violence   Domestic spats are not news, unless they are so violent murder is committed. But when Lorena Bobbitt tired of her husband's mental and physical attacks and cut off his penis. . . . Yes, that was news for several weeks.

In fact, media fascination with the Bobbitt family surgery led Peter Kann, publisher of *The Wall Street Journal,* to condemn "media fascination with the bizarre, the perverse and pathological—Lorena Bobbitt journalism."

But it was over in a month or so, and today few people could identify Lorena Bobbitt and her 15 seconds of media attention. The bizarre has the life-span of a firefly's momentary flash.

To some, though, the attention was important and worthwhile, for the incident made people think about domestic violence and its victims, and in its wake some governors pardoned women imprisoned for killing husbands who had for years tormented and beaten them. Cause and effect? Who can tell?

Mike Roemer

Political Conflict

The opponents on the issue of abortion do battle with placards, parades and politics. This long-running conflict has erupted in violence.

A Lone Man's Plea

As the tanks headed down Cangan Boulevard in their show of strength in Beijing, a young man darted in front of the column. The tanks stopped. The man looked up and called out to the soldiers to stop the killing. The tanks tried to weave around him, easing him aside. He cried out again, pleading for no more violence. Bystanders finally pulled him away, fearing he would be crushed under the treads.

AP Photo by Jeff Widener

A Symbol   The young man who stood alone before a column of tanks on their way to bloody Tiananmen Square struck everyone who saw the photograph and read the accompanying story as so amazing, so wondrous that the act quickly became a symbol: To some, it was a symbol of defiance of tyranny. To others, it was, as the writer and critic Ian Buruma wrote, a symbol "of the futility of empty-handed opposition to brute force."

This tragic figure came to represent the end to the student demonstration in the Square for freedom and democracy. But, some say, the bizarre episode may well symbolize "the beginning of the end of the Communist Party rule in China," as Buruma put it.

7. Currency

Occasionally, a situation long simmering will suddenly emerge as the subject of discussion and attention. Historians might describe the situation as an idea whose time has come. When it does, the media catch up.

In the early 1960s, President Kennedy called attention to the plight of the poor. Then President Johnson declared a "war on poverty." Newspapers responded by covering health and welfare agencies and by going into poor areas of their cities in search of news. Television produced documentaries on the blighted lives of the poor. More than 30 years later, poverty, although as pervasive, receives less attention.

Newspapers and broadcast stations will sometimes make discoveries of their own and push them so that they become current. When a newspaper decides that some facet of community or national life is worth intensive coverage, it may assign a reporter or a team of reporters to dig into the situation. The result, usually a number of stories, is called a *campaign* or a *crusade*. Much of this news has a steamroller effect, and further news is developed because of the sudden currency of the theme or issue.

These seven guidelines do not tell us that one of the most enduring stories is the tale of how humanity prevails—how we live now is a story few have ever been able to resist. Nor do they give us any hints about the realities of the newsroom, how its pressures and its politics influence what and who become news.

News Is Relative

These news values do not exist in a vacuum. Their application depends on some practical considerations. Geography for one. We have seen in the value *proximity* that a leash law in one city is news, but means nothing to those deciding on news in a distant state.

Demography is also a factor. We read about how a newspaper with a black readership played up the death of a black astronaut. A newspaper with a large urban readership put this headline on government statistics:

Blacks make gains in family income

The same government release led to this headline in the *Lakota Times,* whose readership is Native American:

Indians fall in poverty stats

The news flow itself determines what is news. On a slow news day, when there is little news coming out of Washington and the state, and when the local staff has to dig deeply for scraps of news, then the little girl's lost puppy just might be a news item. But when the news overflows, the only people to hear about Wendy's pup are her folks and the neighbors who notice her forlorn signs on trees on the block.

How we define news has changed with the times. There is more news these days about personal matters—how to cope with rebelling teen-agers, how to manage money, weight and the in-laws. And there is more about the personal lives of the rich, famous and political.

Personal Lives Open to View

In this, the Age of Candor, there is hardly anything that is considered off-limits to journalists. It wasn't always this way.

During Franklin Roosevelt's presidency, his affair with Lucy Mercer was considered off-limits for journalists. So was his obvious physical disability. Struck down by infantile paralysis as a young man, Roosevelt could not walk

Changing Times . . . Changing Beats

A century ago, 50 percent of the workforce in the United States made a living from agriculture. Farm news was big news. Today, with 2.5 percent so employed, farm news is important outside agricultural areas only when the cost of food goes up. At the beginning of the 20th century, fewer than 115,000 students attended college and journalists paid little attention to them. Today, more than 50 times as many are enrolled and higher education is a major beat.

James McNulty

Mike Roemer

unaided. He often used a wheelchair. No photographers took pictures of his cumbersome braces, and no mention of his disability was made in print.

John F. Kennedy's sexual activities were a matter of common knowledge to the Washington press corps, but only the most discerning reader could catch a glimpse of this between the lines of carefully written stories.

Enter Bill Clinton, Gennifer Flowers, Paula Jones and Monica Lewinsky. Did he or didn't he? Was that spot on Monica's dress Clinton's semen? The relentless coverage as well as the grand jury inquiry led Clinton to confess his sexual relationship with Lewinsky.

Some media critics, and a good-sized segment of the public, cried, "Enough, already" during the Clinton sex coverage. But others said nothing should be off-limits in the reporting of the powerful, for such reporting informs us of the person to whom we have entrusted authority and power.

For editors, a less theoretical determinant is involved. "When my competition has it, I'll use it," editors say.

The Role of Competition   No editor wants to be accused of protecting someone by not running material that has appeared elsewhere. A few years ago, the mainline newspapers and the networks would not deign to cover a story revealed in the supermarket tabloids. Today, newspapers do so regularly, and the networks have their own versions of the weekly tabloids.

Competition has expanded considerably with the Internet. Here in play daily are rumor, innuendo, gossip and legitimate information put out by news servers. What appears on the screens of millions of Net users cannot be ignored by the older media. After all, it was a Net server who deals in entertainment news and gossip that broke the Clinton-Lewinsky story.

Needs, Nature of the Media

Watch the local evening news on television. Compare the placement and time given news in the broadcast with the play in the newspaper. Some of the news that is emphasized on television is given routine treatment in the newspaper, and some newspaper stories receive slight, if any, mention in newscasts. Obviously, some news is better suited to the newspaper than to television, and television is better able to capture some events than is the newspaper; and neither can compete with online news servers for speedy dissemination of breaking news events.

Television technology and the audience demand pictures, which leads television to lean heavily on action. As Richard Salant, former president of Columbia Broadcasting System News, put it, "You see more fires on local television than you do in the newspapers because fires look better on television."

Online news providers can offer even more information than print publications. Online can do this by linking material to more material.

A news item on CNET, which covers the computer industry, may run a few hundred words. The story will provide links to related material, even items in other news media if they relate to the CNET news story.

Tom Regan, supervising online editor at *The Christian Science Monitor,* sees this as the future for online news providers:

> A reader should be able to come into a news site and see a list of stories, with perhaps a short blurb about each. If the reader so desires he or she should then be able to, as they say, drill down into the story for more information.
>
> Another click brings a longer version of the story. A third click might present additional resources or more photos.
>
> The point is that readers decide how deep they wish to go. If they want a summary, it's there for them. If they want to read a 25-page report referred to in a story, you can provide a link to it.

Economic Pressures

In a newspaper, the space allotted for news usually depends on the amount of advertising that is sold. Unlike radio and television, which have nonexpandable time slots for newscasts, a newspaper may run 32 pages one day and 48 the

Internet Influence. Drudge and other Internet tipsheets reported that a Little Rock prostitute claimed her 13-year-old son was fathered by then governor Bill Clinton. A supermarket tabloid, they reported, would conduct DNA tests on the boy to check the claim. The *New York Post* Sunday final city edition banner headline blared: **Clinton Paternity Bombshell.** The DNA test proved the prostitute's claim false.

next, when department stores place their white-sale advertising. A story that would run half a column on a day when the news hole is tight could be given a full column when ample space is available.

Advertising is the engine that drives the media. When income is down, as it was in the early 1990s, and costs are high, staffs are cut, space and time for news are limited. The media's reliance on advertisers can be even more pernicious. Advertisers can, and do, put pressure on those who decide what's news, even on those who decide on the advertisements the media carry. In Rochester, N.Y., a telecommunications company threatened to pull its commercials unless stations there dropped a union's spots. The union was in a contract dispute with the company. Most stations caved in, but WHAM-AM did not, and the company did indeed pull its commercials.

The annals of journalism have many stories of those who surrender.

Cave In   When the Chinese government was upset by the British Broadcasting Corporation's news coverage of developments in China, it made its displeasure known to Rupert Murdoch, the owner of a massive global media conglomorate that includes large holdings in China. Murdoch's Hong Kong broadcast operation had been airing BBC newscasts that irritated Chinese Communist Party leaders.

Murdoch acted quickly. He eliminated BBC news. He said that using the BBC, considered the provider of the finest broadcast journalism in the world, would jeopardize his business in China.

Murdoch again made the news with a move motivated by his business interests in China. HarperCollins, a book publisher owned by Murdoch, planned to publish a book by Chris Patten, the last British governor of Hong Kong. Patten was an outspoken critic of China's authoritarianism and miserable human rights record. When Murdoch learned of the plans he ordered HarperCollins to drop the book.

A British newspaper published a "private and confidential" memo circulated in the publishing house that set out a strategy to disguise the reason for abandoning the book. The memo, according to the newspaper, "expressed great anxiety over how a 'hostile press' might report the move."

Self-Censorship   Elizabeth Whalen, the executive director of the American Council on Science and Health, was asked by *Harper's Bazaar* to write an article with the title "Protect Your Man from Cancer." Her article began with the link between smoking and cancer. When the editor saw the article, he told a copy editor, "Christ, Jane, I can't open this article with smoking." She moved the material to the end "so it wouldn't jump in the face of every cigarette advertiser," she said.

Whalen was told the cutting was based on her "frequent mention of tobacco and the fact that they (the magazine) ran three full-page cigarette ads each month."

Murdoch's Empire. "Murdoch uses his diverse holdings, which include newspapers, magazines, sports teams, a movie studio and a book publisher, to promote his own financial interests at the expense of real newsgathering, legal and regulatory rules and journalistic ethics. He wields his media as instruments of influence with politicians who can aid him, and savages his competitors in his news columns. If ever someone demonstrated the dangers of mass power being concentrated in few hands, it would be Murdoch."

—*Russ Baker, "Murdoch's Mean Machine," Columbia Journalism Review, May/June 1998.*

Conflicting Goals: Sales vs. Truth

Advertising is the principal source of revenues that supports our media system. That dependence creates an incongruity between the public's preferences and the criteria employed by the people in charge. As consumers of communication, we judge it by its value and meaning for us; advertisers judge it by its efficiency in disseminating what they call "exposure opportunities."

Media content has been driven primarily by the need to maximize audiences for sale rather than by the desire to communicate the truth about our world or express deep thoughts and feelings. To this end, broadcasting and film have vied with each other in pursuit of violence and vulgarity. The largest of our mass media, the daily press, traditionally the forum for contention and irreverence, has undergone a steady attrition of competition and a general retreat to the safety of the middle ground. Left to its own devices, the public persistently drifts toward amusement rather than enlightenment, avoiding confrontation with the pressing, perhaps overwhelming, problems that confront the nation and the world.

—Leo Bogart

Pressures Resisted

For every instance of capitulation to Mammon, there is a positive story that journalists include in their Honor Roll.

No Capitulation   After a Connecticut newspaper printed a front-page story about a kidnapping at a shopping center, the merchants at the center told the publisher that the newspaper's survival depended on the economic health of local business and that such stories would drive shoppers elsewhere. The newspaper replied that crime was always covered by the newspaper and that no individual or group could be given special treatment.

At *The Washington Post,* reporter Leonard Downie had been looking into an arrangement between corrupt real estate speculators and local savings and loan institutions to gouge inner-city residents. The bankers got wind of Downie's checking and told the managing editor that if the *Post* ran the series, they would pull their advertising.

Downie, who later became the *Post*'s managing editor, recalls Benjamin C. Bradlee, his editor, telling him about the visit and the threat. Bradlee looked at Downie and said simply, "Just get it right."

The reporting continued, the series ran and the banks pulled their advertising, costing the newspaper $750,000 in lost advertising revenue.

Tobacco's Dangers   *The Charlotte Observer* carried a 20-page special report titled "Our Tobacco Dilemma." North Carolina's farmers grow two-thirds of the tobacco used for cigarettes and its workers manufacture more than

Mark Sluder, *The Charlotte Observer*

half the almost 700 billion cigarettes made in the United States each year. Tobacco, the state's leading cash crop, brings in $1 billion a year to growers.

Yet the *Observer* did not shrink from putting under the title of its special section this headline:

N.C.'s top crop; part of our lives but bad for health

On the front page next to a picture of a tobacco warehouse was a photograph of James McManus, 62, a former painter and paperhanger, a five-pack-a-day smoker. He was pictured with the tubes from his oxygen tank attached to his nose and mouth. "McManus speaks only with difficulty and needs an oxygen tank to survive," the paper states. He has "smoking-caused emphysema."

The tobacco industry outspends all other national advertisers in newspapers and is second to the transportation industry in magazine advertising. The tobacco industry spends more than $1 billion on advertising cigarettes, about $25 a smoker per year.

Advertising's Positives

Advertisers can also elevate media performance. Increasingly, large retailers are seeking out the quality audience. They are less interested in quantity. They want to reach out to well-educated, discerning and fairly prosperous men and women.

The advertiser who seeks this quality audience wants a quality medium in which to place his ads and commercials. And the advertiser knows that if she were to exercise pressure on the news, the people she is trying to reach with her advertising are the very people who are sure to hear about it.

This takes us to a major determinant in decisions about what is covered and how events are reported and played—the audience.

The Audience

When the TV actress Ellen DeGeneres announced that she is a lesbian, the *San Francisco Chronicle* put the story on page 1 alongside a four-column photo of a crowd in town watching the show on a big screen. *The New York Times* national edition put the story on page 17A. The reason for the difference in play: San Francisco has a large percentage of gay men and women in its population.

Everything media writers do is aimed at an audience, and the nature of that audience may well be the most important influence in media performance.

Look at teen-age magazines. They are preoccupied with romance and dating and personal appearance, not with school or jobs. The news directors of non-commercial television and radio stations lean heavily on analysis and venture into advocacy journalism, whereas the commercial stations with their mass audiences stay close to so-called objective, event-oriented reporting. Reporters for special-interest magazines and alternative newspapers are less sensitive to the needs of the mass audience than are the reporters for daily newspapers.

Newspaper readership studies have shown that young people are interested in stories about music and entertainment and that, as they grow older, marry and purchase homes, they become more interested in local news. Stories about taxes, schools and local politics interest older readers, as do stories about food, health and medicine.

Appealing to the Young

The young and women are increasingly important to advertisers. Both are major spender-consumers. Advertisers are especially interested in reaching the young, whose buying habits are still forming. Advertisers look for the people who buy cars, CDs, stereo units; take weekend jaunts to the Bahamas; buy refrigerators and stoves to set up households. Most of these spenders are young, in their 30s, and their reading and viewing habits are geared to a faster, peppier pace than are those of their elders.

The media have shifted content to attract this younger, on-the-go audience. Profiles of rock groups and movie stars have increased. Stories have been shortened to appeal to an audience said to be too busy to read two columns about the school budget or to devote an hour to a documentary on the rain forest. More illustrations appear in newspapers and magazines, and boxes and other typographic shorthand provide information for readers on the run.

Increasingly, more space is being devoted to sports, style and features, and greater amounts of television time are scheduled for zippy magazine shows. The

The Affluent. *USA Today* devotes plenty of space to its "Money" section. A third of the newspaper's readers have incomes of more than $100,000, the readers that advertisers are anxious to court.

Supermarket Stuff. Sal Ivone, managing editor of the *Weekly World News,* describes the news policy of the tabloid this way: "If someone calls me up and says her toaster is talking to her, I don't refer her to professional help. I say, 'Put the toaster on the phone.'"

traditional news staples—local, national and international news—make up a smaller part of the total news budget.

Special Audiences

As the public has fragmented, so have the media. It is becoming increasingly difficult for a newspaper, magazine or station to appeal to the wide range of interests, tastes, income in the mass audience. The mass media have been joined by specialized media—cable, niche publications, online servers and other media that cater to particular audiences. Actually, this is nothing new, as sports magazines, medical journals, women's magazines, financial publications and the like have been around a long time. But the move toward meeting the needs of special audiences has accelerated.

Newsroom Politics and Ideology

We have to add still another factor in looking at what becomes news, and this is an internal element. We now have to walk into the newsroom to look over the shoulders of reporters and editors and, if we can, figure out why this wire service story about Sen. Roberts' bill will make the news, but Sen. Collins' bill will not.

We see that some editors lean toward features and photos, a sort of news-light, and some prefer the old-fashioned heavy diet of politics, crime and government news. The commitment of a newspaper to a large statehouse staff may mean a lot of news from the state capitol, even at the expense of important international news, because people on the payroll must be put to use.

The politics in the newsroom can affect the news. The power structure, which puts the reporter close to the bottom of the power hierarchy, places decision making in the hands of editors, publishers and news managers who rarely see the events the reporter writes about. Yet they often have firm ideas about what should be covered and how stories should be written, and the reporter is tempted to go along to get along. Some publishers and station owners have pet projects—a favored charity, the downtown business mall—and these will be given special attention. Political and social cronies may be granted time and space disproportionate to their actual news value. And some editors let their ideologies make news.

When Fidel Castro had a swimming accident, the *El Paso Times* ran this headline:

Castro Narrowly Escapes Drowning
Too Bad! Too Bad! Too Bad!

Civil Rights: Not News

During the civil rights movement in the South, when blacks sought an end to discrimination, many newspapers refused to run the growing story.

"Most of the papers in the South blacked out much of what the movement was doing," said John Siegenthaler, who covered the civil rights struggle for *The Tennessean* in Nashville, "even when it was in their own city on their own city square."

Bill Kovach, curator of the Nieman Foundation at Harvard, recalled trying to cover the movement as a young reporter. "The paper I began with in East Tennessee . . . made an arrangement with the Chamber of Commerce not to report on the freedom riders.

"And when I found out, I quit and went to work for the paper John (Siegenthaler) worked for, and we covered the civil rights movement."

The Influence of Owners

The strong publisher determined to influence public policy through his or her newspaper has just about disappeared. But ownership still influences how news is covered and what is published and aired. Without the spur of competition, the monopoly newspaper may become lazy, sitting back to await news rather than going out to dig it up. It may ignore what Benjamin C. Bradlee, the former executive editor of *The Washington Post,* describes as the "special responsibilities" of the monopoly newspaper: "to listen to the voiceless; to avoid any and all acts of arrogance; to face the public with politeness and candor."

Chains The chain newspaper might be light on local news, which is expensive to gather, and heavy on wire news and syndicated material, which requires only editing. An anonymous home office concerned with the profits of the chain may direct the editor of the local newspaper to the bottom line on the ledger rather than to the amount of local news.

The chains are swallowing newspapers at such a rapid rate that four of five newspapers are now within the 170 groups. The chains defend group ownership by contending that the financial strength of groups gives local editors greater resources that enable them to take on the local power structure. But Ben Bagdikian of the University of California, a press critic, disagrees with this optimistic view of chain ownership. He sees the ever-present need for profits precluding the development of quality journalism.

"There's real danger that the number of distinguished papers will decline, because they're part of chains now, too, and the pressure is on them to produce dollars," Bagdikian says.

Leo Bogart, a media research specialist, says that the result of the centralization of newspapers is that "complacent survivors are irresistibly drawn toward the gently flowing mainstream, or even to the shoals of mediocrity, and the public is left without alternative reports and opinions on what's going on."

Tom Wolfe, the former newspaper reporter who wrote *The Right Stuff* and *The Bonfire of the Vanities,* blames newspaper chains for the decline in reporting, which he describes as "the weak link in American journalism right now. And it is, oddly enough, one of the least discussed. But reporting is the heart of everything."

Publisher Power. Arthur Hays Sulzberger disliked modern art, and when he saw a review of Paul Klee's art with an accompanying photo of one of Klee's drawings in his *New York Times,* he exploded: "I don't generally get this positive about things that I don't understand, but I think I am going to say definitely that I don't want anything of this kind in *The New York Times* again."

Threat. "It is daily becoming more obvious that the biggest threat to a free press and the circulation of ideas is the steady absorption of newspapers, television and radio stations, networks and other vehicles of information into corporations that know how to turn knowledge into profit—but are not equally committed to inquiry or debate or to the First Amendment."
—*Reuven Frank, former head of NBC News.*

U.S. Cities with Competing Daily Newspapers

- ● Birmingham (Ala.) News
- ● Birmingham Post-Herald

- ● Tucson Arizona Daily Star
- ● Tucson Citizen
- ● Tucson Territorial

- ● San Francisco Chronicle
- ● San Francisco Examiner

- ■ Denver Post
- ■ Denver Rocky Mountain News

- ■ Washington Post
- ■ Washington Times

- ● Honolulu Advertiser
- ● Honolulu Star-Bulletin

- ■ Chicago Defender
- ■ Chicago Daily Herald
- ■ Chicago Southtown Economist
- ■ Chicago Sun-Times
- ■ Chicago Tribune

- ● Salt Lake City Desert News
- ● Salt Lake City Tribune

- ● Fort Wayne (Ind.) News-Sentinel
- ● Fort Wayne Journal-Gazette

- ■ Boston Globe
- ■ Boston Herald

- ● Detroit Free Press
- ● Detroit News

- ■ Columbia (Mo.) Missourian
- ■ Columbia Daily Tribune

- ● Lincoln (Neb.) Journal
- ● Lincoln Star

- ■ Las Vegas (Nev.) Sun
- ■ Las Vegas Review-Journal

- ■ Trenton (N.J.) Times
- ■ Trenton Trentonian

- ● Albuquerque (N.M.) Journal
- ● Albuquerque Tribune

- ■ New York Daily News
- ■ New York Post
- ■ New York Times
- ■ New York Newsday
- ■ Stater Island (N.Y.) Advance

- ● Cincinnati Enquirer
- ● Cincinnati Post

- ■ Wilkes-Barre (Pa.) Times Leader
- ■ Wilkes-Barre Citizens' Voice

- ▼ York (Pa.) Dispatch
- ▼ York Daily Record

- ■ Kingsport (Tenn.) News
- ■ Kingsport Times-News

- ● Seattle Post-Intelligencer
- ● Seattle Times

- ● Charleston (W. Va.) Gazette
- ● Charleston Daily Mail

- ● Green Bay (Wis.) Press-Gazette
- ● Green Bay News-Chronicle

- ● Madison (Wis.) Capital Times
- ● Madison Wisconsin State Journal

Legend:
- ■ Two separate newspapers
- ● Newspapers under joint operating agreements

Dying Competition

The number of cities with competing newspapers has steadily declined, and the number of chain-owned newspapers has spiraled over the past three decades, the result of declining advertising income and a decrease in the circulation of afternoon newspapers. Twenty-eight states have no competing newspapers.

"The reason that the link has become weak is the fact that there has been such an erosion of competition in the newspaper business. There are many cities where newspapers are, in effect, regional monopolies. This inevitably leads to a reduction in the ranks of reporters."

Eugene Patterson, former editor of the *St. Petersburg Times,* says the concentration of media ownership "has come at the price of commitment to public service. Publicly held chains must pay attention to the sensitivities of securities analysts, and those birds are not overly sentimental about good intentions that might dilute shareholders' profits. Add to the mix competition from new technologies like the Internet, and front offices start trying to count jumping beans."

Some Optimism   This competition from the so-called New Media may well offer the public a wider news and information menu so that the ingredients lacking in the so-called Old Media are increasingly available. The many and diverse voices now at finger-tip availability range from gossip and entertainment information on the Drudge Report to commentaries and controversies on the online magazines, the zines.

When a major network, ABC, owned by Disney plays up or ignores some aspect of Disney's affairs, the reaction is quick and efficient: A scathing report runs on the Net, and a cable outfit delights in reporting the special treatment.

The Changing Nature of News

News, we've seen, is hardly determined in a vacuum. The subjects of journalism change with such a variety of causes it would take many more pages to catalog them. As the economy improved, for example, people had more leisure time and entertainment news increased, as did financial news because working men and women were interested in how to invest their money.

Governmental actions in the 1990s were aimed at decentralizing power, moving decision making from Washington to state capitals and cities. This has meant more coverage at the local level of government activities. The changing face of welfare is now a local story.

The people who decide what is news are themselves hardly representative of the public, and this was evident in the coverage of religion.

News of Religion

Religion, says Terry Mattingly, wasn't news for a long time, despite the clear religious convictions of most people in the United States. He recalls covering the 1984 convention of Southern Baptists, the largest non-Catholic denomination in the United States, when its leadership stated that women should not be ordained because Eve sinned first in Eden. Mattingly, who writes the "On Religion" column for Scripps Howard News Service, learned that moderates in the organization were thinking of forming a breakaway organization and he informed his editor. His story was spiked.

Today, he says, it is "impossible to argue that religion isn't news. Everyone from Billy Graham to Shirley MacLaine has preached sermons to journalists noting that religious groups shape the lives of millions, control budgets containing billions of dollars and play pivotal roles in an unusually high number of gripping local, national and international stories."

TV Coverage   On television, WNET produces the program "Religion & Ethics NewsWeekly," which is dedicated to exploring "the new diversity of America's spiritual life, the beliefs of the major faith traditions, and the profound ethical dilemmas facing us all." The programs have traced the arrival in the United States of new religious traditions brought in by immigrants since the passage of the 1965 Immigration Act. The program looked at Boston, home of

Bob Thayer, *The Providence Journal Bulletin*

Religion Now News

Long confined to back pages and covered with routine notices of services and quotes from sermons, religious news has emerged as a major beat.

Irish Catholics and old-line Congregationalists and Unitarians. Now a Hindu temple attracts thousands of Boston-area Hindus, and an Islamic center serves one of 20 Muslim communities in New England.

It asked seven people from different religious traditions how they blend their religious beliefs with their working lives. Sen. Joseph Lieberman, D-Conn., an Orthodox Jew, will not do routine political work on the Sabbath. But he says that if he has "to make an important decision that affects people of my state, I will take a call on the Sabbath, or walk over to the Senate and cast my vote."

Some newspapers have weekly sections that cover religion, and the intensified coverage has led to many page 1 stories about such issues as the ordination of married men as priests, the split in Baptist seminaries over the interpretation of the Bible, the condemnation by Orthodox rabbis of Reform and Conservative Judaism.

To guide journalists toward informed coverage of religion, The Freedom Forum has issued a booklet "Deities & Deadlines: A Primer on Religion News Coverage" by John Dart, religion reporter at the *Los Angeles Times.* The Religion Newswriters Association gives annual awards for coverage.

Next, two other subjects long ignored by the media.

Environmental Reporting

Journalism was late in examining the disrespect for and the despoiling of land, air and water. Despite public interest in the subject, most newspapers and television stations do not have full-time environmental reporters. The beat isn't sexy, says James Detjen, an environmental reporter now at Michigan State University. Moreover, it's complicated.

"It's tougher reporting than if you go to cover a game or if you are covering City Hall," says Gregory Favre, executive editor of *The Sacramento Bee,* which has three full-time reporters on the beat. "This stuff is not right up there in front, and there are all different kinds of agendas at work and multiple facets of any one story."

Hog Heaven   Despite journalism's tardiness and the complexity of the beat, major stories have been developed about the threat to the environment by accident and design. *The News & Observer* examined an unlikely source of environmental degradation—hog lagoons.

Raising hogs is big business, and the bigger the hog farm the better the business because the slaughterhouse can be next door, eliminating the expense of hauling the hogs to the meat cutters. But the big hog farms—some have a million animals—do the following, the newspaper revealed:

Contaminate Ground Water

Through the emission of ammonia gas into the atmosphere that is returned with rain, streams are being choked with algae.

Waste from the hogs — which produce as much as four times as much waste per hog as do humans — is piling up in open fields.

The series on the hog farms contamination won a Pulitzer Prize.

The Society of Environmental Journalists has a Web page with links to authoritative sources: www.sej.org, and one of the links is to the National Library for the Environment: www.cnie.org/nel/index.shmtl.

Gays and Lesbians

Another subject long ignored by the newsroom was news of the gay and lesbian community. This omission is an exhibit in the case some make against the media, suggesting that most of the media follow because they fear to lead.

Journalists considered such coverage taboo. They were concerned about a backlash from their readers and viewers.

No longer a hush-hush subject, such coverage is routine today, even though some segments of the public continue to object—to little avail.

After the *Florida Times-Union* in Jacksonville ran a profile of gay parents, readers protested in letters and with phone calls. A few threatened to cancel subscriptions.

The newspaper did not publish the protesting letters. Most, said reader advocate Mike Clark, contained profanity and were otherwise unprintable.

"If you do a story about gays and imply they deserve coverage, you get the most extreme reaction from readers. The whole issue of homosexuality is a very powerful one in this town. Emotions kind of go off the chart," says Clark.

"News and feature stories have to cover the real world," he continues. "That includes families that differ from the traditional family unit."

Weather

"Everybody talks about the weather," said Mark Twain, "but nobody does anything about it." That was true of journalism for years. Content to give a few lines to the forecast and coverage of violent weather, the weather was a nonstory.

All this has changed. A mobile society has put grandparents in Miami, a son in Duluth, a daughter in San Diego while the folks are at home in Detroit. And when the folks plan a week's vacation they want to know what the weather will be like for their trip to Tucson.

Commuters want to know, too. Should they take an umbrella when they go into the city?

The response: Color weather maps, an all-weather TV channel and weather reports every eight minutes on all-news radio.

Nancy Pastor

Street Shower

Even 4-year-olds are interested in the weather. A sudden rainstorm gave this youngster a fun bathing, far better than the nightly bath at home.

Information

We have to add another dimension to our discussion of news—information. By this we mean the kind of material that is "useful to everyday living," to quote an executive of Scripps Howard.

"Our papers (and many others) have been paying attention to readership studies that say people want the best of both worlds: the news of the day AND information they can use in their personal lives, such as tips on time-saving and traffic, parenting and personal relationships, money-saving, job-finding," says Susan H. Miller, an executive with the news organization.

"We should be asking ourselves how we can better serve people in a changing world."

News organizations have been doing the asking of the public as well as engaging in soul-searching. They have conducted focus groups of their readers and viewers, and they have established advisory groups. Let's look at one.

Public Participation

At the *Argus Leader* in Sioux Falls, S.D., the editors meet with an advisory board to obtain insights into what people think should become news. (The newspaper also has an Editorial Board Advisory Committee.)

The *Argus Leader* is part of the Gannett newspaper group and has been working with the group's News 2000 program in an attempt to become reader driven. David W. Hawpe, editor of Gannett's *Courier-Journal,* says the program is designed to meet readers' needs and desires, designed to "empower" readers and to sharing "the civic dialogue with them rather than dictating to them."

Vox Populi

The voice of the Sioux Falls public is sounded through *Argus Leader* advisory panels. The people speak; the editors listen. Citizens provide comments on events the newspaper has ignored, criticism of coverage and, occasionally, praise for work well done.

In some cities, the concept of "public journalism" has taken hold. In Norfolk, Va., *The Virginian-Pilot* replaced its beat system with reporting teams organized to cover issues such as public safety and public life, issues, the editors say, that will be covered the way private citizens see them.

Civic Journalism   An outgrowth of public participation has been the development of civic or public journalism in which extensive use of polling and focus groups attempts to determine what's on the mind of the public. The issues that turn up become the subjects of the sponsoring publication or station's news coverage.

Newspapers using the concept have covered elections on the basis of what the public told them should be discussed by the candidates.

Critics have said civic journalism may overlook issues people would prefer not to discuss, and Eugene Patterson, former editor of the *St. Petersburg Times,* calls it a "hand-licking fad."

Most journalists are wary of surrendering their decision making. They contend they know their community's heart and soul and can reflect these in their news decisions. Some journalists go further: They actively set a news agenda for their communities. These journalists can be described as advocates of an activist journalism.

An Activist Journalism

To some journalists, news consists of overt events—an automobile accident, a city council meeting, a court document, the State of the Union Address. Their journalism is denotative, pointing to what has happened.

Necessary as this reporting is, some journalists consider it a passive type of journalism because the journalist essentially is responding to events. They would complement denotative journalism with a more active, seeking-out journalism.

Abortions for All   When Heidi Evans of the *Daily News* was told by a caller that every woman who went to a cash-only abortion clinic was informed that she was pregnant, Evans raced over to the clinic the next day with a urine sample of her own.

"The owner, who did the tests himself, told me I was pregnant and tugged at my arm to have the procedure right then," Evans said.

"The following day, I sent another reporter with a sample from one of our male colleagues. The urine also tested positive." After two more weeks of reporting, in which she showed how poor, mostly immigrant women were herded by the clinic owner to a back room where a fly-by-night doctor operated, the state shut down the clinic.

Evans had been called by the clinic owner's receptionist with the tip because Evans had a reputation as a reporter who could do something, could correct injustice. She had just completed a series after finding that the city had 2,000 unread Pap tests sitting in a box. Thousands more had just been sent out for analysis after sitting in an office for as long as a year unread.

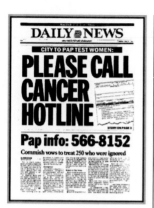

Help Offered

When the *Daily News* prodded the city to act, it set up a Hot Line for women whose Pap tests were ignored.

"The women had been told by clinic doctors to assume their Pap tests were normal if they didn't hear back in six weeks," Evans said. "Ninety three learned later that they had precancerous conditions and 11 had cervical cancer."

The result: The city's testing program was overhauled and women now are given their test results in a week. Four of the officials responsible were fired or demoted. Evans was awarded the prestigious George Polk Award for local reporting for her Pap smear series.

Evans is not reluctant to say that her journalism is an activist, advocacy journalism. She makes news out of the undercurrents and the hidden activities of those in power.

Legitimatizing Issues

Activist journalists seek to place on the public agenda matters that they believe require consideration and action. Social scientists say that conditions usually do not speak for themselves. The sociologist Herbert Blumer states that issues come to public attention, not because of the "intrinsic gravity of the social problem," but because they have been given status by some respected group that has called attention to the problem. These groups can legitimatize an issue as a matter of concern requiring action, Blumer says.

Among those that can legitimatize situations Blumer lists educational organizations, religious leaders, legislators, civic groups and the press. Once legitimatized, the issue may be acted on quickly, as occurred when television showed the starvation in Somalia and the United States sent in troops with food. Or the situation may be unresolved, as has happened despite the efforts of political leaders and the press in the case of poverty, still a problem more than three decades after President Lyndon B. Johnson declared a war on poverty.

Summing Up

Impersonal and objective as journalists would like to make the determinants of news, much of journalism is based on selection, and choice is a highly personal affair. It derives from the journalist's professional background, his or her education and the intangible influences of family, friends and colleagues.

The professional decisions—what people need to know—are framed by other considerations as well: The need to entertain to keep readers and viewers who are constantly being seduced by entertainment media; the pressures of the business of journalism such as budgeting restrictions, meeting the competition, considering the needs of advertisers.

Even more elusive in our search for absolutes in the area of news determinants are the decisions that have their origin in the arena where ambition and conscience battle.

Vague as these influences may be, the reporter must cope with them. Fortunately, the reporter's handiwork is tangible. Once the heat of reporting and writing has cooled, the reporter can examine the story. Then, alone or with a trusted friend or colleague, the reporter can try to pinpoint the reasons for decisions. This self-questioning—directed by some of the principles we have discussed in this chapter and those we'll tackle in Chapter 27 on the morality of journalism—is part of the journalist's continuing education.

Further Reading

Bagdikian, Ben H. *The Media Monopoly.* Boston: Beacon Press, 1987.
Clurman, Richard. *To the End of Time: The Seduction and Conquest of a Media Empire.* New York: Simon & Schuster, 1992.
Gans, Herbert J. *Deciding What's News.* New York: Pantheon Books, 1979.
Roshco, Bernard. *Newsmaking.* Chicago: University of Chicago Press, 1975.
Schudson, Michael. *Discovering the News.* New York: Basic Books, 1978.
Westin, Av. *Newswatch: How TV Decides the News.* New York: Simon & Schuster, 1983.

4 The Tools of the Trade

The telephone . . . a basic reporting tool.

Preview

Journalists rely on a variety of tools to do their work. These include the computer, tape recorder, telephone and many information sources such as census data, polls, reference works, official documents and reports, many of which are available on-line in databases.

The journalist:

- Understands how to use basic references.
- Knows public-record laws.
- Understands how the computer can help to gather and to analyze information for stories.
- Is able to conduct and interpret a public opinion poll.

Journalists use several kinds of instruments for their reporting—pencils, pads, tape recorders and computers. They use reference materials and such analytic tools as mathematics and polling techniques. Then there is the special language the journalist uses to communicate with co-workers.

Learning the language is essential, as the apprentice electrician finds out the first day on the job when he is told to get a bucket of volts, or the chemistry student who is immortalized in the couplet:

Johnny was a chemist; Johnny is no more.

What Johnny thought was H_2O was H_2SO_4.

Newsroom ignorance may not prove fatal, but it can lead to inclusion in journalism's hall of horrors. Take the case of the afternoon newspaper in Walsenburg, Colo., that wanted to carry the name of the winner of the Indianapolis 500 car race in its late edition. The newspaper's AP wire shut off at 3 p.m., too early for the result. So the editor asked the Indianapolis AP bureau to let him know who the winner was by telegram.

The Indianapolis bureau acknowledged the newspaper's request with this message: "Will overhead winner of Indianapolis 500." The AP was telling Walsenburg it would telegram the winner's name. In wire service lingo, the word *overhead* was used for *telegram*.

But the sports department didn't know that, and a reporter who was handed the message wrote this story:

> Indianapolis, Ind., May 30 — (AP) — Will Overhead won the Indianapolis Memorial Day race today. At the two hundred fifty mile post Babe Stapp was leading the string of racing cars, but gave way to Overhead on the last half of the 500 mile grind.

A glossary of journalism terms is provided in the back of the book. When in doubt about any term, consult it. You may want to pencil in additions.

Bannered Blunder

The Tangible Tools

Unlike the reporter's vocabulary, the tangible tools are supplied by the employer:

The **computer** is used to type and to edit stories, to call up background information and to do computer-assisted reporting from databases.

A **pad** with a hard back like a stenographer's notebook is best for note taking. The stiff backing makes jottings clear, and the spiral binding keeps notes in order.

The **tape recorder** is a necessity for the radio reporter, optional for the print reporter. The tape recorder is useful in covering speeches. It is an aid for stories requiring precise quotes. The broadcast journalist may not tape the voice of the source without asking permission.

A **laptop computer** is useful for out-of-office assignments.

The **telephone** is a basic tool of the trade but it cannot substitute for the face-to-face interview. (See Chapter 25 for legal restrictions.)

The **cellular phone** and the computer, powered by battery, allow reporters to send in their stories from any location. The system can be carried in a briefcase.

The **microcomputer** makes charts, graphs and diagrams. With the microcomputer it is possible for even the smallest newspapers and stations to expand their use of visual material produced in the newsroom.

Newsroom Resources

Newspapers and stations subscribe to a variety of news services. The major supplier is the Associated Press. Syndicates formed by large newspapers such as the Los Angeles Times–Washington Post News Service, the Chicago Tribune Press Service, the New York Times News Service and others are increasingly used.

Local reporters use the wire services for special coverage. A newspaper will ask the AP to follow a local team in a national tournament and the service will write a story aimed at that paper's readers. The wire service also will make special checks. A member newspaper could ask the AP to check a senator's vote on a farm bill, for example.

Basic References

Every reporter has a few references handy—the newspaper or station stylebook, a dictionary and the telephone directory. The stylebook assures consistency in spelling, capitalization, punctuation and abbreviation. Is it 18 Fifth Ave. or 18 Fifth Avenue? The stylebook tells us. Do newspapers use postal abbreviations for states? The stylebook tells us to use Calif., not CA. A **Stylebook**, included in this textbook for your use, begins on p. 723.

Reporters use the dictionary to verify spellings and to make certain that the words they want have the shades of meaning they intend.

The cross-indexed or reverse directory, a listing of telephone numbers by address, is invaluable on a late-breaking story when the reporter cannot go to the event but needs details from the scene.

Every reporter should know how to use these references, most of which are available online as well as in print form:

Searching the Past

For her feature on changes in fashions, this reporter turns to the *Reader's Guide* for magazine articles about men's and women's clothing in the 1960s. She could also have used a CD-ROM of the *Guide*.

- **A world almanac.**
- *The Reader's Guide to Periodical Literature.*
- *The New York Times Index.*
- *Bartlett's Familiar Quotations.* Who penned, "How do I love thee? Let me count the ways"? Had a Chicago journalist consulted Bartlett's, the newspaper might have been spared embarrassment. The quotation was used under a large page-1 picture of a couple sitting on a statue of Shakespeare in a Chicago park—with attribution to William Shakespeare. (If you do not know the author, look it up.)
- *National Five-Digit Zip Code and Post Office Directory.* Use this for locating cities in states and for finding the ZIP code.
- **City directory.** Several firms produce directories with information about people living in the community. A typical entry will include correct full name; occupation and employer; complete street address including apartment number; spouse's name and initial; whether the person owns or rents, is retired, is employed, is a student. In the street directory, a reporter can find the name of the resident and his or her telephone number from a given address. Some directories are based on telephone numbers; given a number, the reporter can find the name of the telephone subscriber. The directory companies also make up classified business directories that list, at no charge, all businesses.
- *Who's Who in America.* This resource contains biographical information about 72,000 living North Americans and is an essential source for information about leaders in social, economic, cultural and

ALPHABETICAL DIRECTORY WHITE PAGES

ⓗ HOUSEHOLDER   ⓡ RESIDENT OR ROOMER

correct full name —————————

occupation and employer —————

complete street address
including apartment number ———

student 18 years of age or older ——

cross reference of surnames ———

out-of-town resident employed
in area ——————————

armed force member and
branch of service ——————

wife's name and initial —————

corporation showing officers and
nature of business ——————

suburban designation —————

retiree ——————————

business partnership showing
partners in parenthesis ————

husband and wife employed ———

"r" resident or roomer —————

"h" householders ——————

owner of business showing name
of business in parenthesis ———

bold type denotes paid listing ——

business firm showing name of
owner in parenthesis ————

unmarried and unemployed
resident ————————

more than one adult in household ——

church showing name of pastor ——

Landon Edw G & Charlotte D; servmn B F Goodrich
   h1215 Oak Dr
Landon Fred M & Mary E; supvr Reliance Elec h60
   Norman Av
Landon Kenneth A & Carol L; clk First Natl Bk
   h1400 E Main St Apt 14
Landon Kenneth A Jr studt r1400 E Main St Apt 14
Landon Virginia E r1641 W 4th St
Lane See Also Layne
Lane Allen M & Joan M (Allen's Bakery) h1234
   Grand Blvd
Lane Avenue Restaurant (Ernest G Long) 216
   Lane Av
Lane James M & Betty B; brkmn Penn Central
   ~ Rt 1 Jefferson O
Lane Marvin L USA r1234 Grand Blvd
Lane Robt B & Margt E; retd h1402 N High St
Lane Walter M r1234 Grand Blvd
Layne See Also Lane
Layne Agnes E Mrs v-pres Layne Co h2325
   Eureka Rd
Layne Albert M & Minnie B; slsmn Hoover Co h19
   Bellows Av
Layne Co Inc Thos E Layne Pres Mrs Agnes E
   Layne V-Pres Edw T Layne Sec-Treas bldg
   contrs 100 N High St
Layne Edw T & Diane E; sec-treas Layne Co h140
   Oakwood Dr
Layne Ralph P & Gladys M; formn Layne Co h1687
   Maple Dr
Layne Thos E & Agnes E; pres Layne Co h2325
   Eureka Rd
Leach See Also Leech
Leach Wm E USMC r1209 Ravenscroft Rd (EF)
Lee Alf M & Celia J; retd h2106 Oakwood Dr
Lee Bros (Louis J And Harry M Lee) plmbs 151
   Abbott St
Lee Harry M & Karen L (Lee Bros) h2023 Stone Rd
Lee Louis J & Martha B (Lee Bros) h1616 Fulton
Lee Martha B Mrs ofc sec Lee Bros h1616 Fulton

Lee Minnie M Mrs h87 Eastview Dr
Lee Muriel E r810 LaForge St
Lee Sterling T & Nadine S; mtcemn Eastview Apts
   h202 Wilson St Apt 1
Lee Thos W & Effie M (Tom's Men's Wear) r Rt 23

**LEE'S PHARMACY (Lee A Shaw) Prescriptions
   Carefully Compounded, Complete Line Of
   Toiletries And Cosmetics, Fountain Service,
   Greeting Cards, 1705 N High St (21505) Tel**

Leech See Also Leach
Leech Doris E tchr North High Sch
   h1323 W McLean St
Leech Joseph B & Lucy V; slsmn Metropolitan Dept
   Store h824 Wilson St
Leech Joseph B Jr studt r824 Wilson St
Leech Marcia M clk Community Hosp r1323 W
   McLean St
Lewis Anne M Mrs clk County Hwy Dept h914
   Wilson Av
Lewis Ernest W studt r914 Wilson Av
Lewis Harold G & Anne M; mgr Cooper Paint Store
   h914 Wilson Av
Lewis Robt B lab County Hwy Dept r1410 Union
   Hwy Rt 2
Lewistown Methodist Church Rev John R Allen
   Pastor 515 Maple Valley Rd

R.L. Polk and Company

political affairs. Biographical information is supplied by the person listed. Other biographical directories published by the same firm, Marquis Who's Who Inc., include regional directories and directories on biographees' professions. For biographies of long-dead people, the *Dictionary of American Biography* is useful. For people who have died within the last several years, consult back volumes of *Who's Who, Who Was Who* or *Current Biography.*

Using the Computer

Key Skills. Wendy S. Williams of American University says the basic skills needed for computer-assisted reporting are keyword searching of text files, e-mailing, understanding databases—including their breadth and limitations—and understanding how to use the Internet.

The computer has put information of vast scope at the journalist's fingertips. Through the computer, the journalist can dip into the newspaper or station's library with ease and venture way beyond to commercial online services such as Lexis-Nexis, which supplies stories from hundreds of newspapers and magazines, and to the Internet with its World Wide Web and news groups.

The reach is enormous, and it is ever widening. Every day, journalists use the Internet to obtain material for stories. A reporter in Ohio is checking on local health care and wants to see how other newspapers treated the subject. She calls up stories on the subject. A reporter in North Carolina working on a series on infant mortality needs data about child death in other states. He uses the Web to obtain figures from the Centers for Disease Control and Prevention.

Basic Functions

Smarts. "Tools and technology are important only in reference to their application. A baboon with a computer is a baboon."
Ed Miller, former editor and publisher, The Morning Call, Allentown, Pa.

The computer is also an organizing tool. It can take information fed into it and perform these functions:

• **Alphabetizing:** Similar jobs or similar names can be placed in a series.

• **Rank ordering:** Instructed to put in order any list, the computer will reveal, for example, the highest to lowest infant mortality rates among the cities in a state or among the states in the nation.

• **Correlating:** The computer will match two different databases. A reporter who wants to check whether school hiring procedures are thorough can match a list of the city's schoolteachers against a list of convictions for sex crimes.

Double Pay   Reporters at the *Dayton* (Ohio) *Daily News* fed the names of all county workers into their computer, which made a master alphabetized list that showed that several employees held two jobs and were receiving two salaries. The reporters also learned the names of those receiving unusually large amounts of overtime pay.

Court Racism   The *Los Angeles Times* analyzed criminal court sentences and found that first-offender blacks were much more likely to be jailed than first-offender whites for the same crimes.

Smoke and Drink   Bob Sanders had heard that alcohol and cigarette distributors target minority neighborhoods. To check, he obtained billboard locations from the city planning commission and the minority population concentrations from tract material of the Census Bureau and correlated them. Here is how his story for *The Post-Standard* in Syracuse, N.Y., begins:

Jeff Scruggs has a blue ribbon on his front door on Seymour Street proclaiming his opposition to drugs.

But when he opens that door each day he is confronted by a different message: a long smoldering cigarette gracing a 12-by-25-foot billboard, providing a backdrop on a corner neighbors say is a hot spot for drug dealers. . . .

All up and down Salina Street and Erie Boulevard, outside the mom-and-pop stores on South Avenue and on the near west side, more than half the city's 247 street-level billboards give residents two major messages: smoke and drink.

Weapons   When reports of mass murders with assault rifles became numerous, reporters in the Washington bureau of the Cox Newspapers decided to see whether these weapons were frequently used in crimes. No one had the information tabulated, so they dug into cardboard files for documents—42,758 in all. With a computer program, they organized the voluminous files and they learned that semiautomatic guns were 20 times more likely to be used in a crime than were conventional weapons.

Sex Offenders   The *Star Tribune* in Minneapolis spent nine months making a computer-assisted analysis of the activities of 767 sex criminals. The 30,000 word series of articles by Donna Halvorsen and Allen Short, "Free to Rape," found the state's courts failed to deal effectively with rapists and child molesters and that those who were treated in Minnesota's costly psychological treatment program were more likely to commit new sex crimes than those who were not treated. The reporters also found a far higher rate of repeat crimes than the state's official figures indicated.

Dangers   Reporters in the Washington bureau of the Knight-Ridder newspapers analyzed computerized Medicare records of open-heart surgery to pinpoint unusually high death rates in some hospitals. After three children were killed in school-bus accidents, *The Providence Journal-Bulletin* compared a list of bus-driver licenses to a tape of traffic violations and discovered that some bus drivers had been ticketed as many as 20 times. Some drivers were convicted felons. The state tightened licensing procedures as a result.

Behind the Tests   In the Hartford bureau of the AP, reporters compiled economic factors for Connecticut's 169 cities and towns. Then it obtained tests scores in reading, writing and math. The bureau staff correlated the scores with the economic factors and found a strong relationship. The best predictor of the scores, they found, was the cost of the homes in which the children live.

> **Not Magic.** Computers "will not transform bad reporters into good ones," says Andrew Schneider, prizewinning reporter and director of the National Institute of Advanced Reporting. "If you don't have the basic reporting skills and use them well, a hundred computers won't make a difference."

Online Publications

Another development from the computer revolution has been the creation of online publications. They range from the online versions of newspapers, which number in the hundreds, to "zines," the online magazines that have no print counterpart. There are also daily news servers online.

These new journalistic ventures are providing journalism graduates with jobs at a time the rest of the industry is static.

Let's look closely at some of these resources.

Databases

Information that used to be stored on paper and tape is now being put in databases, and it's all there for the journalist's use in more than 5,000 machine-readable libraries. Local governments put their payrolls in a database; the agencies of the federal government place just about everything—reports, statistics, payrolls—in databases.

The user has to know where to look for needed information, and directories of electronic information providers can be consulted. There are many of these—Yahoo!, www.yahoo.com, AltaVista, www.altavista.com, among others.

The search sites and other websites that have useful material for reporters are listed in **Appendix E: Sources Online.**

Patrick Lee, a business reporter for the *Los Angeles Times,* says he prefers "statistics, official reports, full documents" to the press releases and canned statements of businesses and government. "The advantage of the Internet is that you can go directly to the primary sources without an intermediary."

Three Types

The three types of databases are:

1. **Full text:** Articles from newspapers and magazines and documents.
2. **Bibliographic:** References to full text; summaries of the full text.
3. **Numeric:** Data such as census material.

Collaboration

The Internet allows journalists to get together through news groups, forums and e-mail discussion groups. The Investigative Reporters and Editors, the Society of Professional Journalists and others provide daily exchanges among journalists.

Randy Reddick, director of FACSNET, an information source used by journalists, says, "The 'conversation' may range from how to manipulate government data files to 'Does anybody out there know some good stories on toxic waste?' "

Applications

Let's see how journalists collaborate.

A *Wall Street Journal* reporter who was preparing a story on Parkinson's disease learned that there is an Internet news group made up of people interested in the disease. He put a message out and was able to obtain useful names and information.

Here are two typical exchanges that moved on the Internet:

Query

Does anybody have story ideas for using death-record data? When you used the data in your state, did you get the names and addresses of the dead people? Here in Oregon, they'll only give you a stripped-down database without the names. Thanks for any ideas.

Reply

You could sort out by cause of death or age of victim. Maybe that would come up with an interesting angle. You might find, for instance, that just as many people in their 70s commit suicide as kids from ages 17 to 24. You might find that people of certain ages and ethnicity tend to die of gunshot wounds. You might find that most people who are homicide victims die between 2 a.m. and 6 a.m., while most suicide victims die in the early afternoon. Dunno. I'm just casting about ideas.

After Orange County, Calif., found itself $1.7 billion in the hole and filed for bankruptcy, a reporter for *The Orange County Register* asked, "Does anyone know where I can find a list of the largest bankruptcies in the U.S.?" An answer came quickly: "I'd try Forbes or Barron's."

The Grateful Dead   When Elizabeth Weise covered a story for the AP about the reopening of a remodeled auditorium in San Francisco, she wrote that the Grateful Dead had played the night the hall opened 35 years before. Weise had the bad luck to have an editor in AP's New York headquarters who was a Deadhead. She messaged Weise that the Grateful Dead didn't exist then. Check your facts, she told Weise.

Weise knew that there is a Grateful Dead Usenet news group, and she posted a query on it. She was right, they told her, but at that time the group was using the name The Warlocks.

The Web

Used with care, websites provide quick and useful information, ranging from the general to the specific.

Several organizations provide journalists with background material and access to experts. FACSNET, www.facsnet.org, makes available background papers and documents on public policy issues and has links, organized around beats, to sources for interviews.

ProfNet also provides sources for interviews. ProfNet is a collaborative of 4,000 public information officers linked by the Internet who can provide quick and convenient access to experts. Half the members of ProfNet are colleges and universities. The remainder consist of think tanks, laboratories, government agencies, nonprofit organizations and public relations agencies. ProfNet, www.vyne.com/profnet/, also can be reached by e-mail, profnet@vyne.com

Online Road Map   Each week, Hot News/Hot Research at the Poynter Institute for Media Studies selects a newsworthy topic and provides links to sites useful to journalists writing on the topic. Among the topics Hot News/Hot Research (www.poynter.org/hr/hr_intro.htm) has examined are school violence, media credibility, Martin Luther King Jr. Day. Researcher David Shedden describes the service as a series of road maps that lead the user to information.

Donations   Want to know who donated to a candidate for Congress and how much, consult the Federal Election Commission Reports, www.tray.com/FEC/INFO/index/html-ssi. A Nation of Islam speaker coming to town, you can find information from the organization at www.noi.org/, and if you want comments on the Nation of Islam you can consult Yahoo!, a hierarchical index, www.yahoo.com, or one of the search engines, AltaVista, www.altavista.com, or HotBot, www.hotbot.com. The Anti-Defamation League (www.adl.org) also has material.

Most journalistic Web work involves obtaining material kept by various governmental agencies—city building permits, names of school bus drivers, planning and zoning actions, county tax receipts, election results by precinct and voting district, census data, drunk driving convictions, prison populations, violent and property crimes on campus. The list is longer than imaginable. If there is a document kept by a governmental department, chances are that it is available through the Internet.

Dead Voters

In a close race for attorney general of New York State, the Republican candidate, who had lost, charged that votes had been cast by dead people in New York City. Josh Barbanel of *The New York Times* decided to investigate the claim. He took the registration rolls of all voters in New York City and compared the names with names on a list of 17.4 million people who had died since 1990 that the Social Security Administration provided.

He found that only a scattering of names overlapped, that it amounted to 132 votes, far short of the number the losing candidate needed to overcome his rival in the race.

Barbanel went further than settling for his computer count. He took the names of four of the supposedly dead voters in his tabulations and tried to track them down. He found that three were actually alive, which the Social Security Administration confirmed. The fourth person was indeed dead. But his son, who

The Library of Congress

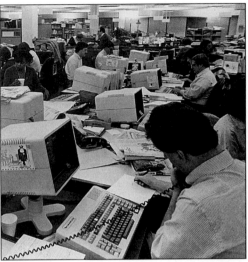

Newsday

The Old . . . and the New Newsrooms

Before the electronic revolution, paper, pencils, glue pots and spikes were the tools of the trade for copy editors. Under the harsh light of bright bulbs overhead, the editors slashed at the copy in front of them. In today's newsroom, computers have replaced typewriters, pencil and paper. Stories are edited on the screen, and no one accidentally jams his or her hand on the spike.

bore the same name, had been voting under his father's name because the son's voting registration card had been destroyed in error.

Shortly thereafter, the Republican candidate dropped his charges and conceded the election.

Helpers

There is so much out there, no journalist can hope to know the extent. Enter the librarians, men and women especially trained to lend journalists a hand in traveling along the cyberspace highway. At the *Daily News* in New York, Russ Buettner is looking into divorce proceedings, why the process is so slow, how judges handle cases, who is favored in monetary awards and custody.

It's a joint venture, Buettner and the newspaper library staff, just as it was when they combined for a major series that revealed the failure of the city's health department to monitor restaurants in New York. Despite citations for unhealthy conditions, few were closed. The series caused tremors among New Yorkers, who are frequent diners at delis, corner cafes and posh restaurants—many of which were in the health department's database as having roaches, mice and assorted vermin in their kitchens.

Cautions and Warnings

Gary Deckelnick, legal affairs editor of the *Asbury Park Press* in New Jersey, advises caution in the use of sources provided by the Internet. "You weigh what they say, evaluate their credentials and act accordingly," he says. "There's no law requiring you to print everything you get from ProfNet or everything you get from interviewing the local mayor."

Neil Reisner, a training director for the National Institute for Computer-Assisted Reporting, says the Internet is "just another tool for journalists. Use the same methods you use to verify any other source."

Revisionists   In *The New Republic,* Brian Hecht says of the Internet, "It is impossible to know where information comes from, who has paid for it, whether it is reliable and whether you will ever be able to find it again. A student looking for information on the Internet about, say, World War II cannot know whether a given 'page' has been posted by a legitimate historian or by a Holocaust revisionist." (Revisionists assert there was no Holocaust in which Nazi Germany murdered millions of Jews, gypsies, the mentally ill, homosexuals and political opponents.)

Polluters   Bill Kovach, curator of the Nieman Foundation at Harvard, worries about the "careless, even ignorant misuse of technology." He says that too many reporters "routinely rummage around in the electronic databases for information which, as often as not, is a public-relations handout, self-serving market tip or other self-seeking, self-serving trash.

"As a result, plagiarism and facile rewriting masquerade as real reporting and further pollute the electronic databases with more useless, inaccurate information." Kovach worries that because databases may not be recharged "with new and important information based on active and aggressive reporting of what is truly new" that the database will grow "more toxic and dangerous to the health of democracy."

Shoe Leather Reporting

As essential as the computer has become to journalism, it does not substitute for the old-fashioned type of reporting described by one of the great practitioners of the trade, Joe Liebling, as "climbing the stairs and knocking on doors."

The reporter may obtain data on the unusually high infant mortality rate in Forsyth County, but these are just numbers. The *Winston-Salem Journal* gave the real dimension of individual tragedy by interviewing the parents behind the statistics.

Louis D. Boccardi, chief executive officer of the Associated Press, says that although the new technology can strengthen news reporting, "the seductiveness of its technology" should not change "the principles of what we do."

Too Distant. "Technology is the knack of so arranging the world that we don't have to experience it."

—*Max Frisch, Swiss playwright.*

Public Records

Reporters should know just what records are available to them on their beats. Among the many records usually accessible to the public are:

- Assessment and tax records, deeds, property transfers.
- Records dealing with licenses—restaurant, dog, liquor, tavern and the many other business and professional licenses.
- City engineer's records—streets, alleys, property lines, highways.
- City building permits, variances, unpaid taxes, liens, violations.
- Automobile ownership.
- Election returns.
- Articles of incorporation. Most states require officers to file their names and holdings in the corporation. Partnerships.
- Bills and vouchers for all governmental purchases. Copies of the checks (warrants) paid out for goods and services.
- Minutes of city council, county commission meetings. All appropriations, budgets.
- Most records in the judicial area—indictments, trials, sentences, court transcripts.
- Wills, receiverships, bankruptcies.
- Most police records on a current basis.

Reporters sometimes discover that they are denied public records. A check of the law helps open them up. All the states have "sunshine laws" that require records to be available for public examination.

Freedom of Information Act

Access to one of the vast areas of information—federal records—was limited until Congress enacted the Freedom of Information Act in 1966. The act, and important amendments in 1975, unlocked millions of pages of federal documents. The FOIA states that the public has the right to inspect any document that the executive branch possesses, with nine exceptions. These exceptions prevent reporters, or anyone else, from examining income tax returns, secret documents vital to national defense or foreign policy, intra-agency letters and other sensitive material.

The 1975 amendments give the federal courts the power to review classified documents to make sure that they are properly classified, and they put a limit on the time an agency can take to reply to a request.

The *Mercury-News* in San Jose, Calif., used a Freedom of Information request to the FBI to obtain material that revealed that President Reagan had been an FBI informer in the late 1940s. The documents obtained by the newspaper identified Reagan as "T-10" and said that he and his first wife had "provided the FBI with names of actors they believed were members of a clique with a pro-Communist line." The *Mercury-News* also learned from FBI files on the author John Steinbeck that the FBI had tracked Steinbeck for years because of his involvement with labor causes. Steinbeck wrote *The Grapes of Wrath*, which won a Pulitzer Prize for literature in 1940.

No Secrets. The journalist's insistence on freedom to seek out information has a distinguished heritage. In 1644, John Milton's *Areopagitica, "A Speech for the Liberty of Unlicensed Printing,"* contended that truth might be learned if all ideas were let loose for discussion. Joseph Pulitzer put the matter in journalistic terms:

"There is not a crime, there is not a dodge, there is not a trick, there is not a swindle which does not live by secrecy. Get these things out in the open, describe them, attack them, ridicule them in the press, and sooner or later public opinion will sweep them away."

To use the act, find out which agency has the records sought. A guide is the *U.S. Government Manual,* which may be obtained from the Government Printing Office. Ask for Stock Number D22-003-00424-8. Requests usually are sent to the Freedom of Information Office of the agency. No reason need be given for the request for information. It sometimes makes the request easier to handle if specific information is requested. Charges are usually nominal. The reporter may ask to be notified of charges in advance.

The letter should state that the request is being made "under the provisions of the Freedom of Information Act, 5 U.S.C. 552." See **Appendix C** for the request procedure and a sample letter.

State Laws: Exceptions

All states have enacted open records and open meetings laws. Usually, these laws presume that everything public and official is open with stipulated exceptions. Most denials of requests for records fall into these categories:

1. **Confidential records.** Records that are exempted by federal or state law such as income tax returns, health and welfare files on individuals.

2. **Privacy.** Records that would allow an unwarranted invasion of an individual's privacy. (Officials have less right of privacy than do private individuals.)

3. **Collective bargaining negotiations.** Disclosure of present or imminent actions in these areas could impair discussions.

4. **Trade secrets.** Information that might injure a person or firm in a competitive situation.

5. **Records compiled for law enforcement agencies.** Records that could impede a fair trial, endanger the life or safety of an agent or an informer.

6. **Interagency memoranda and intra agency reports.** Excludes statistics, policies and instructions to the staff.

7. **Examinations and evaluations.** Materials used in assessing job applicants.

The states' open meetings laws exempt executive sessions that are concerned with collective bargaining; imminent legislation; the medical, financial or credit records of a person or corporation; and any matters made confidential by state and federal law.

Census Data

The census takes the social and economic pulse of 250 million Americans every 10 years. It is used to determine congressional representation and is the basis for the allocation of billions of dollars in federal, state and local funds. The Bureau of the Census breaks down its count into census tracts of around 4,000 people, making vast amounts of information available to the local reporter: How many married women are living with their husbands? How many households are headed by females? What are the median and average family incomes?

The reporter who wants to track social change in his or her community will find census data essential. Working mothers, children in nursery school, shifts in family patterns and demographic changes—data on all this are available. Reporters have used census data to find pockets of the elderly and of ethnic groups. Changes in the racial makeup of neighborhoods can be charted with census data.

For Civic Profiles   For a story about the housing stock in the community, the reporter can find the number of houses that lack toilets, private baths and hot water. The number of people living in housing units (density) also can be determined. By analyzing who lives in a representative's district, it is possible to indicate how he or she is most likely to vote or to determine the pressures exerted on the legislator regarding public housing, Social Security and other social issues. The data also can be used to document depth reporting—the need for additional day-care centers, low cost housing or senior citizen facilities.

Printed census reports are available at public and university libraries and at many local, state and federal agencies. The best place to obtain local census material is the State Data Center, where experts can help with interpretations and make comparisons with previous censuses. Detailed information is available from the centers on computer tapes and floppy disks as well as on CD-ROM (compact disc–read-only memory) and through the Bureau's website, www.census.gov/.

The Bureau takes more than 250 sample surveys a year to monitor trends in employment, population growth, fertility, living arrangements and marriage. It makes surveys of a number of activities every five years, including housing, agriculture, business, construction, government, manufacturing, mineral industry and transportation.

Death and Disease Data

Some of the best-kept official records are those for disease and death. Doctors, clinics and hospitals are required to keep scrupulous records. These are sent to city and county health offices, which relay them to state and federal agencies.

Because this information has been kept for many years, it can provide the journalist with an insight into community health standards. In fact, infant mortality rates are sometimes described as the measure of the civilization of a society.

The United States' infant mortality rate is 23rd among industrialized nations, and the rates in some of its cities are even higher than those in some developing countries.

The figures are highest in urban areas and poor rural areas, and they are unusually high among minority, teen-age, and unwed mothers. Internal comparisons also can be made because most local health agencies break the city into health districts. Districts with low-income residents can be compared with those with middle-income residents, and comparisons can be made between districts with white and nonwhite populations.

Some of the stories developed from infant mortality are stark:

	Black	White
Infant mortality rate	13.7	6.0

Correlations can be made between the infant death rate and such factors as low birth weight, marital status of mother, prenatal care, family income.

Data on death and disease are available from the state health department, which usually has the figures in an available database, and from the Centers for Disease Control and Prevention, www.cdc.gov/ and the National Center for Health Statistics, www.cdc.gov/nchswww/products/htm.

You can see that a lot of the material reporters gather is in the form of numbers, quantitative data. This takes us to another useful tool, but one that makes some journalism students shudder.

Mathematics for the Reporter

The UPI dispatch reads:

The average American who lives to the age of 70 consumes in that lifetime the equivalent of 150 cattle, 24,000 chickens, 225 lambs, 26 sheep, 310 hogs, 26 acres of grain and 50 acres of fruits and vegetables.

A Nevada newspaper reader who saw the story was puzzled. That seemed like a lot of meat to consume in a lifetime, he thought. He consulted his butcher who estimated the dressed weights of the various animals listed in the story.

They came up with a total of 222,695 pounds of meat. The reader wrote the UPI that he had done some figuring. He multiplied 70 years by 365 days to find the total number of days in the average person's lifetime. The figure was 25,500 days. He divided the total meat consumption of 222,695 pounds by 25,500 days. "That figures out to a whopping 8.7 pounds of meat a day," he wrote.

The UPI retired the reference work from which the item was gleaned.

The reporter who handled the story would have avoided embarrassing UPI had he observed Rule No. 1 for numbers: Always check them.

If the reporter who handled the Postal Service food drive story for his Florida paper had checked the numbers he was given, he would have avoided looking as silly as the UPI reporter. He wrote that letter carriers had collected 11 million tons of food last year in three Florida counties. A reader checked: 11 million tons equals 22 billion pounds. Divide that by the U.S. population of 261 million.

The reader calculated that the letter carriers would have had to have collected 84 pounds of food from each man, woman and child in the United States. Hardly likely.

It turns out that it wasn't tons but pounds—11 million pounds. That's still a lot, but it's 1/2,000th of the newspaper's figure.

Percentages

We live in an age of quantification. Numbers surround us, and they reveal a great deal about how we live. The reporter must be able to make simple calculations like the one an Associated Press reporter made for the new census figures. The new U.S. population figure was 249,632,692, but the reporter knew this number alone would be meaningless in the lead. Even the total increase of about 23 million would not make a sharp lead.

What was needed was the percentage increase, which he figured this way:

New	249,632,692	
Old	−226,504,825	
Increase	23,127,867	
Increase	23,127,867	= 10.2%
Old	226,504,825	

Here was the AP lead:

> The Census Bureau today put the population of the United States at 249,632,692, an increase of more than 23 million people, or 10.2 percent, over the total 10 years ago.

One of the most common mistakes in calculating a percentage increase or decrease is putting the difference between the old and the new over the new figure. Wrong. The denominator, the bottom figure in the fraction, is the original or old figure. We are figuring the change—the percentage increase or decrease—from the **old** to the present or **new,** so we use the old as the base.

The police reporter is given the annual report of violent crimes in the city for last year: 17,030. Two years ago, the total was 22,560. The reporter knows that she has to give a percentage decline:

Two years ago	22,560	$\underline{5,530}$	= 24.5 percentage decline
Last year	−17,030	22,560	
Decline	5,530		

The reporter writes:

> Violent crimes in Freeport declined 24.5 percent last year from the previous year.
> The police department's annual survey reveals that 17,030 violent crimes were committed last year, compared with 22,560 the year before, or 5,530 fewer crimes.

Personalizing the Smoker

"An estimated 50 million Americans smoked 600 billion cigarettes last year," the story about a local anti-smoking proposal said. The city editor calls you, the reporter handling the story, to the desk.

"Let's put this and a lot of the other figures into some understandable terms," he tells you. "In this case, why not follow the sentence with one that says, 'This means the average smoker lit up so many cigarettes a day.' "

Back at your desk, you make a few simple calculations: 600 billion cigarettes smoked a year ÷ 50 million smokers = 12,000 cigarettes per smoker a year.

You want average daily use, so you make the next calculation: 12,000 cigarettes a year ÷ 365 days = 32.87 cigarettes per smoker a day.

You round that off to 33—a pack and a half a day. A reader can see the smoker crumpling up a pack and smoking halfway through a second pack for his or her daily dose. This is more graphic than the millions and billions, which depersonalize the story.

Numbers and Rates

New York City is the murder capital of the United States. True or false? True, more murders are committed in New York than in any other city. But raw numbers do not tell the story accurately here and in many other instances.

Let's look at infant mortality data for a minute. California has more infant deaths than any other state, with 3,200. Texas is second with 1,900 a year. Alabama has 600, Mississippi, 400.

Is California five times more deadly than Alabama, eight times more dangerous than Mississippi for infants? Hardly. We know that California is more populous than Alabama and Mississippi, much more. So even with good medical care, the figures would be higher.

To use figures properly, we use rates rather than raw numbers much of the time. Rates take such factors as population into consideration.

When we do this, we find that Washington, D.C., not New York, is the nation's murder capital, its rate almost four times greater. And when we look at infant mortality, we find Alabama at 10.3 and Mississippi at 9.7 have higher rates than California, 6, and Texas, 6.1.

A rate is a relationship of two numbers. In many stories reporters handle, population is one of the numbers. So many robberies, per 100,000 population; so many AIDS deaths per 100,000 population. We talked about murder. What's the state with the highest murder rate?

Murder Rates

California had 2,916 murders in a recent year. Its population is approximately 32,268,000:

$$\frac{2,916}{32,268,000} = .00009$$

We multiply by 100,000 and we reach the rate of 9.

Now, let's look at Louisiana with 762 murders in a recent year, less than a third of California's murder total. But let's take population into consideration:

$$\frac{762}{4,352,000} = .000175$$

We multiply by 100,000 and the rate is 17.5, which, it so happens, is the highest state rate in the nation.

Death Rates for Infants

Let's apply the same approach to infant mortality rates. But here we use a different figure than population. The death rates for infants is figured on a base of so many deaths of children less than a year old per 1,000 live births.

$$\text{California:}\frac{3,200}{533,333} = .006$$

We multiply by 1,000 and the rate is 6.

$$\text{Alabama:}\frac{600}{61,600} = .0097$$

We multiply by 1,000 and get 9.7.

Refining the Data

Unfortunately, just when we think we're getting somewhere, we encounter an obstacle. In this case, our infant mortality numbers and our murder numbers are actually masking something essential to understanding life in the United States. Just as we saw in the case of the computer, machinery without a mind behind it is useless. Here, we have to think about a basic fact of life in the United States, race.

If we break both murder victims and infant mortality deaths into racial categories we find data that tell us more about life in the United States than our averages tell us. When we do this, we find that the black murder victimization rate is 6 to 10 times greater than the white rate, depending on which age groups are compared.

In some states black infant mortality rates are as much as three times as great as those for white infants.

And this takes us to the problem of averages. Darrell Huff, the author of books about mathematics says, "When you are told something is an 'average' you still don't know very much about it unless you can find out what kind of average it is: mean, median, or mode."

Modes, Means and Medians

How would you describe the average salary at J.C. Walnut and Co., an upholstery shop whose employees are on strike? Walnut says it is $31,140, and he has put a sign in his window saying so and telling his customers that the employees are ungrateful.

Here is how the annual salaries for the company break down:

- $72,500 (1) Mr. Walnut
- 59,600 (1) Son Theodore
- 30,500 (4) Master craftsmen
- 25,200 (6) Upholsterers
- 20,600 (3) Laborers

If we add up the salaries, being careful to multiply by the number of workers in each category, we reach a total payroll of $467,100. To find the average Walnut reached, we divide by 15, the total number of people on the payroll. The average is $31,140. So Walnut is right, right? Wrong.

First let's consider the word *average*, which covers three kinds of figures:

Mean: This is the average Walnut used. To derive it, we add up all the figures in our set and divide by the total number of individual components.

Mode: The component occurring most often in a listing of components.

Median: The midpoint in a grouping.

The mean distorts when there are unusually high or low components, as there are here with Walnut and son Theodore's salaries making the average tilt toward the high end.

The mode here is $25,200, which is the most frequently occurring salary.

The median, which is used most often in computing averages, requires you list all the salaries to find the midpoint:

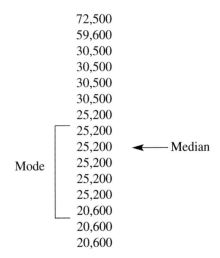

Look at this list of 15 numbers. The midpoint is the eighth on the list because there are seven salaries above it and seven below it. The eighth salary on the list is $25,200, which is the same as the mode.

Our figure of $25,200 is considerably less than Walnut's average of $31,140. And if we use some common sense, we realize that only the employees are on strike, so what is Walnut doing putting his and his son's salaries in the computation?

Take out the top two on the list and we get 13 salaries. The mode and the median are still $25,200. The mean is $25,769.

Let's take this a step further before we leave the delightful realm of mathematics. Let's look behind the median. There's more here than meets the eye.

Analyzing Averages

The federal government announces that the median household income last year was $44,570. Not bad. But wait a minute. Common sense, based on our reading and experience, tells us that income is widely disproportionate in this country among whites, blacks and Hispanics and between men and women. We want a breakdown of the median. Look at what we find:

Household Income

White	$46,865
Black	25,690
Hispanic	31,740

These figures tell us something about the nature of our society: The median family income of blacks is 58 percent that of whites, and the median income of Hispanics is 71 percent of whites.

As for working women, here are the median incomes:

Income of Women

White	$26,470
Black	22,764
Hispanic	19,676

Women of all groups earn 74 percent of the income of men.

Dissecting data gives us specifics, and, as we know, journalism is the art of the specific. The same agency that gave us median income figures reports that 35.5 million people were living in poverty last year, poverty being designated as a household income that is less than $16,400 for a family of four. With each additional family member, the poverty threshold increases by about $2,500.

We ask for particulars. Who are these 35.5 million people? The largest number, 24.5 million, are white and make up two-thirds of the total poor. But if we make a further check to see what percentage of the total number of whites live in poverty, we derive a much smaller percentage, 12.3 percent. Let's make a similar calculation for other groups:

Black:	26.5 percent
Hispanic:	23.4 percent
Asian:	11.9 percent

Censorship Information

When we left Dick in the first chapter, he was beginning to write his story about the request of a local group to ban books they found racist. In gathering information, Dick used the LEXIS®-NEXIS® service.

A NEXIS Search

To provide background for his story, Dick uses the LEXIS-NEXIS® service, which gives him access to a vast number of articles. Dick wants to track developments in recent years, so after clicking the *More Sources* button to access the *Source Selection* hierarchy, he chooses the *News* file folder and then the *News Group File, Most Recent Two Years* source.

After Dick clicks the *OK* button in the lower right corner, his next step is to construct his search, which he does by typing **book censorship** in the Search Request field. After clicking the *x* button, the screen informs him: "153 Documents found." He clicks the *Cite*/display format that lists articles in reverse chronological order, which allows him to choose the material he needs.

He wanted to know which books are the most often censored and banned, and in short order he obtained a list from one of the articles the search turned up:

I Know Why the Caged Bird Sings, Maya Angelou

The Giver, Lois Lowry

The Adventures of Huckleberry Finn, Mark Twain

Of Mice and Men, John Steinbeck

The Color Purple, Alice Walker

The Chocolate War, Robert Cormier

Go Ask Alice, Anonymous

The Catcher in the Rye, J.D. Salinger

A Day No Pigs Would Die, Robert Newton Peck

Native Son, Richard Wright

My Brother Sam is Dead, Christopher and James Lincoln Collier

Bridge to Terabithia, Katherine Paterson

Considerable material shows up in his Nexis search. Too much. He sees that over a long span, Mark Twain has been one of the most frequently challenged authors, as has *The Adventures of Huckleberry Finn.* He also learns that in the last few years the attack on particular reading materials has broadened. A news story refers to an organization called People for the American Way, which issued a report in which it stated that "attempts to censor have given way to broader assaults on the public schools."

The organization also found that "a disproportionate number of books written by African-American women were attacked this year with Maya Angelou's *I Know Why the Caged Bird Sings* being the most frequently challenged book in the country." Is it used in schools here? Dick will check.

Another story refers to a number of attacks on student publications in the high schools. Some states, he reads, have passed laws giving high school students First Amendment rights for their newspapers and magazines. What's the situation in this state? he wonders.

He decides to ask the People for the American Way for its list of challenged books on which Twain's book appears. He finds the organization's website and goes to work (www.pfaw.org/).

Public Opinion Polling

Abortion, prayer in school, gun control, taxes, the budget. And now the president's sex life. Would the voters support or repudiate the president in the upcoming congressional elections?

In the past, the answer derived from taking the political pulse was hardly convincing. Reporters would chat with political leaders, those supposedly perceptive insiders with delicate olfactory nerves attuned to the mildest of political

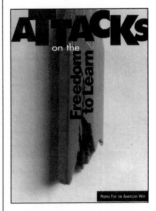

State Breakdowns

Dick notices that the People for the American Way issues an annual report in which book banning and other censorship attempts are broken down by state. He e-mails pfaw@pfaw.org and asks for the book.

breezes. The result might be interesting reading, but it had no predictive value whatsoever.

Now, the science of surveying gives the journalist a surer hand to reach into areas of coverage that before had been handled with impressions and conjecture.

Polls are used for a variety of stories. The well-designed poll can tell with a fair degree of accuracy not only what people think of a president's perform- ance, but also whether a proposed school bond issue is popular in a middle-class section of the community or what types of day care are favored by working mothers. Polls have been used to determine whether Catholics approve of abor- tion, how people feel about the death penalty, what blacks think of affirmative action. *The New York Times* even ran a survey that established that 87 percent of 3- to 10-year-olds believe in Santa Claus.

Recognizing the value of polls and surveys, many newspapers and televi- sion stations have hired pollsters and polling organizations. The reporter is still essential, for the poll can supply only the information. The reporter must make the poll into news. To do this, he or she must understand how polls work and their possibilities and limits.

The poll is a systematic way of finding out what people are thinking at a given time by questioning a sample population. It can provide a fairly accurate stop-action photo of a situation. This does not mean that all polling data should be taken at face value. There are some inherent problems in polling, and there are pollsters whose purpose is to promote their clients. Reporters who under- stand polls know what to accept, what to discard. Reporters who are over- whelmed by data, who believe there is some mystery about figures, will be vic- timized, just as they will be misled by any public relations gimmick.

Polls are "able to establish with great accuracy the extent to which an opinion is held, and they can successfully predict behavior over the short run," writes Sheldon S. Wolin of the Department of Politics at Princeton University. "Once the period is extended," he cautions, "the reliability of the findings dimin- ishes rapidly."

Political Polls

There are hundreds of polling organizations and firms. The majority are local groups that conduct marketing surveys. The big firms—Gallup, Harris, and Roper—handle commercial clients, too, but are best known for their political polls and surveys. It is this political polling that so often finds its way into news- papers and news broadcasts. During a political campaign, as much as one-third to one-half of the news is about the public's reaction to a candidate or an issue.

Unfortunately, the emphasis on predicting winners, on who's ahead, rather than on interpreting the data leads to the waste of huge amounts of fascinating material about how people are voting and why, whether some groups—blacks, Jews, Catholics, farmers—have switched their allegiances.

Although reputable pollsters pretest their questions, ambiguities do creep in. Reporters always should examine the questions behind the polling data to make sure that they are clear and, for polls conducted for private clients, to as- certain whether they are loaded.

Types of Polls

The first check a reporter makes of polling material is a determination of how the poll was conducted. There are a variety of ways to elicit information from the public, some of them unreliable, some less reliable than others.

The coupon poll is just about worthless. People are asked to clip, fill out and mail a coupon that appears in the publication. The results are distorted because the person who goes to all that trouble—including paying for postage—is usually someone with strong feelings about the subject and hardly representative of the general population.

Call-In Poll   The call-in poll, in which readers or viewers are asked to express their sentiments about an issue by telephoning the newspaper or station, is subject to the same criticism as the coupon poll. When the *San Francisco Chronicle* conducted a call-in poll on the death sentence, it headlined the results on page 1. Not surprisingly, three-fourths of those calling favored the death penalty. After *USA Today* reported that its call-in poll showed that Americans loved the financier Donald Trump, it learned that 5,640 of the 7,800 calls came from a single source, another financier. Shamefaced, the newspaper said its polls are "strictly for fun."

The 1-900 call-in poll is useless as a measure of public opinion. "You have to be willing to pay for a phone call in order to participate, and that very seriously limits the representativeness of the people whose responses are being reported," says Harry O'Neill, president of the National Council on Public Polls.

Straw Poll   The straw poll is no more reliable than the other types of polls already mentioned, although some newspapers have been using this technique for many years. For a straw poll, a person hands out ballots at one or more locations. People then drop their ballots into a box at the spot. It is difficult to keep the straw poll from being overrepresented by the people in the one or two locations selected—usually supermarkets, factory gates and the like. The *Daily News,* which conducts straw polls for New York and national elections, uses a professional pollster to organize its straw locations.

Man-in-the-Street Poll   The man-in-the-street poll is probably the poll most frequently used to gather opinions at the local level. Newspapers and stations without access to their own polling apparatuses will send reporters out to interview people about a candidate or an issue. Those who have had to do this kind of reporting know how nonrepresentative the people interviewed are. Reporters may seek out those who look as if they can supply a quick answer, those who do not need to have the question explained to them. Reporters may ignore those who are poorly dressed and members of minority groups.

These polls can be used as long as the story says precisely what they are—the opinions of a scattering of people, no more than that, no more scientific than astrology. The sample of people interviewed in such polling is known as a "non-probability sample," meaning that the conclusions cannot be generalized to the population at large.

Margin of Error. Polls are accurate to a point. The margin of error expresses one of the variables. Depending on the number of persons polled, the margin of error can be as high as 12 percent, as low as 3 percent.

A 3 percent margin of error gives a cushion of 3 percent up or 3 percent down. Thus, in a poll that gives Jones 51 percent and Smith 49 percent of the voters polled, a 3 percent margin of error means the result cannot be forecast with any certainty. Jones' actual result could be 54 percent (up 3) or 48 percent (down 3). Smith could be 52 percent (up 3) or 46 percent (down 3).

Too close to call.

Proper Polling

A good poll should be done at night and over weekends, not just during the workday. It is best to poll people in their homes rather than on the street. Polls that are conducted by home interviews are usually more reliable than the catch-as-catch-can polling techniques of the straw poll or man-in-the-street interviews.

Most polls are done by phone to save time and money, although many of the poor and many members of minority groups do not have phones, and 25 percent of those called refuse to cooperate.

To reach its conclusions about how well adults around the country thought the president was handling his problems, *The New York Times*/CBS News Poll spoke to 1,422 people by telephone. At first glance, this effort seems like madness. To pass off the opinions of fewer than 1,500 people as representative of more than 100 million adults seems folly. Yet if the sample is selected carefully, the questions properly put, the results stated fairly and completely, and the interpretations made with discernment, a sample of around 1,500 people can reflect accurately 95 percent of the time the opinions of people across the country with a margin of error of about 3 percentage points. (See **Appendix B, "Public Opinion Polling Checklist."**)

The Sample   Obviously, if a small group is to speak for many, that group must be carefully chosen so that it is representative of the larger group. The key word here is *representative*.

If we want to know what people think of an incumbent governor, we can interview voters and nonvoters. But if we want to know whether people will vote to re-elect him or her, it is common sense to interview only eligible voters, those who have registered. But we cannot stop there. If we went out in the daytime to supermarkets, laundromats and parks where mothers gather with their young children, our sample would be skewed heavily toward women. That would be a nonrepresentative sample because men constitute a large percentage of voters. Also, because only a third to a half of eligible voters actually go to the polls in most contests, questions must be asked to determine whether the person being polled will actually vote.

Samples are selected in a number of ways. *The New York Times*/CBS News Poll sample of telephone exchanges was selected by a computer from a complete list of exchanges around the country. The exchanges were chosen in such a way that each region of the United States was represented in proportion to its population.

Once the exchanges were selected, the telephone numbers were formed by random digits. This guaranteed that unlisted as well as listed numbers would be included in the sample.

The making of *The New York Times*/CBS News Poll sample demonstrates how pollsters try to eliminate the human factor from the choice of those who will be interviewed. A good sample should give everyone in the population we are trying to learn something about a chance to be represented in the poll. This is what is meant by the term *random sample*. To the average person, the word *random* usually means haphazard, without plan. Pollsters use it to mean that the

---

Polling Problems. When the candidate is black or female, the race or gender of the poll taker can influence results. Also, people will not give "socially undesirable" answers to poll takers, regardless of their true feelings.

Hardly Representative. The stories about French unfriendliness are untrue, said American Express. The proof: A poll of 1,000 Americans who visited France more than once over the last two years (and thus would be inclined to be pro-French). People who lose weight can keep it off, said a diet-products company in a news release. The sample: A group of 20 who went through the company's weight-loss program.

The Exit Poll

Everyone wants to know who won the election and why, as soon as possible. The exit poll provides the information—usually just as the voting ends. For most races, this poll supplies the winners and the reasons voters cast their ballots.

The exit poll is based on interviews with voters as they emerge from polling places. For results of national interest, the AP and the four networks have joined to form the Voter News Service. The VNS uses county-based models to form its polling base. These models allow analysts to call Candidate A a winner even when the vote count shows her trailing Candidate B.

sample guarantees that any of those in the larger population group have as good a chance to be polled as anyone else in that group.

Once the sample has been drawn, it is then weighted to adjust for sample variations. In the *Times*/CBS Poll of the president's popularity, the sample consisted of 445 people who told the pollsters making the calls that they were Democrats, 482 who said they were Republicans and 495 who said they were independents. Using the breakdown in the sample would overrepresent Republicans. To reflect the known proportion of party members in the voting population, the groups of voters were weighted by party identification.

The poll also weighted the results to take account of household size and to adjust for variations in the sample relating to religion, race, age, sex and education. This weighting was done in accordance with what is known of the characteristics of the voting population from the results of the last election, the proportion of men and women in the population, census figures on nationality, religion, income and so on. The raw figures were adjusted to eliminate distortions from the norm.

Despite the inclination to think that the more people interviewed, the more accurate the results, the statistical truth is that it is as much the quality of the sample that determines the accuracy of the poll. After a critical number of interviews have been conducted, little additional accuracy is achieved. Results based on a good sample successfully interviewed are adequate for most purposes.

Two Polling Disasters   The classic example of quantity over quality is the *Literary Digest* poll for the 1936 presidential race between Franklin D. Roosevelt and Alf Landon. On the basis of its 2,376,523 replies, the poll predicted a Landon victory. But Landon was soundly defeated and carried only Maine and Vermont. The reason: The sample was made up of names from lists of automobile owners and telephone users, hardly representative of the general populace, most of which was mired in a deep depression.

The presidential election in 1948 was another disaster for the pollsters. Gallup forecast 49.5 percent for Thomas Dewey, the Republican candidate,

44.5 percent for Harry Truman. The actual result: Dewey, 45.6 percent, Truman, 50 percent. Why? Gallup said he stopped interviewing 10 days before the election, too soon to catch the groundswell for Truman. Today, pollsters go at it until the day before election.

Winners and Losers

Journalists must be careful about their tendency to heed the demands of readers and listeners for definitive opinions and for winners and losers. A poll can only state what people **say** they are thinking or how voters **say** they will vote at the time they are polled, and sometimes even then the contests are too close to call.

Journalists should remember this: People change their minds; polls cannot guarantee that behavior will be consistent with intentions.

Reputable pollsters know just how far they can take their data. But they are often under pressure to pick winners in election contests. When preelection polls indicate a 60–40 percent breakdown, a pollster feels at ease in choosing the winner. But when an editor, reflecting the desire of readers and listeners, asks for a choice in a 44–42 race with 14 percent undecided, then trouble lies ahead.

Although editors and broadcast producers tend to be most interested in the top of the poll—who's ahead—most of the significant material in the poll usually is found in why the candidate is ahead or behind and how the candidate is faring with certain groups. This can make interesting and significant news. There may be a good story in the candidate who does well with a certain religious group and poorly with another because of his or her stand on abortion or prayer in schools.

The Future

We have not covered other tools that the journalist of the future probably will have to master. Tom Regan, supervising online editor at *The Christian Science Monitor* and the technology columnist for *Nieman Reports,* says that versatility will be required of journalists. Not only will they have to master the computer technology, but also the digital camera and video and tape recorders.

Some foresee the journalist of the future going on a story armed with pad, pencil, camera, laptop and other devices. Regan sees "reporter teams where several Web reporters will cover one story, each creating a section of what will become a larger report. One might write the text, another would create video footage, a third might create a photo montage, a fourth an audio version, but all working as a team so that each element complements the other elements."

Regan also sees the journalist of the future more involved with readers. Some newspapers already offer their readers the opportunity to be interactive with staff members, a reaction to the studies that show readers feel disconnected from their sources of information. These newspapers print editors' e-mail addresses in the masthead, and some offer the e-mail addresses of reporters.

Summing Up

Journalists have a vast array of reporting and research resources at their fingertips. Used intelligently, these resources can contribute to making stories accurate and thorough. They also can help journalists develop story ideas that were too time-consuming to pursue before the computer.

None of these tools, however, operates by itself. All must be directed by the human pressing the keys. Journalists not only must know how to use these devices wisely and creatively, they must also have a wide range of knowledge and experience that will generate the ideas to feed into the machines.

Further Reading

Aueletta, Ken. *The Highwaymen: Warriors of the Information Superhighway.* New York: Random House, 1997.

Barzun, Jacques, and Henry F. Graff. *The Modern Researcher.* New York: Harcourt Brace Jovanovich, 1985.

Croteau, Maureen, and Wayne Worcester. *The Essential Researcher.* New York: HarperCollins, 1993. (A one-volume sourcebook for journalists written by University of Connecticut journalism faculty members.)

Huff, Darrell, and Irving E. Gers. *How to Lie with Statistics.* New York: Norton, 1954.

McCormick, Mona. *The New York Times Guide to Reference Materials.* New York: Times Books, 1985.

Meyer, Philip. *Precision Journalism,* 2nd ed. Bloomington: Indiana University Press, 1979.

Paul, Nora. *Computer Assisted Research: A Guide to Tapping Online Information,* 2nd ed. St. Petersburg, Fla.: The Poynter Institute for Media Studies, 1994.

Williams, Frederick. *Reasoning with Statistics.* New York: Holt, Rinehart and Winston, 1968.

5 Story Structure

Richard Ferro, *St. Petersburg Times*

A daring rescue—a single-element story.

Preview

Planning precedes writing. Reporters see the news story as an organized whole. Each sentence, every paragraph is placed to suit a purpose. Even while reporting, reporters try to visualize the shape and content of their stories, especially the beginning, the lead. The lead gives the story its structure.

News stories have a linear structure:

• The beginning includes a summary of the most important material. It tells the reader what to expect.
• The remainder of the story—the body—amplifies, buttresses, gives examples and explains the beginning. It also contains background and secondary material. The ending can sum up the story.

First the idea. Then the words.

As the young reporter struggled with his story, he recalled this advice that his city editor gave him the day before. Having written the obituary of a banker in 45 minutes, he was proud of his speed. But the editor said that the story was disorganized. The reporter read his story carefully, keeping in mind his editor's comment. Yes, he was writing without a firm idea of what he wanted to say and how it would fit together.

Suddenly, he was struck by what he had just told himself: "What do I want to say? Where do I put it?" That was the key to putting his notes into some kind of structured shape.

• What do I want to say?
• Where does it go?

This reporter's discovery is made all the time by young journalists. Usually, it is followed by another revelation: The news story form or structure is simple and most stories fit into the following structure:

• The lead.
• The material that explains and amplifies the lead.
• The necessary background.
• The secondary or less important material.

The Main Idea

The city editor's advice about thinking before writing has been offered to generations of students. As an essay in the *Fifth Reader,* a grade school textbook of the 1880s, puts it, "In learning to write, our first rule is: '*Know what you want to say.*'" (The italics are those of the author of the essay, Edward Everett Hale, the Boston clergyman who wrote the short novel *The Man Without a Country.*) Hale had a second rule: "*Say it.* That is, do not begin by saying something else which you think will lead up to what you want to say."

Every writer who has written about the writer's craft—whether journalist, poet, novelist or critic—has understood these first principles of writing. George Orwell, the British journalist and novelist, was concerned that the English language was being endangered by unclear thinking. In an essay, "Politics and the English Language," he wrote that the first question scrupulous writers ask themselves before writing is, "What am I trying to say?"

The Structure

In *The Elements of Style,* the "little book" that generations of college students have used, authors William Strunk Jr. and E. B. White begin their section on writing this way: "Choose a suitable design and hold to it." They continue: "A basic structural design underlies every kind of writing. . . . The first principle of composition, therefore, is to foresee or determine the shape of what is to come, and pursue that shape."

Henry James, the American novelist, said that without form "there is absolutely no substance." Form, he wrote, "*takes,* holds, and preserves, substance—saves it from the welter of helpless verbiage that we swim in as in a sea of tasteless tepid pudding, and that makes one ashamed of an art capable of such degradations."

Sometimes plans change. A writer may develop new ideas in the act of writing and the original plan has to be discarded. But even then a new plan is substituted.

Nevertheless, many reporters start to write without a plan in mind. As a result, their stories exhibit one of the most common faults of journalistic writing—disorganization or lack of focus. Henry Fairlie, a British journalist, calls this deficiency "shapelessness." He attributes it to "an intellectual inability, on the part both of the reporter and copy editor, to master the story." This mastery, Fairlie says, must be put to use "before writing."

As one journalism teacher has been telling his students, "You can't write if you can't think." Ambrose Bierce, a newspaperman and author of *The Devil's Dictionary,* described good writing as "clear thinking made visible."

Locating the Basic Idea

Almost all writing is based on an observation, an emotion or an opinion that the writer wants to communicate. This basic idea may be put at or near the beginning of the piece as it usually is in a news story, or it may be tacked on at the end, as is a request for money for the flight home at Christmas in a student's letter to his or her parents. The basic idea is *always* there.

The news story has a beginning that sets out the basic idea or theme and a body that elaborates and explains the theme. As the newsroom adage puts it, "The story flows from the lead." When reporters attempt to form ideas for stories, they search for the lead of the piece. Fairlie describes the importance of the lead this way: "Every journalist who has ever struggled with [a lead] knows why it can take so much effort. It is as important to him as to the reader. Writing it concentrates the mind wonderfully, forcing him to decide what in the story is important, what he wants to emphasize, and can eventually give the shape to the rest of the story as he writes it."

Thomas Boswell, columnist for *The Washington Post,* says, "The most important thing in the story is finding the central idea. It's one thing to be given a topic, but you have to find the idea or the concept within that topic. Once you find that idea or thread, all the other anecdotes, illustrations and quotes are pearls that hang on this thread. The thread may seem very humble, the pearls may seem very flashy, but it's still the thread that makes the necklace."

Wandering in Wonderland

The inability to fix on the point causes writers to go on and on and on. They believe that as long as they keep going, they will hit on something newsworthy. They are like Lewis Carrol's Alice in her conversation with the Cheshire Cat:

"Would you tell me, please, which way I ought to go from here?"

"That depends a good deal on where you want to get to," said the Cat.

"I don't much care where—" said Alice.

"Then it doesn't matter which way you go," said the Cat.

"—so long as I get *somewhere,*" Alice added as an explanation.

"Oh, you're sure to do that," said the Cat, "if you only walk long enough."

No editor will permit a writer to wander aimlessly through a story on the way to *somewhere.*

Some Stories

Locating the central or basic idea for the news story or feature begins early in the reporting process, as soon as the reporter is given the assignment. There is always a reason for this particular coverage, and the reason is the guide to the story focus: Two cars collided at Brighton and Roth—an accident story:

That means possible injuries, certainly damage; and we need to know how it happened.

You can see that the thinking begins at once. On the scene, the generalizations take specific form:

A driver suffered a broken leg when he ran a stop sign and collided with a car going through the intersection.

Scholarships   You are assigned to profile three high school seniors who have received college scholarships, an athlete, a musician, a 15-year-old student with a gift for mathematics. Questions immediately come to mind:

Why did you choose this particular school? Who advised you on your choice? Were you recruited heavily by the school you chose? By any other schools? Name them. Is the athlete being given more financial help than the two others?

Because you will have to blend the three interviews into three miniprofiles for one story, you realize that you need to select one of the three students and lead with something about him or her. Or you will have to find an element common to all three and lead with that as the basic idea.

You know that colleges that recruit athletes are required to tell those they are recruiting the graduation rate of athletes. Did our high school senior ask, and if he did, what was it? You know that many Division I schools have low graduation rates for minority athletes. Is he aware of this?

Interview   You are to cover a talk by the congresswoman from the 15th district. She is to speak about campaign finance reform, a topic people are interested in. You know you will interview her after her talk, so you check the files to see how she voted on bills on campaign reform. She opposed most of them. Your line of questions begins to shape up, as does a possible lead—her explanation of her votes.

You know that the basic story design consists of the lead idea and material that explains, supports and amplifies the lead. So you take notes on the bills on which she cast her votes.

Let's look at some basic story forms next.

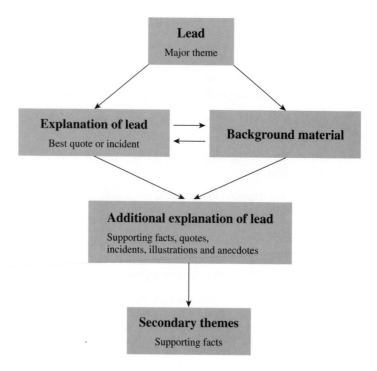

The Single-Element Story

A story that consists of one important action or is based on one major fact or idea is a single-element story. Also known as the single-incident story, it is the story handled most often by beginning reporters. The story requires:

- Lead.
- Explanatory and amplifying material.
- Background (if necessary).
- Secondary material (if any).

The single-element spot news story may contain several themes or ideas, but in this type of story the reporter decides that only one is important. A story of this kind may have the following structure:

- Lead: Idea A.
- Explanatory material. Elaboration of Idea A.
- Secondary material. Subthemes of B, C, D, E.
- Background.
- Further elaboration of Idea A.

Short pieces written this way usually can be cut after the lead or two paragraphs, and longer pieces can be cut after a few paragraphs.

Thieves Get 36 Batteries

Thieves who entered a Charlotte auto parts store stole 36 Delco batteries, police were told yesterday.

Crowell Erskine, 49, manager of the Piedmont Auto Exchange at 410 Atando Ave., told officers the store was broken into between 5 p.m. Tuesday and 8 a.m. Wednesday by thieves knocking a hole in the rear wall of the one-story brick building.

Erskine said the batteries were valued at $539.18.

—*The Charlotte Observer*

Analysis

1. The lead focuses on the basic idea, the theft of a batch of batteries. The reporter knows the reader opens the newspaper each day with the question, "*What* happened today?"

2. The reporter answers what he or she thinks will be the logical questions a reader might ask, "*Where* did the break-in occur? *When* did it happen? *How* was it done?" The answers to these questions explain and amplify the lead.

3. Background is provided. The reporter knows the reader will want to be told the value of the goods stolen.

Other Scenarios

If the parts-store theft had taken place in broad daylight while shoppers thronged the streets, this fact—*when* the theft occurred—would go into the lead.

Had the thief scaled a 15-foot wall to gain entry, *how* the theft was managed would be placed in the lead.

If the thief left a note in the store apologizing for his act and saying he needed the money to pay medical bills for his sick wife, *why* the theft occurred—according to the thief—would be put into the lead.

The most important element always forms the basic idea for the lead. To find that basic element, the reporter anticipates the questions the reader will ask and then answers them. These questions have been summarized as *who, what, when, where, why* and *how*—the Five W's and an H.

Burying the Lead

A student was assigned to interview the chairman of the local United Way Campaign, which was in the middle of a fund drive. The student thought that the midpoint of the drive might be a good time to check progress. Here is the story he turned in:

> The local United Way Campaign today issued its second weekly report in its current campaign to raise $750,000 for next year's activities.
>
> Tony Davis, the campaign chairman, said that donations in the first two weeks had exceeded last year's fund raising at a similar time.
>
> "We've collected $350,000, and that's about $25,000 ahead of last year," Davis said. "Thanks to the work of our downtown volunteers, the local merchants have been canvassed more

thoroughly than ever before, and their gifts have been very generous."

The month-long drive seeks funds for 28 local organizations, including the Big Brothers, Senior Citizens House and a new program to aid crippled children.

The story is clear but it has a glaring fault: What should have been the basic idea or theme was placed in the second paragraph. Occasionally, a reporter will intentionally delay the lead, usually for dramatic effect. This was no such instance. The most significant fact the student reporter gleaned from his reporting was that the campaign was running ahead of last year's receipts. And because this is a straightforward or spot news story, the progress report should have been placed in the lead. Given this advice by his instructor, the student rewrote the story:

The United Way Campaign to raise $750,000 is running ahead of last year's drive at the midway point.

Tony Davis, the campaign chairman, said today that in the first two weeks of the month-long fund drive, $350,000 had been collected. That is $25,000 ahead of last year's collections at this time.

"Thanks to the work of our downtown volunteers, the local merchants have been . . ."

The same set of facts was given to a reporting and writing class. Here are some of the leads that emerged:

Tony Davis, the chairman of the United Way Campaign, reported today that the fund drive is running ahead of schedule.

The United Way Campaign has collected $350,000, which is $25,000 ahead of last year's drive at this time.

Local merchants were credited today with helping to push the United Way Campaign closer and faster toward its goal of $750,000.

In each of these leads, the basic idea is the same: Collections are ahead of those of last year. This is the most important element and it must be the basis of the lead.

The Multiple-Element Story

Multiple-element stories are written the same way as the single-element story. The difference is that we put more than one basic idea high up in the story.

An event that has two or more major ideas or themes calls for a multiple-element story. The structure of the multiple-element story is:

- Lead: Idea A, Idea B.
- Explanatory material. Elaboration of Idea A, Idea B.

- Secondary material. Subthemes C, D, E, F.
- Background.
- Further elaboration of Idea A, Idea B.

Two-Element Story

Here are 12 paragraphs from an election story that appeared in the *Daily News*. Seemingly complex, the story has a simple structure that is based on the two major story ideas: (A) rejection of the bond issue and (B) Republican control of the legislature.

Gov. Hughes Loses Bonds & Legislature
by Joseph McNamara

(1) New Jersey Gov. Richard J. Hughes took a shellacking all around in yesterday's statewide election. The voters rejected the $750 million bond issue proposal on which he had hung much of his political prestige, and the Republicans gained control of both houses of the Legislature.

(2) Hughes, who had warned during the campaign that if the bond issue were defeated he would ask the Legislature in January for a state income tax and sales tax to meet the state's financial needs, announced early today that he "may have to do some rethinking" about the size of the need. And he made it clear that the "rethinking" would increase his estimate of the amount required.

(3) "I accept the verdict rendered by the people," he said in a written statement.

Behind from the Start

(4) The bond issue proposal, which was broken into two questions—one on institutions and the other on roads—trailed from the time the polls closed at 8 p.m. With the count in from 4,238 of the state's 4,533 districts, the tally early today was:

(5) Institutions: No, 868,586; Yes, 736,967.

(6) Highways: No, 866,204; Yes, 681,059.

(7) As a measure of Hughes' defeat, in the Democrats' Hudson County stronghold—where the Governor had hoped for a plurality of 150,000—he got only a 100,501 to 64,752 vote in favor of the institutional bonds and 93,654 to 66,099 in favor of the highway bonds.

(8) He had promised that if the bond issue were defeated, he would go before the Legislature in January and ask for a state income tax and a state sales tax to meet the state's obligations.

(9) Four other referendums had no great opposition, and passed easily. They were on voter residency requirements, a tax break on farm land and a change in exemptions from the ratables to the finished tax for both veterans and the elderly.

(10) The Republicans have controlled the State Senate for the last half century, and smashing victories yesterday in crucial Essex, Burlington and Camden Counties increased their majority—which had shrunk to a hairsbreadth 11–10—to two-thirds.

(11) Democrats swamped in the avalanche included Gov. Hughes' brother-in-law Sen. Edward J. Hulse of Burlington County. He was unseated by Republican Edwin B. Forsythe who ran up a convincing 6,000-vote majority.

(12) In populous Essex County, Republican C. Robert Sarcone defeated Democrat Elmer M. Matthews—who conceded shortly after 11 p.m. without waiting for the final count. And in Camden County, Republican Frederick J. Scholz unseated incumbent Joseph W. Cowgill. . . .

(1) The lead contains a colloquial phrase in the first sentence that the reporter believed would attract readers. The second sentence summarizes the two themes, A and B.

(2–8) These seven paragraphs refer to theme A. In 2, the reporter gives a possible consequence of the loss of the bond issue.

In any election, vote tallies are essential, and the reporter supplies them in 5 and 6, which set up a good example in 7 of the extent of the governor's shellacking. In 8, the reporter gives a bit of background to A.

(9) Secondary information about other items on the ballot.

(10–12) Elaboration of theme B. Examples of specific races are given.

Three-Element Story

The following is an example of a story that begins with a three-element lead. The reporter would have singled out one element had she thought that one was the most important of the three. She decided the three were of equal importance.

Study Links 3 Factors to Heart Ills

By Jane E. Brody

(1) A new study conducted among 110,000 adult members of the Health Insurance Plan of Greater New York has once again demonstrated that smoking, an overweight condition and physical inactivity are associated with a greatly increased risk of death and disability from heart disease.

(2) The study, published yesterday in the June issue of The American Journal of Public Health, reported that men and women who smoke cigarettes face twice the risk of suffering a first heart attack as do non-smokers.

(3) The annual incidence of first heart attacks among pipe and cigar smokers was also found to be higher than among non-smokers, but not as high as among cigarette smokers.

(4) Men who are "least active," both on and off the job, are twice as likely as "moderately active" men to suffer a first heart attack and four times as likely to suffer a fatal heart attack.

(5) Men who were classified as "most active" showed no advantage in terms of heart attack rate over men considered "moderately active." The authors reported that other differences between active and inactive men, such as the amount they smoked, could not account for their different heart attack rates.

(6) The heavier men in the study had a 50 percent greater risk of suffering a first heart attack than the lighter-weight men. An increased risk was also found among women who had gained a lot of weight since age 25.

(7) None of the differences in risk associated with weight could be explained on the basis of variations in smoking and exercise habits, the authors stated.

(8) The incidence of heart attacks was also found to be higher among white men than among non-whites and among Jewish men than among white Protestants and Catholics. But the heart attack rate among Jewish women was not markedly different from that among non-Jewish women.

—The New York Times

Some reporters might have found a lead in the information Brody places in the last paragraph. Although most events have obvious leads, a number do not. News judgment is essential on multiple-element stories, and judgments differ. Brody was on target. The last paragraph is secondary.

Brody's story also illustrates another basic guideline for structuring a story: Put related material together.

Story Units

In organizing their stories, news writers move from one theme to another in the order of the importance of the subjects or themes. The lead is elaborated first, and then the next-most-important theme is stated and then elaborated and explained. The rule of thumb is this: Put everything about the same subject in the same place.

When his editor explained the rule "like things together" to the journalist Dwight Macdonald, his first reaction was, "Obviously." His second, he said, was, "But why didn't it ever occur to me?" His third was, "It was one of those profound banalities 'everybody knows'—after they've been told. It was the climax of my journalistic education."

The Inverted Pyramid

The story structure explained in this chapter—important elements at the beginning, less important at the end—has for decades been taught to students as the "inverted pyramid" form. The term can be misleading. An inverted pyramid is an unbalanced monolith, a huge top teetering on a pinpoint base. It is a monstrous image for journalists, for the top of a story should be deft and pointed. Discard the picture of this precariously balanced chunk and remember that all it means is that the most important material is usually placed at the beginning of the story and the less important material is placed at the end.

The news story takes its shape from the requirements and limitations of the craft as measured by the clock—a silent but overwhelming presence—and the available space and time for copy. Given these realities, most stories must be written in such a way that they can be handled quickly and efficiently. If the 10 inches of available space suddenly shrinks to 8 and the 40 seconds of air time to 20, no problem. The story structure makes it possible to cut the bottom two paragraphs without losing key information.

If the only justification for the standard news story form were its utility to the people writing and editing the news, it would not have stood up over the years. The form has persisted because it meets the needs of media users. People usually want to know what happened as soon as the story begins to unfold. If it is interesting, they will pay attention. Otherwise, they turn elsewhere. People are too busy to tarry without reward.

Sometimes the pleasure may come from suspense, a holding of the breath until the climax is revealed deep in the story. When the reporter senses that this kind of structure is appropriate for the event, a delayed lead will be used.

Memorable Parts   Research tells us that structure can help increase the veiwer's and reader's understanding of the story and his or her involvement in it. For those who stay with the story from beginning to end, the start and the conclusion seem to be the best-remembered portions of the piece. Now that page layout can be more precisely designed, the reporter can put a kicker or summary at the end of a story without worrying that it might be squeezed out.

News forms may be said to be utilitarian or pragmatic, in the tradition of the hustle and bustle of American life. But there is also an aesthetic component in the standard news form that its detractors sometimes fail to detect. If the expression "form follows function" implies beauty in the finished work, then the news story is a work of art, minor as it may be. The news story meets the demands of art: It reveals a harmony of design.

Storytelling Form

Editors are concerned about the failure of the newspaper to attract new readers. They believe that the standard fare and form are unappetizing, that a generation reared on MTV, 15-second TV commercials, rock music and docudramas seeks more excitement than most newspapers have been offering. As a consequence, there is increasing use of the storytelling or narrative form. The reader is invited into the story with an interesting, amusing or exciting incident. The story then builds to a climax.

Scene Setting Here is how Jere Downs of *The Philadelphia Inquirer* began a story:

Driving to Easter services yesterday about 1:45 p.m., James Freeman saw a man standing on the South Street bridge.

"I knew he wanted to jump," said Freeman. "I made a U-turn right on the bridge and stopped traffic."

Freeman left his wife, his granddaughter and four foster children — all dressed in their Easter finery — watching from their minivan. Then, Freeman walked toward the lone figure staring down into the Schuykill 60 feet below.

The reader is hooked. Will Freeman talk the would-be suicide into backing off? Downs lets Freeman show us what happened:

"I've been where you want to go," Freeman said he told the man. "Whatever it is, it's not worth it."

Freeman said the man, in his mid-40s, looked at him with a pinched face lined with tears.

Then the man looked back across the river toward the University of Pennsylvania campus.

"I gotta do it," Freeman recalled saying. "Nobody loves me. I'm a Vietnam vet. My being here is like a burden on everybody."

Downs has used a column of type to this point, and she goes on to describe how others stopped their cars to help. A minister approached the distraught man and said to him, "You're looking down when you should be looking up to God."

The Climax Finally, in the 24th paragraph, the man climbs down from the concrete abutment.

(Postscript: A few days later, Downs received a handwritten note in the mail. "I enclose a check which I made out to you. Would you possibly be able to funnel this money in some way to allow Mr. X to receive some quality psychotherapy. I must remain anonymous. My reasons for doing this are (1) I was once where Mr. X was. (2) I have come back and am a successful businessman. Thank you for writing a terrific article." The check was for $1,000.)

Structure Necessary

At first glance, this storytelling form seems to release the writer from the task of structuring carefully. Not so. As we will see in the next chapter, the storyteller is just as scrupulous in the choice of material for the beginning of the piece as is the user of the traditional form. Both forms require the writer to identify the major theme and to make clear at the outset that the story will be concerned with that theme. The incident or example selected to begin the storytelling article must fit neatly into the theme of the piece.

That theme may come in the first paragraph, the third paragraph or the last. The ending is as carefully crafted as is the beginning. In all cases, the writer must first identify the theme and then decide where it will be placed in the piece.

Look at a story a reporter wrote about the search for a new city hall. She began with a general observation and then moved into the significant action:

> Modern buildings of glass and steel mark the downtown section.
>
> But the city's business is conducted in an old brick building that many residents liken to a warehouse.
>
> Last night, city officials went shopping for a new city hall. They looked at a modern 10-story office building. . . .

The third paragraph contains the news element, the lead idea. The first two paragraphs take the reader to the theme in an interesting way.

But suppose the reporter is covering a fire in city hall that led to two deaths. This story must begin with the news of the deaths. That news cannot be delayed. The story's structure takes its shape from the nature of the event.

Story Necessities

Take any event and play the reporter's game. What are the necessary facts for an automobile accident story, a fire story, an obituary? Let us say an automobile hits a child. What must the story include? It will have to contain the child's name, age and address; the driver's name, age, address and occupation; the circumstances and location of the accident; the extent of the child's injuries; the action, if any, taken against the motorist. Any other necessities?

Given an assignment, the reporter has in mind a list of necessities for the story. The necessities guide the reporter's observations and direct the questions he or she will ask of sources. But there can be a problem.

Unless the reporter can spot the significant differences between stories of a similar type, one accident story will be like another, one obituary like a dozen others. The reporter on the "automobile hits child" story tries to discover the unusual or unique aspects of the event that should be given priority: Was the youngster playing? If so, was he or she running after a ball, playing hide-and-seek? Was the child looking for a dog, cat, younger brother? Was the child crossing the street to go to school? How seriously was the child injured? Will the youngster be able to walk normally?

Once the reporter has (a) thought about the necessities of stories he or she is assigned and (b) sought out the facts that differentiate this story from others like it, the story is on its way to being organized. The final step is to construct a lead around the important or unique element. There is no simple formula for determining what should go into the lead. The criteria for news we developed in Chapter 2 are helpful.

Basically, news judgment is an exercise in logical thinking. When a fire destroys a hotel worth $30 million and takes 14 lives, the reporter focuses the lead on the lives lost, not the destruction of the hotel, no matter how costly. The reporter reasons that a life cannot be equated with money. If no one was killed or hurt in the fire, then the significance may well be that it was a costly structure, not a three-story hotel for transients that had seen better times. If there were no injuries and the hotel had some historical interest, the lead might be that a landmark in town was destroyed by fire. Finally, if no one was hurt and the hotel was a small, old building like many others in town, the fire would rate only two or three paragraphs and a single sentence, maybe two, on the 11 p.m. newscast.

The thinking process that underlies writing news stories is precisely the same as the thinking process that guides reporting. Reporting and writing are inextricably bound together, and when done properly they provide the ingredients for the well-organized story.

Covering a Strike Threat

Let's watch a reporter assigned to the education beat. Told to check a report that public school teachers might not report for work next fall, she thinks of several essential questions:

- Is the report true?
- How many teachers are involved?
- What are the reasons for the strike?
- When will the decision be made about whether to strike?
- What are the responses of authorities to the threat?
- What plans are being made for the students should there be a strike?

The answers to these questions and other observations made during her reporting are the building blocks for the story. The reporter knows what her lead will be from the minute she receives the assignment—the possibility of a teacher strike and schools not opening. She has a simple formula for finding the basic theme: What do I know today that I did not know yesterday and that everyone would like to know?

These are the first few paragraphs of the story she writes:

Teachers in all 15 public schools in the city today threatened to strike next September unless they are given an 8 percent wage increase in next year's contract.

Spokesmen for the local unit of the American Federation of Teachers, which represents 780 Freeport school teachers, said the strike threat will be presented to the City Board of Education at Thursday's negotiating session.

"Without a contract that contains pay levels reflecting the increased cost of living, we will not report for work in September," said Herbert Wechsler, the president of the local unit. "No contract, no work."

If the Thursday session leads to no resolution of the issue, the reporter's story about this development will begin this way:

> The possibility of a strike of public school teachers next September loomed larger today when six hours of contract talks failed to settle the wage issue.
>
> The teachers' union seeks an 8 percent pay increase over the current pay levels for next year's contract. The school board has offered 4 percent.
>
> The nonstop discussion between the union and the city school board failed to produce a settlement, said Herbert Wechsler, the president of the local unit of the American Federation of Teachers. The union, which represents the city's 780 public school teachers, issued its strike threat Tuesday and presented it formally at today's session.
>
> Joseph Foremen, the state superintendent of education, who is attending the contract talks at the invitation of both sides, said:
>
> "The two groups are widely separated. We need a cooling-off period. Unless one side or the other makes some kind of concession, we may have no teachers in the schools Sept. 9. And a concession is the last thing on their minds now."

The General, Then the Specific

The best advice she received from an editor, a reporter remarked, was "Follow every generality with a specific."

Every story has a logical structure, the editor told her, of general to specific. For example, when a council member says that next year's budget will set a record high, the reporter asks how high that will be, what the amount will be:

> Riggio said next year's budget will set "a record high." He estimated it would amount to $725 million.

Here's another example:

> Miles said, "Vince Lombardi was wrong when he said that winning is everything." It's more important, Miles said, to develop an athlete's sense of fair play and his or her love of sport.

DAD: Dialogue, Action, Description

To the news writer, form and content are one. Each reinforces the other. We've already noted that no matter how well-reported a story is, if it zigs here and zags there, the reader or viewer will not bother to try to make sense out of the chaos. But let's pause a moment to look at the perfectly organized story: If it lacks dialogue, action or description, the bored reader will also move on.

Dialogue, action, description: DAD. Let's look at a story that contains these essential elements, a religion story. Back in Chapter 3, we said that journalists came late to the topic of religion despite the great interest many people have in it. This story by Jena Heath that appeared in *The Charlotte Observer* stirred a tempest.

Letters showered down on the newspaper for a month, and Heath received calls of support and outrage from Virginia and the District of Columbia as well as from North Carolina after the piece was put on the Knight-Ridder wire and run on the front page of the religion section of *The Washington Post.*

Women Priests

Heath, who now works for *The News & Observer* in Raleigh, N.C., initiated the story. She thought it was time to write something about the role of Catholic women in their church. Her editor suggested she talk to women who want to be priests. Newsroom colleagues came up with names of sources.

Heath worked on the story for two weeks. The story ran at the top of page 1 of the Sunday newspaper. Look at how Heath blends description, action and dialogue in these opening paragraphs:

It was seven winters ago, but Sister Carol Symons hasn't forgotten.

She was ministering to the sick in Boone. The day the call came, the town's only priest was away. Sister Carol raced the seven minutes from her home to the hospital, where she found anguish. A Mexican migrant worker had given birth to a stillborn girl.

As she entered the dimly lit recovery room, the nun murmured to the woman's husband, tears glistening on his face. She walked across the room and took the woman's hand. Looking up from her stretcher, the woman choked out the words in Spanish.

Quiero confesar mis pecados, she pleaded. I want to confess my sins.

Sister Carol couldn't help. In the Roman Catholic Church, only priests can offer the peace of absolution.

"For me, the heart of the story is that there I was, a person in ministry and I couldn't help her," Sister Carol said. "I would be ordained if I could."

Change is coming for Catholic women, not fast enough for some, too fast for others. One door, though, remains firmly shut: the door to the priesthood.

The image of a female priest at the altar is an emotional one for Catholics. Traditionalists say Jesus chose 12 men as his disciples, that Jesus himself was a man and that the church's long history of an all-male clergy means the priesthood was never intended for women.

Many Catholic women, meanwhile, have seen female priests in the Episcopalian Church since 1976, when it began ordaining women. They've seen female rabbis since 1972 and a host of female ministers, including Southern Baptists, since 1964.

Yet Catholic women who feel called to the priesthood say they must live with the pain of knowing they cannot serve God as their hearts dictate.

Robert Lahser,
The Charlotte Observer

Sister Carol Symons

Summing Up

A lot of work goes into writing a news story. As a reporter with more than 30 years of experience on California newspapers put it to a beginner, "Those of us who survive work on our stories from the minute we get the assignment." The work the reporter was talking about takes the form of projecting at each level of reporting and writing the story as it will appear in its final form.

Reporters try to visualize and structure their stories at these stages:

- Immediately on receiving the assignment.
- While gathering material at the event.
- Before writing.
- During writing.

It is time to examine in detail the most important step in the writing process—creating the lead.

Further Reading

Scanlan, Christopher, ed. *How I Wrote the Story*. Providence, R.I.: Providence Journal, 1983.

Snyder, Louis L., and Richard B. Morris. *A Treasury of Great Reporting*. New York: Simon & Schuster, 1949.

Wilson, Ellen. *The Purple Decades: A Reader*. New York: Farrar, Straus and Giroux, 1982.

6 The Lead

Al Ransom,
San Antonio Light

Flood rescue—a direct lead.

Preview

The lead gives the reader the sense of the story to follow. There are two basic types of leads:

• **Direct:** This lead tells the reader or listener the most important aspect of the story at once. It is usually used on breaking news events.

• **Delayed:** This lead entices the reader or listener into the story by hinting at its contents. It often is used with feature stories.

The lead sentence usually contains one idea and follows the subject-verb-object sentence structure for clarity. It should not exceed 35 words.

The effective story lead meets two requirements. It captures the essence of the event, and it cajoles the reader or listener into staying awhile.

We slept last night in the enemy's camp.
—By a correspondent for the *Memphis Daily Appeal,* after the first day of the Civil War Battle of Shiloh.

Millionaire Harold F. McCormick today bought a poor man's youth.
—Carl Victor Little, UP, following McCormick's male gland transplant operation in the early 1920s. UP's New York Office quickly killed the lead and sent out a sub (substitute lead).

The million-to-one shot came in. Hell froze over. A month of Sundays hit the calendar. Don Larsen today pitched a no-hit, no-run, no-man-reach-first game in a World Series.
—Shirley Povich, *The Washington Post & Times Herald,* on the perfect game the Yankee pitcher hurled against the Brooklyn Dodgers in 1956.

"I feel as if I had been pawed by dirty hands," said Martha Graham.
—Walter Terry, dance critic of *The New York Herald Tribune,* after two members of Congress denounced Graham's dancing as "erotic."

What price Glory? Two eyes, two legs, an arm — $12 a month.
—St. Clair McKelway, *Washington Herald,* in a story about a disabled World War I veteran living in poverty.

Snow, followed by small boys on sleds.
—H. Allen Smith, *New York World-Telegram,* in the weather forecast.

Rule Breakers, but Memorable

These leads defy almost every canon decreed by those who prescribe standards of journalistic writing. The first lead violates the rule demanding the reporter's anonymity. The UP lead is in questionable taste. Povich's lead has four sentences and three clichés. Terry's lead is a quote lead, McKelway's asks a question—both violations of the standards. Smith's weather forecast is a little joke.

Yet, the leads are memorable.

They work because they meet the requirements of lead writing: They symbolize in graphic fashion the heart of the event, and they entice the reader to read on. Here are two leads from New York City newspapers that appeared the morning after the mayor announced his new budget. Which is better?

Mayor Lindsay listed facilities for public safety yesterday as his top spending priority for next year, shifting from his pledge of a year ago to make clean streets his first objective in capital expenditures.
—*The New York Times*

Mayor Lindsay dropped his broom and picked up the nightstick yesterday, setting law enforcement facilities as the top priority in the city's construction plans for the coming fiscal year.
—*Daily News*

Great Beginnings

The business of luring the reader into a story is hardly confined to journalistic writing. Andrew E. Svenson, the prolific author of many of the Nancy Drew, Bobbsey Twins and Hardy Boys juvenile books, said that the trick in writing is to set up danger, mystery and excitement on page 1 to convince the child to turn the page. He said he had rewritten page 1 as many as 20 times.

Plato knew the importance of the first words of a written work. "The beginning is the most important part of the work," he wrote in *The Republic.*

The Old Testament begins with simple words in a short sentence: "In the beginning God created the heavens and the earth."

Everyone remembers great beginnings:

> It was the best of times, it was the worst of times, it was the age of wisdom, it was the age of foolishness, it was the epoch of belief, it was the epoch of incredulity, it was the season of Light, it was the season of Darkness, it was the spring of hope, it was the winter of despair.

As most high school students know, that is how Charles Dickens began *A Tale of Two Cities.* Another book, written 92 years later, is also familiar to high school readers, possibly because of the beginning that trapped them into reading further:

> If you really want to hear about it, the first thing you'll probably want to know is where I was born, and what my lousy childhood was like, and how my parents were occupied, and all that David Copperfield kind of crap, but I don't feel like going into it, if you want to know the truth.

The writer—J. D. Salinger. The book—*Catcher in the Rye.* Another great beginning:

> It is a truth universally acknowledged, that a single man in possession of a good fortune, must be in want of a wife.

That's the way Jane Austen began *Pride and Prejudice.*

Finding the Lead

New Yorker writer John McPhee says, "The first part—the lead, the beginning—is the hardest part of all to write. I've often heard writers say that if you have written your lead you have 90 percent of the story." Locating the lead, he says, is a struggle.

"You have tens of thousands of words to choose from, after all—and only one can start the story, then one after that, and so forth. . . . What will you choose?" McPhee asks.

But before the words can be selected, the facts must be sorted out. How does the reporter select the one or two facts for a lead from the abundance of material he or she has gathered? What's the focus of the story?

As we saw in Chapter 5, the fact sifting begins well before the reporter sits down to write. Experienced reporters agree with journalists John W. Chancellor and Walter R. Mears who say:

> We have found that a way to write good leads is to think of them in advance— to frame the lead while the story is unfolding.

The Five Lead Questions

We can begin our examination of the lead-writing process by looking into the thinking of news writers. Their first step consists of answering two questions:

1. *What* was unique or the most important or unusual thing that happened?
2. *Who* was involved—who did it or who said it?

After answering these questions, the reporter seeks words and a form that will give shape to the responses by asking three more questions:

3. Is a direct or a delayed lead best? (Does the theme of the story go in the first sentence or somewhere within the first six paragraphs?)
4. Is there a colorful word or dramatic phrase I can work into the lead?
5. What is the subject, and what verb will best move the reader into the story?

Pregnant Teen-Agers

Let's accompany Sarah as she works on a story about a talk she has just covered. A Harvard sociologist spoke about teen-age pregnancy to a campus audience. He said that the bill for social services, special schools, lost work hours and hospital care for the infants, who are often born prematurely, adds up to several billion dollars a year.

"Last year," he said, "about 375,000 unmarried teen-agers gave birth, and almost as many teen-agers had abortions. The dollar costs have been enormous, to say nothing of the social costs."

Sarah is writing for the campus newspaper. She has a couple of hours before deadline. If she were working for a radio or TV station, she would not have the luxury of time to think about her lead and story. As Chancellor and Mears state in their book *The News Business:*

> When you've got to run to a telephone to start dictating, or when you've got to go on camera and start talking, the one thing you really need is to have a lead in your head. It doesn't have to be fancy, but if you frame it properly, the rest of the story will flow from it in a natural and graceful way.

Sarah knows that if she can identify the heart of the talk, her story will just about organize itself because the next several paragraphs after the lead will consist of quotes that buttress and amplify the lead material she has selected. Easier said than done, she muses.

Well, what's her lead? She had better start writing, and she does:

A Harvard sociologist studying teen-age pregnancy gave a speech last night to more than 200 students and faculty members in Hall Auditorium.

Sarah isn't happy with her lead. She talks to herself:

> Trouble. That's called backing into the lead. All this kind of lead tells the reader is that the speaker spoke to an audience, which is hardly unique and certainly not interesting or important enough to merit anyone's attention. He did say something interesting—in fact, he made several interesting points.

Sarah had been surprised by the large number of teen-agers who gave birth and the number of abortions among these young women. Lead material?

Not really, she reasons, because the speaker devoted most of his talk to the cost of teen-age pregnancy. This information was clearly the most important. She could work the figures into the second and third paragraphs to explain the reasons for the high cost. Sarah writes:

> A Harvard sociologist said last night that teen-age pregnancy is costing the country billions of dollars a year.
> Gerald Cantor told 200 students and faculty members in Hall Auditorium that the annual costs associated with the pregnancies of almost 750,000 unmarried women under the age of 20 "are vastly greater than we had thought."
> He attributed the costs to social services. . . .

Sarah pauses to read what she has written. She is satisfied that she has found the most important part of the talk for her lead, that she has identified the speaker properly and placed the talk. . . . Wait. She isn't happy with the word *said* in her lead. Not very exciting.

> Should I make it *warned?* Or is that too strong? He really didn't warn. I'll leave it as is.

Sarah has answered the first three of our five questions for lead writing:

1. **What:** The high cost.
2. **Who:** Harvard sociologist.
3. **Direct or delayed:** Direct.

We take leave of Sarah as she ponders the fourth and fifth questions. If you wish, lend her a hand.

A Race for Congress

Here is a lead a reporter wrote about a congressional race. He thought he had answered the first two questions writers ask themselves when writing a lead:

> Replies of Rep. Ronald A. Sarasin and William R. Ratchford, candidates in the Fifth Congressional race, to a Connecticut League of Women Voters questionnaire were released today.

He did include *what* had happened and *who* was involved. But he did not make his answer to the first question sufficiently specific. What did they say in their replies? The reporter reached this answer down in the story, but his editor pointed out that voters want to know the opinions and positions of their candidates quickly in stories about politics. Such events do not lend themselves to delayed leads.

A better lead for the political story might have been:

> Ronald A. Sarasin and William R. Ratchford, candidates for Congress in the Fifth District, agree that financing Social Security is the major domestic issue facing the nation.

The next paragraph might have included the background information that the reporter had mistakenly put into his lead:

> Their positions on Social Security and on other issues were released today by the Connecticut League of Women Voters. The League had sent its questionnaires to all major candidates for office.

The subsequent paragraphs would expand the Social Security theme and introduce additional material from the replies of the candidates.

Kickers

All these leads are direct leads for breaking or hard news stories. But there are times when writers back into the lead on a breaking news story—intentionally. Edna Buchanan began a story for *The Miami Herald* this way:

> Bad things happen to the husbands of the Widow Elkin.
>
> Someone murdered husband No. 4, Cecil Elkin, apparently smashing his head with a frying pan as he watched "Family Feud" on TV.
>
> Husband No. 3, Samuel Smilich, drowned in a weedy South Dade canal.
>
> Husband No. 2, Lawrence Myers, cannot be found. . . .

Anyone out there who isn't hanging on every word? Notice the detail Buchanan supplies: It was not just any pan but a frying pan with which No. 4 was dispatched. And he wasn't just watching television but "Family Feud." The canal where No. 3 was found was "weedy."

Buchanan goes on to write about Widow Elkin and then concludes the piece:

> It is the murder of her fourth husband that got Margaret Elkin in trouble. She is accused of trying to hire a beekeeper to kill him. The trial is set for Sept. 9.

The prosaic way to have started this story would have put the date set for the trial in the lead. But Buchanan's reporting turned up a remarkable series of events, and she gave us a modern morality tale with a climax.

Journalists call these lead-type endings *kickers,* probably in recognition of the jolt the climax gives the reader.

Types of Leads

Beginning journalists often are offered lists of leads. They are told about the who, what, where, when, why and how leads; the anecdotal, clause, contrast, direct address, staccato, gag, shotgun and quote leads; and a score of others.

This categorizing may be useful for a research project, but the lists are of little use to the working reporter. No reporter looks at his or her notes and thinks, "Well, this looks like a *who* lead here. Or maybe it's a *what* lead."

What ran through the mind of the reporter who wrote this lead?

> NORFOLK — Charley Greene has hit the roof in an effort to prove that he isn't six feet under.
> —*The Virginian-Pilot* (Norfolk, Va.)

Is that a *who* or a *what* lead? What is the difference and who cares? The reporter learned that a retired Navy warrant officer had not been receiving his retirement pay because the government thought him dead. The situation seemed humorous enough for feature handling. Then the reporter played with some words that would express the plight of a man caught in coils of red tape. The reporter decided on a delayed lead.

There are only two basic leads, direct and delayed. All the others fall under these two types.

Direct Lead

The direct lead is the workhorse of journalism, the lead that is used on most stories. As we have seen, the direct lead focuses on the theme of the event in the first paragraph. The surest way to test a reporter's competence, editors say, is to see whether his or her leads on spot news events move directly to the point and are succinct and readable.

Here are some direct leads:

WASHINGTON—The House of Representatives voted today to impeach President Clinton.

A local couple was awarded $150,000 in damages yesterday in Butte County Court for injuries they suffered in a traffic accident last March.

LONDON — Ginger Spice said Sunday she is leaving the Spice Girls, but the all-girl pop group will continue to perform with four members.

SPENCER — Shocked survivors wandered their ripped-apart community Sunday, searching for tornado-scattered belongings and mourning six neighbors who died.

Another in a series of snowstorms is expected to hit the Sierra today.

SAN FRANCISCO — The California Supreme Court ruled today that newspapers and television stations can be held liable for news-gathering techniques that intrude on privacy.

WASHINGTON — The U.S. Senate this afternoon acquitted President Clinton of the two impeachment charges brought against him by the House of Representatives. The vote on both charges fell far short of the two-thirds required for conviction.

Lively Leads   Direct leads need not be dry and dull. Here's a direct lead by Aljean Harmetz of *The New York Times* for a business story, which we usually think of as a dry subject with prose to match:

> Two veteran motion picture industry
> executives were chosen today by the board
> of Walt Disney Productions to head the
> troubled company a mouse built.

When a fire struck a high-rise apartment building in Queens, New York, the AP put this lead on its story:

> A late-morning fire in the upper floors
> of an 18-story apartment building in the
> Lefrak city project in Elmhurst, Queens,
> killed three people Thursday, the Fire De-
> partment said.

Now look at how the *Daily News* began its story about the same fire:

> Strong winds combined lethally with a
> fire in a Queens high-rise building yesterday,
> creating a "blowtorch" that roared through an
> apartment building and into a hallway,
> killing three people and injuring 22.

The image of a blowtorch searing its way through the building is powerful. A battalion fire chief used that word in an interview and the reporter had the good sense to put it in the lead. Good reporting makes for good writing.

Four Essentials   Looking back at the direct news leads in this section, we can generalize about their essentials.

First, we notice that each lead has something *specific* to tell the reader. The reporter moved directly to the heart of the event.

Next, the *time* element is almost always in the lead. Then, there is usually a *source* of the information or action, and the source is often identified. And finally, the *place* of the action usually is included.

Delayed Lead

The delayed lead is often used on features and news features, the kinds of stories that are not about developing or fast-breaking events. The delayed lead usually sets a scene or evokes a mood with an incident, anecdote or example.

Here is a delayed lead on a feature about a man who runs a demolition company. It was written by AP Newsfeatures writer Sid Moody:

> Jack Loizeaux is a dentist of urban
> decay, a Mozart of dynamite, a guru of
> gravity. Like Joshua, he blows and the
> walls come tumbling down.

Retribution. When *The Washington Times* began publication, many of its staffers were members of the Rev. Sun Myung Moon's Unification Church. One of them turned in this lead for a fire story:

A 39-year-old Fairfax man was punished by God Thursday night for smoking in bed by burning to death.

Notice that the reader does not know from this lead just what Jack Loizeaux does—the delayed lead does not reveal essential information to the reader. The suspense is part of the attraction of the delayed lead.

Features, profiles, investigative reporting, series—these usually take delayed leads. Here is how an investigative reporter for the *Chicago Tribune* began a series of articles exposing corruption in Chicago's ambulance services:

> They are the misery merchants and they
> prowl the streets of our city 24 hours a day
> as profiteers of human suffering.

News Magazines   The delayed lead is a favorite approach of the news magazines for events that readers are already familiar with through newspaper and broadcast coverage. Here is how *U.S. News & World Report* began its long piece on the week's big story:

> He had a temper so combustible that he
> once ejected Lana Turner and Ava Gardner
> from his Palm Springs house, screaming
> "Out, out, out!" and then hurling Gardner's
> cosmetics, clothes and records into the
> driveway. His buddies included mobsters
> and thugs, and he divided the world, Sicil-
> ian style, into friends—recipients of lavish
> gifts—and enemies. Face to face, the blue
> eyes could drill through you, and he could
> be unpredictable, foul-mouthed and crude,
> taking swings at anyone who got in his way.

Compare this beginning with the AP's direct lead on the same event:

LOS ANGELES (AP) — Frank Sinatra, the dashing teen idol who matured into the premier romantic balladeer of American popular music and the "Chairman of the Board" to his millions of fans, died Thursday night of a heart attack. He was 82.

On Track   Just any incident or anecdote will not do for the delayed lead. The lead must be consistent with the news point, the theme of the story. It must *lead* the reader straight to the heart of the event. Notice how John Rebchook of the *El Paso Herald-Post* takes this delayed lead to the news point in the fourth paragraph, the current status of the drive to collect unpaid traffic fines. Rebchook illustrates his point about unpaid traffic warrants by using in his lead a specific driver who has avoided paying:

> In less than three miles, Joseph L. Jody
> III ran six stop signs, changed lanes im-
> properly four times, ran one red light, and   **Example**
> drove 60 mph in a 30 mph zone — all
> without a driver's license. Two days later,
> he again drove without a driver's license.

This time he ran a stop sign and drove 80 mph in a 45 mph zone. For his 16 moving violations Jody was fined $1,795.

He never paid. Police say that Jody has moved to Houston. Of the estimated 30,000 to 40,000 outstanding traffic warrants in police files, Jody owes the largest single amount.

Still, Jody's fines account for a small part of at least $500,000 owed to the city in unpaid traffic warrants.

In February, Mayor Jonathan Rogers began a crackdown on scofflaws in order to retrieve some $838,000 in unpaid warrants. As of mid-March, some $368,465 had been paid.

News point (Theme)

Leads on News Features

As the movement of news and information speeded up with all-day, all-news radio and TV stations and the Internet, print publications with a much slower access to readers turned to writing techniques to attract readers who already had some idea of the event. One of the techniques is the news feature. The writer "featurizes" the breaking news event by putting a delayed lead on the story. We've already seen how news magazines do this. Newspapers do, too.

By the time *The New York Times* was on newsstands and doorsteps, everyone knew the end to a legal battle over custody of 2 1/2-year-old Jessica. The

Don't Delay Too Long

Unless the writer intends to build to a last-paragraph climax, the sooner the news point is reached after a delayed lead the better. Here's a good example by George James of *The New York Times* in which the lead is in the second paragraph:

Sheila Maria Boyd and Jerry Conner, both of Brooklyn, were married yesterday in Queens Borough Hall. Afterward, they celebrated at Cobblestone's Restaurant, a few blocks away at 117–18 Queens Boulevard in Forest Hills.

Among the uninvited guests were nine police officers from the 112th Precinct, who gave them handcuffs and arrested them on 18 counts of robbery.

"I think they were having our famous baby back ribs," said Pete Massaro, the owner of the Cobblestone's, "and the white house wine."

Ms. Boyd, 23 years old, of 32 Lincoln Avenue, and Mr. Conner, 27, of 1765 Prospect Place, were wanted for the robbery of 13 patients and 5 employees in the office of Dr. Arnold. . . .

Supreme Court had dashed the hopes of Jessica's adoptive parents to keep her. This meant the child would have to be turned over to her biological mother, who had given her up for adoption shortly after Jessica was born.

Don Terry put this lead on his news feature:

> BLAIRSTOWN, Iowa, Aug. 2 — When she is grown up, maybe Jessica De-Boer will understand why the adults in her young but complicated life have caused so much hurt in the name of love.
>
> But starting today, the 2 1/2-year-old has more immediate lessons to learn, namely how to live without the only people she has ever known as Mommy and Daddy, Roberta and Jan DeBoer of Ann Arbor, Mich.

The Associated Press, which takes a conservative approach to newswriting, put this beginning on a murder story:

> DECATUR, Ga., Jan. 26 (AP) — Aster Haile, an Ethiopian immigrant, was delighted when her cousin arranged a marriage for her — so excited that she bought clothes for her first date with the man and showed them off.
>
> But the day after the date, Ms. Haile called a friend and said that the man was too old and that she could not marry him. A day later, she was found dead along an Atlanta highway, shot in her head.

In the third paragraph is the arrest, which in times past would have been the lead to this story.

> The police have charged the man who set up the date, Arega Abraha, with murder. Mr. Abraha was arrested on Friday at the Cincinnati-Northern Kentucky International Airport on a Federal charge of unlawful flight to avoid prosecution.

When the House of Representatives voted to impeach President Clinton, the *St. Louis Post-Dispatch* put this lead on the momentous story:

> New York Democrat Charles Rangel rose Saturday to utter one of the rare sentences on which both sides of the House of Representatives could agree: "Mr. Speaker, the whole world is watching."

President Clinton's name was not mentioned until the fifth paragraph, and the actual vote was near the bottom of the 34-inch story. The editor, Cole C. Campbell, explained the choice of a delayed lead: "We knew people would know the outcome of the vote when they picked up the paper, so we wanted to do a story that conveyed the historicity of the moment."

In Rwanda

Early in his coverage of the slaughter in Rwanda, the AP's Mark Fritz understood that the battle between the Hutus and Tutsis had to be put in human terms. He had to put faces on the carnage. Numbers alone would only numb readers.

Health centers were set up in Rwanda in an attempt to lure refugees back to their country from neighboring Zaire, to which they had fled. Fritz began his news feature about the centers this way:

GOMA, Zaire (AP) — Bernard Sebazzogue watched as cholera killed his daughter on Monday, his wife on Tuesday and his grandmother Thursday. By week's end, he gathered up his three remaining children and fled for help. To Rwanda.

What lay before him, rising from the dirt over the first 50 miles into his country, were five hospitals that began springing up just a few days before Sebazzogue's family began dying.

These outposts at Goma's doorstep are part of a quick and somewhat haphazard effort to create a corridor of health care in Rwanda from which more than 1 million people fled over several panicked days in early July.

Note that a direct lead could have been fashioned out of the material in the third paragraph. Fritz chose to featurize the story, and the impact is obvious. His coverage included feature stories and straight news accounts as well as news features. His work was recognized with the Pulitzer Prize for International Reporting.

A Story of Drugs

At first glance, the death record that police reporter Robert Popp of the *San Francisco Chronicle* saw in the police file seemed routine. But rewriteman George Williamson, copy editor Jim Toland and Popp turned it into a sad tale. Here is their news feature:

Small Boy's Big Loss to Drugs

Johnny B., 6, awoke at a pre-dawn hour yesterday and saw his fully clothed mother lying on the floor next to the bed they shared in the Roy-Ann Hotel at 405 Valencia Street.

Her nose was bleeding badly. Johnny got up, found some tissues, and wiped her face clean. Then he went back to sleep.

When he awoke again at 8:30 a.m., Anne B., 25, was still on the floor. Her face was covered by new blood.

Johnny dressed himself neatly — as usual — and groomed his Dutch boy haircut before going downstairs to tell the hotel clerk about his "sick" mother.

The coroner's office later determined that she had died from an overdose of an undetermined drug.

Johnny recounted that the night before, two men had visited the studio apartment in the Inner Mission District. He said he asked one man why he was using a rubber cord to make his arm veins bulge, and the man responded that he was taking a blood test.

The men left some time after Johnny went to bed.

Postscript: Jim Toland had given students in his newswriting class at San Francisco State University the facts taken from the police report. One student, curious to see if there is such a place as the Roy-Ann Hotel, drove by. She found the *Chronicle* had misspelled the name of the hotel. It was the Royan.

Dr. Ruth's Blooper

In her story for *USA Today,* Barbara S. Rothschild describes a sex therapist's boo-boo with this delayed lead:

There may finally be a question that embarrasses Dr. Ruth Westheimer. It's about the accuracy of her book.

Teens who read the new sex book coauthored by the USA's best-known sex therapist could get more than they asked for.

A baby, perhaps.

First Love: A Young People's Guide to Sexual Information, by Dr. Ruth and education professor Nathan Kravetz, has a major error on page 195.

In a chapter on contraception, the $3.50 book says it's "safe" to have sex the week before and the week of ovulation.

It should read "unsafe" — since those are the times a woman is *most* likely to become pregnant. . . .

Direct or Delayed?

As should be clear by now, there are no absolute rules about when the direct or the delayed lead should be used. True enough, on large-scale events the direct lead is usually called for, and on features the delayed lead works best. But the lines tend to blur between these extremes.

Usually, publications, stations and the online servers establish a style their reporters follow. When a study of bank lending practices found that whites are more likely than blacks to receive mortgage money, Michael Quint of *The New York Times* began his story with a direct lead:

WASHINGTON, Oct. 21 — The most comprehensive report on mortgage lending nationwide ever issued by the Government shows that even within the same income group whites are nearly twice as likely as blacks to get loans.

Jim Hughes, *Daily News*

Adrift

The storm was expected, but it seemed to catch everyone by surprise, from motorists to city emergency officials. Direct or delayed lead on the story? Here's how the *Daily News* began its story:

Didn't anyone see this coming? And were emergency officials caught napping?

These questions surged to the top in the wake of the raging storm that caught most New Yorkers by surprise and produced startling scenes of motorists nearly drifting into the East River.

City officials were warned and should have passed their alert on to the public, the National Weather Service said last night.

For its page 1 story the same day, *The Wall Street Journal* writer John R. Wilke preferred a delayed lead that focused on the effect of the discriminatory practices on an individual. Here is how his story began:

> BOSTON — When Sterling Saunders needed a home-repair loan, he turned to two of New England's largest banks, Shawmut Bank and Bank of Boston. He had a steady job, equity in the house and little debt, but they turned him down.
>
> In desperation, he arranged a $35,000, two-year loan from a small Massachusetts mortgage lender, Resource Equity Inc., at a stratospheric 34.09% interest rate. When Resource wouldn't refinance Mr. Saunder's loan he fell even deeper into debt through refinancings with other high-rate lenders. Now the 42-year-old city employee, his wife and three daughters face eviction from their home of 16 years by a third lender.
>
> "This might never have happened if we'd been able to find a bank loan in the first place," Mr. Saunders says. The banks decline to address specifics of his case, but judging by recent studies of lending patterns, one reason he couldn't get bank loans may have had to do with his address: He lives in a low-income, mostly black Boston neighborhood with few bank branches. A big survey by the Federal Reserve and analyses by others show these areas get a disproportionately small share of mortgage money from banks. . . . **Theme**

The *Journal* also ran a direct-lead story reviewing the study inside the newspaper.

The Dangers

The narrative style has influenced papers across the country, but the style sometimes has spread by contagion rather than by healthy example. The delayed lead requires a talented hand. Moreover, it cannot be used at the reporter's whim.

In an attempt to sell their editors on their stories, ambitious reporters use delayed leads on routine news stories, and some reporters play with delayed leads when they are unable to write direct news leads. By taking the narrative or chronological approach or by focusing on an individual or an incident, they hope that the reader will somehow figure out just what the news point is.

Editors are aware of these tactics and the abusers of the delayed lead find themselves confined to taking scores from the local bridge and bowling leagues and explaining to the wrestling promoters why the sports editor doesn't consider wrestling results worthy of space.

The Combo Lead

Some reporters have mastered a technique that combines the direct and delayed leads. The story begins with a few general sentences. Then the reporter hits the reader with a karate chop at the end of the first paragraph. Edna Buchanan, the Pulitzer Prize-winning police reporter for *The Miami Herald,* is master of this kind of lead. Here are two typical Buchanan leads:

The man she loved slapped her face. Furious, she says she told him never, ever to do that again. "What are you going to do, kill me?" he asked, and handed her a gun. "Here, kill me," he challenged. She did.

On New Year's Eve, Charles Curzio stayed later than planned at his small TV repair shop to make sure customers would have their sets in time to watch the King Orange Jamboree Parade. His kindness cost his life.

Direct, with a Difference Buchanan covered a story about an ex-convict, Gary Robinson, who pushed his way past a line at a fried-chicken outlet. He was persuaded to take his place in line, but when he reached the counter there was no fried chicken, only nuggets, whereupon he slugged the woman at the counter. In the ensuing fracas, a security guard shot Robinson. Buchanan's lead was:

Gary Robinson died hungry.

Buchanan says her idea of a successful lead is one that could cause a reader who is breakfasting with his wife to "spit out his coffee, clutch his chest, and say, 'My god, Martha. Did you read this?' "

For her lead on a story about a drug smuggler who died when some of the cocaine-filled condoms that he had swallowed began to leak in his stomach, Buchanan wrote:

His last meal was worth $30,000 and it killed him.

A Difficult Choice

Let us listen to Margaret as she mulls over the notes she has taken at a city council meeting:

There were 13 items on the agenda. Well, which were the important ones? I'll circle them in my notes—
• General traffic program to route heavy trucks to Stanley Street and keep Main for lighter traffic.
• 56 stop signs to be bought.
• Paving program for Kentucky Street that will later fit into the bypass.
• OK'd contract to White Painting Co. to paint City Hall, $28,000.
• Hired consulting firm for traffic study.

Clearly, I need a direct lead here. Four of them seem to deal with traffic. Should I summarize them or should I pick out the truck route or the traffic study? They seem equally important, so maybe I'll play with a summary lead. I'll drop the stop signs way down and then go into the painting contract.

She writes:

The City Council today took three significant actions to cope with the city's downtown traffic congestion.
The Council:
1. Approved the employment of Rande Associates, a consulting firm from Burbank, Calif., to make a study of traffic patterns.
2. Called for bids on paving 12 blocks of Kentucky Street, which is planned as part of a downtown bypass.
3. Endorsed the city traffic department's proposal to route heavy vehicles to Stanley Street before they enter Main Street.

At this point, some doubts assail Margaret. She remembers that the truck traffic issue has been argued for several months. Downtown merchants complained to the mayor about the truck traffic, and Stanley Street home owners petitioned the Council to keep the trucks away. The local newspaper and radio station have editorialized about it. In her haste to structure a complicated story, her news judgment went awry, she thinks. She writes:

The City Council today decided to route truck traffic to Stanley Street and away from downtown Freeport.

The city hall reporter is pleased with the lead she has written. But then more doubts. Maybe the overall pattern is more important than the single item about Stanley Street. After all, she thinks, the Council's three major actions will affect more people than those involved in the Stanley Street situation. Margaret decides that she needs some advice and she shows the city editor both leads.

"That's a tough one," he tells her. "Sometimes you flip a coin. Why don't you use your first lead and move up the third item, the one on Stanley Street, and put it first in the list?"

If we look closely at the two leads Margaret prepared, we notice that the single-element lead about the routing of truck traffic to Stanley Street denotes a specific action the council took. The summary lead about the council taking three "significant" actions to "cope with" traffic congestion is the reporter's conclusion or interpretation. The *Daily News*'s summary lead on the New Jersey election in Chapter 5 also contains an interpretation that the governor "took a shellacking all around in yesterday's statewide election." Editors allow experienced reporters to interpret the news.

Good Reporting Equals Good Leads

Many weak leads are the result of inadequate reporting. Consider this lead:

Barbara Elizabeth Foster, 19, St. Mary's University sophomore, will be queen of the city's Rose Festival.

Immediately, the city editor knows he is in for a tedious trek through the copy. The reporter failed to single out an interesting characteristic of the new queen to add to her age and year in school. Glancing through the copy, the editor notices that her mother was named Maid of Cotton 25 years ago. At the end of the story, there is a fleeting mention that her father enjoys gardening.

The editor runs his fingers through thinning hair. Masking his exasperation, he circles two sections and suggests to the reporter that there just might be a lead in the mother-daughter relationship and that a logical question to have asked the new queen was whether her father grew roses. Without good reporting no story can shine, much less be complete.

Color and S-V-O

Next, to the fourth and fifth of our five guides to writing leads. The fourth question the reporter has to answer is, "Is there a colorful word or dramatic phrase that I want to work into the lead?"

When Florida conducted the first execution in the United States in a dozen years in which a person was put to death, many reporters were assigned to the event. The nation had engaged in a debate about the morality of the death penalty. How best to put the Florida execution into words? Here is the lead Wayne King wrote for *The New York Times:*

> STARKE, Fla., May 25 — The state of Florida trussed Arthur Spenkelink immobile in the electric chair this morning, dropped a black leather mask over his face and electrocuted him.

A Poet's Perception. "Reduced to its essence, a good English sentence is a statement that an agent (the subject of the sentence) performed an action (the verb) upon something (the object)."

—John Ciardi

The choice of the verb "trussed" is inspired. Not only does it mean to secure tightly, its second definition is "to arrange for cooking by binding close the wings or legs of a fowl."

The fifth guide takes us directly into the construction of the lead—the selection of the subject and verb for the lead.

The basic construction of the lead should be subject-verb-object, S-V-O. That is, the lead should begin with the subject, should be closely followed by an active verb and should conclude with the object of the verb.

The S-V-O structure has an internal imperative: It directs the reporter to write simple sentences, sentences with one main clause. This kind of construction keeps leads short, another major requirement for a readable beginning.

Here are two direct leads:

> In the past decade, David Blake has overpaid the city $7,635 in property fees on his small pharmacy in East Harlem.
> *—Newsday*

S = David Blake; V = has overpaid; O = the city.

SAN FRANCISCO — A federal judge has ordered the City of San Francisco to hire 60 women police patrol officers within the next 32 weeks.

—UPI

S = judge; V = has ordered; O = San Francisco.

The S-V-O construction is the staple of journalistic writing. Three-fourths or more of the sentences a reporter writes follow this pattern. Most direct news leads—whether for print or broadcast—have this construction. It parallels the usual pattern of discourse and conforms to the command, "Write as you talk." Also, the S-V-O construction is functional. It is consistent with the thinking pattern of the reporter as he or she structures the lead. It is the most direct way of answering the first two questions the reporter asks when trying to find the lead: What happened? Who was involved?

Actors and Writers. Actors are told, "Act the verb." The same advice helps writers: "Write the verb." The verb gives life and energy to the sentence.

Variety Is Possible

Although the S-V-O guideline may seem rigid, it does permit a variety of styles. Let us look at several leads written the night of a famous heavyweight championship fight:

BULLETIN

CHICAGO, Sept. 25 (UPI) SONNY LISTON KNOCKED OUT FLOYD PATTERSON IN THE FIRST ROUND TONIGHT TO WIN THE HEAVYWEIGHT CHAMPIONSHIP OF THE WORLD.

M950ct

CHICAGO, Sept. 25 — Nobody got his money's worth at Comiskey Park tonight except Sonny Liston. He knocked out Floyd Patterson in two minutes, six seconds of the first round of their heavyweight title fight and took the first big step toward becoming a millionaire.
—Robert L. Teague, *The New York Times*

CHICAGO, Sept. 25 — Sonny Liston needed all of two years to lure Floyd Patterson into the ring and only two minutes, six seconds to get him out of it in a sudden one-knockdown, one-round-knockout at Comiskey Park last night.
—Jesse Abramson, *The Herald Tribune*

CHICAGO, Sept. 25 — Floyd Patterson opened and closed in one tonight. It took Sonny Liston only 2:06 to smash the imported china in the champ's jaw and, thereby, record the third swiftest kayo in a heavyweight title match — a sudden ending that had the stunned Comiskey Park fans wondering wha' hoppened. The knockout punch was there for everyone to see. It was a ponderous hook on Patterson's jaw. But the real mystery was what hurt the champ just before that; how come he suddenly looked in trouble when Liston stepped away from a clinch near the ropes?
—Leonard Lewin, *The Daily Mirror*

CHICAGO, Sept. 25 — It was short, sweet and all Sonny Liston here tonight. The hulking slugger with the vicious punch to match his personality teed off on Floyd Patterson, knocked the champion down and out at 2:06 of the first round and won the world heavyweight championship without raising a bead of sweat on his malevolent countenance.
—Gene Ward, *Daily News*

All the reporters agreed on the news angle or theme—Liston's quick knockout of Patterson. The thinking of these reporters was along the S-V-O line: S = Liston; V = knocked out; O = Patterson.

The first lead, written for the UPI, whose reporters are told to remember that there is a deadline every minute, has little more than the S-V-O structure in the lead. Written within seconds of the 10-count, the story was designed to meet the needs of newspapers and broadcast stations on deadline.

The other reporters, who worked for New York City newspapers when the city had four morning dailies, were under less pressure and were able to fashion more distinctive leads. Some put personal observations and their interpretations into the leads—a practice permitted byline reporters.

Obituary Lead   When Thurgood Marshall died, the leads were also basically the same:

Retired Supreme Court Justice Thurgood Marshall, the first black to serve on the nation's highest court and a key figure in the civil rights movement, died yesterday of heart failure at 84.
—Phil Mintz, *Newsday*

WASHINGTON — Thurgood Marshall, who championed the causes of the downtrodden, the imprisoned and the defenseless in almost a quarter-century on the Supreme Court, died yesterday at the Bethesda Naval Medical Center near here. He was 84.
—*The Boston Globe*

WASHINGTON — Thurgood Marshall, one of the most influential Americans of the 20th century and the first black to be elevated to the U.S. Supreme Court, died Sunday at the Bethesda Naval Medical Center in suburban Washington. He was 84.
—Glen Elsasser and Nicholas M. Horrock, *Chicago Tribune*

WASHINGTON — Retired Justice Thurgood Marshall, the first black to sit on the U.S. Supreme Court and a towering figure in the civil rights movement, died Sunday of heart failure. He was 84.
—The Associated Press

Lead Length

When a reporter writes a lead, he or she navigates between divergent currents. One pull is toward writing a longer-than-average sentence, as the lead must offer significant information. The other is toward a short sentence because short sentences are more readable than long ones. The long sentence may be difficult to grasp; the short sentence may be uninformative or misleading.

Lead sentences should adhere to a 35-word limit whenever possible, for visibility as well as readability. Long leads occupy so much of the narrow newspaper or online column that they appear forbidding. For broadcasting, all sentences tend to be short for quick comprehension.

The AP tells its reporters, "When a lead moves beyond 20–25 words it's time to start trimming." Some of the extra baggage that can be jettisoned:

- Unnecessary attribution.
- Compound sentences joined by *but* and *and*.
- Exact dates and times unless essential.

This means that the AP and other news organizations never run long leads, right? Wrong. When the occasion demands full information in the lead and the news writer is adept at constructing a sentence that has rhythm and balance, long leads are given a green light. Look at this lead by Peter Coy of the AP:

NEW YORK (AP) — The stock market plunged out of control Monday in a selling panic that rivaled the Great Crash of 1929, pushing the Dow Jones average down more than 500 points, draining more than $500 billion from the value of stocks and sending shock waves around the world.

That's 46 words, a blockbuster, but so was the event. Despite its length, the lead is not hard to read. One of the reasons is the writer's use of action verbs that propel the reader through to the end.

Momentous Lead   When an event is compellingly important, all rules and guidelines are tossed aside and the writer is allowed to jam the facts into the first sentence. Look at this lead from *The Washington Post* that runs 39 words long:

Five men, one of whom said he is a former employee of the Central Intelligence Agency, were arrested at 2:30 a.m. yesterday in what authorities described as an elaborate plot to bug the office of the Democratic National Committee.

Not much artistry here, just the facts. But what facts. This was the opening salvo in the *Post*'s exposure of the Watergate scandal that led to the resignation of Richard Nixon from the presidency.

Leads for Folos

When the Supreme Court ruled that principals can censor high school newspapers, *The Christian Science Monitor,* the *Kennebec* (Maine) *Journal, The Augusta* (Ga.) *Chronicle* and scores of other newspapers around the country assigned staff reporters to find out what effect the ruling would have on local high schools.

These local stories are known as *folos.* The *folo* can run alongside the major story, or it can be published a day or so after the major piece has run.

The lead to a *folo* includes some information from the major piece:

Local high school principals say they will continue to allow student journalists a free hand, despite a Supreme Court decision that gives them the power to censor school publications.

Updated or freshened stories fall into the category of the *folo* story. Usually, it is possible to find someone to comment on a new development or to track down people affected by a new program or policy.

Causes and consequences are useful for leads to these stories:

> Service and maintenance workers were
> returning to their jobs today following a
> vote to end a 10-day strike against three
> Baltimore-area hospitals.
> —*The Baltimore Sun*

Disasters are updated without difficulty. If the cause of the airplane crash is unknown, investigators can be asked about the progress of the inquiry. If there were serious injuries, the condition of the victims can be checked, and if there are additional fatalities, a new death toll can be used as the basis of the lead, which we saw the AP do in Chapter 1 as reporters covered the Jonesboro school shooting.

Readability

A reporter handed in this lead:

> The city planning office today recommended adding a section
> to the zoning code regulations on classification for residential
> use of property.

The editor puzzled over it and then instructed the reporter to say specifically what the proposed section would do. The reporter tried again.

> The city planning office today recommended that property
> zoned for two-acre, one-family dwellings be rezoned to allow the
> construction of cooperative apartment houses for middle- and
> low-income families.

The city editor looked this over and seemed pleased. "Let's take it a step further," he said. "What's the point of the recommendation?" He answered his own question. "To change the code so ordinary people, not only the rich, can move into that wooded area north of town near the Greenwich Estates section. Let's try to get people into the lead." The reporter returned in 10 minutes with these two paragraphs:

> Low- and middle-income families may be able to buy
> apartments in suburban areas north of the city.
> This is the intention of a proposal made today by the city
> planning office. The recommendation to the city council would
> rezone property in the area from the present restrictions that
> permit only single-family dwellings on two-acre lots.

In this process of writing and rewriting, the reporter went from a jargon-loaded, impenetrable lead to one that stated succinctly and clearly what the proposed regulation was intended to bring about. Accuracy was not sacrificed for simplicity and readability.

Readability Components

Readability stems from the ideas that make up the sentence, the order in which they are written and the words and phrases chosen to give the ideas expression:

Ideas: When possible, the lead should contain one idea. "The sentence is a single cry," says Sir Herbert Read, the British critic and author, in his *English Prose Style.* Too many ideas in a sentence make for heavy going. Also, the idea selected should be easy to grasp; complexities should be simplified.

Sentence order: The subject-verb-object construction is the most easily understood.

Word choice: Because the lead moves on its subject and verb, the choice of nouns and verbs is essential for readability. Whenever possible, the subject should be a concrete noun that the reader can hear, see, taste, feel or smell. It should stand for a name or a thing. The verb should be a colorful action verb that accelerates the reader to the object or makes the reader pause and think. It is not so much the presence or absence of the verb that matters, but the choice between a transitive and an intransitive verb.

Don't Write Writing

Immersed in words, the reporter is tempted to write writing, to make meaning secondary to language. This is fine when a poet plays with words, but it is dangerous for a journalist, whose first allegiance is to straightforward expression. Word play can lead to tasteless flippancies such as this lead:

> JACKSONVILLE, Fla. — Like justice,
> the new judge of the Duval County Court
> is blind.

Some reporters seem to think that using a direct quotation in the lead or injecting *you* into the lead makes for classy writing. They're wrong. Editors consider this weak writing. When you are tempted, consider this lead and imagine the editor's explosion when it popped out on his screen:

> You don't have to go to a doctor to find out whether you are pregnant. Test kits can be bought over the counter.

Good journalism is the accurate communication of an event to a reader, viewer or listener. As Wendell Johnson, a professor of psychology and speech pathology at the University of Iowa, put it, "Communication is writing about something for someone . . . making highly reliable maps of the terrain of experience." Johnson would caution his students, "You cannot write writing."

The reporter who puts writing before fact gathering will achieve notoriety of a sort, if he or she is clever enough. Such fame is fleeting, though. Editors and the public eventually flush out the reporter whose competence is all scintillation.

This is not a red light to good writing. In fact, the fashioning of well-written stories is our next objective.

Summing Up

Good leads are based on the writer's clear understanding of the theme of the story. All else follows. This is why finding the theme is No. 1 in our list of guidelines for writing readable leads:

1. Find the essential element(s) of the story.
2. Decide whether a direct or a delayed lead better suits the event.
3. If one element is outstanding, use a single-element lead. If more than one is, use a multiple-element lead.
4. Use the S-V-O construction.
5. Use concrete nouns and colorful action verbs.
6. Keep the lead short, under 30 or 35 words.
7. Make the lead readable, but do not sacrifice truthful and accurate reporting for readability.

Further Reading

Howarth, W. L. *The John McPhee Reader.* New York: Vintage Books, 1977.
Murray, Donald. *Writing for Your Readers.* Chester, Conn.: The Globe Pequot Press, 1983.
Roberts, Gene, and David R. Jones. *Assignment America.* New York: Quadrangle/Times Books, 1974. (An anthology of good writing by correspondents for *The New York Times.*)

7 The Writer's Art

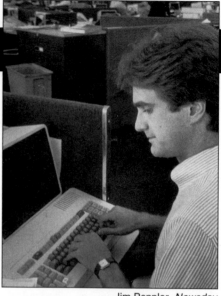

Jim Peppler, *Newsday*

Putting notes into story form.

Preview

Well-written stories have these qualities:

• They show the reader the event or individual through anecdotes, quotations and incidents.
• Quotations and human interest are placed high in the story.
• The language is precise, clear and convincing.
• Sentences are short. Transitions take the reader smoothly from one theme to another.
• The writing style is appropriate to the event.

Good writing depends on reporting that turns up relevant information. The story flow is aided by the use of the narrative structure. Language is simple and direct.

Whether three-paragraph item or feature, the story is carefully put together. The rudiments of the well-crafted story are:

• **The structure:** The lead states the essential elements of the event. The body amplifies and expands the lead.
• **The content:** Facts, derived from direct observation or reliable sources, are accurately presented and used to show and tell the viewer, reader or listener what happened, who was involved, when and where it happened, and the causes and possible consequences of the event—its how and why.

But more is expected of the journalist. The story should be well-written. Readers and viewers are not passive recipients of news. They demand that it be presented in an interesting way, or they will move on to another story or station.

The well-written story is clear, easy to follow, easy to understand. Good writing helps the reader see the event the reporter is trying to describe. George Orwell said, "Good prose is like a window pane."

The window pane, unlike the stained glass window, does not call attention to itself. Good writing calls attention to the people in the story, the event, the information.

Writers Write . . . and Read, Too

The men and women who write for a living—whether journalists, poets, novelists or essayists—work at learning and mastering their trade. They have an "idea of craft," as the writer-teacher Frank Kermode puts it, a drive toward "doing things right, making them accurate and shapely, like a pot or a chair."

Stephen King, the prolific writer of best-selling horror stories, says, "Writing is a matter of exercise . . . if you write for an hour and a half a day for ten years you're gonna turn into a good writer."

Every writer is familiar with the agony of chasing elusive words. The writer knows that words can be brought to life only by strenuous and continued effort. The aim is perfection of expression, the absolute fit of words to the event. Walt Whitman described the writer's goal this way:

> A perfect writer would make words sing, dance, kiss, do the male and female act,
> bear children, weep, bleed, rage, stab, steal, fire cannon, steer ships, sack cities. . . .

Creative workers and craftsmen and craftswomen know that the path to individuality begins with emulation. In teaching students at the Royal Academy, Joshua Reynolds, an 18th-century English painter, advised, "The more extensive your acquaintance is with the works of those who have excelled, the more extensive will be your power of invention, and the more original will be your conceptions." Journalists read widely to master style and technique, to learn the tricks of the writer's trade.

Poet or police reporter, the writer is engaged in a struggle to find words and phrases to match his or her observations. When Hemingway covered the police court for the *Kansas City Star,* he would take his notes home and work over them hour after hour to simplify the testimony of witnesses until he had captured in a few words the essence of the evidence. He would use the language he had heard in court. This practice, as much as the influence of Ezra Pound and Gertrude Stein, may have been responsible for Hemingway's objective prose, what the critic Maxwell Geismar called "his famous flat style: the literal, factual description of the 'way things are.' "

This style, more brother than cousin to journalism, is evident in the ending to *A Farewell to Arms.* Frederic has just pushed the nurses out of the room where Catherine has died so that he can be alone with her:

> But after I had got them out and shut the door and turned off the light it wasn't any good. It was like saying good-bye to a statue. After a while I went out and left the hospital and walked back to the hotel in the rain.

> **Reach the Reader.** "The key questions are: Is this stuff interesting? Does it move, touch, anger, tickle, surprise, sadden or inform? If it does you are in for a treat, a good read."
> *—Thomasine Berg, The Providence Journal*

Doing It Right—in a Hurry

Novelist or journalist, said Hal Boyle, for years one of the AP's top reporters, the writer has the same task: "The recognition of truth and the clear statement of it are the first duties of an able and honest writer."

Unlike the novelist, the journalist cannot spend hours in the search for the right word, a couple of days to devise a beguiling beginning.

The journalist is asked to write—and to write well—now, quickly, before the clock's hands sweep to the inexorable deadline. No other writer is asked to perform with such speed. Yet journalists manage to do the job, creating stories that are, in Kermode's words, "accurate and shapely."

Before we find out how this is done, let's consider a few housekeeping details first.

Preliminaries

It is impossible to write for the public unless you understand what you are writing about. Comprehension precedes clarity. You cannot "be wholly clear about something you don't understand," says John Kenneth Galbraith, the Harvard economist whose books and articles about what is called "the dismal science" of economics are models of clarity.

Next, you have to be in command of writing mechanics, which cover a wide field from being at ease with language to the ability to organize material into a story to spelling. A study of working journalists showed that those considered superior by their editors were the reporters whose writing mechanics were in high gear.

A reminder: Don't write writing. Don't make the purpose of your writing clever prose. Your job is to communicate information. "I never heard a reader praise the quality of writing," says Henry McNulty, for many years the ombudsman for *The Hartford Courant*. "They are only interested in the facts in a story and their accuracy." Write well, the best you can to attract and retain readers, listeners and viewers. But never at the expense of a truthful telling of the story.

And some solace: Don't worry if glittering copy doesn't spin from your keyboard. "I don't know anybody who writes well who writes easily," says Joan Beck, a columnist for the *Chicago Tribune*. After journalism school, she went to work at the *Tribune* and was, she says, "surprised to see people whose bylines I had admired for a long time sitting there, head in hand, trying to write. It was a great revelation to me that writing did not come easily to anybody I know."

And last: Writers who try to write well are always asking themselves whether the words they are using make their stories clear, succinct, direct. When they are dissatisfied with the answer, they revise and rewrite. As Ernest Hemingway told an interviewer who asked him what the problem was that caused him to rewrite the last paragraph of *A Farewell to Arms* 39 times: "Getting the words right."

Current-Day Newswriting

Newswriting nowadays is much different from the writing of a few decades ago. *Lean and tight is right* might be the contemporary newswriter's axiom. Look at how Phoebe Zerwick begins a series on infant mortality for the *Winston-Salem Journal:*

The first baby who died in Forsyth County in 1995 lived only an hour and 16 minutes. He was born premature, with a defect in his spinal cord.

A 2-month-old baby boy died two days later of sudden-infant-death syndrome. Twelve days later, 13 more infants were dead, including a set of triplets, each of

---

Technique. "Sometimes the eye too narrowed on technique misses the point of purpose and content."
—*William Safire.*

"Technique holds a reader from sentence to sentence, but only content will stay in his mind."
—*Joyce Carol Oates.*

whom died within two hours of birth. By the end of March, five more babies were dead. And by the end of the year, the county's infant death toll reached 53.

The deaths of these young children — some so small and weak they barely cried — haunt their parents, whose grief lasts far longer than their children's lives.

"I would have given my life for him and there was nothing I could do," said Wednesday Scott, whose son Stephen died last November an hour after birth. "Here was this little boy living and so rambunctious and I couldn't keep him from dying."

This writer is not *writing*. She is letting the numbers and one heartbroken father tell the story.

Purple Prose   Not so in the old days. Few nouns were unaccompanied by an adjective, and most verbs were propped up by adverbs. Here's a story from the *Philadelphia Bulletin* that brought to an end one of the most intensely covered events of the 1930s, the kidnapping of the 20-month-old son of Charles Lindbergh, the first man to fly solo across the Atlantic Ocean and a national hero:

Trenton, April 4 — Bruno Richard Hauptmann has kept, at long last, his rendezvous with death. At 8:43 o'clock last night, in the death house of the New Jersey State Prison, there shot through his stalwart frame the first of three shattering stabs of man-made lightning.

At 8:47, the incisive voice of Dr. Howard Weisler, the prison physician, sounded through the awful hush that sat upon the close-packed ranks of witnesses:

"This man is dead."

Thus an obscure German carpenter paid his debt to society for one of the most infamous crimes of all time, the kidnapping and murder of Charles A. Lindbergh Jr., and thus was written "curtain" to at least one act of the tragic Lindbergh drama. . . .

Compare that ornate writing with this execution story six decades later:

JARRATT, Va. (AP) — A parolee convicted of killing a convenience store clerk in 1991 was executed by injection Monday night.

Johnile DuBois, 31, was pronounced dead at 9:09 p.m. at the Greensville Correctional Center.

DuBois, who received no visits from relatives on Monday, smiled at prison guards as he entered the death chamber and spoke briefly to a minister before making his final statement.

"I send love to my family and friends and everyone who knows them. That's it," he said. . . .

Terse, to-the-point, S-V-O sentences.

Show, Don't Tell

In our effort to find some guides to help us write well, we might start with Leo Tolstoy who, in describing the strength of his masterwork *War and Peace,* said, "I don't tell; I don't explain. I show; I let my characters talk for me."

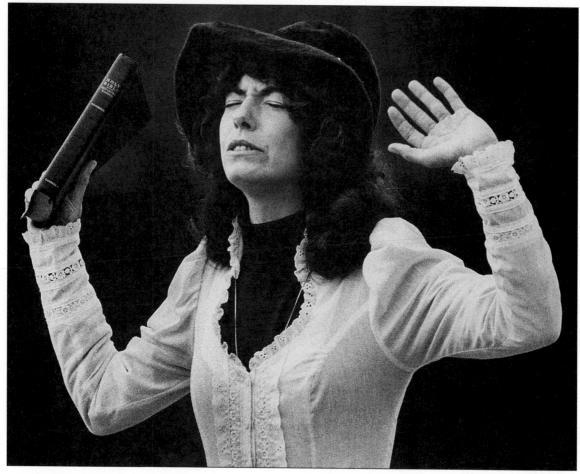

© Greg Lovett

Taking the Gospel to College Students

The careful reporter listens closely to the message of this young evangelist as she proclaims the gospel at the University of Arkansas. The writer quotes her, describes her intensity, watches students' reactions. The reporter also interviews the students to whom she is preaching and talks to the evangelist about her successes and failures.

Consider the science reporter who wanted to describe the size of a small worm. She wrote, "Although they strongly caution against inferring too much about human life spans from worms no bigger than a comma at the end of this clause, they say that evolution. . . ." That's showing.

If one of the writer's most impelling directives is to make the reader see, then the science writer did just that. Show, don't tell. Telling not only makes for dull reading, it makes readers passive. Showing engages readers by making them visualize, draw conclusions, experience insights.

Let Them Talk, Act

"Isn't anybody in this town can beat me. I'm invincible." This is Bella Stumbo of *The Los Angeles Times* quoting a politician. She doesn't have to tell us the man has a gigantic ego.

Good writers let the words and the actions of their subjects do the work. John Ciardi says, "Make it happen; don't talk about its happening."

When the reporter makes it happen, the reader moves into the story. The writer disappears as intermediary between the event and the reader.

Covering the funeral of a child killed by a sniper, a reporter wrote, "The grief-stricken parents wept during the service." Another reporter wrote, "The parents wept quietly. Mrs. Franklin leaned against her husband for support." The first reporter **tells** us the parents are "grief-stricken." The other reporter **shows** us the woman's grief.

In a movie review, Stanley Kauffman of *The New Republic* writes, "We are told later that he (George C. Scott) is a cool man—which, presumably, is why his wife left him—but we are only *told* it; it's characterization by dossier, not by drama."

To show the effects of the disappearance of dairy farms in the northeast, the reporter wrote of the farmers who stick around after selling their farms and can be seen "in the general store buying their morning beer."

Details show us more than generalities do. A story about a former Minnesota beauty queen pleading guilty to shoplifting described her loot as "several items." When the story reached an AP editor, she found out what had been stolen and put the items in the story—a swimsuit, silk scarves and hairpieces.

Teen Priorities   In a three-sentence paragraph, Sam Blackwell of the Eureka, Calif., *Times-Standard* shows us a lot about teen-age romance:

> They had met cruising the loop between Fourth and Fifth Streets in Eureka. She fell in love with Wes' pickup truck, then fell in love with Wes. Wes gave her an engagement ring the day she graduated from high school.

Louis Lyons, a Boston newspaperman and later curator of the Nieman Foundation for journalists at Harvard, never forgot the lesson his night editor taught him. "When I was a cub reporter I had a story to do on the quarterly report of the old Boston Elevated system, whose history then as now was a nearly unbroken record of deficits," Lyons recalled. "This time they were in the black. I knew just enough to know how extraordinary that was.

"I wrote: 'The Boston Elevated had a remarkable record for January—it showed a profit. . . .'

"The old night editor brought my copy back to my typewriter. He knew I was green. In a kindly way, quite uncharacteristic of him, he spelled out the trouble.

32,000 Times Better. Henry James, the writer, advised young writers that "an ounce of example is worth a ton of generalities."

Ten Guidelines for Writing the News

1. Understand the event first. Then write.
2. Write when you know what you want to say.
3. Show, don't tell.
4. Put good quotes and human interest high in the story.
5. Put relevant illustrations or anecdotes up high in the story.
6. Use concrete nouns and colorful action verbs.
7. Avoid adjectival exuberance and resist propping up verbs with adverbs.
8. Avoid judgments and inferences. Let the facts talk.
9. Don't raise questions you cannot answer in your copy.
10. Write simply, succinctly, honestly and quickly.

"He pointed out that the word remarkable 'is not a reporting word. That is an editorial word.'" Then he advised Lyons to write the story so that the reader would say, "That's remarkable."

One way journalists show their readers is through reporting the effects on people of the situation about which they are writing. The Department of Health and Human Services reported that 1.1 million minors run away or are thrown out of their homes every year. Most runaways are physically or sexually abused by a parent. About a third have an alcoholic parent, and many are from foster homes.

Troubled Teens   To give the report life and meaning, Sonia L. Nazario of *The Wall Street Journal* found some troubled teen-agers in California. Her account begins:

HOLLYWOOD — Five teen-agers crouch over a candle in a dark, fetid cavern under a busy roadway. Around them, the dirt floor seems to move as rats look for food. As the teen-agers pass around a half-gallon bottle of Riesling, they talk about their latest sexual scores. This is the place the teens call, simply, the Hole. "This is my home," reads a graffito scrawled on a concrete wall.

Here at the Hole, an ever-changing group of about 30 teen-agers, who have run away from home or been thrown out, have banded together to form a grotesquely modern kind of family. Predominantly white, middle-class and from troubled backgrounds, the "Trolls," as they call themselves, come to the Hole to find empathy and love. They have adopted a street father, a charismatic ex-con named John Soaring Eagle, or "Pops" to his flock. In return for his affection and discipline, the Trolls support Pops — and themselves — by panhandling, prostitution and mugging.

Good Quotes up High

The reporter is alert to the salient remark, the incisive comment, the words of a source that sum up the event or that will help the reader visualize the person who is speaking. Also, a person's words help achieve conviction, the feeling of truth. After all, if these are the words of a participant, the reader reasons, the story must be true. The higher in the story the quote appears, the better, although good quote leads are rare.

Notice the use of the poignant remark of the child in the second paragraph of this story:

> Mary Johnson, 9, lay alongside the bodies of her slain family for nearly two days. She believed she, too, would die of the bullet wounds inflicted by her mother.
>
> But Mary lived, and told ambulance attendants on her way to the hospital yesterday: "Don't blame mother for the shootings."

In an interview with an opponent of the U.S. government's policies in El Salvador, a reporter used this quote high in her story:

> "Why are we on the side of those who are killing the nuns?" he asked.

Reporters have an ear for the telling quote. In a story about the record number of murders in Miami-Dade, Edna Buchanan of *The Miami Herald* quoted a homicide detective as saying, "In Dade County, there are no surprises left."

The astronomer James Jeans provided a startling image of the universe: "Put three grains of sand inside a vast cathedral and the cathedral will be more closely packed with sand than space is with stars."

The actress Farrah Fawcett was quoted in a story, "The reason that the all-American boy prefers beauty to brains is that he can see better than he can think."

Unprintable   Unfortunately, some of the best quotes never make it into print or to broadcasts. But they live on in journalism lore. There's the story about Frank Sinatra and the 1952 Democratic national convention, where, after Sinatra sang the national anthem, the audience erupted. Sam Rayburn, Speaker of the House of Representatives and the convention chairman, walked across the platform toward Sinatra.

Rayburn, a towering figure in politics and in demeanor, reached out to shake Sinatra's hand. As Rayburn put his left arm around Sinatra's shoulder, Sinatra snarled:

"Get your hands off me, you creep."

Adored by his fans, Sinatra was known to journalists as much for his nasty temper as for his generosity to friends. But the nastiness rarely emerged in stories about Sinatra.

Next, to another working rule for newswriters.

Quote Them. "Realistic dialogue involves the reader more completely than any other single device. It also defines character more quickly and effectively than any other single device. (Dickens has a way of fixing character in your mind so that you have the feeling he has described every inch of his appearance—only you go back and discover that he actually took care of his physical description in two or three sentences; the rest he has accomplished with dialogue.)"
—*Tom Wolfe*

Human Interest up High

As with good quotations, we try to place as close to the lead as possible the high-quality example, incident or anecdote that spotlights the theme of the story:

The steady increase in tuition is driving some students away from the colleges of their choice and keeping them in schools close to home.

Ralph Cramer, a high school senior, was admitted to an Ivy League college, but the $22,000-plus tuition was out of his family's reach. . . .

As you see, the example amplifies and humanizes the story theme. When delayed leads are used, the human interest incident begins the story. With direct leads—which often stress the formal aspect of the event—the human-impact illustration or example should be close to the lead.

We are all a little like Alice (of *Alice's Adventures in Wonderland*). " 'What is the use of a book,' thought Alice, 'without pictures or conversations?' " The reporter lets the anecdotes serve as pictures, and the quotations as conversations.

Mark Twain's Principles

Mark Twain had volunteered to read the essays submitted for a writing contest by the young women at the Buffalo Female Academy. He was delighted by what he read, and in his report to the Academy he pointed out the virtues of the two prize essays. He described them as "the least artificial, least labored, clearest, shapeliest and best carried out."

The first-prize essay "relates a very simple little incident in unpretentious language," he said. It has "the very rare merit of *stopping when it is finished.*" (Twain's emphasis.) "It shows a freedom from adjective and superlatives, which is attractive, not to say seductive—and let us remark, in passing, that one can seldom run his pen through an adjective without improving his manuscript.

"We can say further that there is a singular aptness of language noticeable in it—denoting a shrewd facility of selecting just the right word for the service needed, as a general thing. It is a high gift. It is the talent which gives accuracy, grace and vividness in descriptive writing."

Four Principles   Good writing has four characteristics. It is:

• **Accurate:** The language fits the situation. This is what Twain means by "accuracy of wording," "using just the right word."

• **Clear:** Through proper use of form and content, the story is free of vagueness and ambiguity.

• **Convincing:** The story is believable. It sounds true.

• **Appropriate:** The style is natural and unstrained. In Twain's words, "unpretentiousness, simplicity of language . . . naturalness . . . selecting just the right word for the service needed."

The four principles are not islands unto themselves. Causeways connect them. If we write that a congressman "refuted" charges that his proposal will cause unemployment, when he actually "denied" the charges, the language we use is inaccurate and the story is not clear. When we quote people as they use the language—not in the homogenized dialogue that passes for the spoken word in too many news stories—the language is appropriate and our stories are more likely to convince readers they are true.

Before we go on, a reminder and a qualifier.

The reminder: A great deal of work is done before the reporter writes. Good journalistic writing is the result of good reporting and clear thinking. Clever writing cannot conceal a paucity of facts, stale observations or insensitive reactions to people. But bad writing can nullify superior reporting.

The qualifier: In the rest of this chapter—and in other chapters, too—rules, formulas and injunctions are presented. They are offered as guidelines, as ways to get going. They should not be considered inviolate laws. But it is best for the beginner to accept them for the time being, until his or her competence is proved. After this apprenticeship has been served, the experienced journalist can heed Anton Chekhov's comments about writing in his play *The Seagull.* "I'm coming more and more to believe that it isn't old or new forms that matter. What matters is that one should write without thinking about forms at all. Whatever one has to say should come straight from the heart."

Accuracy of Language

The city editor of a medium-size Iowa daily stared at the lead in disbelief. A reporter who had covered a city commission meeting the night before had written that the commission adopted a controversial resolution "with one descending vote." The proper word is *dissenting,* the city editor informed his errant reporter.

Without accuracy of language, the journalist cannot make the story match the event. The obvious way to check words for accuracy is to use the dictionary. But reporters who misuse language often do so without knowing their words are misfits. They could be saved from embarrassment by widening their reading.

Writers struggle to find the words with just the right shades of meaning for the situations they are describing. The handwritten manuscript of *The Great Gatsby* reveals that F. Scott Fitzgerald worked unceasingly to find the accurate word, replacing *looked* with *glanced* in one place, changing *interrupted* to *suggested* in another. Fitzgerald knew Tolstoy's rule: Show, don't tell. He eliminated sections in which he told the reader about his characters and instead let the action and dialogue do the work.

Ernest Hemingway's writing was simple, but it was not simplistic. He shaved language to the bone, but at no sacrifice to meaning. This required hard work. Reaching for a baseball metaphor, Hemingway said of the writer that "he has to go the full nine even if it kills him."

Talk of the Town

A young reporter assigned to the police beat used his enterprise to develop a story about youth gangs for the *Omaha World-Herald.* The editor told Charles Robins that his story had more impact on the community than any other in months. The editor outlined the reasons:

1. It began with a "vivid, graphic description of specific, real-life events, things that happened to real people." He said too many enterprise stories use pseudonyms, "losing at least 50 percent of their effectiveness when they do.

2. "The story had a hard-news peg. A man had just been mugged.

3. "It had confirmation from named sources.

4. "You used direct quotations, but you were selective in what you used. You weren't just a stenographer tapping out everything your sources said in long, repetitive quotations.

5. "You used specific, colorful description. You noted the color of their (the gang members') 'uniforms,' including the color-coded shoelaces, the $300 jogging suits and the cellular telephones.

6. "The story was told economically in 24 inches. There were other angles you probably could have gone after, but doing so might have delayed publication and made the story more difficult to digest."

Ever since the day the story was printed, the editor said, it has been Topic No. 1 "in every age and demographic group in Omaha."

Use Words with Referents

An accurate vocabulary comes from a feel for words, for the way people use language, which sometimes differs from dictionary usage. "The true meaning of a term is to be found by observing what a man does with it, not by what he says about it," says the scientist P.W. Bridgeman.

Journalists use words that correspond to specific objects and identifiable feelings and ideas. When the journalist writes about the state treasurer's annual report, she is describing a specific person who has issued a document that can be examined. But when the reporter takes it upon herself to describe the report as *sketchy* or *optimistic,* she is moving into an area in which there are no physical referents. She may use such words in an interpretative story, but only if she anchors them to specific facts and figures.

Words such as *progress, freedom, patriotism, big business, militant, radical* cause trouble because they float off in space without being anchored to anything specific, concrete or identifiable. Reporters will quote sources who use these words and phrases, but they ask sources to explain just how they are using these vague terms.

Unwary reporters can become accomplices in brainwashing by using vague language. When an oil company distributed a press release announcing

Avoid. *Jargon:* The specialized language of a profession or trade few outside it understand. *Gobbledygook:* Words for the sake of words piled up to obscure the fact the writer doesn't have a clue as to what he or she is saying. *Purple prose:* Inflated language used to impress, as *hydraulic specialist* for *plumber.*

the construction of an "oil farm" outside a Massachusetts town and the reporter dutifully wrote in her lead that the "oil farm will occupy a tract southeast of the city," the reporter was not only using language inaccurately, she was helping the oil firm obscure the truth. The so-called "farm" was to be used for oil storage tanks, which have a grimy image. A farm, with visions of white barns and green pastures, is what the oil company wanted readers to imagine so that potential opposition would be diverted. *Farm* as used by the oil company and the reporter is a euphemism.

Let us leave the topic of word usage with two comments about words from Mark Twain:

> A powerful agent is the right word. Whenever we come upon one of those intensely right words . . . the resulting effect is physical as well as spiritual, and electrically prompt.
>
> The difference between the right word and the almost right word is really a large matter—the difference between lightning and the lightning bug.

Euphemisms

When Congress was discussing *taxes,* it sought to soften the impact of that dread word by substituting the words *revenue enhancement.* In Northern California, where marijuana is a major agricultural product, the polite term for its cultivation is *cash-intensive horticulture.* A company does not demote an employee; it hands him or her a *negative advancement.* When the *Challenger* shuttle exploded, the bodies were placed not in coffins but in *crew transfer containers.*

When a pleasant word or phrase is used in place of one that may be grim, the substitute is called a *euphemism.*

Some journalists may consider themselves compassionate for letting euphemisms slip by. After all, what is the harm in permitting people who work with convicts to describe prisoners as the *consumers of criminal justice services?* What, for that matter, is wrong with *senior citizens* for older people or *sight deprived* for the blind? Surely, these euphemisms hurt no one.

Actually, they do damage us because they turn us away from reality. If the journalist's task can be reduced to a single idea, it is to point to reality. Words should describe the real, not blunt, blur or distort it.

Some years ago, a Chicago police reporter who was covering a rape was reminded by his desk of the newspaper's prohibition of what the publisher considered earthy language. *Rape,* he was told, was taboo. In his second paragraph, he wrote, "The woman ran down the street screaming, 'Help, I've been criminally assaulted! Help, I've been criminally assaulted!' "

Veiling Reality. The State Department said that it would no longer use the word *killing* in its reports on human rights. In its place, the department said, will be "unlawful or arbitrary deprivation of life."

For its program to train dolphins to kill enemy swimmers, the Navy said the purpose was "swimmer nullification."

Said

These misuses of language are dangerous shoals on which many reporters have run aground. If we could mark the reefs that threaten writers, the most dangerous would be where reporters have gone under while fishing for synonyms for the verb *to say.*

The newswriter wrote that the party treasurer "disclosed" that Jones had received donations from foreign businesses, a violation of the law. The word *disclosed,* his editor told the reporter, "suggests that we believe the assertion. Make it *said,* a neutral word."

Let it be said at once, loud and clear, the word *said* cannot be overused for attribution. If tempted to replace it with *affirmed, alleged, asserted, contended, declared, pointed out, shouted, stated* or *whispered,* see the dictionary first. Better still, recall Ring Lardner's line: "Shut up he explained."

Facts First, Words Second

One of the impediments to accuracy stems from the reporter's unceasing desire for language that will perk up the reader. The desire is healthy, but it can lead to the selection of words—as well as facts—that are more colorful and exciting than the event merits. Reporters sometimes are so stimulated by the urge to be creative that their language and their stories diverge from the reality that inspired them. As writers, they believe that an occasional liberty with facts and language should be granted them. In his novel *The Deer Park,* Norman Mailer describes the lure of a well-crafted story for a movie director, Charles Eitel. Mailer indicates the corruption of such temptation: "The professional in Eitel lusted for the new story . . . it was so beautifully false. Professional blood thrived on what was excellently dishonest."

To some writers, words are ends in themselves. But the objective is to communicate information accurately, not to display technical brilliance with the zoom lens or tape splicer, not to play with words. Technique has its place; its proper role is to aid in accurate communication. As Pauline Kael, the movie critic, put it, "Technique is hardly worth talking about unless it's used for something worth doing."

Good writing follows good reporting. William Burroughs, the novelist, said of the writer, "Generally speaking, if he can't see it, hear it, feel it and smell it, he can't write it."

Spelling

A few words about the bane of the copy editor, the misspelled word. A word incorrectly spelled is a gross inaccuracy. It is like a flaw in a crystal bowl. No matter how handsome the bowl, the eye and mind drift from the sweeping curves to the mistake. A spelling error screams for attention, almost as loudly as an obscenity in print.

Maybe not. These days we see *alright* for all right, *its* for it's, *cemetary* for cemetery. Even *The New York Times,* surely one of the most scrupulously edited newspapers, has its share of misspellings. A story about nuns who support the ordination of women stated, "They want nuns to have a visible role at the *alter.*"

Some reporters put their trust in computer programs that check spelling. But such programs will not flag correctly spelled words that are misused, such as *alter* for altar. The program was of no use to *enRoute,* the flight magazine for Air Canada in its Trivial Pursuit Quiz:

> 11. What city was the *sight* of the last
> Moorish kingdom in Spain?

The computer won't catch misspelled plurals such as the one a reporter used for a newspaper we shall not name: "He said that although the testes were hard, he managed to pass them."

Intelligent reporters—good spellers or bad spellers—use the dictionary. Many editors associate intelligence with spelling ability because they consider the persistent poor speller to be stupid for not consulting the dictionary—whatever his or her native intelligence.

The saying has it that doctors bury their mistakes and architects cover them with ivy. Journalists have no such luck. Their blunders are forever committed to public view:

> Letters must be signed and should include address and phone number. The Monitor reserves the right to edit letters for spelling, grammer and punctuation, as well as possibly libelous material.
> *The Monitor*

Question is, how to tell roommates your gay
—Forum (Fargo, N.D.)

Blind girl servives first round of bee
—Gazette (Indiana, Pa.)

Clarity

The words and phrases the journalist selects must be put into a setting, into sentences and paragraphs that make sense to readers. "If you're going to be a newspaper writer you've got to put the hay down where the mules can reach it," said Ralph McGill of the *Atlanta Constitution.* Although his reporting ranged over subjects as complex as race relations and foreign affairs, McGill wrote for ordinary people. His journalism was never vague. A reader of the King James version of the Bible, he learned early the strength, vigor and clarity of the precise word in the simple declarative sentence.

So There. When Harvard awarded Andrew Jackson an honorary degree, John Quincy Adams boycotted the ceremonies, describing Jackson, known as the people's president, as "a barbarian who could not write a sentence of grammar." Jackson replied, "It is a damn poor mind indeed which can't think of at least two ways to spell any word."

Internet Spelling. Patricia T. O'Conner, author of a grammar book *Woe Is I,* trolled Internet newsgroups to check on spelling and grammar. She landed a boatload. "Leaving aside the misuse of *its,* the misspelling of *grammar* seemed to be the most common mistake of all," she says.

"A word fitly spoken is like apples of gold in pictures of silver," McGill said of the journalist's craft, quoting from Proverbs in the Old Testament. We know several ways to make these pictures—these sentences and paragraphs—clear to our readers.

Grammar

First, there are the essentials of grammar and punctuation. In our grandparents' day, students stood at the blackboard and diagrammed sentences. They broke sentences down into nouns, verbs, pronouns, adjectives, adverbs, prepositions, conjunctions and interjections. From there, they went into phrases—verbal, prepositional, participial, gerund and infinitive. Then they examined clauses—main and subordinate. This is how they learned sentence construction. In most schools today, the only grammar students learn is taught in foreign language classes. For a journalist, this is inadequate training.

One way the beginning journalist can cope with this inadequacy is to invest in a handbook of grammar. It will not only solve grammatical problems quickly, but also help expand the student's writing range.

Punctuation

Punctuation is the writer's substitute for the storyteller's pauses, stops and changes in voice level. The proper use of punctuation is essential to clarity. Misuse can change emphasis or meaning:

She could not convince him of her innocence, however she tried.

She could not convince him of her innocence; however, she tried.

Punctuation Pains. It is said of the novelist Gustave Flaubert that he spent an entire morning laboring over where to place a comma, then took the afternoon to fret about whether to remove it.

James Thurber, the great *New Yorker* writer, said of his editor Harold Ross, "He used to fuss for an hour over a comma. He'd call me in for lengthy discussions about the Thurber colon."

We know that readers pause at the ends of sentences and paragraphs. These short intervals in the flow of the story help readers absorb what they have read. Broadcast copy needs even shorter sentences, because the listener cannot reread unclear material. Even Gertrude Stein, the author of nonstop prose ("Rose is a rose is a rose is a rose"), came to recognize the value of the period. In *Lectures in America,* (Boston: Beacon Press, 1957), p. 217, Stein wrote:

> When I first began writing, I felt that writing should go on, I still do feel that it should go on but when I first began writing I was completely possessed by the necessity that writing should go on and if writing should go on what had colons and semi-colons to do with it, what had commas to do with it, what had periods to do with it. . . .
>
> What had periods to do with it. Inevitably no matter how completely I had to have writing go on physically one had to again and again stop some time then periods had to exist. Besides I had always liked the look of periods and I liked what they did. Stopping sometimes did not really keep one from going on, it was nothing that interfered, it was only something that happened, and as it happened as a perfectly natural happening, I did believe in periods and I used them. I never really stopped using them.

Sentence Length

Spurred by an anxiety to cram facts into sentences, some inexperienced reporters write blockbusters that send the reader down line after line in increasing confusion. When you have a sentence running three lines or more, think of the self-editing of Isaac Babel, a Russian writer whose short stories are highly polished gems:

> I go over each sentence, time and again. I start by cutting all the words it can do without. You have to keep your eye on the job because words are very sly. The rubbishy ones go into hiding and you have to dig them out—repetitions, synonyms, things that simply don't mean anything.
>
> Before I take out the rubbish, I break up the text into shorter sentences. The more full stops the better. I'd like to have that passed as a law. Not more than one idea and one image to a sentence.
>
> A paragraph is a wonderful thing. It lets you quietly change the rhythm, and it can be like a flash of lightning that shows the landscape from a different perspective. There are writers, even good ones, who scatter paragraphs and punctuation marks all over the place.

The maxim that each sentence should, if possible, carry only one idea has been assumed to be an injunction limited to journalism. Not so, as we see from Babel's comment. Good journalistic writing is based upon the principles of good writing. Journalism is a part of the world of letters.

Guide   The press associations have concluded after a number of studies that one of the keys to readable stories is the short sentence. Here is a readability table:

Average Sentence Length	Readability
8 words or less	Very easy to read
11 words	Easy to read
14 words	Fairly easy to read
17 words	Standard
21 words	Fairly difficult to read
25 words	Difficult to read
29 words or more	Very difficult to read

This table refers to average sentence length. One sentence after another under 17 words would make readers and listeners feel as though they were being peppered with bird shot. The key to good writing is variety, rhythm, balance. Short and long sentences are balanced. A long sentence that is well-written can be as understandable as an eight-word sentence, if it is broken, usually by punctuation, into short clauses and phrases.

Transitions

Some reporters have trouble writing short sentences because they cannot handle transitions, the links between sentences and paragraphs. Because these reporters have no mastery of the device that enables a writer to move smoothly from sentence to sentence, their tendency is to think in large clots of words. The journalist with control of transitions thinks in smaller sentence clusters.

There are four major types of transitions:

1. **Pronouns:** Use pronouns to refer to nouns in previous sentences and paragraphs:

> *Dr. Braun* began teaching history in 1977. *He* took *his* Ph.D. that year. *His* dissertation subject was the French Impressionists.

2. **Key words and ideas:** Repeat words and ideas in preceding sentences and paragraphs:

> He has been accused of being an *academic purist. Those words* make him shudder.
> "*Academic purist* is made to sound like an epithet," he said.

3. **Transitional expressions:** Use connecting words that link sentences. A large array of expressions function as connectors. Here are most of the major categories of conjunctions and some of the words in each category that can be used as transitions:

> **Additives:** again, also, and, finally, furthermore, in addition, next, thus, so, moveover, as well.
> **Contrasts:** but, however, nevertheless, instead, on the other hand, otherwise, yet, nonetheless, farther.
> **Comparisons:** likewise, similarly.
> **Place:** adjacent to, beyond, here, near, opposite.

A Pulitzer Prize Story: Workings of the Brain

Here is the beginning of the first story in a series by Jon Franklin that won a Pulitzer Prize for explanatory journalism for *The Evening Sun.* The word count in these 12 sentences runs 16, 24, 34, 9, 13, 18, 14, 21, 19, 5, 13, 21. The average sentence length is 17 words, standard reading fare. Notice the way Franklin varies the length of his sentences to set up a rhythm—long, short. The longest sentence in the sample—the third, 34 words—is followed by a short sentence—9 words.

Since the days of Sigmund Freud the practice of psychiatry has been more art than science. Surrounded by an aura of witchcraft, proceeding on impression and hunch, often ineffective, it was the bumbling and sometimes humorous stepchild of modern science.

But for a decade and more, research psychiatrists have been working quietly in laboratories, dissecting the brains of mice and men and teasing out the chemical formulas that unlock the secrets of the mind.

Now, in the 1980s, their work is paying off.

They are rapidly identifying the interlocking molecules that produce human thought and emotion. They have devised new scanners that trace the flickering web of personality as it dances through the brain. Armed with those scanners, they are mapping out the terrain of the human psyche.

As a result, psychiatry today stands on the threshold of becoming an exact science, as precise and quantifiable as molecular genetics. Ahead lies an era of psychic engineering, and the development of specialized drugs and therapies to heal sick minds.

But that's only the beginning: The potential of brain chemistry extends far beyond the confines of classic psychiatry.

Many molecular psychiatrists, for instance, believe they may soon have the ability to untangle the ancient enigma of violence and criminality.

Time: afterward, in the meantime, later, meanwhile, soon.

He tried twice to obtain permission to see the paintings in the private museum. *Finally,* he gave up.

Dr. Braun's *next* project centered on the music of Berlioz. *But* his luck remained bad. An attempt to locate a missing manuscript proved a *similar* failure.

In the meantime, he continued his study of Spanish so that he would be able to do research in Spain.

4. **Parallel structure.** Sentences and paragraphs are linked by repeating the sentence pattern:

No one dared speak in his classes. *No one* ventured to address him in any but the most formal manner. *No one,* for that matter, had the courage to ask questions in class. His lectures were nonstop monologues.

Transitions are used after the reporter has planned his or her piece by blocking out the major sections. Transitions link these blocks as well as the smaller units, the sentences. Transitions are the mortar that holds the story together so that the story is a single unit.

Logical Order

A news story should move smoothly from fact to fact. When natural sequence is disrupted, the story loses clarity. Here are two paragraphs from a story in an Oklahoma daily newspaper:

> "There is nothing new in the allegations," Bartlett said. "We've heard them all before."
>
> "When we first heard them we thought there was nothing to it, but then we had a second look," Tillman said.

Although the first paragraph is closed by quotation marks, which means that the speaker (Bartlett) is finished, most readers jump ahead to the next quote and presume that Bartlett is still talking. They are jolted when they find that Tillman is speaking. The solution is simple: When you introduce a new speaker, begin the sentence or paragraph with his or her name. Also, jumps in time and place must be handled carefully to avoid confusion:

NEW YORK (April 13) — A criminal court judge who last month ruled that a waiter had seduced but not raped a college student sent the man to jail for a year **yesterday** on a charge of escaping from the police after his arrest.

On March 19, Justice Albert S. Hess acquitted Phillip Blau of raping a 20-year-old Pembroke College student. The judge said a man could use guile, scheme, and be deceitful, but so long as he did not use violence, rape did not occur.

At that time, women's groups protested the decision.

"Despite the protests of outraged feminists who demand your head, or other and possibly more appropriate parts of your anatomy," the judge told Blau **yesterday,** "I shall punish you only for crimes of which you have been found guilty."

The changes in time are clearly indicated at the start of the second and third paragraphs. From "yesterday" in the lead, the reader is taken to "March 19" in the second paragraph and is kept there in the third paragraph by the transition "At that time" beginning the paragraph. When the quote begins the fourth paragraph, the reader is still back in March with the women. Midway through the paragraph the reader suddenly realizes the judge is speaking and that he spoke yesterday. The jolts in time and place could have been avoided with a transition at the beginning of the fourth paragraph:

> In sentencing Blau **yesterday,** Justice Hess commented on the protests. He said: . . .

This may seem to be nitpicking. It is not. The journalist knows that every sentence, every word, even every punctuation mark must be carefully selected. Readers read from word to word, and are maneuvered, teased, pushed, sped and slowed through the story by the way it is written. Major disturbances of logic and order in the story confuse readers, just as a quick jump cut on television can destroy the continuity of the event for the viewer.

Chronological Order   Logical order is based upon the organizing concept that the reporter selects. The most frequently used organizing principle is chronology, a narrative device that is particularly useful on longer pieces.

The chronological approach has two forms. The writer can use the storytelling approach by beginning sometime before the climax:

Two college sophomores began the day yesterday in a hurry.

Judy Abrams had studied late the night before and had slept late. She gulped her breakfast of coffee and jumped into her car, five minutes before her 9 a.m. class.

Franklin Starrett did not have time for breakfast before he, too, sped off in his car for the campus. He had an appointment with his English instructor at 9 a.m.

Within minutes of their departures, the cars they were driving collided on Stanford Avenue south of the campus. . . .

Or the writer can put a direct news lead on the story and then, a few paragraphs down in the story, begin the chronological account:

Two Mallory College students were critically injured when the cars they were driving collided head-on yesterday morning on Stanford Avenue south of the campus.

Community Hospital officials said the students suffered multiple fractures and internal injuries. They called on students to volunteer blood for transfusions.

The students began the day in a hurry. . . .

Movement

Stories must move, and the nature of the event determines the pace at which the story progresses. A story about a tornado or hurricane striking a community will move at the speed of the wind, but the piece about the burial service for the victims will follow the deliberate cadence of the prayers of the minister as he speaks of those called too soon to their maker.

Fast or slow, the story has to move along. It cannot stop to explore secondary roads. Stan Grossfeld, associate editor of *The Boston Globe,* profiled the filmmaker Spike Lee as he taught a class at Harvard. In one of the class sessions, Lee describes how he edited the opening scene of *Jungle Fever:*

In the opening scene, which was shot but later cut, he descends in front of the Brooklyn Bridge on a crane and announces, "All you people who think I'm anti-Semitic can kiss my black ass two times."

Lee said the scene was extraneous: "When you write a script, you think every-thing's gonna be great, but once the film is shot and put together, sometimes a lot of the stuff is redundant. We had a whole subplot between me and my wife, eight scenes that had to go, 'cause it wasn't moving the plot forward. It didn't matter that I was in the scene, the [expletive] had to go."

AP Photo by Jerome Delay

Mourners

Schoolchildren weep outside St. Martin Bascilica in Liege, Belgium, for two slain classmates who were kidnapped by a child rapist. The story of the funeral had longer-than-average sentences, muted verbs.

Conviction

Some people find the news they read, hear and see as unconvincing as some of the advertising that accompanies it.

"What's the real story?" reporters are asked, as though they were prevented from revealing the truth by powerful advertisers or friends of the publisher or station manager. These pressures rarely influence reporters. More often, the pressures of time and the inaccessibility of documents and sources impede truth telling, and just as often, reporting and writing failures get in the way of the real story. Here are the components of a story that is accurate, complete and credible:

Reporting:

1. Relevant factual material from personal observation and physical sources. Details, specifics.

2. Authoritative and knowledgeable human sources for additional information.

3. Significant and complete background information.

Writing:

1. Simple language.

2. Illustrations, examples and quotes that document the lead.

3. Human interest.

4. Appropriate style.

Let's examine these story necessities.

Relevant Material

The journalist uses details just as any writer does—to build a picture that shows us what is going on and that convinces us of the truth of the account. The journalist's eye catches the tears of the child whose puppy takes third place instead of first at the dog show. Such specific observations convince the reader that the reporter's account can be trusted.

The journalist is conscious of the backdrop, the scene. It may be that the news conference took place in the mayor's office, the rescue made in a calm sea at dusk. Then the particulars: The mayor spoke from his desk, with seven microphones from radio and television stations in front of him and a dozen journalists in attendance; the Coast Guard boat was manned by six seamen and an officer.

A journalism teacher, a veteran of many years on newspapers, still shudders at his recollection of the night he was sent out to the suburbs by a San Francisco newspaper. Fumes from an unvented heater had poured through a house, killing the entire family. Only the dog survived. The reporter gathered the relevant information—names and ages of the victims, occupation of the father, approximate time of death, schools the children attended, how long they had lived in the house, whether the vent was legal and even the name of the dog (taken from its collar). Racing to a pay phone to make the final edition, he was dictating the story when he was stunned by the rewriteman's question: "What kind of house was it? Wood? Stucco? Brick?" The reporter had no idea, and there was no time to dash back to the house to find out.

Authoritative Sources

Here are the first four paragraphs of a speech story:

This country must return to law and order if America's free institutions are to survive, Lexington businessmen were told Monday night.

And, it is the responsibility of businessmen on the local level to educate Americans, particularly the youth, in the importance of these free institutions and what they mean.

Speaking at a general membership meeting of the Greater Lexington Area Chamber of Commerce, Dr. Kenneth McFarland, author, educator and businessman, said that the current situation must be turned around.

"We can no more co-exist with this than we can co-exist with a cancer," he said. "We've got to take the handcuffs off the police and put them back on the criminal where they belong."

These are serious statements, and we wonder who is making them. We are given the source's background in the third paragraph. But the identifying material raises more questions than it answers: Author of what? Educator where? What kind of business? Does he own or manage the business?

Because the story is so vague about the qualifications of the source, readers will be reluctant to accept his analysis. He may be qualified, but the story does not give his qualifications.

Readers and listeners find some news unconvincing because the sources that journalists use are officials or so-called experts who have not experienced the situations they are describing. A local story about unemployment that quotes only officials and data is inadequate. Unemployment is more than figures released by an official sitting at a desk. It is men and women standing idle on street corners or waiting anxiously in front offices day after day for job interviews.

It is, of course, easier for a reporter to call an official for material than it is to seek out people affected by events. The result is education stories written without interviewing students, public health stories that lack comments from those who use clinics and emergency rooms.

Complete Background

In an AP story about the Army's pleasure over an unusually heavy crop of volunteers, the "story cited every factor except the main one: The economy was down, unemployment up, and enlistments always rise under those circumstances," said Jack Cappon, AP's general news editor.

An event that is not placed in context lacks meaning. Context can provide the how and why of the event. As Cappon put it, "In news writing, nothing is more basic than making sure that any event, speech, situation or statistic is reported in sufficient context to fix the meaning accurately."

Simple Language

One of the biggest best sellers in this country's history was a political treatise, *Common Sense,* by Thomas Paine. Within three months of its publication in 1776, 120,000 copies were sold in the Colonies, whose population was about 2.5 million. Today, a book selling as well would reach 10 million readers in this country. Paine used the language of the people. He began his pamphlet, "In the following pages I offer nothing more than the simple facts, plain arguments, and common sense."

The good reporter is firmly rooted in the language of ordinary people, which, because it is comprehensible, has the ring of conviction.

Look at the power of this section of a speech given by Sojourner Truth, an abolitionist and an advocate of equality for women. This is from her talk on women's rights, given in 1867:

> I am above 80 years old; it is about time for me to be going. I have been 40 years a slave and 40 years free, and would be here 40 years more to have equal rights for all. I suppose I am kept here because something remains for me to do; I suppose I am yet to help to break the chain. I have done a great deal of work; as much as a man, but did not get so much pay. I used to work in the field and bind grain, keeping up with the cradler; but men doing no more, got twice as much pay. . . . We do as much, we eat as much, we want as much. I suppose I am about the only colored woman that goes about to speak for the rights of the colored women. I want to keep the thing stirring, now that the ice is cracked. . . . I am glad to see that men are getting their rights, but I want women to get theirs, and while the water is stirring I will step into the pool.

Quotations

Wallace Stevens, the insurance company executive who wrote poetry that influenced a generation of poets, commented with some incredulity on events that were swirling around him: "In the presence of extraordinary actuality, consciousness takes the place of imagination." Fact has supplanted fiction.

Why, then, is so much journalism dull and unconvincing? Possibly because writers do not use in their stories what they see and hear. They paraphrase good quotes. They explain instead of letting the example show the reader.

Here are two paragraphs from a book by Studs Terkel, *Working: People Talk About What They Do All Day and What They Think of While They Do It.* Terkel, a radio reporter based in Chicago, interviewed a 14-year-old newsboy, Terry Pickens:

> I don't see where being a newsboy and learning that people are pretty mean or that people don't have enough money to buy things with is gonna make you a better person or anything. If anything, it's gonna make a worse person out of you, 'cause you're not gonna like people that don't pay you. And you're not gonna like people who act like they're doing you a big favor paying you. Yeah, it sort of molds your character, but I don't think for the better. If anybody told me being a newsboy builds character, I'd know he was a liar.
> I don't see where people get all this bull about the kid who's gonna be president and being a newsboy made a president out of him. It taught him how to

handle his money and this bull. You know what it did? It taught him how to hate the people on his route. And the printers. And dogs. . . .

No paraphrase or summary would have the impact of Terry Pickens' own words. For that matter, few psychologists with their understanding of the problems of adolescence can express so succinctly and convincingly—and with such emotion—the realities of growing up. Journalists can.

When the Virginia State Bar Association voted to admit its first black member despite a determined effort by some senior members to block the move, a news story quoted a Richmond lawyer as praising the applicant as a "commendable person with a high standing as a lawyer." Then the story quoted him as adding, "But he is a Negro and therefore I am opposed to accepting him as a member of this association. . . . I have a good many Negro friends, but I don't invite any of them to my home or club to socialize with me."

In three sentences, the reporter crystallized an aspect of racism by letting one of the participants speak.

Distant Judges   Sara Grimes covered juvenile court in Philadelphia. The judges were generations away from the reality of street life. Here are sections of a story Grimes wrote to show the distance between the court and the young offenders. A judge is speaking to two boys in court:

"You should stand still and be respectful when approached by a police officer. Then the officers will respect you. . . .

"I imagine they roughed you up a little bit, huh? I'd have given you a couple of good ones, too, before I took you in.

"In the old days, we used to have Irish policemen and we'd get it over the legs and then we'd get it again at home when the police took us to our fathers.

"We didn't call it police brutality then, and I'm concerned about the disrespect shown here for the policemen. . . .

"The next time you see a policeman, think positively. You can even say, 'Officer, what can I do for you?' The police are paid to protect us. When I see them I feel safe.

"You work, you pay taxes, the police are there to protect you."

Slaughter's Witness   Let sources talk and you often will find a vivid image, a colorful phrase, a passionate vehemence, a deep sadness. After a riot at the New Mexico State Penitentiary during which 33 prisoners were beaten, burned and hacked to death by fellow inmates, a reporter asked what it had been like inside as prisoners wielded blowtorches, hammers and hacksaws. An inmate replied:

> Man, what can I tell you? It was like
> the devil had his own butcher shop and
> you could get any cut you wanted.

In her story in *The Washington Post* about depression among youngsters, Laura Sessions Stepp balances the statements of authorities with the comments of adolescents like Darrell.

"Right over there," she quotes Darrell as he points across the street, "some boy got shot. I was at the skate rink across the street when it happened. You

Mark Henle,
The Phoenix Gazette

'Magical Door'

"With envy, I listen to my grandchildren and greatgrandchildren speak the beautiful language. Speaking English is like a magical door to anywhere for them." —Irene Begody, 77, Navajo Reservation.

never know when it's going to be pointing your way. You shouldn't have to worry about getting shot when you're a kid."

Caution: Important as quotations are, it is improper to put into direct quotation what has been heard second- or thirdhand. This device, used by "imaginative" reporters influenced by the New Journalism, is unethical. Reconstructed quotes are best left to the novelists.

Human Interest

When a television reporter returned with a feature about a local store that was selling books, posters, pictures and other material based on television's "Star Trek," his editor praised his enterprise. But the tape concentrated on the material sold. There was little about the customers, the "Star Trek" fans.

"We missed," the editor said. "We should have followed a customer around and used him as the center of the story."

Frederick C. Othman, a veteran reporter for UPI, advised reporters to put as many personal references as possible into each sentence, "he, she, King George, uncle, boy, girl or any such word describing a human being. The more such words, the more interesting the story."

Here is some more advice from Othman: "If a gent wears a dark-brown coat, say it's chocolate-colored. Not only is that descriptive, but it gets food into the story. Any word connoting food adds interest value.

"Tell about the taste of things and, especially, smells. Both good and bad. Take the man smoking a Turkish cigarette; it smells like burnt chicken feathers. Say so."

Sometimes reporters fail to personalize events that easily lend themselves to human interest. When a puppy fell into the shaft of an abandoned well in Carlsbad, N.M., the rescue operation became a front-page story in many newspapers. One press service story that used the name of the puppy, Wimpy, was widely preferred to the competition's story that lacked the pup's name.

Dull

Interesting

Compare these versions of another story:

I

All doctors hope their patients never have occasion to use the Poison Control Center recently established in the emergency room of the Community General Hospital. However, it should be reassuring to citizens, particularly parents, to know the center exists for use in an emergency.

Springfield is one of only eight cities in the state which have official "recognized" centers to handle poisoning cases. The other seven cities are . . .

II

A frantic mother called her physician and cried that her two-year-old had been at the oven cleaner. The child's lips were smudged with the liquid.

The label said poison. What should she do?

Her call set in motion a series of checks and other calls. In a short time her physician knew precisely what chemicals were in the cleaner, which were poisonous, and what should be done.

The child was treated and beyond a few small burns on the lips and tongue the toddler is doing well.

This happened the other day, and it was the first case for the Freeport Poison Information Center in the Community General Hospital.

The journalist who wrote the second piece did a better job of writing because his reporting was superior. Also, he contributed a greater public service because the picture he painted of a mother and child is etched in the minds of parents. The second story is also more appropriate to the event—it *shows* what the Center does.

The style of the second piece is consistent with the event. The average sentence length of the first five sentences, which describe the poisoning incident, is around 11 words. The next three average 21 words because the reporter was seeking to give an air of calm after the frenzy of the incident. This brings us to the fourth and last of our guidelines for good journalistic writing.

Appropriate Style

The story began this way:

It was in midtown Manhattan, one of those new high-rises where the lobby rug is so thick you trip over it, and the walls are so thin you can hear the plumbing rushing. The office was on the 21st floor, at the end of a long corridor. I knocked on a door. The man who opened it looked like a private investigator. That was O.K. by me. I was there to write about private investigators.

"Joe Mullen," the man said. He stuck out a paw and I pumped it. He looked to be in his early 40s, medium height, silver hair. His eyes went with the hair, only darker. . . .

No, this isn't the beginning of one of Dashiell Hammett's hard-boiled detective novels. It's the way Carey Winfrey began his story about a real private investigator for *The New York Times*.

Every event has its own tone, texture and pace that writers try to reflect in their stories. The way a story is written is known as its *style*. An understanding of style might start with Cicero, the Roman statesman and orator: "Whatever his theme he will speak it as becomes it; neither meagerly where it is copious, nor meanly where it is ample, not in this way where it demands that; but keeping his speech level with the actual subject and adequate to it."

This congruity between theme and speech is what the writer means by fitting the story to the event. Cardinal John Henry Newman in his book *The Idea of a University* wrote, "Matter and expression are parts of one; style is thinking out into language."

Every creative person tries to match expression with content. Spike Lee says he filmed *Malcolm X* in three different styles. Each represented a distinct period in Malcolm's life.

In the following story of a murder, the short sentences reflect the starkness of the event:

Fight for Hat Cited as Motive in Boy's Slaying

Sixteen-year-old Kenneth Richardson was killed Thursday over a floppy brown hat, police said.

"It was just a plain old hat," Metro Homicide Detective Hugo Gomez said.

Richardson was wearing it. Someone tried to take it. Richardson refused.

Others entered the fray. The youth ran. They chased him.

"It was a running and shooting type thing. They were shooting directly at him," Gomez said.

Richardson still had the hat when taken to International Hospital, where he died in surgery. Dade's 554th homicide this year.

He was shot in the parking lot of the Miami Gardens Shopping Plaza at 12:15 a.m., soon after the nearby Gardens Shopping Skating Center closed for the night, police said.

No arrests have been made.

"They were all Carol City kids," Gomez said. "There was talk of several guns."

About 25 youths were in the area at the time, police say. "But there was nothing but the dust settling when we got there," Gomez said.

—*The Miami Herald*

Making Words Fit the Event

Because journalists are obliged to tell their stories briefly, they must choose words that count, words that quickly and efficiently paint pictures. The story is most effective when the journalist selects words in which the denotative and connotative meanings, the explicit and implicit meanings, mesh.

When New York City was close to bankruptcy, the city appealed for federal aid. President Ford brusquely said no, that the city's profligacy and incompetence had caused its fiscal misery and that it had to put its house in order itself. Pondering the story on the president's refusal, William Brink, the managing editor of the *Daily News,* cast about for the five or six words he could fit into the *News'* page 1 headline for the story. He tried:

FORD REFUSES
AID TO CITY

Colorful. Columnists are allowed more leeway than newswriters, but sometimes they are checked, even when their reputations are based on straight talk. Molly Ivins, whose column is written from Texas, wrote of a local politician that "if his IQ slips any lower, we'll have to water him twice a day." But when she wrote of "a fella . . . havin' a beergut that belongs in the Smithsonian," her editors made it read, "a man with a protuberant abdomen."

The headline was dull, and the top line was half a unit too long. He tried again:

FORD SAYS NO
TO CITY AID

This fit, but it was as dull as the first. Brink recalls that in the back of his mind was the idea that "Ford hadn't just declined to help us. He had, in effect, consigned us to the scrap heap." He then wrote two words on a piece of copy paper. After a few moments, he put three other words above them.

The headline in the margin here was instantly famous. Television news stations displayed it that night, and *Time* and *Newsweek* ran it in their summaries of the city's plight. It not only presented the information succinctly (denotative), it also suggested the president's disdain for New York (connotative) in language New Yorkers understand. The headline was appropriate to the subject.

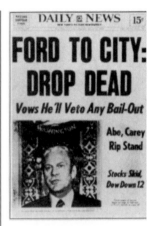

Vocabulary Helps   The key to stylistic excellence is a wide vocabulary and a sensitivity to language that guides word choice. For instance, when the treasurer of a large utility is convicted of stealing $25,000 in company funds, a reporter can write:

- The *employee* was xxx.
- The *official* was xxx.
- The *executive* was xxx.

Each noun has a different connotation. *Employee* would be appropriate for a lower-ranking worker. Although he is an *official* of the company, the word usually is used in connection with public officials. *Executive* seems most appropriate.

Let us look at some verbs:

- He *pilfered* $25,000 xxx.
- He *took* $25,000 xxx.
- He *appropriated* $25,000 for his own use.
- He *embezzled* $25,000 xxx.
- He *stole* $25,000 xxx.

Pilfered seems to trivialize the event. *Took* is prosaic: We *take* a rest, *take* cream in our coffee. *Appropriated* suggests an official action: Congress *appropriates* funds. *Embezzled* and *stole* are strong words and probably the best to use.

Good writing is anchored in control, but sometimes the words take off on their own:

Thoughts flew like spaghetti in his brain.
"Marvin," she hissed.
The muscles on his arms rose slowly, like a loaf of bread taking shape.

The Stylist

The stylist is prized in every newsroom, just as an individual style is valued in every field. Yet reporters often are unimaginative in their selection of facts, and their writing is uninspired. A vapid writing style begets stereotyped observations and vice versa. Compare these two stories about Memorial Day. Which one is more appropriate to the event?

Topeka Reminded of Debts to Dead

An Army general officer and a Navy lieutenant commander reminded Topekans of their debt and responsibility to America's war dead in two Memorial Day services Tuesday morning.

Brig. Gen. John A. Berry, commanding general of Fort Riley, spoke to representatives of 18 veterans organizations at ceremonies at Mount Hope Cemetery.

Earlier, Lt. Cmdr. John G. Tilghman, U.S. Navy Reserve, talked briefly at services on the Topeka Avenue Bridge.

"It is good for us to gather this morning to think of — and thank — those men and women who gave their lives in wars past that you and I may have the full benefits and privileges and responsibilities of our American heritage," said Cmdr. Tilghman.

"Many men in our wars did not always understand all the causes behind the war in which they fought, but they were sure they wanted those of us at home to continue to enjoy the birthright and heritage which is ours, and gave their lives that we might do so.

"You and I must realize our responsibilities in making sure our children and those to come in future generations will be sure of the same promise.

"Today, thousands are fleeing from those who would take away their birthright and their heritage. You and I may someday join their flight unless we get off the fence and take a stand for that which is right — morally right and right patriotically."

Tilghman told his audience protection of its heritage may not always be in combat dress and on a battlefield.

—The State Journal

Fresno Rites Honor Fallen War Heroes

Walk with me early this Memorial Day through the Liberty Cemetery before the ceremonies begin and a thousand feet scatter the dust over these quiet gravestones.

Here are the dead of many of our nation's wars.

A Flag flutters beside each grave and flowers grace them all. No one is forgotten.

Some died in uniform. Others, like Sergeant William J. Dallas of the 2nd Tennessee Infantry in the Spanish-American War, went to war and returned to live a long life — 80 years long.

Many stones stand upright, their marble veined with the passage of time. What stories lie behind some of these stones? The passerby cannot tell. The inscriptions simply say:

Michael O'Connor, US Navy, Spanish-American War. Or, in the Civil War section: Isaac N. Ulsh, Company B, 13th Kansas infantry.

Other markers do tell their stories:

Jack T. Martin, Jr., 1922–1942, USS Langley, Lost At Sea.

James S. Waggoner, CEM, USN, USS Kete, 1917–1945, Lost At Sea.

Sergeant Keith A. Matthew, 877th Bomber Squadron, USAAF, 1918–1945, Lost At Sea.

Two Petersons

Side by side are these two:

T. Sergeant Maurice Peterson, 9th Air Corps, 330th Bomber Group, 1917–1944, Ploesti, Roumania.

Sergeant Sterling Peterson, Airborne Infantry, Company B, 1919–1944, Normandy, France. . . .

The sun rises higher and friends and relatives of the dead come bearing flowers.

Families come and decorate graves with snapdragons, roses, stocks, hydrangea, marigolds and others. While the adults place the flowers, the children roll in the grass and shout to one another.

Then the ceremonies begin.

Veterans organizations march to the cemetery, and the Colors are massed at the War Veterans Memorial Shaft.

"Let us pray that we may always honor those who have given the last full measure of devotion to their country," Dean Emeritus James M. Malloch says.

"Let us pray that the United States may ever be the land of the free and the home of the brave and the advocate of peace in the councils of nations."

Pay Tribute

At the Belmont Memorial Park, military units stand at attention while tributes are paid to the dead.

Mayor C. Cal Evans reminds the quiet crowd Memorial Day has a new significance, paying "homage to the heroes of peace as well as to the heroes of war."

The main speaker, Legislative Commissioner Ted C. Wills, says:

"Although the bodies of our loved ones are consigned to the earth, their souls have winged their way to the Father in Whose house there are many mansions, where, for all eternity, theirs will be the fullness of joy."

The oratory is carried to the treetops and fades away and the soldiers march off.

—*The Fresno Bee*

The first story is like dozens of Memorial Day stories. The oratory, although perhaps passionately uttered, has little emotional impact because it ignores those the event commemorates—the victims of war. The second story teeters on the edge of sentimentality in the lead, but soon settles into understated narrative that seeks to match the solemn nature of the event.

New Journalism

The antecedents of the journalist's relaxed, nonstilted writing style are the nonfiction novel of the 1950s and the New Journalism of Tom Wolfe and others in the 1960s. In a *Wall Street Journal* review of an anthology of Wolfe's works, *The Purple Decades: A Reader,* Ellen Wilson describes Wolfe's inspiration for this new way of writing:

In the early Sixties, Tom Wolfe went to the New York Coliseum to cover a Hot Rod and Custom Car show, and came back with the New Journalism. As he tells it in the introduction to "The Kandy-Kolored Tangerine-Flake Streamline Baby," he felt frustrated by his inability to recreate the atmosphere of the show, with its "nutty-looking, crazy baroque custom cars, sitting in little nests of pink angora angels hair," in standard journalese. He needed a style flexible and uninhibited enough to capture everything a straight news story would miss: the carnival atmosphere and the thoughts and emotions of the participants.

He came up with a style incorporating slang and contemporary speech patterns, stream of consciousness and abrupt switches in perspective. The first step was painstaking research and close attention to detail. After that, he was free to select from the novelist's whole bag of tricks.

Journalism historians say the roots of New Journalism actually go back a century. One of the founders of the school was Richard Harding Davis, a war correspondent of the late 19th century. His biographer, Arthur Lubow, points out in *The Reporter Who Would Be King* (New York: Scribner's, 1992) that Davis followed a maxim included in a popular journalism correspondence course of the day: "Truth in essentials, imagination in non-essentials is considered a legitimate rule of action in every office."

When Davis was reporting for the *Evening Sun,* he covered the story of a physician accused of killing a young woman in a botched abortion and of secretly burying the body. We pick up Davis' account as a gravedigger discovers the woman's body:

> He had struck a nickel-plated screw of the coffin, and at that moment the bell over the superintendent's house began to toll. They were very near your secret then, Dr. McGonegal — very near. And the bell that tolled for the funeral passing through the gate of the cemetery was just a coincidence, but it sounded like a knell, Dr. Mc-Gonegal — very like a knell.

The doctor was found guilty and at 70 began a sentence of 14 years at hard labor.

Writing for the Medium

A lot of what we have discussed so far concerns the requirements of writing for print. There are other media, of course, and these have special needs the newswriter must master.

Radio newswriting is more condensed than writing for print. The reader can always go back and reread something she was unclear about. The radio listener has to grasp meaning on his first and only hearing. The radio news writer will not have much detail, few nuances.

The television news writer often writes to pictures, which are left to speak for themselves. The TV news writer has a more complicated script than the radio news writer because the TV writer is usually jumping back and forth—the interviewer, the burned-out family being interviewed, the house in flames, back to the studio.

We will go into greater detail about broadcast newswriting in Chapter 9.

Online Writing

Writing for the Internet also answers to the special needs of the medium, in this case a screen, usually with material on one or both sides of the news text. Most of those who work in online journalism agree with Mark Fitzgerald of *Editor & Publisher* who says, "The computer screen is notoriously inhospitable to long stories. Even a story that amounts to just 10 inches on the newspaper page seems endless on a computer."

Ruth Gersh, editor of multimedia services at the Associated Press, says the screen—its size or the need to scroll—gives readers "a sense of movement or impermanence that seems to beg for a simpler writing style." She says the broadcast style of newswriting works best.

The AP provides an online news service, the *Wire*. Readers can get to it through a link on their newspaper's Web page. The *Wire* uses radio style newswriting.

Reading for Writers

"You can't write well if you don't read," says veteran reporter Joe Galloway, who covered the Vietnam War and put in stints as a foreign correspondent. "Don't show me your resumé," he says of job applicants. "Show me your library card." Wide reading—novels, essays, the work of journalists—helps writers learn to write, a task that is never-ending. The writing coach Don Murray says, "Professional writers never learn to write; they continue to learn writing all their professional lives. The good writer is forever a student of writing."

One journalist whose work would repay study is Ernie Pyle, a Scripps Howard newsman who wrote features for the news organization, then requested to be sent to cover World War II for the United Press.

Reporter's Reporter

Pyle was loved by the soldiers he accompanied to battle. One of Pyle's memorable dispatches was of the death of Captain Waskow during the Italian campaign of 1944. It has become a journalistic classic. Here is part of Pyle's story:

Then a soldier came and stood beside the officer, and bent over, and he too spoke to his dead captain, not in a whisper but awfully tenderly, and he said:

"I sure am sorry, sir."

Then the first man squatted down, and he reached down, took the dead hand, and sat there for a full five minutes, holding the dead hand in his own and looking intently into the dead face, and he never uttered a sound all the time he sat there.

And finally he put the hand down, and then reached up and gently straightened the points of the captain's shirt collar, and then he sort of rearranged the tattered edges of his uniform around the wound. And then he got up and walked away down the road in the moonlight, all alone.

The Army Signal Corps operator who sent Pyle's dispatch over shortwave radio to United Press headquarters in New York told Pyle's biographer, "I had to struggle through that piece to make my voice override my tears." (*Ernie Pyle's War: America's Eyewitness to World War II,* James Tobin.)

With the Troops Murray Kempton, the reporter and columnist admired by many journalists for his dogged reporting and distinct writing style, paid homage to Pyle who, Kempton wrote, "stands above the rest because he most fully incarnated what a reporter ought to be. Pyle went again and again wherever the worst extremes waited, the unconscripted man bound by conscience to the comradeship of the conscripted and enduring by free will what they were compelled to endure by necessity."

Pyle understood the use of understatement. Reread the four paragraphs about Captain Waskow's death. The emotion comes from you, the reader. When he went ashore with the troops on D-Day, Pyle wrote of what he saw strewn on Omaha Beach as men were mowed down—socks, sewing kits, family pictures. The details gave a personal cast to the body counts.

Jack Foisie, also a World War II combat correspondent, said of Pyle that he "seldom injected himself into his writings. He never mentioned his own close calls with death, although he had a number of them."

With the Navy   When the war in Europe ended, Pyle went to the Pacific to cover the sea war against Japan. There, Pyle felt uncomfortable about what he saw as the Navy caste system.

Soon after he was aboard a ship he found that his dispatches were being censored. The names of the sailors he had written about were deleted and only the names of high-ranking officers were left untouched. He also balked at the system that relegated black sailors to serving in the food services. Pyle was able to change the first by threatening to abandon Navy coverage for the Marine and Army GIs, and the Navy gave in and stopped censoring his stories.

But he could not change the discrimination against black servicemen. That took three more years and the action of President Truman in 1948.

The Pyle Style   Malcolm W. Browne, who served as a war correspondent in Indochina, Pakistan and the Persian Gulf, says that Pyle was "a master of language, the equal of any first-rank novelist. He constantly struggled for the precise phrase and the telling verb; whereas a less careful correspondent might write that a shell 'howled' or 'screamed' overhead, Pyle wrote that it 'rustled.' "

The writer John Hersey said of Pyle that he was "the great artist" of the "human aspects of warfare—of bravery, loss, wounds, humor, self-sacrifice, pain and yes, death—and, by the way, he always added the name and home address of the person he was talking about."

The End   The death of good men haunted Pyle, and when he was shot by a sniper on Ie Shima in 1945, the soldiers who had risked their lives to bring back his body found in his pocket a column he had written for the end of the fighting in Europe. Here is some of it:

> Those who are gone would not wish themselves to be a millstone of gloom around our necks.
>
> But there are many of the living who have had burned into their brains forever the unnatural sight of cold dead men scattered over the hillsides and in the ditches along the high rows of hedge throughout the world.

Dead men by mass production—in one country after another—month after month and year after year. Dead men in winter and dead men in summer.

Dead men in such familiar promiscuity that they become monotonous.

Dead men in such monstrous infinity that you come almost to hate them.

Pyle is buried beside GIs in the Punchbowl Cemetery in Hawaii.

The Bard and the Bible

A study of writing can begin with this advice in Sir Herbert Read's *English Prose Style:*

> The great strength of the English language lies in its splendid array of transitive verbs drawn both from the Anglo Saxon and Latin. Their power lies in their recognition of nature as a vast storehouse of forces. . . . Shakespeare's English is immeasurably superior to all others. . . . It is his persistent, natural and magnificent use of hundreds of transitive verbs. Rarely will you find an *is* in his sentence. A study of Shakespeare's verbs should underline all exercises in style.

Abraham Lincoln, who had little formal education but wrote forceful and compelling prose, read Shakespeare and the Bible. John McPhee, the *New Yorker* writer many journalists read with admiration, says he returns regularly to Shakespeare for replenishment and instruction. Writers admire Shakespeare's use of action verbs:

- Every cloud engenders not a storm.
- We are advertis'd by our loving friends.
- An honest tale speeds best being plainly told.
- The grass stoops not, she treads on it so light.
- The labour we delight in physics pain.
- Policy sits above conscience.

Few journalists realize how much they owe the King James Bible. Almost every virtue of the prose style the journalist uses can be traced to its influence: direct simplicity, exactness and economy of language, rapid pace, even the S-V-O construction. The writings of John Bunyan, Emily Brontë and scores of others were influenced by the Bible. The novelist Willa Cather said she read passages from the Bible to be in touch with good prose before she wrote. Peter Abràhàms, a South African author, said he had a teacher who "whenever I used big words or made clumsy and almost meaningless sentences, sent me to the Bible. I read the Bible and I saw."

This is no place to make a plea for taking up the Bible. But look at these sentences and consider the possibility of some extracurricular reading:

- For many are called, but few are chosen.
- Who is this that darkeneth counsel by words without knowledge?
- We all do fade as a leaf.

- Man shall not live by bread alone.
- A word spoken in good season, how good it is.
- The rich rules over the poor, and the borrower is the slave of the lender.
- How forcible are right words.
- Let thy words be few.

Gilbert Millstein, a network television newswriter, recommends reading Hawthorne, Melville and Nathanael West. Of West's novels he says:

> For example, any television newswriter who reads *Miss Lonelyhearts* or *The Day of the Locust* by Nathanael West would find in them an economy and vividness of language achieved without adjectives that would surprise the life out of him. I would offer those two books as models for any person who wants to write factual news. The economy of *Miss Lonelyhearts* is unbelievable. There isn't a single word that could be dropped. The same is true for *The Day of the Locust*. But young people appear not to read these kinds of books anymore.

Write, Write and Rewrite

Look at an author's manuscript; you'll be surprised by the extent of the revisions. In a review of an exhibit of the manuscripts of major American and British authors, the reviewer wrote that "the single unifying link is revision. From Nathaniel Hawthorne and Charles Dickens to Virginia Woolf and Saul Bellow, the lesson goes: writing is rewriting, leaving out more than putting in, always trying to simplify and clarify."

Much of what we've said presumes a rational, disciplined approach to news writing. Sometimes, diligent thinking and careful planning are of no avail. The right lead will not come; the exact words lurk just beyond our reach; sentences stumble over each other; and the whole business looks a mess.

Then—only minutes before the edition closes or the newscast is to go on—the story comes together. The theme of the piece is clear. There it was, hiding in the fourth graf. And there, that quote in the fifth graf, the perfect second graf. We toss out 50 lines. Adrenalin flows and the words fly. Everything fits. On deadline, too.

Every writer has gone through this scene. Sean O'Faolain, the Irish writer, points out that ideas sometimes become clear "by, and only by, the very act of writing."

Some writers can function only under this kind of pressure. Given a day to do a story, they dillydally until the deadline is an hour off. Then they can write. True enough, they rarely miss their deadlines. But the wear and tear they undergo and the anxiety they inflict on their editors is frightening to behold. Better to develop good writing habits now, gradually and without too much pressure, so that on-the-job writing most often is a calm, deliberate process. That means writing, seeing your mistakes and rewriting.

The Round File. "The wastepaper basket is the writer's best friend."
—*William Kerrigan.*

Mencken on Writing

H.L. Mencken was a master of prose. A columnist for *The Baltimore Sun,* his columns often began with a flourish:

Whoever it was who translated the Bible into excellent French prose is chiefly responsible for the collapse of Christianity in France.

He was also a master of invective, and never so masterfully abusive as when skewering writing he considered contemptible. Here is perhaps the most famous writer-bashing on record. Mencken is commenting on the writing of President Warren G. Harding:

I rise to pay my small tribute to Dr. Harding. Setting aside a college professor or two and a half a dozen dipsomaniacal newspaper reporters, he takes the first place in my Valhalla of literati. That is to say, he writes the worst English that I have ever encountered. It reminds me of a string of wet sponges; it reminds me of tattered washing on the line; it reminds me of stale bean-soup, of college yells, of dogs barking idiotically through endless nights. It is so bad that a sort of grandeur creeps into it. It drags itself out of the dark abysm (I was about to write abscess!) of pish, and crawls insanely up to the topmost pinnacle of posh.

Someone said nothing good was ever written as a first draft. Journalists often do not have the leisure of a second look at their copy. Too often, the job requires writing on the run, doing a story with facts gathered close to the deadline. Nothing can be done about that. But when there is time, the rewrite is almost always a good idea and usually necessary.

With practice, writing comes easier and is accomplished with less anguish and more speed. But every writer knows that his or her work can be improved with rewriting, and even the veteran journalists rewrite when they have time. The discipline of editing your own words is handy. When Jan Wong was writing a book about her experiences in China, *Red China Blues,* she was worried about putting together her many experiences.

"As a reporter, I sometimes got bogged down structuring a thousand-word article. Would I be able to put together 150 times that much—and still make the words flow?" she wondered.

Not to worry. She wrote . . . and rewrote. "I rewrote some chapters many times," she says. "But I enjoyed that. Rewriting was a skill I had honed as a journalist."

Let's see if we can wrap up this long chapter with a few conclusions about the art of writing.

Word Choice

Here is some practical advice from John Ciardi, poet, essayist and writer on writing:

Count the adjectives and verbs; good writing (active writing) will almost invariably have more verbs. . . . A diction in which every noun is propped up by an adjective may be almost flatly said to be a bad one.

Mark Twain advised, "Whenever you see an adjective, kill it." And that vast source of material, Anonymous, is quoted on writing as saying, "The adjective is the enemy of the noun."

As for verbs, the action verb is our object. Mervin Block, the television writing coach, received a script with this lead: "The Dow was down more than 62 points." Block commented: "The verb *was* is a linking verb and doesn't convey any action. The writer needs a vigorous verb like *fell.* Or *sank.* Or *slid.* Or *skidded.* Or *dropped.* Or *plunged.* Or *tumbled.* But *was* doesn't move."

Block's point is that there are plenty of action verbs available to the writer.

Sentences

Red Smith's teacher at Notre Dame, John Michael Cooney, wanted sentences from his students that were "so definite they would cast a shadow." He was an enemy of vague writing and began class by intoning, "Let us pray for sense."

Sense for whom? Harold Ross, the founder and longtime editor of *The New Yorker* wanted his magazine never to contain "a sentence that would puzzle an intelligent 14-year-old."

The sentences should be put to good use, and that means using them for quotations, anecdotes and illustrations. Donald Murray, the writer and writing coach, comments on the use of examples, illustrations and anecdotes:

You tell them the anecdote and they say, "Boy, this is a bad situation." That's the art in it—not to tell the reader how to think, how to feel, but to give the reader the old Mark Twain thing, "Don't say the old lady screamed. Drag her on stage and make her scream."

Lamentation

Perhaps the next to last word should be given to the copy editor. Here's Joel Rawson's lament about the copy he sometimes reads at the *Providence Journal Bulletin:*

The thing that I resent most is sloppiness. I resent getting a story with misspellings in leads and errors of fact, and I resent getting a story that I know somebody didn't sit down and reread. Even on deadline I expect somebody to go back and reread that story and fix up what is obviously wrong with it. You're taking up a lot of people's time and you're also ruining your credibility and mine if work like that goes through the copy desk or other editors on this newspaper. And if somebody else doesn't catch (the mistakes) and they go into print, it hurts us all.

Summing Up

Journalistic writing, whether for a magazine, a newspaper, an online publication or a broadcast station is part of the world of letters. Those of us who write for a living strive to blend information-giving with artistry if we can. So it's natural here to turn to a writer who wrote well and thought a lot about the writing craft.

Robert Louis Stevenson was the author of highly readable novels—*Treasure Island, Kidnapped* and *The Strange Case of Dr. Jeykll and Mr. Hyde* among the many—as well as essays, poetry and travel accounts. Here's what he had to say about writing:

- **Accuracy:** ". . . there is only one way to be clever and that is to be exact. To be vivid is a secondary quality which must presuppose the first; for vividly to convey a wrong impression is only to make failure conspicuous. . . ."
- **Brevity:** ". . . the artist has one main and necessary resource which he must, in every case and upon any theory, employ. He must, that is, suppress much and omit more. He must omit what is tedious or irrelevant. . . . " But he must retain the material essential to the "main design."
- **Language:** The words with which the writer works should be from "the dialect of life."
- **Structure:** ". . . every word, phrase, sentence and paragraph must move in a logical procession." No word or phrase is selected unless it is "what is wanted to forward and illustrate" the work.

> **How Long?** A reporter asked his city editor how much he should write on a piece he was doing. The reply: "Keep on writing as long as it's interesting."

Further Reading

Breslin, Jimmy. *The World According to Breslin.* New York: Ticknor & Fields, 1985.

Clark, Roy Peter. *The American Conversation and the Language of Journalism.* St. Petersburg: The Poynter Institute for Media Studies, 1994.

Ghiglione, Loren, ed. *Improving Newswriting: The Best of the American Society of Newspaper Editors.* Washington, D.C.: ASNE Foundation, 1982.

Ivins, Molly. *Molly Ivins Can't Say That, Can She?* New York: Random House, 1991.

Kluger, Richard. *The Paper: The Life and Death of The New York Herald Tribune.* New York: Random House, 1987.

Ross, Lillian. *Reporting.* New York: Dodd Mead & Co., 1981.

Scanlan, Christopher, ed *Best Newspaper Writing.* Chicago: Bonus Books; St. Petersburg: Poynter Institute for Media Studies.

Terkel, Studs. *Working: People Talk About What They Do All Day and What They Think While They Do It.* New York: Pantheon, 1972.

Terkel, Studs. *The Good War: An Oral History of World War Two.* New York: Pantheon, 1984.

Tobin, James. *Ernie Pyle's War: America's Eyewitness to World War II.* New York: Free Press, 1997.

Anita Henderson,
Beloit (Wis.) *Daily News*

Features make us laugh and cry.

Preview

Features are written to entertain. The writer lets the actions and comments of the personalities carry the story. Features usually begin with a delayed lead—an incident or anecdote that illuminates the point of the feature. The body contains additional incidents, many quotes and the news peg. The ending may summarize the piece or provide a climax.

Long stories are written to provide readers with information about a complicated idea or situation. The reporter outlines the theme before reporting so that material relevant to it can be gathered. In writing, a tone or style appropriate to the main idea is adopted, and ample quotes and incidents are used to keep the story moving.

Series are written when the subject is too complex for the long story format. Each article has a major theme; sidebars may be used to develop subthemes.

Some editors say there are three types of news stories. Although there are no precise lines that can be drawn to separate the three, they can be distinguished as follows:

Spot news story: Contains material of such significance that it must be reported immediately to the public.

News feature: Uses information that supplements the spot news, usually by providing the human element behind the breaking news event or by giving background through interpretation and explanation.

Feature: Aims to entertain and/or inform with writing that emphasizes storytelling.

The Feature

The feature has had a reputation much like Canadian mining stock, slightly suspect. Although it has worthy antecedents in the satire and parody of poets and essayists who used the pen to attack individuals in public and private life, the feature was approached gingerly by editors. Many editors subscribed to the philosophy of Richard Draper, who wrote in his Boston *News-Letter* in the 18th century that he would use features only when "there happens to be a scarcity of news."

At First Distasteful

Conservative editors of the 19th century reacted with distaste to the features published by the penny press from the 1830s to the Civil War. Directed to the working class, which had been enlarged by the country's industrial revolution, these inexpensive newspapers ran stories about domestic tragedy and illicit sex, stories that editors such as Horace Greeley found unworthy of journalism. When he established the *Tribune* in New York in 1841, Greeley announced that his newspaper would avoid the "immoral and degrading Police Reports, Advertisements and other matters which have been allowed to disgrace the columns of our leading Penny Papers." But Greeley was soon running the kind of material he had condemned.

The feature story was a weapon in the great circulation wars between Pulitzer and Hearst in New York at the turn of the 20th century. Crime stories, sports, society news, science news—all of it embroidered with sensational details often as much invented as factual—were used to attract readers. This type of feature became synonymous with Yellow Journalism.

The Hearst newspapers were perhaps the most successful of the sensational and flamboyant papers of their day. W. A. Swanberg, in his biography *Citizen Hearst,* describes them:

> They were printed entertainment and excitement—the equivalent in newsprint of bombs exploding, bands blaring, firecrackers popping, victims screaming, flags waving, cannons roaring, houris dancing and smoke rising from the singed flesh of executed criminals.

A reporter for a Hearst newspaper described a typical Hearst paper as "a screaming woman running down the street with her throat cut." The Chief, as Hearst was known to his employees, had the man fired.

In the days of Front Page Journalism, the feature writer's job was to wring tears from the bartender, smiles from the policeman and gasps of wonderment from the tenement dwellers. The tales of the city, as spun out by the feature writers of the day, were long on drama, short on fact.

Tale of the Cat   During the circulation war between the Hearst and Pulitzer papers, a reporter for Pulitzer's *New York World* who covered shipping described what happened when reporters tried to make features of straight news:

One of those wrecked ships had a cat, and the crew went back to save it. I made the cat a feature of my story, while the other reporters failed to mention the cat and were called down by their city editors for being beaten. The next time there was a shipwreck, there was no cat but the other ship news reporters did not wish to take chances and put the cat in. I wrote the report, leaving out the cat, and then I was severely chided for being beaten. Now when there is a shipwreck, all of us always put in a cat.

The Decline   As the United States grew into a world power and its citizens had to confront the consequences of World War I and then a pervasive depression, some of the press graduated to more serious pursuits. The feature came to be seen as too frivolous for the responsible newspaper. Newspapers that held on to the old formulas declined in popularity. The Hearst chain dwindled from 22 newspapers to 8.

In 1947, when Joseph G. Herzberg, city editor of *The New York Herald Tribune,* put together a series of essays by *Tribune* staffers for the book *Late City Edition,* not one of the 29 chapters was devoted to the feature story.

Now Thriving

Nevertheless, the feature thrives today. First, editors discovered that serious journalism does not have to be abstract. They rediscovered the fact known to Greek playwrights 2,300 years ago—events have a human dimension. Indeed, it is the human aspect of the event that makes it worth communicating. In his play *The Frogs,* Aristophanes has the playwright Euripedes say, "I made the drama democratic. I staged the life of every day, the way we live." This is an excellent description of our approach to the feature today.

The contemporary journalist tries to present the full dimension of how we live now, from how we are governed, make a living, raise a family and spend our money to the ways we entertain ourselves and make our way through the trials and terrors life holds for us. The feature has proved a useful writing tool to tell many of these stories. So useful, in fact, that in 1979, after many years of ignoring the feature, the Pulitzer Prize board established a category for a distinguished example of feature writing, "giving prime consideration to high literary quality and originality."

The Somber   This is the more serious face of features. The Prize has gone to Lisa Pollak of *The Baltimore Sun* for her "compelling portrait of a baseball umpire who endured the death of a son while knowing that another son suffers from the same deadly genetic disease." The Prize has honored features about inner-city youngsters' determination to succeed and personal accounts by journalists, one a reminiscence by Howell Raines of *The New York Times* about Raines' childhood friendship with his family's black housekeeper. The first Prize in the new category went to Jon Franklin for a story about brain surgery, which we will be looking at in a few pages.

The Cheerful   But an unvarying diet of the somber does not tell the full story of how we live now. Also, any mass medium given over to a steady diet of the serious will be rejected by the mass audience. So the media offer a variety, and one of the items is the entertaining feature.

The news story might be a piece from Washington, D.C., about a sudden rise in the cost of living. The feature writer will use that as a takeoff for a feature about how the candy bar he used to buy for a nickel now costs more than 10 times as much. Where, he wonders, do kids these days get the money for a Babe Ruth or a Mars bar? He lurks around candy counters to find out.

A Feature: A Man Beset

By making every word count, a reporter for *The Fresno Bee* captured the mood of a man with a problem:

Ben Karp is a patient man. Like most of us he can shrug off life's little onslaughts in hopes of a better day.

But Karp has been shrugging and dodging and hoping for six months now, and his patience finally snapped. He called the *Bee* and asked for a reporter to see him at his general merchandise business at 1837 Mariposa Street.

"Very important," he said. On the scene, Karp whipped off his hat, pointed a slightly trembling finger at a brownish spot the size of a half dollar on it and then wordlessly pointed skyward.

There, cooing happily and roosting comfortably in corners and on window sills, were pigeons. Dozens of pigeons.

"I've called the mayor, the public works commissioner, the health department," Karp said. "They promised me to do something. Nothing is done. It's ruining my business. People don't like to walk in here past that line there.

"I'd like to get a shotgun and scare them off. But you can't shoot a gun in the city. The health department says it can't do anything because it can't prove pigeons carry disease. The humane society says I can't trap or poison them. The mayor's office says he was going to have a meeting on it. Nothing happened.

"This is bad for the city. I tell you. Thousands of people go in and out of the bus depot and they see this and I hear them say to each other, 'Fresno can't be such a clean city. Look at this.'

"I don't blame people for not wanting to come into the store. What can I do about it?"

And Karp looked up at his feathered friends and shrugged.

What he learns astounds him. Some youngsters are rolling in dough. Even poor kids are sporting $125 athletic shoes, he notices. One story begets another. But first, for the candy bars. It won't be nominated for a Pulitzer Prize, but that's all right. It's a fun story to write. And, he hopes, for people to hear about.

Caution: Some young reporters say they prefer to write features rather than hard news because the feature is easier to handle. This is the blather of the uninformed. The momentum of the news event carries most spot news stories. True, it is not easy to learn to organize a tight news story, and the skill to devise succinct leads that quickly take the reader to the news point is not easily mastered. But the feature writer must carry these burdens and more.

The feature is an exception to some of the writing rules, and this imposes on the writer the task of pioneering in each piece, beginning anew to find a form, a story tone, the appropriate words and the telling scenes for this particular story. Readers demand more of feature writers than of straight news writers and so do editors.

Guidelines

The few guidelines for feature writing cut to the heart of writing itself:

- Show people doing things.
- Let them talk.
- Underwrite. Let the action and the dialogue carry the piece.
- Keep the piece moving.

Few writers have gone wrong by making the individuals in their stories carry the action. This requires a discerning eye to see the telling action and a discriminating ear to catch the illuminating quote.

Frontier Nurse   Showing people doing things and letting them speak requires that the reporter be on the scene. Jim Warren of the *Lexington Herald-Leader* accompanied Glenna Allen of the Frontier Nursing Service as she made her rounds in the eastern Kentucky mountains. His story begins this way:

> HYDEN—The road that snakes up from Coon Creek is hard-packed dirt in some places and bottomless mud in others, all of it pitted with cavernous potholes.
>
> Slide one way and you hit a mountain wall; slide the other and you go off a cliff into space.
>
> Driving is tricky, especially when a mountainous coal truck—in this case a Tennessee Orange Mack with a full load of bituminous coal—looms around a blind curve.
>
> Glenna Allen handled the situation with skill that comes from long practice, steering her battered tan Toyota almost to the drop-off at the right edge of the road. . . .

Warren lets Allen talk:

> "My mother hates it that I'm doing this," Miss Allen said with a laugh. She left Dayton, Ohio, to work in the mountains. "She thinks I'm going to get myself killed by a rattlesnake or run over some cliff, and she keeps asking when I'm coming home. . . ."

Conforming Kids   Lena H. Sun, *The Washington Post* Beijing bureau chief, took her readers into a kindergarten to show how Chinese children are made into conforming, obedient citizens:

> BEIJING—It is a playtime at the Tongren Kindergarten. As 3-year-olds run relay races in the schoolyard, the teacher suddenly calls out to one girl.
>
> "You didn't run on the dotted line," the teacher says disapprovingly. The girl, pigtails bobbing, immediately retraces her steps on faded red spots painted on the concrete. The teacher smiles and nods. No one else makes the same mistake.

"Show people doing things," our first guideline, is the thrust of Sun's lead.

Tom Woods II, *The Lexington Herald-Leader*

Backwoods Care

Gambling Woman   When reporters were assigned to cover the opening of an off-track betting parlor in a suburb of New York City, most were content to report such obvious facts as the size of the crowd and the name and address of the first bettor on line. Leonard Levitt of *Newsday* resisted the routine and did some checking about the 62-year-old grandmother who was first in line. He refused to settle for the obvious. As good feature writers know, snappy writing cannot sustain the underreported feature.

Through interviews with the woman, her husband and children, Levitt learned that she was a chronic gambler who bet $50 and $100 a day. Her husband told Levitt, "It was hard when the kids were growing up. I used to hold three jobs." The woman told Levitt, "My husband doesn't approve of my betting. Neither do my kids. None of them bets. But they love me." In these few quotes, a family's tragedy is unfolded.

Sleepers   The feature writer also sees the absurd and hears the preposterous. In his piece about the Southern Furniture Market in High Point, N.C., where the new styles in furniture are previewed each year, Lew Powell tells us about Dr. Samuel Dunkell, "psychotherapist and author of the best-selling 'Sleep Positions.' " Just to make sure we know this event is hardly the stuff of which significant news is made, Powell sets the mood in the first paragraph:

> Today in Washington reporters are awaiting Koreagate revelations. In Memphis, the latest on Elvis. In Minneapolis, the Billy Graham audit. In High Point we're crowded into a mattress showroom waiting for the inside poop on sleep positions.

From the serious to the silly. Powell does this in a few sentences. The words "inside poop" tell the reader that what follows is going to be fun:

Enrico Caruso slept with 18 pillows. Neil Sedaka rubs his feet over each other. The late Hannah Arendt, author of "The Origins of Totalitarianism" and not someone you'd expect to be spilling this kind of stuff, favored the "water wings" position.

And have we got a photo opportunity for you! As Dunkell discusses the "royal" position, the "flamingo," the "mummy," the "sphinx" and the "swastika," model Norma demonstrates. Her yellow sleep-shirt keeps riding up, ensuring undivided attention. When she's joined by a male model for the "hug" and "spoon" position, a sock-footed TV cameraman clambers onto an adjacent Maxipedic for a better angle.

"Republicans sleep face down, Democrats on their backs," Dunkell says. Scribble, scribble. "Surprisingly few people fall out of bed—perhaps 20 percent in their lifetime." Scribble, scribble. . . .

The feature writer sees universals as well as aberrations. What is there about that pianist, this drummer with dreams that strike chords common to all of us? The feature writer knows that great writers inspire us to see ourselves in Tolstoy's Natasha, Fitzgerald's Nick Carraway and Melville's Captain Vere. The feature writer must be open to human experience. It was said of Rembrandt that he rejected nothing human. Neither does the feature writer.

Planning

Frank Barrows of *The Charlotte Observer* says careful planning of the feature is essential. "Simply because a feature is not written to be cut from the bottom—as a news story might be—does not mean that the material can be randomly set down on paper.

"For a feature to be something other than puffery, you must do the type of serious preparation and thinking that lead to organization. For instance, you might not want to put all the straight biographic data in one place."

Barrows knows that such material is usually tedious. Beginners tend to bunch up background. More experienced hands break up background such as biographical material and place bits and pieces into the moving narrative. For example, he says, when a reporter comes to a place in the story where she is showing how the subject's hometown influenced his life, that is the place to put something about his birthplace and a few other routine details. In other words, the necessary background is spotted or blended into the ongoing story.

Another fault of beginners is the leisurely pace they set at the outset of the piece, as though they are feeling their way toward the theme of the story.

"Too often in features the writer does not tell his reader soon enough what he is writing about," Barrows says.

Truck Stop   Look at how Eric Lawlor of the *Houston Chronicle* slides the reader right into his piece about a truck stop outside town. He sets a scene in the first paragraph, pulls us into the restaurant in the second and in the third we meet Tina who introduces us to a dialogue that gives us a good idea of what's going on:

The truck stop on the North Freeway is ringed with rigs. Trucks glide past one another with the grandeur of sailing ships: 16-wheel galleons bearing—not spices from the Indies or gold from the New World—but auto parts and refrigerators.

Truckers weave as they enter the restaurant; like sailors on shore leave, they are still finding their legs.

Tina Hernandez, an 18-year-old waitress here, serves an order of ham and eggs.

"Where are my grits?" asks the recipient.

"You don't get grits unless you ask for them," she tells him. "If you want grits, you gotta say, 'I want grits.' "

If this sounds unnecessarily acerbic, it's not, in fact: Tina and her customers are actually fond of one another. An affection that masquerades as good-natured abuse.

"Give me a bowl of split-pea soup," says a man whose face looks curiously flat.

Perhaps someone sat on it. "Is there any meat in there?"

"There's meat in there all right," says Tina. "The problem is finding it."

"How are you and Billy (not his real name) doin'?" he wants to know.

"We don't talk anymore," says the waitress. "He got scared. Just checked out."

"Oh, I don't believe that. I'll bet you are goin' out and just don't want anyone to know about it."

"I'm tellin' ya: that man is scared of women."

"Maybe, he just doesn't like YOU," offers Myrtle, another waitress.

At a nearby table, a driver is telling a colleague about a recent fling.

"I had to leave her finally because she was so cold-blooded. You could get pneumonia sitting next to a woman like that."

Using All the Techniques

In his feature about a school for bartenders, Lawlor gets down to business at once, taking the reader into the classroom in the lead:

> K. C. Stevens is explaining the difference between a godfather and a godmother.
>
> "To make a godfather," she tells her class at the Professional Bartenders School, "use amaretto and scotch. A godmother, on the other hand, combines amaretto and vodka."

Then Lawlor steps back for a few paragraphs to let the reader survey the scene, telling us something about the teacher and her students:

> K. C., a onetime barmaid, has been teaching people to mix drinks for four years now.
>
> "I didn't want to find myself at the age of 40 wearing orthopedic shoes behind some crummy bar," she says. "Being a bartender is a young person's game."
>
> Her class nods agreement. If that isn't to exaggerate this barely perceptible movement of heads. This is a pretty lethargic group. They slump at the school's mock bar as if drink had ravaged them. They wouldn't look out of place in Pompeii.
>
> It's hard to imagine these people doing anything as animated as tending bar. Indeed it's hard to imagine them doing anything as animated as standing up.
>
> K. C., a good soul, is inclined to agree.
>
> "A lot of them are spaced off somewhere," she says. "I was telling a couple of them just this morning, 'Look, you're gonna have to put more time into studying.' But once they get the picture, things usually work out. Many people come in here expecting to party. They don't realize there's a lot of work involved."

Steve Campbell,
Houston Chronicle

Learning the Trade

K. C. Stevens displays the proper blend of savvy and cordiality as she instructs budding bartenders. Then her students take over.

From the first sentence, the reader is hooked on this story, a story that occupies a full column of type. Every line was read. Why? If we can answer the question, perhaps we will make a start toward understanding what makes a good feature.

First, the subject is interesting. Even if you can't tell a Hot Toddy from a hot buttered bun—and care less—you wonder about these people who are able to throw together scores of different concoctions from their amazing array of bottles.

Second, Lawlor knows what he is doing. The most interesting subject in clumsy hands will be dulled. Let's analyze Lawlor's craft:

- The story moves quickly.
- The quotations are vivid.
- The characters interact. They talk, do things.

Tone and Style

In any discussion with feature writers, the words *tone* and *style* always come up. A feature writer uses one tone—one kind of voice—for a piece about a classical guitarist, another for a guitarist with a rock group. Tone is established by selection of facts, quotes, illustrations, by word choice, length of sentences, even by the length of paragraphs. The rock musician may be quoted in short, one- or two-sentence paragraphs to match the rock beat, whereas the classical musician's quotes may run on longer to give the reader the sense of the sonority of classical music.

The Monster

The new field of neuroscience interested Jon Franklin, chief science writer for *The Evening Sun* in Baltimore. Franklin had been talking to Dr. Thomas Ducker, chief of neurosurgery at the University of Maryland Hospital, about brain surgery, and Ducker had agreed to call him the next time he planned an especially difficult surgical procedure. When Ducker called, Franklin set out to follow the story of Edna Kelly, who was afflicted with what she called her "monster," a tangled knot of abnormal blood vessels in the back of her brain. She was born with the malformation, but in recent years the vessels had ballooned inside her skull and were crowding out the healthy brain tissue.

Kelly agreed to be interviewed, and she allowed Franklin to use her name. She also permitted Franklin to watch the surgery. Ducker agreed to cooperate.

Preparation   Here is how the first story in Franklin's two-part series begins:

In the cold hours of a winter morning, Dr. Thomas Barbee Ducker, University Hospital's senior brain surgeon, rises before dawn. His wife serves him waffles but no coffee. Coffee makes his hands shake.

Downtown, on the 12th floor of the hospital, Edna Kelly's husband tells her goodbye.

For 57 years Mrs. Kelly shared her skull with the monster. No more. Today she is frightened but determined.

It is 6:30 a.m.

"I'm not afraid to die," she said as this day approached. "I've lost part of my eyesight. I've gone through all the hemorrhages. A couple of years ago I lost my sense of smell, my taste, I started having seizures. I smell a strange odor and then I start strangling. It started affecting my legs, and I'm partially paralyzed.

"Three years ago a doctor told me all I had to look forward to was blindness, paralysis and a remote chance of death. . . .

Operation   Franklin's intentions are made clear at the outset. This is to be a detailed account of the confrontation between a skilled surgeon and disease. Franklin takes the reader into the operating room:

Now, at 7:15 a.m. in Operating Room 11, a technician checks the brain surgery microscope and the circulating nurse lays out bandages and instruments. Mrs. Kelly lies still on a stainless steel table.

A small sensor has been threaded through her veins and now hangs in the antechamber of her heart. Dr. Jane Matjasko,

the anesthesiologist, connects the sensor to a 7-foot-high bank of electronic instruments. Wave forms begin to move rhythmically across a cathode ray tube.

With each heartbeat a loudspeaker produces an audible popping sound. The steady pop, pop, pop, pop isn't loud, but it dominates the operating room.

Dr. Ducker enters the operating room and pauses before the X-ray films that hang on a lighted panel. He carried those brain images to Europe, Canada and Florida in search of advice, and he knows them by heart. Still he studies them again, eyes focused on the two fragile aneurisms that swell above major arteries. Either may burst on contact.

The one directly behind Mrs. Kelly's eyes is the most dangerous, but also the easiest to reach. That's first.

Ducker has managed to find and clip off one of the two deadly aneurisms. The next article begins with Ducker peering into the neurosurgery microscope in search of the second. The going is slow, dangerous.

Problems Five hours into the operation there is trouble and Ducker worries that his patient's heart has been slowed too many times. He decides not to continue. If she recovers, he says, he will try again.

If she survives. If. If.

"I'm not afraid to die," Mrs. Kelly had said. "I'm scared to death . . . but . . . I can't bear the pain. I wouldn't want to live like this much longer."

Her brain was too scarred. The operation, tolerable in a younger person, was too much. Already, where the monster's tentacles hang before the brainstem, the tissue swells, pinching off the source of oxygen.

Mrs. Kelly is dying.

The clock in the lounge, near where Dr. Ducker sits, says 1:40.

"It's hard even to tell what to do. We've been thinking about it for six weeks.

But, you know, there are certain things . . . that's just as far as you can go. I just don't know. . . ."

He lays the sandwich, the banana and the fig newtons on the table before him neatly, the way the scrub nurse laid out instruments.

"It was triple jeopardy," he says, finally, staring at his peanut butter sandwich the same way he stared at the X-rays. "It was triple jeopardy."

It is 1:43, and it's over.

Dr. Ducker bites, grimly, into the sandwich.

The monster won.

Franklin holds the reader in suspense until the jolting final sentences. The three sentences are short, quick—consistent with the abrupt end of Mrs. Kelly's life.

You might want to go back to our four rules for writing the feature and note in the margins of the sections from Franklin's pieces where he follows these guidelines.

The News Feature

The news feature usually has its origins in some news event. When Carl Hiassen of *The Miami Herald* dug into the court case involving a doctor and his millionaire wife, he came up with a tale of greed preying on loneliness. His story begins:

To Dr. Edward Gordon, love meant never having to say he was out of money.

Six years ago, the solicitous Miami Beach physician married a patient who was worth more than $8 million. Her name was Elizabeth Buffum, and she was a lonely alcoholic.

With Gordon, she stayed lonely and she often stayed drunk. She just barely stayed wealthy.

Today, as lawyers doggedly try to retrieve her scattered fortune from all over the globe, the former Mrs. Gordon lies in a Fort Lauderdale nursing home, permanently brain-damaged. Relatives say her life was destroyed by four ruinous years as the doctor's wife. They say it wasn't a marriage, it was a matrimonial Brink's job.

"Unbelievable," says one son, Peter Beaumont. "It's sort of a classic: elderly lady with lots of bucks heads down to Retirement City and gets fleeced by local doctor."

It began as a September love affair. He was 62, silver-haired and single, with a new medical practice in Florida. She was 60, a bit overweight and twice divorced, given to irascibility and depression. . . .

The lead is inviting. Nobody, every writer knows, ever tires of reading about love, money and violence.

The second and third paragraphs are like the coming attractions at a movie, or the come-on advertising of television.

The fourth paragraph drives home the theme: A woman ruined by her marriage. And in the fifth paragraph, a quote is used to sum up the theme. The sixth paragraph introduces us to the chronological narrative the writer will spin.

Feature Ideas

The advertisement read:

> **HEARTBROKEN** Anyone who purchased (at my Garage Sale last week) a small white canister with blue flowers, please call me. It contains remains of a dearly departed family member.

There's a story in that canister. How did it find its way into the garage? Who bought it? Was it returned? And if so, where will the dearly departed be placed now?

Changes make for good stories, especially those that come about over resistance. When Orthodox Jewish women in a Queens, N.Y., women's prayer group met to read from the Torah, they were told by a rabbinical group to disband. Prayer groups of women and reading from the Torah by women breach the boundaries of Jewish tradition, they were told. The differing roles of men and women in the Orthodox branch of Judaism made for a long feature.

Similar stories about the refusal of women to accept traditional roles have been written by feature writers.

Feature stories originate in many ways—through reading widely, gumshoeing around town, personal experience. Shopping in a supermarket, a reporter notices the stacks of items near the checkout counter and wonders:

> How important is impulse buying? How do merchants determine what goes on the bottom shelves, on the top shelves? How much do people spend on junk food? What is junk food anyway? Do students really spend a lot of money on chips, soda and beer?

And there the reporter's train of thought stops and abruptly shifts:

> Does anyone go to the kitchen faucet and drink water anymore? Or is everyone going to the fridge for a bottle or can?

James J. Malloy, *The Providence Journal*

Saying Goodbye to a Good Buddy

The story of the teen-ager's funeral begins with a lead-in paragraph: "Tommy DeGrafft, 15, is remembered as a good boy and an outstanding athlete who died because he was in the wrong place at the wrong time. A priest calls for an end to the anger and hatred that has given way to shootings in the past year." (The youth was killed in a drive-by shooting.) Then, reporter W. Zachary Malinowski begins his story from the funeral site, Pawtucket: Tears streamed down Wayne Tucker's face as he led the funeral procession down the center aisle at St. Teresa's Church yesterday. Behind Tucker stood eight teen-age pallbearers in black sweatshirts and loose-fitting jeans, bearing the silver casket holding their friend, Tommy DeGrafft, who died in a barrage of gunfire last weekend. In Tucker's hands was a basketball covered with the scrawled signatures of DeGrafft's former teammates. One said simply, "To Tommy from All of Us."

Ideas are everywhere. A letter writer to Ann Landers says that college students consume an average of 34 gallons of alcoholic beverages a year and quotes the chancellor of the University of Wisconsin as saying that the biggest problem on campus today is alcoholism. A reporter wonders:

What's happening on the local campus?

Be Alert, Aware

Just look around. Notice that group sitting in the cafeteria, those high school students? They are griping. About what? Listen in: His mother doesn't like his girlfriend: "She thinks I'm too young to be going steady. She thinks I should spend my time on school work. But me and my girl were meant for each other."

A young woman says to no one in particular, "I don't fit in, not even here. I don't think I look good enough. I don't like the way my body is. Everyone else is popular. Not me."

Another teen-ager says he just had some good news that has relieved him after a couple of weeks of stress: "I thought that my girlfriend was pregnant. Lost a lot of sleep, and weight. I just found out she isn't."

Death in a Dumpster

Read the newspaper closely, even the smallest items. It was a short, horrific story that caught Jules Loh's attention: A homeless drifter had sought a night's peace in a Dumpster. As the man slept, a garbage truck making its rounds picked up the Dumpster. . . . In a pocket of the mangled body was an army discharge paper with the name Gregory DeGregorio.

That was all Loh, an AP special correspondent, had to go on when he decided to investigate DeGregorio's short life. The story, when Loh finally finished his extensive reporting involving interviews around the country and a long session at the keyboard, ran more than 150 paragraphs. Yet many papers ran all of it, the story of a Vietnam veteran, a drunk, a petty criminal and a schizo-phrenic. It moved on AP's wires on Veterans Day with an editor's note that pointed out that "among the heroes are the homeless. . . . How could a society so proud of its safety nets so completely overlook one of its most helpless?"

The story, crammed with details, begins:

> Verlin Bell's routine began, as usual, in pitch darkness. His last stop, still an hour before sunup, was in the parking lot behind the Southern Paint Co. store on Seagrave Street.
>
> He nudged his big green garbage truck with practiced accuracy up to the Dumpster and slid its two steel lifters into sleeves on either side. He levered the Dumpster noisily up and over the cab, tilted its contents into the brightly lit truck bed, then lowered it back in place.
>
> As he backed away, he shoved the compactor blade in gear and glanced at the mirror.
>
> "I always check the mirror. I look through the window in back of the cab to make sure the hydraulic hoses are clear. This time . . . well, this time I saw the top half of a man. He was caught between the blade and the roof, hanging over the blade, facing me."

Detail Essential   Why so many details? Loh says, "The reader gains confidence because the writer knows so many specifics, knows I was there. I re-quired myself to be as specific as I could, and that required extra reporting. I wanted the reader to know an awful lot about this guy. All this detail gives the reader the sense of being able to believe everything."

Loh takes the reader back to the dead man's birth:

> He was born in Philadelphia and baptized 10 weeks later at Annunciation Church on South 10th Street, the spiritual anchor of a neighborhood where they still hear confessions in Italian. His parents, Frank and Mary DeGregorio, named the boy Gregory John. He was their only child.
>
> His father was a large, friendly, 35-year-old veteran of World War II, a tile setter by trade. Around the union hall they called him Big Frank. Mary was five years younger and according to friends as gregarious and optimistic as her husband. Both doted on their son.

To Vietnam:

> After six months in the field, on July 17, DeGregorio arrived on a stretcher at the 3rd Field Hospital near Saigon, bleeding from his stomach. A shrapnel wound. They patched it, leaving a jagged scar.
>
> But they did not send him back to his own infantry outfit. Instead they assigned him to a security unit in Saigon. There, by the only observation available, "DeGregorio sort of went berserk." Four days later, at a hospital in Japan, the diagnosis came down: chronic schizophrenia.

Key Interview   To a homeless shelter in St. Petersburg where Loh interviewed the man who ran it with his wife:

"Greg would come in the morning for coffee and doughnuts, maybe take a shower," Jerry Styles recalled. "He was never dirty. His clothes were not the best, secondhand but clean. He never looked run down or scuzzy or shaggy.

"But I knew he had mental problems. We feed about 80 men in the morning. They sit at the picnic tables out back or stand in groups, but Greg stayed apart. He sat by himself on a bench against the house as far as he could get from the others. He was totally quiet, just sat and stared. He was never loud or violent. In fact he was quite docile. He was not unfriendly, just indifferent. He didn't choose to mix."

Indifferent?

"That's what he was," said Styles, "indifferent."

Loh comments on this interview:

The reason the high school transcript gave for Gregory's dropping out was "indifference." It was a real stroke of luck—for me, anyhow—when Jerry Styles used the same word. So that the reader wouldn't miss that, I made Jerry repeat it by repeating it myself. Finding Jerry Styles and his wife, Camille, who ran the homeless shelter in St. Petersburg, turned out to be a godsend not just in reporting the story but writing it as well."

Loh wanted to end with the "two elements of Gregory's story. The first is the irony of one last mix-up by the record keepers":

Anyone who would care to visit the grave should be forewarned:

In the cemetery's alphabetical visitors' directory Gregory's name is not there. Like his missing Army record, it has been misfiled. Someone divided his last name, DeGregorio, into two words and you will find him listed under the G's. His grave is number 573 in section 104.

Then to the second element, the grave itself in a National Cemetery near Tampa:

He rests in a sweet and silent bivouac of the dead 10 ranks back from the smooth curve of a blacktop road and 15 files east of two live oak trees that shade his tombstone in the late afternoon.

His epitaph reads vertically in eight lines:

GREGORY

DeGREGORIO

PVT

US ARMY

VIETNAM

JULY 15 1947

NOV 12 1992

PURPLE HEART

AP-NY-1215EST

Steve Ueckert,
Houston Chronicle

Duck Talk

"You've got to tell those ducks what they want to hear," says Jimmy Goddard, a master duck caller Eric Lawlor interviewed for his piece about that fine art.

Lawlor let Goddard speak:

"Talk to them the way you'd talk to your lady. Say 'I love you honey, please come on back. . . .' You have to mean everything you say.

"Nothing alive spots a fraud faster than a duck. . . . You must be able to tell a duck's mood. I watch the bird. If he's happy, I'm happy. I tell him, 'If you'll just come on down here, the two of us can have a fine old time.' That's if he's happy. If he's lonesome, then you have to be lonesome. Ask him if he'd like to cry on your shoulder."

The last paragraph, Loh says, evokes "the one contribution he made in his life—his military service—by using soldierly words: 'bivouac,' 'ranks,' 'files.' And I allow myself a soothing alliteration—'sweet,' 'silent,' 'smooth'—in contrast with the turmoil of his life and the violence of his death."

Avoiding the Pitfalls

The following suggestions are from a dozen feature writers around the country:

- "Good stories come from good material. Good material comes from good reporting—and that is just as true if not more so with feature writing as with news writing," says Sheryl James of the *St. Petersburg Times.* As Tom Wolfe puts it, "Style can't carry a story if you haven't done the reporting."
- Single-source stories are not as good as multisource stories. No one cares to read about the author who talks about his life unless his personal account is supplemented by interviews with fellow writers, critics, his family, friends, even some readers.
- Do not have such a love affair with quotes that you fail to paraphrase routine material. Worse: Do not use quotes chronologically from the interview as a prop for failing to organize the piece. Good features can be written that are almost all quotes, but the quotes in these stories are usually rearranged.
- Know what you are going to say and the tone in which it is to be said before starting. Otherwise, the story will never get off the ground.
- Develop an enthusiasm for the piece. Features can be marred by an objectivity that keeps the reader at a distance. "The idea of a feature is to

involve the reader," a reporter said. "This is often taken to mean good craftsmanship through colorful writing. That's not enough. The writer needs to take a point of view, not simply to say, 'Look at this guy who was put into an institution for the retarded at the age of six, and when he was 18 some worker in the place saw that the kid wasn't retarded at all but had a learning disability.'

"The writer of this kind of piece has to be indignant at the tragedy. How can you be objective about this kind of inhumanity? A reader should be moved to indignation—not by the reporter's sounding off. We don't want that. But this kind of piece has to have the kind of facts and a story tone that gives a strong sense of human waste and bureaucratic inefficiency."

• Make sure the story has a good plot and is unusual enough to hold our interest. This means the central idea should have possibilities for drama, conflict, excitement, emotion.

• Don't tell us when you can show us people doing things.

• Avoid first-person stories. They are usually less interesting than you think. There are exceptions, of course:

I don't drive a Mercedes. I don't smoke Cuban cigars, or drink Dom Perignon (unless you're buying). I'm more likely to dine at Burger King than a four-, three-, or two-star restaurant. But I do have one thing higher rollers would envy. I own a racehorse.

No, I don't own the horse by myself. I have a few partners; there are an even dozen of us, actually. We're not the types you'd expect to be in this game. We're a locksmith, an investment banker, a journalist, the director of a rape crisis center, a retired businessman, two therapists, a prosecutor, three lawyers in private practice, and a law student. Four of us are women.

David Hechler's experience as a horse owner lasted a year or so. Gypsy Flame proved to be nice to look at but slow afoot.

Brights

The *bright* is to the feature what the short story is to the novel—a distillation, a tightly written gem that brightens the reader's day. The bright can be one paragraph or several. The following article is about as long as a bright should run:

POOLE, England — (AP) — "It was God who took out my tonsils," the little boy told his mother after his operation at Poole General Hospital.

"When I was taken into the big white room, there were two lady angels dressed in white. Then two men angels came in. Then God came in."

"How did you know it was God?" the mother asked.

"Well, one of the men angels looked down my throat and said, 'God, look at that child's tonsils.'

"Then God took a look and said, 'I'll take them out at once.' "

The conversation was reported by the hospital's staff newsletter.

The last paragraph is an anti-climax. It belongs in the running story, probably at the end of the second paragraph. Then the reader would be left with that wonderfully innocent quotation from the child.

The Long Story

Despite the pressure on news writers to compress, to boil down the already distilled, long stories are being written all the time, even online. Some events and situations are so complicated, only a lengthy treatment suffices. Or the situation may be so interesting that length is an asset. Readers and viewers and listeners will stay with it all the way through, fascinated by every twist and turn.

Broadcast journalists work on documentaries and print journalists are called upon to dig deeply into a subject for extended treatment.

Gang Rape

When Berkley Hudson learned that a UCLA student who had complained she was gang-raped by three fraternity members told the district attorney she did not want the case prosecuted and the DA dropped the case, Hudson realized that telling the story would take time, in the reporting and in the telling. Such incidents are increasing on college campuses, and the situations have a startling similarity.

A fraternity throws a party. There is binge drinking and pot smoking. A woman passes out and is the victim of sexual intercourse. The men claim the sex was consensual, the woman says she was in no condition to assent or deny. Prosecutors are in a quandary.

The scenario played out in Hudson's story for the Los Angeles *New Times.* Hudson begins his lengthy account this way:

> Sometime near dawn on June 1, a UCLA sorority sister sat in a Palm Springs hospital, bleeding from her vagina and weeping. The hospital summoned police, and the woman reluctantly told a cop that she'd been gang-raped by three fraternity men from her school.

Background   The story describes lawsuits brought by victims of campus rape, efforts by campus authorities to cope with the problem, the reaction of fraternities to growing numbers of such incidents, and the comments of "rape experts." Most, he writes, say "UCLA didn't take a tough enough stand following the Palm Springs party."

Hudson examines the police report and finds this by an investigating officer:

> It became apparent that she was worried that if she pursued the matter she would be looked down upon by the fraternity and sorority.

He ends the article with a visit to the ZBT house. One of the members answers Hudson's question about his feelings toward the woman: "The only thing I know is, my three friends were on the news. She wasn't. She ruined their lives for a while. I have no personal feeling toward her."

The Necessities

No reader, viewer or listener will stay with a long story or a documentary unless the reporting develops interesting material and the writing is a cut above that acceptable for shorter pieces. The long article also must be well-organized to carry the reader or viewer through the long journey.

John McPhee, whom many consider one of the best reporters writing, had a formula when he wrote long pieces for *Time* magazine. "Each had to have a beginning, a middle and an end, some kind of structure so that it would go somewhere and sit down when it got there," McPhee says.

Border Patrol For her story about the objections of local people to border checkpoints set up near Nogales, Ariz., Miriam Davidson begins her account with scene-setting:

A spring shower has just ended, and as the sun sets over southern Arizona, five United States Border Patrol agents work quickly to reopen a traffic checkpoint on the main highway north from Nogales. The checkpoint, which is taken down during bad weather to prevent accidents, has been closed for about an hour.

"The smugglers know when the checkpoint is down, and that's when they send their loads through," says agent Sonya Ealey, as her fellow agents place cones and signs on Interstate 19 to divert traffic up on to an overpass. "We always catch a bunch when we reopen after being closed for a while."

Then in her article for *The APF Reporter,* Davidson writes:

Sure enough, after a little more than an hour, eight illegal Mexican immigrants are standing by the roadside, waiting for a ride back to the border. All of them have been plucked from the passengers in taxis and shuttle vans that run between Nogales and Tucson, 60 miles north.

Despite the arrests, many people in the Nogales area are fed up with the activities of the Border Patrol. In her swing or transitional paragraph, Davidson takes us to the heart of her piece:

But a small, dejected group of aliens isn't all the agents catch this evening. They also catch flak from dozens of local residents who are angry about being stopped and asked for their citizenship. Some people roll their eyes or flash dirty looks. Others express their displeasure by speeding

© Jeffry D. Scott

Illegals

away from the checkpoint in a squeal of tires. Ealey and the other agents say drivers honk, yell, and curse at them. They have been called "Nazis."

To end her article, Davidson quotes both sides, the Border Patrol agreeing to move the portable checkpoint from place to place so that it is not a permanent point of contention, and the protesters who "say they intend to make sure the checkpoint keeps moving."

Time and Labor   The long story travels on the legs of the reporter. Hudson put in weeks reporting his gang-rape story.

"The first point about reporting a depth story," says Jeffrey Tannenbaum of *The Wall Street Journal,* "is that it usually requires a lot of work. For a profile of Rockefeller University, I conducted at least 20 interviews in person, and the typical interview lasted 90 minutes. I also did several more interviews by phone and read a great deal of background material."

Balance   The long story, he says, "is an interplay between the specific and the general." By "general" he means the key points or themes that the reporter has selected as the basis of the piece. A story about a breaking news event may have one or two points. The long story may have half a dozen. "Specific" refers to the details that illustrate and amplify the general points.

"For every generalization in the story," Tannenbaum continues, "there should be specific illustrations to buttress it. This means the reporter has to identify the themes and then must dig out the proof for them. The more specific and colorful the details that are used as proof or buttressing material, the more effectively the generalization or theme will be brought home to the reader."

© Jeffry D. Scott

'No Mas'

Protesters take their complaints to Border Patrol headquarters in Tucson.

Early Planning   Like all experienced journalists, Tannenbaum tries to sketch out his major ideas or key points as early as possible. This may come before any reporting is done, or soon after the reporting begins. A theme can come from a tip, an editor's assignment, the reporter's hunch. Or it may simply be the logical step following a series of developments on a beat.

"For each key point, I want two things: Good quotes stating the point and colorful illustrations, anecdotes, examples," he says. "I know exactly what I am looking for from each interview subject."

In the reporting, additional points often will develop, and these, too, must be buttressed with specific quotes, illustrations, data and anecdotes.

Organizing the Story

The major difficulty writers have with the long story is controlling its several major points, the half-dozen building blocks that must be arranged in logical and interesting order. It is not easy. McPhee says he goes "nuts trying to put it all in focus."

McPhee's first step is to structure the piece by typing up his notes and organizing them by subject or theme. He types the themes on index cards and tacks them to a bulletin board. Some reporters spread their cards on a flat surface. The story is plotted by arranging the cards in the order that seems best for the story.

By attaching the notes to the appropriate cards with the thematic material, the reporter has the story laid out in a form easy to scrutinize and to rearrange if necessary. This physical arrangement tends to give the reporter a sense of control over the story, and control of themes and reporting detail is the key to mastering the long piece. The long article must move logically and coherently from beginning to end, from idea to idea.

"Strange as it may seem to the beginner anxious to set words to paper, structuring the story challenges a reporter's creative talents as much as the writing. What's most absorbing is putting these stories together," says McPhee. "I want to know where I'm going from the start of the piece. It's my nature to want to know."

The following system is useful to organize the long article:

1. Identify all themes. Summarize in a sentence or two.
2. Place each summarized theme on a separate index card. Put the cards in the order that the themes will follow in the story.
3. Cut up notes by theme and place them next to theme cards. Reread and again arrange cards and notes in the order in which they will be written.
4. Look through the cards for the major theme that will serve as the lead or the integrating idea for the article. Write it on another card.

Writing Preparations

As the notes are lined up (Step 3), a reporter may discover a lack of adequate documentation or illustrative material to buttress some of the themes. More reporting will be necessary.

Reporters check their notes at this stage for the high-quality quotes and illustrations that can be placed high up in the various sections of the story. One might be used to begin the article if the piece lends itself to a delayed lead. Some reporters use a colored pencil or pen to mark these high-quality quotes, anecdotes and incidents to call them out for use.

Caution: Resist the temptation to use a dramatic quote or telling incident simply because it is attention getting. The material must illustrate the theme it accompanies. If the fit is loose, put the example with a more appropriate theme or toss it out—however much work went into digging it up, however exciting the material.

Remember: Keep clearly in mind or in view the major theme for the piece (Step 4). Toss out any material that is irrelevant to this integrating idea.

The Magazine-Story Formula

The most common problem that Art Carey, associate editor of *The Philadelphia Inquirer Magazine*, finds with long stories is poor organization. "So many writers, it seems, sit down with no plan, no idea of how to arrange the mass of information they've assembled in an understandable and engaging way."

He says that over the years the magazine has developed "a reliable magazine-story formula." This is it:

- A scene-setter lead that introduces the story's protagonist in a colorful situation that seems to epitomize his or her character or the quest, adventure or trend in which the protagonist is involved.
- A "nut" section or "hoohah" that explicitly states the premise of the story, outlines the major points and sells the story by tempting readers with some of the most engaging quotes, tidbits of information and previews of coming attractions.

  This section should also tell readers why the story is so important, or new or different. There should be enough fanfare about the story's significance to convince readers that it's well worth the investment of the next 20 minutes of their lives.
- A background section that explains how the main character got to be the way he or she is or how a certain situation or controversy evolved.
- Several sections dealing in detail, and in an orderly progression, with the meat of the story and the themes heralded earlier.
- A concluding "kicker" section that packs some dramatic wallop, wraps everything up in a neat bow, tells the reader what it all means and perhaps leaves the reader with something profound to ponder.

Changing Directions

Once the story is organized, do not assume that the structure cannot be changed. If the piece does not seem to be flowing properly, shift some of the elements around.

Some of the other problems that come up are:

• A theme has too much material to organize: Divide it into subthemes that can be handled more easily. Consider dropping, or at least drastically subordinating, some themes.

• A theme is too minor to be worth the space being given it: Blend it into another theme or discard it.

• The transition from one theme to another is awkward: To go from one theme to another smoothly, reorder the themes so that the linkage is more natural.

• A long block of background material does not move; it impedes the flow of the article: Break up this background, history, explanatory material and blend sections into the narrative.

A Television Documentary

Everyone who writes for a living goes through the anxieties of cutting back, of discarding quotes, of tossing out details that get in the way of the theme and that impede the flow of the story. But this cannot be done until the theme is clearly identified. Let us watch the producer of a television documentary as he tries to focus on a theme for his subject—the decline of many of the country's older cities—and then makes changes in his script.

The deterioration of the inner city has had the attention of planners, politicians and journalists since the 1950s. If the city is the heart and brain of civilization, then the troubles afflicting the city cores of Denver, Detroit, Cleveland, Philadelphia, Boston, Baltimore, St. Louis, Los Angeles, New York and dozens of others threaten a way of life—cultural, commercial, educational, religious. For in the heart of the cities are the opera houses and philharmonic halls, the factories and the offices, the schools, and the temples and the cathedrals. The city gives a center to modern life.

To make journalism out of the tribulations of the large city is no easy task. The decline is the result of complex social, political and economic forces. Reporters with a national audience cannot write about all the cities in trouble. They must make one or two illustrate the plight of the many. They must draw common elements from the tangled problems of many cities and then find a city that symbolizes most of these elements.

The Racial Factor

Howard Weinberg, a producer of "Bill Moyers' Journal," decided to look at the problems of the inner cities, and he cast about for some central themes and a city to symbolize them. Weinberg first defined the scope and limits of his piece. He then settled on a point of view. His idea was to show the forces, especially racism, at work in causing neighborhood deterioration.

"I went to Chicago," Weinberg says. "My associate and I spent a week there, interviewing realtors, mortgage bankers, open housing leaders, community leaders, journalists, government officials and others on the south, west, north sides of Chicago."

When he returned to New York he felt frustrated. He had no idea how he would tell such a complicated story in half an hour. Tentatively, he decided to use the neighborhood of Austin on the West Side where black and white community groups had organized to preserve and improve their neighborhood. Also, one organizer, Gale Cincotta, lived in Austin, and Weinberg wanted to have a person as a focus for the program.

"In discussions with Bill Moyers, I was forced to rethink and refine my outline," he says. In looking back at his original outline, Weinberg found he had written, "It is beginning to be understood in communities of the inner cities that deterioration is not an accident, it is the inevitable result of a lack of faith. Expect deterioration—and you'll get it."

Redlining

This idea of a self-fulfilling prophecy kept coming back to Weinberg, and he continued to do more reporting. Gradually, a theme and a strong point of view emerged. "It became clearer that 'redlining' was the story I wanted to tell, not the FHA abuses, not the efforts to relocate blacks in the suburbs or to 'stabilize' a threatened neighborhood."

Redlining takes its name from the red circles that banks and other lending agencies reportedly draw on maps around certain neighborhoods. The banks decide that people in these neighborhoods will not be given mortgage money because the banks consider the neighborhoods to be deteriorating. The practice makes it difficult for residents to improve their homes or for buyers to move into the neighborhood. Further deterioration results.

Weinberg was struck by the material he turned up in his reporting. "A savings and loan association was licensed to serve a neighborhood—and clearly, it was not doing that when it openly admitted that it received 80 percent of its deposits from its neighborhood and reinvested 20 percent in its neighborhood," Weinberg says.

Weinberg visualized the booming suburbs—which the savings of inner-city residents were helping to build—and the deteriorating inner city. This would make for dramatic pictures.

He decided to shift the main focus from Austin to Rogers Park, which was beginning to go the way of Austin. Here is how the script of "This Neighborhood Is Obsolete" begins:

BILL MOYERS: The skyline of Chicago thrusts a handsome profile above the shores of Lake Michigan, suggesting the serene self-assurance of a city and its architecture, its wealth and its power and its tolerance for new ideas in urban living. But opulent skylines point up and away from the reality in their shadows. And in Chicago, as in every large American city, the grand vista is misleading.

Out beyond the soaring, secular temples of commerce, before you reach the shopping centers of suburbia, the future of Chicago is being decided every day in less spectacular surroundings: in neighborhoods where drugstores and delicatessens, taverns, laundromats, barbershops, and small churches on treelined corners express a lifestyle in danger of extinction.

For the way the economic game is played these days, these neighborhoods hardly have a chance. There's a profit in moving people out and hang the human cost.

In the next half hour, we'll look at two Chicago neighborhoods where the neighbors are fighting back.

I'm Bill Moyers.

This neighborhood is obsolete.

The people who live here don't think so, but some of the banks and savings and loan associations do. They stopped lending money because they believe the community's deteriorating and the risk is too great. But without money to improve people's homes or to give them a chance to buy another, the decay speeds up and the fear becomes a self-fulfilling prophecy.

In this and similar neighborhoods in Chicago, people accuse the savings and loan associations and the banks of redlining. Redlining means an entire geographic area can be declared unsuitable for conventional loans and mortgages. A redline is, in effect, drawn like a noose around a neighborhood until for want of good housing the working and middle classes are driven to the suburbs and the neighborhood is left to the very poor.

A side effect of redlining is something called disinvestment. You probably haven't heard of that term before. I hadn't until I came here. Disinvestment is a process of collecting deposits in one neighborhood and investing them somewhere else. The lending agents say it's necessary to spread the risk, but it leaves a neighborhood like this short of capital and hope. Gasping for its very life.

The people who could afford to, move on. And that's what the savings and loan associations would like to do. After they've helped to build up the suburbs and make them affluent and attractive, they want to move there, too, or at least to open a suburban branch. Only then does an old neighborhood like this discover where its money has gone, but by then it's too late.

The Results   Like much good journalism, the documentary and the campaigns of local stations and newspapers had results. The month after the Moyers documentary, the Illinois Savings and Loan Commissioner issued a regulation against redlining that prohibits savings and loan associations from refusing to lend money in a neighborhood because of its age or changing character. The following year, Congress passed two pieces of legislation to end redlining by banks.

Notice that Weinberg had to reduce his ideas to the dimension of his program. Like the writer of a 300-word story or a 30-second news item, he had to focus on a single theme and toss out all extraneous material. The journalist never escapes the chore of boiling down material, of eliminating anything not related to the theme.

That basic theme can always be expressed in a simple sentence or two. David Belasco, the American theatrical producer, once remarked, "If you can't write your idea on the back of my calling card, you don't have a clear idea."

The Series

Some subjects are too broad, too deep, too complex for even the long story. Faced with such a problem, the reporter finds that the series of articles is the way out. When Sam Roe of *The Blade* decided to examine the decline in Great Lakes shipping, he knew that he could not handle the topic in a single article. Only a series would do the job.

Roe's task was to show how the collapse of the steel industry struck lake shipping with devastating effect. Most of the ships served U.S. steel firms, carrying iron ore to the giant plants. Toledo's port on Lake Erie handled 43.8 million tons of cargo in 1966. Two decades later, it handled 17.9 tons.

"To capture and hold a reader's attention throughout a series is no easy task," Roe says. "That's why it is important to have stories with action, particularly in the first installment." Roe's first part in his four-part series begins with a delayed lead:

ABOARD THE AMERICAN REPUBLIC—"Damn! She's swinging too wide."

Capt. Robert Tretter cuts the throttle, curses the current, and prays that the *American Republic,* a freighter longer than two football fields, can negotiate one final hairpin bend on the Cuyahoga River. A strong current is denying her a lefthand turn and is pushing her toward a concrete embankment.

"You got 12 feet over here," says wheelsman John Norton. "She'd better not get closer."

The men on the bridge are as tense as sailors aboard a battleship in combat. For the past two hours, the *Republic,* carrying 21,000 tons of iron ore from Lorain, has inched her way down the narrow river toward Cleveland's inner docks.

Just what does this have to do with his theme, the decline of Great Lakes shipping? In a deft maneuver, the journalistic equivalent of Capt. Tretter's handling of his freighter, Roe sets his story in the right direction:

Now, just when it appears the *Republic*'s port side will ram the embankment, the current lets her go. . . .

This time, the *American Republic* prevailed.

But ahead of her lies a far more formidable obstacle, one that her crew and all others in the shipping industry fear they can't beat: the relentless decline of Great Lakes shipping.

Numbers tell the story. This year there were only . . .

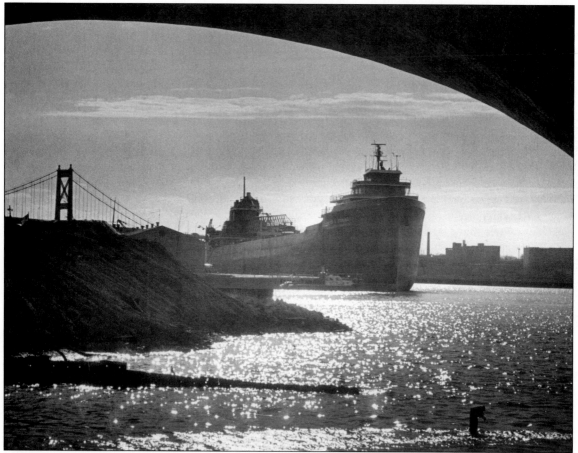

Tom O'Reilly, *The Blade*

A Port's Relentless Decline

As the steel industry collapsed, Great Lakes shipping went into decline. For the main story in his series on the slump in shipping, Sam Roe of *The Blade* went aboard a freighter and accompanied the crew on its voyage.

"This lead is more captivating, I thought, than diving into the statistics," Roe says.

Roe says he finds it useful to "walk the reader through" main stories. "For example, the main Great Lakes story was reported and written from the vantage point of a single ship on a single voyage.

"A cook in the mess talking about tough times allowed me to cite unemployment figures. Two decks below, in the cargo holds, an engineer pointing out new equipment allowed me to discuss technological changes in the industry. And so on. The story never really had to move off the ship."

Outlining

Roe says an outline ensures a successful series. As soon as he has in mind a clear picture of what he wants to say, the outline is written. Too soon and the reporter cannot single out what is significant. Too late and the reporter will waste time gathering information irrelevant to the theme.

The outline helps the reporter see holes in the reporting before writing begins. It also has a practical use. "A solid, detailed outline helps a reporter sell a series to editors," Roe says. Editors are reluctant to give the OK to a reporter who has in hand only an idea and some scattered notes. Series require a large amount of space, and editors won't provide it unless they have some assurance of the probability of a successful series.

Roe suggests writing nut grafs, the paragraphs that contain the basic idea, for each story. "Keep in mind when writing them: Why is this story significant? What am I trying to say?"

Organizing and Writing

Outline in hand, the reporter then divides his or her notes in the appropriate sections, according to the outline.

"I read through all the notes on a particular story," Roe says. "I think along the way: Does this information belong in this story? Is more reporting needed?"

To organize each piece, Roe uses color markers, red for all the material that pertains to the lead, green for statistical information and so on. This makes it possible to link similar material quickly. Items that do not fit his pattern are moved to another story or scrapped.

"This process requires a lot of room," he says. He spreads his notes out. "Take time to see everything you've collected," he advises.

Roe's series, "Struggling to Stay Afloat," won first place in an AP contest for enterprise reporting among newspapers with circulation greater than 75,000.

Tecumseh Street

For his two-part series on children living amid poverty, violence and parental neglect—an increasingly grim prospect for youngsters growing up in large cities—Roe focused on a single street in Toledo. "At first glance," he says, "it seemed to be a lifestyle piece. But more than anything it was a records-search project. I spent several weeks gathering material from documents—juvenile court and police records and census tract records."

Many of the records were not computerized and he had to go through thousands of individual cards to carry out his idea that developed from a figure he had seen: Each year, 400 local youngsters are sent off to state prisons, more than one a day.

Perhaps, he reasoned, he could find a street from which an unusual number of youngsters graduate to state prison. He found one, Tecumseh Street, which in 18 months sent off eight youngsters. Roe looked at the general picture, and then he zeroed in on particulars.

The general:

- Four of five children are born out of wedlock.
- Median income is $10,856, and in one section of the 1 1/2 mile street, the income is $4,448.
- The street is one of the most crime-ridden in Toledo.

Case Studies   For the particulars, he looked at the eight youngsters who went off to prison: Five grew up without fathers and four of them "saw one of their parents sent to prison," Roe said. He tracked down families to show that the problems ran through five generations—poverty, school dropouts, teen-age pregnancies.

Here is how his first piece began:

There, in that house, lives a family so poor that the 11-year-old daughter once was arrested for shoplifting socks and underwear. A few years later she was arrested again, this time for selling her body.

Down the street lives a boy who at age 14 was recruited by drug dealers to traffic cocaine. Now he's 17 and doing time at a state youth prison.

Further down lives a boy who says the only time he sees his mother is when she comes into the neighborhood to buy drugs. He's been arrested for receiving stolen property, robbery, and the rape of a 13-year-old girl.

Welcome to Tecumseh Street, perhaps the most difficult place to grow up in Toledo.

"It's rough," says 17-year-old Tecumseh resident Mandrell Walker. "And it's at its roughest point."

Mandrell is awaiting trial on charges that he shot a man in the back of the head.

It's just one street. But this one street in the Central City owns burdensome numbers:

▲ Court records show that in the last 18 months, officials have sent eight children living on Tecumseh to state juvenile prisons—the most from any street in Toledo.

▲ Another seven kids are suspected of being members of gangs such as the Bloods, the Buck Street Gangsters, and the Avondale Posse.

▲ And over the last five years, the street has seen a dozen child-abuse and child-endangering cases.

On top of that, the street lies in one of the poorest, most crime-ridden neighborhoods in town.

"It almost seems that some kids are doomed before they even start," says Keith Zeisloft, assistant administrator of the Lucas County Juvenile Court.

Alan Detrich, *The Blade*

Real-Life Games

Tecumseh Street children share their street with drug dealers and the customers of the dealers. The youngsters often witness drug busts. Here, 7-year-old Tracy ties up his 5-year-old sister Rebecca in a game of drug dealer. He is playing the arresting officer, his sister the arrested dealer. Luckey, 9, is a witness for the arresting officer. Tracy says that across the street from their play area is a real drug house.

Neglect   For his second piece, Roe focused on a young man awaiting trial for aggravated robbery, a youth who "has been arrested 15 times, suspended from school 14 times, detained at the juvenile jail six times and sent to state youth prisons twice." Roe continues:

Sounds like a rotten kid.

But what is remarkable is that he is not worse.

Court records show he has only seen his father three times in his life, and his mother is an admitted crack addict who abandoned him when he was 7.

Before she did, the boy says, she and her boyfriends—men he never really knew—put welts on his legs by whipping him with an extension cord.

And the mother—now serving 3 to 15 years in a Cleveland prison for burglary—tells Lucas County Juvenile

Judge James Ray in a recent letter that two men once physically abused her son in her apartment building.

"I was there," she writes, "but I was so drunk I didn't hear my son's screams."

There may be problem kids on Tecumseh Street, but often the problem is the parents.

"It's terrible," Judge Ray says. "Actually, I'm amazed at the number of kids who survive those situations."

The Aftermath

Predictably, there was an angry reaction. "Many Tecumseh Street residents were furious, believing their street had been unfairly singled out," Roe said. A petition with 180 signatures was sent to *The Blade* demanding that the story be redone and that Roe be banned from any future stories about the area. The editors refused, and residents responded by planning a march on the newspaper.

"They enlisted a civil rights leader to help. But he was acquainted with my previous work. In fact, his group had given me an award several months earlier for a series on police corruption. He urged the residents to attack the problem, not the messenger." They did.

They met with the mayor, city manager, police chief. And soon after, the police stepped up patrols, the city cleaned alleys and fixed street lamps. City officials vowed to fight drug dealers and gang members, and residents extended their Block Watch program.

Alan Detrich, *The Blade*

Problem Parents = Problem Kids

"When your parents don't care about you, you don't care about yourself," says this young man, a product of Tecumseh Street, awaiting trial on a robbery charge. He has been arrested 15 times.

Series: Reading by 9

"Millions of students read poorly, not because they can't learn, but because schools aren't teaching them properly. The good news: The problem can be fixed by proven methods."

The problem. The solution.

This was the basis of a large-scale investigation that *The Sun* in Baltimore undertook to see why so many youngsters do not learn to read and how the situation can be changed. Eight reporters were assigned to the project that was titled "Reading by 9."

The first installment sets the high stakes: "Research shows that most children who haven't learned to read properly by third grade, usually age 9, are likely to be poor readers their whole lives. With that failure often comes a lifetime of disappointment and privation—and burdens for society."

Few Readers in the City

An examination of Baltimore city schools showed that whereas one of three third-grade students statewide read at a satisfactory level, and in some counties one of two, only one of nine of the third-graders in city schools read satisfactorily on the state School Performance Assessment Program test. In some city schools, the reading test showed only one or two children in a class could read.

The *Sun* reporters concluded that the solution lay in abandoning the "whole language" teaching method and returning to phonics and in better teacher training. Reaching that conclusion was not easy for the reporters, said Maryland editor Robert Benjamin. Reporters had to "pierce the confusion, jargon and imprecision that clouds the issue of reading instruction. The reporters worked very hard at clear-headed analysis and lucid writing."

Readers React   Benjamin says more than 600 *Sun* readers called the newspaper about the series. The newspaper's Internet site received 15,000 to 20,000 hits each of the days the series ran.

"I thought it would be an eyes-glaze-over series," said Mike Bowler, veteran education writer who worked on the series. "But we were overwhelmed with feedback. Reading, it turns out, is heavily laden with emotion. People cried on the phone. I heard it myself."

Schools React   The response of the school system was to pay greater attention to the phonics method of teaching reading, and there were curricular changes in teacher training.

The series, which won the Sigma Delta Chi Public Service Award, was the first of a planned five-year examination of education. "We are continuing to address the issues raised in the two initial series with aggressive reporting," Benjamin said.

A Serial

Most series consist of long individual pieces. Roy Peter Clark, a longtime writing coach at the Poynter Institute for Media Studies, had an idea for a different approach, and in his series "Three Little Words" for the *St. Petersburg Times* he wrote 29 short pieces—chapters, he calls them—of about 1,000 words each. The story is about a family's struggle with AIDS.

Clark says the idea originated in his childhood reading of the Flash Gordon and Hardy Boys stories that ran in parts. He took the concept, he says, "and squeezed it tighter." He made his chapters "a five-minute read. A cup of coffee. Your breakfast serial."

"Three Little Words" was followed by another serial, this one more personal, "Sadie's Ring: A Journey of the Spirit," that describes Clark's experience as a young Catholic man exploring his Jewish roots. His self-discovery began, as did the first of the 11 chapters in this serial, this way:

> One cold and sunny morning, back in
> 1958, a tall lady with steel-gray hair came
> out of Sunday Mass, spat at my mother
> and called her "that Jew."

Clark, parochial school student and altar boy, was confused. "I was almost sure we were Catholic, not Jewish," the first part goes on.

The Form

Each chapter, says Clark, focuses on one important scene or key issue. "The dead limbs are pruned. The chapters have a stand-alone quality. And yet, when possible, they end with a cliffhanger. It's one of the oldest tricks in the book: 'To be continued. . . .' "

People, he says, "will come back day after day to follow a good story—if you give them a reason." He found that when people left town they continued to follow Sadie's Ring on the website.

Clark found objections to his serial form. "I heard from inside and outside the newsroom that the chapters were too short, the series too long, that the story of 'Three Little Words' was not news.

"I agree that this form invites the writer and reader to bend traditional definitions of news, but not in a negative sense. In the way that a musician bends a note to achieve a certain sound."

A Student Series

The days when cotton was king are long gone, but King Cotton's legacy lingers in the Alabama Black Belt. In this region, a series in *The Mobile Register* points out, the plantation way of life survives in several ways. As the editor Stan Tiner states in his introductory article for the *Register*'s Special Report, "Social institutions are crumbling, the economy is stagnant, and many of the Black Belt's brightest are fleeing to more promising destinations."

Tiner also describes the Report as a "journalistic landmark." The reason: The 20 pages are the work of journalism students from the University of Alabama. Under the direction of their instructor H. Bailey Thomson, the students spent six months in the field reporting and photographing people and places. They found "an agrarian mindset, class and racial divisions, a reverence for tradition."

A Travelogue

Daniel Cusick takes the reader into some of the area's small towns:

Michael Palmer

A Past Recalled

Once, acre on acre blossomed white with cotton. Today, this cotton plant on a Demopolis street corner is a reminder of time past.

If you've heard anything about the Alabama Black Belt lately, chances are that the news wasn't especially good or uplifting.

Top stories from the region tend to be disheartening: church burnings, poverty, joblessness, voter fraud, government bankruptcy.

Given the Black Belt's banner events—the ones important enough to make headlines in the big newspapers—it's easy to accept the conventional wisdom about the place.

The Black Belt, so the wisdom goes, is Alabama's poor and undernourished stepchild, a region so backward that it's easier to ignore the place than to care about it. While the rest of Alabama grows healthier, the wisdom continues, building high-tech automobile factories and rocket plants, the Black Belt weakens, remaining doggedly rural and fiercely resistant to change. Some even say the region is the antithesis of progress.

As you drive through the Black Belt's wide-open spaces, it's hard not to feel sadness, like you might feel about some acquaintance who has a terminal illness. . . .

Cusick stops in the town of Eutaw. He chats with Greene County Sheriff George Hall who is "cooking up a batch of cane syrup in his backyard off Gainesville Road. He'd be happy to sell you a take-home jar, but he's just as likely to give you a sample for the asking. That's the Black Belt way, where graciousness runs slow and steady like pure cane syrup."

Then to the county weekly newspaper:

Over at the offices of The Greene County Democrat, editor and co-publisher Carol Zippert can give you the week's news. There's a lot more in this weekly newspaper than social calendars and a roll of out-of-town visitors. Zippert's is a strong and passionate voice for Greene County. A Louisianan by birth, she came to the Black Belt in the 1970s with political and social reform on her mind. She's still fighting to make it happen. And don't be surprised if Zippert asks you to wrestle with Greene County's problems. She wants more than anything to get black folks and white folks talking to each other. Fresh ideas, she says, are something in short supply in Greene County.

Long-Time Friends

In Newbern, H.B. Phillips, left, and his buddy Hersey Bryant pose for photographer Michael Palmer.

Investigative Series

Some series are so complex that their writers have trouble putting the material in focus, an essential step before a lead can be written.

When Donald Barlett and James Steele investigated a new federal tax law that exempted many rich individuals and a number of large corporations, they found they had seven themes, one for each piece in the series. They then started to write. But as they moved along they had trouble distilling some of the pieces into leads.

Rather than stop their writing, they continued with the series. They would write the leads later.

Their editor, Steve Lovelady, was looking over the third of the articles, soon to appear in *The Philadelphia Inquirer.*

"What does this mean to the average reader?" he asked himself. And he answered—"That you'll never get a break"—unlike the well-connected taxpayers the reporters had uncovered.

Lovelady showed Barlett what he had scribbled on an envelope, and Barlett said, "Forget part three, this is now part one."

Barlett and Steele worked it over, polished it. Here is the lead for the series they came up with:

Imagine, if you will, that you are a tall, bald father of three living in a Northeast Philadelphia row house and selling aluminum siding door-to-door for a living. Imagine that you go to your congressman and ask him to insert a provision in the federal tax code that exempts tall, bald fathers of three from paying taxes on income from door-to-door sales. Imagine further that your congressman cooperates, writes that exemption and inserts it into pending legislation. And that Congress then actually passes it into law. Lots of luck.

Reaching into the Past for a Feature

Features based on historical material in libraries and letters make for good reading, especially if there are interesting photographs to accompany the article. This photograph of a homestead in Wyoming reveals a lot about the roles of men and women on the frontier. The head of the household is seated comfortably at the center, and around him the women are shown with the tools of their work. One poses with her spinning wheel, and grandma is shown knitting. To the man's left a young woman poses with the butter churn, and to her left a mother fans a child in her lap.

Long. Very long. The reader is directly addressed twice in the first few words. But it works. The series had an enormous readership, and the newspaper was swamped with requests for copies.

Summing Up

The feature, long story and series join the direct or hard news story as the staples of journalistic writing. Despite criticism of the longer forms, if they are interesting, clear, well-organized and written with vigor they are read. The *Inquirer*'s lengthy tax series was read. Avidly. The *Oregonian* in Portland picked it up from the Knight-Ridder News Service. John Harvey, the *Oregonian*'s news editor, said:

> Your series touched off the greatest response of any series I have ever run in the *Oregonian*. Our readers were outraged. Were a certain senator on the ballot this year I doubt he could be reelected. Congratulations on a first-class job of reporting.

The book from the series became a big seller.

Further Reading

Buchwald, Art. *You Can Fool All of the People All the Time.* New York: Putnam, 1985.

Halberstam, David. *The Powers That Be.* New York: Knopf, 1979.

Mitchell, Joseph. *McSorley's Wonderful Saloon.* New York: Grosset & Dunlap, 1943.

Moffitt, Donald, ed. *The American Character: Views of America from* The Wall Street Journal. New York: George Brogiller, 1983.

Swanberg, W. A. *Citizen Hearst.* New York: Scribner, 1961.

Swanberg, W. A. *Pulitzer.* New York: Scribner, 1967.

Note: Ben Hecht's book of the rough-and-tumble Chicago journalism period, *Gaily, Gaily,* is no longer in print, but copies can be found in libraries. It was published by Doubleday in 1963. Also hard to locate is *The Front Page,* a play about the same period written by Hecht and Charles MacArthur.

Broadcast Newswriting

Ken Klotzbach,
Argus Leader

**Tornado strikes . . . saturation
coverage.**

Preview

Broadcast stories are written to be easily understood. Radio and television writers should:

- Use everyday language.
- Write short sentences.
- Limit every sentence to one idea.
- Use the present tense whenever appropriate.
- Usually confine their stories to one major theme.

In addition to writing local stories, broadcast writers rewrite into broadcast form the stories they obtain from news wires. The material is compressed, sentences are shortened and tenses are changed.

Television journalists must cope with a technology that emphasizes the image. What is written and how it is written often depends on the available video.

Broadcast news is written to be read aloud by newscasters and to be heard or seen by listeners or viewers. Stories are written according to rules different from those for print journalism.

Watch the evening news, stopwatch in hand. Most of the *tell* stories on television—brief items read by an anchor without tape—run two to five sentences for 10 to 30 seconds. Few broadcast stories run more than 90 seconds. If all the news on a half-hour newscast were to be printed, it would not fill two-thirds of a page of a standard-size newspaper.

Broadcast news serves a purpose different from that of the newspaper. Its intent is to provide the public with basic information quickly and succinctly. The broadcast writer's job is to get the story idea across without detail. To communicate events in such short bursts to an audience that cannot read or hear the material again, the broadcast journalist follows a special set of guidelines.

Like the jockey or the weight watcher who thinks twice about every slice of bread, the broadcast journalist examines every word and idea. Too many words and the story may squeeze out another item. Too many ideas and the listener or viewer may be confused.

Broadcast newswriters set their writing rhythm to a series of rules: Keep it tight. Write simple sentences. One idea to a sentence. When attribution is necessary, begin the sentence with it.

An Early Guide

When the United Press hired reporters they were handed a green booklet about the size of a small greeting card. It was titled *United Press Radio News Style Book* and was written by Phil Newsom, the UP Radio News Manager.

Though more than 50 years old, and written before the days of television, Newsom's advice holds up today. Here are some of Newsom's guidelines:

To write effectively for radio you must unlearn the prose writer's rules about sentence structure. Disregard such forms as dependent clauses and balanced sentences. You can even forget the first grammatical rule you ever learned—that a sentence must have a subject and a verb.

Some of radio's most effective sentences are not complete sentences at all. They are descriptive phrases. They save a lot of words and go over very smoothly on the air.

Ordinarily, short sentences are the best for radio. But the real test is whether they can be read aloud, whether the announcer finally can arrive at the end without gasping for breath.

Don't try to tell too much in your opening sentence. The radio listener requires a little time to get adjusted after each story. We call it "warming up the listener."

Never lead into a story with a question. The similarity between such leads and commercials is apt to be confusing.

There has always been a rule in radio news reporting against hanging phrases, since they break up the flow of thought. For example, a newspaper lead might say:

"Fourteen persons were killed today in an explosion at King's Powder Mill, state police announced."

The radio news report would say:

"State Police announce that 14 persons have been killed in an explosion at the King's Powder Mill."

These days we would not have the state police "announce" the 14 deaths. If it's an established fact, we would not even have to attribute the deaths.

Newsome suggests that broadcast writers study their notes for the "most interest-compelling angle" and use it for the lead. He goes on to advise writers to emphasize the aspects of the event that affect people personally. Stories written with people in mind hold their attention, he says.

Rewriting the Wires

Most of radio's nonlocal news is rewritten from the news wires. The wire stories are condensed and simplified. On television, most of the brief items—the *tell* stories—are also taken from the wires and rewritten. Let's see how this is done.

News Wire

SAN FRANCISCO (AP) — Leaders of the University of California on Thursday voted to drop race-based admissions following a tumultuous meeting in which Jesse Jackson and other demonstrators drove the panel from its meeting room.

The 14–10 decision by the UC Board of Regents was a major victory for those working to roll back affirmative action programs around the nation, including Republican Gov. Pete Wilson, who has made that fight the key plank of his presidential campaign.

"It means the beginning of the end of racial preferences," said Wilson, who grabbed the national spotlight from his vantage point as president of the regents. "We believe that students at the University of California should achieve distinction without the use of the kind of preferences that have been in place."

Jackson said after the vote, "California casts either a long shadow or a long sunbeam. This is a long shadow. July 20 will live a long time in California history."

(Ten more paragraphs follow.)

Radio Wire

[San Francisco] — The University of California Board of Regents voted tonight to end race-based preferences in school admissions.

The vote came soon after demonstrators interrupted the regents' meeting, singing "We Shall Overcome." The regents were forced to another room to vote on the admissions policy.

Earlier tonight, the regents voted to eliminate the school's affirmative action-based policies on the hiring of faculty and contractors.

Let's watch Mervin Block rewrite a wire story for a 20-second tell story for network television news. Here is the wire copy Block had before him:

News Wire

Yorba Linda, Calif [AP] — Construction of the long-delayed Richard M. Nixon presidential library and museum will require the demolition of the home of a 93-year-old widow who doesn't want to move, officials say.

"I love my house. I don't want them to take it from me," said Edith Eichler, who knew Nixon as a boy here and supported him for president.

"Why should I have to move into a more crowded, dinky retirement place away from my family and friends? Do you think Richard Nixon would want his mother to move?"

Yorba Linda, Nixon's birthplace 30 miles southeast of Los Angeles, was chosen for the $25 million library last month after a nine-year search. Years of delays by San Clemente city officials forced Nixon to give up building the library in that coastal community, where he kept the western White House during his presidency.

At a news conference Monday night, city officials said they would appraise Eichler's one-story, wood-frame cottage within a month and make her an offer.

Eichler, a former schoolteacher who has lived in the house for 65 years, will be the only person displaced by the museum.

Eichler said she knew the Nixon family well.

"Richard was a nice enough little boy, always running around like any other kid. Who would believe he would become a president?

"And who would ever imagine they'd want to build this big library for him right in my own back yard?" she asked.

Here is Block's story:

Broadcast Version

They're putting up a library for former President Nixon near Los Angeles, but they say they first have to tear down the home of a 93-year-old widow. She says she loves her home and does not want to move. Officials of the city of Yorba Linda say they'll appraise her wood-frame cottage and make her an offer. The woman says she knew Nixon as a boy and supported him for president.

Here is how Block, now a broadcast writing coach, thought the story through:

I tell news writers, "Avoid premature pronouns." Yet I started my script with "they." Why? Although I refrain from starting a story with a pronoun, I know that in conversation we often start tidbits with "they." F'rinstance: "They say onions and garlic are good for you—but not for your companions."

I certainly don't want to start with a yawner: "Officials in Yorba Linda, California. . . ." In the first sentence, I want to mention *Nixon, library* and *L.A.,* but I don't see how I can sensibly start with any of them. So I turn to our old friend "they." I make it clear that it's "they" who say the home must be torn down.

I don't use the widow's name because it doesn't mean anything outside Yorba Linda. I defer mentioning the name of the town, because it's not widely known. I save words wherever I can: I don't call it a *presidential* library; what other kind would they put up for a former president? And I'm just as stingy with facts: I don't mention San Clemente, the western White House, the widow's background and other details in the wire copy.

"Newsbreak"

"Newsbreak" runs on the CBS television network several times a day. In less than a minute, several major stories are read. One day, Block compressed seven wire stories into 50 seconds. Here are three items from the script and his explanation of how he wrote them:

Script	Explanation
A former employee of the Westchester Stauffer's Inn, near New York City, was arrested today and charged with setting the fire that killed 26 corporate executives last December.	Rather than start a story with a place name, "In White Plains, New York," I always try to fix the place up high but unobtrusively. In the fourth line, I wrote "outside," then realized that "near" is closer and shorter. I didn't use his name because he was an unknown and his name wouldn't mean anything to anyone outside White Plains, which is largely unknown itself except as the site of a Revolutionary battle.

The government's index of leading economic indicators last month rose slightly, one-point-four percent. The increase reversed three straight months of declines.

To save words, I didn't say the U.S. Department of Commerce issued the statistics. It's sufficient to say "the government." I originally wrote, "rose slightly last month." Then I caught myself, remembering Strunk's rule to "place the emphatic words of a sentence at the end."

A British truck driver admitted today he was the "Yorkshire Ripper," pleading guilty to manslaughter in the deaths of 13 women. By not pleading guilty to murder, Peter Sutcliffe could be sent to a hospital for the criminally insane—and not prison.

This is a simple, straightforward, no-frills account of a dramatic development in a sensational story. But there's no need here for any supercharged language to "sell" the story. (As the architect Ludwig Mies van der Rohe used to say, "Less is more.") My second sentence gives the "why" for his plea. I underlined "murder" because I thought it was a word the anchor should stress. (Some anchors welcome this. In any case, in the pressure-cooker atmosphere of a network newsroom, the stress is usually on the writer.)

Voice-Over Videotape

Television writing is complicated by the need to write to visuals. Block was told to write a lead-in and 20 seconds of voice-over videotape for the "CBS Evening News" from this wire service story:

CRESTVIEW, Fla. [AP] — Tank cars carrying acetone exploded and burned when a train loaded with hazardous chemicals derailed here today. Thousands were evacuated as the wind spread thick yellow sulfur fumes over rural northwest Florida.

Only one injury was reported. A fisherman trekking through the woods near the wreck inhaled some of the fumes and was hospitalized for observation.

Oskaloosa County Civil Defense director Tom Nichols estimated that 5,000 people had fled homes or campsites in the 30-square-mile evacuation area, which included several villages and about half of Blackwater River State Forest.

"It's a rural area and houses are scattered all through it," said Ray Belcher, a supervisor for the Florida Highway Patrol. "It's about half woods, half farms."

Civil Defense officials put the approximately 9,000 residents of nearby Crestview on alert for possible evacuation as approaching thunderstorms threatened a wind-shift that would push the fumes in that direction. . . .

Block was writing "blind" in the tape. That is, he did not have access to the videotape his copy would refer to. Here is Block's thinking:

First, I see the dateline, Crestview, Fla., and I know that in writing for broadcast I have to put the dateline up near the top as unintrusively as possible. It has to be done deftly.

When I started writing for broadcast, I was told by an editor that it's inadvisable to begin a story by saying, "In Crestview, Florida. . . ." The editor told me that was a lazy man's way of starting a story. In London today . . . in Paris today. . . . He didn't say never. But in 90 or 95 percent of the cases, it's best not to begin that way.

We see in the first line of the AP story that one of the trains is carrying acetone. My reaction is that most people don't know what acetone is. That probably is a reflection of my ignorance. If we were to use it on the air, it could sound like acid-own. In any case, there's no need to identify the chemical, or any of the chemicals, perhaps. The most important element is the explosion and the evacuation.

In the second paragraph of the story, it says that only one injury was reported. I didn't mention the injury. It seems slight. The third paragraph gives the name of the county. In writing news for broadcast, you have to eliminate details and focus on the big picture.

In my script, beginning with the second paragraph, I had to write 20 seconds of voice-over. As so often happens, I had no chance to see the videotape in advance, so I had to write in a general way without getting specific. I made an assumption at this point, and although it's dangerous to assume, I have seen so many derailments on TV films or tape that I figured the opening shot would be of derailed cars. So I presumed my paragraph covering the tape of the accident would be appropriate.

I was looking for facts in the AP story that would be essential in my script. As you can see, my script consists of about a five-second lead-in and 20 seconds of voice-over for the tape. Within the tight space, I can use only the most important facts because a script cannot consist of a string of dense facts.

Here is the script as Block wrote it:

mb	A tank car
DEAN	explosion in the
	Florida Panhandle
	today led to the
	evacuation of about
	five-thousand people
⑦	from their homes.
SIL/VO	The explosion was
:20	one of several that
	ripped through 18 cars
	that derailed at
	Crestview, Florida.

Several were carrying toxic and explosive chemicals.
Because of the danger of various fumes and the chance of further explosions,
officials ordered the evacuation of one-fourth the population of the county.

⟨20⟩

Rewrite. Looking over his handiwork a few years later, Block regretted burying a good verb in a noun. He should have made it: "A tank car exploded in the Florida Panhandle today and caused the evacuation of about five thousand people from their homes."

Sentence Structure and Language

From our window into the thinking of a broadcast newswriter, we can generalize about writing for the ear.

Write short, simple sentences. Use everyday language. Make the structure of most sentences conform to the S-V-O rule (subject-verb-object). Keep one idea to a sentence. Here are some other guidelines and examples:

- **Begin sentences with a source, with the attribution, if needed:**
  WRONG: The city needs new traffic lights, the mayor said.
  RIGHT: The mayor says the city needs new traffic lights.
- **Avoid starting a story with a participial phrase or a dependent clause:**
  WRONG: Hoping to keep the lid on spiraling prices, the president called today for wage-price guidelines for labor and industry. (Participial phrase.)
  RIGHT: The president is calling for wage-price guidelines to keep prices down.
  WRONG: When the bill was passed, he was absent. (Dependent clause.)
  RIGHT: He was absent when the bill was passed.
- **Use ordinary, one-syllable words whenever possible:**
  WRONG: The unprecedented increase in profits led the Congress to urge the plan's discontinuance.
  RIGHT: The record profits led Congress to urge an end to the plan.
- **Use vigorous verbs.** Avoid adjectives and adverbs:
  WEAK: He made the task easy for his listeners.
  BETTER: He simplified the task for his listeners.
  WEAK: She walked slowly through the mud.
  BETTER: She trudged through the mud.
- **Use the active, not the passive, voice:**
  WEAK: He was shown the document by the lawyer.
  BETTER: The lawyer showed him the document.
- **Use familiar words in familiar combinations.**
- **Write simply, directly.** Omit useless words.
- **Write in language that can be read easily.** The writer should test his or her writing by reading it aloud. Not only will the reading catch sounds that do not work, it will reveal whether a newscaster can read one idea in a single pulse. The newscaster must be able to breathe, and each breath closes out an idea.

Simple, direct writing can be elegant. This is the language of Mark Twain, Charles Dickens, and Edward R. Murrow. Here is a lead by Charles Kuralt, a correspondent for CBS television who was doing a piece about exploitation of the environment:

Men look at hillsides and see board feet of lumber. Men look at valleys and see homesites.

- **Use a phrase to indicate someone is being quoted:** as he said, as he put it, and these are his words. For routine quotes, paraphrase.

> WEAK: He said, "I am not a crook."
> BETTER: He said, and these are his words, "I am not a crook."

- **Place titles before names.** Spell out all numbers through 11. (Why 11? Because it resembles two l's.) Do not use initials for agencies and organizations unless they are widely known, such as FBI and CIA. Use contractions for informality. Paraphrase quotations unless they are essential or unusual. Keep sentences to fewer than 20 words.

Tenses

The anchoring tense for broadcast copy is usually the present or the present perfect tense:

> The state highway department **says** it will spend six million dollars this year improving farm-to-market roads.
>
> The state highway department **has announced** it will spend six million dollars this year improving farm-to-market roads.

When the present tense is used in the lead, the story often continues in that tense. When the present perfect tense is used in the lead, the story shifts to the past tense to indicate when the event occurred:

> A federal judge **has issued** a temporary order stopping efforts to put a reservist on active army duty because he refused to shave off his beard.
>
> Yesterday, the judge **gave** the army ten days to answer a suit filed by the American Civil Liberties Union for the reservist.

Following the past tense, the story can shift back to the present perfect or even to the present tense if the writer believes the situation is still true or in effect. The AP radio story continues:

> The ACLU **filed** the suit on behalf of a high school teacher, John Jones of Bristol, Rhode Island.
>
> The suit **asks** the court to declare unconstitutional a regulation forbidding beards and **claims** the teacher was marked absent from several drills that the suit **says** he attended.

Watch Out. There is a False Present, says Block, that broadcast news writers sometimes fall victim to under the pressure to put the present tense in their copy. An example: "An earthquake shakes California and sends dozens of people to hospitals today." Use of the False Present, Block says, is artificial and wrong.

Attribution

Broadcast copy places attribution at the beginning of sentences. This makes for clarity.

News Wire

ALBUQUERQUE [AP] — The death of a man whose body was found set in 500 pounds of concrete in a 55-gallon drum may be connected to a counterfeiting case, a federal agent says.

"I believe there is a connection. We won't be 100 percent certain until we know if the guy is who we think he is," said David Saleeba, special agent in charge of the U.S. Secret Service office in Albuquerque. . . .

Broadcast Wire

(Albuquerque) — A federal agent says the death of a man whose body was found set in 500 pounds of concrete in a 55-gallon drum may be connected to a counterfeiting case. Albuquerque police and federal agents say they believe the body recovered is that of 21-year-old Derek Suchy.

More on Writing

Block conducts broadcast workshops around the country, scrutinizes news scripts and, in his column for the *RTNDA Communicator,* he examines bloopers, blunders and questionable writing. "Too many of us think we're not only the messengers but also part of the message," he writes. For example:

> Carrollton police tell us one person was injured during a car chase overnight.

Sometimes, the broadcast writer will introduce the station into copy, or the media, as this Nebraska news writer did:

> It was a full-fledged media event that brought every TV station in the state to northwest Nebraska today.

"The media are not the story," says Block. "The *story* is the story."

In one of his columns, Block culled these sentences from clips. Look at the words in italics:

- The attorney for defendant Henry Watson *dropped a bombshell* in his closing argument.
  - City officials and union leaders have been *burning the midnight oil.*
- The workers were *visibly shaken* but not hurt.
- Lopez was sitting with friends on a courtyard bench at the Marlboro Houses in Coney Island when *shots rang out* Sunday.

Yes, you are right. They are clichés, the "language of newspeople churning out copy in a race against the clock," Block says. And he goes on to quote

Who Is *She?* A feature about a mail carrier who found a puppy inside a mail box ends:

She took the terrier-mix puppy to the humane society. She's being treated for dehydration and parasites but is expected to be just fine.

George Orwell's warning to writers: "Never use a metaphor, simile or other figure of speech you are used to seeing in print."

The Lead

Some events are too complex to plunge into immediately. Or there may be a confusing array of personalities or numbers. The listener then has to be set up for the theme of the piece.

Newspaper Lead

As Gov. Alfred Caster neared the end of his seven-day working vacation aboard a riverboat today, his aides said that he was unconcerned about some editorial criticism that he had become an absentee governor whose administration was adrift.

Broadcast Lead

Some newspaper editorials have criticized Governor Caster as an absentee governor. But officials aboard a riverboat with the governor say that the criticisms don't bother him. He is nearing the end of his seven-day working vacation on the boat.

Broadcast Reporting

Let's look at how broadcast reporters work. First, we go to an all-news radio station.

Each evening, the news director makes up an assignment sheet for reporters for the next day. The editor goes through the futures file, notes continuing stories and consults the wire services' schedules of stories. About 6 a.m., reporters begin to check with the editor for their assignments.

In the field, the reporters, who carry tape recorders, may each cover three or four stories—a feature, a running story from city hall, a talk by a congressman and a traffic accident that tied up a major artery. For each, the reporter phones the editor, who decides whether the reporter should go on live or be recorded.

If the reporter is to go on live, the editor places the reporter on a newscast. If recorded, the reporter talks to an aide, who makes sure the material is being recorded properly by an engineer. The recording, called a *cart* (for *cartridge*), is labeled by slug and time and given to the editor.

Radio reporters cannot rely on pictures, so they supply much of the descriptive material for their stories. Sound bites from their interviews are essential to give the listener a sense of immediacy and participation. The radio reporter develops a keen ear for the high-quality quote, the quotation that sums up the situation. The rest is ruthlessly discarded.

One of the most important tasks of the broadcast journalist is to ask relevant questions. Good interviews are made by the right questions.

As tape can be edited, the reporter can ask a question again if the answer is too long or complicated.

The television reporter works with a more complex technology than does the radio journalist. The TV reporter is always aware of the need for the picture.

Cover shots (see **Glossary**) may be needed to cover the sound track. If the story is about nutritious breakfasts, a cover shot of people shopping for cereal might be appropriate. Words augment the picture.

Here is how the script of ABC's "World News Tonight" began when a hostage was released in Beirut. See whether you can decipher the left-hand column:

0	LS, David Jacobsen and Terry Waite	Peter Jennings V/O:	This is the picture that David Jacobsen's family has been waiting to see. The former hostage alive and well and on his way home.
8	LS, ABC studio	Announcer:	From ABC, this is World News Tonight with Peter Jennings.
14	CU,	Jennings O/C:	Good Evening. The former hostage, David Jacobsen, once told his family that his job as administrator at the American University Hospital in Beirut was the most

Newsreaders. "Most local television stations hire readers, not journalists or newspeople. Local anchors are hired for their personalities or their looks, good hair, for instance. . . . They should be called newsreaders, as they are in Europe."
—*Walter Cronkite.*

			satisfying one he'd ever had. He had gone to the Middle East in 1984 for a change of pace, some change. As of yesterday, he'd been a hostage for 17 months. Tonight he's in West Germany and the doctors there say he is in remarkably good condition. Here's ABC's Pierre Salinger:
41	LS, helicopter	V/O:	The first leg of freedom. The helicopter from Beirut set down in Cyprus bringing back David Jacobsen. But it was obvious that release was a bittersweet experience for him.
47	LS, helicopter		
50	CU, Jacobsen		
52	CU Jacobsen	SOT:	"My joy is somewhat diminished by the fact that other captives are still being held in Lebanon."
1'05	CU of Jacobsen on videotape	V/O:	It was only a month ago that Jacobsen appeared on this videotape released by his captors criticizing the Reagan Administration.
1'12		SOT:	"Mr. President, are you going to make another mistake at the cost of our lives? It seems that you are continuing to make mistakes in our situation."

In case you couldn't figure out the abbreviations: LS, long shot; CU, close-up. Often used, though not here, is ECU, extreme close-up.

Reporting and Writing to Tape

The feature or timeless piece may include an interview, voice-over silent tape, or tape with sound of an event and the reporter's summarizing the event. The story may take days of planning and hours of shooting, editing and writing, and then when it is finally broadcast it may run for only a minute and a half.

For a story on a new reading program in the city schools, an interview with the superintendent of schools may set out the intent of the curriculum change. Additional interviews will allow viewers to hear the specific plans of teachers. School children will be interviewed. Locations might include classrooms, teachers discussing the program, the superintendent in his office.

The producer will want a variety of shots—medium, close-up and cutaway—to build a picture story to accompany the reporter's narration and interviews.

Stories for newspapers usually follow a straight-line form—most important material at the beginning, least important at the end. But for longer broadcast pieces, the form is a circle because the ending usually has a reminder of the theme.

The reporter's task is to marry natural sound, visuals and interviews. Sometimes the reporter muffs the opportunity. In a piece about a cloistered order of nuns who vow perpetual silence, the reporter wrote a narration with no pauses. He wrote about silence but never stopped talking. In effect, the viewer could not hear the silence. The event would have been captured had he stopped talking in some places, a few seconds at a time, to allow viewers to hear the clatter of knives and forks at a silent dinner, the footsteps of nuns in darkened hallways. The tone of the story should match the event.

Top Tips of the Trade

1. Start strong. Well begun is half done.
2. Read—and understand—your source copy.
3. Underline or circle key facts.
4. Think. Don't write yet. Think.
5. Write the way you talk.
6. Apply the rules for broadcast newswriting.
7. Have the courage to write simply.
8. Refrain from wordy warm-ups.
9. Put attribution before assertion.
10. Go with S-V-O: subject-verb-object.
11. Limit a sentence to one idea.
12. Use short words and short sentences.
13. Use familiar words in familiar combinations.
14. Humanize your copy. And localize it.
15. Activate your copy: use active voice—and action verbs.
16. Avoid a first sentence whose main verb is any form of *to be: is, are, was, were, will be.*
17. Avoid *may, could, seems.*
18. Put your sentences in a positive form.
19. Use present tense verbs where appropriate.
20. Don't start with a quotation or a question.
21. Use connectives—*and, also, but, so, because*—to link sentences.
22. Put the word or words you want to stress at the end of your sentence.
23. Use contractions—with caution.
24. Pep up your copy with words like *new, now, but, says.*
25. Watch out for *I, we, our, here, up, down.*
26. Omit needless words.
27. Hit only the highlights.
28. Don't parrot source copy.
29. Place the time element, if you need one, *after* the verb.
30. When in doubt, leave it out.
31. Don't raise questions you don't answer.
32. Read your copy aloud. If it sounds like writing, rewrite it. The art of writing lies in rewriting what you've already rewritten.

Adapted from Block, Mervin, *Writing Broadcast News—Shorter, Sharper, Stronger,* 2nd ed. (Chicago: Bonus Books, 1998).

Packaging Short News Features

Let's accompany a television news student, Cathy, as she puts together a news feature. The story is about a program designed to prevent children from committing crimes when they grow up. Cathy has an interview with the psychologist who developed the program. She also has videotaped the children in the program as they talk to the psychologist and play. Cathy has interviewed the children for their reactions to the program.

After her reporting, Cathy has 40 minutes of tape. On her way back to the station Cathy starts blocking out her story:

> I'll tell the editor to start with pictures of the children in a circle for 20 seconds while in my script I'll give some facts about the project.
>
> Then a 20-to-30-second sound bite from the psychologist explaining the "substitute family" technique. As he talks about the substitute parents, the editor will show pictures of the children and parents greeting one another affectionately.
>
> Then I'll write a short transition into the interviews. I think that to get into this section I'll pose the question, "But does the program work?" and have three or four short interviews with the answers.

She'll close with a quote from the psychologist and then her own wrap-up from the scene to answer questions she thinks have been left unanswered. She estimates the feature will run from 2:30 to 2:45, just what the producer wants.

Interviewing

Much of what Cathy did was the result of planning. For her interviews, she devised questions that sought to get to the heart of the story quickly. Interviews have to be kept short, to the point. This requires gentle but firm direction by the reporter. Here are some interviewing guidelines:

1. Don't ask questions that can be answered yes or no.
2. Don't ask long, involved questions.
3. Don't suggest answers to interviewees.
4. Build on the subject's answers—don't ask questions just because you prepared them. Listen to his or her answers and ask questions about what he or she says.
5. Ask only one question at a time. Don't ask multiple questions.
6. Develop a sense of timing. Cut in if the subject starts to be repetitive or long-winded. Don't cut the subject off just when he or she is about to say something important.

Advice. Studs Terkel, for 45 years a major figure on National Public Radio whose interviews have won prizes and acclaim, advises: "Listening leads to truth. . . . You can't fake interest. . . . Let the little guy tell his tale. . . . Stay patient."

7. Make the subject comfortable before shooting the interview.

    a. Describe the general area your questions will cover, but don't tell the subject exactly what the questions will be. The first, spontaneous response to a question is often the truest.

    b. Explain the setting—which mike the subject should speak into and so on. Tell him or her to look at *you* or other questioners—not the camera—unless he or she is going to show the audience how to do something that requires direct communication between speaker and audience.

    c. Before the interview chat easily to dispel any nervousness. Show an interest in the subject's area so he or she will gain confidence.

    d. Don't act like you know it all. *Prepare* so you *do* know enough and so that your subjects believe you understand what they say.

    e. Know what you are looking for. Most short news items must be carefully focused because of time limits.

8. Try to stick to one topic.

9. Adjust the tone of the questions to the interviewee's experience. A politician may need to be pushed and asked direct questions.

Long Pieces

Most broadcast stories, as we have seen, are short. The better stations give their staffs the time to do longer pieces and series. Public broadcasting stations have a commitment to long-form television, as do several commercial stations such as WCCO-TV (Minneapolis), WBRZ-TV (Baton Rouge) and WSMV-TV (Nashville).

WSMV-TV has won many awards for its in-depth pieces. One of its prizewinning series was "A Matter of Taste." It was a penetrating examination of whether Tennessee was losing its natural beauty to development.

"Visual Chaos"

"When we started brainstorming about the series, the first location that came to mind was Pigeon Forge," says Don Heider, the writer for the WSMV-TV series. "This community had seen a remarkable amount of development in a short time, primarily due to its strategic location as an entry way to the Smoky Mountains. It was obvious this was a place where there had been unchecked development."

Heider needed someone to express those concerns, and he thought an artist would see the situation from a visual perspective. He also needed someone who would speak in support of the path the town took to its newfound prosperity. The Pigeon Forge Chamber of Commerce supplied some names. He also found an architect who was with a group pushing for stronger sign laws in the state.

"Key to the success of the piece," says Heider, "was a lot of set-up time on the front end, interviewing a number of people over the phone until I knew I had the right people to tell the story, and also ensuring that we had strong visuals.

"Also essential was good communication between myself and the photo-journalist." They discussed ideas before Heider made his first calls, and the discussion continued throughout the planning and shooting. "We were still talking about what the story should say and look like when we edited it."

Here is the beginning of Heider's script:

SLUG ANCHOR   WRITER   WSMV-TX NEWS   STATUS TIME
TACKY #1   HEIDER   MON JUL 25 09:02   READY 4:54

NAT SOUND

SOUNDBITE 4/10:43 LEE ROBERSON/ARTIST [I SUPPOSE MOST PEOPLE WHO LIVE HERE KIND OF TAKE IT FOR GRANTED BUT I NEVER REALLY HAVE. I'M HERE BY CHOICE. I LIVE ADJACENT TO THE SMOKY MOUNTAINS NATIONAL PARK AND THAT'S BECAUSE I WANTED TO, IT'S **JUST NOT** SOMETHING THAT HAPPENED.]

NESTLED AWAY IN A SMALL COVE NEXT TO THE SMOKIES LIVES LEE ROBERSON.

SOUNDBITE 4/11:53 LEE [THESE MOUNTAINS ARE LIVEABLE AND THEY'RE HOSPITABLE AND THEY'RE COMFORTABLE, THEY KIND OF WELCOME YOU.]

LEE IS AN ARTIST. HE DRAWS HIS INSPIRATION FROM THIS LAND WHERE HE WAS RAISED.

SOUNDBITE 4/12:24 LEE [MY GRANDPARENTS LIVED IN CADE'S COVE.]

WHERE LEE LIVES, IT'S PEACEFUL . . . QUIET . . . RESTFUL.
BUT JUST A FEW MILES AWAY, THINGS ARE DIFFERENT.

NAT SOUND—PIGEON FORGE

SOUNDBITE 2/13:34 LEON DOWNEY/PIGEON FORGE [IT IS A BOOM TOWN, SURE, AND IT HAS BEEN A BOOM TOWN FOR THE PAST SEVERAL YEARS.]

IT'S TENNESSEE'S NEWEST MECCA FOR TOURISM. PIGEON FORGE.

NAT SOUND

PIGEON FORGE IS A PUTT-PUTT PARADISE. A GO-CART KINGDOM. A UTOPIA FOR ANYONE UNDER THE AGE OF 15.

SOUNDBITE 2/17:27 DOWNEY [WHEN A FAMILY COMES IN HERE WITH A CARLOAD OF CHILDREN, WITH ONE OR TWO CHILDREN OR WHATEVER, THEIR HEADS ARE ON A SWIVEL AS SOON AS THEY GET HERE. THEY JUST CAN'T BELIEVE

ALL THE FUN THINGS THERE ARE TO DO IN PIGEON FORGE.
IT'S SORTA LIKE MYRTLE BEACH IN THE MOUNTAINS.]

THIS IS A COMMUNITY DESIGNED AROUND THE NEEDS AND WANTS OF CHILDREN. CHILDREN WHO CAN TALK THEIR PARENTS INTO SPENDING MONEY.

PIGEON FORGE WAS A GROWING TOURIST TOWN UNTIL 1986. THAT WAS THE YEAR DOLLY PARTON CAME BACK TO EAST TENNESSEE. SHE CONVERTED AN OLD AMUSEMENT PARK INTO DOLLYWOOD. THE PARK AND THE TOWN TOOK OFF.

NAT SOUND

IN JUST A YEAR DOLLYWOOD DOUBLED ITS ATTENDANCE. IN 1987, THE YEAR AFTER DOLLYWOOD OPENED, COMMERCIAL CONSTRUCTION IN PIGEON FORGE QUADRUPLED.

PIGEON FORGE ISN'T JUST A TOURIST TOWN NOW. IT'S A PHENOMENON. DEVELOPMENT HAS BEEN GOOD FOR BUSINESS. BUT DEVELOPMENT ALSO THREATENS SOMETHING HERE.

SOUNDBITE 4/17:04 ROBERSON [WHILE THERE'S NOTHING WRONG WITH PROVIDING ACCOMMODATIONS AND ENTERTAINMENT AND THE VARIOUS THINGS PEOPLE ARE LOOKING FOR I GUESS WHAT WE'RE A LITTLE CONCERNED ABOUT IS THAT WE MIGHT LOSE SIGHT OF WHY THEY COME HERE. NOW IF WE ALLOW WHY THEY CAME HERE AND COME HERE TO BE DESTROYED, WE ALL LOSE.]

PIGEON FORGE GOT ITS START AS THE GATEWAY TO THE SMOKIES. A STOPOVER POINT AS YOU ENTERED ONE OF THE SOUTH'S MOST SPECTACULAR NATURAL WONDERS.

BUT NOW AS YOU DRIVE THROUGH PIGEON FORGE YOU CAN BARELY SEE THE SMOKIES. THE VIEW IS BLOCKED BY SIGN AFTER SIGN.

SOUNDBITE BURR/5:14 EUGENE BURR/ARCHITECT-PLANNER [IT'S ESSENTIALLY A VISUAL CHAOS.]

EUGENE BURR IS A KNOXVILLE ARCHITECT AND PLANNER WHO HAS ALSO NOTICED SOME OF PIGEON FORGE'S GROWTH PROBLEMS.

SOUNDBITE BURR/2:56 BURR [YOU DON'T HAVE A SENSE OF CITY WHEN YOU ENTER PIGEON FORGE, THERE'S THIS WALL OF GARISH ADVERTISING WHERE EACH BUSINESS IS TRYING TO COMPETE WITH THE NEXT.]

BURR BELIEVES IF THE CITY DOESN'T TAKE STEPS TO IMPROVE ITSELF, ITS GROWTH MAY NOT LAST LONG.

Shifting Emphasis

More stations and the networks are blending the day's headlines with features and theme stories. Some of this shift has been toward more coverage of entertainers, but a significant amount has been toward substantive topics such as poverty, the homeless and problems of race and class.

Juvenile Crime

"The CBS Evening News" began one of its in-depth pieces this way:

RATHER: In the streets of America, those domestic priorities include what to do about the plague of violent crime by the young against the young. Dallas today became the latest city to turn to one increasingly popular and controversial solution. Scott Pelley has a report.

SCOTT PELLEY: Each night the body count grows— American teen-agers victims of gangs, drugs and violence. It is a deadly trend that is prompting a growing number of cities to impose curfews on youth.

AL LIPSCOMB (Dallas city councilman): The figures are astoundin' on young people—the killin', the maimin'.

PELLEY: Dallas City Councilman Al Lipscomb is sponsoring a curfew measure.

LIPSCOMB: Since we cannot have any type of a curfew on parents, who cannot control their youth, we have to do the next best thing.

PELLEY: The proposal says kids under 17 must be home by 11, unless they work. Parents could be fined. Businesses that let kids in after the curfew face fines up to $2,000.

SARAH SLOBEN (dance-club manager): It's—it's solving a problem with a chain saw that needs to be dealt with with a scalpel.

PELLEY: Sarah Sloben manages a dance club for teenagers.

SLOBEN: It's an infringement of the rights of teen-agers. It's an unnecessary burden on business owners, and it's gonna tie up the police. The police are not baby-sitters. They're policemen.

Sexual Harassment

KTRH NewsRadio in Houston had cultivated sources in the Houston Police Department over the years of covering its activities. One of its sources told a KTRH reporter that women officers and other workers who complained of harassment suffered retaliation.

Stephen Dean investigated and verified the tip. Some women officers were transferred to desk jobs or to distant posts. Nothing was done to the officer against whom the complaint was filed.

Here's the lead-in to the first story:

Charges of retaliation and unfair treatment are raised by cops who claim they are victims of sexual harassment on the job. NewsRadio's Stephen Dean has the results of an exclusive KTRH investigation.

Dean then picks up the story:

Women who wear Houston police badges find themselves quickly transferred to desk jobs or cross-town assignments when they file sexual harassment complaints.

Some say they're treated harshly by supervisors and co-workers as the complaints are being processed.

Internal Affairs Sergeant Patsy Chapman filed a complaint against an office supervisor, saying he made repeated advances and stuck his tongue in her ear. When she turned him away, overtime requests she turned in for his approval suddenly disappeared. She was out $800 of pay.

So her last resort was a written complaint, and she says it caused her life to get even worse.

She was quickly transferred to another part of the city, while the supervisor was able to stay put in his job.

Attorney Cathy Butler is handling two cases of harassment in the department.

NewsRadio finds at least four cases within the past year where the victims claim they were forced to transfer after filing complaints.

And one female officer says she'd rather be touched all the time than go through the hassles in her new job.

Butler says if the department handled crime the way they handle sexual harassment, they wouldn't be catching many criminals.

Disappearing Songbirds

As cities expand into the countryside and as industry replaces forest and grassland, the environment changes. Pavement replaces grass, duplexes and factories rise where pine and birch once grew. KOTV in Tulsa wondered whether in this changing environment the songbird would be silenced.

It embarked on a documentary, an "ecocampaign," the station called it, to alert viewers to the plight of grassland songbirds. One of the imperiled birds is the state bird, the scissortailed flycatcher. The reporting and filming took more than three months of arduous work.

"For those who've never noticed, once a songbird alights on a perch, it generally doesn't stay very long," says Scott Thompson, the reporter for the documentary. "We would spend hours in nearly inaccessible prairie draws and sloughs and desolate mesa plateaus, waiting for a chance encounter with a songbird or raptor."

The photographers shot vast amounts of videotape to be able to capture a few seconds of usable footage.

Result   The public responded. KOTV distributed more than 12,000 viewer guides, and proceeds from the sale of videotapes went to a research center.

"Songs of the Prairie" is unusual for television, judges for Sigma Delta Chi's annual awards stated, although the subject "is just as important as it was when Rachel Carson published *Silent Spring*. The writing, photography were excellent, practically lyrical. The videography deserves special recognition."

The documentary won the Public Service Award.

KANU-FM photo

Pervasive Prejudice

Public radio station KNAU-FM in Flagstaff, Ariz., used "real people and real voices," the judges said in awarding the station a prize for its documentary about persistent "tension and discrimination" in the cities bordering the Navajo and Hopi reservations. Producer Sandy Tolan (shown here) included a first-person narrative on what it's like to grow up Navajo in Flagstaff alongside the dominant white culture. His goal, he said, was to stimulate discussion of the issue.

A Dozen Deadly Don'ts

Thou shalt not:
1. Scare listeners.
2. Give orders.
3. Start a story with
   - "as expected."
   - "in a surprise move."
   - "a new development today."
   - "our top story tonight is."
   - *there is* or *it is.*
   - a participial phrase.
   - a personal pronoun.
   - a question.
   - a quotation.
   - an unknown or unfamiliar name.
   - someone's "making news" or "making history."
   - *another, more* or *once again.*
4. Characterize news as "good" or "bad."
5. Use any form of *to be* as the main verb in your lead.
6. Bury the verb in a noun.
7. Use *yesterday* or *continues* in your first sentence.
8. Use *no, not* and negatives in your first sentence.
9. Use newspaper style, language or rituals.
10. Cram too much information into a story.
11. Lose or mislead a listener.
12. Make a factual error.

Adapted from Block, Mervin. *Writing Broadcast News—Shorter, Sharper, Stronger,* 2nd ed. (Chicago: Bonus Books, 1998).

Copy Preparation

Copy is written to give the newscaster as much help as possible. The rules for copy preparation differ from station to station. Some require the slug in the upper left-hand corner and the time it takes to tell the story above it.

Copy for television is written on the right half of the page. The left half is kept open for technical instructions. Some stations also ask that radio copy be written this way, but most radio copy is written across the page.

A line of 45 to 50 characters will take four seconds to read. By keeping lines to the same length, it is easy to estimate the time it will take to read the story without the use of a stopwatch.

End each page with a full sentence. Better still: End on a paragraph. Do not leave the newscaster hanging in the middle of a sentence or an idea as he or she turns the page. Keep paragraphs short.

Each page should be slugged. For pieces running more than one page, each page should be numbered, and the writer's name or initials should appear on all pages.

Place the word *more,* circled, at the bottom of stories of more than one page, and use a clear, large-end mark—30, #, END—when finished.

Copy should be written in cap and lowercase. For television, visual directions should be written in all caps.

Telling the Whole Story

Little of what goes through the broadcast station's editing rooms reaches the public. Interviews are ruthlessly cut as editors search for the brief sound bite. Background material, if any, is compressed. Sometimes, the meaningful shades of gray that make the story complete don't make the broadcast, especially when they complicate the theme or story line.

Critics have accused broadcast journalists of allowing office holders and candidates to pass on to the public what one disparagingly described as "sound bites that were simply advertising."

A Conveyor Belt

People in public life have long considered broadcast news a more direct route to the citizen and a more congenial medium than print. Franklin D. Roosevelt was famous for his radio fireside chats in which he soothed a country mired in a deep depression. Dwight D. Eisenhower began the televised presidential news conference to reach the public directly, without the interpretations and possible criticism of the print press. Eisenhower used television, historian Stephen Ambrose wrote, to "set the national agenda" and also to "obfuscate an issue when he was not sure how he would deal with it."

Mario Cuomo of New York, when governor, told newspaper reporters, "Don't flatter yourselves into thinking you're the best way to reach the public.

"When I go to you, I don't reach the public directly; you do. When I go electronically, I reach the public. If I want to reach the public, I shouldn't be talking to you. I should be talking to a radio microphone."

Cuban Complications   A.M. Rosenthal, former executive editor of *The New York Times* and now a columnist for the newspaper, was angered by a segment on the TV program "60 Minutes" in which the Cuban ballerina Alicia Alonso explains how she protested the brutality of the dictator Batista by refusing to dance for several years. When Fidel Castro came to power, she was placed in charge of the national ballet company.

"Not one word," comments Rosenthal, about how she feels about Castro's "imprisonment of poets, painters and writers. An unquestioning plug for Mr. Castro and a rewriting of history by omission."

Rosenthal asked Morley Safer, who did the segment, about this omission. "He told me that he did indeed ask the ballerina about Castro tyrannies," Rosenthal writes. "But she was wordy and polemical so he thought he would cut that part. It made for a better show, he said. A judgment call, he said."

Ethical Imperatives

Broadcast journalists are aware of attempts to use them as the conveyors of messages, and they are as careful of being exploited as are print journalists. Although broadcast journalists operate within tighter deadlines and are called on to be more concise than print journalists, they try to give fair, well-rounded and accurate accounts of events.

The TV camera has enormous power, and its users are conscious of this. When they were slow to arrive in Somalia, a CBS medical reporter said, hundreds of thousands of starving people died.

Local News: Mostly Crime

Studies of local news on TV stations show that they are the number one source of news for the public. But the studies also show that most of the news focuses on crime and little on social issues, education, race relations.

A study of local TV news by eight journalism schools found almost a third of news time went to crime and criminal justice stories, and a sixth to government and politics. Education averaged a miniscule one-fiftieth of news time. A study of 100 local TV newscasts by the Rocky Mountain Media Watch found crime took up 30 percent of newscast time.

Patricia Dean, head of broadcast journalism at Northwestern University, said, "What was surprising to me was what wasn't being reported at all, education and race relations especially." She said these were "very big issues" in the eight markets studied: Austin, Chicago, Indianapolis, New York, Syracuse, Eugene, Miami and Los Angeles.

KVUE-TV   The exception to the large amount of time devoted to crime was in Austin. There, KVUE-TV instituted "community standards" guidelines for deciding whether to broadcast a story about a local crime. Under the direction of Carole Kent Kneeland, vice president for news, the station decided it would use a crime story if news executives could answer yes to questions such as: Is there an immediate threat to public safety? Is there a significant community impact? Do viewers need to take some kind of action?

Austin was recorded in the study as devoting 5.7 percent of airtime to crime, whereas Indianapolis devoted 36.7 percent of airtime to the subject. KVUE has held the top ratings position for news in the Austin area for several years.

The Power of TV. In 1958, Edward Murrow said, "This instrument can teach, it can illuminate, yes, and it can even inspire. But, it can only do so to the extent that humans are determined to use it to those ends. Otherwise it is merely wires and lights in a box. There is a great and perhaps decisive battle to be fought against ignorance, intolerance and indifference. This weapon of television can be useful."

Today, the United States is the only Western nation without a network newscast in the prime-time evening hours.

A TV Newsman's Critique

The power of television to inform and influence the public worried Charles Kuralt, a veteran network reporter and writer. He thought too many stations follow the advice of news consultants who "would cut the Iliad or King Lear to 90 seconds." He was disturbed by the inadequate news training of the "earnest young man or woman" who opens the six o'clock news: " 'Good evening, here is the news.' This is said very urgently and with the appearance of sincerity—most often by an attractive person who would not know a news story if it jumped up and mussed his or her coiffure."

In a talk at the University of Nevada-Reno, he told journalism students and their instructors:

> The real rewards—both in the giving and the receiving—are in the patient, hard work of the careful writer who seizes a fact or an event out of the air as it flashes past and hammers it like a blacksmith on his anvil, and tempers it, and dissatisfied, discards it and rekindles the fire in the forge, and comes back to it until at length it becomes a useful and pretty thing—and a bit of truth. Television news is papier-mâché. Real writing is wrought iron.

The Reason   Marty Haag, senior news vice president for the A.H. Belo stations, says that "covering crime is the easiest, fastest, cheapest, most efficient kind of news coverage for TV stations. News directors and station owners love crime because it has a one-to-one ratio between making the assignment and getting a story on-air."

Improvement   Some cable stations, which have smaller geographical boundaries than the major local TV stations, are offering excellent local coverage in Washington, D.C., Cape Cod, Orange County, Calif., and elsewhere.

Comments: Pluses and a Few Minuses

Dan Rather, anchor, "CBS Evening News": The feel-good alleged news correspondents, the good-news pretenders are a dime a dozen and on every station. They're everywhere now. . . . One of the reasons, Dear Listener, is that not enough of you care, nor of us, those of us still in the craft, in the profession of what is supposed to be the public service of broadcast news.

Joan Barrett, KVUE-TV, Austin, Tex.: One of the first questions we ask at our morning meeting is, "What are people talking about today?" And then it's, "What do people need to know? What should they know? What do they want to know?" You know, producers play a key role in our shop. Yet we don't get many students who say "I want to be a producer." But they're the ones shaping the decisions in the newscasts for the most part.

See Appendix D for the Code of Ethics of the Radio-Television News Directors Association.

Andrew Lack, president, NBC News: We are spawning a generation of reporters and news directors who no longer place any value on the written word, the turn of phrase, the uncut, long, hard question. All we care about are the almighty pictures, the video, the story count—and that it moves like a bat out of hell. We barely listen to what is said any more.

Tom Bettag, executive producer, "Nightline": I like to think of Nightline as a broadcast that attempts to illuminate the major issues of our time. They turn on Nightline to find out if there's something they need to know, if there's something people are going to be talking about in the morning. They aren't interested in being entertained. Nightline has its largest audiences when there is real news.

Kirk Winkler, KTVK-TV, Phoenix, Ariz.: The most important problem (among journalism students) is a simple lack of curiosity. One in ten students now graduating has enough of it to make it as a successful reporter. Also: They do not know how to report on deadline and some don't know what a city directory is and don't read a daily newspaper.

Walter Cronkite, "CBS Evening News" anchor and managing editor for 19 years: Some anchorpersons are inadequately educated and poorly trained. Their only qualifications seem to be pretty clothes and stylish hairdos—and this applies to both sexes. Too many are interested in becoming stars rather than journalists. They aren't interested in news except as it resembles show business. However, a talented generation of young people is coming out of journalism schools with the hearts and guts—and educational background—to be called journalists.

Summing Up

Preparation: Examine notes and all material for the broadcast to determine the key material. Highlight it. Know the time allotted for the segment you are writing. Decide on the lead.

Writing: Begin with the best. Make it short, to the point, interesting. Use S-V-O construction, present tense, familiar words and phrases.

Last-minute check: Read what you have written. If you sound too formal, stumble on a word or run out of breath, then rewrite.

Further Reading

Arlen, Michael J. *The Camera Age: Essays on Television.* New York: Farrar, Straus & Giroux, 1981.

Auletta, Ken. *Three Blind Mice: How the TV Networks Lost Their Way.* New York: Random House, 1991.

Bliss, Edward, Jr. *Now the News: The Story of Broadcasting.* New York: Columbia University Press, 1991.

Block, Mervin. *Writing Broadcast News—Shorter, Sharper, Stronger.* Chicago: Bonus Books, 1987.

Block, Mervin. *Rewriting Network News: WorldWatching Tips from 345 TV and Radio Scripts.* Chicago: Bonus Books, 1990.

Block, Mervin. *Broadcast Newswriting: The RTNDA Reference Guide.* Chicago: Bonus Books, 1994.

Cloud, Stanley, and Lynne Olson. *The Murrow Boys: Pioneers on the Front Lines of Broadcast Journalism.* Boston: Houghton Mifflin, 1996.

Cronkite, Walter. *A Reporter's Life.* New York: Knopf, 1996.

Ellerbee, Linda. *And So It Goes: Adventures in Television.* New York: Putnam, 1986.

Hewitt, Don. *Minute by Minute.* New York: Random House, 1985. (Hewitt is the executive producer of "60 Minutes.")

Kimball, Penn. *Downsizing the News: Network Cutbacks in the Nation's Capital.* Washington: Woodrow Wilson Center Press; Baltimore: Johns Hopkins University Press, 1994.

Persico, Joseph E. *Edward R. Murrow: An American Original.* New York: McGraw-Hill, 1988.

Smith, Howard K. *Events Leading Up to My Death: The Life of a Twentieth Century Reporter.* New York: St. Martin's Press, 1996.

Smith, Sally Bedell. *In All His Glory: The Life of William S. Paley, the Legendary Tycoon and His Brilliant Circle.* New York: Simon & Schuster, 1990.

Sperber, Ann M. *Murrow: His Life and Times.* New York: Freundlich Books, 1986.

Note: For an insight into the status of network news see:

Boyer, Peter J. *Who Killed CBS?* New York: Random House, 1988.

Frank, Reuven. *Out of Thin Air: The Brief, Wonderful Life of Network News.* New York: Simon & Schuster, 1991.

Joyce, Ed. *Prime Times, Bad Times.* New York: Doubleday, 1988.

10 Digging for Information

Susan Pollard,
Contra Costa Times

Backgrounding a kidnapping.

Preview

The reporter's job is to gather information that helps people understand events that affect them. This digging takes the reporter through the three layers of reporting:

1. **Surface facts:** source-originated material—press releases, handouts, speeches.
2. **Reportorial enterprise:** verification, investigative reporting, coverage of spontaneous events, background.
3. **Interpretation and analysis:** significance, causes, consequences.

The reporter always tries to observe events directly rather than rely on sources, who sometimes seek to manipulate the media. One common tactic of sources is the media event, an action staged to attract media attention.

Verification, background checking, direct observation and enterprise reporting amplify and sometimes correct source-originated material.

Reporters are allowed to interpret events when appropriate.

The reporter is like the prospector digging and drilling the way to pay dirt. Neither is happy with the surface material, although sometimes impenetrable barriers or lack of time interfere with the search, and it is necessary to stop digging and to make do with what has been turned up. When possible, the reporter keeps digging until he or she gets to the bottom of things, until the journalistic equivalent of the mother lode—the truth of the event—is unearthed.

The reporter, like the prospector, has a feel for the terrain. This sensitivity—the reporter's street smarts or nose for news—helps unearth information for stories. Equally helpful is the reporter's general knowledge.

Let's watch a reporter for a Florida newspaper do some digging.

Finding the Winner

The word from Tallahassee was that the single winning ticket in the $5 million Florida lottery had been sold in Port St. Lucie. Sarah Jay, a reporter for *The Port St. Lucie News,* had heard rumors about the winner—that someone in a meat market knew the winner's name; that the winner could be found by talking to someone in the Roma Bakery. Jay tried the market. No luck. She fared better at the bakery, where a woman told Jay that her niece was the winner.

She gave Jay the woman's name—Pat Lino—but no phone number or address. Jay checked the telephone company—the number was unlisted. But she did find some Linos in the directory and called, thinking she might reach a relative.

"One guy was totally unrelated," Jay says. "Another was the winner's brother-in-law, and although he wouldn't give me her phone number he did mention that she lives in St. Lucie West, a new housing development."

Knowing that property tax records that list addresses are available, Jay checked the files for Pat Lino. She found the address and drove to the location, only to find no one there.

"It was all locked up. It looked as though I'd hit a dead end, but just to be sure I talked to a neighbor. He didn't know them, he said. Nor did another. But then I tried one more neighbor, and she knew Pat Lino. She had Pat Lino's daughter's phone number."

The neighbor called and Pat Lino was there. But she said she didn't want to be interviewed. "I told the neighbor that I only wanted to speak with her for a minute, that I'd been looking for her all day," Jay said. Lino gave in.

"In this small bedroom community, the naming of a $5 million lottery winner was the talk of the town. And we had it first."

Using the Computer

Next, let's move north to examine the work of a team of reporters at *The New York Times* who combined shoe-leather reporting with computer-assisted digging, the traditional and the new technology. The subject of the four-member team was a major hospital chain in the growing health care industry, Columbia/HCA Healthcare Corp.

Columbia had been praised as a model of the industry in magazines and newspapers. It was, *Time* magazine reported, a boon to patients and to the corporation's shareholders.

At the *Times,* Martin Gottlieb, the projects editor, decided to look at Columbia as representative of the vast changes sweeping through the health care industry. Gottlieb and business reporter Kurt Eichenwald set out to find out how Columbia could be making so much money (its profit had jumped from $120 million to $1.5 billion in five years) when the health care business was struggling. Why? What was happening?

Columbia said that because it ran more than 300 hospitals it could purchase by volume and receive discounts. Eichenwald was dubious, and Gottlieb, who had reported on health care before, knew that others in the field had been making volume purchases and had not achieved the profits of Columbia.

Database Check   Gottlieb knew that government agencies keep good records on hospitals. He asked Joshua Barbanel of the *Times* staff to help with database analyses. Tamar Lewin was added to the team as the story became a major investigation.

Barbanel looked through his data and discovered that Columbia's patients were the victims of more serious illnesses than patients in other hospitals, and thus Columbia was receiving more money from government agencies. As he went through thousands upon thousands of records in databases, Barbanel made significant other discoveries. One was that despite its claim of quality care at low cost, Columbia's hospitals were actually more expensive than comparative facilities. The cost to Medicare in Texas was "at least $48 million more than if the care had been billed at the state average," the *Times* reported.

The combined traditional and new technology reporting resulted in a four-part series that led to major reforms in the health care industry. The full story is told in the July/August 1998 *Brill's Content* by Roger Parloff.

The Reporting Process

As reporters go about their work of digging up information, they are guided by an understanding of the nature of reporting: Reporting is the process of gathering relevant material through a variety of means (direct observation, interviews, study of reports and documents, use of databases and Internet resources) and subjecting the material to verification and analysis. When assembled, the material gives the reader, listener or viewer a good idea of what happened.

The Layers

Sometimes, the reporting process involves using source-originated material. The state's senior senator is planning to give a talk tomorrow at a fundraising dinner for the state Republican Party. The story that gives the time, place and purpose of the senator's talk is a Layer I story. That is, it simply relays information from a source.

If the reporter handling this story were to dig a bit deeper and ask the senator's press secretary whether the senator will support a particular gubernatorial candidate in the party primary, we can say that the reporter is now operating at a deeper layer, Layer II. We have seen how Sarah Jay worked Layer II by not waiting for the state to announce the winner of the lottery. And we saw how a team of reporters investigated a supposedly successful health care giant by digging beneath the laudatory press releases (Layer I) to find serious shortcomings in the company's performance (Layer II).

The News Story and Its Layers of Truth

Layer I—Handouts, press conferences, speeches, statements.

Layer II—Reportorial enterprise, verifying material, background, reporter's observations, spontaneous events.

Layer III—Significance, impact, causes, consequences, analysis, interpretation.

I Source-Originated Material

II Spontaneous Events

Reportorial Enterprise

III Interpretation and Explanation

The Story

Digging for the Story

As we move on in our examination of journalistic work we will meet reporters who are allowed to interpret their findings, to find causes and consequences of the events they examine. They work in Layer III.

Most journalists say that their most important task is to look beneath the surface for the underlying reality. Lincoln Steffens, the great journalist of the muckraking period, said the reporter's task is "the letting in of light and air." Reporters base their work on the same conviction that guided Steffens. Their job is to seek out relevant truths for people who cannot witness or comprehend the events that affect them.

Layer I Reporting

Layer I reporting is the careful and accurate transcription of source-originated material—the record, the speech, the news conference. Its strengths and its limitations are those of objective journalism.

Layer I is the source for the facts used in most news stories. Information is mined from material that originates with and is controlled by the source. Fact gathering at this level of journalism may involve going to the mayor's office to pick up a transcript of the speech he is to deliver this evening or it may involve calling the mortuary holding the body of the child who drowned last night. The stories based on these facts rely almost wholly on information the source has supplied.

Fact gathering at Layer I is the journalistic equivalent of surface mining. The reporter sinks no shafts into the event but is content to use top-layer material, some of which is presented by public relations and information specialists. Much of the reporter's task is confined to sorting out and rearranging the delivered facts, verifying addresses and dates and checking the spelling of names. Most stories appearing in newspapers and on radio and television are based on source-originated material.

Essential Information   Despite criticism of it, Layer I reporting serves an essential function. At its most basic level, it gives the community information about the happenings in the community. The local newspaper will publish photos of dogs awaiting adoption at the County Animal Shelter and tell parents that the school lunch on Monday will be hot dogs, junior salad bar, veggie dippers and fruit salad. Tuesday, meatball sandwich, salad, buttery corn and raisins. . . .

The newspaper also will provide an hour-by-hour police incident report:

> 1:03 a.m.: A loud party was reported on Lincoln Street. On request, the responsibles agreed to quiet down.
> 2:24 a.m.: William Young of 42 Broadway was arrested for driving under the influence of alcohol. He was booked in the county jail. . . .

In Layer I, journalists report city council meetings, legislative hearings, United Way fund raising, street closings, traffic accidents, basketball games, appointments of the new university president and human rights commissioner, the verdicts at trials—an enormous range of activities. These stories tell people what's happening and to whom. Such coverage is essential, especially in the area of public affairs. The public must have access to the statements and activities of its officials, and these officials must have access to the people so they know what's on the mind of the public. This give and take makes responsive, consensual government possible.

Manipulation and Acceptance

News organizations, as well as sources, have thrived under the arrangement implicit in Layer I journalism. Material for news can be obtained quickly and inexpensively by relying on source-originated information. Sometimes, it is impossible to dig any deeper.

In totalitarian countries journalists are restricted in coverage, as they are during wars and armed conflicts. The pictures journalists drew of these countries were often exactly the opposite of the grim reality. John K. Fairbank, an esteemed scholar of Chinese history who at one time wrote that the Chinese peasants had found Mao's revolution "a magnificent achievement," admitted later, "Our reporting was very superficial. As has been pointed out it was mainly through the English language, it was seldom from a village, and I don't recall ever talking to a peasant in the three or four years I was in wartime China."

Steven Mosher, a historian, says in his book *China Misperceived: American Illusions and Chinese Reality* that while journalists were sending back glowing reports of the progress in reducing crime and massive improvement in health, millions were dying of starvation.

Despite considerable coverage of the Soviet Union, its swift collapse came as a shock to newspaper readers and television viewers. They were surprised by the revelations of the ruinous state of the economy and the pervasive hatred of the Communist Party among the people. There was no indication of this in many reporters' accounts of Soviet life. The manipulators of the media had been able to hide the true state of affairs in these repressive societies.

But there is no excuse for accepting Layer I material when verification is possible.

Pseudo-Events

As the mass media, particularly television, became the dominant dispensers of experience in American life, sources sought to manipulate reality to accommodate the media, especially television's need for pictures. The information sources realized that press releases and announcements unaccompanied by visual material of events would not merit more than 20 seconds on most newscasts, if that. As a result, sources learned to stage events for the press that resembled spontaneous events (Layer II) but were, in fact, as much under the control of the source as the press release and the prepared speech. These staged events are known as *media-events* or *pseudo-events.*

The press could use the stories and pictures of the first female window washer in San Francisco, even if the event had been dreamed up to publicize the availability of rental space in a new office building. By providing the media with an endless stream of events, the managers of staged events enable the 11 p.m. news to be different from the 7 p.m. news and the afternoon newspaper to take the morning news a step further. The flow of contrived events feeds the insatiable news maw, for the public has been conditioned to demand vivid, dramatic news with every newscast and edition. Television stations—creating and responding to the demand—devised news programs with titles such as "Eyewitness News" and "Action News."

Following a presidential State of the Union speech, Russell Baker of *The New York Times* asked one of the president's advisers if the speech "was not mostly a media event, a nonhappening staged because reporters would pretend it was a happening."

"It's *all* media event," the adviser replied. "If the media weren't so ready to be used, it would be a very small splash."

Daniel J. Boorstin, the social historian, originated the term *pseudo-event* to describe these synthetic occurrences. He says that a "larger and larger proportion of our experience, of what we read and see and hear, has come to consist of pseudo-events." In the process, he says, "Vivid image came to overshadow pale reality." His book about image making opens with this short dialogue:

ADMIRING FRIEND: "My, that's a beautiful baby you have there!"
MOTHER: "Oh, that's nothing—you should see his photograph."

Boorstin says the pseudo-event has these characteristics: "It is not spontaneous, but comes about because someone has planned, planted or incited it. . . . It is planted primarily (but not always exclusively) for the immediate purpose of being reported or reproduced. Therefore, its occurrence is arranged for the convenience of the reporting or reproducing media. . . . Its relation to the underlying relativity of the situation is ambiguous. . . ."

Media Manipulation

The orchestration of events for public consumption is a frequent occurrence in government and politics. Needing public attention and approval, politicians often resort to media manipulation, and they often get away with their contrivances.

Perhaps one of the most dramatic pictures of the civil rights movement in the South in the early 1960s showed a determined Gov. George C. Wallace blocking the entrance to a University of Alabama building, refusing to allow two black students to enroll. For Wallace, a symbol to southerners of resistance to federally imposed desegregation, this was a powerful image. He refused to give way when confronted by federalized National Guard troops with a court order.

Grudgingly, however, in the face of firepower, he stood aside.

The reality was far different: In secret meetings, the Justice Department and Wallace had worked out a scenario that would make President John Kennedy and Wallace look good. Wallace would be allowed to take a stand

Spinsters. People, wrote Walter Lippmann in his 1922 book *Public Opinion,* do not react rationally to information but respond to the "pictures inside their heads." This marked "the birthing moment of spin," says Stuart Ewen, Hunter College historian and author of *PR! A Social History of Spin.* "We live in a world where everyone is always battling for the public mind and public approval," Ewen says. "I think the public believes there is no truth, only spin—in part because much of the educated middle class spins for a living."

against desegregating the university but would permit the black students to enroll under the Guard's protection.

Wallace thus was able to make political capital in the South, and Kennedy appeared decisive to people who wanted the country to move faster toward desegregating its educational system.

Another well-plotted scenario developed during the 1972 Republican presidential convention. But this pseudo-event was exposed by enterprising reporters.

Presidential Plotting   Because President Nixon was certain to be renominated, Republicans faced a publicity problem: How could reality—the routine renomination of the president—be made exciting? If there were no drama, how then would the White House press managers keep the public tied to the television screen and how would they be able to provide the raw material from which reporters could fashion their stories?

The GOP's solution was to override reality with a staged event of enormous dimension. The White House wrote a 50-page scenario for the convention, a full script that called for "impromptu remarks" from delegates, "spontaneous" shouts of "Four more years," and allotted—to the minute—screams of enthusiasm. At the moment the president would be renominated, the chairman was instructed to attempt "unsuccessfully" to quell the "spontaneous" cheering.

The script fell into the hands of the press. *The Wall Street Journal,* among others, ran news stories on how the White House had organized the convention for television viewers. As the *Journal*'s reporter, Norman C. Miller, put it in his story, the "convention was perhaps the most superorganized ever . . . the delegates' only function during the formal proceedings was to serve as a necessary backdrop for the TV show."

Miller went offstage and tried to dig up the real story—Layer II. He interviewed delegates, watched a pep rally for Republican women and found no one had showed up at the "Poor People's Caucus."

Campaign Consultants   The manipulation of political conventions is matched by the strategies of campaign consultants and media handlers to keep the press from direct access to the candidates. Press handouts and daily telegenic events are common fare for campaigns. In presidential campaigns, political pros usually call the shots in campaign coverage. Some examples:

In 1988, George Bush went to Disneyland where he met U.S. Olympic athletes and some Walt Disney characters. That night, television had colorful pictures. NBC showed Bush talking to the athletes: "You're representing the country of the little guy. No matter what the circumstances of your birth and background, you can go anywhere and do anything."

In another visual, Bush was shown unloading fish at a San Diego cannery. And so it went. Dukakis' media chiefs tried to match these visuals when they realized they were being overwhelmed on the evening television news. The Democrats put Dukakis in an Army tank, but the visual was a flop: It showed the head of a diminutive Dukakis peeping out of the turret.

In the 1992 presidential campaign, the Democrats faced a serious problem: A poll showed that 40 percent of the voters considered Bill Clinton a "wishy-washy" politician who would not "talk straight." They disliked Hillary Clinton even more, describing her as "being in the race for herself, going for power," a wife intent on "running the show."

Clinton had already been battered by talk of an extramarital affair. Something, his advisers agreed during the summer of 1992, would have to be done to keep the campaign from disintegrating.

Behavior Modification   The result was a 14-page outline of behavior modification and media manipulation. Clinton was to be made into an ordinary guy. Hillary Clinton was to be less aggressive, the couple "warm and cuddly."

The image construction was necessary, Democratic strategists reasoned, because the Republicans were sure to emphasize Bush "family values" and imply the Clintons lacked these values.

But by the time the Republicans "made their move, the program of image-modification drafted by Clinton's consultants had so changed the Clintons' public persona that the feared attack failed to wound him at all," *The New York Times* reported. Clinton had become just plain Bill, even "Bubba," as a friendly talk show host described him.

Clinton made the news by playing the saxophone on one of the late-night shows. He turned a sanctimonious assertion that he had tried marijuana as a student but had not inhaled into a joke, making fun of himself. His handlers had found through focus groups that people viewed Clinton sympathetically when he talked about his mother and the alcoholic stepfather who abused his brother and his mother.

On talk shows and in interviews, Clinton presented what his strategists had worked out as "the human side, the real Bill Clinton." As for Hillary Clinton, they made her speak out on family issues.

The results included a *People* cover story, "At Home with the Clinton Family," and a *U.S. News and World Report* story, "The Bill Clinton Nobody Knows."

During Clinton's administration, Hillary Clinton emerged as a powerful spokeswoman for health care reform. Again, pollsters found that some people wanted her less visible, and the White House took notice. But in the 1996 presidential campaign, Hillary Clinton re-emerged, speaking often, traveling widely.

History may have taught the Clintons something. During Franklin Roosevelt's presidency, his wife Eleanor was an outspoken advocate of causes—racial justice, strong unions, international cooperation. The criticism was loud, continuous and sometimes vicious, all to no avail. Mrs. Roosevelt continued to travel widely and to speak out. President Roosevelt supported her. Mrs. Roosevelt remained the most popular woman in the country, and her husband was elected to four terms in the White House.

Sex in the White House   After his re-election, Clinton faced another attack on his personal life, again because of an extramarital affair, this one occurring in the White House with a young intern attached to his staff. His advisers knew that Clinton's personal popularity could carry him through the rough seas if he continued to demonstrate strong leadership. He did just that, ordering an air attack on terrorists in Afghanistan and the Sudan, traveling to Russia to help Boris Yeltsin weather a political and economic storm, promising to keep Social Security adequately funded, making sure the economy continued strong.

Clinton's media handlers also had turned Clinton into a man of the political middle, neither liberal nor conservative.

The public rewarded Clinton with a 60 percent-plus standing in the polls despite his sexual liaison with the young intern and his impeachment in the House of Representatives.

Trial Balloons

One of the ways government officials manage the media is through the floating of trial balloons. The technique involves letting reporters in on inside information, usually about an appointee or a new program. The material is to be used without attribution. The information is published or used on television, and public reaction is gauged. If the public rejects the idea floated, no one can be blamed as there is no source named. If there is acceptance, the nominee may be named, the program adopted.

Early in his administration, President Clinton floated several nominees before the public. One, a candidate for attorney general, pulled out when negative response developed. The administration also leaked the possibility of freezing cost-of-living increases for Social Security recipients. When the reaction was negative, the administration sent up another balloon—increasing the taxes on Social Security benefits. That met with less opposition.

Dangers of Layer I

When reporting is confined to Layer I, the distinction between journalism and public relations is hard to discern. The consequences for society can be serious, as Joseph Bensman and Robert Lilienfield, sociologists, explain:

> When "public relations" is conducted simultaneously for a vast number of institutions and organizations, the public life of a society becomes so congested with manufactured appearances that it is difficult to recognize any underlying realities.
> As a result, individuals begin to distrust all public facades and retreat into apathy, cynicism, disaffiliation, distrust of media and public institutions. . . . The journalist unwittingly often exposes the workings of the public relations man or information specialist, if he operates within a genuine journalistic attitude.

Tom Wicker of *The New York Times* said that the press—because of its concentration on Layer I—has been weak at picking up new developments before they have become institutionalized, and their sponsors have learned to stage media events to attract attention.

Conduit. "Increasingly, information is generated by those who wish to promote something or someone—a product, a cause, a political candidate or officeholder—without arguing their case on its merits or explicitly advertising it as self-interested material either. Much of the press, in its eagerness to inform the public, has become a conduit for the equivalent of junk mail."
—*Christopher Lasch.*

Worthwhile Information

Some staged events do produce news—the civil rights demonstrations in the 1960s, picketing by the local teachers union. Certainly, dozens of source-originated events are newsworthy—the text of the mayor's speech, the details the mortuary supplies about the child's death, the announcement that the university football program has been placed on probation for booster activities that included payment to athletes.

A Hospital Closes Good reporters can show initiative in Layer I reporting, as did Jere Downs when she covered Montgomery County for *The Philadelphia Inquirer.* Downs had heard that the Sacred Heart Hospital in Norristown was about to close its doors. But when? Downs says she "crept into the hospital and went to the boardroom." She had been told that the closing was imminent, perhaps that day. Yes, she learned, the board members were being told of the immediate closure.

This was big news. The hospital was the borough's fourth-largest employer with 870 full- and part-time employees, and almost 100 patients would have to be transferred.

Downs had a few hours to make the morning newspaper with her story.

First, she talked to board members. Then she interviewed employees "who had just learned that this shift would be their last. I knew many people who worked at the hospital and called them from a nearby pay phone for quotes.

"My best break came through a retired policeman who was working as a security guard at the hospital. He told me that 85-year-old Jimmy Caiola, who helped found the hospital in the 1930s, was a patient on the fifth floor.

"I knew Jimmy and called up to his room about 9:30, just in time to put the finishing touch on the story that I then dictated over the phone."

Downs' story made page 1. An *Inquirer* editor called her work the "finest deadline reporting" in years. The story begins:

The financially troubled Sacred Heart Hospital in Norristown abruptly announced last night that it will shut down today, transferring 97 patients and laying off 870 full- and part-time employees.

Hospital president J. Russell Walsh made the announcement shortly after 9 p.m., following a vote to close by the board of directors.

"Despite aggressive cost-saving measures and months of extensive review of operating alternatives," Walsh said, "resources will not be available to sustain the services necessary to guarantee quality care for our patients, and we must take the necessary steps to not place them in jeopardy." He said the hospital had an operat-

ing deficit of $2.2 million for the first quarter of this year. In recent years, he said, the hospital had instituted layoffs and significant cost-cutting measures.

The 270-bed nonprofit hospital and rehabilitation center, at DeKalb and Fornance Streets, was founded in 1936 by the Missionary Sisters of the Most Sacred Heart, a Catholic order based in Reading, Pa.

Hospital officials said the transfers and discharges of patients would begin this morning and were expected to be completed by the end of the day. They said nurses were visiting patients last night, informing them of what was in store this morning.

Handling the Handout

"Don't be a handout reporter," Harry Romanoff, a night city editor on the *Chicago American,* would tell young reporters. One of Romanoff's charges was Mervin Block, who recalls an encounter with Romanoff:

I remember his giving me a fistful of press releases trumpeting movie monarch Louis B. Mayer's expected arrival at the Dearborn Street Railroad Station. An hour later, Romy asked me what time Mayer's train would be pulling in. I told him, and when he challenged my answer, I cited the handouts: one from the Santa Fe, one from Mayer's studio (MGM), and one from his destination, the Ambassador East Hotel. All agreed on the time. But that wasn't good enough for Romy.

"Call the stationmaster and *find out.*"

More Costly   When handouts from food chains in Chicago announced price cuts on thousands of items, the Chicago newspapers bannered the stories on their front pages. One such headline:

Inflation Breakthrough—Food Prices to Drop Here

Despite the rash of stories about how the shopper "may save 15% in price battle," as one paper said in a headline over one of its stories, consumers were actually paying more on a unit, or per-ounce, basis.

The Chicago commissioner of consumer affairs demonstrated that the city's consumers were being misled by the store announcements and consequently by the newspaper stories that took the handouts at face value. Many of the items that were reduced in price were also reduced in weight. Peanut clusters went from 72 cents a packet to 69 cents, an apparent saving of 3 cents. But the packet went from 6 ounces to 5 1/4 ounces. With a little arithmetic, a reporter could have figured out that this was actually an increase of 6 cents a packet. Some items were publicized because they stayed at the same price "despite inflation," according to the handouts and the stories. True enough. A 70-cent can of beef stew was still 70 cents. But the new can contained half an ounce less than the old can.

The moral of this little tale of the peanut clusters and beef stew is: Even when operating in Layer I, check and check again.

The Internet as Source

Journalists mine the Internet for background information, as a tip source for stories and as a communication channel with other reporters and with sources. The Internet extends the reach of the journalist enormously. A reporter with *The Knoxville News-Sentinel* says he refers to the World Wide Web "as much as to the city directory, telephone book and the newspaper morgue."

But there is a difference between the material obtained via the Internet and that from standard references. The references are checked and verified. When the journalist turns to the Web, often as not he or she is operating in Layer I with unverified, source-originated material—and sometimes the source may be spurious.

Let's look at what happened when a reporter discovered what she thought was a lead to a fabulous feature.

The Backyard Archaeologist

The material looked promising:

Subject: a nutball
Date: Monday, April 13, 1998 10:33AM

The story behind the letter below is that there is this nutball who digs things out of his back yard and sends the stuff he finds to the Smithsonian Institute, labeling them with scientific names, insisting that they are actual archaeological finds. This guy really exists and does this in his spare time! Anyway . . . here's the actual response from the Smithsonian Institute.

Smithsonian Institute
207 Pennsylvania Avenue
Washington, DC 20078

Dear Sir:

Thank you for your latest submission to the Institute, labeled "93211-D, layer seven, next to the clothesline post, Hominid skull."
We have given this specimen a careful and detailed examination, and regret to inform you that we disagree with your theory that it represents conclusive proof of the presence

of Early Man in Charleston County two million years ago. Rather, it appears that what you have found is the head of a Barbie doll, of the variety one of our staff, who has small children, believes to be "Malibu Barbie."

It is evident that you have given a great deal of thought to the analysis of this specimen, and you may be quite certain that those of us who are familiar with your prior work in the field were loathe to come to contradiction with your findings. However, we do feel that there are a number of physical attributes of the specimen which might have tipped you off to its modern origin:

1. The material is moulded plastic. Ancient hominid remains are typically fossilized bone.

2. The cranial capacity of the specimen is approximately 9 cubic centimetres, well below the threshold of even the earliest identified proto-homonids.

3. The dentition pattern evident on the skull is more consistent with the common domesticated dog than it is with the ravenous man-eating Pliocene clams you speculate roamed the wetlands during that time.

This latter finding is certainly one of the most intriguing hypotheses you have submitted in your history with this institution, but the evidence seems to weigh rather heavily against it. Without going into too much detail, let us say that:

A. The specimen looks like the head of a Barbie doll that a dog has chewed on.

B. Clams don't have teeth.

It is with feelings tinged with melancholy that we must deny your request to have the specimen carbon dated. This is partially due to the heavy load our lab must bear in its normal operation, and partly due to carbon dating's notorious inaccuracy in fossils of recent geologic record. To the best of our knowledge, no Barbie dolls were produced prior to 1956 AD, and carbon dating is likely to produce wildly inaccurate results. Sadly, we must also deny your request that we approach the National Science Foundation Phylogeny Department with the concept of assigning your specimen the scientific name Australopithecus spiff-arino. Speaking personally, I, for one, fought tenaciously for the acceptance of your proposed taxonomy, but was ultimately voted down because the species name you selected was hyphenated, and didn't really sound like it might be Latin in origin.

However, we gladly accept your generous donation of this fascinating specimen to the museum. While it is undoubtedly not a Hominid fossil, it is, nonetheless, yet another riveting example of the great body of work you seem to accumulate here so effortlessly. You should know that our Director has reserved a special shelf in his own office for the display of the specimens you have previously submitted to the Institute, and the entire staff speculates daily on what you will happen upon next in your digs at the site you have discovered in your back yard.

We eagerly anticipate your trip to our nation's capital that you proposed in your last letter, and several of us are pressing the Director to pay for it. We are particularly interested in hearing you expand on your theories surrounding the transpositating fillifitation of ferrous ions in a structural matrix that makes the excellent juvenile Tyrannosaurus rex femur you recently discovered take on the deceptive appearance of a rusty 9-mm Sears Craftsman automotive crescent wrench.

Yours in Science,

Harvey Rowe
Curator, Antiquities

Check It   Great stuff. But our reporter Clara is not about to jump to the keyboard. She recalls reading about some credulous broadcasters who aired a story that ostensibly moved on the AP wire that Bill Gates of Microsoft had bought the Vatican. And she has heard about the thousands of people who sent their beaten-up old sneakers to the Nike factory in Wilsonville, Ore., when a report on the Internet stated that the company would redeem the old shoes with new ones.

Clara looks at the material again and suddenly is suspicious. She notes that the sender refers to the "Smithsonian Institute." Actually, it's the Smithsonian *Institution.* She wonders:

Maybe that's his error. But look at the reply. That also says *Institute.* Let me check the address in *The World Almanac.* It's on Jefferson Drive. But maybe Pennsylvania Avenue is the executive office of The Smithsonian.
This story is really too good to be true.
I'd better check with the Curator of Antiquities, Harvey Rowe.

Clara places a person-to-person call to Rowe. No such person exists at the Smithsonian, the operator tells her. Clara asks for the Curator of Antiquities. A pause. A long pause. Finally, the operator returns, "I'm sorry, there is no such title at the Institution."

So much for the backyard archaeologist. By moving deeper than Layer I, Clara saved herself from embarrassment. By engaging in the checking, the verification of the information, Clara was working in Layer II.

Layer II Reporting

When reporters initiate information-gathering and when they add to Layer I material, they are digging in Layer II. We could say that the ordinary beat reporting that journalists engage in has much of Layer II involved. When sports reporters cover a game, they are working in Layer II, for example.

Whenever the situation moves beyond the control of those trying to manage it, the reporter is working in Layer II.

The transition from Layer I to Layer II can be seen at a news conference. The reading of a statement provides the source-originated material (I). The give-and-take of the question and answer period is spontaneous (II). When the source declines to answer questions, the reporter should understand that he or she is back in Layer I, dealing with material controlled by the source.

The reporter who seeks verification from a second source that the governor will appear at the Lions Club ceremony is moving into Layer II. So is the reporter who, after she is told by the police that the hotel was burglarized at 5:46 a.m., looks up the time of sunrise that day. Her enterprise enables her to write, "The holdup man left the hotel in early morning darkness."

The reporter who writes that the state purchasing agent has awarded to a local dealer a contract for a fleet of automobiles is engaged in Layer I journalism. The investigative reporter who digs into the records to learn that the contract was awarded without bids is working at the second level.

Checking a City Proposal

When an official of a city undergoing a recession recommends a city-financed plan that he says will increase employment, the reporter will ask him for precise details, questions that belong mostly in Layer I reporting. Then the reporter will check the data the official has supplied. He will look into the program the official said has been working in another city in the South. This checking moves the reporter into Layer II. Finally, the reporter will seek comments from other city officials about the feasibility of the proposal and its prospects for adoption.

Untold numbers of stories have been written about proposals that went nowhere because they were badly drafted or were introduced or recommended by people with no influence. Local newspapers usually play up a legislator's proposals or intentions, but give no attention to the fact that he is a freshman with no influence, a member of the minority party, or that the committee chairwoman has vowed never to let such legislation move through her committee.

Normal Procedure   If we look back at the reporters at work in Chapter 1, we can see how often journalists move from Layer I to II:

• Much of the work Dick did on his story about the Black Parents Association after receiving the handout from the group was on his initiative.
• The investigative stories by Cammy Wilson, Heidi Evans and Carolyn Tuft were carried out entirely in Layer II.

These reporters moved beyond merely relaying information originated and controlled by a source. Each checked the information, supplied missing facts, explained complicated details. None of these efforts is the activity of a reporter content with Layer I information. When they have time, reporters usually move from I to II.

Let's look at some other examples of Layer II reporting.

Mark Avery

Seeking Out Dissidents

Jan Wong of *The Globe and Mail* of Toronto maintained contacts with those working for a democratic China in the face of suppression and prison. To avoid wiretaps and inquisitive police, she would meet in public places.

The Cost of the Gender Gap

After California passed a law prohibiting gender price discrimination, reporters for KRON-TV in San Francisco checked to see whether it was being complied with. The law had come about after a survey by a legislative office showed that women paid on average $1.79 more to launder an identical shirt than men, that they paid $5 more for a similar haircut and that clothing alterations were considerably more costly for women than for men.

KRON-TV reporters found "women were still being taken to the cleaners." Emerald Yeh and Christine McMurry found that of 30 hair salons in San Francisco, a third quoted higher prices for women than for men. When a woman took in a size 4 men's style shirt to be cleaned, she was charged $2.50. When a man took in the same shirt, he was charged $1.

Car Leasing   The TV team did a similar investigation on the hidden costs of car leasing. They found a couple that had signed a lease for a Toyota Corolla that would end up costing them more than twice a cash purchase would have cost them. They investigated "the seductive pitch of leasing—more car for less money" and they found high costs for those who lease. They found lease agreements do not have to state the price of the car on which monthly payments are based. Hidden charges such as extra mileage could cost thousands extra, they reported.

Women for Sale

When Lena H. Sun, *The Washington Post*'s correspondent in China, heard of the practice of selling women to men seeking wives, she looked for a victim so she wouldn't have to rely on secondhand accounts. On the outskirts of Beijing, she found Ma Linmei who was, Sun wrote, "a virtual prisoner. The main road is more than an hour away by foot, down a steep, rocky path. She has no money, and she can barely speak the local dialect. No one will help her escape."

Her husband had been unable to find a bride locally and traveled thousands of miles to Yunan Province in southwestern China to buy a wife.

Sun interviewed Ma, who told her, "I miss my home. I miss my mother. I'm always sick. If I had money I would run away."

But in a way, Ma was luckier than many women, Sun found. Thousands of others "are abducted by traders in human flesh, who trick them with promises of good jobs and a better life far from home. The traffickers often rape and beat the women before selling them into virtual bondage, often with the full knowledge and cooperation of local Communist Party officials. . . ."

Some of the victims, she reported, are as young as 14. Some are locked up, others shackled to keep them from running away. "Some have had their leg tendons cut to prevent them from escaping," Sun reported.

Deadly Plumes

The Massachusetts Military Reservation occupies 22,000 acres on the island of Cape Cod, and despite the $165 million spent over 15 years to clean the

Lena H. Sun,
The Washington Post

Sold for $363

Although Ma Linmei is far from home and is married to a man she does not like, she is luckier than most bought wives. Many are brutalized, kept in virtual captivity.

site, it continues to send toxic clouds into the air and over the land. The plumes aroused the interest of the *Cape Cod Times,* which found they had polluted 66 billion gallons of water sources on the large island.

Its six-part series presented this picture of irresponsibility by the government:

In what our grandchildren will judge the crime of the century on Cape Cod, poisons from our past are robbing us of our future.

And those people charged with protecting us—the military, politicians and government regulators—have been incapable of stopping the mushrooming environmental disaster.

Eleven fingers of toxic-waste plumes continue to stretch ever-outward from their points of origin on the Massachusetts Military Reservation, preying on the health and security of nearby residents and stealing from the Upper Cape's precious water supply.

Checkup

The Rev. Louis Farrakhan, leader of the Nation of Islam, told the National Press Club that he did not believe news stories about the existence of slavery in the Sudan. He challenged the press to go to the country and prove it. *The Baltimore Sun* sent two reporters to check. The reporters bought two small boys for $1,000 from Arab slave traders and wrote the story. (They returned the boys to their father.)

Computer-Assisted Reporting Projects

Journalists who use the computer to analyze material work in Layer II. When he was database editor of the *Austin American-Statesman* Jeff South teamed up with reporters to write informative stories. Here's how one begins:

Some of the highest-paid employees of Austin city government aren't doctors, lawyers and department heads. They're electricians, water workers and mechanics who add thousands of dollars to their salaries through overtime.

Dozens of city employees regularly earn more than $15,000 a year in overtime. Ninety have received more than $50,000 in overtime pay over the past four and a half years, and two-thirds of those employees work for one department: the electric utility.

By examining city payroll records, South and Mike Todd found the city had paid out more than $8 million in overtime in a year. A union official said the amount raises questions about proper staffing, equity in salaries and safety.

Dams, Drivers, Teachers In other computer analyses of database and other material, South found 402 dams in Texas "could collapse" with heavy rains, that despite the law a sixth of Texas drivers do not have auto insurance, and a fourth of Texas public schools had no black or Hispanic teachers.

South, now teaching journalism at Virginia Commonwealth University, said computer-assisted reporting widens the reporter's scope.

"When a bureaucrat announces the bottom line—appraisals went up 5 percent—the CAR-savvy reporter knows the real story is in the details." The announcement is Layer I journalism. The details take the reporter into Layer II. South asks:

"What was the biggest appraisal increase? Where did appraisals go down? Who owns those homes? Can we map changes by neighborhoods?

"Hey, let's run the appraisal database against the list of City Council members and appraisal office employees."

Notice the way Layer II journalism encompasses the watchdog function of the press.

Usually, such journalistic revelations lead to remedial action. But sometimes, the anger at Layer II journalism by those in power can be overwhelming to a journalist. Raymond Bonner of *The New York Times* paid a high price for his reporting of the El Mozote massacre in El Salvador.

Questioning Authority

In January 1982, Bonner found the charred skulls and other remains of dozens of men, women and children in a village in El Salvador. His story began, "From interviews with people who live in this small mountain village and surrounding hamlets, it is clear that a massacre of major proportions occurred here last month." Bonner described bones scattered through the El Mozote area. Hundreds were killed, he reported, quoting those who said they had witnessed government troops killing with abandon.

Bonner quoted Rufina Amaya, a survivor. She said she had hidden in trees when the soldiers arrived at El Mozote. They killed her blind husband and her four children, ages 9, 5 and 3 years and 8 months.

The story appeared at a time U.S. foreign policy supported the military regime in El Salvador. Worried by the leftist Sandinista government in nearby Nicaragua, the Reagan administration wanted to contain guerilla movements in Central America. El Mozote was the key to a guerilla stronghold.

The Reagan foreign policy was under attack as supporting the El Salvadoran military regime's abuse of human rights, and Bonner's story in the prestigious *Times* threatened to undermine the policy still more.

Denials and Accusations

The government said no massacre had occurred. *The Wall Street Journal*'s editorial page, which was a strong supporter of the Reagan foreign policy, described Bonner as "overly credulous," and "a reporter out on a limb," that he had been taken in by a rebel "propaganda exercise." In a 36-inch editorial titled "The Media's War," the *Journal* editorialized:

> Much of the American media, it would seem, was dominated by a style of reporting that grew out of Vietnam—in which Communist sources were given greater credence than either the U.S. Government or the government it was supporting.

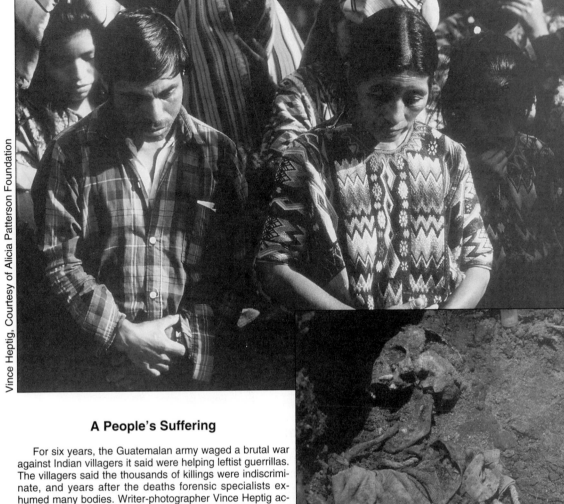

A People's Suffering

For six years, the Guatemalan army waged a brutal war against Indian villagers it said were helping leftist guerrillas. The villagers said the thousands of killings were indiscriminate, and years after the deaths forensic specialists exhumed many bodies. Writer-photographer Vince Heptig accompanied forensic anthropologist Luis Minguel Alonso as he dug up remains. In *The APF Reporter,* Heptig tells the story simply and directly. Here are some excerpts:

Layer by layer, Luis brushed away the rich soil to reveal what the onlooking people already knew—the boy had been shot in the head. As he continued, Luis revealed the rope that tied the young boy's hands behind his back had also reached around his neck.

Luis deducted that the boy had been killed by "tiro do gracia," or a shot to the head at close range. The other twelve bodies the anthropologists unearthed suffered similar fates.

This mass grave contained 13 skeletons, bringing the total number of bodies exhumed in this tiny village to 26.

A Boy's Death: Hands Tied, Shot in Head ▶

The ambassador to El Salvador described Bonner as an "advocate journalist," meaning Bonner had a desire to see events to fit a social or political agenda.

The *Times* buckled under the pressure. It ordered Bonner home and put him on the business desk.

Vindication

In time, Bonner was proved right. A team of forensic archaeologists dug into the ruins of El Mozote in 1992 and uncovered dozens of skeletons, most of children. They found shell casings and other indications of a massacre.

After reading Mark Danner's book *The Massacre at El Mozote: A Parable of the Cold War, New York Times* columnist Tony Lewis wrote, "After the Danner report, no rational person can doubt that Salvadoran forces carried out a massacre. They killed hundreds of people in El Mozote and other hamlets nearby: men, women, children, infants. They killed with a savagery that is hard even to read about." Lewis wrote that the incident proved "again how essential it is to be skeptical of convenient government denials."

At *The Washington Post,* its reporter Alma Guillermoprieto had written a report similar to Bonner's. *Post* editor Ben Bradlee did not back down in the face of pressure. Bradlee supported his reporter.

In an article in *Harper's* 10 years after the Bonner story and his recall, Michael Massing asked, "Did the *Times* bow to pressure from the government? When does official criticism of a reporter amount to a threat? What happens to a reporter when his or her interpretation of events contradicts that of the powers that be?"

After Bonner's exile, a new editor at the *Times* restored Bonner as a foreign correspondent.

Similarities in Guatemala

This was not the first time that the *Times* acceded to government pressure in placing foreign correspondents. In 1954, the publisher of the newspaper agreed with the CIA to keep Sydney Gruson out of Guatemala. The CIA suggested that Gruson was "politically suspect." At the same time the CIA was clearing Guatemala of an inquisitive reporter, it was planning a coup to overthrow the elected president.

The coup was successful and the country began a slide into oppressive right-wing rule that led to a lengthy guerilla war with government troops engaging in the same kind of village cleansing as took place in El Salvador.

Investigative Reporting

Those who dig deepest in Layer II are called investigative reporters. They check on illegal activities such as awarding government contracts to politically connected insiders in violation of purchasing laws. They also look into systemic abuses such as those conducted by the Brownsville Revival in Florida that attracted the attention of the *Pensacola News Journal.*

Miracles or Hokum? The Revival had mixed notices. "If believers of the Brownsville Revival were correct—that this might be one of the signs that Jesus Christ is ready to return to earth—it would be the religion news story of the decade and probably of the century," said Executive Editor Teresa Wasson. "At the same time, there were many other people who had serious questions about the revival and what its leaders were doing."

The newspaper decided to investigate and assigned 10 of its staff of 70 to look into the Revival. It set out to answer some questions:

> The numbers are amazing: millions of visitors, millions of dollars, thousands of souls. The claims are heart-warming: crime curtailed, addiction overcome, sickness healed. The leaders are captivating: an ex-convict-junkie converted to evangelism; a visionary and prophet dedicated to revival. But how true is it all? Is Pensacola's Brownsville Revival all that its leaders say it is? Are the leaders who and what they say they are?

Distortion, Manipulation After a four-month inquiry, the newspaper published a five-part series that proved that little of the millions of dollars donated by the faithful went to charity, missions, the poor or to legitimate church and revival expenses. The reporters found no miraculous healings.

The religious message, the newspaper reported, consisted of "distortions of Scripture and sharp departures from Pentecostal teachings and practices" in the course of manipulating believers.

Victimizing the Poor

Another investigation that comes under the heading of checking a systemic abuse began when Judy Johnson of *The Anniston Star* heard that some people in an Alabama community were having trouble getting credit from banks and finance companies. She decided to investigate. She spent months examining records of mortgages and land transfers. "I compiled them into lists year by year, looking for patterns, building a history," she said.

She talked to people turned down by banks. Through the years of borrowing from a local businessman, one woman had accumulated $50,000 in loans. Among her loans was one for a four-year-old car she and her husband had bought from the businessman's used car lot. The model she bought cost her slightly less than a new car would have cost her.

Johnson showed how the poor, who cannot obtain credit from large lending institutions, are victimized by private lenders. Her series won national recognition.

A Tax Giveaway

As soon as the massive Tax Reform Act was passed by Congress and signed by the president, Donald L. Barlett and James B. Steele of *The Philadelphia Inquirer* began to examine it. They discovered hundreds of tax breaks for corporations and specific individuals. But the language was so intricate that identities were hidden.

Here is a typical provision:

> The amendments made by Section 201 shall not apply to a 562-foot passenger cruise ship, which was purchased in 1900 for the purpose of returning the vessel to United States service, the approximate cost of refurbishment of which is approximately $47,000,000.

The two investigative reporters set out to find who was profiting, why they were being helped and what the cost would be to taxpayers. They searched through financial disclosure statements by members of Congress, looked at documents of the Securities and Exchange Commission, used databases to examine thousands of newspapers, magazines, newsletters and government reports.

The digging took 15 months, and Barlett and Steele found that Congress had made the largest giveaway in the history of the federal income tax. (The beneficiaries of the provision involving the 562-foot passenger cruise ship, incidentally, were a group of wealthy investors in the *S.S. Monterey* who were given an $8 million tax break.)

They named the people and the companies that had been allowed to escape taxes by a law that stenographic journalists working in Layer I had hailed as a "tax reform." The rich were being helped by the new law at the expense of the average taxpayer.

In the face of massive public reaction—the lengthy series was reprinted around the country—Congress shelved its so-called reform legislation and passed a new tax bill without a single tax break for an individual or company. Barlett and Steele won the Pulitzer Prize for national reporting for their seven-part series.

Illegalities

Shortly after his graduation from journalism school, James Dwyer of *The Dispatch* in Hudson County, N.J., was checking the bids of merchants hoping to sell supplies to a vocational school. His instructor had told Dwyer that bids sometimes are manipulated and that looking them over can be rewarding.

Strange Bids   Dwyer noticed that some seemed to be typed on the same typewriter. He also noticed that the prices for ladders, dust cloths, shovels and other items were high. Even when the supplies were purchased in quantity, prices were higher than they would have been for goods sold as individual items in hardware stores. For example, the school paid $564 for ladders that local stores sold for $189. He visited the school and found enough dust cloths to keep the school's furniture glowing for a couple of centuries.

Dwyer tried to locate the firms that made the unsuccessful bids. He could not find them. He theorized that the agent through whom the goods were sold had invented bidders, and using these fake firms to enter high bids on faked stationery, the agent made his firm the low bidder. Dwyer's investigation confirmed his theory and a grand jury took over after his stories appeared.

Abortions to All   Next, to a clinic in Norfolk. "Are you going to perform an abortion?" Ellen Whitford asked the doctor who had just given her a pelvic examination. Whitford, a reporter for *The Virginian-Pilot* in Norfolk, had gone to the clinic to investigate statements women had given her of unusual activities there. Whitford was not pregnant, but the doctor said he would do an abortion.

Whitford had the proof she needed—that the clinic was performing unnecessary abortions. Her series of stories about the clinic led to the George Polk award for local reporting.

CAR Project   Finally, in this quick tour, back north to New York where a reporter had been told by an out-of-office politician that some city workers were political appointees who never showed up for work. An idea: Examine parking tickets in resort areas issued to vehicles with New York license plates. He compared the names on the tickets with names on the city payroll—possible with the computer and city payroll tapes. Lo and behold, he found tickets for city employees on days they were supposed to be working.

Finding Sources

As you may already have gathered, there are two basic types of sources, physical and human. Physical sources range from databases of political campaign donations to the minutes of city council sessions. They include census data and crime statistics. We will be looking at sources in greater detail in Chapter 13, but we'll pause a moment here to look at how a veteran reporter handles human sources.

Jeffrey A. Tannenbaum of *The Wall Street Journal* puts the names of the most helpful sources in his files. "Someday, they may come in handy," he says. But what about finding sources for a subject entirely new to the reporter?

"First, look for institutional sources," Tannenbaum says. "If you're writing about pizzas, there's a national association of pizza chefs." For his story about the growing power of the states' attorney generals, he asked the New York attorney general if there was an association of all 50 officers. He was given a telephone number.

In gathering information from news sources, he says, "One source leads to another. Perhaps only the seventh one in the chain has what you need."

When do you know you have gathered all you need? "Only after the information the sources have provided is getting redundant, and the sources are failing to supply new sources."

For his piece on the attorney generals, a source told him about the Pennsylvania AG's refusal to support the application of a Moose Lodge for renewal of its liquor license. The Lodge, Tannenbaum was told, had been rejecting black applicants for membership and had refused to serve drinks to blacks even when they were brought as guests. That situation became the basis of the lead to his story.

Getting Answers

Most sources are cooperative. But some make life difficult for the digging journalist. The source unaccustomed to being interviewed who shies away from questions requires time to soothe and reassure. Some sources simply refuse to talk to reporters. The public official or boardroom general who refuses to cooperate must be pressed for answers to legitimate questions affecting the public.

Reporters have a few techniques to make reluctant sources open up to their questions. When a public official will not respond to legitimate questions about public events and issues, the reporter can tell the source that the public has a right to expect openness from those its taxes support.

For those in private life who exercise power—media company heads, utility directors and the like—the refusal to reply can be met with the reporter's, "Fine. I'll just say that you 'refused to answer' this question." Faced with a non-responsive response, the reporter counters, "OK. I'll just say that you 'did not explain your answers.'"

When nothing works, reporters usually turn to other sources to try to obtain the needed information. And when there is demonstrable falsification by a source, the reporter is free to say so in the story.

Correcting Sources

The reporter moves from Layer I to Layer II reporting when he or she refuses to allow incorrect information to reach the public. In an interview with *The New York Times,* a financier said he wanted upbeat news in the newspaper he was trying to save from failing, the *New York Post.* He said the *Post*'s founder, Alexander Hamilton, "wasn't into printing negative things." The story continued:

> "He was up about the country; he wasn't looking for the bad," Mr. Hoffenberg said. (In fact, Hamilton's newspaper was known for publishing scathing editorial commentary as well as juicy tidbits about the sex life of Hamilton's rival, Thomas Jefferson.)

The reporter didn't wait for or seek out another source to deny the source's assertion about Hamilton. She corrected it on her own in the same story in which the misstatement was made.

Caution: Journalists cannot expect public support in their persistence in digging for information. "The press in America is operating in an environment of public opinion that is increasingly indifferent—and to some extent hostile—to the cause of a free press in America," George Gallup, the pollster, concluded after measuring public attitudes toward the press. He found that 37 percent of his respondents said curbs on the press were "not strict enough," whereas 32 percent said they were "about right" and only 17 percent said they were "too strict." The others had no opinion.

A reason for this anti-press sentiment from the public may be found in another set of questions Gallup asked. The poll found that only 24 percent of those asked knew "what the First Amendment to the U.S. Constitution is or what it deals with." Less than half, 42 percent, of the college-educated answered correctly.

Layer III Reporting

People are not content with knowing only what happened. They also want to know how and why it happened, what it means and what may occur as a result—causes and consequences. When the story is important, reporters should mine Layer III, the area of interpretation and analysis.

Layer III reporting tells people how things work and why they work that way, or why they don't work. When President Bush announced two legislative actions with political overtones during the 1992 campaign, he did so, *New York Times* reporter Andrew Rosenthal wrote, "after the network news programs had already been prepared. The hour of disclosure assured that they would receive minimum press exposure. . . ."

Layer III reporting moves into the area of judgment and inference. Obviously, this kind of journalism requires reporters who have command of their subjects as well as a mastery of the craft.

The need for interpretative and explanatory journalism in a complex society emerged at the same time the preparation of journalists was becoming more formal and less insular. Before World War II, most journalists came up through an apprenticeship system. Hired as copyboys—almost all were male—they learned the processes and procedures of the newsroom, which were the sum and substance of the education of most reporters and editors.

When the GI Bill of Rights produced a sea of education-hungry young men and women after World War II, journalism schools expanded. They offered more than trade-school training. The result was a new generation of journalists who had studied sociology, geography, foreign languages. Editors, in time, respected this background and gradually began to allow their reporters greater leeway in reporting. Reporters are now allowed to point, explain, lead.

Easy Credit The AP story from Chicago began:

> William Rodriguez trudged home through rain and snow and wee-hour darkness.
> He was only 23, in good health and known as a happy-go-lucky fellow.
> Yet he would be dead before sunrise.

Rodriguez had purchased rat poison on his way home from work, and as he walked he ate the poison. Why? the AP assigned two reporters to find out. Their digging turned up the answer—easy credit. Rodriguez owed $700 to merchants for furniture, clothing, a television set. He couldn't meet the payments, and the creditors were threatening to tell his employer.

The story galvanized the city's enforcement agencies. Rodriguez had been sold low-grade merchandise and had been given credit at usurious rates. The legislature reacted by lowering interest rates. The resulting law is known as the "Rodriguez Law."

Voter-Conscious   When the New Jersey state legislature passed a bill banning state Medicaid payments for abortions, it ignored nine federal district court decisions in eight states that ruled similar bills were unconstitutional. The reason for the legislators' action was described in this Layer III sentence from *The New York Times:* "Approval of the measure reflects the influence of the Catholic Church, which opposes abortion, in New Jersey: About 55 percent of the state's registered voters are Catholic."

The battle over the need for interpretative reporting has long been over, although some newspaper and broadcast station editors are adamant about its dangers and rarely permit it. Dangers there are, but the risks are only slightly greater than those inherent in other areas of journalism. The benefits to the reader outweigh these risks.

Putting I, II and III to Work

Let us watch a reporter mine these three layers for his story.

City Planner Arthur calls the local stations and newspaper to read to reporters a statement about a new zoning proposal. The release contains facts 1, 2 and 3. At the newspaper, reporter Bernard looks over the handout, tells his city editor that 1 and 2 are of no news value but that 3—elimination of two-acre zoning north of town—is important and worth exploring in an interview with Arthur. The editor agrees and assigns Bernard to the story.

Before leaving for the interview, Bernard checks the newspaper library for a story about a court decision he recalls that may be related to the proposed regulation. He telephones another city official and a real estate developer to obtain additional information. With this background and Arthur's statement, Bernard begins to develop ideas for questions. He jots down a few, 4, 5 and 6.

During the interview, City Planner Arthur repeats 1, 2 and 3. Reporter Bernard asks for more information about 3, the elimination of the minimum two-acre requirement for home building. Bernard also brings up his own subjects by asking questions 4, 5 and 6. New themes develop during the interview: 7, 8 and 9.

Back in the newsroom, Bernard looks over his notes. He sees that his hunch about 3 was correct. It was important. Arthur's answer to question 5 is newsworthy, he decides, and fact 7—the possibility of low- and medium-cost housing in the area—which developed during the interview, may be the lead, especially because the broadcast stations probably will not have it. Bernard needs comments on the impact of 7 from developers. A couple of calls and the possible consequences, 10, emerge. The developers confirm their interest in building inexpensive housing. Looking over his notes, he spots background from the library, 11, that is now relevant and also will go into the story.

The story will contain facts 3, 5, 7, 10 and 11. Bernard decides he will fashion 7 and 10 into a lead, and he worries about how to blend 11 into the story at a fairly early stage without impeding the flow of Arthur's explanation. Background is important, but sometimes it is difficult to work smoothly into the story. He writes this lead:

A proposed change to eliminate the two-acre zoning requirement for home building north of town could open the area to people who can afford only low- and medium-cost housing.

Bernard's story will consist of the following:

Facts	Layer
3	I
5, 7, 11	II
10	III

Bernard has used almost all the techniques reporters have at their command to gather facts for stories. He was given information by a source. Then he used the newspaper library—a physical source—for background. He then interviewed his original source—a human source—and made independent checks by calling up additional sources.

Now that we have sketched out the layers of reporting, it is time to turn to the process itself, which we can summarize here before we go on:

- Know what to look for.
- Gather the information.
- Record it accurately.
- Weigh the information.

All this precedes writing.

Summing Up

Here is some down-to-earth advice about reporting from working reporters:

- Stay ready for any breaking news story by keeping up-to-date on developments in the community.
- There is a story behind almost any event. Remember, it was a third-rate break-in in a Washington building that began the Watergate revelations and ended in the resignation of a president.
- Always check all names in the telephone book, the city directory and the library to make absolutely sure they are spelled correctly.
- Follow the buck. Find out where money comes from, where it is going, how it gets there and who's handling it. Whether it is taxes, campaign contributions, or donations, keep your eye on the dollar.
- Be counterphobic. Do what you don't want to do or are afraid to do. Otherwise you'll never be able to dig into a story.
- Question all assumptions. The people who believed the emperor was clothed are legion and forgotten. We remember the child who pointed out his nudity.
- Question authority. Titles and degrees do not bestow infallibility.

Further Reading

Behrens, John C. *The Typewriter Guerrillas.* Chicago: Nelson-Hall, 1977.

Boorstin, Daniel J. *The Image: A Guide to Pseudo-Events in America.* New York: Atheneum, 1961.

Crouse, Timothy. *The Boys on the Bus.* New York: Random House, 1973.

Hersey, John. *The Algiers Motel Incident.* New York: Knopf, 1968.

Hess, Stephen. *The Washington Reporter.* Washington, D.C.: Brookings Institution, 1981.

McGinniss, Joe. *The Selling of the President 1968.* New York: Pocket Books, 1973.

Weir, David, and Dan Noyes. *Raising Hell: How the Center for Investigative Reporting Gets the Story.* Reading, Mass.: Addison-Wesley, 1983.

11 Making Sound Observations

Michael Norcia,
Daily News

Twelve stories high—a dramatic rescue.

Preview

To gather the reliable and relevant information essential to a story, the reporter must:

- Know what readers and listeners are interested in, what affects them and what they need to know.
- Find a theme for the story early in the reporting.
- Look for the dramatic, the unusual, the unique aspect of the event that sets it apart from other events like it.

Reporters face restraints on their fact gathering. Time is always limited; it is not always easy to find vantage points from which to see the event; sources will not cooperate.

For some stories, journalists use unobtrusive observation (the identity of the reporter is unknown to those being observed) and participant observation (the reporter becomes part of the event being reported).

The Congo was torn by civil war. Because the war had serious international implications, the United Nations dispatched a peacekeeping force and sent Secretary-General Dag Hammarskjold to the African republic to try to arrange a cease-fire.

At dusk, reporters at the Ndola airport in Northern Rhodesia awaiting Hammarskjold's arrival saw a plane land and a fair-haired man emerge. The reporters, who had been held behind police lines a hundred yards away, ran to file bulletins on the secretary-general's arrival. Anticipating Hammarskjold's next move, the press associations soon had stories describing Hammarskjold's conferring with President Moise Tshombe about a cease-fire. Many of these stories ran in early editions of the next day's newspapers.

But the man the reporters saw disembark was not Hammarskjold. He was a British foreign affairs official on a fact-gathering tour. At the time the reporters were filing their stories, Hammarskjold was aboard another plane that later crashed in a forest 10 miles north of Ndola, killing the secretary-general and the others on board.

The UPI reporter told his boss later, "I saw a man I thought looked like Hammarskjold. Other reporters claimed they were sure it was. After comparing notes, we all agreed to file stories."

293

The incident reveals some of the problems reporters face in covering spot news stories. To make sound observations, the reporter has to see and hear the event clearly, but this is not always possible. In this case, rather than wait to be certain of their man's identity, the reporters did what reporters do when their observations are uncertain and they are under pressure—they made an inference.

Because the man had light hair and his build approximated that of the secretary-general, the reporters jumped to the conclusion that he was Hammarskjold. They had violated the reporter's maxim, "Beware of inferences. Do not jump from the known to the unknown."

To guard against individual error, they checked with each other and formed a consensus. The difficulty in covering events often causes journalists to consult each other for reassurance, which leads to what is known as *herd* or *pack journalism.* Reporters tend to chat about the lead, the credibility of the source, the reliability of the documentation they have been offered. They seek agreement in resolving the uncertainties.

Accurate observations are the basis of news stories and features. Learning how to report accurately—more difficult than it seems—begins with an understanding of the methods that are used in the search for relevant information for the task of truth telling.

The Art of Observation

In his short story, "The Murders in the Rue Morgue," Edgar Allan Poe has his character C. Auguste Dupin expound on the art of observation as Dupin goes about solving the grisly murders of Madame L'Espanaye and her daughter, which have stumped the Parisian police. He dismisses the way the police work:

> There is no method in their proceedings, beyond the method of the moment. . . . The results obtained by them are not unfrequently surprising, but, for the most part are brought about by simple diligence and activity. When these qualities are unavailing, their schemes fail.

Although hard work is essential to good reporting, activity is not enough. A method is essential. Dupin says that the detective makes "a host of observations and inferences. So, perhaps, do his companions; and the difference in the extent of the information obtained lies not so much in the validity of the inference as in the quality of the observation. The necessary knowledge is of *what* to observe."

In other words, the vacuum-cleaner collector of information wastes time. Dupin says the proper method is to follow "deviations from the plane of the ordinary." This is how "reason feels its way, if at all, in its search for the truth. In investigations such as we are now pursuing, it should not be so much asked 'what has occurred,' as 'what has occurred that has never occurred before.' "

France's Fiction = New York's Fact

Dupin may be Poe's invention, but his method of observation is as real as the gunslingers on New York city streets. Robert T. Gallagher, a private detective who spent 18 years on the New York City police force, disarmed more than 1,200 gun-toting thugs before they could draw their weapons. He had, everyone on the force agreed, an uncanny ability to spot people carrying guns on the street. How did he do it?

"If you're not looking for the clues you don't notice them," Gallagher said. "But if you're looking for them, they're so obvious they begin to jump out at you."

The easy one, "the classic bulge," Gallagher dismisses. He knew that most street criminals stick their guns in their waistbands. As a consequence, when they walk the leg on the gun side takes a shorter stride and the arm a shorter swing.

Another clue: the "security feel." Those carrying guns unconsciously reach to touch the weapon. They also adjust it after getting out of a car, going up or down stairs and stepping off a curb.

He notices the way jackets hang in the front. Buttoned, one side clings more tightly to a thigh than the other.

Like Dupin, Gallagher looks for the different, the unusual, what Dupin calls the "deviations from the plane of the ordinary." Dupin talks of seeing the "matter as a whole," and Gallagher's procedure is to examine the clothing, the gait, the mannerisms of his suspect. Out of this picture may emerge the clue for Gallagher, the deviation for Dupin and the lead for the journalist.

The Reporter's Task   For the reporter, every assignment is a mystery to be unraveled. With a method of observation, the reporter can find the significant information that becomes the core of the story. What makes this basketball game decided in the last 30 seconds different from the dozens of others that are also won with a last-second basket? How does this school board meeting differ from the last one, and the one before that? What is the outstanding evidence in the prosecution's case, who among the many is the defense's key witness, the judge's most significant quote in his sentencing comments?

The journalist cannot leave it up to the reader, viewer or listener to decide. By knowing how to make the important, the pertinent, the relevant observation the reporter provides the public with insight.

'Make Me See'

When reporters see clearly and see as a whole, they are on their way to communicating not only truthfully, but graphically. Gene Roberts, former managing editor of *The New York Times,* learned this on his first job as the farm columnist for the 9,000-circulation *Goldsboro News-Argus* in Wayne County, N.C. Roberts' editor was Henry Belk, who was blind.

Mourner

For the reporter who seeks out the unusual, the sting of defeat may make as good a theme as the joy of victory.

The unusual is not always at center court. It may be on the sidelines where the losers bury their heads in grief. It could be found in the half-hidden gesture of capitulation when the candidate betrays a bold front. It could be buried in the small print in a document, the last sentence in a press release that begins with optimism and self-congratulation but ends with the admission of an unprofitable business year.

Looking deeply, listening intently, the reporter discovers truths that fascinate readers and viewers.

© Gregg Lovett

Roberts recalls that when he showed up for work in the morning, Belk would call him over and inform the young reporter that his writing was insufficiently descriptive.

"Make me see," he would order.

Roberts says, "It took me years to appreciate it, but there is no better admonition to the writer than 'Make me see.' There is no truer blueprint for successful writing than making your readers see. It is the essence of great writing."

Relevant Observations

The reporter on assignment is confronted by a flood of facts. A meeting can last two hours, cover seven different topics and include four decisions. A speaker may deliver an address containing 4,500 words. To handle these stories, the reporter may have at most a column for each story, about 750 words, or 90 seconds on a newscast.

There are three guides to the selection of relevant facts:

1. **Know the community:** Develop a feeling and understanding of what readers need and want to know.

2. **Find the theme:** Carefully identify the theme of the story as soon in the reporting as possible. This way facts that support, buttress and amplify the theme can be gathered, the rest ignored as irrelevant.

3. **Look for the dramatic:** Develop a sensitivity to the unique, the unusual, the break from the normal and routine.

Know the Community

In Chapter 2, we saw that material that is relevant to readers in one area may be unimportant to readers elsewhere and that the article that fascinates viewers here may bore others there. Journalists have to know what interests and affects their readers or viewers. This news sense is part intuition, part common sense and part knowledge acquired from living and working in the community.

Reporters who move from one area to another often have trouble adjusting to their new readers and listeners. The story is told about the veteran reporter for a Chicago newspaper who decided to forsake the big city for a more relaxed life in Texas. He accepted a job as the city editor of a west Texas daily newspaper. One day a fire broke out in town and the reporter's blood stirred in the city editor. He decided to go out on the story himself.

On his return, he batted out a story, Chicago style—dramatic and well-written. The managing editor was pleased with his city editor's handiwork except for one hole in the story.

"How much water did they use to put out the fire?" he asked. In parched west Texas, that fact was as important to readers as the number of fire units answering the call would have been to Chicago readers.

Find the Theme

Our second guideline is based on the form of the news story, which places certain demands on the reporter that he or she must satisfy in fact gathering. We know that the story consists of the statement of a central theme or idea (the lead) and the elaboration of that theme or idea (the body). The reporter must find the theme quickly so he or she can ask the relevant questions and make the appropriate observations to flesh out the story.

The sociologist Irving Kristol observed, "A person doesn't know what he has seen unless the person knows what he is looking for." In his book, *The Art of Scientific Investigation,* the British scientist W.I.B. Beveridge writes that developing ideas or hypotheses helps a person "see the significance of an object or event that otherwise would mean nothing."

When the Salvation Army dispatched 4,000 of its soldiers to New York City to do battle against "sin and evil," a reporter for *The New York Times* accompanied some of the troops through the streets. Impressed by the work of the Army men and women, the reporter decided early in her reporting to emphasize their dedication and singled out this detail in her account to illustrate her theme:

Bob Thayer,
The Providence Journal

Turning Point?

Did the steal open up a big inning? Or did the second baseman's grab of a poor throw keep the runner at second and prevent a rally? This play could be the lead for the game story.

"The Army believes in total abstinence," a young soldier was saying to a disheveled-looking man, whose breath reeked of alcohol. "You are the temple of the Lord and if you destroy yourself, you're destroying Him."

"Am I?" the older man asked, as they stood in front of the entranceway of the Commodore. "No, I'm not."

"Sure you are," the soldier replied, resting his hand on the man's shoulder. The man reached out his hand, too, and began to cry. So did the Salvation Army soldier.

This approach—confining observations to the theme—is not unique to journalism. All writing intended to communicate information is written with the theme clearly in mind. Irrelevant details are gravestones marking dead writing.

But if the reporter discovers facts that contradict the basic idea, then the idea is discarded and a new theme is adopted. In this way, the reporter is like the scientist whose conclusion can be no stronger than his or her evidence.

Of course, some events will have secondary themes. The same rule about gathering only material that buttresses the theme applies to the secondary ideas.

Devising Themes   Experienced reporters almost always have a theme or tentative idea as soon as they receive an assignment or at the outset of a story they originate. If a reporter is sent to cover a fire in a college dormitory, the reporter immediately thinks of deaths and injuries and the cause as the theme or possible lead. If the assignment is about the rescue of a drowning man, the lead could be the courage or ingenuity of the rescuer. Six youths die in an automobile accident; the reporter cannot help but immediately think of alcohol and drugs or speeding.

As soon as the Bethesda Naval Center announced that Supreme Court Justice Thurgood Marshall had died, reporters knew the theme of their story and the direction it would take. The fact that a Supreme Court Justice had died was not the theme but that the first black to join the Court and a leading figure in the civil rights movement had died. And that is just how the AP story began:

> WASHINGTON—Retired Justice Thurgood Marshall, the first black to sit on the U.S. Supreme Court and a towering figure in the civil rights movement, died Sunday of heart failure. He was 84.

Reporters knew what to write because of their knowledge of Marshall and his career.

These themes or ideas tell the reporter "what to observe," to use Poe's language. They guide the reporter in asking questions, in doing background checks. In short, they allow the reporter to structure the reporting.

The theme or idea is fairly broad. Usually, it comes to the reporter's mind almost as soon as he or she is given an assignment or senses a story. The idea originates in the reporter's experience, knowledge of the subject, understanding of the essentials or necessities for this kind of story and in a vague area we can only describe as the reporter's feel for the subject.

Intuition   Some reporters call these ideas or insights hunches. (We will discuss hunches and reportorial intuition in Chapter 17.) Ideas also can originate in a reporter's prejudices or biases.

"Look, I have advance prejudices," says Seymour Hersh. "Any reporter who says he doesn't is kidding. But that doesn't mean I would deliberately report something wrong or not tell the truth about something. I would not change a story to make it fit what I think.

Science in the Newsroom. O.K. Bovard, the great editor of Pulitzer's *St. Louis Post-Dispatch,* was said to take a scientific approach to news. He would advance a theory or hypothesis on the basis of a bit of information and then prove or disprove it through reporting. He said he and his staff used the approach "all day long in this room. The imaginative reporter does it when he refuses to accept the perfunctory police view of the mystery and sets himself to reason out all the possible explanations of the case and then adopts a theory for investigating the most likely one."

"I spent an incredible amount of work—dozens of interviews—digging into a number of allegations by a number of people that the American military was involved in the overthrow of Allende (president of Chile). I did a lot of work and I couldn't find it. It's not there. I'm not going to write that story. It's gone, kaput," said Hersh.

"As long as I can make these kinds of judgments I'm okay."

The reporter's theme or idea throws a broad shaft of light on the subject, allowing the reporter to see his or her way through the dense undergrowth of material. Reporters know that they also need to make a pencil-light penetration of the material to come up with the specific news pegs or news angles for their stories. To do this they fall back on their knowledge and experience to help them distinguish the new from the old, the unusual from the usual, the unexpected from the routine.

These "deviations from the plane of the ordinary," as Poe put it, provide the newsworthy element for the story, the lead.

The reporter can spot these deviations, these interruptions in the expected, by knowing a lot about the situation that is being reported. The extraordinary shouts out for attention to the reporter who is open to the significant, the novel.

Look for the Dramatic

Learning to distinguish the unique from the routine is difficult enough, let alone for the sports reporter covering her 33rd basketball game, the education reporter covering his fifth school board meeting. Events seem to settle into a familiar pattern. Spotting differences is difficult. We grow up seeing likenesses, similarities. How many can distinguish the Jonathan from the Delicious, the Jersey from the Guernsey? To most of us, all apples are alike, and cows are just cows.

But journalists see differently. They learn early on to look at the world through the eyes of the innocent child while applying the discerning eye of the wise elder who can distinguish between the significant and the unimportant, the dramatic and the routine.

Red Smith, a sportswriter who covered so many baseball games he lost count, explained the basis of the journalist's artistry: "Every ball game is different from every other ball game—if the reporter has the knowledge and wit to discern the difference."

When Gustave Flaubert, the French novelist, was teaching Guy de Maupassant to write, he told the young man to pick out one of the cab drivers in front of a railway station in Paris and to describe him in a way that would differentiate him from all the other drivers. To do so, Maupassant had to find the significant details that would single out that one man. The moustache? No, four others have one. That slouch? No, they all seem to be collapsing. Ah, one has a red beret. The others are wearing black hats. Also, he is the only one without a cigarette dangling from his mouth.

Little differences can make for big stories.

Carlos Antonio Rios,
Houston Chronicle

Different Reason

Thousands cross the Rio Grande in search of work, but this pregnant woman wants her child born in the United States.

Individuality

Experienced reporters usually agree on the themes of the stories they cover. Beyond that, each reporter puts his or her individual stamp on the story. Some of that individuality comes from writing style. Much is based on the particular observations the reporter makes. What is relevant to one reporter may be irrelevant to another.

When Homer Bigart, the winner of two Pulitzer Prizes and one of the country's great reporters, was sent to cover the military trial of Lt. William Calley, who had been accused of murdering civilians in the My Lai massacre during the Vietnam War, Bigart observed how Calley was brought into court. He linked this observation to his observations at another army officer's trial he had covered, and he wrote:

> Although he had just been found guilty of twenty-two murders, Calley was treated far more gently than was Army doctor Captain Howard B. Levy four years ago after receiving a sentence for refusing to give medical training to Green Berets on the grounds that the training would be used unlawfully in Vietnam.
>
> Unlike Levy, Calley was not handcuffed and left the court unfettered. An officer explained: "His conduct has been exemplary throughout and he'll continue to be treated as an officer."

Bigart's editors at *The New York Times* apparently considered his references to the Levy trial to be irrelevant, for the section read simply:

> Lieutenant Calley was not handcuffed
> when driven to the stockade.

Whose judgment was better, Bigart's or his editors'? Bigart's reference to the Levy trial provides the reader with some idea of the intense feeling of the military against the peace movement—of which Levy was a symbol—and its consideration for the accused murderer of civilians, a career army man.

Looking, Listening

A journalist may be sharp of sight, acute of hearing and blessed with wide experience and the best of news sense. But unless that journalist is in a position to see and hear what is happening, all these qualities are meaningless. Good observation begins with good vantage points. This usually means being close to the action.

At a news conference, Gov. Kirk Fordice of Mississippi told reporters, "The United States of America is a Christian nation. . . . The less we emphasize the Christian religion the further we fall into the abyss of poor character and chaos in the United States of America."

Gov. Carroll A. Campbell Jr. of South Carolina differed, he wanted reporters to know. "The value base of this country comes from the Judeo-Christian heritage that we have and that is something we need to realize." Richard L.

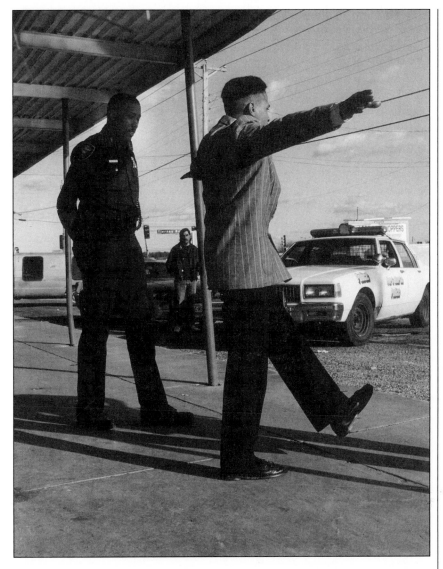

Berke, who covered the conference for *The New York Times,* watched Campbell as he returned to his seat on the dais next to Fordice.

"I just wanted to add the 'Judeo' part," Campbell told Fordice. Berke then writes, "Mr. Fordice responded tartly, 'If I wanted to do that I would have done it.' "

The exchange, brief as it was, provided a shaft of light for the reader, an insight into the positions and the feelings of the conservative and center factions of the Republican Party.

Berke had positioned himself so that he could overhear the conversation of the governors.

Sometimes finding a vantage point from which to see and to hear is difficult and the reporter has to shoulder his or her way to the front of the crowd.

Hearing Problems   A reporter for a college newspaper was unable to find a seat near the front of the lecture she was assigned to cover and took a place in the back of the room. The subject was political satire, and the speaker seemed to be outspoken in his summary. The reporter wrote this lead:

> "Political satire of today stinks," Den-
> nis Quinn, assistant professor of English,
> said at yesterday's Poetry Hour.

A few days later, the newspaper received a letter from Professor Quinn. With some restraint, he wrote that he had actually said, "Political satire is practi-cally extinct." The *University Daily Kansan* printed his letter, and despite the re-porter's embarrassment she stayed in journalism and went on to do distinguished work as an AP correspondent.

The *Asbury Park Press* reported that sewage effluent was being tested by placing "mice and shrimp" in the liquid for four days. If half survived, the efflu-ent would be considered harmless.

No, no, moaned the source for the story when he saw the article in the New Jersey newspaper. "I said, mysid shrimp," he told the managing editor.

Seeing for Yourself   Direct observation is the surest guarantee of ac-curacy. When a young reporter covering the Vietnam War rewrote an army press release, Homer Bigart was annoyed that the reporter had swallowed a fiction and passed it on to his readers. He took the reporter to the front. "That's what I wanted you to see—it isn't here," *The New York Times* correspondent told the reporter.

But even when direct observation is possible, journalists sometimes give a quick look-see and leave. A reporter who visited a monastery was taken to task by the sisters who said she had not spent enough time "to hear how loudly the si-lence speaks. . . ."

Wrong Turn

A reporter decided to visit the site of a reception center where he had been in-ducted into the Army 40 years before, which was now being used by a national re-search laboratory. In his story in *The New York Times,* the reporter described the "barrackslike buildings with no windows" and "locked gates" that reminded him of the isolation he felt as a young soldier.

A laboratory employee, puzzled by the description that bore no relationship to the place in which he worked, followed the reporter's route as outlined in the story. The reporter, it turned out, had made a wrong turn off the parkway and had driven to the back entrance to a racetrack. The "barrackslike buildings with no windows" were stables.

Checking It Out

So, not only get up close, but when what you think you've heard sounds strange, check it out. No source should be allowed to back away from a statement, but sometimes what we think we've heard needs verifying.

Verify that seemingly wild statement, rumor or situation. Don't write it off. The reward could be a footnote in journalism history, or a Pulitzer Prize.

Editors attending a luncheon at a convention of the American Society of Newspaper Editors were astonished when they saw Fidel Castro, the guest of honor, reach across the table and swap plates with the president of the Society.

Had an editor acted on that astonishment at the 1961 banquet and done what reporters are supposed to do—ask why—that editor might have been informed that Castro feared assassination. And that editor might have had a major story. For in 1975, the Central Intelligence Agency admitted that during the administrations of presidents Eisenhower, Kennedy and Johnson the United States government had indeed tried to murder Castro.

Down the Drain   No one could believe the rumors: The Internal Revenue Service was botching a huge number of returns. Some weren't being examined, some were tossed away. Arthur Howe of *The Philadelphia Inquirer* decided to check the rumors and he learned that the IRS had mishandled one of three returns for the previous year. In Atlanta, a worker flushed returns down a toilet. In Memphis, complicated returns were destroyed.

The IRS denied it all. But Howe persisted, and he corroborated everything. He was awarded the Pulitzer Prize for National Reporting.

Unbelievable   Deborah E. Lipstadt maintains in her book *The American Press and the Covering of the Holocaust* that many newspapers refused to publish reports of the Nazi Final Solution because the reports of death squads and gas chambers were "beyond belief." If the newspapers and radio stations had been less skeptical of the reports of refugees, she writes, they might have had an accurate description of Hitler's rise to power and his policies. Even when faced with government reports of Nazi atrocities, the press maintained a "persistent incredulity," says the author. The accounts of eyewitnesses seemed too horrifying to be believed.

Lipstadt holds the press "ultimately as culpable as the Government" for failing to report on the Holocaust. She does recognize a few journalists, among them Edward R. Murrow, who did spot the dangers of the Nazis early and were inclined to believe what happened later.

The Holocaust and the Castro incident point to an unseen dimension of reporting. Although the reporter is guided by logic, he or she must be open to the most implausible facts and observations. Time after time reporters find aberrant facts and extraordinary observations and put them aside as too unusual for further examination. No report should be dismissed—no matter how outlandish it seems—without at least a quick check.

> **"Skepticism** is the chastity of the intellect, and it is shameful to surrender it too soon or to the first comer."
> —*George Santyana*

Caution: Notice the word *check*. The journalist's term for this is verification. By verification journalists mean direct observation and when that is not possible they mean statistical data, documents, reports, some kind of physical evidence. An anecdote or an isolated incident is not verification. These serve to buttress the observation and the evidence, give it a human dimension.

When physical evidence is impossible to obtain and direct observation is blocked, then human sources are acceptable if there is confirmation from several such sources.

Limitations of the Story

Although we may agree that the reporter's task is to continue the search for relevant facts until the theme is adequately supported, we also must admit that the search can never be completed, that there are facts beyond the reporter's reach. Just as a map can never be the complete guide to a territory, so a news story is rarely the definitive statement of reality.

Here are some of the obstacles reporters face:

- The deadline.
- The source the reporter cannot locate.
- The missing record, document or newspaper clipping.
- The incident the reporter cannot see or hear properly.
- The facts the source will not divulge.
- The material the copy editor cuts out of the story.
- The reporter's own limitations.
- The book or magazine the reporter fails to read. Yesterday's newspaper left unread beyond page 1.
- The phone call not returned.
- The question not asked.
- The appointment missed.

For those who like ideas expressed in formulas, we can represent the concept of the limitations of the story with the Reporter's Equation:

$$\textbf{Truth} = \textbf{Story} + \textbf{X}$$

Actually, the capital letter X represents a series of small x's—those that we have listed as the obstacles reporters face.

From our quick trip into the realm of math, let's take a turn down the hall to talk to a semanticist about truth and certainty.

Certainty's Boundaries

As the semanticist Wendell Johnson put it, "There is always at least a small gap between the greatest probability and absolute certainty." But we can be certain, Johnson does say, about some statements.

"It is certain that 2 = 2," Johnson says, "because we say so. We agree to treat it as certain." But there is no certainty that two lawyers equal two lawyers. "No two things are the same, and no one thing stays the same," he says.

This concept is helpful to the journalist, for it guarantees—if it is followed—the reporter will take a fresh eye to people and events, that the first impression is helpful but not decisive.

"In the realm of direct experience," Johnson says, "whether we look backward in memory or forward in anticipation, nothing is absolutely certain. Each new situation, problem, or person is to be approached, therefore, not with rigidly fixed habits and preconceived ideas, but with a sense of apparent probabilities."

We will be discussing how journalists formulate "apparent probabilities" in Chapter 17 when we examine hunches, feelings and thinking patterns. But it should be said here that reporters covering their 5th football game, 10th basketball game, 15th city council meeting or 20th speech need to keep Johnson's advice in mind: (1) no two things are the same and (2) approach a reporting situation with an open mind but with some idea of the story.

Red Smith, whom many consider the best of all the sportswriters, went to every game. "He was horrified that someone might actually cover a game by watching TV or listening to radio," Gene Roberts said. Smith "needed the material, the sense of being there," Roberts said. It was his "being there" that gave Smith material that made his story of **this** game different from the story about yesterday's game.

Smith also approached each game with some idea of "probabilities," which he derived from the names of the starting pitchers, the possible continuation of streaks, animosities left over from the last time the teams played and a dozen other factors.

The Tyranny of Time

The clock is the journalist's major obstacle. Unlike the historian or the sociologist, who face few daily or weekly deadlines in their work, the journalist submits to the requirements of publication and airtime while still seeking to present a complete and accurate account.

Complex events require the time to find relationships that link seemingly disparate events. The reporter may find that the newspaper or station will not provide time. Discouraged, the reporter sometimes settles for a rudimentary form of truth, the recital of what sources declare (Layer I journalism), which is truth of a sort.

Style as a Barrier

The journalistic style also may obstruct truth. The journalist is instructed to tell a story in simple, dramatic, personalized prose. Some important events are complicated. The reporter who seeks to make these events—usually ideas, trends, concepts—come alive may distort them by using exciting details that are colorful but misleading. For years, the newsmagazines emphasized this kind of detail. Their correspondents named the wines the diplomat drank, counted the cigarettes he smoked during a tense hearing. The significance of the event often was lost in the human-interest trivia.

The Reporter as Intruder

The act of reporting can itself be an impediment to accurate observations. Walter Lippmann characterized the journalist as a "fly on the wall," a detached observer whose presence does not affect the event being observed. But if reporting requires close-at-hand observation, scrupulous note taking, photographs, or tape, how unobtrusive can the reporter be? The fly descends and buzzes around the event.

We know what happens when a television crew arrives at an event. Drones become animated. Reserved people begin to gesticulate. Reality is altered.

At a political rally in Central America, a reporter noted the calm, almost serene atmosphere. Even when a speaker released a dove from the center of the plaza, the crowd was hushed. Then the television and still photographers arrived, and the event suddenly took another shape. Fists were shaken. A Cuban flag was unfurled for the photographers, and revolutionary slogans were shouted into the recording equipment. When the photographers departed, the rally returned to its placid state. In the next day's newspaper, accompanying the reporter's story of a quiet protest against United States policy, was a shot of what seemed to be a fist-shaking mob.

Even the reporter's pencil and paper can distort the event. Every reporter experiences the trying moment when, after chatting with a source to put him or her at ease, it is time to reach for a pencil and notepad. In an instant, the mood changes. The simple tools of the reporter's trade have spooked the source.

Unobtrusive Observation

This type of reaction can be avoided by nonreactive or unobtrusive observation, methods that have the merit of allowing the reporter to be a fly on the wall. Let us follow a reporter as he uses this reporting technique.

Among the dozens of reporters gathered in central California to attend a Republican state conference was a reporter who wanted to prove to his editor that he could handle politics. The newspaper's political reporter was assigned to the main political story. The reporter we are following was to do sidebars.

Unlike the other reporters at the convention, our man was unknown to the delegates. He was able to mix freely, smiling and shaking hands with delegates. He knew he was being mistaken for a young delegate, and when one of the central committee secretaries told him there was an important meeting, he went along with her. They walked into the meeting together, and he sat near her, apparently doodling absent-mindedly on a pad in front of him.

All day long he moved in and out of caucuses, meetings and powwows. He heard Orange County delegates denounce the president, a Republican, as a liberal, a spendthrift, an enemy of the party's conservative principles. He listened as deals were made to try to attract labor and minority votes.

His story, played prominently on page 1, was exclusive and other newspapers were forced to quote from it. Republican leaders were chagrined. Our young reporter was jubilant.

The week before when another political group—a national organization of right-wing partisans—held a convention, the reporter had plumped down in a soft chair in the lobby of the hotel and listened. He had heard delegates talk about bringing back the gold standard, the threat of communism from minorities, the radicalism of the labor movement and the dangers of sex education in the public schools.

Ethics Debated

Some journalists condemn this kind of reporting. Their criticism stems from their concern about widespread intrusions into privacy by insurance firms and credit investigators. The federal government has poked into people's lives through wiretaps and mail openings. What right, then, do journalists have to do what they condemn others for doing?

The journalist defends prying on the ground that the search for truth justifies the means if the story reveals wrongdoing or aids the public in decision making. As for a check on the prying journalist, the reporter would have none but his or her conscience. "Let me use my judgment," the journalist says. "I will not use material irresponsibly."

Opponents of the ends-justify-the-means argument contend that reporters cannot adopt methods they condemn, that they cannot set themselves apart from the rules that apply to others.

We do know that the Census Bureau, health and welfare departments and other agencies collect material for the common good but intrude on privacy. Can journalism use this defense of its methods?

Is there a link between the journalist's unobtrusive observation and governmental inquiry, or are some areas clearly off-limits for the journalist? **A guideline:** For private activities, think twice; for official activities held in private, act in the public interest.

Journalistic ethics are discussed further in Chapter 27.

Participant Observation

Another research method—participant observation—links social science and journalism strategies. An Oregon reporter who managed to fold his six-foot frame into a third grader's seat at school was a participant observer. The reporter who worked as a telephone operator and then wrote a series of articles based on her observations was basing her stories on personal experience. At the simplest level, a reporter can spend a day with a meter reader, a public health nurse. Mary Voboril of *The Miami Herald* took an exercise class with Jane Fonda.

In participant observation—the opposite of unobtrusive observation—the reporter discards his or her role as the uninvolved, detached observer and joins the activity of the person or group he or she is covering. The newspaperman who became a third-grader for a story participated in the children's school work, ate lunch with them and played ball at recess. The school children took him for a friend, a bit older and awkward about some things, but a companion neverthe-less. They talked to him as an equal. His relationship with the students enabled

Charles Buchanan, *Winston-Salem Journal*

Going Along for the Morning Collection

For her story about sanitation men, Phoebe Zerwick of the *Winston-Salem Journal* rides along on the orange garbage truck as the men make their morning rounds. She absorbs the sights and the sounds—and the smells, too. "A mist lingers on an unusually cool August morning. A few dogs bark, lunging at fences. Once in a while someone starts a car engine and backs out of a driveway. . . . The smell, sometimes sweet, sometimes sour, is still faint at 8 a.m. before the heat of the day cooks up stronger odors." She observes the workers: "The men keep up a furious pace, with Casey, 28, taking long strides in knee-high rubber boots and McLaurin, 34, running."

him to gather material that the usual interview and observation techniques would not have revealed.

News vs. Reality

William Foote Whyte, in his classic study of an Italian-American slum, *Street Corner Society* (Chicago: The University of Chicago Press, 1943), talks about the difference between the traditional perception of what is news and the reality of the way people live, which participant observation allows the reporter to view:

> If the politician is indicted for accepting graft, that is news. If he goes about doing the usual personal favors for his constituents, that is not news. The newspaper concentrates on the crisis—the spectacular event. In a crisis the "big shot" becomes public property. He is removed from the society in which he functions and he is judged by standards different from his own group. This may be the most effective way to prosecute the lawbreaker. It is not a good way to understand him. For that purpose, the individual must be put back into his social setting and observed in his daily activities. In order to understand the spectacular event, it is necessary to see it in relation to the everyday pattern of life. . . .

Whyte learned how to be accepted by the street corner people. "If you ask direct questions, people will just clam up on you," he writes. "If people accept you, you can just hang around, and you'll learn the answers in the long run without even having to ask the questions."

When Whyte used some obscenities to try to gain acceptance, one of his new friends advised him, "Bill, you're not supposed to talk like that. That doesn't sound like you." Whyte had to be careful about influencing the group he was observing. "I tried to be helpful in the way a friend is expected to be helpful." The results of his observations allowed the reader to have a moving picture of the street corner society, not the still photograph that the brief glimpse allows.

New Directions

The influence of social scientists like Whyte, Margaret Mead and others who studied people in their settings influenced journalists. Traditionally, journalism focused on centers of authority with their formalities—ceremonies, meetings, announcements. This was insufficient, journalists came to realize. They realized that they were not describing the reality of human experience and they became anxious to develop techniques that enabled them to expand their reporting. Sara Grimes, a reporter in Philadelphia, said after she had been covering the juvenile court for a year, "I wonder why so many reporters insist on quoting people in positions of power rather than observing people who are affected by power."

Listening to Youngsters   She listened closely to the young defendants in court, and she sought to understand the effect of the system on youngsters by talking to them. One day she learned that an 11-year-old boy—who was brought into court in handcuffs—had been held in a detention center for nine months although he had not committed a crime. He was a runaway. Grimes asked to talk to the youngster, who had been sent to foster homes after his parents were judged neglectful. He had not liked the foster homes and had run away. Here is part of the story she wrote:

"Jones, Jones," the guard's voice could be heard as he walked up and down the cell-block. Amid a few undistinguishable low grumblings behind the rows of bars came a small, high voice. "Yes, that's me."

Johnny was brought out to an anteroom. No longer crying, he sat with downcast eyes in dungarees and a gray sweatshirt. Quietly and slowly he answered questions.

He wished he had somebody to bring him soap because the institutional soap gives him a rash. He would like to leave YSC (Youth Study Center) and would go "any place they send me."

How does it feel to be handcuffed? In a barely audible voice, he answered: "It makes me feel like a criminal."

It was a natural step from this kind of reporting to participant observation, for the only way the reporter can understand some situations is to experience them. Without this personal experience, some reporters contend, the people they write about become cardboard figures.

Among the Navajos Reporters for *The Albuquerque* (N.M.) *Tribune* spent eight months with Navajo Indians in and around Gallup, N.M., which has the highest rate of alcohol-related deaths in the United States. The series by David Gomez and Patricia Guthrie showed death, disease and despair.

The six-part series also revealed the failure of officials to deal with the problem. The series won a George Polk award for local reporting.

With an Addict Loretta Tofani of *The Philadelphia Inquirer* watched as the young woman dropped her maternity pants past her swollen stomach. The woman, eight months pregnant, picked up a syringe and injected heroin into her right calf.

"He won't stop moving, this baby," the woman told Tofani. "When he moves a lot it means he's sick. He needs a fix."

Tofani stayed with the 30-year-old addict for months, watched her wheedle money from relatives for her drugs, stayed in her kitchen when she entertained a visitor for the $20 she needed for a fix.

And she stayed through the birth of the baby and watched the woman fight to retain custody of her daughter, who was born addicted to heroin, methadone and a pill the woman was popping before the birth.

Going behind the Doors

These reporters who contend that journalism has not dug deeply enough into the lives of people would agree with Chekhov's observation in his short story "Gooseberries":

We see the people who go to market, eat by day, sleep by night, who babble nonsense, marry, grow old, good-naturedly drag their dead to the cemetery, but we do not see or hear those who suffer, and what is terrible in life goes on somewhere behind the scenes. Everything is peaceful and quiet and only mute statistics protest: so many people gone out of their minds, so many gallons of vodka drunk, so many children dead from malnutrition. And such a state of things is evidently necessary; obviously the happy man is at ease only because the unhappy ones bear their burdens in silence, and if there were not this silence, happiness would be impossible. It is a general hypnosis. Behind the door of every contented, happy man there ought to be someone standing with a little hammer and continually reminding him with a knock that there are unhappy people, that however happy he may be, life will sooner or later show him its claws, and trouble will come to him—illness, poverty, losses, and then no one will see or hear him, just as now he neither sees nor hears others. But there is no man with a hammer. The happy man lives at his ease, faintly fluttered by small daily cares, like an aspen in the wind—and all is well.

Some reporters see themselves as the man behind the door. Their hammer is pad and pencil, camera and tape recorder. Let's look closely at a journalist who devoted considerable time to such reporting.

A Ghetto Family

Leon Dash, a reporter for *The Washington Post,* spent several years with a woman and her family in a relationship so close that he was able to gather the most intimate details of their lives. Although sympathetic to the family, Dash was unsparing in his presentation of a family wracked by poverty, drugs, prostitution, crime and illiteracy.

The book Dash wrote later is dedicated to "unfettered inquiry."

The head of the family, Rosa Lee, in her 50s on welfare and food stamps, supports herself through shoplifting and drug dealing. She has eight children by five different men. Dash shows her strengths as well as her weaknesses—her love for her children, aspiration to a decent life, resourcefulness. But he is no soft touch for the tales his sources tell him. Ducky, Rosa Lee's youngest son, informs Dash that he has had a religious conversion and will hereafter serve Christ.

Dash tells Ducky, "You cook powdered cocaine into crack for New York City dealers . . . and you have been addicted to crack for some time now."

Drugs emerge as the major destructive force in the life of the family Dash portrays. Two sons manage to escape from the dysfunctional home life, and Dash says three factors were involved: They attended school longer than their brothers and sisters; an adult became concerned about them (one a school teacher, the other a social worker), and each was able to obtain a full-time job.

The Live In

Dash's extended participant observation can also be described as a Live In, a reporting technique introduced 30 years ago at the Graduate School of Journalism at Columbia University. Based on the work of Mead, Oscar Lewis and Robert Coles, the Live In sends students into homes and workplaces. To move closer to their sources, students have tutored addicts in drug rehabilitation centers and children in schools. They have slept on the floors of mission houses in the Bowery, in sleeping bags at a residence of the Catholic Workers and on cots in shelters for the homeless.

Students have walked the beat with police officers, gone on home visits with social workers and accompanied ambulance drivers on their calls. These experiences were not one-shot affairs. Students met the policeman's family, talked to the welfare mother's children and went into wards to talk to patients.

The Students

Charles Young, a white, middle-class student from Wisconsin, did his Live In at a junior high school in West Harlem in New York City. Let's join Young while he waits for the assistant principal in his office. The room is filled with students. Young describes the scene at the beginning of his Live In:

Gus Marinos, known simply as "Marinos" to everybody, a Greek immigrant in his twenties with dazed but kindly eyes beneath his Coke-bottle glasses, returns to his office on the fourth floor. The room erupts with a deafening chorus of his name.

"MAH-*REE*-NOS! HER FINGERNAILS BE POISON!" a girl screams, holding up her scratched right hand.

"So die," says Marinos, examining some smudged papers on his desk.

"WHY 'ON'T CHEW DIE!"

"You wanna go home?"

"YEAH, BUT CHEW CAN'T TELL ME HER NAILS AIN'T POISON!"

"So go home."

"HER NAILS GOT DIRT AN' SHIT IN 'M!" The girl leaves with a pass home.

"MAH-*REE*-NOS!" another girl demands, "GIMME A PENCIL!" He hands her a pencil from his desk. "I 'ON'T WANT NO PENCIL LIKE THAT! I WANNA BLACK PENCIL!"

"This *is* a black pencil."

"I MEAN A YELLOW PENCIL THAT WRITES BLACK!"

"We don't sell those here."

"I 'ON'T WANT TO BUY NO PENCIL! I WANT CHEW TO GIMME IT!" She grabs the pencil from his hand and in the process drops a textbook. "NOW SEE YOU MADE ME DONE DIRTY MY BOOK!"

"I made you done what?"

"DIRTY MY BOOK!" She leaves for class.

These girls read an average of two years below the national norm for their grade level (slightly ahead of the boys), but the ghetto has already taught them how to get what they want from life: yell until somebody gives it to you. The lesson is apt, because when they are graduated in three years or so, they won't be equipped to do anything anyway.

That these girls (all sent to the office for disciplinary reasons) want something is obvious. What they want is less obvious and increasingly important as the market for unskilled labor dries up.

The first step in finding out what they want is learning a new vocabulary, some of which would be useful to define here. To "come out your mouth" is to communicate. "On time" is an adjective or adverb of approbation meaning you have done something according to socially accepted procedure. "On cap" is synonymous with "in your head," referring to intelligence. . . .

The Disciplinarian

Young interviewed the assistant principal in charge of discipline, who, he writes, "carries a cane in one hand and a leather whip in the other when she wades into a group of warring Dominican and Puerto Rican youths."

His description continues:

She resembles an army tank—solid, low-to-the-ground, unstoppable, paradoxically maternal.

She is in fact known as the mother of the school. Teachers speak with awe of the dedication that brings her to the otherwise deserted building on weekends and vacations. Students speak with equal awe of her omniscience. Because they trust her, she knows exactly who is pushing what drugs and who is fighting with whom.

Standing at the main entrance to the building at 3 o'clock one Friday afternoon in anticipation of a gang fight, Williams catalogues a gathering of a dozen or so Puerto Rican school alumni.

"That one is on parole now. . . . That one is pushing. Look at his station wagon. . . . That one has a sawed-off .38 in his pocket. We'd tell the police about it, but it will pass fifty hands by the time they can react. . . ."

On Thursday, one of their little brothers dropped a piece of chalk from the fourth floor that hit a Dominican on the head. In the ensuing melee, another Puerto Rican was badly cut on the arm with a broken bottle. The Puerto Ricans seek vengeance.

Having no stake in the matter, the blacks are blasé and leave the area immediately. They've seen it all before and even the prospect of serious violence is a bore. The Hispanics gather in groups along the sidewalk and buzz with rumors, with more energy than they have shown all day in class.

Williams crosses the street and puts her arm around one of her former students who has an Afro bigger than the rest of his body. She makes small talk for a couple of minutes, then kisses him on his pockmarked cheek as the gang scatters off down the street. A group of Dominicans, observing the enemy from a block away, disappears to its lair on 133rd Street.

The aborted fight is typical of junior highs anywhere in that the participants seem willing to do battle over nothing. What is frightening is that the involved alumni range in age from 16 to the mid-twenties. They never grew up, just became better armed. They are the fruit of the American system of education.

"Even five years ago they at least expressed an interest in college," says Williams back in the dormitory-room-sized office which she shares with three other school officials and usually seven or eight students who have been thrown out of class. . . .

The Basketball Player

Young befriended a bright young black student in the school. After Young graduated and went to work for *Rolling Stone,* he decided to look up the youngster for a story for the magazine about his dream of becoming a basketball star.

He found the youth in high school, playing basketball, struggling with his classes and still filled with hope. Young's piece, "Above 125th Street: Curtis Haynes' New York," begins:

"I'm growin' plants all the time," says Curtis Haynes, pouring half a glass of water over a geranium. The floor and window ledge of his bedroom are covered with leafy pots. "Plants are everything. They give us oxygen and food. They also a home for insects." He brushes an aphid off a leaf. "Insects gonna inherit the earth."

He continues the tour of his room—recently painted electric blue by his mother—by pulling a picture off a shelf full of basketball trophies. Judging by his fleeting eyes and reticent tone of voice, he doesn't know what to make of me—a pale, white, 26-year-old, bearded magazine editor with thick glasses from a myopic childhood of too much TV watching and book reading in Madison, Wisconsin. Nor do I know what to make of him—a handsome, ebony-skinned, 16-year-old, short-haired high-school student with sharp vision from a childhood spent on the basketball courts of Harlem. "This is my brother, Footie," he says, holding a blurred photograph of a teenager bearing a strong resemblance to Curtis. "Remember, remember, remember . . ." is inscribed around the margins. "We named him that because he had such big feet," he says. Curtis' Pro Ked basketball shoes equal my own 11 1/2 Adidas—and I am 6' 2" while he is just 5' 10". "He died in a fight two years ago. Puerto Rican friend got in an argument at a party and the other dude pulled a gun. My brother jumped between them. I never go to parties no more."

Problems of Involvement

Participant observation can cause problems. In addition to the possibility that the reporter's presence may affect the event, the participant observer can become too deeply involved with his or her sources, risking the possibility that feelings may override responsibility to the facts.

Participant observation also has been criticized as exploitation of the source. After all, the journalist is using the lives of people as the basis of a story, which could lead to the reporter's acclaim, help him or her win a pay raise and possibly a promotion. But the alcoholic, the addict, the welfare mother and the police officer are not reimbursed for their contributions. Nor is much done about the problems that overwhelm some of these people.

The journalist James Agee agonized over prying into the lives of Southern sharecroppers. He and the photographer Walker Evans were assigned to do an article on cotton tenantry, the system by which farmers worked the fields of landowners in return for a share of the crop less what was advanced to them for seed, living quarters and tools. The sharecroppers were poorer than dirt poor, for not even the earth they tilled was theirs. The magazine article was not published, but in 1940 the work became a book, *Let Us Now Praise Famous Men*. Agee knew the justifications for his intimate observations, but they did not console him. Early in the book, he describes his reservations:

It seems to me curious, not to say obscene and thoroughly terrifying, that it could occur to an association of human beings drawn together through need and chance and for profit into a company, an organ of journalism, to pry intimately into the lives of an undefended and appallingly damaged group of human beings, an ignorant and helpless rural family, for the purpose of parading the nakedness, disadvantage and humiliation of these lives before another group of human beings, in the name of science, of "honest journalism" (whatever that paradox may mean), of humanity, of social fearlessness, for money, and for a reputation for crusading and for unbias which, when skillfully enough qualified, is exchangeable at any bank for money (and in politics, for votes, for job patronage, abelincolnism, etc.). . . .

In Defense of Prying

In rebuttal to these criticisms, reporters who use the technique say that public awareness is increased by stories about the lives of people. They say this awareness can lead to reform by involving the public emotionally in the situations described by the reporter.

Steven Almond, a reporter for the *Miami New Times,* spent weeks at the James E. Scott housing project to reveal "what life is really like for the women and children living in Miami's inner city." Almond said he was bothered by one aspect of his work:

> By far, the most difficult aspect of the work was realizing that I was merely another male figure who would eventually abandon the kids that I had befriended. And facing that, in some deep sense, I was exploiting the kids by using their lives as journalistic fodder. It was betrayal.
>
> Hopefully, The Canyon managed to convey a little bit about what it is like, day to day, for women and children who live in inner-city housing projects. That's not a story often told.

A Corrective for Detachment

Also, participant observation can help correct a detachment that can lead to callousness. A student who said he considered drug addicts weak and worthless conducted a Live In with a young female addict. The woman's daughter was being put up for adoption because the mother had been judged unfit to raise her. The woman's agony at the prospect of losing her daughter—which the student felt intensely—led him to do a series of revealing articles about the city's adoption laws.

The experience of participant observation allows the reporter to step outside routines and familiar environments to achieve new insights and to avoid another trap—the tendency to stereotype. Working under pressure, reporters fall back on stereotyping people, which permits them to simplify complicated events and to communicate complexities in easily understood terms. Forgetting that life is endless variety and change, some reporters look at the world through a kaleidoscope that is never turned. As a consequence, their observations reflect only a narrow, static vision. In Chapter 17, we will examine these stereotypes and the ways of thinking that determine how reporters look at events.

Postscript: Some 50 years after Agee and Evans interviewed and photographed the poor in the rural South, a Harvard student read their book and decided to make it the focus of his senior thesis. The student, Bill Berkeley, went to Alabama to interview some of those Agee had talked to.

He found a few who remembered the Agee-Evans team. One woman, who had been photographed as a child for the book cover, asked Berkeley, "What right did that man have to put my picture on the cover of his book?" She was pictured wearing a potato sack.

Berkeley decided on journalism as a career, and, after working on an Alabama daily, became a free-lance foreign correspondent. His reporting in Liberia on human rights abuses led to a warning that he would be killed if he returned to Liberia, and in Zaire he and his wife were arrested, questioned for 48 hours and ordered to leave the country immediately because of "unauthorized reporting."

Everyday Reporting

Whether the reporter is involved in participant observation or covering a city council hearing, the principles and the methods of reporting are the same.

The reporter has a sense of what is newsworthy from his or her familiarity with the community and the beat. On assignment, the reporter tries to come up with a story idea quickly. Then the reporter documents the idea.

But the reporter is not so transfixed by the broad theme that he or she ignores details. When Christopher Ringwald of the *Watertown Daily Times* covered the disappearance of a young mother, he noted in his story, "The only item missing with Miss McDonald was a quart bottle of Bacardi rum." She had taken nothing else with her when she left.

Six weeks later, a partially decomposed body was found in a remote area. The identity was uncertain, and the police were not talking. But Ringwald did learn one fact that made his story have some certainty about the identification of the woman:

> To the side of the corpse, which was found in a reclining position as if the woman had fallen asleep there, according to Chief King, was a quart bottle of Bacardi rum.

Ringwald said that when he interviewed the family he asked what the woman took with her. On learning it was rum, "it seemed unnecessarily nosey to ask what brand. But I did."

Not only do reporters ask questions that they think will elicit useful replies, they note relevant and specific physical characteristics: Are there fewer spectators than anticipated? Were the bookcases empty? Is the block on which the murder took place a quiet residential street? Was the highway slick with rain when the accident occurred? Was it dark or dusk when the game ended?

They note whether the bird in the cage of the apartment in which the crime took place was a parakeet, canary or parrot. And they listen if it was a parrot. A reporter for a California newspaper put up high in his story the cries of the parrot at the scene of a suicide-murder: "Where's mommy? Where's daddy?"

Summing Up

The key to first-rate observation is the quality of the theme the reporter has in mind. The reporter's theory or idea—call it the possible lead to the story—"suggests and coordinates observations," says the scientist and teacher-writer Stephen Jay Gould of Harvard. "Theory can prod, suggest, integrate and direct in fruitful ways."

But it "can also stifle, mislead and restrict," Gould adds. He calls the business of devising themes as a prelude to making observations the "double-edged

Charlie Starr, *The San Diego Union-Tribune*

Looking for—and Finding—the Different Angle

Journalists seek out the new and different. If it's routine, it isn't newsworthy. On assignment from his newspaper to find a feature photo, Charlie Starr thought a shot of baseball's All Star game from a hillside in the twilight would be interesting.

When he made it up the hill, he found a group set up to enjoy the game with their own tailgate party. Starr waited for the light from the TV screen to be about the same level as the light from the stadium. This is the result.

sword . . . as both liberator and incarcerator. . . ." It is liberating when the theme is borne out by information gathered on the basis of detached observation. It is incarcerating when the reporter's observations are made with eyes and ears determined to see and hear on the basis of hope and belief that the theme or lead is on target.

In the next chapter, we will look at how reporters build the background on which they structure sound observations for their stories.

Further Reading

Agee, James. *Let Us Now Praise Famous Men.* Boston: Houghton Mifflin, 1960.

Beveridge, W.I.B. *The Art of Scientific Investigation.* New York: Vintage Books, 1962.

Dash, Leon. *Rosa Lee: A Mother and Her Family in Urban America.* New York: Basic Books, 1996.

Lipstadt, Deborah E. *The American Press and the Covering of the Holocaust, 1933–1945.* New York: Free Press, 1985.

Sanders, Marlene, and Marcia Rock. *Waiting for Prime Time: The Women of Television News.* Urbana: University of Illinois Press, 1988.

12 Building and Using Background

Todd Panagopoulos,
The Star,
Chicago Heights, Ill.

The shooting is set against mounting school violence.

Preview

Journalists are always at work building two kinds of background knowledge:

• **General:** The overall knowledge that the reporter takes to the job. It is based on wide reading and general experience.

• **Specific:** The specialized information that helps the reporter handle his or her beat. It includes, for example, knowing about one judge's preference for jail sentences and another's for probation, or the mayor's determination to reassess property values to increase revenues.

A command of background allows the reporter to see connections among facts and incidents; this grouping of material may lead to stories that are more revealing than is the bare recital of the news event.

The journalist is expected to know it all. An error, a missing fact or a misinterpretation cannot be explained away.

Demanding as this may seem, it is the lot of the professional to be unfailingly certain in performance. The doctor is expected to identify the ailment that plagues the patient. The attorney is an authority on the law. The teacher is a wise, unfaltering guide who takes students through the complexities of phonics, irregular French verbs and William Blake.

But we know professionals are fallible. Doctors misdiagnose, and sometimes their operations fail. Lawyers lose cases they should win. Teachers are human, too, like the grade school teacher who assigned her class the task of writing sentences containing words from a list she supplied. One youngster, who consulted his collection of baseball cards for inspiration, chose the word *cap,* and he wrote, "Catfish Hunter wears a cap." The teacher returned the boy's paper with the sentence corrected: "A catfish hunter wears a cap."

Should the teacher have known Catfish Hunter was a baseball player? Well, perhaps we do make excuses for teachers, as well as for doctors and lawyers. But we do not excuse the journalist who errs through ignorance.

Should the journalist really be expected to know everything? "Yes," said the reporter Murray Kempton. "When you're covering anything, and you're writing about it at length, you use everything you know. And in order to use everything you have to be interested in an extraordinary range of things."

Twain's and Mencken's Complaints

In Mark Twain's *Sketches,* he describes his experiences as a newspaper-man in "How I Edited an Agricultural Paper." Twain is telling a friend that little intelligence is needed to be a newspaperman:

I tell you I have been in the editorial business going on fourteen years, and it is the first time I ever heard of a man's having to know anything in order to edit a newspaper. You turnip! Who write the dramatic critiques for the second-rate papers? Why, a parcel of promoted shoemakers and apprentice apothecaries, who know just as much about good acting as I do about good farming and no more. Who review the books? People who never wrote one. Who do up the heavy leaders on finance? Parties who have had the largest opportunities for knowing nothing about it. Who criticise the Indian campaigns? Gentlemen who do not know a war whoop from a wigwam, and who never have had to run a foot race with a tomahawk, or pluck arrows out of the several members of their families to build the evening camp-fire with. Who write the temperance appeals, and clamor about the flowing bowl? Folks who will never draw another sober breath till they do it in the grave.

H.L. Mencken, a journalist whose prose skewered presidents, poets and bartenders with equal vigor, used some of his most choice execrations to denounce his fellow journalists. In an editorial in the *American Mercury,* October 1924, he wrote of journalists:

The majority of them, in almost every American city, are ignoramuses, and not a few of them are also bounders. All the knowledge that they pack into their brains is, in every reasonable cultural sense, useless; it is the sort of knowledge that belongs, not to a professional man, but to a police captain, a railway mail-clerk or a board boy in a brokerage house. It is a mass of trivialities and puerilities; to recite it would be to make even a barber or a bartender beg for mercy. What is missing from it is everything worth knowing—everything that enters into the common knowledge of educated men. There are managing editors in the United States, and scores of them, who have never heard of Kant or Johannes Müller and never read the Constitution of the United States; there are city editors who do not know what a symphony is, or a streptococcus, or the Statute of Frauds; there are reporters by the thousand who could not pass the entrance examination for Harvard or Tuskegee, or even Yale. It is this vast ignorance that makes American journalism so pathetically feeble and vulgar, and so generally disreputable no less. A man with so little intellectual enterprise that, dealing with news daily, he goes through life without taking in any news that is worth knowing—such a man, you may be sure, is as lacking in true self-respect as he is in curiosity. Honor does not go with stupidity. If it belongs to professional men, it belongs to them because they constitute a true aristocracy—because they have definitely separated themselves from the great masses of men. The journalists, in seeking to acquire it, put the cart before the horse.

GBS: Two Views

The practice of journalism arouses considerable passion among outsiders, sometimes leading them to excesses of inconsistency. George Bernard Shaw, the eminent playwright and critic, was of two minds regarding journalism. In a note to a journalist, he wrote:

> Dear Sir,
> Your profession has, as usual, destroyed your brain.

But he also wrote:

> Journalism can claim to be the highest form of literature. For all the highest literature is journalism, including Plato and Aristophanes trying to knock some sense into the Athens of their days and Shakespeare peopling that same Athens with Elizabethans. Nothing that is not journalism will live as long as literature or be of any use while it does live. So let others cultivate what they may call literature. Journalism for me.

Improvements?

These comments were made years ago. Journalists are now college trained, often in schools of journalism (a hopeful sign, Mencken said in the same editorial we have quoted from). And yet: What are we to make of the current generation, one of whose representatives wrote in a college newspaper about a presentation of *The Merchant of Venus,* instead of *The Merchant of Venice?*

And what can we say to the journalism student who wrote of the sculptor Michel Angelo? Or to the reporter who wrote when crimes in town doubled that they went up 200 percent?

Should the journalist be expected to know the plays of Shakespeare, the world of art and the names of baseball players? And how to derive a percentage, calculate a ratio and find the median in a group of figures? Would it terrify would-be journalists to suggest that the answer has to be yes?

This storehouse of knowledge is the reporter's background. As Kempton, Twain and Mencken suggest, it should be kept full and constantly replenished. Reporters need to have at their fingertips a wide assortment of information: They should know dates, names, policies made, policies defeated, what leads the best-seller list and what agency compiles the list of the 10 most-wanted criminals. All of this has to be put into some kind of schematic, some kind of pattern, or reporters will eventually see themselves in the sad comment of T.S. Eliot, "We had the experience but missed the meaning."

Background Defined

The term *background* has three definitions:

- A reporter's store of information. This knowledge may be amassed over a long period or picked up quickly in order to handle a specific assignment. Without background knowledge, a reporter's fact gathering can be nondirected.
- Material placed in the story that explains the event, puts it into perspective. Without background, a story may be one-dimensional.
- Material a source does not want attributed to him or her. It may or may not be used, depending on the source's instructions.

Here, we are dealing with the first two meanings.

The Contents of the Storehouse

Reporters have a deep and wide-ranging fund of knowledge. Much of this stored information concerns processes and procedures: the workings of the political system; the structure of local government; arrest procedures; government finance. The good reporter is aware of the past and its relation to the present. The *Dred Scott* and the *Brown* v. *Board of Education* Supreme Court decisions are kept in mental drawers, ready for use. When a political candidate refers to the New Deal, the reporter knows what is meant.

General Knowledge

The knowledge of how things work can turn a routine assignment into a significant story. When a reporter for a Long Island newspaper was sent to cover a fire in a plastics factory, she noticed that the plant was located in a residential zone. On her return to the office, she told her editor, "I've got the information on the fire, but I want to check out why that factory was built there in a residential zone. Was it zoned industrial when the factory was built, or did the company get a variance?" The reporter knew that variances—exceptions to general zoning patterns—are sometimes awarded to friends or political donors. Although the reporter was not a city hall reporter or a specialist in real estate, she knew about zoning through her overall understanding of city government. Her curiosity and knowledge led to a significant story.

We can describe this wide-ranging storehouse of information as general background knowledge. It is the result of reading, experience and schooling.

A frequent criticism of U.S. journalists is that although their mastery of the journalistic craft is unexcelled, their general knowledge is limited. American journalism lacks a tradition of scholarship, critics contend.

Such knowledge is important because it is the bedrock on which news stories are built. The American philosopher John Dewey said, "We cannot lay hold of the new, we cannot even keep it before our minds, much less understand it, save by the use of ideas and knowledge we already possess." Irving Kristol, a

---

What They Don't Know

The National Assessment of Educational Progress tested 8,000 17-year-olds of different races, both sexes and all regions of the United States.

Some of the findings:

- 20 percent or fewer could identify Joyce, Dostoyevsky, Ellison, Conrad or Ibsen.
- 36 percent knew Chaucer is the author of *The Canterbury Tales.*
- 37 percent could equate Job with patience during suffering.
- Fewer than 25 percent knew that Lincoln was president between 1860 and 1880.
- 32 percent could place the Civil War between 1850 and 1900.
- 57 percent could place World War II between 1900 and 1950.
- 30 percent could identify the Magna Charta.

Their elders didn't do much better: 63 percent of those 18 to 24 could not find France on an unmarked map, more than half couldn't locate New York City and one in seven couldn't point to the United States on a world map.

And What They Do Know

John Treacy, professor of economics at Wright State University in Dayton, Ohio, asked 109 students to identify Adam Smith, the father of economic study, who was discussed in their reading, and Spuds McKenzie, a dog used in a television commercial for beer. The results:

- 29 percent identified Adam Smith correctly.
- 95 percent identified Spuds McKenzie correctly.

Vacuums. ". . . while they may be trained to write and while they may be trained to articulate what is written, the fact remains that many who call themselves journalists and are employed in local stations have no notion whatsoever about history, geography, political science, economics and other things about which an informed individual should have some grasp."
—Frank Magid, CEO, Frank N. Magid Associates, TV consultants to 140 local stations

writer on social and political affairs, says, "When one is dealing with complicated and continuous events, it is impossible to report 'what happened' unless one is previously equipped with a context of meaning and significance."

Specific Knowledge

Journalists also have a stockpile of specific knowledge, the information that is useful for their beats. Every journalist should know the difference between a stock and a bond, but only the business reporter need know the difference between a stock's yield and its price-earnings ratio.

Let's look at how four journalists applied their specific knowledge.

The Clone   When Gina Kolata, science reporter for *The New York Times,* was thumbing through her copy of *Nature,* a magazine for scientists, she came across an article titled "Viable Offspring Derived from Fetal and Adult Mammalians." She leaped up.

"It didn't say the word clone and there was no clue in the article that there was anything interesting," she said. "People missed this story because they had to be able to understand the title and the abstract," which, she says, "was in the most abstruse scientific language in the whole world."

But she immediately called her editor and said, "Do you know what? I think they have actually done something amazing. I think they've cloned an adult."

Kolata's understanding of the abstruse technical article led to an exclusive page 1 story.

Covering the 500   When Joe Munson, a photographer for *The Kentucky Post* in Covington, Ky., was covering the Indianapolis 500, the daring tactics of a driver caught his eye. Munson knew that there is an imaginary line that race car drivers must follow around bends in order to keep their cars under control.

"I noticed driver Danny Ongais straying six inches from that imaginary line and I suspected he was destined for a crash," Munson recalled.

"So I kept my camera focused on him."

Munson was ready when Ongais lost control and his car cracked into the wall. Munson was able to gun off 20 shots of the fiery crash that seriously injured Ongais. One of them took first place in the sports category of a National Press Photographers Association regional competition.

Joe Munson, *The Kentucky Post*

Cutting the Turn Too Closely: Crack-up at the 500

Bills 17, Jaguars 16   When the Buffalo Bills quarterback Doug Flutie scored a last-seconds touchdown, the AP sportswriter recalled a similar desperation play Flutie made that won a college game years before. This led to the lead:

> Doug Flutie did it again. This time with
> his legs, not his arm, and on a broken play.

After giving the score of the game he watched, the writer amplified his lead by recalling that Flutie "is famous for his last-second desperation pass while at Boston College that defeated the University of Miami in 1984."

Now for a specific knowledge quiz: What is the descriptive name given to the type of pass Flutie threw in that game long ago?

Wait, you say. "I am not interested in sports. I don't have to know that," you say. Sorry. You want to be a journalist, you have to know everything. It's called the "Hail Mary" pass, and it has become general usage for a last and desperate try. During the Senate trial of President Clinton, a Democratic senator described the House impeachment team's request to question witnesses again as a "Hail Mary try to salvage its case."

Knowing the Records   Marcia Chambers, who covered the Criminal Courts Building for *The New York Times,* scored many exclusives because she had mastered the procedures of the criminal justice system. Chambers used files, records and background that led to an exclusive she wrote on the arrest of a mass-murder suspect. Without her background knowledge, her arrest story would have had some interest but little significance. Here is her description of how she went about digging up the information for her story:

> On the day Calvin Jackson was arrested, I covered the arraignment where the prosecutor announced that Jackson had been charged with the murder of one woman and had "implicated himself" in several others. At the time, we wanted to find out more about Jackson's prior criminal record, but given the hour—5:30 p.m.—we couldn't get the information. In a sidebar story that appeared the next day, Joe Treaster, the police reporter, said Jackson's previous arrest had occurred 10 months before. But the disposition of the case, the story said, was unknown.
>
> From my experience, I knew that nearly all cases are disposed of through plea bargaining, the process whereby a defendant agrees to plead guilty in exchange for a lesser charge. Several weeks before I had obtained from the Office of Court Administration data that showed that last year only 545 out of 31,098 felony arrests went to trial, including drug cases. The rest were plea bargained.
>
> On Monday, at 10 a.m., I went to the court clerk's office. My premise was that Jackson's last arrest, like the thousands of others that pass through the criminal court system, had probably involved plea bargaining, a reduction of charges and a minimal sentence.
>
> From the docket book, I obtained the docket number of the mass-murder case, and since case records are public information, I asked the clerk for the case. I took it to the side of the room, and quickly copied the file that contained information about his previous arrests. (In addition to carrying change and a phone credit card for phone calls, reporters should carry at least two dollars in change at all times for the copying machine as well as a backup pen or pencil.)

> **Lost.** "The unprepared mind cannot see the outstretched hand of opportunity."
> —*Alexander Fleming,*
> *discoverer of penicillin*

Jackson's previous arrests (listed on what is called a rap sheet) were described by penal code designations, which sent Chambers to the newspaper's library to check the numbers in one reference and then to another reference to see what the maximum penalty was for the felonies for which he was convicted.

She found Jackson had been convicted of two felonies for which the punishment was up to 15 years in prison. By then it was 5:15 and Chambers started to write for the 7 p.m. deadline.

Suspect in Slaying Once Got 30 Days Instead of 15 Years

By Marcia Chambers

Calvin Jackson, who is said by the police to have "implicated himself" in the murder of at least nine women, was arrested in Manhattan 10 months ago on felonious robbery and burglary charges that could have sent him to prison for 15 years, an examination of court records disclosed yesterday.

Instead, the 26-year-old former convict was sent to jail for 30 days after the felony charges against him and two others were reduced to misdemeanors.

He had pleaded guilty in plea bargaining in Criminal Court to the lesser charges, which arose from the robbery last November of a young man, a resident of the Park Plaza Hotel, where Mr. Jackson lived and where six of his alleged victims were killed.

Mr. Jackson's experience is no different from that of thousands of others who yearly pass through the city's court system.

. . . the year of Mr. Jackson's last arrest, there were 31,098 felony arrests in Manhattan, according to the crime analysis unit of the Police Department. Of these, only 545 cases went to trial on the original felony charges, including possession or sale of narcotics.

Four out of every five of the 31,098 felony arrests were subject to plea-bargaining and were disposed of at the very outset of the court process—at arraignment before a Criminal Court judge or at a subsequent hearing. That is what happened in the Jackson robbery case. . . .

—*The New York Times*

Blundering in Print

Reporters with ample background knowledge do not embarrass themselves or their editors by blundering in print or on the air. Witness these bloopers, the result of a lack of specific knowledge:

- In one of her columns, Harriet Van Horne referred to Canada as having a "tough and happily homogeneous population. . . ." (The columnist ignored the large Indian and Inuit populations and the almost six million French-speaking Canadians. Not only is the country not homogeneous, the French- and English-speaking Canadians are hardly happily ensconced together. Many of the French-speaking people contend that they are second-class citizens, which has led to the separatist movement in the province of Quebec.)

- When the basketball coach at Boston College accepted the head coaching job at Stanford, a CBS sports announcer said that the coach had "followed Horace Mann's advice to go west." (The advice is attributed to Horace Greeley, founder and editor of *The Tribune:* "Go west young man." Horace Mann was an educator.)
- In a feature on food served during the Jewish holidays, a reporter for the *Press-Enterprise* in Riverside, Calif., described Yom Kippur as "marked by rich, indeed lavish meals." (Yom Kippur, known as the Day of Atonement, is the most solemn of all Jewish holy days and is observed by fasting.)
- A New York Times Story of mourning for victims of a terrorist bombing in Jerusalem said the mourners' clothing was "rented." (In funerals, clothing is *rent*—torn—not rented.)
- During a televised National Basketball Association game, a player let the man he was covering drive past him for a basket. The player looked disgusted with himself, and from the broadcast booth the sportscasters could see his lips moving. "What do you think he's saying, Bill?" one asked his colleague, Bill Russell, one of the great defensive stars in basketball and the first black coach in the NBA.

Russell replied, "I know how Walt feels. I can hear him muttering a four-syllable word." Russell's colleague laughingly corrected him, "You mean four-letter word, Bill." Slowly, deliberately, Russell said, "No, I mean four-syllable word."

There was a long pause, a smothered gasp and then a commercial. (Russell's long playing career had given him a vast store of knowledge about the game, from strategy to the obscenities players use.)

Amassing Background

Specific and general knowledge are gained in many ways. Education is a major contributor. Well-rounded high school and college curricula usually provide the knowledge and tools with which journalists must be equipped, from history and geography to foreign languages and mathematics.

A study of editors of newspapers with circulations between 25,000 and 90,000 by Mike Shelly, Traci Carson and Liz Russell of the Department of Communication at Illinois State University showed that the editors recommended for future journalists the following minors with a journalism major (in percent of editors polled):

Political science	23 percent
History	18 percent
Economics	17 percent
English	14 percent
Business	12 percent

The Past Illuminates the Present

To those who despair over today's racism and environmental damage, a knowledge of the past provides perspective. For years after gold was discovered in California, mining companies used hydraulic water cannons to wash down mountains for the gold ore they contained. Silt clogged once pristine rivers, causing floods downstream and irreparable damage was done to the terrain. After considerable public pressure, the practice was outlawed.

Now only a fringe movement of the far right, the Ku Klux Klan once elected governors and paraded its cause down the main avenues of cities and state capitals. Klanswomen even paraded down Pennsylvania Avenue in Washington, D.C.

Top photo: Plumas County Museum. Bottom photo: National Archives in Washington, D.C.

Continuing Education

Education does not stop with a degree. Journalists read widely and continue their studies in various ways. But not all knowledge comes from books.

The young men and women who are determined to be journalists are alert to the world around them. They make friends with all sorts of people, and they welcome new ideas, new ways of seeing events. They are interested in history, current affairs and what makes people and organizations tick. They speculate about what motivates people, they wonder about the role of money in society, and they are interested in how geography, history and the weather affect what people think and do. Although they are present oriented, they know something of the past. They learn by going to roller rinks and museums, from talking to third-graders and pensioners, by watching fishermen and street vendors.

They also learn by attending seminars and conferences for journalists, by obtaining material on a wide variety of subjects from groups that dispense background matter. One such organization, the Foundation for American Communications, sponsors conferences and issues background material. Funded by the Ford Foundation, FACS' address is 3800 Barham Blvd., Suite 409, Los Angeles, Calif., 90068, (213) 851-7372, www.facsnet.org/.

Pairing Facts at the State Pen

Good reporters collect stray pieces of background that often have no particular use at the moment. Sooner or later, another bit of information will come along that when paired with the first will make a good story.

For example, a reporter who made it his business to look in on the state penitentiary every few weeks was talking to a guard one day when an old man walked by. He was an inmate with a long record, the guard said. Swindler, thief and bad-check artist, he was always in trouble, and now he was in the pen for life. A few weeks later, the reporter was chatting with the warden about another prisoner. Despite a long record of violent crime, he was in for an eight-year term, which meant he would be out in a little more than four years.

The disparities in sentences interested the reporter, but he did little with the information. Such disparities were not new to him. Well-to-do defendants were infrequently convicted for drunken driving but instead were allowed to plead to reckless driving charges; the poor were usually convicted of drunken driving. He had done a story on that. The short prison terms usually imposed on white collar criminals was also an old story.

Every so often, the reporter would go through the penitentiary's records of the arrests, convictions and sentences of the inmates for possible features. One day, while leafing through the record book, he noticed that the elderly swindler had been sentenced under something called the "habitual criminal law," which required stringent and specific sentences for frequent offenders, known in some states as the "three strikes and you're out" law. The reporter checked all the habitual criminal convictions and found that there was no consistency in sentences. The reporter's interest was piqued.

The convict with a long record of violent crimes was not sentenced under the habitual criminal law, despite the mandatory law. Putting these facts together, he wrote a series of articles pointing out that judges and district attorneys throughout the state were ignoring and misapplying the habitual criminal law. As a result, of the 72 frequent offenders in the state penitentiary who should have been sentenced under the law, only 14 were doing time under its provisions.

Many Prosecutors and Judges Ignore New Mexico Habitual Criminal Laws

(New Mexico has a stringent law concerning habitual criminals. But a Journal survey has shown that it is being consistently ignored by law enforcement officers. This is the first in a series of articles on this important law.)

SANTA FE, Jan. 4 — New Mexico's habitual criminal laws, which were designed to increase punishment for the frequent offender, are ignored, inconsistently used, and misunderstood by many of the state's law enforcement officers and judges, a study of official records disclosed today.

Although the laws are clearly mandatory and require district attorneys to bring charges under the act when they can be applied, few district attorneys follow the statutes.

The habitual criminal laws apply to persons who have been found guilty of more than one felony.

Yet of the 72 men now behind bars at the state penitentiary who have committed three or more felonies, only 14 were sentenced under the habitual criminal act. The number of second offenders who could have been sentenced under the law but were not were too numerous to check.

In a few cases where men have been convicted under the law, district judges have handed down illegal sentences and have not applied the law consistently.

For some time the legal profession has been aware of these facts, but little has been done either to repeal the laws or to make them work fairly.

The habitual criminal act was passed in 1929 and establishes a table of increased prison sentences for law violators who have committed more than one felony. . . .

—*The Albuquerque Journal*

Always Use Background

Few stories are complete without some background information. Reporters who disregard this advice do so at the peril of inadequately informing their readers and listeners. Events have causes and consequences.

When Sen. Robert Dole was seeking the 1996 presidential nomination, the Kansas Republican announced that he would try to block President Clinton's choice for Surgeon General. The nominee, the head of a medical school, had performed abortions during his career as a physician. The Associated Press report of Dole's opposition included this background sentence about the nominee:

His nomination is vehemently opposed by Christian right organizations, groups Mr. Dole has been courting in his presidential bid.

Anticipatory Journalism

A solid grasp of the past and the present is essential to a growing area of reporting—*anticipatory journalism*. It consists of spotting trends, identifying movements in their earliest stages, locating individuals with an important message.

Journalism has not been good at this kind of reporting. It ignored the feminist movement, was late to sense the civil rights surge, was hesitant about the lifestyle changes of teen-agers.

But anticipatory journalism need not confine itself to trends and movements to be useful. It can be as simple as making journalism out of the realization that the city's revenues are inadequate to meet expenses and that payrolls and services will have to be cut or taxes increased. With this knowledge, the reporter can interview the mayor, city council members and community leaders about what solutions they recommend.

This is public service journalism, for its practice gives the public ample time to discuss and decide issues rather than having to react to decisions already made.

An essential to the practice of anticipatory journalism along with a grasp of background is a good string of sources, a subject we shall next look into after a final doleful note.

Summing Up

The best journalists know a lot. They know the past as well as the present. They are exceptions to the charge leveled by *The New York Times* columnist Bob Herbert who describes the United States as "a nation of nitwits." As evidence, he cites a Gallup Poll that found:

- Sixty percent of Americans are unable to name the president who ordered the atomic bomb dropped on Japan. (Truman)
- One of four didn't know Japan was the target of the bomb.
- A fifth didn't know that such an attack had occurred.

"We are surrounded by a deep and abiding stupidity," he writes.

To ply their trade well journalists know that they must be informed. Otherwise, they are a menace to their readers, listeners and viewers.

Further Reading

Lewis, Anthony. *Gideon's Trumpet.* New York: Random House, 1964.
Steel, Ronald. *Walter Lippmann and the American Century.* Boston: Atlantic Monthly Press, 1980.
Ullmann, John H. *Reporter's Handbook: An Investigator's Guide to Documents and Techniques.* New York: St. Martin's Press, 1983.

Finding, Cultivating and Using Sources

Chris Hardy,
San Francisco Examiner

Sources come in all sizes.

Preview

The reporter relies on three types of sources:

• **Human sources,** which consist of authorities and people involved in news events. They can be less reliable than physical sources because some may have interests to protect or are untrained observers. When using human sources, reporters find the person most qualified to speak—an authority on the subject, an eyewitness, an official, a participant.

• **Physical sources,** which consist of records, documents, reference works, newspaper clippings.

• **Online sources,** which include a vast array of human and physical sources, from academicians to government data.

Journalists have a saying that a reporter can be no better than his or her sources. These sources include officials, spokesmen and -women, participants in events, documents, records, tape recordings, magazines, online search engines, libraries, films and books. The quality of the reporter's story depends on the quality of the sources.

Reporters spend a lot of time looking for and cultivating people who can become sources and contacts. A county courthouse reporter in California puts in a couple of hours a day passing time with his sources. He also chats with guards, secretaries, elevator operators, all of whom he describes as contacts, people who can provide tips for stories. An elevator operator tipped him off about a well-known businessman who had been summoned by a grand jury and was taken to the jury room by a back elevator.

Making Nice at the Courthouse

Jeff Klinkenberg of *The St. Petersburg Times* shows us Milt Sosin, the Associated Press courthouse reporter in Miami, at work:

He pokes his head into offices and makes small talk with secretaries. He chats with a lawyer in an elevator. He shares respectful words with a newspaper reporter outside a courtroom. With a charming smile, he even opens a hallway door for a sweaty man in a three-piece suit.

For Sosin, who is probably the best reporter you *never* heard of, charm is part of his giant bag of journalist's tricks. His job is getting information. Being chummy, though it may come unnaturally, could pay off one day: He may need these courthouse people to provide news that might lead to an Associated Press exclusive.

"It's no big deal," Sosin says later, sounding almost embarrassed. "They're just sources. You treat them right. You stop by and ask them if anything is going on, that's all. If they give you something you can use, you protect them. You never betray their confidences."

Sosin's way with sources pays off. One of his biggest scoops was the indictment of Gen. Manuel Noriega of Panama for drug crimes. All the major newspapers were working on the story.

Klinkenberg writes:

> "I was sure he had been indicted," Sosin says now. "But the U.S. attorney was keeping it secret. He wanted to announce it at a press conference. I made a few phone calls. All my sources said Noriega's name was on the indictment. I told AP to go with the story."

During his first weeks covering Congress for *The Wall Street Journal*, Fred L. Zimmerman learned that finding and cultivating sources and contacts is essential. "If you can establish a friendly relationship with a committee chairman's secretary, she will tell you where he can be found in a hurry," Zimmerman says. "Or she will put you through on the phone sometimes when she wouldn't do it for a reporter she doesn't know."

Reliability of Sources

The distinction between human and physical sources, and their relative reliability, was nicely put by Sir Kenneth Clark, the British writer and critic: "If I had to say who was telling the truth about society, a speech by the Minister of Housing or the actual buildings put up in his time, I would believe the buildings."

The difference is often on the reporter's mind, for even though much of his or her work depends on interviews, the reporter seeks physical evidence whenever possible. This kind of material includes newspaper clippings, books, records and documents as well as the reporter's direct observation.

Because of the possibility of hoaxes, rumor passed as fact and old information, reporters are careful about using online material. It is verified before use.

Human Sources

A person with information the reporter needs for a story or for background is called a *source*. Sources include the woman who saw an airplane fall short of the landing strip and Deep Throat, the informant who cooperated with *Washington Post* reporters Woodward and Bernstein on their Watergate investigation. The stockbroker friend of a reporter who explains complicated financial matters is a source, although his name may never appear in a story.

Arthur L. Gavshon, the diplomatic reporter for the AP, defines a source in an article on sources in the *AP World Magazine:*

> To me anyone on the inside of any given news situation is a potential source. But they only turn into real sources when they come up with a bit, or a lot, of relevant information.

Gavshon says he finds sources anywhere and everywhere. He develops his sources "just as you would get to know a friend and nurture a relationship in everyday life (always assuming you can live a normal life as a journalist)—through the exercise of patience, understanding and a reasonable capacity to converse about shared interests."

Authoritative Sources Sometimes an assignment is so complex or so unfamiliar that a reporter hardly knows where to begin. The clips on the subject prove to be too sketchy, and the references presume some knowledge of the subject. The reporter needs a crash course in the topic, but the assignment is due and there is no time for in-depth research.

On her second day as the marine news reporter for *The Gazette* in Montreal, Jan Wong was given an assignment and told to handle it quickly because her editor had another story for her to cover.

Wong did what reporters do in such circumstances. She turned to people who know, authoritative sources:

"I must have called 20 people," she says. "I called everyone I could find in the marine directory. People were very helpful."

Sources need not be mayors or directors of companies. The city hall reporter knows that the town clerk who has served a succession of mayors has a comprehensive knowledge of the community and the inner workings of town government. The courthouse reporter befriends law clerks, court stenographers and security guards. Business reporters cultivate switchboard operators, secretaries, mailroom help.

Tactics Reporters have gone out of their way to do favors for their sources. At one newspaper in California, the reporters who handle obituaries send birthday candy and flowers to the mortuary employees who call to report the deaths of important people. A death called in near deadline means the newspaper or station telephoned first will have that much more time to write the obituary. A difference of two minutes can be the difference between making or missing the last edition or the 6 p.m. newscast.

Some reporters cultivate sources by reversing the news-gathering process. One Midwestern newsman says that instead of always asking sources for news, he puts his sources on the receiving end. "I see to it personally that they hear any gossip or important news. When I want news, I get it," he says.

The source needed for information on a single story need not be cultivated with the care reporters lavish on sources essential to a beat. But courtesy and

Wayne Miller

Dual Purpose

Human sources supply specific information for a story and are quoted. Or they can provide background material to help the reporter understand the event.

consideration are always important. In speaking to a source for the first—and perhaps the only—time, the reporter identifies himself or herself immediately and moves to the questions quickly. A different pace is necessary for the source essential to a beat. Gavshon cautions:

> Don't ever rush things. Don't make the ghastly mistake of thinking only in terms of tomorrow's headline. . . . One-night stands rarely satisfy anybody.

Be Careful

Under pressure, reporters often must rely on human sources who seem trustworthy. Sometimes they are not what they seem. When a federal agency called for a moratorium on silicon-gel breast implants, a woman made herself available to reporters, saying she was a breast cancer patient and had implants. She said she was satisfied with them. Three local television stations and *The Boston Globe* used her comments.

Terry Schraeder of WCVB-TV in Boston checked out the woman and found she was a paid spokeswoman for Dow Corning, manufacturer of the implant material, which had provided her with training in handling the media and a list of reporters to contact.

Pseudo-Sources

Then there are the sources who are hardly qualified to speak on a subject but appear authoritative. When some members of Congress wanted to find out the plight of farmers hard hit by rising costs and falling income, they called Sissy Spacek and Jane Fonda to testify. The women had played the wives of farmers in films.

Tips

"It was not the pink leather sofa ($3,070), the trip with seven aides to Puerto Rico ($16,000) or the chartered helicopter to Atlantic City ($1,500) that precipitated Laura D. Blackburne's fall from the chairmanship of New York City's Housing Authority last week. It was her abrupt, often harsh treatment of subordinates—who then opened the door for reporters who had been tipped to what they would find."

This is the beginning of Calvin Sims' account in *The New York Times* of the toppling of a major city official.

Disgruntled employees in Blackburne's office supplied reporters with lists of trips, lavish spending and the dates. The reporters then filed Freedom of Information Act requests and obtained the records.

"We vowed to get her back, and we did," said one source.

Tips come from whistle-blowers—people who are angry at what they consider incompetence and violations of the law—as well as from disgruntled workers. We saw in Chapter 1 how a city employee tipped Heidi Evans to the failure of the city health department to renew Pap smear testing, and how that tip opened up a scandal. Her source was a whistle-blower.

Tobacco Insider   For several years, a paralegal worker at the Brown and Williamson Tobacco Corporation in Louisville copied the company's secret files. Scientific studies in the early 1950s had shown lung cancer was 50 times higher in smokers than in nonsmokers, and the rate of disease was directly proportional to the number of cigarettes smoked per day. The tobacco companies denied the hazards of smoking but at the same time did research to see whether they could eliminate the dangers involved in smoking.

The research showed that the companies could never make a safe cigarette, unless they could sell one that did not burn tobacco. The research was kept secret, and it was this material that the paralegal worker was copying. He took about 4,000 pages of documents out, and in the mid 1990s they found their way to reporters. Other whistle-blowers began to supply documents as well.

A sidelight: The papers were first offered to ABC News, whose lawyers confiscated them and ordered reporters not to work on the story. Philip J. Hilts of *The New York Times* was then shown the material, and even the *Times* was reluctant to use the information. Finally, the *Times'* Science Department insisted on using Hilts' material for a story.

Tips Worth Checking   Tips come in all shapes and sizes, not only as revelations of wrongdoing. A member of the local university's social science department tells a reporter on the university beat that he read a study that found that the favorite newspaper reading of those 21 to 25 years of age are the comics, television and movie listings and the classified ads. Maybe there's a story there, he suggests to the reporter.

A city hall employee tells the beat reporter that anticipated property tax revenues have failed to materialize and the city may be caught short at year's end. A service station owner tells the radio reporter who stops by for gas that he has heard the street will be widened and many merchants on the three blocks to be widened plan to protest at the next meeting of the city planning and zoning commission. A woman working in a drugstore tells a customer—a TV reporter—that her daughter is excited about "the new reading program." The reporter checks the information and breaks a story about the city schools switching from the whole language approach to teaching reading with the old-fashioned phonics method.

Keeping the Source

The source is the reporter's life blood. Without access to information through the source, the reporter cannot function. The reporter is just as necessary to most sources, for without the journalist the source has no access to the public. Sources in the public sector need reaction to their ideas and policies.

Out of this mutual need a source-reporter relationship develops: The source will provide the reporter with information and will brief him or her on developments. In return, the reporter will write a fair account of the material.

As events become more complex, the reporter's dependence on sources increases. When a reporter learns of a probable future event, such as the presentation of the municipal budget to the city council, he or she may ask a source for background so that the difficult story can be written authoritatively. The courthouse reporter who learns through the grapevine that the grand jury is about to return an indictment against the city clerk will ask the district attorney for a briefing, promising not to break the story before the indictment is returned. Sources usually are happy to comply because they prefer an accurate story to a rush job.

Bob Greene of *Newsday* says that it's necessary to build a "personal bond" with sources to keep them. "Show an interest in them, their work, their activities, their family. Get the names of children, husbands, wives, and use them. Every now and then, say, 'Let's have dinner, breakfast.' "

When something happens on a beat that could cost a reporter his or her source, another reporter usually is assigned to the story. "In sports, we'd rather have an investigative reporter come in and do our tough reporting," says Mary Kress of *The Florida Times-Union* in Jacksonville, "so that the sports beat reporter doesn't get into trouble with the coach or the players."

Protecting Sources

Sometimes a reporter is asked to protect a source's identity. An investigative reporter learns from a police officer that a convict serving a life term for murder was convicted on perjured police testimony. In return for the tip about the frame-up, the reporter must promise not to name the source.

The reporter can make this promise because shield laws in most states protect confidential sources. All states have some kind of protection, but in some states, a reporter who tries to protect a confidential source may face contempt charges and jail. State press associations usually distribute pamphlets about reporters' rights.

Sometimes reporters have to overcome their reluctance to embarrass a friendly source with a tough story. Walter Lippmann said there must be a "certain distance between the reporter and the source, not a wall or a fence, but an air space." Once a friend becomes an official, he said, "you can't call him by his first name anymore."

Some reporters protect their sources. Jack Anderson, a Washington columnist who specializes in inside information, states his philosophy as follows: "We will give immunity to a very good source as long as the information he offers us is better than that which we've got on him."

The inexperienced reporter has still another problem that sometimes leads to the overprotection of sources. Mixing with the kinds of people the reporter had once only read about or seen on television—governors, movie stars, generals—can be a heady affair. As a consequence, the reporter may lose objectivity. Veteran reporters may suffer from another form of this ailment. They become source oriented. Forgetting that they are responsible to the general reader, they write copy for their source's approval.

James Woodcock,
The Billings Gazette

She Knows Best

For a story on crowded classrooms, the best sources are the teachers and the students, not the president of the board of education.

The Expert

Who knows the most about any given subject? The expert, of course. As obvious as this is, reporters sometimes use sources because of who they are, what they are, not because of what they know.

People tend to believe those in authority. The more impressive the title, the higher the social position, the more prestigious the alma mater, the more faith people have in the expert or authority. This trust in authority is known as the "hierarchy of credibility"—the higher on the scale the authority is, the more believable the source is thought to be. When the journalist surrenders to this tendency, he or she allows those in power to define events and situations.

Reporters must be careful to use sources only within their areas of expert knowledge. Asked questions within the narrow range of their expertise, sources are useful. A banker can talk about banking, a general about the strategy and tactics of war. But it is dangerous to rely on a banker for comments on the nation's economy or on a general as an authority on international affairs. They may be less useful than the lesser-known labor department area representative or the assistant professor of international affairs at a local college.

A reporter's best sources are those who have demonstrated **their knowledge** and competence as accurate observers, interpreters and forecasters of events. Reporters should drop sources who are proved wrong in their observations and assessments, whether they served in the president's cabinet, ran a multimillion-dollar import business or graduated *summa cum laude* from Harvard.

Sources to Beware

Then there are those who twist, distort and obfuscate. We have space here for three of the species that the reporter fishing for information may encounter, the liars, the hoaxsters and the promoters.

The Liars   Sometimes, sources lie. Some lie because they want the publicity a story-starved reporter will give them. Pete Hamill recalls one incident early in his journalism career: "Years ago I published a column based on a horrific story related to me by a man in East Harlem; three weeks later someone sent me a copy of a 30-year-old short story on which the lie was based."

He recalls another columnist's piece about a man who described his heroism in a fire. The next day, says Hamill, "this splendid gentleman was arrested for setting the building on fire."

These are the kooks and sad sacks. There are others—professionals, office holders, politicians—who lie as part of their jobs. A prominent criminal lawyer told journalists at a national convention, "If I give you deliberate misinformation on behalf of a client and you print it, that's your problem."

He said that he routinely and successfully manipulates reporters so that they write stories favorable to his clients. Some cases, he says, create a "feeding frenzy" among the press. "It's frightening . . . the hunger that's out there, whether it's the print media or television," he says. "I have found, to some extent, that media people can be used."

The Hoaxsters   Then there are the hoaxsters, some of them engaging in sick humor, such as those who call newspapers to report the deaths of people very much alive. Obituary writers are vulnerable to the caller who says he or she is telephoning from a distant city about the sudden death of a local person. Editors caution those new to this beat to verify all deaths with a relative, a local mortuary, some official source.

Some hoaxsters are harmless, even hilarious. No journalism survey is complete without a salute to the inimitable Joe Skaggs, a teacher of media communication and a genius at staging events for a gullible press.

At one news conference, crowded with reporters and television crews, Dr. Josef Gregor announced that he had distilled cockroach hormones into a pill so potent it would make people immune to ailments as diverse as acne and menstrual cramps. His study group, the "Metamorphosis," distributed the scientific literature to reporters who reported his discovery.

At another packed news conference some time later, Joe Bones announced he had formed the Fat Squad for people who needed help dieting. For a fee of $300, the Squad—a group of burly enforcers—was prepared to use physical force if necessary to keep clients on their diets. The story was carried on network television and in major newspapers around the country.

Outside the Democratic convention in New York City, the Rev. Joseph sat quietly on his bicycle. Behind him, attached to the bike, was a handsome oak portable confession booth, the Portofess, the Rev. Joseph told the curious.

Some delegates, too hurried to walk to a church a few blocks away, took advantage of the service.

The Portofess attracted the press, and stories were carried by the AP and Reuters. CNN and CBS. Scores of other stations and newspapers featured the Portofess with its gold lettering that advertised Father Joseph's good office.

Gregor-Bones-Joseph was, of course, Joe Skaggs, who says he stages these elaborate scenes to show how careless the media are in checking sources. "Aren't they also susceptible to more dangerous manipulation?" he asks.

The Promoters   Our third type is the source with something he or she is pushing. It may be a commercial venture or product, a political candidate, a policy. *The Washington Post* business pages ran a long story about a new shopping center a developer was working on. Even with this free publicity, nothing came of the venture.

Court documents in Minnesota's tobacco trial revealed that the tobacco industry paid scientists more than $155,000 to write letters to *The Wall Street Journal* and scientific publications that discredited a federal report linking secondhand smoking to cancer.

In some cases, the evidence indicates that tobacco law firms wrote the letters for the scientists to sign. In all, 13 scientists took tobacco money, one receiving $25,000 to write an article.

The lesson here: When using a so-called expert source, it's a good idea to ask if he or she is on retainer or has received any fees from anyone associated with the event or issue being reported.

Leaks

Officials and agencies, departments and cabinet members, mayors and council members—everyone leaks information to reporters, and no one wants his or her name, agency or department attached to the information as a source. The other common characteristic of the leak is that it serves the leaker's purpose.

A list of the evils of the leak would be longer than the companion list of the good the leak serves. Officials can hide, float trial balloons, and plead innocence if the material backfires. But the leak also can be the avenue of communication for the whistleblower. It can be a route along which classified or secret material reaches the public. The reporter has to walk a thin line between serving the source's purposes and serving the public's needs. But walk it the reporter must, because the leak is more than here to stay; the leak thrives and will continue to do so.

Presidents take office vowing to stem the tide of leaks. Ronald Reagan urged lie detector tests for those suspected of leaking, and before he took office, George Bush threatened reprisals against those leaking material to the press. He said that leaks reflected a lack of discipline among officials that could lead to problems such as the disclosure of security information.

Leaks can be wildly inaccurate and sometimes damaging to the subjects of the leaked material. Elie Abel of Stanford University has some guidelines for the use of such material:

Indicted. During the grand jury investigation of President Clinton's affairs, leaks poured forth. One, picked up by stations and newspapers, said Hillary Clinton would soon be indicted. Like many of the other leaks, this one came to nothing.

• Be skeptical about the motives of the person leaking the information. "The leaker's interest should be identified, even when he cannot be named," Abel says.

• Editors should ask reporters questions about the material, and reporters "who expect to be trusted by their editors ought to show comparable trust in the discretion of their editors."

• Editors should require that at least two independent sources confirm leaked material.

Online Cautions

Liars, hoaxsters, promoters and leakers thrive on the Internet. "You can't be sure of any of it," says Henry Stokes, managing editor of *The Commercial Appeal.* "You can't even be sure that the person or institution you think you are dealing with is genuine or fake."

Elizabeth Weise of *USA Today* double-checks everything she obtains from anyone unknown to her. She says that people fake e-mail material, Web addresses, identities. We've already seen a classic fake, the letter from the "Curator of Antiquities" at the Smithsonian Institution.

Fallable Humans

Beat reporters find that their sources have interests they wish to protect, programs they want to push, enemies they want to punish. But even the best-intended can be unreliable.

The reporter who has to rely on transient sources for quick information on a breaking story knows that most people are notoriously inaccurate observers. A woman who says she saw an airplane crash "in a ball of fire" may not be relaying what she saw but what she has seen in the movies.

An eyewitness can seduce a reporter by the sheer drama of his or her story. Instead of being enthralled, reporters should be cautious, for their knowledge of human nature should tell them that most people tend to overdramatize events.

Erving Goffman, the sociologist, says everyone is a performer trying to put his or her stamp of individual identity on things. Individuals find it hard not to exaggerate their observations or feelings when they know that the more dramatic their account the more likely they will appear on TV. People also remember selectively, recalling mostly that which fits their preconceived notions or that which they find pleasant or exciting.

Reliability Tests

For sources on the beat, those the reporter is in touch with on a regular basis, reliability is usually determined by consistency. That is, the source is considered reliable if in the past the information he or she supplied proved accurate.

For transient sources, those interviewed for a particular story, the test is more complicated:

- Was the person an observer of the incident, or did he or she hear about it from someone else?
- Is the person a competent observer? An airline employee would be a better source for information about an airplane crash than would a student or a salesperson.
- Can the source supply precise details that have the ring of truth and seem consistent with the facts?
- Are several sources offering the same information? Generally, when several people provide the same version of an event, chances are good that the accounts are reliable.

Increasingly, as journalism covers complex events, experts are called upon as sources. These can be academicians, scientists, financial analysts and so on. As we have seen, not all are independent, down-the-middle in their expertise. The university scientist who issues skeptical reports about what he calls the "so-called greenhouse effect" may have his research funded by coal and oil interests. This funding does not necessarily mean the information is slanted, but a reporter would be wise to find someone without industry funding for research in this area.

Chris Bowman of *The Sacramento Bee* suggests these checks on the scientific expert:

Where does the funding come from for his or her research?
Is this original research, or material from some outside source?
Does the expert distinguish between his or her scientific observations and personal beliefs?

Gavshon uses a fairly simple device to test reliability. "My own rough-and-ready rule is to test out the new-found source with questions to which I already know the answers."

Online Checks Those who use the Internet—and few journalists do not—are cautious. They know that Web pages can remain for years without being updated and that little is available about events before 1995 because it was then that material began to be placed on the Web. And, as we've seen, the journalist cannot be certain of the authenticity of the source of the material.

"Check and confirm before using Internet material," says Weise. To confirm, Weise will check with someone she knows to be reliable or make a telephone call to the source to verify the information. "Unless the person is already known to you, as a general rule never quote an individual without speaking to him or her on the phone to confirm his or her identity."

Despite these tests and checks, journalists know that unless they observe the event themselves they are relying on someone else, that person's observations or recollections. In the case of documents, journalists also know that recording errors can be made. Reporting is made even more complicated by the profusion of interest groups, some of which disguise their agendas to seek to appear as disinterested and independent organizations.

Let's look at the Population Research Institute whose press releases and news conferences have made news on network TV, in *The Wall Street Journal* and on the AP wire.

The Institute and the Bureau Family planning is a controversial issue that is debated on the floor of Congress, in the halls of international conferences and at school board meetings. The words *sex education* and *abortion* are red flags to many. Journalists looking for some middle way to find reliable information have to move carefully.

The Population Research Institute seems a straightforward organization. But a check of Internal Revenue Service files discloses that the Institute is a public relations arm of Human Life International, a partisan anti-abortion organization. It is headed by Paul Marx, whose book *Confessions of a Prolife Missionary* contains this sentence: "Note the large number of abortionists (consult the Yellow Pages) and pro-abortion medical professors who are Jewish."

The foreign advisor to Human Life International is Dr. Siegfried Ernst, about whom a German court stated: "The things he says are so racially discriminating that any impartial observer can see parallels to the ideology of the Third Reich."

Why, then, the media's use of Institute material? Possibly because journalists confuse the Population Research *Institute* with the authoritative and independent Population Research *Bureau*.

On issues like abortion, gun control, school prayer and others that have divided the country, it is important that journalists not pass on to the public propaganda in the guise of information from an independent source.

"The motives of those who press their views upon journalists must be routinely examined and, where appropriate, revealed to the reader," says Dr. Judith Lewis Herman of the Harvard Medical School. Also, she warns against relying on anecdote and speculation in reporting on controversial issues. Anecdotes and personal experiences do not constitute proof.

Physical Sources

The range of physical information is enormous. The availability of physical sources is limited only by the reporter's knowledge of their existence.

Databases provide quick access to dozens of excellent sources, from census material to local arrest records. Donald Barlett and James Steele turned to *The Philadelphia Inquirer* databases for material for their prize-winning series about the federal Tax Reform Act. "Once you would come up with a name of somebody, you could go right to one of these databases and see what was known about him very quickly," Steele said. The database made it possible to pack large amounts of convincing detail into their stories, such as the description of the widow who inherited $4 million more from her late husband's estate under the giveaway terms of the act.

Not All Sources Are Equal

Not all physical sources are of equal reliability. Tables of vital statistics are more reliable than the city official's summary introducing the tables. The world almanac is more reliable than a newspaper clipping of the same event, for the almanac is usually the work of professional researchers, and the news story may have been written in a hurry before all the facts were in.

The Spy Who Wasn't

Art Jester of the *Lexington Herald-Leader* used physical and human sources to puncture the dramatic story of a public speaker, Col. John Cottell, who passed himself off as having served as a spy for the British and told tales of being parachuted behind Nazi lines, being imprisoned in Moscow's dreaded prison, Lubyanka, and being the model for John Le Carré's novels, *The Spy Who Came in From the Cold* and *Tinker, Tailor, Soldier, Spy*. He gave 70 to 75 talks a year at $2,500 each.

The tales were just too dramatic, Jester felt, and he started to dig. His conclusion in a copyrighted story: "Much, if not all, of his story is fiction."

- Le Carré denied any knowledge of Cottell. "I'm getting fairly irritated by the man. I've never heard of him, and there's no question of him being the basis of characters in my work. He is either mad or a fraud."
- Cottell said he was in a spy exchange at the Berlin Wall in 1957. The Wall was built in 1961.
- He claimed he was an ordained Anglican priest, and in his talks he often wore clerical garb. An Anglican bishop Jester contacted said, "Cottell has no connection with this diocese and we believe him to be a fraud." In answer to Jester's questions, Cottell acknowledged that he only holds a mail-order ordination certificate from the Universal Life Church Inc., which sends out certificates to anyone who mails a fee.
- His birth certificate listed him as two years younger than he claimed, which would have made him 16 years old when, he asserted, Winston Churchill sent him to parachute behind German lines in World War II.

Paper Trail

Much can be learned by tracking a person through the many documents he or she leaves behind. Such searches are described as "following the paper trail." The trail is strewn with material: a birth certificate, hospital records, school records, real estate transfers, marriage and death certificates.

The material can be found in newspaper clippings, court records, reference works and government agency files. Two examples of what can be learned:

Home: What it cost; what was paid and what was borrowed for the down payment; who holds the mortgage and how much it amounts to; liens on the property; the amount of property taxes paid and any delinquencies.

Automobile: Registration number; title information; name and model of vehicle; year of manufacture; license plate number. Automobile records also include data on the owner—name, age, height, weight, offenses.

Digging into Databases

Increasingly, reporters are using the computer to locate and to process information for stories. The procedure is called computer-assisted reporting (CAR), and it has proved effective for almost every beat. Jeff South, former database editor at the *Austin American-Statesman,* says newsrooms use computer research to "mine political campaign records, crime statistics, census demographics and other data for stories."

All levels of government are putting their records in a form easily available to reporters engaging in CAR.

Drunk Drivers   When the Paddock papers in the Chicago area wanted to know what happened to people arrested for drunk driving, reporters fed into the computer 1,500 drunk driving arrests and their dispositions. The finding: More than two-thirds of those arrested avoided conviction. Only 1 in 15 was jailed or fined heavily. The *Atlanta Constitution* used local bank records to show a pattern of racial discrimination in housing loans, and it won a Pulitzer Prize for its stories.

Led to Slaughter   Martha Mendoza of the AP used the computer to track the handling of a multimillion dollar federal program designed to protect thousands of wild horses on public lands. Under the direction of the Bureau of Land Management, the program allows individuals to adopt up to four horses each and care for them. After a year, the adopters are given legal title to the animals. At that point, Mendoza found, many of the owners, some of them BLM employees, were selling the horses to slaughterhouses—at a profit of $700 a horse. After her revelation, the BLM admitted that about 90 percent of the horses in the program were sold for slaughter.

Overtime   For his examination of overtime payments to city employees, Mike Trautmann obtained the city payroll. For one of his stories in a series for the *Argus Leader,* Trautmann put the mayor's salary into the computer to find out if anyone in the city's employ was earning more. The story he wrote began:

> When does an assistant make more than the boss? When he works for the city of Sioux Falls.
>
> Last year, the city paid three employees more than Mayor Gary Hanson's $77,250—including his chief of staff, Dean Nielsen.
>
> Three other employees earned nearly as much.

School Inspections   For his two-part series on the lack of adequate fire inspections of South Dakota schools, Trautmann developed a database for the more than 800 school buildings. His first story began:

More than half of South Dakota's schools have not had fire inspections in the past two years, as state law requires, making it uncertain whether some of those schools are fire safe.

Officials with the state fire marshal's office acknowledge that inspections have seriously lagged for many public and private schools. They say they will institute wholesale administrative changes to catch up.

"It's an embarrassment," said Mike Mehlhaff, director of the Division of Commercial Inspection and Regulation, the office responsible for overseeing school inspections.

Approximately 430 of the state's 850 public and private school buildings have not been inspected within the two-year legal requirement. Some haven't been inspected for as long as 10 to 15 years, according to inspection reports filed in the state fire marshal's office.

More than two dozen schools have no record of ever being inspected.

His second set of stories dealt with the specific hazards in the schools and the reasons they exist. In these stories, Trautmann blended physical and human sources. One story begins:

HARTFORD—Deputy Fire Marshal Paul Coon tugged on the exit door leading from West Central High School's home-economics classroom.

It didn't budge.

He tried using both hands, bracing his feet against a concrete slab outside the door. Grunting with the effort, he pulled again.

Nothing.

Three more sharp tugs, each harder than the last.

Nothing. Nothing. And nothing.

Frustrated, Coon turned away and shook his head, wondering when the same exit might be the only escape for some frantic high-schoolers trying to escape a fire.

Jammed exits, bolted doors, water-logged basements and dangling fire escapes are just a few of the fire hazards inspectors encounter weekly as they try to examine more than 800 school buildings across South Dakota.

Hazards can be as simple as burned-out bulbs in exit signs, and as severe as fire escapes held in place by bolts shimmying loose from the concrete.

CAR projects can be devoted to features, too. For one, we go west to San Francisco where Elizabeth Weise has an idea for an April 1st story for *USA Today*. Weise covers the computer industry in Silicon Valley for the newspaper.

Computer Viruses   Weise began to think about the prevalence of virus warnings online, "and especially how they seem to increase around April Fools Day." Most of the warnings, she knew, are fakes. "But I realized that many readers probably didn't."

Here is how she went about gathering material for her story:

First I called CERT, the Computer Emergency Response Center at Carnegie Mellon University in Pittsburgh, Penn. Then I did a search on the Web for Fraud pages, found several, one of which proved to be run by Rob Rosenberger, who runs the Computer Virus Myths site and proved to be an excellent interview.

Here is how her story began:

> With *April Fools'* Day on Wednesday, computer security experts have but one plea: Don't believe everything you read in e-mail.
>
> The Internet is awash in warnings about viruses that don't exist and scams that don't work, created by the malicious and passed on by the innocent, who think they're helping the Internet by spreading the word. With the day of tricks here, experts expect the river to turn into a flood.
>
> "It's amazing what people will believe because they got it over the Internet," says Rob Rosenberger, who runs the Computer Virus Myths site (*kumite.com/myths*). "Be sure to add fresh batteries to your clue meter come *April Fools'*."

Here is how Weise ended the piece:

> Finally, there's a simple test you can use to detect almost every deceptive message, says Bill Orvis, a security specialist with the Department of Energy's Computer Incident Response Advisory. "You can tell a *hoax* because it always ends with 'Tell all your friends.' "

For a listing of sources on the Internet, see **Appendix E, Sources Online.**

How Reporters Use Sources

Let us accompany some reporters as they work with various kinds of sources for their stories. The first story is the type that puts reporters on their mettle, the late-breaking event that must be handled quickly and accurately.

A Fatality

The story takes us to a New Jersey newsroom where a reporter is making late police checks, which consist of calling area police departments not personally covered by the police reporter. Here, the reporter must rely on human sources. There is little opportunity to examine police records.

The reporter is told that a car plowed into a motorcycle at a stoplight and the two young people on the motorcycle were killed. The driver was arrested three miles down the highway and charged with drunken driving. The reporter knows this is a good story, but little time remains before the last edition closes. The rule in the newsroom, she remembers her editor telling her, is simple: "In baseball, if you get your glove on the ball and don't handle it cleanly, it's an error, no matter how hard it's hit to you. If you get a story before deadline and don't have it written for the next edition, you're not a reporter."

She has seen baseball games in which fielders managed to touch a ball but were not given errors when they failed to throw the batter out. But she had not called that to her editor's attention. She knows better.

Basic Information   She quickly learns the names of the victims and the driver as well as the location and circumstances of the accident. Knowing that the investigating officers are still writing their report, she asks if they are available at the station. They will have details she needs, especially about the chase for the driver. She then calls the mortuary to obtain background about the victims. Mortuaries usually have the exact spelling of a victim's name, and his or her age, address and occupation.

She glances at the clock to see whether she has time to call the parents of the victims for more precise information. Also, relatives often are around after an emergency to help out, and they might be able to tell her something about the deceased. But she decides that first she will see whether the victims' names are in the newspaper library.

During her interviews with the investigating officers, one of them mentions that this was the third motorcycle accident in the last month. She notes that on her pad for a quick check in the library, too.

The check of the library discloses this was actually the fourth motorcycle accident in the county, one of the others having been fatal to a young man. She also finds a story about the young woman who was killed. She was the daughter of a prominent local family, and the story indicates she used a middle name, which was not in the reporter's notes.

The reporter then decides to locate the parents of the man who died in the accident. She realizes that she had decided not to make those calls because of her distaste for intruding on the family's tragedy. At some newspapers, reporters do not have to make such calls, she recalls a colleague telling her, but that is not the case at this one. The younger sister of the man answers the telephone and is able to supply some details about him.

The reporter used physical and human sources. One key to the story is her knowledge that the investigating police officers might be at the police station writing up the report of the accident. She knows that the best sources are those close to the scene. Although they had not seen the accident, they had arrived quickly and had conducted the investigation. The names of the officers will add authenticity to the story.

She begins to write, some 20 minutes before the last edition closes. She knows she has time because she had been organizing her notes as she was reporting.

A Shooting

Although reporters sometimes use the telephone when they should be on the street talking to people or at meetings observing the give-and-take of open debate, there are times when direct observation is impossible. We have just seen a reporter handle a fatal accident by telephone. When the deadline is imminent and the source or the event is more than a short walk or trip away, the only recourse is the telephone.

Using the telephone can be an art. Properly used, it is a boon to reporting. Let us watch a television news reporter cover a shooting 50 miles north of her station, WKTV in Utica, N.Y.

Early one fall evening, Donna Hanover is told by a cameraman that he has picked up an interesting police report: Two people had been shot in separate incidents as they drove past an Indian encampment near the town of Big Moose. Hanover knows immediately this is a big story. Some Mohawk Indians had moved onto state-owned land in the Adirondack Mountains six months before and had refused to leave.

Hanover's major problem is her impending deadline and the distance to Big Moose. Her newscast is at 11 p.m., which gives her no time for the trip up, reporting and the return trip. She has to use the telephone.

By 10:15 p.m., her calls to the state police have turned up little information—a few details on the shooting and the names and ages of the injured. Apparently both were wounded by shots fired at the cars in which they were riding. Hanover then calls a medical center near Big Moose to check the condition of the victims, a 22-year-old man and a 9-year-old girl. She also hopes to learn something more about the incident. She is told that the young man was taken to a hospital in Utica and that the girl is on her way.

Hospital Check   She asks for the names of the relatives of those who were injured, and a hospital attendant gives her the name of the injured man's father. She then calls "information for the home telephone number, hoping that some member of the family would have stayed at home in Big Moose," Hanover says.

She is lucky. The father is not there, but the victim's brother answers her call, and he had been riding in the car with his older brother at the time of the shooting.

This piece of good fortune enables Hanover to use an eyewitness, a better source than someone with a secondhand account. He tells Hanover that they had been fired at twice by the Indians. The first time the shots missed. But on the return trip, the car had come under heavy fire and his brother was hit in the shoulder.

The girl was in a car that passed by the Indian encampment a few hours after the boys were fired at. One bullet entered the trunk, went through the rear seat and struck the girl in the back.

As a result of her calls, Hanover is able to make the 11 o'clock news with a report of the incident. She does not have all the information she needs, but she does have the interview, information from the state police, the condition of the 22-year-old and the name of the 9-year-old girl who was also injured.

To the Scene   The next day, with plenty of time, Hanover and two photographers drive to Big Moose to do an on-the-scene report. She interviews the injured man's brother again, this time in front of a camera, photographs the damaged automobile and interviews local residents and the state police.

"The interview with the brother was important," Hanover says later, "because he was a primary source. The police report wasn't, and our job is to give our viewers the best and most accurate information about what has happened." The interview also added an essential ingredient for television news—visual identification.

"I always try to make the viewers feel close to the scene, to make them feel they were there as it happened," says Hanover.

One patrolman was photographed indicating bullet holes in the car. The Mohawk Indians were not available for interviews. Later, they told her they had been shot at and were returning the fire.

Her script begins:

New York state police are manning roadblocks near Eagle Bay and are escorting cars on Big Moose Road where two people in passing cars were shot Monday. Nine-year-old April Madigan of Geneva, New York, is in critical condition at St. Luke's Memorial Hospital Center. . . .

An Enterpriser

We turn from these spot news stories to a story that begins with a chat between friends.

Jeffrey A. Tannenbaum, a reporter with *The Wall Street Journal,* is in the newsroom when a call comes in from a former college classmate, Ralph Sanders.

Sanders, who is blind, tells Tannenbaum he is active in an organization called the National Federation of the Blind and that the group is planning a demonstration. Sanders says that the blind are tired of being denied rights granted to sighted people.

Sanders suggests the demonstration will make a good story. Sensing a broader story than the coverage of an event that is being staged for the media, Tannenbaum arranges to have lunch with Sanders.

"I was fascinated with the possibility of writing a story about the blind comparable to early stories on the civil rights movement," Tannenbaum says later. "In the course of a long interview, Sanders provided the theme for the story. I used it in the sixth paragraph of the finished story.

"What I needed to do after the interview was to document the central thesis. I needed to find examples of ways in which blind people are discriminated against. And I needed to find cases of discrimination in which blind people were militant."

At lunch, Sanders provides some sources and examples of militancy. Tannenbaum finds other examples by calling organizations of the blind. He learns about discrimination by checking with social agencies and human rights commissions. He is able to find more than a dozen examples of discrimination.

Examples   "As a rule of thumb," Tannenbaum says, "I like to have half-a-dozen highly readable, colorful, to-the-point examples in a story. Each

THE WALL STR

VOL. CLXXXVI NO. 7   ★ ★   EASTERN EDITION   THURSDAY, JU

New Crusaders

Angry Blind Militants, Seeking 'Equal Rights,' Try Tougher Tactics

---

Sightless Stage Walkouts, Sue Landlords, Bosses, Reject 'Excessive' Pity

---

The Fight With Sky Glider

By JEFFREY A. TANNENBAUM
Staff Reporter of THE WALL STREET JOURNAL

Keith and Elizabeth Howard were all set to board an Allegheny Airlines flight from Washington, D.C., to Philadelphia. The airplane wasn't fully booked. Yet an airline official suddenly insisted they must take separate flights.

The reason: The Howards are both blind.

The couple say they were told the pilot didn't want more than one blind passenger on the flight because he assumed that blind people might cause a safety problem or require extra service. While his wife went on ahead, the 43-year-old Mr. Howard waited for the next flight.

Far from being helpless nuisances, the Howards both successfully manage their own lunch counters in Washington. They angrily protested to Allegheny, which confirms their story. Allegheny apologized, and says that Ransome Airlines, which operated the flight under contract, has changed its policies to prevent a repeat of the incident. But the Howards figure their problems are far from over. They say the airline incident was typical of the "common discrimination—a normal thing" that society practices almost routinely against the blind.

But nowadays, blind people like the Howards are moving with increasing fervor to protest such discrimination. They are voicing complaints, turning to the courts and even staging strikes and demonstrations. As a result, employers, landlords and businesses generally are finding they must either change their policies or face protests and lawsuits.

"A Dash of Leprosy"

"Society will give charity to the blind, but it won't allow us to be first-class citizens," charges Ralph W. Sanders, president of the Arkansas unit of the National Federation of the Blind. "Like the blacks, we've come to the point where we're not going to stand for it anymore," he adds.

Ironically, this militancy occurs at a time when conditions for the blind are improving significantly, particularly in the realm of jobs. Several states in recent ~~days~~ ~~approve~~ ~~broad~~

What's News—

* * *

Business and Finance

OIL'S EXPORT PRICE was cut by Ecuador in what may be the first major crack in the oil cartel's pricing structure. Ecuador's cut was through a reduction in the income-tax rate charged oil companies.
(Story on Page 3)

* * *

A tax on most crude oil and refined petroleum products of up to three cents a barrel was proposed, as expected, by President Ford to help pay for damages caused by oil spills.
(Story on Page 3)

* * *

A Honduran commission urged steps to nationalize the concessions and property of units of United Brands and Castle & Cooke to increase that country's participation in the banana-export business.
(Story on Page 2)

* * *

Developing nations' efforts to negotiate new international agreements fixing commodities prices will be resisted by the U.S., a top Treasury official said.
(Story on Page 2)

* * *

General Motors is being countersued by a former dealer for $33 million in connection with a tangled series of criminal and civil cases involving alleged warranty fraud. Separately, GM said its supplemental benefit fund for laid-off employes could soon resume payouts for a brief period.
(Stories on Page 4)

* * *

Ford Motor confirmed that it quietly paid for repairing about 69,000 rust-damaged 1969-73 models even though normal warranties had expired.
(Story on Page 4)

* * *

Great Atlantic & Pacific Tea reported a $6.5 million loss, less than predicted, for its May 24 first quarter; a year earlier it earned $10.3 million.
(Story on Page 4)

* * *

International Paper's second quarter earnings slid 37% to $47.2

World-Wide

A MIDEAST AGREEMENT isn't "anywhere near," Kissinger said.

The Secretary of State, beginning a European trip during which he will meet with Israeli Prime Minister Rabin, said reports that an Egyptian-Israeli accord had been all but wrapped up are "totally wrong." Hearst Newspapers quoted Egyptian President Sadat as indicating that basic terms of a new interim Sinai agreement had been worked out. But Prime Minister Rabin said some key issues remain to be settled.

Sources suggested that an agreement would involve an electronic surveillance system, operated by the U.S., to warn of any attack through the Gidi and Mitla mountain passes in the Sinai.

Rabin conferred with West German Chancellor Schmidt in Bonn, who urged the Israeli premier to take advantage of the current chance for a settlement with Egypt. Kissinger arrived in Paris and will meet with Soviet Foreign Minister Gromyko in Geneva before seeing Rabin Saturday in Bonn.

The Palestine Liberation Organization said in Beirut that it had failed to win the release of an American Army colonel kidnapped last week. It said the colonel was being held by two radical Palestinian groups that don't belong to the PLO. The deadline the abductors set for the U.S. to meet their ransom demands passed.

* * *

A TURKISH-ARMS COMPROMISE was offered to the House by Ford.

After meeting with 140 House members, the President proposed legislation partially lifting the ban on military aid that was imposed after Turkey used U.S. weapons in invading Cyprus. Under the plan, undelivered arms already paid for by Turkey would be shipped and more weapons could be bought for cash, but Turkey wouldn't be eligible for grants. Ford would report to Congress every two months on arms sales and on the chances for a Cyprus settlement.

The three leading House opponents of arms for Turkey weren't invited to the meeting with Ford. One of them, Rep. John Brademas (D., Ind.), denounced the proposal as a fraud.

Speaker Carl Albert predicted the House would approve Ford's plan. The Senate last month voted 41-40 to end the arms embargo. Turkey has demanded that negotiations on the status of U.S. bases begin next Thursday if the embargo hasn't been lifted by then. It wasn't known whether Turkey would accept Ford's compromise.

* * *

PORTUGAL'S ARMED FORCES will form local units bypassing political parties.

An Enterpriser: A Reporter-Initiated Story

one should illustrate a different aspect of the general problem, buttressing the main theme but not duplicating one another."

He checks with people who might have another point of view on what the blind charge is discrimination. Tannenbaum says, "More than fairness is involved here. A good reporter knows that the best stories are multidimensional. Conflict and controversy do make a better story, but they also accurately reflect reality."

Tannenbaum now has sources with specific complaints and incidents. He has a feeling an incident at a Washington, D.C., airport described by Keith and Elizabeth Howard should be well up in his story, perhaps the lead.

He interviews the head of Sanders' organization and a blind professor of American history at Seton Hall College in New Jersey, who provides an excellent quote that gives an overview. He consults some references for data about the blind. He has now interviewed 40 people and is ready to write.

Tannenbaum finds the writing goes quickly. "A well-reported story—one reported logically with a central theme in mind—tends to write itself," he recalls an editor telling him. He begins with the Howards in a delayed lead and presents the theme in his words in the fifth paragraph and then in Sanders' words in the sixth paragraph. The next two paragraphs are background.

Tannenbaum's first version had the blind professor's quote lower in the story, but he remembered the guideline that good quotes should be put up high in a story and so he raised the quote as high as he could.

Do Jane and Johnny Read?

The reporter, Mullins, is told by his city editor to find out whether people "are reading as much as they used to." It's a vague assignment, but Mullins thinks he knows what his editor has in mind. The editor has talked often about "cretinization by television," and recently he walked through the newsroom brandishing a photo from a college newspaper of roommates talking to each other on their computers. The photo shows them three feet apart.

"It says here that college students spend three to four hours a day surfing the Internet," he exploded. "No wonder they don't know anything. They have no time to read."

The reading scores in local schools have been declining in recent years, and the newspaper has played up those stories. So Mullins decides to pass on the Net surfers and look at the young readers.

First, he wants to compare local reading scores with those of other school systems in the state and with national reading scores, which will take him to databases. He makes a note to do that. Maybe this is not just a local situation.

"If you find anyone is still reading, tell us what's being read," is the editor's parting comment as Mullins leaves the newsroom.

So his first stop will be a nearby library and another near a grade school.

He will also want to talk to some teachers. A reporter on the newspaper whose wife is a fourth-grade teacher told him that she is convinced her students cannot spell because they rarely read outside class and are unfamiliar with words. "Nobody can spell," Mullins told her, having put in time on the copy desk.

Ken Elkins,
The Anniston (Ala.) *Star*

Pitts?

Library Users   In one library, he notices some youngsters chatting at a table near the window. Unobtrusively, he moves over to listen.

"What did you find out about the clipper ships?" one of the boys asks another. A few minutes later, a girl asks the boy next to her if he knows when the first transcontinental railroad was completed. Apparently they are doing research for an assignment on transportation. Mullins asks one of the boys, and he is told the work is for an honors history class in one of the local high schools. That is worth noting, Mullins decides.

As he passes three other students, he glances at the books they are reading—Jack Kerouac's *On the Road,* Hermann Hesse's *Demian,* and a book that appears to be about race car driving, judging by its title. That, too, goes into Mullins' notes. Suddenly, it strikes him that this is just what he needs to be doing, to rely on his observations and to support them with interviews of library users.

Mullins strolls around the library. As he passes one shelf, he observes that most of the books, which bear numbers ranging from 200 to 300 on their spines, are hardly used but that a few are well-worn. The well-read books are on eastern religions. He jots down their titles, and he makes a note to look into that by talking to the librarian. She might have some of the titles of the books that have been borrowed frequently.

Older Readers   The physical evidence seems to show that youngsters on school assignments are major library users, as are older people with time on their hands. The older readers congregate around the newspaper rack, and much of their borrowing and reading is of the historical romances, adventure novels and mysteries. Considerable activity by all age groups focuses on the how-to books that offer instruction on investments, gardening, home repair and sex. He learns videotapes are a big item with library users.

Mullins' story is a blend of human and physical sources, the one supplementing the other. His observation of the library users injects human interest into the story. He *shows* his readers students and adults using books, newspapers and magazines, and he names these publications, remembering the guideline that journalism is the art of the specific.

Births and Deaths

As you have seen, journalists who combine enterprise with a knowledge of how to use various sources are able to develop good stories. One of the themes increasingly being developed by public service–oriented journalists is the high infant mortality rate in the United States. Why is it, these journalists are asking, that in this the richest of Western industrialized nations the infant mortality rate is highest?

The experts in the health field say that some of the causes are lack of prenatal care, low birth weight of the infant, births to teen-age mothers and births to unmarried women. Drug use and smoking also are factors, they say.

You want to check this out with records and documents. Fortunately, government databases in the public health sector are excellent. You turn to the National Center for Health & Human Services, its Centers for Disease Control and Prevention's National Center for Health Statistics whose website is www.cdc.gov/nchswww/fastats/infmort.htm and the data pour out.

The states with the highest infant mortality rates are Mississippi, North Carolina, Alabama, Louisiana, Maryland, South Carolina, Tennessee, Arkansas, Kentucky and Delaware. You check the data the CDC has supplied for the four factors and you do see correlations.

A Red Light But as you go through your lists of rankings you have made from the data your eye catches figures that are way out of the range for even the highest states—figures for the District of Columbia. The nation's capital is—and there seem to be no other words for it—a disaster area. (The CDC and other federal government listings for states also include the District of Columbia.)

The infant mortality rate for the District of Columbia is 12.0, well over Mississippi's 10.9; 11.8 percent of the mothers had late or no prenatal care, compared to the national average of 4 percent; 14.3 percent of the infants were born with low birth weight, compared to the national average of 7.4 percent and to the highest-ranking state, Mississippi with 9.9 percent.

The teen-age birth rate, which is figured as the number of births per 1,000 population in the teen-age group (15 to 19 years of age), for Washington, D.C., was 102.1, almost twice the national average and much higher than the first-ranked state, Mississippi with 75.5. In Washington, D.C., two of three of the births in the year studied (66.1 percent) were to unmarried women, twice the national percentage of 32.4 and much higher than the percentages in Mississippi (45 percent) and Louisiana (43.4 percent).

Racial Breakdowns You also note that the figures are broken down by race and ethnic groups, and it is clear that the rates are highest among black and Hispanic groups. The infant mortality rates for blacks in some states are twice to three times the rates for white infants, and the same ratio exists in low-birth-weight infants.

Blending Human, Physical Sources

All this data may give you a headache, but it does point to worthwhile public service stories, and several newspapers and stations have burrowed into the data to call attention to problems in their states. The *Winston-Salem Journal* in North Carolina has done prize-winning series on its infant mortality rates that through the years have been among the highest in the country. Black infants die at a rate two to three times the white rate. In the *Journal*'s home county the black rate was 23.1 for every 1,000 live births, more than twice the state average.

The *Journal* staff understood that numbers alone do not tell the story. Behind every child's death is a story of sadness and pain. It told these stories, and it wrote of ways experts suggested to make pregnancy and birth joyous.

Here is the beginning of one of the stories in the series by Phoebe Zerwick:

It's 3:45 on a Thursday afternoon and the newest admission to the intensive-care nursery weighs in at 875 grams, or 1 pound, 14 ounces.

The baby can't breathe on her own. Her lungs collapse every time she takes a breath.

She lies flat on her back, with her arms and legs flailing beneath bright lights. Born 13 weeks too soon, she doesn't have the muscle tone to curl herself up for comfort. Her skin is so sensitive that the touch of a nurse's hand hardly soothes. She can barely cry.

Three nurses, two doctors and a respiratory therapist hover around her open bassinet. The trip from the delivery room to the nursery was harrowing. Even with a ventilator filling her lungs, the oxygen level in her blood fell dangerously low.

Mothers told their stories. Here is Yvette Johnson's:

Yvette Johnson took her punishment for smoking crack day after day as she watched her 3-pound son struggle to live.

"Even today, after being clean for four years, I still remember those months," Johnson said.

"Seeing this baby suffer, seeing those needles and tubes and seizures, I really felt it was my fault," she said. "The only way I could say I was sorry was to go there every day and stay clean.

"Basically my son died about 10 times in the hospital. That was the worst punishment that I could actually say a person could have given me. Jail wouldn't have done no good. A whipping would have done no good.

"For the first three-and-a-half months I didn't do nothing. I just sat there and looked at my baby and cried."

Johnson said that she smoked crack throughout her pregnancy, knowing it could damage her baby but unable to stop.

"I prayed and asked God to please let my baby be OK," Johnson said. "If my stomach cramped or I spotted I'd be scared to go to the emergency room because I was afraid they would detect cocaine."

She would try to stay clean for two or three days before doctor appointments. If she slipped, she would skip the visit.

Once, she went into labor and hemorrhaged. Her relatives sent her to Forsyth Memorial Hospital, where doctors stopped her labor, put her on bed rest and tested her positive for cocaine.

A few days later she was back in the hospital, bleeding again. Again, doctors stopped her labor, put her to bed and tested her positive for cocaine. This time hospital social workers took her through the intensive-care nursery.

"I remember seeing the babies hooked up. It scared me. I'll never forget it," Johnson said. "They wouldn't point, but they said, 'These babies are born to cocaine users, heroin users.'

"I remember crying and saying, 'I surrender. I need some help.' "

Johnson went into treatment and hasn't smoked crack since then, she said. But it was too late to prevent the damage she'd already done.

Eddie was born three-and-a-half months premature. Like other babies his size he wasn't ready to breathe on his own. Frequently he stopped altogether. His liver didn't work well so he was jaundiced. He took medicine for his lungs. And he had surgery on his esophagus.

After two months his mother mustered the courage to reach into his incubator and touch his hands. After three months she held him. After five months he went home, with an oxygen tank and a heart monitor.

That was four years ago. Johnson now works as a security guard and maintenance worker at a church. And Eddie has finally caught up to other children his age, she said.

Summing Up

Good reporters rely on human and physical sources. A study by Kathleen A. Hansen of the University of Minnesota journalism faculty found that Pulitzer Prize winners used a greater variety of physical sources in their stories than did nonwinners. The winners used more documents, reports, books and other printed matter and fewer interviews than did the nonwinners.

Yet many reporters rely on the interview for almost all their reporting. Stephen Hess found in his study of Washington reporters that journalists used no documents in almost three-fourths of their stories. When reporters are given more time to do stories, he says, "they simply do more interviews."

The reporters we have been studying know the value of physical and human sources, and they know their limitations. We also can make these generalizations about reporters:

- They make direct observations whenever possible.
- When it is necessary to use secondhand accounts, they find the best human sources available, backed by physical evidence.
- They understand that the official version is not necessarily the true account, so they seek verification.
- They know the limitations of human and physical sources.

Interviews are, of course, essential to reporting. We will next examine how to conduct them and we will consider their place in the reporter's arsenal of methods for digging out useful and relevant material.

Further Reading

Abel, Elie. *Leaking: Who Does It? Who Benefits? At What Cost?* Winchester, Mass.: Unwin Hyman, 1987. (This is a 20th Century Fund study that examines leaks and their consequences to government and to journalism.)

Downie, Leonard J.V. *The New Muckrakers.* Washington, D.C.: New Republic, 1976.

Sigal, Leon V. *Reporters and Officials.* Lexington, Mass.: Heath, 1973.

14 Interviewing Principles

Preview

Reporters conduct two kinds of interviews:

- **News interview:** The purpose is to gather information to explain an idea, event or situation in the news.
- **Profile:** The focus is on an individual. A news peg often is used to justify the profile.

For effective interviews, reporters prepare carefully, and they ask questions that induce the source to talk freely. Questions are directed at obtaining information on a theme that the reporter has in mind before beginning the interview. If a more important theme emerges, the reporter develops it.

The reporter notes what is said, how it is said and what is not said. Sources are encouraged by the reporter's gestures and facial expressions to keep talking.

NBC News photo

"Why do you think he's a good candidate?"

In the stadium locker room, the half-dressed hurdler was stuffing his warm-up suit and track shoes into a battered black bag. Seated on a bench nearby, a young man removed a pencil and a notepad from a jacket pocket.

"I'm from the paper in town," the young man said. "You looked sharp out there. Mind if I ask you some questions?"

The athlete nodded and continued his packing.

"First time you've been to this part of the West or this city?" the reporter asked. Another nod. This was not going to be easy, the reporter worried. The editor had told him to make sure he brought back a good story for tomorrow's paper, the day the National Association of Intercollegiate Athletics would begin its outdoor track meet at the local college. The tall, lithe young man standing in front of the bench was a world record holder in the hurdles, the editor had said, and worth a story for the sports section.

The reporter tried again. "What do you think of our town?" The athlete seemed to see the reporter for the first time.

"I don't know anything about this town," he replied. "I'm here to run. I go to the East coast, the West coast, here. They give me a ticket at school and I get on a bus or a plane and go. My business is to run." He fell silent.

Rebuffed, the reporter struggled to start the athlete talking again. In the 20-minute interview, the hurdler never really opened up.

Four Principles

Back in the newsroom, the reporter told the editor about his difficulties. They seemed to begin with his first question about whether the athlete had been to the town before, he said. His boss was not sympathetic.

"First, you should have checked the clips and called the college for information about your man," the editor said. "That way you could have learned something about him, his record or his school. You might have used it to break the ice. Or you could have asked him about the condition of the track, something he knows about."

Then the editor softened. He knew that interviewing is not easy for young reporters, that it can be perfected only through practice.

"I think you have a good quote there about the business of running," he told the reporter. "Did you get anything else about the places he's been? That could make an interesting focus for the piece."

Yes, the reporter said, he had managed to draw the hurdler out about where he had been in the last few months. With the editor's guidance, the reporter managed to turn out an acceptable story.

This incident illustrates the four principles of interviewing:

1. Prepare carefully, familiarizing yourself with as much background as possible.
2. Establish a relationship with the source conducive to obtaining information.
3. Ask questions that are relevant to the source and that induce the source to talk.
4. Listen and watch attentively.

Because much of the daily work of the journalist requires asking people for information, mastery of interviewing techniques is essential. The four principles underlie the various techniques the reporter uses. Clearly, the sportswriter's troubles began when he failed to prepare by obtaining background about the athlete he was to interview. Lacking background, the reporter was unable to ask questions that would draw out his source. Furthermore, he had failed to establish a rapport with the hurdler, so that the session was more like dentistry than journalism, with the reporter painfully extracting bits and pieces of information from an unwilling subject. Fortunately, the reporter had listened carefully so that he managed to salvage something from the interview.

If we analyze news stories, we will see they are based on information from several kinds of sources: physical sources, such as records, files and references; the direct observations of the reporter; interviews with human sources; online sources. Most stories are combinations of two or three of these sources.

Glance at today's newspaper. Listen carefully to tonight's evening newscast. You will be hard-pressed to find a story that lacks information from an interview. A front-page story about a court decision on welfare assistance, for example, has a quotation from the governor about the consequences of the decision. A story about the city's plan to put desk officers on the street quotes the police chief. An obituary contains an employee's comments about the generosity of his late boss.

Straight news stories seem to consist of physical sources and observations. Yet if you examine them closely, you will more often than not find information a source has supplied through an interview, brief as that interview may have been.

Let's examine in detail the four principles of interviewing that we mentioned following the young reporter's frustrating interview with the hurdler.

Preparation

There's a saying in newsrooms that good interviews follow the two "P's"—persistence and preparation. Persistence is necessary to persuade people to be interviewed, and it is essential in following a line of questioning that the subject may find objectionable.

Preparation may consist of a few minutes spent glancing through a story in last week's newscast before dashing out to interview a congresswoman on a flying visit to look at the local Veterans Hospital where cutbacks have affected care. It may be a prolonged examination of clippings, material from Nexis and articles that databases have turned up for a profile of the new university president.

Clyde Haberman, a *New York Times* columnist, says "exhaustive research is the basic building block of a successful interview."

Research

A.J. Liebling, a master reporter who moved from the newspaper newsroom to *The New Yorker* magazine, is quoted in *The Most of A.J. Liebling*, edited by William Cole: "The preparation is the same whether you are going to interview a diplomat, a jockey, or an ichthyologist. From the man's past you learn what questions are likely to stimulate a response."

Research begins with the library's clippings about the subject. If the topic has more than local importance or if the interviewee is well-known, *The New York Times Index, Facts on File* or a database may have a reference that can be useful. *The Readers' Guide to Periodical Literature* may list a magazine article about the topic or the person. *Who's Who in America* and other biographical dictionaries can be consulted. Most of these reference works are on CD-ROM and are accessible online. People who know the interviewee can be asked for information.

These resources provide material for three purposes: (1) They give the reporter leads to tentative themes and to specific questions. (2) They provide the reporter with a feel for the subject. (3) They provide useful background.

Rapport

This was the fifth session Claudia Dreifus was spending with Dan Rather for a profile, and she knew a mile-high barrier separated them. Finally, she told Rather, "This isn't working." Rather agreed and he invited Dreifus to accompany him in his pickup from Sam Houston State University in Hunstville, from which he graduated, south to Wharton, where he was born, and then over to Austin for dinner.

Back home, Rather relaxed and opened up, complaining about his ill-fated pairing with Connie Chung on "The CBS Evening News" and worrying about the cost-cutting that has affected news coverage.

"At CBS News, we're down to the bone, past the bone, and we've been there a long time," he told Dreifus.

With experienced subjects, interviews usually go smoothly as both stand to gain from the interview: The subject will have his or her ideas and comments before the public, and the reporter will have a story.

But with less-experienced sources or with those who are reluctant to speak to the questions the reporter is there to ask, there can be tension. The reporter has to find ways to reach the source.

Give and Take   The early stage of the interview is a feeling-out period. The interviewee balances his or her gains and losses from divulging information the reporter seeks, and the reporter tries to show the source the rewards the source will receive through disclosure of the information—publicity, respect and the feeling that goes with doing a good turn.

When the source concludes that the risks outweigh the possible gains and decides to provide little or no information or is misleading, the reporter has several alternatives. At one extreme, the reporter can try to cajole the source into a complete account through flattery—or by appearing surprised. At the other extreme, the reporter can demand information. If the source is a public official, such demands are legitimate because officials are responsible to the public. The reporter can tell the source that the story—and there will be some kind of story—will point out that the official refused to answer questions. Usually, the source will fall into line.

A public official cannot evade a question with a plea of ignorance. A city controller, whose job it is to audit the financial records of city agencies and departments, told a reporter he had no idea whether a bureau had put excess funds in non-interest-bearing bank accounts. Told by the reporter it was his business to know that and that the story would state so, the controller supplied the information.

The Questions

Careful preparation leads the interviewer to a few themes for the interview, and these, in turn, suggest questions to be asked. But before the specific questions are put to the interviewee, a few housekeeping details usually are attended to, vital data questions. For some interviews, these may involve age, education, jobs held, family information. For well-known people, the questions may be about their latest activities.

Questions of this sort are nonthreatening and help make for a relaxed interview atmosphere. Also, they are sometimes necessary because of conflicting material in the files, such as discrepancies in age or education.

People want to know these details. Harold Ross, the brilliant and eccentric former newspaperman who founded and edited *The New Yorker,* slashed exasperatedly at the pages of profiles and interviews that lacked vital data. "Who he?" Ross would scrawl across such manuscripts.

Even the obvious questions about background can result in fascinating and revealing answers. For a personality profile, the interviewer asked Whoppi Goldberg why she adopted Goldberg as her stage name. She replied:

"It was my mother's idea. It's a name from the family past. There are lots of names hangin' on our family tree, Jewish, Catholic, Asian. . . . Black folks, white folks. I'm just the all-American mutt."

Simple question. Fascinating quotation.

Direct Questions   Most questions flow from what the reporter perceives to be the theme of the assignment. A fatal accident: Automatically, the reporter knows that he or she must find out who died and how and where the death occurred. The same process is used in the more complicated interview.

A reporter is told to interview an actor who had been out of work for two years and is now in a hit musical. The reporter decides that the theme of the story will be the changes the actor has made in his life. He asks the actor if he has moved from his tenement walk-up, has made any large personal purchases and how his family feels about his being away most nights. These three questions induce the actor to talk at length.

Another reporter is to interview a well-known entertainer. The reporter decides to ask about the singer's experiences that led him to write songs that call attention to war, poverty, sexism and racism. "Bread," says the singer in answer to the first question the reporter asks. "Money," he explains. There is a good market in such songs. The reporter then quickly shifts themes and asks questions about the economics of popular music and the singer's personal beliefs.

Open- and Closed-Ended Questions   When the sportswriter asked the hurdler, "What do you think of our town?" he was using what is known as an *open-ended question,* which could have been answered in general terms. The sports editor's suggestion that the reporter ask the athlete about the condition of the track would have elicited a specific response—fast, slow, or slick—as it was a *closed-ended question.*

The open-ended question does not require a specific answer. The closed-ended question calls for a brief, pointed reply. Applied properly, both have their merits. Two months before the budget is submitted, a city hall reporter may ask the city manager what she thinks of the city's general financial situation—an open-ended question. The reply may cover the failure of anticipated revenues to meet expectations, unusually high increases in construction costs, higher interest rates and other factors that have caused trouble for the city. Then the reporter may ask a closed-ended question, "Will we need a tax increase?"

As we have seen, reporters often begin their interviews with open-ended questions, which allow the source to relax. Then the closed-ended questions are asked, which may seem threatening if asked at the outset of the interview.

Television and radio interviews usually end with a closed-ended question because the interviewer wants to sum up the situation with a brief reply.

The reporter who asks only open-ended questions should be aware of their possible implications. To some sources, the open-ended question is the mark of an inadequately prepared reporter who is fishing for a story.

Some television reporters tend to ask open-ended questions, even when a specific one is more appropriate. A Chicago TV reporter in an interview with orphans asked a youngster, "Do you wish you had a mother and father?" The most familiar of all these open-ended questions asked by poorly prepared TV reporters is, "How do you feel about . . . ?"

Good questions are the result of solid preparation, and this requires more than reading the local newspaper and chatting with authorities. Reporters who hold to these narrow confines usually operate only in a linear fashion. That is, today's coverage is built on yesterday's newspaper stories and the council meeting of the day before. Good stories—informative journalism—are spurred by the questions that break the chain of events. Remember Copernicus. All he asked was what would happen if the sun and not the earth were the center of the universe, and centuries of linear thinking shot off onto a new plane.

Tough Questions   Sometimes a young reporter finds that posing the right question is difficult because the question might embarrass or offend the interviewee. There is no recourse but to ask.

Oriana Fallaci, an Italian journalist famous for her interviews, says that her success may be the result of asking the world leaders she interviews questions that other reporters do not ask.

"Some reporters are courageous only when they write, when they are alone with their typewriters, not when they face the person in power. They never put a question like this, 'Sir, since you are a dictator, we all know you are corrupt. In what measure are you corrupt?'"

Remarkably, heads of state, kings and guerrilla leaders open up to Fallaci. One reason for this is her presumption that the public is entitled to answers and her unwillingness to be treated with indifference. When the heavyweight champion boxer Muhammad Ali belched in answer to one of her questions, she threw the microphone of her tape recorder in his face.

Another reason for her effectiveness is "her talent for intimacy," as one journalist put it. "She easily establishes an atmosphere of confidence and closeness and creates the impression that she would tell you anything. Consequently, you feel safe, or almost safe, to do the same with her," writes Diana Loercher in *The Christian Science Monitor*.

Kissinger the Cowboy In her interview with Henry Kissinger, the U.S. secretary of state at the time, Fallaci had him admit that his position of power made him feel like the "lone cowboy who leads the wagon train alone on his horse." His image of himself as the Lone Ranger caused an embarrassed Kissinger to say later that granting Fallaci the interview was the "stupidest" act in his life.

A political reporter who accompanied Sen. Don Nickles on a tour of Oklahoma towns noticed an apparent inconsistency in Nickles' public statements. Nickles often described himself as a conservative who was tough on federal spending. Yet in Eufaula, Nickles announced "good news" from Washington, a commitment of federal funds for a new housing project.

The reporter then asked if the Republican senator's approach was consistent—condemning government spending in one place and welcoming it in another. Nickles' answer: He would vote against federal housing funds but as long as they were available, "I will try to see that Oklahoma gets its fair share."

The quote ends the story, and the reader is left to decide whether the senator is an opportunist.

Some reporters gain a reputation for asking tough questions and not wasting time on preliminaries. When Jack Anderson, the Washington columnist whose specialty is exposés, calls a congressman, the politician knows that he is unlikely to be asked for the text of a speech he is to give in Dubuque. Anderson is after meatier game.

Intrusive Questions Still, there are questions that few reporters like to ask. Most of these concern the private lives of sources—the mental retardation of a couple's son, the fatal illness of a baseball player. Some questions are necessary, some not. The guidelines for relevance and good taste are constantly shifting, and reporters may find they are increasingly being told to ask questions that they consider intrusive. This is the age of intimacy.

Reporters who dislike asking these questions, preferring to spare sources anguish, are sometimes surprised by the frank replies. A reporter for *Newsday*

Sandpaper Sam. Some viewers find the questions of Sam Donaldson of ABC abrasive. He defends his tough, boring-in style:

There's a perception that I'm always asking some rude or confrontational question. That's absolutely wrong. I'm not trying to make the president say something foolish or trip him up. But I think it's proper to ask him a question that confronts him with the critics of his policy.

was assigned to follow up on an automobile accident in which a drunken youth without a driver's license ran a borrowed car into a tree. One of the passengers, a 15-year-old girl, was killed. In doing his follow-up story, the reporter discovered that most of the parents were willing to talk because, as one parent said, the lessons learned from the accident might save lives.

Junk Questions   Wendell Rawls Jr., a veteran newsman, describes his interviewing technique:

> Don't tell people what you know. Ask questions. Then back off. Use diversion. I love to do that—talk with people about things you're not there to talk to them about. You ask a question that may be very meaningful. Then you move away from it. I do it sometimes even if the person doesn't get particularly fidgety, because I don't want him to think that I think what he has told me is necessarily important to me. I'll move to another question and say, "What is that on the wall? That's an interesting sort of. . . ." Whatever. Anything that will divert him, and he will start talking about that. And then maybe ask two or three questions about junk, and then come back and ask another very pointed question.

Listening, Watching

"Great reporters are great listeners," says Carl Bernstein of the Woodward-Bernstein reporting team that exposed the Watergate cover-up that led to President Nixon's resignation.

The good listener hears good quotes, revealing slips of the tongue, the dialect and diction of the source that sets him or her apart.

In an interview with Luis Manuel Delgado whom Diana Griego Erwin encounters at a motor vehicle office in Santa Ana, Calif., she finds Delgado unable to tell the English-speaking clerks what he needs. Does that bother him? Erwin asks. Here is an excerpt of their conversation from *The Orange County Register:*

"I should know how to speak English," he said with a quiet simplicity. "This is the United States."

"My kids are very good," he said. "They get good marks in school. They speak English. No accent. One wants to be a doctor. When they first came here I told them to study English and learn it well. Don't let them treat you like a donkey like they treat your papa."

I asked him if it didn't hurt, being treated "como un burro," as he said.

"No, I am not a donkey and my children know it. They know I do all this for them.

"They are proud of me. Nothing anyone else says or does can make me sad when they have pride in me.

"And they will never be donkeys."

Sometimes, a single quote can capture the person or illuminate the situation the interview is about. In an interview with a former governor of Arkansas, Sid McMath, a single quotation told a great deal. First, the background.

School Desegregation   In 1957, Gov. Orval Faubus defied a federal court order to desegregate Little Rock's Central High School. Although President Eisenhower responded by ordering the 101st Airborne to enforce the court order, Faubus had legitimatized resistance and there was mayhem when the few black students tried to enter the high school.

Faubus was a small-time politico when McMath plucked him out of Madison County.

After the Little Rock spectacle, McMath was asked about Faubus and he replied: "The sorriest thing I ever did as governor was to build a paved road into Madison County so Orval Faubus could come down it."

School Cruelty   Listen to Wendy Williams, a bright 13-year-old, talk to a reporter. She lives in a trailer park in Dixon, Ill. Her teacher recommended her for an advanced math class, but she said no. "I get picked on for my clothes and for living in a trailer park," she said. "I don't want to get picked on for being a nerd."

Types of Interviews

The major story on page 1 of a September issue of *The Hawk Eye* in Burlington, Iowa, was about a three-alarm fire that destroyed a two-story building that housed an automobile sales agency and a body repair shop. The reporter interviewed several people for information to supplement his observations. Here are the people he interviewed and a summary of their comments:

- **The owner:** 15 cars destroyed; exact loss as yet unknown.
- **A fire department lieutenant:** The building could not have been saved when firefighters arrived. They concentrated on saving the adjoining buildings.
- **An eyewitness:** "I didn't know what it was. It just went all at once. I seen it a-burning and I was scared to death."
- **The fire chief:** The state fire marshal will investigate the cause of the fire.

News Interview

Although the reporter was not present when firefighters battled the fire during the early morning hours, the interviews with the lieutenant and the eyewitness give his story an on-the-scene flavor. Because these interviews help explain the news event, we describe them as *news interviews.*

Another local front-page story also relies on a news interview. A head-on automobile crash on Iowa Route 2 near Farmington took the life of a Van Buren County woman and caused injuries to four others. The story is based on an interview with the Iowa Highway Patrol.

Personality Interview

The other type of interview story is the *profile* or *personality interview* in which the focus is a person rather than an event or situation.

Phoebe Zerwick of the *Winston-Salem Journal* frequently writes profiles for a feature called "Tarheel Sketch." In one, she profiled a federal district judge with a reputation as a hero to the disadvantaged.

JAMES McMILLAN

Big Mac's understanding of the Constitution
made him into a champion of the oppressed

By Phoebe Zerwick
JOURNAL REPORTER

CHARLOTTE — Something about the way the attorney was arguing his case didn't sit too well with Judge James B. McMillan.

The case before McMillan, a federal judge in the Western District, concerned a judge who had been opening court with prayer.

The judge, H. William Constangy, said that prayer helped him set a dignified tone for the day's proceedings and also expressed his reverence for the Lord.

But five public defenders in Charlotte were offended by the prayer. They thought that it came too close to government endorsement of religion and violated the First Amendment to the Constitution. Several weeks ago they brought their complaint to McMillan.

As McMillan said afterward, the case was riveting. The evidence was succinct, and the attorneys were well organized. But still, as Constangy's attorney delivered his closing argument, McMillan kept interrupting, fixing on a seemingly minor detail, the possessive pronoun his.

"I'm interested in the theory that it's his courtroom," McMillan asked, at least four or five times, each time raising more extreme examples. Does the judge have a right to pray even though he offends some and bores others? What if he wanted to turn toward Mecca and kneel upon a prayer rug? Does he have the right to do that?

Looking up from the bench, McMillan said, "It's not my courtroom. It's a place where I work."

McMillan's place of work is the federal courthouse in Charlotte, which faces Trade Street, a broad, tree-lined avenue that runs into the city's downtown. He works in a courtroom on the second floor.

Over the past 20 years, advocates for black children sent to inferior schools, poor people awaiting public assistance, disabled people who have been kicked off the Social Security

---

RESUMÉ

FULL NAME:
James B. McMillan.

AGE: 73.

PUBLIC POSITION:
U.S. District Court judge in the Western District.

BIRTHPLACE:
McDonald, Robeson County

EDUCATION:
B.A., University of North Carolina at Chapel Hill; Law degree, Harvard University.

FAMILY:
Married to Holly Neaves McMillan; one son, one daughter.

---

rolls, and mentally disturbed children locked away in state hospitals have climbed the stairs to that courtroom. And over the years, McMillan has provided them with relief.

In 1970, he ordered the Charlotte-Mecklenburg Board of Education to bus black children into schools in white neighborhoods and white children into schools in black neighborhoods. The case was the first busing case to be upheld by the U.S. Supreme Court and led to the desegregation of schools across the state and nation.

That was the first major case McMillan heard, and no case since then has triggered the kind of controversy that raged around him during those years. But since then, he has become a kind of hero among advocates for the poor by ruling in favor of the disadvantaged in numerous lesser-known cases.

Theodore O. Fillette, the deputy director of Legal Services of Southern Piedmont, said, "I can say without a doubt he has had the greatest impact on improving the rights of low-income people than anyone else in the state. I would include people without power, racial minorities, prisoners, and physically and mentally handicapped people."

In 1975, McMillan ordered the N.C. Department of Human Resources to process applications for welfare and Medicaid, the federal insurance program for the poor, within the required 45 days.

Some applicants were waiting as long as six months. During that time, some were evicted because they couldn't pay their rent. Others went hungry or cold.

The state is still under court order,

See McMILLAN, Page A20

Chapter 14

"Over the past 20 years," Zerwick writes, "advocates for black children sent to inferior schools, poor people awaiting public assistance, disabled people who have been kicked off the Social Security rolls, and mentally disturbed children locked away in state hospitals have climbed the stairs to that courtroom. And over the years, McMillan has provided them with relief."

Before we examine the two types of interviews in detail, let's look over some of the rules under which interviews are conducted.

The Interviewer's Ground Rules

Both parties in an interview have certain assumptions and expectations. Generally, the reporter expects the interviewee to tell the truth and to stand behind what he or she has told the interviewer. The interviewee presumes the reporter will write the story fairly and accurately. Both agree, without saying so, that the questions and answers mean what they appear to mean—that is, that there are no hidden meanings.

Having said this, we must admit to the exceptions. Sources may conceal, evade, distort and lie when they believe it is to their advantage. The reporter must be alert to the signs of a departure from truth.

The rules that govern the reporter's behavior in the interview can be detailed with some certainty. Reporters, too, conceal, mislead and, at times, lie. Few reporters justify these practices. Most agree the reporter should:

1. Identify himself or herself at the outset of the interview.
2. State the purpose of the interview.
3. Make clear to those unaccustomed to being interviewed that the material will be used.
4. Tell the source how much time the interview will take.
5. Keep the interview as short as possible.
6. Ask specific questions that the source is competent to answer.
7. Give the source ample time to reply.
8. Ask the source to clarify complex or vague answers.
9. Read back answers if requested or when in doubt about the phrasing of crucial material.
10. Insist on answers if the public has a right to know them.
11. Avoid lecturing the source, arguing or debating.
12. Abide by requests for nonattribution, background only or off-the-record should the source make this a condition of the interview or of a statement.

Reporters who habitually violate these rules risk losing their sources. Few sources will talk to an incompetent or an exploitative reporter. When the source realizes that he or she is being used to enhance the reporter's career or to further the reporter's personal ideas or philosophy, the source will close up.

Sources also risk trouble when they exploit the press. Reporters understand that their sources will float occasional trial balloons and give incomplete, even misleading, information. But constant and flagrant misuse of the press leads to retaliation by journalists.

Earning Trust

When Sheryl James of the *St. Petersburg Times* was interviewing sources for her prize-winning series on abandoned infants, she realized that many of those she was interviewing were unaccustomed to talking to a reporter. "I was dealing with good but somewhat unsophisticated people," she says, "who would have been easy to manipulate. It was a challenge to be sure they understood what I was doing and to keep promises made during the reporting process that I could have broken with impunity."

James focused on a woman who was charged with leaving her baby in a box near a dumpster. She had to develop a relationship with the woman. "I simply tried to be straightforward about what I was doing," James said, "and get her to trust me, to know that I would keep my word to her.

"Aside from that, when I finally did interview her, I felt as I do with many people I interview—I try to establish a relaxed rapport, to be human myself so that they know I'm not a media monster."

The News Interview

The extended news interview can provide readers and listeners with interpretation, background and explanation. When Douglas Watson, a *Washington Post* reporter, was covering the extortion and tax evasion trial of a Baltimore County official, he heard the testimony of a stock manipulator who was a confessed white-collar criminal and political fixer. Watson was told that the witness was being held by the United States Marshal's Service in a special facility while testifying for the government. Watson learned there were several of these facilities—known as "safe houses"—and he decided to do a story about them. After the trial, he spent several hours talking to officials.

"In the interviews, I learned about other interesting and unreported aspects of the organization besides 'safe houses.' " Watson said. "One of the Service's activities is giving new identities to people who had been government witnesses. This enables them to start new lives in another part of the country."

Here is how Watson's story begins:

"Restricted Area—U.S. Govt. Training Center," says the sign on the barbed wire-topped fence surrounding a barracks at Ft. Holabird on the edge of Baltimore.

The sign doesn't say it, but the barracks is one of several "safe houses" that the U.S. Marshal's Service operates for the special care and feeding of very important prisoner-witnesses such as Watergate conspirator E. Howard Hunt, political saboteur Donald Segretti and stock manipulator Joel Kline.

Three to five "safe houses" have been in existence around the country for about a year, usually holding about 50, mostly white collar, "principals," as they like to call themselves. They are federal prisoners who usually were involved in organized crime and who are considered too valuable as government witnesses or too endangered by threats to be incarcerated in the usual prison. . . .

On the Scene

A radio reporter interviews a speaker following his address at a campus rally to protest alleged unfair hiring practices.

Bomb Designer   The news interview can emphasize an aspect of a continuing story that the reporter considers to have been overlooked or neglected. When the debate over nuclear weapons heated up, Jimmy Breslin of the *Daily News* interviewed I.I. Rabi, one of the nuclear physicists who built the first atomic bomb.

Breslin wondered if Americans weren't too casual about nuclear weapons. A master journalist, Breslin let Rabi speak:

"You're a Queens Catholic. Get on your knees and pray," Breslin quoted Rabi as telling him.

"Nuclear weapons are entirely beyond the people in our government today. It doesn't take much to know that."

Rabi recalled that during the 1980 Reagan-Carter debate, Carter had talked about his daughter Amy's concern over nuclear weapons. "The newspapers said it was stupid," Rabi said. "I never did. It was the little girl who was going to be killed. . . ."

Rabi is quoted extensively because he has something to say, has the authority to say it and says it well. Young reporters are often surprised at how eloquent the subjects of interviews can be if they are encouraged to speak.

The Profile

The profile should be seen as a minidrama, blending description, action and dialogue. Through the words and actions of the subject of the profile, with some help from the reporter's insertion of background and explanatory matter, the character is illuminated. Profiles should include plenty of quotations.

For a retrospective piece on the 1980 championship University of Georgia football team, *U.S. News & World Report* interviewed the starting offense and the punter in the team's Sugar Bowl victory over Notre Dame. The magazine found: 9 of the 12 did not graduate; none of the 6 black starters received degrees.

In a series of miniprofiles, the magazine reported on the players' careers in school and later. Herschel Walker, the star of the team, left the team after three years. "I had to worry about what was best for Herschel—and leaving school was best for Herschel," he is quoted as saying. He was signed for a reported $5.5 million by a professional team.

Not so fortunate was Walker's gridiron blocker, Jimmy Womack. Like Walker, he did not graduate. But he had no professional career and regrets his role in Walker's shadow. "If I had gone to Florida State, I could have been in the NFL somewhere," he said. There were, the magazine reports, "compensations . . . in the form of wadded-up $100 bills, passed along in 'padded handshakes' from alumni and boosters." Off the field, he remembered, there were "these girls that liked football players, not one at a time either."

Nat Hudson, who went on to play in the NFL for five years, says that when he goes to a Georgia game or to the athletic area, he feels "like a social outcast." The attitude, he says, is that "we've exploited your talent and we're through with you, so you go back to your business." Racism, he says, is the source of his cool reception.

Ingredients

The profile consists of:

- The person's background (birth, upbringing, education, occupation).
- Anecdotes and incidents involving the subject.
- Quotes by the individual relevant to his or her newsworthiness.
- The reporter's observations.
- Comments of those who know the interviewee.
- A news peg, whenever possible.

Interviewing only the source will lead to a thin, possibly misleading story. When a young *New York Times* reporter turned in a piece about an alcoholic nun who counsels other similarly afflicted nuns, the story did not move past Charlotte Evans, an editor.

"As it stands," Evans told the reporter, "all you have is a moderately interesting interview with Sister Doody. You sat in a chair, and she sat in a chair and you had a chat. That's not very good, considering the story material.

"Did you talk to any nuns in treatment or just out of it?

"Where is the anguish, the embarrassment, the guilt?

"It doesn't sound as if you had done any real reporting, digging, pushing. Where are the people, the quotes, the color?"

For her profile of Les Brown, a black preacher and radio personality, Itabari Njeri of *The Miami Herald* talked to other ministers, a community activist and the directors of the local chapters of the Urban League and the National Association for the Advancement of Colored People, as well as to Brown. Assessments of Brown diverged widely: "I will not allow anyone to manipulate or prostitute the black community, and that is what Les Brown is doing to the nth degree," an Urban League official said. The activist had a different view: "He is different . . . he's got guts. He is a challenge to the traditional black leaders here."

Reporting Is the Key

Reporting makes the profile. Joseph Mitchell, whose profiles for *The New Yorker* are considered the standard for the form, is described by Brendan Gill in *Here at The New Yorker,* a history of the magazine, as having had the ability to ask "just the right questions." The questions would open up his sources, and Mitchell would closely attend their recollections and reflections. He encouraged sources to a loquacity no one suspected they possessed. Mitchell knew that everyone has a good story and that good reporting will flush it out.

In the dedication of one of his books, Calvin Trillin, a *New Yorker* writer, wrote, "To the *New Yorker* reporter who set the standard, Joseph Mitchell." Note Trillin's description of Mitchell as a "reporter." Trillin, like all good writers, knows that reporting is at the heart of the journalist's work.

The Miniprofile

When Mark Patinkin and Christopher Scanlan were assigned to profile the black community in Rhode Island for *The Providence Journal-Bulletin,* they focused on individuals—the people who symbolize the facts and figures they were gathering.

For a story about the high rate of unemployment among blacks, they talked to a black man who was looking for work:

Voices: Stephen Gordon on Unemployment

"I felt like everything I was trying to build was worthless," said Stephen Gordon. "I was back at the bottom. Quite a few times, I'd just break down and cry. I couldn't even get a job on a garbage truck. I felt less than a man."

Stephen Gordon sits in the darkness of his kitchen in a Newport housing project, speaking of being black and jobless.

Back from Vietnam in 1971, he had gone through three years of the hardest of times. He had no high school diploma. He had no job. He had two children. His family survived on welfare.

Then came a federal job program that reached out and gave him hope, gave him training as a welder. He was a tradesman. For nine months, he strove to build the good life.

He was fired. He appealed the firing to the State Human Rights Commission, which found the company guilty of racial discrimination. That was two years ago, but the case remains on appeal. Meanwhile, Gordon went on unemployment, then welfare. He remembers the feeling.

"My inspiration was destroyed again," he said. "It was the same old rut."

Recently, he climbed out of the rut by finding a job as a cook in a Newport inn. For other black adults in the state, joblessness remains chronic.

Unemployment among Rhode Island blacks is higher than for any other group. There were 8,880 blacks in the labor force. . . .

There is hope in the black community, however, and with the careful use of quotes and the selection of incidents, Patinkin and Scanlan showed black success:

Voices: Ed Blue on Moving Up

"I wanted the good life," said Ed Blue. "I wasn't going to settle. I figured, I'm a citizen, I'm a taxpayer. I have as much a right as anybody else. Just give me a chance."

Twenty-eight years ago, Ed Blue came to Rhode Island with a suitcase and $300, another poor black immigrant from a small town in the South. Today he is the state's chief bank examiner and lives with his family in the state's wealthiest suburb, Barrington. Barbara, his wife, is running for Town Council.

For most blacks, Rhode Island has not been a place of opportunity. It wasn't for Ed Blue either. It was a place of slammed doors.

They slammed as soon as he got out of college. One large retailer put an "X" on his application for a clerk's job. He demanded to know why. The interviewer admitted it was to mark black applicants. Next he went to a bank. The bank told him he'd never be anything more than a guard.

Ed Blue saw other blacks told the same thing and saw them accept it. Don't bother, they told him, you won't make it, they won't let you make it. Blue would not accept that. "I was new here," he recalled, "I figured hell, I'll give it a shot. I'm going to break that down."

He put his shoulder against the door and he pushed hard. And when it finally gave, and a higher door slammed, he broke that one, too. He did it, he said, by proving he was so qualified they had no choice but to hire him. Ed Blue made it because he believed in Ed Blue.

"This is one of the things I've instilled in my children," he said. "Don't say you can't. I don't want to hear 'You can't.' "

For their report on crime in the Providence ghetto, the reporters interviewed a prostitute:

Voices: Debbie Spell on Hustling

"Being a hooker is all I know," said Debbie Spell. "It's how my mother supported me. That's all I seen when I was a kid, broads jumping into cars. Put me in a factory and I just couldn't hack it."

In poor neighborhoods, where unemployment and welfare rates are high, many blacks turn to hustling to survive. Debbie Spell turned to prostitution. Although she is 20, she looks 15. She is already the mother of three children. She normally works on Pine Street in Providence, where most of her customers are white.

"If it wasn't for them, then I wouldn't have food for my kids," she said, "or Pampers for my baby." Nor would she have her color television and living-room furniture.

"I'm not proud of it," she added, "but it's the way I make a living. Why should I work in a factory for $100 a week when I can make that much on a Thursday night?"

Although blacks make up only 3.4 percent of the population in Rhode Island, they make up 24 percent of the population at the Adult Correctional Institutions and 7.5 percent of admissions to state drug abuse programs.

In Providence, blacks account for about 10 percent of the population, but a much higher percentage ends up in the city's arrest books. Last year, of the 243 juveniles Providence police arrested for major crimes, 37 percent, or 90, were black. As blacks get older, their arrest percentage grows. . . .

The story about Debbie Spell has a tragic epilogue. A year after she was interviewed, she was arrested on charges of assault and loitering for prostitution. Two days after her arrest, she hanged herself in the shower room of the jail.

Scanlan returned to the streets that Debbie had walked to find out more about this woman who became a hooker at 12, was a drug addict, had three illegitimate boys, and was dead at 22.

"What I found were two grief-stricken women who told me an illuminating story about life on the streets," he said. His interview with Debbie's friends begins:

PROVIDENCE—It's a little after 5 on a Friday afternoon. Pine Street, between Pearl and Portland Streets, is a desolate stretch littered with broken glass, where young women wait on the sidewalks for men who drive slowly by to stop and pick them up for a few minutes of sex.

This part of South Providence was where Debbie Spell used to wait, too—until last Wednesday when the police arrested her. On Friday, she hanged herself at the Women's Prison in Cranston.

Maurine sits in the doorway of a vacant building, a tired-looking woman in her early twenties, wearing shorts and a halter top.

"Sometimes it's not even worth the money to me," she said. "I got stabbed three times. I got busted in the face with a bottle. Just crazy guys. I told the police, but they didn't do nothing. I even got his

Andy Dickerman, *The Providence Journal-Bulletin*

plate. They still didn't do nothing. They said, 'If that's the type of life you want to lead, you got to take the bitter with the sweet.' "

Last summer, Debbie Spell told a reporter that she was a prostitute because the money was good. But times have changed, Maurine said.

"Hmph," she snorted when a reporter told her what Debbie had said. "Ain't no money here. Too many girls now. Some girls bring their little sisters down here, underage girls, 11 or 12 years old, some of them."

A young man approached and slowed his car.

"Wanna go?" Maurine asked half-heartedly. He looked at her, shook his head and drove on.

Another young woman came up. A few minutes before, Tammy had been dropped off by a trick, and now she was back on the corner. She said she was Debbie's best friend. On her way to Pine Street, she learned that Debbie was dead. She spoke bitterly, her voice husky with grief, sharp with anger. Tears shone in her eyes. Like Maurine, she did not want her real name used.

"This was Debbie's life, right here on Pine Street," Tammy said. "This is all of our lives, right here."

She too was bothered by all the younger girls on the streets, but for a different reason.

"They don't know what they're getting into," she said. "This is no game. It's just step up and make money. But they don't know that yet." A man stopped his car at the corner. She talked to him for a while, leaning on his car door, but he, too, drove away. . . .

Quotes, Quotes

Look back and you'll notice that your interest perked up when you saw quotation marks. As the novelist Elmore Leonard says, "When people talk, readers listen." In interviews, the writer listens for the telling remark that illuminates the person or the situation. Leonard says he lets his characters do the work of advancing his story by talking. He gets out of the way.

"Readers want to hear them, not me."

Listen to the singer Lorrie Morgan talk about her problems: After her husband, the singer Keith Whitley, died of alcohol poisoning, Morgan was only offered slow, mournful ballads by her songwriters, she said in an interview with *The Tennessean* of Nashville.

"I mean, it was all kinds of dying songs," she said. But then she fell in love with Clint Black's bus driver, and she decided to change her tunes.

"I said, 'I'm not going to do that. I'm not basing my career on a tragedy.' I live the tragedy every day without it being in my music." Her life, she said, has turned around, thanks to her new love. "He's a wonderful, wonderful guy. This guy is very special, and I'm into him real bad." However, not too long afterward Lorrie's love life took a detour—her affections switched to a politician.

For reasons unknown, reporters have a tendency to paraphrase rather than to quote directly. In fact, several articles have appeared in journalism publications advocating paraphrasing as an efficient way to tell a story. Efficient? Maybe. But so are telegrams. For reader interest, for enthralled reading and viewing, direct contact with the individual interviewed is best achieved by letting interviewees speak.

Research shows that quotations are useful. S. Shyan Sundar of Pennsylvania State University found "the credibility and quality of stories with quotations to be significantly higher than identical stories without quotations."

"Bess" Recalls

Barry Singer of *The New York Times* lets Anne Wiggins Brown talk, and she has plenty to say. Brown was the original Bess in George Gershwin's famous folk opera *Porgy and Bess.* The first African-American vocalist admitted to the prestigious Juilliard School of Music, she was a graduate student when at the age of 21 she heard that Gershwin was writing an opera "about Negroes in South Carolina." She applied and was called for an audition at which she sang Brahms, Schubert and Massenet for Gershwin, who then asked her, "Would you sing a Negro spiritual?" She flared at the request. She explains:

I was very much on the defensive at that age. I resented the fact that most white people thought that black people should or only could sing spirituals. "I am very sorry," I said, "but I haven't any of *that* music with me." And then I broke out, "Why is it that you people always expect black singers to sing spirituals?"

He just looked at me. He didn't say anything or do anything at all; he didn't appear angry or disturbed. But I saw that he understood my reaction. And as soon as I saw that, my whole attitude just melted away and I wanted more than anything else to sing a spiritual for this man. I said, "I can sing one spiritual without an accompaniment, if that's O.K." He told me it was. And I sang "City Called Heaven." It's a very plaintive, very melancholy spiritual. And I knew when I finished that I'd never sung it better in my life, because I was so emotionally involved at that moment.

He was very quiet for some time. Finally he spoke: "Wherever you go, you must sing that spiritual without accompaniment. It's the most beautiful spiritual I've ever heard." And we hugged one another.

Next, we watch Brown become reflective, and we also can tell that her interviewer has been watching her intently. His observations influence his writing.

Observation

As Brown looks back on her long career, she is thinking of what might have been:

> "If I had been born 20 years later, I might have sung at the Metropolitan Opera," she mused.

Notice the word *mused*. The interviewer has caught Brown relaxed and contemplative. She goes on:

> "I might have marched for civil rights. I would have been here for that. I would certainly not have lived in Norway and my life would have been very different."
>
> "Of course," she conceded, her eyes bright, "I would not have met Mr. Gershwin and that would have been a shame."

Actions Can Be Revealing

Watch the dean of students as he discusses a student disciplinary case. As he answers your questions, is he fiddling nervously with a paper clip, leaning back in his chair, looking at the papers on his desk? Is he tense, relaxed?

Do the quarterback's fellow players joke with him in the locker room, or do they avoid his company?

Does the grief seem genuine or forced?

Sometimes, sources reveal themselves as much, perhaps more so, in their actions as they do in their statements.

The revealing profile blends background, quotations and observations.

Diversity

We live in an entertainment-driven period, and the media reflects this preoccupation. Look at the covers of magazines. Most of them display a popular personality. (A side comment: In order to be able to profile these stars, the magazine usually allows the personality to choose the questions that will be asked, is given approval rights over the photos to be used and often is shown the piece before publication.)

The journalist who wants to show the diversity of American society has a more fascinating story to tell.

Listen to Linda Raisovich-Parsons, one of the first women to go into the coal mines, talk to Bharati Sadasivam:

> I went into the mines when I was 18 years old and had just finished high school. There was not a whole lot of career opportunities for a girl back then in West Virginia. My father was a coal miner. He had multiple sclerosis and I didn't want to burden him with the expense of a college education. . . .
>
> Initially, he didn't like the idea because he didn't want his daughter working in that kind of environment. But when he saw that I was not just testing the waters and was determined to make a go of it, he taught me the ropes and looked out for his baby daughter. . . .
>
> There was a lot of heavy lifting and carrying to do and that was what I found the most difficult. Most of the men took the position that well, if you're here, you've got to pull your weight and I was determined that no one was going to prove that I wasn't able to do the job.

Sadasivam's magazine article consists entirely of direct quotes. She allows Raisovich-Parsons to tell her story. After several years in the mines, the United Mine Workers union offered her a job as a mine inspector. She would have been the first female inspector. At first, it was not easy.

> There were some safety committees that simply couldn't accept a woman and would bypass me and go to my male co-workers. And I often got the same reactions from the coal companies. But there were others that were more accepting of me. I found the older miners more helpful and respectful than the younger ones. Sexual harassment was a problem initially but we've grown with these men and I think we're just one of the crew now.
>
> I found women on the whole more safety-conscious than men. They took all precautions, made sure that all the equipment was working properly. You find a very low accident rate among women.
>
> I'm comfortable here, but there are times when I've felt like a token woman. But the few women that are there are very outspoken, the type of people who get out and get involved because they've had to be fighters and scrappers to get the job. I have a button from a women miners' conference that says, "Just Another Mouthy Union Woman."

Sadasivam wrote the story just this way, a first-person account.

Summing Up

Good interviews make for good stories. They provide insights into people and events. Here is some advice from practitioners of the trade.

Helen Benedict, author of a book on writing profiles, says: "People who are interviewed a lot get tired of the same old questions. You want to stand out as an interviewer and get a good story, and that depends on preparation and intelligence."

Bharati Sadasivam

Working People

The diverse ways people make a living are worth chronicling: The Indian jewelry craftsman, the coal mine inspector, the railroad worker, the sign painter. Each has a fascinating story to tell.

Joseph Noble, *The Stuart* (Fla.) *News*

Mike Roemer

Benedict writes out her questions and takes her list with her to the interview. During the interview, she gently guides her subject after establishing his or her trust. "Don't interrupt too much, and don't challenge too early so the person is put on the defensive. Don't talk too much."

She likes to interview in her subjects' homes so she can observe their clothes, objects on walls and desks—their taste. She watches their mannerisms, how they move, sit, drink their coffee, answer the phone, speak to others.

To get at the person behind the personality, good interviewers talk to the friends, associates, relatives of the subject. Samuel Johnson, the brilliant 18th-century English writer, advised writers that "more knowledge may be gained of a man's real character by a short conversation with one of his servants than from a formal and studied narrative, begun with his pedigree and ended with his funeral."

Some Guides

Fred L. Zimmerman, a *Wall Street Journal* reporter and editor, suggests the following:

1. Almost never plunge in with tough questions at the beginning. Instead, break the ice, explain who you are, what you are doing, why you went to him or her. A touch of flattery usually helps.

2. Often the opening question should be an open-ended inquiry that sets the source off on his or her favorite subject. Get the person talking, set up a conversational atmosphere. This will provide you with important clues about his or her attitude toward you, the subject and the idea of being interviewed.

3. Watch and listen closely. How is he or she reacting? Does he seem open or secretive? Maybe interrupt him in the middle of an anecdote to ask a minor question about something he is leaving out, just to test his reflexes. Use the information you are obtaining in this early stage to ascertain whether your preinterview hunches about him were right. Use it also to determine what style you should adopt to match his mood. If he insists upon being formal, you may have to become more businesslike yourself. If he is relaxed and expansive, you should be too, but beware of the possibility the interview can then degenerate into a formless conversation over which you have no control.

4. Start through your questions to lead him along a trail you have picked. One question should logically follow another. Lead up to a tough question with two or three preliminaries. Sometimes it helps to create the impression that the tough question has just occurred to you because of something he is saying.

5. Listen for hints that suggests questions you had not thought of. Stay alert for the possibility that the theme you picked in advance is the wrong one, or is only a subsidiary one. Remain flexible. Through an accidental remark of his you may uncover a story that is better than the one you came for. If so, go after it right there.

6. Keep reminding yourself that when you leave, you are going to do a story. As she talks, ask yourself: What is my lead going to be? Do I understand enough to state a theme clearly and buttress it with quotes and documentation? Do I have enough information to write a coherent account of the anecdote she just told me?

7. Do not forget to ask the key question—the one your editors sent you to ask, or the one that will elicit supporting material for your theme.

8. Do not be reluctant to ask an embarrassing question. After going through all the preliminaries you can think of, the time finally arrives to ask the tough question. Just ask it.

9. Do not be afraid to ask naive questions. The subject understands that you do not know everything. Even if you have done your homework there are bound to be items you are unfamiliar with. The source usually will be glad to fill in the gaps.

10. Get in the habit of asking treading-water questions, such as "What do you mean?" or "Why's that?" This is an easy way to keep the person talking.

11. Sometimes it helps to change the conversational pace, by backing off a sensitive line of inquiry, putting your notebook away, and suddenly displaying a deep interest in an irrelevancy. But be sure to return to those sensitive questions later. A sudden pause is sometimes useful. When the subject finishes a statement just stare at her maybe with a slightly ambiguous smile, for a few seconds. She often will become uneasy and blurt out something crucial.

12. Do not give up on a question because the subject says "no comment." That is only the beginning of the fight. Act as if you misunderstood her and restate the question a little differently. If she still clams up, act as if she misunderstood you and rephrase the question again. On the third try, feign disbelief at her refusal to talk. Suggest an embarrassing conclusion from her refusal and ask if it is valid. Later, ask for "guidance" in tracking down the story elsewhere, or suggest nonattribution, or get tough—whatever you think might work.

13. Occasionally your best quote or fact comes after the subject thinks the interview is over. As you are putting away your notebook and are saying goodbye the subject often relaxes and makes a crucial but offhand remark. So stay alert until you are out the door. (Sid Moody of the AP says that interviewing gems can come after the notebook is snapped shut. "I've found almost as a rule of thumb that you get more than you've gotten in the interview.")

These are starting points only, not absolute rules. They, and the material in the next chapter, will get you going. After a while, you will develop your own interviewing style. Zimmerman says, "Pick the techniques you think you can use and then practice them. Eventually, they'll become so natural you won't have to think about them."

Further Reading

Benedict, Helen. *Portraits in Print: The Art of Writing Profiles.* New York: Columbia University Press, 1990.

Capote, Truman. *In Cold Blood.* New York: New American Library, 1971.

Fallaci, Oriana. *Interview with History.* Boston: Houghton Mifflin, 1976.

Garrett, Annette. *Interviewing: Its Principles and Methods.* New York: Family Association of America, 1982.

Kadushin, Alfred. *The Social Work Interview.* New York: Columbia University Press, 1983.

Mitchell, Joseph. *Up in the Old Hotel.* New York: Vintage Books, 1993.

Note: The books by Garrett and Kadushin, which are used in schools of social work, are excellent guides for journalists.

15 Interviewing Practices

Speaking for attribution.

Preview

Sources respond to interviewers they consider trustworthy and competent. They pick up cues about the reporter from the reporter's appearance, behavior and questions.

A successful interview depends on:

• Questions that put the source at ease, show the source the reporter knows the topic and elicit information that supports the story's themes.

• Role-playing by the reporter. The reporter may adopt a personality with which the source feels at ease.

• Patience and accurate observations. The reporter lets the source talk while he or she observes the physical surroundings and any revealing interactions between the subject and third parties.

When A. J. Liebling interviewed the jockey Eddie Arcaro, the first question he asked was, "How many holes longer do you keep your left stirrup than your right?"

"That started him talking easily, and after an hour, during which I had put in about twelve words, he said, 'I can see you've been around riders a lot.'

"I had," Liebling said later, "but only during the week before I was to meet him." In his preparations, Liebling had learned that most jockeys on counterclockwise U.S. tracks help balance their weight and hug the rail by riding with the left stirrup longer than the right. A rail-hugging journey is the shortest distance from start to finish.

Starting Off Right

Careful preparations such as Liebling's enable reporters to establish an open, friendly relationship with sources, who are pleased that reporters took time to learn something about them.

Usually, it is not necessary to spend much time on the preliminaries with sources the reporter knows. But people who are infrequently interviewed—the atomic physicist in town for a lecture at the university, the engineer sent out by the company to survey the area north of town for industrial development—must be put at ease.

Reporters use all sorts of techniques to start interviews. One reporter usually glances around the source's home or room upon arriving. He tries to find something about which he can compliment the source. Before one interview, he noticed an ivy growing up one wall of the source's office.

"How do you keep the leaves against the wall?" he asked. "Magnets and small clasps," she replied, and she talked about her plants for several minutes.

Who's in Control?

Some sources take over the interview situation, and if they supply the needed information, the reporter should be willing to assume the passive role. Most sources, unaccustomed to being interviewed, need guidance with explanations, helpful questions, encouraging gestures and facial movements.

The source who dominates the interview and intentionally or inadvertently avoids the issue in which the reporter is interested is a challenge. The reporter must wrest control, subtly if possible. Control need not be overt. Indeed, a reporter bent on demonstrating that he or she is in charge will fail to achieve the balance of listening, watching and guidance that is necessary for the successful interview.

A subject may allow the reporter to direct the interview on the strength of the reporter's reputation or on the basis of his or her experience with the reporter. Some first-time sources consider reporters to be authority figures and become submissive. Generally, a source's cooperation and willingness to be guided depend on the immediate reaction a source has to the reporter's demeanor and first questions. Some of the questions that the interviewee may ask himself or herself are:

- Why is the reporter talking to me?
- What is her purpose? Is she here to hurt, embarrass or help me?
- What sort of story does she intend to write?
- Is she competent, or will she misunderstand and misquote me?
- Is she mature, trustworthy?
- Is she bright enough to grasp some of the complexities, or should I simplify everything?
- Will I have to begin at the beginning, or does she seem to have done her homework?

Appearance and Behavior

One afternoon a journalism student cornered his instructor.

"Professor X (and here he named the journalism school's senior professor) told me I had better get my hair cut," the student said. "He said I would offend people I'm sent to interview."

The student's hair was long. "Have it cut and stop worrying," the instructor replied. "Most of the people you will be interviewing will be very proper people."

Intrusion. "Reporting never becomes any easier simply because you have done it many times. The initial problem is always to approach total strangers, move in on their lives in some fashion, ask questions you have no natural right to expect answers to, ask to see things you weren't meant to see, and so on. Many journalists find it so ungentlemanly, so embarrassing, so terrifying even, that they are never able to master this essential first move. . . ."
—*Tom Wolfe*

The student nodded dejectedly. "But it will ruin my love life," he said.

The instructor and the student thought over the problem, the student in deep despair.

"Why not have it trimmed, and see what happens?" the instructor suggested.

The student took an inch or so off his locks and had no further trouble with Professor X. Nor, presumably, did his love life suffer, for there were no further anguished visits from the young man, who, after graduation, became a long-haired and successful rock music critic for *The Village Voice.*

A few years later, when the hirsute look had become common on assembly lines and in offices and faculty clubs, the issue became women in pants. And so it goes: Youth expresses its independence through dress and grooming. And traditionalists—who usually are the majority and always in authority—take offense and condemn the new ways, until sometimes they join in and the fad becomes a trend and later a tradition. Until then, reporters in the vanguard risk offending sources, most of whom are traditionalists in politics, social activities, business and education.

A carefree, casual attitude and dress can tell a subject that you, the reporter, do not take him or her seriously. Hair and dress, tone of voice, posture, gestures and facial expressions convey messages to a source. Anthropologists say that what people do is more important than what they say, and the first impressions the reporter conveys with his or her dress, appearance, posture and hand and facial movements may be more important than anything the reporter says.

A reporter can choose his or her garb, practice speaking in a steady, modulated voice and learn to control gestures. But age, race, sex and physical characteristics are beyond the reporter's control, and some sources are affected by these.

Where there is identification with the reporter, the source is much more likely to speak freely than he or she is with an interviewer of another sex, race, religion or age. People feel comfortable with those who are like them.

Most small- and moderate-size newspapers and stations are staffed by young reporters, and it may well be that the prejudice among sources against youth is the most pervasive. Youth must prove itself. And until a source is sure that a young reporter can be trusted, the source may be uncooperative.

Reporters have prejudices and biases that can impede their work. One of the most common antagonisms among the young is hostility to authority. There is value in the maxim that it is always wise to question authority, but sometimes youth moves beyond skepticism to cynicism.

Role-Playing

Sent to interview a pioneer developer of the polygraph, a reporter sensed that the man was easygoing and relaxed. In an attempt to be humorous, the reporter's opening remark was, "You're described as the country's leading polygraph expert. That's a lie detector, right?"

Interviewing Klansmen

Peter Francis of *The Stockton* (Calif.) *Record* questions two leaders of the Ku Klux Klan about their plans to organize additional California chapters. The KKK national leader (with cigar) and the head of the California Klan said their program, which included racial segregation, was attracting new members "every day." Although the men were wary of the reporter's intentions, Francis was able to draw them out about their plans for enlarging their base in California.

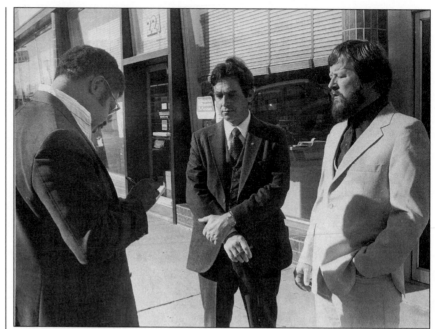

Rich Turner, *The Stockton Record*

The interviewee suddenly stiffened. "If that's all you know, I'm going to call your city editor and have him send someone else over," he said. The reporter apologized, adopted a matter-of-fact approach, and the interview was conducted satisfactorily for both of them.

The reporter was intelligent and had carefully prepared for the interview, but had decided to appear naive to open up the source. He was role-playing, and although this interview just narrowly averted disaster, role-playing is generally successful if the reporter acts out a role appropriate to the subject and situation. Experienced sources expect a neutral, businesslike attitude from their interviewers. Sources who are unaccustomed to being interviewed respond best to the stereotypical journalist they see on television or in the movies, the knowledgeable expert. Some talk more freely to the opposite type, the reporter who confesses he or she needs help from the source.

Obviously, the best role for the journalist is the one he or she finds most comfortable, which for most journalists is the impersonal, unemotional and uninvolved professional. Sometimes, the reporter finds that he or she must become involved or the story will slip away. When one reporter was assigned to cover the rush week activities at a local college, she was struck by the depression of the young women who were rejected by sororities. She felt she was unable to break through the reserve of the young women until she remarked to one of them, "I know how you feel. I went through the same thing in school."

From Friend to Authority Figure

Reporters can adopt the role of friend, confidant and companion when sources appear to need boosting before they will talk. When a source indicates he will cooperate only if he is sure that he will benefit from the story, the reporter is reassuring, promising that her story will be fair and balanced and that this kind of story can only be helpful.

Some stories require pressing sources to the point of discomfort or implying a threat should they fail to respond. Journalism often becomes the business of making people say what they would prefer to keep to themselves. Much of this is properly the public's business, and the reporter who shifts roles from friend to authority figure or threatening power figure may justify his or her role as being in the public interest.

Compassionate Listener

The compassion and understanding that Diana Sugg of *The Sacramento Bee* took to the police beat resulted, she says, in "incredible stories about ordinary people."

She wrote about Connie Cornelius, a 44-year-old mother of four who was a girl scout troop leader, PTA member and volunteer school worker. One night, returning from a high school alcohol-free party for seniors, Cornelius drove her car into an intersection at the same instant a speeding car driven by a drunken driver careened through. Cornelius died instantly. Sugg interviewed family members and friends for her story of a tragic loss.

The suicide of a homeless man, Joseph King Jr., recorded in a brief note in the police reports, interested Sugg. "The detective who had worked the case knew me, and he told me how sad it was because before the suicide King and his friend had been talking about trying to get jobs." Sugg tracked down King's friend. "He told me how shy and skinny King was, and that he always needed protection. 'I wasn't finished teaching him yet about how to live on the streets, about how to deal with the cold,' his friend said."

Sugg began her story of the death of an anonymous street man this way:

Joseph King Jr. was a tall guy, but he wasn't a fighter, and on the streets where he lived, his best friend had to watch out for him.

Even in the Sacramento parks where they sometimes slept, King was in the middle, with a friend on either side of him as protection through the night.

But the 49-year-old man was weary, friends said. Tired of moving from homeless shelter to homeless shelter. Tired of missing his former wife.

About 7 p.m. Thursday, after discussing with his best friend ways to get a job, the homeless man dove 20 feet over a ledge behind the Sacramento Memorial Auditorium.

With his buddy crying at his side in the dark loading area, King died.

"He was my best friend. That was the only friend I ever had that was something to me," said Michael Lockhart, 31, who had been living on the streets with King for the past four years.

Attention to the Victims   Sugg says good police reporting should focus on the victims, make them "the human beings that they are." To accomplish this she devotes time to extensive interviews with friends, relatives, investigating officers. "If we can give readers some sense of the loss, if we can give them some insight and context into what is going on out there they might not become so callous. They might better understand why there are so many shootings and stabbings. And they won't be able to dismiss these victims as anonymous faces."

Sugg spent two hours interviewing the family of a youngster who had died. When Randy Ray Harlan was four weeks old, his father—strung out on drugs and alcohol—had beaten Randy mercilessly. Since that beating, the child had been blind and brain damaged. Randy's grandmother provided constant, loving care. Now, Randy could fight no longer. Five years after he was beaten so badly, he died.

As Sugg drove back to the newsroom, she passed the funeral home. She knew she had little time to write. But she was unsure of just how to handle the story. Maybe stopping here would help. She eased her car to the curb.

She recalled her interview with Randy's grandmother:

"He was beautiful before all this happened," the grandmother told Sugg, "perfect in every way." When Randy's sister asked, "Where's Randy? Where's Randy?" Sugg noted the grandmother's reply: "I told you, he's in heaven." Then the grandmother turned to Sugg and said, "He was very special to Carrie. She would hold onto him and hug him and kiss him, but she knew he couldn't do it back. All we could do was tell her he was sick."

Again, the grandmother recalled Randy:

"That little boy was a real fighter. I can imagine what he would have been like if this had never happened. He would have gone places.

"But it happened."

Sugg got out of her car and walked over to the funeral home. She went in:

Pushing the doorbell and peering through the lace curtains, I realized that the viewing hours had started only minutes before. A man in a suit silently motioned me past the blank guest book. I turned the corner and found myself alone, staring at the baby blue coffin. It was small. I could have reached out and carried it away.

But I stood back, several feet from the open casket, noticing the music that hummed lightly in the background. The song sounded like it was coming from a music box in a nursery two or three rooms away. Pushing my fingers deep into my palms to avoid getting upset, I didn't want to get any closer.

Already I could see Randy's skin was tinged the grayish color I had faced too often. I was angry at myself for intruding into this peaceful place, for thinking that Randy was somehow going to tell me what I should feel, what I should write. Several minutes went by before I walked up slowly to his coffin.

Dressed in dark blue pants and a matching blue tie, his arms were wrapped around his teddy bear. Long, brown lashes hung heavy over his eyes. Looking down at him, I felt I owed him an explanation. Randy Harlan deserved to know why his father got strung out one afternoon on Jack Daniels and methamphetamine and began throwing him—a four-week-old infant—against the nursery walls. But I was lost. I didn't know what to say.

For a second, I thought I could almost see his chest move. I wanted to believe that maybe Randy was only sleeping in that white satin, and I stayed by his side for several minutes, watching him. I fought back an urge to reach out and pick him up, to hold him and rock him, make him forget about the pain he had endured in only five years of life.

This little boy is finally resting, I thought.

Here is how her story began:

A little boy rests at last.

Randy died shortly after dawn Sunday, at age 5. His foster mother was rocking him when the blind boy opened his eyes wide.

"He looked straight up at her, as if to say, 'I gotta go. I can't hang on any longer,' " said his grandmother, Velda Wills.

Randy let out a sigh, his thick, long lashes closing over his blue eyes. His short

life was over — a life of pain and seizures, of barely hearing and never seeing. He couldn't hold his head up; he couldn't move his arms or legs.

Wednesday, Randy lay in a small, blue coffin, looking as though he had just fallen asleep in his church clothes. His arms were wrapped around his small teddy bear.

"Most of these people don't understand, but they don't have a 5-year-old baby to bury because of drugs," Wills said.

And here is the ending:

"That little boy was a real fighter," his grandmother said. "I can imagine what he would have been like if this had never happened. He would have gone places."

"But it happened."

Wednesday night, in his coffin, Randy was dressed in blue pants and a matching bow tie.

Long, brown lashes hung over his eyes, and just for a second his chest seemed to move — as if he were only sleeping.

Randy's funeral will be held at 11 a.m. Friday at the New Testament Baptist Church in North Highlands. The family has asked that any donations be made to child-abuse and drug-abuse prevention programs.

Limits to Role-Playing

The line limiting how far a reporter can go before role-playing becomes unethical is difficult to draw. There is a line between a reporter posing as a coroner to speak with the widow of a murder victim and a reporter feigning ignorance in an interview, a common tactic. Yet, in both cases the reporter is lying. What is the difference?

One well-known Washington reporter said she did not mind letting a senator pat her on the fanny if it meant he would be more inclined to give her a story—an attitude many of her female colleagues find abhorrent. But is that much different from some role-playing that is considered acceptable?

There are other questions. How well, after all, can a reporter assess a source so that role-playing is useful? We saw how one reporter failed. Even psychiatrists admit to no special ability to make lightning diagnoses.

The answers to these questions reside in the personal ethic of the reporter, which we will deal with in Chapter 27. Here, we can say that lying and deception are unacceptable but that the reporter is no different from the physician or the lawyer who is not obligated to tell patient or client all he or she knows in the professional relationship.

Sensitive Questions

For his series "Unmarried . . . With Children," Sam Roe had to touch on touchy subjects. He wanted to know about the birth control practices of the single mothers, "not the most comfortable topic to be discussing with a male reporter," he says.

"Instead of blurting out, 'So, were you using birth control? What kind? What happened?' I said: 'Some women say they were using birth control and got pregnant anyway; others thought they were safe; still others say they just didn't think about it. What was the situation in your case?' "

Roe has found that "being polite, friendly, compassionate, honest helps. There is no substitute for being likeable."

The goal of the interview, Roe says, "is to get your subjects talking and to build up their confidence in you." He says that in his work with youngsters for his stories about Tecumseh Street (See Chapter 8), his first questions were "easy ones." He would phrase his first question as though he were seeking the advice of the youngster: "Before we start, I was hoping you could clear something up for me. I have been talking to a lot of guys in your neighborhood about the gang situation and some say that gangs are a thing of the past, while others say they are just less visible. What do you think?"

Roe said he used this tactic on a 17-year-old awaiting trial for shooting a man in the back of the head. "By the end of the interview he was acknowledging that he only had himself to blame for his problems—a rare admission for a kid.

Roe subscribes to the "share-the-pain" interviewing strategy. When the reporter talks about a similar painful event in his or her life, the reporter is seen to be human and compassionate. "The interview can then work toward being a conversation between two people."

Besides, he says, "If you ask people to spill their guts, you can spill some of your own."

He always leaves his name and phone number, so that "if they want to talk further they can call at any time. This lets them know they are important to you."

Despite the sensitivity of some questions, Roe asks them all. "It never ceases to amaze me what strangers will tell you if you just ask."

Tough Questions

Reporters who work on investigative stories use a reporting technique that requires a straight face and a knowing tone of voice. Bruce Selcraig, a special contributor to *Sports Illustrated,* calls this the "assumed-truth question."

"You're trying to confirm whether the FBI has begun an investigation at Steroid University," he says. "You may get nowhere if you simply ask an agent, 'Can you confirm this or that?' Instead, try: 'What's the bureau's jurisdiction in this case?' 'Which agent will be supervising the investigation of the university?' "

Selcraig suggests reporters watch how their subjects handle questions:

> Notice stress indicators like frequent crossing and uncrossing of legs, constant handling of desk items (paper clips, pencils), picking at one's clothing, and obvious signs like sweating or stuttering. He may not be lying yet, but you may be getting uncomfortably close to the right question. Try asking: "Have I made you nervous?" or "You seem bothered by something today."

With difficult stories and closed-mouthed sources, Bob Greene of *Newsday* takes an approach he calls "building a circle." He will conduct many interviews for his investigative stories. The first one, he says, is general, "far off the goal. Then you move closer and closer until the person you are checking becomes tense. He or she is then primed for the final interview." Along the way, Greene says, a subject hears that you have been calling on people to check him. "He suggests that you might want to come over and talk to him."

"Interviewing is intimidation. Do they or you have the edge? But be cooperative. Say things like, 'We want to be right. Maybe we're wrong, but we've drawn this conclusion. You can see how a reasonable person can come to this conclusion, can't you?'

"Then they will admit about 80 percent of what you're alleging. They'll gradually back down. You can say, 'Please, give us something that proves we are wrong.' "

Greene follows these rules:

- Never debate or argue.
- Never make statements.
- Ask brief questions that are based on evidence.
- Be cooperative.

The Careful Observer

You are entering the office of the chairman of the English department. You had telephoned to ask if you could interview him about the department's plans to cope with the increasing numbers of high school graduates who arrive on campus poorly trained in reading and writing. He had told you to drop in about 3 p.m.

As you enter, you notice two paintings of sea scenes on a wall and two novels, a dictionary and a world almanac on his desk. Books in a floor-to-ceiling bookcase line one wall. These impressions do not particularly concern you because this will be a news interview focused on the situation, not the individual. Nevertheless, the setting could provide an occasional break in the quest for facts.

The chairman is worried, he says, about the growing numbers of students unable to understand college-level material. The chairman pauses often in his answers and occasionally goes to a shelf to take down a book that he reads to amplify a point.

"A friend of mine calls this the cretinization of American youth, and I used to laugh at him," he says. He reads from a copy of *McGuffey's Readers*.

"This grade-school material is now at the high school level," he says. "I wonder if anyone cares." He then reads from a Wordsworth poem that he says used to be memorized in grade school. No more, he says.

As the interview proceeds, you notice that the chairman is toying with what appears to be a battered cigarette lighter. You wonder whether to ask about it.

The Human Element   Suddenly, you decide that the interview should include more than the plans of the department to offer more courses in remedial writing and grammar. The story will include the chairman's personality as well as his plans and ideas. That will help personalize it, to make it more readable.

Quickly, you reexamine the office to make note of the artists of the paintings, the titles of the books on the desk, and you ask about the cigarette lighter. (You learn the chairman uses it to relieve tension; he is trying to stop smoking.)

As the chairman talks, you note his mannerisms, his slow speech, his frequent stares out the window. A student enters the office and asks for permission to drop a course, and you watch him persuade the freshman to give the course another week.

Noticing the family pictures on the chairman's desk, you ask for their identities. Smiling, the chairman complies and then says, "You must be a believer in Whitehead's remark that genius consists of the minute inspection of subjects that are taken for granted just because they are under our noses."

You make a note of that, too, more for yourself than for the story.

Back in the newsroom, the editor agrees that the story is worth two columns, and he sends a photographer to take a picture of the chairman.

Details, Details

The reporter was acting in the best reportorial manner by noting specific details of the setting and the interviewee's mannerisms as well as watching for any interaction with third parties. In looking for details, the reporter was seeking the material that gives verisimilitude to an interview.

It was not enough to say that the chairman toyed with a cigarette lighter. The reporter wrote of the "lighter that he fingered to remind him of his no-smoking pledge." The reporter did not write that the chairman had read from an elementary school reader used in U.S. schools generations ago. He gave the book's title. The reporter did not merely quote the chairman when he spoke about the low scores of entering freshmen on the English placement test. The reporter noted the dejected slope of the chairman's shoulders, and he checked with the college admissions office to obtain the scores.

Too much for you, these warnings to be alert to every little detail? Then ponder the bewilderment of the *Baltimore Sun* reporter who turned in a story about a murder and was asked, "Which hand held the gun?"

The question is asked in newsrooms when a reporter writes a story that lacks convincing detail.

Listening and Hearing

There is an adage that says most people hear but few listen. Words assail us on all sides: Newspapers on the porch every day, magazines in the mail, books to be read, the omnipresent radio and television sets, and the questions, advice and endless chatter of friends, neighbors, relatives and teachers. It is a wonder that anyone hears anyone amidst the clatter. But reporters must hear, must listen carefully. Their livelihood depends on it.

So many people are talking and so few listening with attention and courtesy that the reporter who trains himself or herself to hear will find people eager to talk to someone who cares about what they are saying.

To become a good listener:

- Cut down your ego. You are in an interview to hear what others say, not to spout your opinions.
- Open your mind to new or different ideas, even those you dislike.
- Grant the interviewee time to develop his or her thoughts.
- Rarely interrupt.
- Concentrate on what the person is saying and make secondary the person's personality, demeanor or appearance.
- Limit questions to the theme or to relevant ideas that turn up in the interview.
- Don't ask long questions.

Good listeners will have in their notes the quotations that give the reader or listener an immediate sense of the person being interviewed—what are known as high-quality quotes. Oscar Lewis, the anthropologist who wrote about Spanish-speaking peoples, began his article, "In New York You Get Swallowed by a Horse," about Hector, a Puerto Rican, this way:

A Beatle Talks. *Interviewer:* What do you call your haircut? *George Harrison:* Arthur.

We had been talking of this and that when I asked him, "Have you ever been in New York, Hector?"

"Yes, yes, I've been to New York."

"And what did you think of life there?"

"New York! I want no part of it! Man, do you know what it's like? You get up in a rush, have breakfast in a rush, go to work in a rush, go home in a rush, even shit in a rush. That's life in New York! Not for me! Never again! Not unless I was crazy.

"Look I'll explain. The way things are in New York, you'll get nothing there.

But nothing! It's different in Puerto Rico. Here, if you're hungry, you come to me and say, 'Man I'm broke, I've had nothing to eat,' and I'd say, 'Ay, Benedito! Poor thing!' And I'd give you some food. No matter what, you wouldn't have to go to bed hungry. Here in Puerto Rico you can make out. But in New York, if you don't have a nickel, or twenty cents, you're worthless, and that's for sure. You don't count. You get swallowed by a horse!"

Alert Listening

The reporter may seem slightly passive in the interview, but in fact he or she is working hard, checking the incoming information against his or her preconceptions of the story. Is the source confirming or contradicting the reporter's ideas? Or is he avoiding them for some reason? Or is the source providing better thematic material than the reporter's? Just what does the source mean? What is he trying to say? Does he have any self-interest that affects his statements?

Some people will skirt a topic, and the reporter has to hear what is meant as well as what is said. The concealed meanings can be found by noting gestures, facial expressions, slips of the tongue, half-uttered remarks and the peculiar uses of words. Good listeners pick up the source's inconsistencies. And they are alert to the undercurrents that may be more important than the torrent of information the source seems only too willing to provide.

Taking Notes

Most interviews provide much more material than can be used. Experienced reporters note only the salient facts and the high-quality anecdotes, quotes or incidents that will illustrate them. No reporter can keep up with the source's flow of information and still retain some control of the interview unless the reporter constantly filters the information.

A source, seeing the reporter stop his or her note taking, may be discouraged from continuing. To avoid this, the reporter may want to seem to keep up note taking while the source is supplying nonessential material. Actually, the reporter will be writing about the setting or the ideas he or she has from statements made earlier in the interview. With sources who inadvertently say more than they want to reveal, the reporter slows down note taking or seems disinterested so that the source is not alerted to the significance of his or her remarks.

Before leaving, or during the interview, the reporter may ask the source to repeat something to make certain the quotation is precise or the meaning is clear. When a source contends that he or she meant something else, the reporter must take time to determine whether the source is backtracking.

Early Impressions   The adage that first impressions are the best usually works for the reporter. Lillian Ross, the brilliant *New Yorker* writer whose profiles are studied for their understated yet incisive perceptions, says that "first impressions and first instincts about a person are usually the sound reliable ones that guide you to the rest of what the person has to offer." These early impressions can give the reporter a sense of the entire scene, the whole person, whereas the later impressions tend to be narrower, to focus on details and particulars.

The fresh observation is unimpeded by preconceptions. The reporter new on the scene will sometimes out-report the old-timer who has formed notions and drawn conclusions after repeatedly seeing the same events and persons.

To Tape or Not to Tape?

The tape recorder can provide large chunks of quotes, and the quotes will have the flavor of the person's speech. The tape recorder also protects against charges of misquotation. However, some sources freeze in front of a recorder or become so careful the interview is stilted.

Cautions. Studies of memory and the use of handwritten notes show that those who rely on their memories may omit some material, but copious note takers sometimes irritate sources or influence their responses.

The author Truman Capote said that note taking makes people say "what they think you expect them to say." Annette Garrett, author of a book on interviewing, said that note taking can interfere with the interviewer's participation in the interview. Experienced reporters rely on notes to jog their memories, but few take verbatim notes.

One technique, suggested by a magazine interviewer for subjects who do not mind being taped, is to put the machine out of sight so that the subject is not conscious of the merciless machine with its ability to record every word.

"I tape, therefore I am," says Studs Terkel, whose radio programs and books utilize the tape recorder. For his books, Terkel, an excellent interviewer, transcribes his taped material, then edits it carefully. "It's like prospecting," he says. "The transcripts are the ore. I've got to get to the gold dust. It's got to be the person's truth, highlighted. It's not just putting down what people say."

Lillian Ross has no use for the tape recorder and says flatly, "Do not use a tape recorder. The machine, surprisingly, distorts the truth. The tape recorder is a fast and easy and lazy way of getting a lot of talk down. . . . A lot of talk does not in itself make an interview. . . . A writer must use his own ears to listen, must use his own eyes to look."

Retroactive Requests

Sometimes a person being interviewed will suddenly stop and realize that he has said something he does not want to see in print or hear on television or the radio.

"Please don't use that," he will say. "It's off-the-record."

Should the reporter honor that request? It depends: If the source is a good contact and the material is not crucial to the story, the reporter probably will go along, particularly if the source is not a public figure or official. However, if the source has said something important, or the information is of concern to the public, then the reporter will usually reply that because the source knew he was talking to a reporter, he cannot suddenly go off-the-record retroactively.

When Jessica Mitford was interviewing Bennett Cerf, one of the owners of the Famous Writers School, he chatted freely with the amiable but sharp-penned writer. In the middle of his discourse, Cerf realized he sounded contemptuous of the people who took the school's correspondence course.

Here is how Mitford describes what happened, in her *Atlantic Monthly* article "Let Us Now Appraise Famous Writers":

While Mr. Cerf is by no means uncritical of some aspects of mail-order selling, he philosophically accepts them as inevitable in the cold-blooded world of big business—so different, one gathers, from his own cultured world of letters. "I think mail-order selling has several built-in deficiencies," he said. "The crux of it is a very hard sales pitch, an appeal to the gullible. Of course, once somebody has signed a contract with the Famous Writers School he can't get out of it, but that's true with every business in the country." Noticing that I was writing this down, he said in alarm, "For God's sake, don't quote me on that 'gullible' business—you'll have all the mail-order houses in the country down on my neck!" "Then would you like to paraphrase it?" I asked, suddenly getting very firm. "Well—you could say in general I don't like the hard sell, yet it's the basis of all American business." "Sorry, I don't call that a paraphrase, I shall have to use both of them," I said in a positively governessy tone of voice. "Anyway, why do you lend your name to this hard-sell proposition?" Bennett Cerf (with his melting grin): "Frankly, if you must know, I'm an awful ham—I love to see my name in the papers!"

When the source states beforehand that something is off-the-record and the reporter agrees to hear it on that condition, the material may not be used. Never? Well, hardly ever. Witness how Clifford D. May handles his source in this article, "Whatever Happened to Sam Spade?" in the *Atlantic Monthly.* A private detective, Jeremiah P. McAward, has been describing his difficulties in shadowing people:

"It's harder than you'd think," McAward continues. "Don't print this, but I once lost a pregnant Indian who was wearing a red blanket and had a feather in her hair, in Macy's." I reply that he cannot tell me something like that and expect that I won't use it. "Really?" he asks. I nod. "All right, then." There is a pause and then he adds. "But she just evaporated. A two-hundred-pound Indian."

Confidences

Reporters develop a sense of when to quote someone and when to consider the material off-the-record. The objective of the reporter is to gather important information for the public, not to embarrass or intimidate individuals. A reporter suggests this guideline:

A public official who talks to a reporter about public matters is presumed to be on-the-record. A person who has little contact with the press—even though he or she may be a public employee—should be presumed to be speaking off-the-record during a chat. Where there is uncertainty by the source or by the reporter, set the situation straight.

Reporters always keep in mind the fact that they rely on their sources, and a minor story that is based on quotes that the source presumes are off-the-record may shut off that source for good. However, no reporter will allow an official or a public figure to presume what he or she says is off-the-record unless that is clear at the outset of the interview.

Using and Abusing Quotes

Many reporters cleanse the language of free-speaking sources before putting their quotes into stories. They also correct grammatical errors and ignore absurd and meaningless statements that are not central to the story.

When the Canadian track star Donovan Bailey defeated the American Michael Johnson, Bailey was quoted in *The New York Times,* "He's afraid to lose. We should run this race again so I can kick his rear one more time." A reader e-mailed the newspaper to say that he had heard Bailey on Canadian TV and that Bailey had actually said, ". . . so I can kick his ass one more time." In a note to the staff, an editor wrote, "We shouldn't have changed it to 'rear.' We don't change quotes. (Since we also wouldn't want to use the word 'ass,' the proper course would have been a paraphrase.)"

On the other hand, several newspapers quoted Rep. Patricia Schroeder's response when she was asked how her congressional colleagues treat women. She replied, "A lot of men still don't know that harass isn't two words."

Use It, or Fix It?

When an exact quote is ungrammatical and may cause the source embarrassment, do we rephrase it? Can we eliminate three or four sentences between the two that are relevant?

"You ain't did nothing wrong," the mother was quoted in the first edition as telling her son. In the next edition, it was paraphrased: Telling her son he had done nothing wrong. . . .

When the exact quotation captures the character of the speaker, most writers let it stand. Speaking of the blues, the musician John Lee Hooker said, "Since I was a kid it's been a healing force for me. Since I was 12 years old. The blues done followed me. And I'll never get out alive."

Carol McCabe of *The Providence Journal-Bulletin* says, "I feel very strongly that it is condescending to make everyone sound as if they're speaking Standard English when they're not."

Legal Angle

Alice Neff, a media lawyer, has these suggestions about quotations in the light of court decisions:

- If you use a tape recorder, listen to it to verify quotes.
- Corrections of grammar, syntax, stuttering and filling in explanatory words are all acceptable changes to quotations.
- It is acceptable to edit out irrelevancies and wandering.
- It is acceptable to substitute words, without changing the meaning.
- If you do make changes, consider the whole. Have you conveyed accurately what you think the person meant to say?

The Tabloid Approach

Compare these approaches to quotations with that of the weekly supermarket tabloids. Listen to Jack Alexander of the *Weekly News* describe his interviewing technique:

I always tell them I'm doing a series of articles, that I'm a religious editor or a travel editor. That puts them at ease. I say I'm with *The News* in Palm Beach and I try not to say more than that. I want to put questions in (the source's) mouth, so he just says "yes" or "no." Then we will quote him as saying that. (I ask the source,) "Could this happen?" He says, "Oh yeah." Then as far as we're concerned, it did happen.

Wendy Henry, editor of the *Globe,* explains the philosophy of these newspapers: "The great thing about working here is the simplemindedness that sales are everything, and a great honesty about what sort of paper we are and who we are aiming at."

Holy Writ or Amendable?

"We regard quotations as absolutely sacrosanct. If there is any reason at all to be tempted to change them, then you take the quotation marks off and paraphrase it."

—*The New York Times*

"Quotations should be exact. The words should not be rearranged for more felicitous phrasing."

—*The Washington Post*

"We can trim quotes to fit stories. The biggest problem . . . is how you use quotes and how you edit quotes in the story. . . ."

—*Newsweek*

The magazine engages in "what is commonly known as cleaning up the quotes."

—*The New Republic*

"(W)riters and reporters by necessity alter what people say, at the very least to eliminate grammatical and syntactical infelicities. If every alteration constituted the falsity required to prove actual malice, the practice of journalism, which the First Amendment standard is designed to protect, would require a radical change, one inconsistent with our precedents and First Amendment principles."

—Justice Anthony Kennedy, U.S. Supreme Court

Literal Quotes

To some sources, reporters apply the whip of exact quotations. They know the validity of the statement by Arnold Gingrich, former editor in chief of *Esquire* magazine, "The cruelest thing you can do to anybody is to quote him literally."

One of the delights for the reporters covering Chicago Mayor Richard Daley was quoting him exactly as he spoke. Angry at being attacked, Daley was quoted as saying, "They have vilified me; they have crucified me—yes, they have even criticized me." And, on another occasion when he sought to inspire the citizens of his city, he said, "We will reach greater and greater platitudes of achievement."

Daley had an uneasy relationship with reporters, who frequently pointed to corruption in his administration. Once, while lecturing reporters, he said that "the policeman isn't there to create disorder; the policeman is there to preserve disorder." Reporters delighted in quoting Daley's introduction of the poet Carl Sandburg as Chicago's "poet lariat."

Chicago journalists are equal-opportunity quoters—everyone is fair game. When a candidate for mayor attacked aides of an opponent for visiting a "house of prosecution," he was quoted as he spoke. And when another candidate remarked that he would be a "drum major for education" and would "get out in front and beat the banner," he, too, was quoted as he misspoke.

Here is a section from a piece in *The New Yorker*'s "Talk of the Town." It is about a press conference attended by entrants in the Miss Universe beauty contest. Miss U.S.A. has just been introduced to reporters and is telling them that the Miss Universe contest has helped her express her feelings and widen her knowledge:

"For instance, Miss India has a red spot on her forehead. And do you know what? She says it's an Indian custom. . . .

"One of the experiences I've had was just this morning," Miss U.S.A. says. "I'm rooming with Miss South Africa, and I just saw their money. You see people, but you never realize their money was different."

The reporters try to think of another question. Finally, one of them says, "What do you think of the feminist movement?"

"Oh, I think femininity is the best thing on this earth," she says.

"What about masculinity?"

"That's just as wonderful."

Lest you conclude from all this that reporters are always intent on humiliating their sources and that you are much too compassionate to join this cutthroat company, here's evidence to the contrary:

When a politician took the microphone at a meeting to defend a fellow political candidate and said, "He is not the orgy some people think he is," reporters did substitute *ogre* for *orgy*. When Sen. Dennis DeConcini of Arizona endorsed a balanced budget amendment to the Constitution at a news conference by announcing, "It's going to be a great day because we're going to finally wrestle to the ground this gigantic orgasm that is just out of control, that absolutely can't put itself together."—well, what would you have done?

Anonymous and Confidential

Sources do not always want to be identified, for a variety of reasons. The low-level official whose boss demands all material from the office go out under his name requests anonymity for the information she provides. The whistleblower does not want to endanger his job by being identified.

As the press digs deeper to get to the truths of events, anonymous and confidential sources increase. People with information demand they not be named. The most notable example of an unknown source is Deep Throat, the source for a considerable amount of information about Richard Nixon during his presidency. The reporters who handled the Watergate revelations, Carl Bernstein and Bob Woodward, never disclosed the identity of this key source—if indeed it was one person. Some reporters believe that Deep Throat actually was a convenient way to handle a number of sources who demanded anonymity as the price for information.

The use of anonymous sources is much debated.

"No newspaper worth its name could fulfill its mission without using confidential sources," says Harry M. Rosenfeld, editor of the *Times-Union* in Albany, N.Y. "Without them, much of the very best in journalism would not be possible. At the same time, nothing so much brings our blood to boil. We decry their use and we despair of their ubiquity."

Joel Kramer, executive editor of the Minneapolis *Star Tribune,* says, "Anonymous sources are like fireworks. Used properly, they can produce a spectacular display. But they can also explode in one's pocket."

On the other hand, *USA Today* will not use such sources: "Unidentified sources are not acceptable at *USA Today*," a policy memo states.

Michael Gartner, editor of the *Ames Daily Tribune* in Iowa and former president of NBC News in New York, likes the *USA Today* policy. He worries that "the anonymous source is taking over journalism, that it is appearing even in innocuous stories about obscure newspapermen. It's a lousy trend that is eroding the credibility of newspapers and adding to the unresponsibility of newspapers."

In a study made of such sources for the ethics committee of the American Society of Newspaper Editors, the journalists who participated were unsure of the terms themselves. *The Wall Street Journal* defines an anonymous source as someone whose name will not be used in the story by agreement "but whose identity we may later need to disclose—in the event of a libel suit, for example—in order to show that we had good reason for using the information.

"A confidential source is one whose name isn't published and whose identity we are pledged to keep secret, even if that means losing a lawsuit or going to jail."

Some Guides

Some suggestions:

• Sources should be told exactly what is being promised them in terms of anonymity or confidentiality.

• Use of anonymous and confidential sources should be avoided if at all possible.

• Anonymous sources must not be used to criticize a person's character or credibility. The exception is rare, and then only with the permission of the editor.

• A source should be told that although his or her name will not appear, the reporter is obligated to give the source's name to the editor.

A Television Interview

Let us watch a television reporter as he puts into practice some of the principles and techniques we have been discussing in this and the preceding chapter on interviewing.

It is 6:30 a.m. and we are in an automobile with J. J. Gonzalez, a reporter for WCBS-TV, in New York City. Gonzalez and the crew are driving to J. F. Kennedy International Airport. Louis Treitler, the electrician, is at the wheel. Gonzalez is next to him. William Sinnott, the soundman, and Joe Landi, the cameraman, are in the back seat.

Gonzalez unfolds the typewritten note from the assignment editor and reads it again: "Go to Overseas National Headquarters at 175th St. off Farmers Blvd. (Right near the airport.) We will be able to get interviews with the passengers. Afterwards, we were told, we would be able to get on the runway to film the boarding which has been delayed until 8:30 or 9. Crew should arrive 7:30 a.m."

The passengers the assignment refers to are airline personnel who had been on a DC-10 the previous week en route to the Middle East. Their plane had

Burning Jetliner

Clouds of black smoke rise from the burning fuselage of a jetliner when its takeoff was aborted. Ten crew members and 139 passengers scrambled to safety before the airplane erupted in flames. A television reporter used tape of the burning wreckage in his follow-up piece the next day when the passengers were interviewed as they resumed their trip to Saudi Arabia.

run into a flock of seagulls on the runway, an engine ingested several of the birds, and before the plane could take off, one engine stopped turning over and dropped to the ground. The pilot managed to stop the plane and quickly ordered everyone out. Within seconds, the 10 crew members and 139 passengers were spilling out of the exits and down the escape chutes. The plane caught fire and in five minutes was a charred hulk. No one was injured. But if those aboard had been the usual run of passengers, Gonzalez says, there might have been a catastrophe. The metropolitan editor had instructed Gonzalez to find out how the airline personnel felt about taking off a second time.

The Planning

It is a 45-minute drive to the airport, and Gonzalez and the crew have plenty of time to chat about the assignment. They will be going to three locations—first, to the airlines building where the passengers will be assembling, then to the airplane the passengers will board and finally to a runway to watch the plane take off. Film of the plane heading off into the rising sun will make a good closing shot, they agree. But they are not sure that they will be allowed on a runway, and they discuss going to the airport control tower. Sinnott doubts that the tower will be available either, and they talk about using the public observation platform.

Gonzalez knows there is tape at the station that was shot of the burning plane the previous week. He will want to insert some of that dramatic tape into what he anticipates will be unexciting tape from today's assignment.

"This is really a bunch of talking heads," Gonzalez says. He means that the tape shot today will show individuals talking for the camera.

Gonzalez will need a number of transitions, or bridges, to move the viewer from one place to the next smoothly. Gonzalez begins to think of possible bridges—long shots of the airport, the passengers milling about.

Gonzalez makes mental notes of the questions he will ask. If he is lucky, he will be able to interview the pilot of the plane that burned. He knows the pilot will not be on this morning's flight, but if he should happen to be around the airline office, an interview with him could liven up the story. It also would be useful as a transition to the tape of the burning plane and might even carry through as a voice-over (VO) of the firefighters battling the flames.

On the Scene

Fortunately for Gonzalez, the pilot is there, and after chatting with him to obtain some background about the first flight, Gonzalez asks him, "What went through your mind at this time?"

The pilot answers, "Basically, I thought we should be doing it some other way."

His reply makes everyone in the office laugh and it seems to break the tension.

"It's the understatement of the week," mutters a young woman who was aboard the first flight. But when Gonzalez and the crew look toward her she has put on a sparkling smile. In answer to Gonzalez's question about the mood of her fellow passengers, she says that as professional airline people they are not too nervous.

Gonzalez is excited about his interview with the pilot. "This is the only real news here," he says. "No one else has had an interview with the pilot."

In his interviews, Gonzalez did not ask many questions. He knew that viewers are more interested in the interviewee than the interviewer. To keep from intruding when a source began to slow down in the interview, he would encourage the source with a smile or a head shake.

"I also use facial questions a lot," he remarked later. "When someone tells me something that is unclear or hard to believe, I will look incredulous or give the person a blank stare. This encourages them to go on and talk.

"Sometimes, the best question you can ask is one word, a simple 'Why?' "

On the drive to the airport, Gonzalez had estimated the story to be worth "a pound and a quarter," a minute and 15 seconds. But it is Saturday, usually a dull news day, and there may not be many other local stories to compete with this story, so Gonzalez interviews several of the waiting passengers.

"How do you feel about taking the flight now? Uneasy?" he asks a young woman.

"No, I feel good," she answers as the cameraman shoots her reply. "I just want to get going."

Back in the newsroom, Gonzalez engages in another set of preparations. Before he writes his script, he jots down what he has on tape and the voices that will accompany it. In one column, he lists the order in which he thinks the tape will be put together and in another column, he indicates the lead-in for the anchorman, his own voice and those of the interviewees.

Later, Gonzalez learns his hunch about the length of the story was correct. There are few breaking news stories, and CRASH, as he slugged it, is given more than two pounds on the 7 o'clock news.

Summing Up

A pleasant appearance, a neutral first question, a willingness to listen usually put an interviewee at ease. Jules Loh of the AP says the first question he asks is, " 'When were you born?' He replies, '1945.' I say, 'What date?' He says, 'October 1.' Now you pull the notebook out.

"You're getting a matter of fact. Then a couple more questions like that. This impresses the subject that you are interested in accuracy. The first thing they've heard about reporters is that they get everything wrong."

Sometimes you deliberately avoid taking notes, says Dan Wakefield, journalist, novelist and screenwriter. "If people were saying something I thought really embarrassing I would try not to be writing because I didn't want them to see my hand moving and clam up," he says. "I would wait until they said something kind of innocuous and that's when I would write down the awful thing they said."

Studs Terkel, the master radio interviewer and author of books of interviews, puts people at ease by saying, " 'Oh yeah, that happened to me.' If I bring some of my own stuff in, maybe that person will feel more akin."

Sometimes, the results can be a disaster for the source . . . and troubling for the reporter. Here's the experience of Emily Yoffe, senior editor of the *Texas Monthly:*

> Once I did a story about congressional press secretaries. And one of the press secretaries I interviewed lost his job over the story. I felt absolutely awful; it was never my intention to have anyone lose his job and, in fact, he lost his job because he was being too honest about what it was he did and because it made his boss look like the publicity hound he was.
>
> It was a case where I was sitting there interviewing him, thinking, "I can't believe you are telling me this stuff." And he was very young and I was very young. If I were doing such a piece now and it was someone very young, I don't know if I'd warn him—through the tone of my questions—about what he was saying.
>
> But then again, what he did was describe his job and I just wrote down what he told me. It was his boss who fired him—simply for telling the truth—not me.

Further Reading

Cole, William, ed. *The Most of A. J. Liebling.* New York: Simon & Schuster, 1963.

Mitford, Jessica. *Poison Penmanship.* New York: Vintage Books, 1980.

Webb, Eugene J., et al. *Unobtrusive Measures: Nonreactive Research in the Social Sciences.* Chicago: Rand McNally, 1966.

16 Speeches, Meetings and News Conferences

Robert Kollar

The point is . . .

Preview

• **Speech** stories include the name and identification of the speaker, the theme of the talk, the setting and ample quotations. When a prepared text is used for the story, it is checked against the actual delivery.

• **Meeting** stories usually begin with the major action taken. They include the purpose of the meeting, background to the major action and quotations from those who spoke, including comments by the public.

• **News conference** stories begin with the major point made unless a better lead turns up in the question-and-answer period. Stories include background and topics from the question-and-answer period.

Speeches

"Ours is not to wonder why but to cover the speech or die," the reporter muttered as he put on his overcoat and stepped into the cold for a three-block walk to a downtown hotel where a testimonial dinner for the mayor was to be held. "I'll bet it's creamed chicken again," he said to himself.

The reporter's exasperation was caused as much by the fare he thought the speaker would offer as by the menu.

Speeches, hardly the most exciting stories a reporter covers, are a major part of the journalist's day-to-day work. Realizing that not every speech can be covered, speakers and organizations often deliver a prepared text to the newspaper and broadcast station ahead of time so that the story can be written in the office. (The reporter inserts the phrase, "In a speech prepared for delivery tonight . . ." or something similar.)

Speeches by prominent people are usually covered, whatever the subject. Nothing could have been more mundane than the testimonial dinner set for Betty Ford, wife of President Ford, at the New York Hilton one warm June evening. She was to be honored at the dinner launching a $6 million fund drive for an American Bicentennial Park in Israel. Her remarks were expected to be routine. Indeed, as the evening wore on, reporters became restless. A few of them left, asking those who remained to cover for them should anything unusual turn up.

Naturally, the unusual did occur, and it was front-page news in newspapers around the country and a major item on evening newscasts.

As Mrs. Ford was being introduced, the president of the Jewish National Fund of America, who had just finished speaking, slumped down in his chair at the head table.

In the confusion, Mrs. Ford went to the microphone and spoke to the stunned guests: "Can we bow our heads for a moment and say a prayer for Rabbi Sage," she said. The New York *Daily News* began its story this way:

> First lady Betty Ford led a stunned benefit dinner audience in prayer at the New York Hilton last night for a Zionist leader who collapsed at the affair honoring Mrs. Ford, and died of an apparent heart attack at a hospital a short time later.

Basics for the Speech Story

Every speech story must include:

- What was said: speaker's main point.
- Who spoke: name and identification.
- The setting or circumstances of the speech.
- Any unusual occurrence.

Any of these can provide the lead and theme of the story, although most speech stories emphasize what was said. Itabari Njeri of *The Greenville* (S.C.) *News* began her story with a delayed lead and moved to the speaker's main point in the second paragraph:

The three greatest lies, according to Dr. Eula Bingham, assistant secretary of labor: "The check is in the mail; Darling, I haven't looked at another woman in 27 years; and, I'm from the government and I'm here to help you."

The punchline got the desired laugh. But Dr. Bingham, who also directs the Labor Department's Occupational Safety and Health Administration, said she really is trying to help business and labor by eliminating or streamlining unnecessary government health and safety regulations.

Addressing the annual spring meeting of the South Carolina Occupational Safety Council, the former college professor and zoologist said: "We are attempting to revamp regulations that are burdensome and not meaningful. Our mandate is to protect the health, life and limb of working men and women. We are not interested in harassing or catching anybody."

Locate the Theme   The most important task the reporter faces is finding the theme. A tip-off to the theme may be the title of the speech. Often, speakers will use forensic devices to drive home their major points—pounding the podium, raising the voice, suddenly slowing down the delivery, the summary at the end.

When the reporter is unsure of the theme, it makes sense to interview the speaker after the talk. When combining material from a speech and an interview, the journalist should tell the reader or listener where the information came from.

Otherwise, those who attended the speech or heard it on radio or television will find the report puzzling.

Occasionally, a reporter will find a lead in what the speaker considers a secondary theme. Then, the reporter should lead with what he or she considers the more important element but summarize high in the story what the speaker considers the major theme.

For example, the president of a large investment firm is speaking to a local civic club about the role of the small investor. The morning papers have a story from New York about a sudden selling wave on the stock exchange late yesterday that sent prices tumbling. The speaker sticks to his subject that noon but in a digression predicts that the bottom of the market has not been reached. Obviously, the lead is his prediction of a continued decline. The reporter will probably want to ask the speaker after his talk for his comments on the market decline to give still more information to readers about his newsworthy prediction.

A speech consists of spoken words. So must the story. Unless there is an incident during the talk that would make the circumstances and the setting the most newsworthy item, the story will emphasize what was said with ample quotations at the top of the story. But writers will resist the quote lead unless there is a highly unusual statement.

Tough to Handle

Now and then a reporter sits through an incoherent speech in which illogic and vagueness prevail. What should he or she do—confuse the reader with an accurate account? The reader will only blame the reporter.

The reporter should seek out the speaker and attempt to clarify the confused points and ask others who know about the situation the speaker tried to discuss. If these tactics fail, the only recourse is to write a brief story.

John R. Hunt, who turned from prospecting in the wilds of northwestern Quebec to newspapering, has been covering the North country of Ontario for the *North Bay Nugget* for 40 years, "As a small-town newspaperman, I have covered hundreds of speeches," Hunt says.

"It is an interesting fact that a dull and boring speech can often become an interesting story. But I don't know of anything more difficult to write about than a funny speech." The best tactic is to use plenty of quotations and hope the humor carries through.

Off-the-Record

Reporters have the right to be present at an official, public meeting and can use anything they see and hear there. But they have no legal right to attend a meeting or talk by a private group, and they have to leave if asked. But the reporter can report what he or she learns from those who were there. A talk heard by dozens of people cannot be kept confidential, and the reporter usually points this out to those making the request for confidentiality. He or she also points out that because those attending the session will talk to the reporter about the speech,

Washington Post Policy. In a gathering of a private organization, where the reporter is present as a reporter and guest, he or she must protest any attempt by the speaker to go off-the-record. The reporter should point out that the meeting was open to the press and should declare that he or she will not be bound by the limitation.

the speaker may find the material somewhat garbled in the telling and should welcome an accurate report. This argument usually wins the reporter's battle.

Remember, the reporter is not bound by requests for off-the-record status of any item if the request is made after the information has been disclosed.

Meetings

Meetings provide newspapers and broadcast stations with enormous amounts of news. Public bodies—school boards, city councils, legislatures, planning and zoning commissions—conduct much of their business at open meetings. Then there are the meetings of private groups—baseball club owners, the directors of corporations, protesting citizens.

On her first day as writing coach at the *Winston-Salem Journal,* Phoebe Zerwick encountered a reporter who confessed to her, "I think meetings are dull." Zerwick decided to find out the reason for this resistance and then to compile a tip sheet for "turning dull meeting stories into gems."

The Basics

At the outset of her investigation, Zerwick says she "found that reporters aren't doing some of the things that need to be done." She listed them:

Check the clips.

Obtain the agenda ahead of time.

Write out questions for interviews.

At the meeting, look for the offbeat and unusual.

Think about the people affected by a decision or policy.

In examining past stories on subjects the meeting will consider, reporters accumulate background that can put the issues in perspective. Also, the clips may lead to additional sources and to people affected by an item on the meeting agenda.

A *Journal* reporter confessed to Zerwick that he missed a good story by ignoring an item on the agenda of the zoning board of adjustment. People in Boone complained about a sign advertising a flea market. The sign was in the shape of a lion, and people in Boone were angered by the size of the lion's penis.

"Not bad for a zoning story," Zerwick comments.

Checklist: Meetings

The essentials of meeting stories are:

- Major business transacted: votes, decisions, adoption of policies.
- Purpose, time and location of meeting.
- Items on agenda.
- Discussion and debate. Length of session.

- Quotes from witnesses and experts.
- Comments and statements from onlookers, authorities and those affected by decision, vote or policy.
- Background.
- Unusual departures from agenda.
- Agenda for next session.

Not all meeting stories will contain every one of these items. Notice the items stressed in the first five paragraphs of this meeting story from *The Brattleboro Reformer* of Brattleboro, Vt. The reporter used a delayed lead to emphasize the unusually large number of people who turned out. The first paragraph sets the scene for the major business transacted by the town school board, which is described in the second paragraph:

Public Protests Budget Cuts In Elementary Programs
By Gretchen Becker

Nearly 300 people came to an emotional Brattleboro Town School Board meeting at Green Street School Tuesday night to protest proposed cuts in the elementary school art, music, and physical education programs. — **Purpose Time Location**

Caught between the strong public opinion at the meeting not to make these cuts and a strong Town Meeting mandate to cut 5 percent from their budget, the school directors reluctantly approved almost $35,000 in budget reductions. — **Major business transacted**

Approved were elimination of the elementary art instructor's position, the second physical education position, a part-time vocal instructor's position, the fifth and sixth grade basketball program, and rental of space at Centre Church.

The board took no action on the administration's proposals to eliminate the instrumental music position and the part-time principal's position at Canal Street School. Approval of these cuts would have brought the total cuts to $46,000.

Salary Controversy

At Town Meeting March 22, the representatives voted to cut 5 percent, or $74,200, from the elementary budget. Those urging the cuts requested that teachers' salaries be frozen. However, WSESU Superintendent James Cusick has noted several times that the proposed budget included only $25,000 for increases in salaries. . . . — **Background**

Most often, the lead will focus on the major action taken at the meeting, as in this lead:

City Councilwoman Elizabeth T. Boskin persuaded council members to approve additional funds for the city police department last night.	**Major action taken**
The council had been cutting requested funds for the 1999–2000 budget because of anticipated declines in tax revenues.	**Purpose of meeting**
But Boskin said violent crimes had increased 18 percent last year.	**Amplification of major theme that includes direct quote on theme**
"The only way to handle this is with more police officers," she said.	
The department had asked for a 15 percent increase in funds over the current year's allocation for hiring an additional dozen officers.	**Background**
The council has been making cuts in the requests of city departments and agencies ranging from 10 to 20 percent.	
Boskin's plea was persuasive, and the council voted unanimously to approve the request for an additional $287,000, an increase of 14 percent.	**Amplification of theme**
Then the council returned to wielding the hatchet. . . .	**Transition to other actions**

Sometimes a meeting continues past the reporter's deadline, and the reporter has to make do with what he or she has. It is possible, however, to catch the sense or drift of a meeting, as Robert T. Garrett did in this story in *The (Louisville) Courier-Journal:*

LEXINGTON, Ky. — The Fayette county school board appeared likely last night to reject the teaching of "scientific creationism" alongside the theory of evolution in local science classes.	**Probable major action**
The five-member board, which had been deadlocked 2-2 on the issue, heard opposing views from residents for several hours last night before a packed house at school headquarters.	**Setting**
The board had taken no vote as of 11:15 p.m.	
But the fifth and previously undecided member of the school board, Harold Steele, hinted that he would vote against the proposed "two-model" science curriculum.	**Buttressing of lead with quotes and paraphrases**
Steele said he had concern that "very definite parameters will endure" that ensure the separation of church and state.	

As the school board prepares to face the question of tuition tax credits in coming weeks, it must remember that public education "is not permitted to teach sectarian courses," Steele said.

Before last night's debate, school board Chairman Barth Pemberton and board member Carol Jarboe were on record opposing introduction of creationism in the schools.

Probable position of others on major action

Board members Mary Ann Burdette and David Chittenden had said they support the teaching of creationist views. Mrs. Burdette moved that the creationist proposal be adopted, and Chittenden seconded it.

Scientific creationism is a theory closely aligned to the biblical account of creation.

Background

It holds that man and the Earth were created by an outside force, such as God, in a short span of time less than 10,000 years ago and have changed little since. . . .

The school board did vote 3-2 to reject creationism in classrooms.

News Conferences

The UPI Day Book, a listing of daily events used by New York City newspapers and broadcast stations as an aid in making local assignments, carried this item one Wednesday evening:

> Manhattan District Attorney Robert Morgenthau holds news conference
> to produce evidence that confirms existence of ancient civilization in Israel
> between 2000–1500 B.C., 155 Leonard Street 10:30 A.M.

To local editors, it sounded like a good yarn. Moreover, many New Yorkers feel a kinship with Israel. So, when the district attorney began his conference, half a dozen reporters and two television crews were on hand.

The reporters were told that a Manhattan school teacher visiting Israel had taken a clay tablet out of the country. The tablet was later found to be an antiquity. Under Israeli law, no historical objects may leave the country, and the teacher was therefore in possession of stolen property, a criminal offense.

The DA's Compassion

But the district attorney had decided not to prosecute. He had worked out an arrangement between the teacher and the Israeli government. Although all of this could have been announced in a press release, a news conference was called so that the district attorney could play midwife in the delivery of an important historical tablet to an Israeli representative. The district attorney, an elected official, would appear to the public as a man of compassion and wisdom. The reporters would profit, too, for the story and photograph would get good play.

The incident illustrates the mutuality of interests that the news conference serves. It permits an individual, group or organization to reach many reporters at one time with an announcement that will receive more attention than a press release because of the photo possibilities and the staging, and it is an efficient and economical way for the press to obtain newsworthy material.

Usually, the news conference has a prescribed form. A prepared statement is read or distributed to the reporters beforehand. (See Figure 16.1 below.) Then reporters ask questions.

Figure 16.1

DISTRICT ATTORNEY—NEW YORK COUNTY

For Release: November 20

Contact: Gerda Handler
732-7300
Ext. 603/4

Robert M. Morgenthau, District Attorney, New York County, announced today the recovery of a priceless antiquity from ancient biblical times. The object is a sherd—a fragment of a clay tablet—bearing a cuneiform inscription of unique archaeological significance.

Mr. Morgenthau today returned this antiquity, dating from between 1500 and 2000 B.C., to Amos Ganor, Acting Consul General of the State of Israel.

The sherd was originally found at the site of the archaeological excavation of the ancient city of Hazor, located about ten miles north of the Sea of Galilee in Israel.

It was removed from Israel in violation of that country's Antiquities Ordinance, which requires the finder of any antiquity to notify the Government of the discovery and afford it an opportunity to acquire the object. A complaint was filed with the District Attorney by the Government of Israel through Dr. Avraham Biran, former Director of the Department of Antiquities in Israel. An investigation was undertaken by the District Attorney which resulted in the recovery of the sherd.

The sherd records a case of litigation, conducted in the presence of the king, concerning real estate in Hazor. It is of great historical value because it confirms that the excavation, begun in 1955 near the Sea of Galilee, is the ancient city of Hazor. According to Professor Yigal Yadin, who headed a four year archaeological expedition at Hazor, the sherd is a major link in the identification of the excavation as the ancient city of Hazor, that was mentioned in the Egyptian Execration Texts of the 19th Century B.C., the Annals of the Pharaohs Thut-mose III, Amen hotep II and Seti I and in several chapters of the Bible.

Press Release

District Attorney Robert Morgenthau's press release on the recovery of an antiquity by his office. Compare this with the story a reporter wrote that was based on the release and additional information provided at the news conference.

At the district attorney's news conference, reporters wanted to know the size of the tablet, when it was discovered, how it was recovered and other details. The news stories that appeared differed substantially from the press release.

Here is how Marcia Chambers began her account that appeared in *The New York Times*. Note that some material in the lead is not contained in the handout and was obtained through questioning. Also, the story places the district attorney in the third paragraph, whereas the press release begins with the district attorney's name:

A fragment of a clay tablet 3,500 to 4,000 years old that confirms the existence of the biblical city of Hazor in Israel was returned yesterday to the Israeli Government after a teacher who smuggled it out of Israel agreed to surrender it to avoid prosecution.

The odyssey of the 2-by-2-inch fragment, with a cuneiform inscription, began last year when the young teacher was on his honeymoon. The teacher, an amateur archaeologist, found the tablet at the site of an archaeological excavation some 10 miles north of the Sea of Galilee.

It ended yesterday, at a news conference, when Robert M. Morgenthau, the Manhattan District Attorney, turned over the priceless piece to Amos Ganor, Israel's acting consul general here. . . .

Checklist: News Conferences

The essentials of news conference stories are:

—Major point of speaker.

—Name and identification of speaker.

—Purpose, time, location and length of conference.

—Background of major point.

—Major point in statement; major points in question-and-answer period.

—Consequences of announcement.

Panel Discussions

In symposia and panel discussions, the presence of several speakers can pose a problem. But experienced reporters usually make their way through the tide of talk by emphasizing a thematic approach. They will find a basic theme—often an area of agreement—and write a summary based on that theme:

Four members of the local bar agreed last night that probation is no longer a useful means of coping with criminal offenders.

Although the speakers disagreed on most matters at the symposium on "How to Handle Increasing Crime," they did agree. . . .

AP photo by Mike Wintroath

Even when there is disagreement, a summary lead is possible, for disagreement is a theme, too. Here is such a lead:

There was no accord at the College Auditorium last night as four faculty members discussed "Discord in the Middle East."

The political scientists and historians disagreed on the causes of unrest in that troubled area, and they disagreed on solutions.

All they agreed upon was that the situation is thorny.

"We really don't know whether peace will break out tomorrow, or continued conflict is in the offing," said Professor Walter. . . .

After the theme is developed for a few paragraphs, each speaker is given his or her say. Obviously, the more newsworthy statements come first.

When one speaker says something clearly more interesting than what the others are discussing, the newsworthy statement is the lead rather than a general theme. Here is how such a story runs:

A California research team may have found a potent opponent of the virus that causes the common cold sore.

The information was disclosed today at a discussion of bioscientists and physicians at the School of Public Health on the campus.

Dr. Douglas Deag, a naval biochemist, said that the enemy of the herpes simplex virus (types 1 and 2) may well be the popular seafood delicacy, seaweed. The red

variety — known as Rhodophyta — contains a species that has an active agent that prevents the herpes virus from multiplying.

Herpes is responsible for keratitis — a severe eye infection — and a genital disease as well as the cold sore. But the research is in the early stages, Dr. Deag said.

He was one of five speakers who discussed "Frontiers of Medicine," which was concerned primarily with careers in the medical sciences. . . .

Bob Thayer,
The Providence Journal

Multiple-Element Leads

Stories involving several speakers will sometimes require multiple-element leads. However, it is generally best to avoid them because the number of speakers and multiplicity of themes can be confusing. Obviously, when necessary to the accurate retelling of the event, a multiple lead will be used.

Space exploration can be man's salvation, a physicist said today, but an astronomer worried that man might overreach himself and pollute the universe as well as his own planet.

The disagreement was voiced at a symposium last night, on "Space Travel," sponsored by the Science Club and held in the Civic Auditorium. More than 250 people turned out, obviously drawn by the promise of hearing one of the speakers discuss Unidentified Flying Objects.

But if they came expecting to hear a defense of UFO's they were disappointed, for Dr. Marcel Pannel said flatly, "They do not exist."

Summing Up

Here's a guide to establishing a procedure for covering speeches, news conferences and panel discussions:

1. What's the **subject?** The title is an indicator.
2. What's the **purpose?** Generally, the speaker will be trying to report, explain or persuade, perhaps all three.
3. What's the **main idea?** Here we get to the specific point that will constitute your lead.
4. What's the **evidence** used to prove the point? This provides the body of the story.

Remember: These stories are based on spoken words. Your story must include plenty of quotations. The story always matches the nature of the event.

17 Hunches, Feelings and Stereotypes

John Walker
The Fresno Bee

**Compassion can lead
to good stories.**

Preview

Reporters rely on hunches and feelings as well as rational, disciplined thinking:

• Hunches and intuition spring from the interaction of new information with the reporter's accumulated knowledge. Hunches lead reporters to seek relationships among apparently unrelated facts, events and ideas. The patterns the reporter discovers help readers move closer to the truth of events.

• Feelings and emotions can motivate the reporter to seek out systemic abuses and illegalities.

But hunches and feelings can distort reporting, as can a reporter's stereotypes.

Reporters go about their work in a rational, almost scientific manner. They cover events with detachment, break down their observations and weigh them against their general knowledge and the background of the event and then draw conclusions on the basis of their observations, not in accordance with their hopes and beliefs. Then they reconstruct these observations in coherent, logical stories.

Analysis and synthesis, the application of reason to experience—these are the processes that underlie the journalist's work.

Yet, this summary is misleading. It ignores hunches and intuition and emotional reactions that include feelings such as prejudice, hatred, friendship and love.

Hunches and Intuition

Every reporter has had the experience on assignment of intuitively sensing the meaning of an event, of suddenly seeing through the thicket of details to the underlying concept that shapes the event. Some reporters seem to possess an extrasensory perception that enables them to detect the real story, the actuality that lies beneath surface details. "I can smell something a mile away. It's just a fact of life," says Seymour Hersh, whose stories of the My Lai massacre by U.S. troops in Vietnam was the first of his many investigative stories.

413

Hunches, guesswork and intuition come into play as soon as the reporter is given an assignment. Before leaving the newsroom, before gathering information, the reporter has feelings and insights about the story, and these shape the reporter's coverage of the event.

There is nothing wrong with this. These intuitive concepts are sound starting points for reporting. "Feelings are not only reasonable but are also as discriminating and as consistent as thinking," said the psychiatrist Carl Jung. Even scientists admit the nonrational to their universe. Albert Einstein wrote approvingly of "intuition, supported by being sympathetically in touch with experience."

Hunches Lead to Stories

Murrey Marder of *The Washington Post* glanced at the check-in book at the State Department one Saturday evening. Strange, he thought, two people from the CIA (Central Intelligence Agency) had just checked in. On a Saturday night? Marder had a hunch: A crisis was at hand. But where?

He noticed the only lights on that late were in the Latin American Bureau and the Bureau of International Organization Affairs. As he raced around the building, Marder came upon Harlan Cleveland, who was attached to the International Bureau.

Katherine Graham, publisher of the *Post,* recalls what happened:

Marder had to think quickly of a question that might elicit a useful answer, which an open-ended one like, "What's going on?" clearly would not. So he asked, "How bad does it look to you, Harlan?" to which Cleveland replied, "Well, pretty bad."

Marder felt he was on to something big. But what? He knew the United States was at sword's point with Cuba, then on intimate terms with the Soviet Union. Marder had his question. It was about "this Cuban thing," whether the administration was confronting Cuba. Cleveland responded, "I think we are."

With a little more checking, Marder had an exclusive story—the onset of what was to become the Cuban Missile Crisis.

The Kennedy Assassination   When President Kennedy was assassinated in Dallas, Tom Wicker of *The New York Times* and other reporters heard reports they had no time to check. They had to make quick decisions. Wicker said rumors flew through the city and that he had to go on what he knew of the people he talked to, what he knew about human behavior, what two isolated facts added up to—above all on what he felt in his "bones."

In looking back years later, Wicker said, "I see that it was a hard story to put together, but at the time it was all so compelling that you really didn't have much time to think about what you were doing. You just had to do what you could do.

"In a crisis, if a reporter can't trust his instinct for truth, he can't trust anything."

The Agnew Payoffs   Jerry Landauer, a superb investigative reporter for *The Wall Street Journal,* had a gut feeling when he first saw Spiro Agnew, then being nominated for vice president:

> There was something too tanned, too manicured, too tailored for the guy to
> have been living on a governor's salary, with no other known source of income. So
> I started going down to Towson, seat of Baltimore County, the bedroom
> community where Agnew got his political start; talked to lawyers who frequently
> appeared to be on the losing side of zoning cases, to engineers who didn't seem to
> be getting a fair share of state business. After a couple of visits some started
> talking.

Landauer was told Agnew was receiving payoffs.

Hunches Develop from Experience

We have watched four reporters develop big stories from feelings, hunches, intuition. But if we look closely at their reporting another pattern emerges. Marder and Landauer noticed a break in the normal, the expected, the routine. Wicker had experience with the people he was interviewing, and Hersh had learned that official versions cover up untidy and embarrassing truths.

In other words, experience and prior knowledge provided them with the mind set or memory to put the new material in perspective. They built the new on a foundation of the old, what they already had experienced, what they knew.

What seem to be intuition, hunches and luck are the crystallization of what was already known, a leap from the reporter's storehouse of knowledge to a higher plane of insight. A new situation, fact, observation or statement suddenly fuses with material from the storehouse.

In a review of R. A. Ochse's *Before the Gates of Excellence: The Determinants of Creative Genius,* Mary L. Tenopyr, testing director of AT&T, wrote of intuitive breakthroughs: "Nothing that was not already in the creator's mind comes forth, but what is produced is old information put to a new use or configured differently than it was before."

Reporters store thousands of facts about people, events, policies and the many incidents of their daily experience. This vast storehouse is organized subconsciously. When a new piece of information strikes the reporter as important, it triggers the subconscious into releasing related material.

Hunches and instinct usually work for the good reporters, rarely for the lazy or the talentless.

Gretzky's Genius   Ability plus practice and experience equals excellence in all fields. During the 1982 hockey season, a talented young center for the Edmonton Oilers set records no one thought possible. Wayne Gretzky had fans comparing his feats with those in other sports. His goals, 82, and his assists, 120, for the season were the equivalent of a .425 batting average in baseball, 55 points a game over a basketball season, 3,000 yards gained in a season of professional football.

Pure instinct, said those who watched him. Not so, says Gretzky.

"Nine out of ten people think my talent is instinct," he said. "It isn't. It's all practice. I got it all from my dad."

When Gretzky was a 3-year-old in Brantford, Ontario, his father iced down the backyard and had the youngster practicing. At the age of 10 he was skating five hours a day.

Good reporters make use of this same combination of talent, hard work and experience.

Reporters who rarely develop good stories attribute the success of their colleagues to luck. It doesn't work that way. "Luck is what happens when preparation meets opportunity," says Raymond Berry, a former coach of the New England Patriots.

Awed by a technological society in which computers and data processing machinery seem to minimize human ability, reporters should retain their faith in the mind. "The largest computer now in existence lacks the richness and flexibility in the brain of a single honeybee," writes Peter Sterling, a brain researcher at the University of Pennsylvania Medical School.

Einstein's Model for Thinking

This diagram is a way of looking at the kind of thinking we have been describing.

Albert Einstein drew this diagram for a friend who asked the famous physicist to explain the roles of experience, intuition and logic in making discoveries or in formulating a theory. Einstein did not limit his ideas about thinking to science. The "whole of science is nothing more than a refinement of everyday thinking," he said.

Einstein's diagram shows a cyclical process. The process begins and ends at **E,** of which Einstein says, "The **E** (experiences) are given to us." **E** represents the range of sense experiences and observations that Einstein referred to as a "labyrinth of sense impressions," a "chaotic diversity."

Out of this plane of experiences a curved line rises toward **A** at the top of the model. This leap is the intuitive reach of the thinker, the reporter's hunch, the scientist's sudden breakthrough.

"**A** are the axioms from which we draw consequences," Einstein said. "Psychologically, the **A** are based upon the **E**. There is, however, no logical path from the **E** to the **A,** but only an intuitive (psychological) connection, which is always subject to revocation."

In his first paper on relativity, Einstein referred sketchily to some experiments and then wrote that they "lead to the conjecture," which he called the Theory of Relativity. "There is no logical path to these elementary laws; only intuition, supported by being sympathetically in touch with experience."

In the diagram, lines lead downward from **A** to **S′, S″, S‴**. These are deductions from the central idea, and they can be tested in the plane of experience.

Still Better. Four years later, Gretzky did even better, breaking his 202-point total with 215 on 52 goals and 163 assists. Still later, he became the first National Hockey League player to record 2,500 points.

Everyday Thinking

Scientist or shopkeeper, mechanic or journalist . . . we all think this way, making the leap to some conclusion from our experiences. Einstein said the leap follows no logic, "only intuition." The more diverse the experience, the more insightful the theory or hunch for a story.

This model and Einstein's concepts are useful to the journalist, for they illustrate in simple fashion the reportorial process. Reporters develop ideas, **A,** based on their experiences, observations and readings symbolized by **E.** From **A,** reporters draw consequences, **S', S'', S'''**—which we can call leads or story ideas. These leads or themes are the basis of reporting, which is the validating or disproving of the leads in the plane of experience, **E.**

Application   This discussion of Einstein's theory about thinking may seem theoretical to you. The fact is that reporters apply it often. Look at how Marder developed his exclusive story about the sudden worsening in U.S.-Cuban relations.

He made the leap to **"A"** from his experiences, **"E,"** as a State Department reporter: the unusual Saturday night meeting; the fact that it was taking place in the Latin American Bureau; his knowledge that relations between the two countries was strained.

Once he concluded that the meetings might involve Cuba, he devised a story lead, **"S',"** that the situation had become serious. He tested this idea or story theme by asking an official questions based on his theory. The replies confirmed Marder's hunch.

Feelings

Reporters usually welcome their hunches and intuitive guesses, but they are less cordial toward their feelings—that uncontrollable emotion that can hold us captive without warning, lift us to ecstasy at a glance or a touch and plunge us to bleakest despair with a word or a gesture.

This wilderness of feeling frightens most people, and it terrifies those who depend on their rationality, as reporters do. But reporters are human and must function within the limitations of the rationality of human behavior.

Feelings, in fact, can be an asset. "How can you write if you can't cry?" asked Ring Lardner. The poet Robert Frost commented, "No tears in the writer, no tears in the reader." Feelings help us develop value systems and keep them nourished. Moral indignation can direct a reporter to crowning achievements. The muckrakers, whose journalism may well have been the supreme journalistic achievement in this century, were propelled by a monumental moral indignation. Anyone who reads their work can sense the intensity of feeling behind it.

Exploited Women   One muckraker wrote of a girl of 17 who had been working in department stores for three and a half years. Uneducated, from a poor family, the girl worked at a New York City department store "at a wage of $2.62 1/2 a week; that is to say, she was paid $5.25 twice a month. Her working day was nine and a half hours long through most of the year. But during two weeks before Christmas it was lengthened from twelve to thirteen and a half hours, without any extra payment in any form. . . ."

The Library of Congress

Ida Tarbell

One of the band of muckrakers who exposed the monopolistic practices of big business, Tarbell revealed the ruthless drive to power of John D. Rockefeller and his Standard Oil Company. She and Lincoln Steffens ran *American* magazine from 1906 to 1915 and attacked municipal and federal corruption and the robber barons of industry.

Rheta Childe Doar described maids' quarters that consisted of a den partitioned off from the coal bin; a maid's bed that consisted of an ironing board placed over a bathtub. Maids were rarely let out of the houses in which they worked.

Mary Alden Hopkins described unsafe factories in which women worked . . . and died. In Newark, N.J., 25 young women died when a fire broke out in a factory. Some leaped out of their top-floor workplace. Some stayed and died. "They lost their lives because they worked in a building that was not decently safe for human beings to work in," wrote Hopkins. She said there were at least 100 more unsafe factories in Newark, some without fire escapes.

Child Labor   The exploitation of child labor was another theme of the muckrakers. Edwin Markham wrote in *Cosmopolitan* of Helen Sisscak, who worked in the silk mills in Pennsylvania, "a girl of eleven who had for a year worked nights in the mill, beginning at half-past six in the evening and staying till half-past six in the morning. Haggard, hungry, and faint after the night's work shifting and cleaning the bobbins, this child had an hour's walk in the chill of the morning over the lonesome fields to her home." Her pay: three cents an hour.

Then there was Annie Dinke, a silk-twister, 13, who worked on her feet 13 hours, and Theresa McDermott, 11, whose wage was $2 a week.

John Spargo wrote in *Bitter Cry of the Children* of the 12- and 13-year-olds who worked for 50 and 60 cents a day in West Virginia coal mines:

> Crouched over the chutes, the boys sit hour after hour, picking out the pieces of slate and other refuse from the coal as it rushes past the washers. From the cramped position they have to assume most of them become more or less deformed and bent-backed like old men. . . . The coal is hard and accidents to the hands, such as cut, broken, or crushed fingers, are common among the boys. Sometimes there is a worse accident; a terrified shriek is heard, and a boy is mangled and torn in the machinery or disappears in the chute to be picked out later, smothered and dead.

This strong emotional reaction to the abuses of power of public officials and the titans of commerce and industry propels investigative reporters to their discoveries. The Teapot Dome scandal was exposed by a reporter for the *St. Louis Post-Dispatch* who spent years gathering evidence to prove that powerful oil interests had bribed the secretary of the interior in the Harding administration. The reporter, Paul Y. Anderson, was driven throughout his journalistic career by the need to expose wrongdoers.

Today's Crusaders

These feelings—compassion, indignation at injustice, the need to right wrongs—constitute a powerful, continuing force in journalism. Look at the photograph that opens this chapter and the one on the next page. The photos are from a series in *The Fresno Bee* titled "Children: The Forgotten Farmworkers." The opening photo shows Aida Cruz Sanchez. Hardly more than a child herself,

The Library of Congress

Boys in the Coal Pits

the 6-year-old was left at the migrant labor camp to care for her 10-month-old brother while her parents worked in the fields. In the photo here, 4-year-old Melissa Hernandez gathers onions for her parents who cut off the tops.

Alex Pulaski, who wrote the articles, describes the children he has watched working in the fields as "part of a work force intentionally ignored by federal lawmakers, who have carved out exemptions for agriculture. They allow children to labor in the fields at a younger age, in more hazardous jobs and for longer hours than their counterparts at fast-food outlets, retail stores and nearly every other business."

The newspaper estimates that 100,000 children "labor illegally in U.S. fields, forgotten because their sweat keeps down the price of the raisins, chilies and pickles we buy at the grocery store." These children work "in the cucumber fields of Ohio, the chili fields of New Mexico and the onion fields of Oregon and Idaho." Melissa was photographed in an onion field near Ontario, Ore.

John Walker,
The Fresno Bee

4-Year-Old Field Worker

Auditing Feelings

Despite the usefulness of strong feelings, the reporter is wise to check his or her emotions every so often, for they can distort observations and impede the processes of analysis and synthesis that are the foundation of reporting and writing.

A city hall reporter who finds the personal lifestyle and ideas of a council-woman abhorrent may discover he is looking only for negative facts about her. A political reporter whose personal allegiance is to the Democratic Party may find she is overly critical of the Republican Party and its leaders. The idea of welfare payments to the able-bodied poor—or subsidies to farmers—might so violate a reporter's beliefs that his coverage is distorted.

Here are some questions a reporter might ask himself or herself every so often:

- Have I so committed to myself to a person, an organization or an idea or belief that I ignore negative information about the person or group?
- Does my need for ego gratification—which runs high among journalists—lead me to see an event a certain way? (The blandishments of governors and presidents can lead to a journalism of cronyism and self-censorship. Clever sources know how to play to a reporter's need for praise.)
- Does my need for immediate and frequent reward—a byline, a front-page story, the lead on the evening news—make me write a story before all necessary facts are gathered? (The journalist often must write before every fact is in. Journalism is legitimately described as history in a hurry or, more poetically, "Journalism is history shot on the wing," says E. B. White. But sometimes reporters make stories from skimpy material, particularly when they have not had a good story in a week or two.)
- Is my competitive drive so great that I will ignore, underplay or try to knock down another reporter's legitimate story on my beat?

Cautions Reporters cannot be neutral about life. Nor should they be. Enthusiasms, feelings, generalizations can be useful, as we have seen. But all reactions that swing to an extreme should be examined carefully for their causes. Reporters must watch for uncritical enthusiasm and unreasonable hostility.

Some reactions may be based on what the semanticists call "short-circuited responses," ideas that burst forth without thought. A reporter may be positive about doctors or judges and negative about salespeople or stockbrokers without distinguishing among the individuals in these groups. This kind of thinking is known as *stereotyping,* a dangerous way to think, particularly for a reporter.

Stereotypes, Biases, Fears

We like to think that we are reasonable, modern folk. Unlike our distant ancestors who resolved issues through violence, we turn to reasoned argument, to evidence, physical proof. Yet, what are we to make of the fact that while viewing the same television programs, reading the same newspaper accounts of the O. J. Simpson civil trial, 74 percent of white Americans agreed with the verdict that held Simpson liable for murdering his wife and her friend, whereas only 23 percent of black Americans agreed with the verdict?

Racism. In 1902, President Theodore Roosevelt invited Booker T. Washington to the White House and people were scandalized that a black man was being entertained by the president. Not until 1930 was another black person invited to the White House.

The fact is that we carry with us attitudes, assumptions, biases, fears, desires, inclinations and stereotypes from an early age. We see the world the way our parents, friends, schools and racial and religious communities have defined it for us. We are also creatures of the culture that surrounds us—our jobs, the reading we do, the television programs we watch and our government and economic system.

All these influence the way we think and how we see and hear. And the way we think, see and hear affects the accuracy of our journalism. In a famous experiment, journalism students were shown to have made more errors when they wrote stories about a report that was contrary to their biases and predispositions than they did when the report supported their feelings.

The journalist sees much of the world through lenses tinted by others. The maker of images and stereotypes, the journalist is also their victim.

Victim of Images

Since Plato's time, philosophers have speculated about how and what people see. In the "Simile of the Cave" in *The Republic,* Plato describes a cave in which people are shackled so that they can only look straight ahead at one of the walls in the cave. They cannot see themselves or each other. Outside, a fire burns, and between the fire and the cave dwellers there runs a road in front of which a curtain has been placed. Along the road are men carrying figures of men and animals made of wood, stone and other materials. The shadows that these figures cast upon the wall are all the cave dwellers can see.

"And so in every way they would believe that the shadows of the objects we mentioned were the whole truth," Socrates says of what the prisoners can see.

The parable is striking, almost eerie in its perception of image making. It takes little imagination to replace the cave with the movie theater or to visualize the shadows on the wall as the images on a television or computer screen.

Plato goes still further with his insight into how images pass for reality. He examines what happens when the prisoners are "released from their bonds and cured of their delusions." Told that what they have seen was nonsense, they would not believe those who free them. They would regard "nothing else as true but the shadows," Socrates tells us. The realities would be too dazzling, too confusing.

The Seduction of Stereotypes

Now let us jump ahead some 2,250 years to the speculations of Walter Lippmann, whose classic description of how people see is contained in his book *Public Opinion*. Here is that description:

> For the most part we do not first see, and then define, we define first and then see. In the great blooming, buzzing confusion of the outer world we pick out what our culture has already defined for us, and we tend to perceive that which we have picked out in the form stereotyped for us by our culture.

Lippmann says that the "attempt to see all things freshly and in detail rather than as types and generalities is exhausting. . . ." Stereotypes allow us to fit individuals into categories defined for us, categories that are comfortable because they save time in a busy life and defend our position in society, Lippmann

Shadow Reality. A woman customer of a dating service that uses videotapes tells this story: She was reading the biographies of men in the service's reading room when she saw a young man who obviously was the man she was reading about. He seemed eminently suited for a young woman also in the room, and the woman whispered to the young man that he ought to introduce himself to the young woman. He did, and he spoke to the young woman for some time. When he suggested a date, she replied, "Oh no. Not until I see your videotape."

says. They also "preserve us from all the bewildering effects of trying to see the world steadily and see it whole," he writes.

But the reporter must try to see it whole. When a student movie reviewer at Barnard College saw a film made by Luis Buñuel, she wrote, in amazement, "How Buñuel at age 70 can still direct such marvelous, memorable, intelligent and worthwhile films is beyond me." Her comment illustrates one of the stereotypes common to youth, the belief that with age comes decrepitude.

Stereotypes are held by every age group, by religious groups, nationalities and the sexes.

We have a long history of stereotyping those unlike ourselves by race, religion, ethnic group, tribe, nationality. The payoff has been murderous wars in Africa, endless strife in the former Yugoslavia, racial and religious discrimination everywhere.

Racial, Religious Stereotyping

The most persistent stereotyping in the United States has been directed at Jews, African Americans, Native Americans and Spanish-speaking people. Newspapers and broadcast stations have lent themselves to this stereotyping.

In the 1900s when mass migration brought many Jews to the United States, anti-Semitism spread rapidly, and newspapers were no deterrent. It was not unusual to see a criminal suspect described as a Jew or Jewish. "Jew banker" and "Jew peddler" were common descriptions, as was "Jew store." Bargaining was known as "Jewing down."

This persistent stereotyping had tangible consequences. In 1942, during World War II, a public opinion poll asked which groups menace the country most. Jews were third, just behind Germans and Japanese. Hotels and restricted neighborhoods carried signs, "No Jews or dogs allowed."

The media no longer set Jews apart in derogatory fashion, but other minorities contend they are stereotyped. Jesse Jackson accused the media of projecting black people in "five deadly ways every day. It projects us as less intelligent than we are, as less hard-working than we are, as less patriotic than we are, as less universal than we are, as more violent than we are. . . ."

Native Americans

"If Indians want to get the media's attention, they should focus on issues much more important than whether a team has an Indian for a mascot or over a beer named Crazy Horse." The advice stunned the audience of Native Americans. It was offered by the host of a major television network news show at a conference on the American Indian and the media.

The advice, well meaning though it may have been, revealed the insensitivity of whites to the feelings and frustrations of minority groups, in this case Native Americans.

"It has to do with self-esteem," said Tim Giago, publisher of *Indian Country Today,* a national weekly published in Rapid City, S.D. "It has to do with

Give the Relevance.
The New York Times stylebook on mention of race, religion or ethnicity states:

Race should be specified only if it is truly pertinent. The same stricture applies to ethnic and religious identifications.

Since that guideline was established, the newspaper has added another rule: The relevance of race, religion or ethnicity must be made explicit in the article itself.

children growing up believing they are better than mascots." Crazy Horse, Giago said, is a spiritual leader of the Lakota.

"What would happen if this company named a beer Martin Luther King Jr. malt liquor?" Giago asked. He went on, "Sure, there are more important issues facing us, but if we can't be treated as human beings in the small things, we will never be heard when it comes to the big things." Giago concluded his newspaper column with this warning:

"Like the blacks who were forced to sit in the back of the bus, we will no longer serve as mascots for the sports fanatics of this nation. We refuse to move to the back of the bus anymore."

Curtis Zunigha, an Indian activist, said, "I'm sure the mascot issue is perceived as sensational. But to many Indian people, it represents the core of institutional racism. As long as we tolerate these types of images, attitudes towards jobs, social welfare, progress, and important issues will continue to be dealt with at a surface level."

Some protests paid off: Nike agreed to discontinue an advertisement that described the Mayans as "crazed, savage warriors" and "delirious, blood-thirsty spectators." In Minneapolis, the *Star Tribune* does not use nicknames for American Indians in its sports reporting. Braves, Chiefs, Tribe, Redmen, Skins are out. Tribal names, such as Seminoles, continue to be used. The newspaper asked teams to provide it with suitable replacements.

Sexism

One of the most persistent stereotypings has been that of women. They have been seen as emotional and dependent, whereas men are stoic and self-sufficient. They have been accused of being intellectually inferior.

Jeanette Rankin, the first woman elected to Congress, voted against the United States entering World War I, which led *The New York Times* to comment that her vote was the "final proof of feminine incapacity for straight reasoning."

That same year, 1917, the *Times* was upset when suffragettes picketed the White House for the right to vote. The *Times* described the women's picketing as "monstrous." By the way, the women were arrested and jailed for six months without trial.

Those days are past, but sexism persists in some ways, one of them in media writing that identifies women through their relationships with men. Our language itself often reflects male-centered thinking. The column on the left contains what is considered to be sexist language. The column on the right contains nonsexist forms:

Sexist	Preferred
policeman	police officer
fireman	firefighter
postman	letter carrier
newsman	reporter

How to Tell a Businessman from a Businesswoman

An acute observer of the office scene compiled this telling commentary:

A businessman is aggressive; a businesswoman is pushy.

He is careful about details; she's picky.

He loses his temper because he's so involved in his job; she's bitchy.

He's depressed (or hungover), so everyone tiptoes past his office; she's moody, so it must be her time of the month.

He follows through; she doesn't know when to quit.

He's firm; she's stubborn.

He makes wise judgments; she reveals her prejudices.

He is a man of the world; she's been around.

He isn't afraid to say what he thinks; she's opinionated.

He exercises authority; she's bossy.

He's discreet; she's secretive.

He's a stern taskmaster; she's difficult to work for.

There are also inconsistencies in referring to men and women:

Sexist	Nonsexist
man and wife	husband and wife
men and ladies	men and women
Jack Parsons and Ms. (Miss, Mrs.) Burgess	Jack Parsons and Joan Burgess
Parsons and Joan	Jack and Joan (or) Parsons and Burgess

Gay and Lesbian Stereotyping

Some of the most pervasive stereotyping has been directed at the gay and lesbian community. The Gay and Lesbian Alliance Against Defamation (GLAAD) made the media a "major target of gay activists because of the often derogatory images of gays and lesbians in mainstream media content," says Jack Banks of the University of Hartford. "These activists charge that such portrayals have nurtured homophobic attitudes in society at large and fostered self-loathing by gays and lesbians."

GLAAD and other organizations conferred with TV producers and moviemakers, conducted letter-writing campaigns, sit-ins and boycotts. This activism has been fairly successful, and yet the stereotyping persists in some areas. Recently, People for the American Way reported that the media's tolerance for gay themes has aroused a counterattack from some groups.

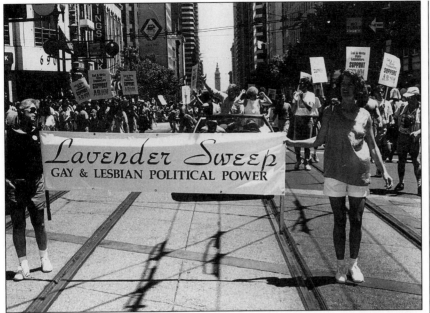

© Mark Geller

Out of the Closet—but Still Attacked

The drive by gays and lesbians for acceptance and political power has stirred resistance. Religious leaders condemn homosexuality as sinful and anti-gay legislation has been introduced in some states.

"When you present information about the contributions of famous gay, lesbian and bisexual people, you are promoting," said a minister opposing a proposal for Des Moines schools. In reply, 30 local ministers said, "To the extent that homosexuality is a factor in people's lives, in history, in the arts, in politics, and in relationships, it should be presented realistically and honestly as part of the way the world is."

GLAAD reported "a proliferation of websites devoted to hate and anti-gay rhetoric."

Substitutes for Observation

A news story grows out of the interaction between reporters and events. If reporters see the event in prefixed forms, they will prejudge the event, making it conform to the stereotyped pictures they carry. Robert L. Heilbroner describes an experiment performed with college students that shows how powerful these pictures can be. The students were shown "30 photographs of pretty but unidentified girls, and asked to rate each in terms of 'general liking, intelligence, beauty' and so on," Heilbroner says.

"Two months later," he continues, "the same group were shown the same photographs, this time with fictitious Irish, Italian, Jewish and 'American' names attached to the pictures. Right away the ratings changed. Faces which were now seen as representing a national and religious group went down in looks and still farther down in likability, while the 'American' girls suddenly looked decidedly prettier and nicer."

Stereotypes are, as the semanticist S. I. Hayakawa points out, "substitutes for observation."

Journalists who settle for stereotyped responses to events might heed the warning of F. Scott Fitzgerald: "Begin with an individual and before you know it you have created a type; begin with a type and you have created—nothing."

Patterns and Relationships

John Dewey said that "the striving to make stability of meaning prevail over the instability of events is the main task of intelligent human effort." These meanings are the patterns that establish relationships among facts and events. The great journalist of the muckraking period, Lincoln Steffens, said that his thinking about reporting was transformed by a prosecuting attorney during his investigation into municipal corruption in St. Louis.

"He was sweeping all his cases of bribery together to form a truth out of his facts," Steffens wrote later. "He was generalizing . . . he was thinking about them all together and seeing what they meant all together." Steffens said that this thinking led the prosecutor to conclude that the corruption was systemic.

Or, as the poet Robert Frost put it, thinking "is just putting this and that together."

Causal Relationships

The causal relationship is one of the most common patterns we form. We see a situation (a child cries) and we look for the cause (he is hungry). Journalists are told not to be satisfied with the event alone but to seek its causes and possible consequences.

The first state-by-state comparison of how public schoolchildren do on national tests showed that only one in seven eighth graders is proficient in mathematics. Why? Authorities said the data showed:

> The states whose students had the best performances are also states with the lowest proportion of families headed by single parents.
>
> Students with the worst performances came from southeastern states where poverty is high and from states with large, disadvantaged urban areas.
>
> The top 10 states in student performance were also the 10 lowest-ranked states in the percentage of students who reported watching more than six hours of television a night.

Here we have to be careful. Just because a situation occurs before or in tandem with an event does not qualify the situation as the cause of the event. Scientists worry about ozone depletion in the atmosphere, but they don't think beer consumption is the cause although it has been shown that the decline in the ozone parallels the increase in beer drinking.

Causal relationships are less certain in human affairs than they are in the world of mechanics and dynamics, where physical forces have visible consequences.

Inferences OK   However, when a reporter has enough facts to indicate a relationship exists, he or she should be willing to make an inference on his or her own. The reporter will be cautious, for he or she knows that ultimate truths are rarely available to a reporter. Nevertheless, risks can be taken. Reporters for the *Minneapolis Tribune* came up with proof that the milk producers' lobby had

---

Cause and Effect. In a traffic fatality roundup in a San Francisco newspaper, the reporter made clear the causal relationship:

Ten lives in 10 hours. Such was the appalling toll yesterday of two head-on crashes that chalked up the grimmest period in Bay Area traffic history.

Not one person in the four cars involved survived. An entire family of five was snuffed out. That family, and a sixth individual, were innocent victims.

Speed was the killer. And liquor a confederate.

Three died in an explosive, flaming smashup on the Bay Bridge at 11:40 p.m. yesterday. The killer car was going 90 miles an hour.

Just 10 hours earlier, at 1:40 p.m., seven met death in a jarring smackup. . . .

channeled hundreds of thousands of dollars into the Republican Party treasury through dummy committees. Following these contributions, the reporters wrote, the White House decided to increase milk support prices.

There was no absolute proof that the contributions had caused the policy decision. But the reporters decided that the suggestion of a causal relationship was legitimate.

In the obituaries of Joe Pyne, a television and radio talk show host, and Hal March, a master of ceremonies on television quiz shows, *The New York Times* reported the men died of lung cancer. Then the stories noted that Pyne had been a "heavy smoker" and that "Mr. March had smoked two packs of cigarettes a day for many years." There was no proof their cigarette smoking had caused their cancer, but the data collected by the surgeon general's office had indicated a high probability of such a relationship, and the newspaper was willing to suggest the cause-and-effect relationship for its readers.

Making causal relationships in print or on the air represents a certain risk to the reporter, but experienced reporters know when to take risks. In fact, risk taking may be one of the marks of a successful journalist. The British mathematician G. B. Hardy remarked that high intelligence is not important to the success of most people. No one, he said, can make the most of his or her talents without constant application and without taking frequent risks.

Polar Alternatives

Another potentially dangerous line of thinking common among harried reporters is the polar alternative. For instance, the reporter may think. "Either the Black Parents Association is right or it is wrong in its stand on school books." This either-or thinking can save the reporter time and energy, but it can lead to superficial journalism.

The reporter who looks only for the black and white of situations will be limiting observations to the most obvious elements of the event. The world is hardly bilateral and the reporter should resist what is called *bilateral consciousness* by being aware of the infinite colors and shades between black and white.

Linking Facts

Confronting this multitude of facets, faces and facts is half the task. The reporter's most difficult job is to put them into some meaningful pattern, to synthesize them in a story. But that is what journalism is about—linking facts to make stories.

As we have seen, these leaps to significant relationships are launched from solid ground. They are based on experience and the logical thinking of the kind described by the philosopher Isaiah Berlin: "To comprehend and contrast and classify and arrange, to see in patterns of lesser or greater complexity is not a peculiar kind of thinking, it is thinking itself."

This ability to arrange and rearrange, to categorize and recategorize, to pattern and to organize is recognized by scientists and poets as well as by philosophers. Israel Rosenfeld wrote, "We do not simply store images or bits but become more richly endowed with the *capacity to categorize* in connected ways. . . . Human intelligence is not just knowing more, but reworking, recategorizing, and thus generalizing information in new and surprising ways."

The technique of patterning is described by T. S. Eliot, the poet, this way: "The poet's mind is a receptacle for seizing and storing up numberless feelings, phrases, images, which remain there until all the particles which can unite to form a new compound are present together." In describing the emotion in a poem, he says it "is a concentration and a new thing resulting from the concentration, of a very great number of experiences which to the practical and active person would not seem to be experiences at all; it is a concentration which does not happen consciously or of deliberation."

There is not much difference in the ways poets and journalists think, indeed in the ways all creative people think. The ability to pattern observations and feelings is the mark of the thinking person, whether we look at a reporter covering a story or a composer at her piano.

The good reporter has what the philosopher Alfred North Whitehead describes as an "eye for the whole chessboard, for the bearing of one set of ideas on another." In his book *The Powers That Be,* David Halberstam describes "the great reporter's gifts" as "limitless energy, a fine mind, total recall and an ability to synthesize material."

Finding the Links

Reporters are always looking for facts that relate to each other. The obituary writer wants to know the cause of death, especially if the death is sudden, unexpected.

A reporter covering such a death was given the explanation—accidental gunshot wound. But the reporter wonders. The death seems staged. Could it have been a suicide? That's playing games, he says to himself. Still, the death looks like that of a character in a novel. Thinking of this sort led the reporter to report that Ernest Hemingway had killed himself, contrary to the explanation put out by the authorities, who had agreed to cover up the truth to save the family from embarrassment.

A reporter assigned to write a year-end summary of traffic fatalities begins with the data the police department has supplied. As she scans the figures of deaths and injuries on city streets, she notices that pedestrian deaths and injuries are up 16 percent, whereas the overall increase over the previous year is 8 percent. She decides to concentrate on pedestrian accidents.

A Story Possibility   Further examination indicates that most of those killed and injured were 14 years old and under. The reporter recalls that some months ago a parents' organization petitioned the city council to provide more play streets for the warm-weather months in areas where there is a heavy concentration of low-income families and few open spaces. She wonders whether the number of children who were killed and hurt in traffic accidents was high in the summer. She also checks the location of the accidents. A pattern is beginning to take shape. Now she must determine whether the facts support her ideas.

As she moves through the data, she notices the traffic department lists the times at which deaths and injuries occurred. She is surprised at the number of children who were killed or hurt in the evening. Well, she reasons, perhaps that is logical. Where else can kids play on hot summer evenings, especially youngsters from homes without air conditioning? She looks at her newspaper's clip file to check her recollections of the city council meeting. All this takes less than an hour. Next, she makes several telephone calls to gather additional information.

A reporter's approach to the story is as important as the fact gathering. She could have settled for Layer I reporting. Had she done so, her story might have begun this way:

> Pedestrian deaths and injuries in the city last year were 16 percent higher than the previous year, a year-end summary of traffic accidents disclosed today.

Dangerous Streets   Instead, after her first hour of thinking and checking the clips and another 45 minutes of calls, she is ready to write a story that she begins this way:

> For 10 of the city's children the streets they played on last summer became a death trap.

She then gives the total figures for all deaths and injuries to children under 14 and the total traffic deaths for the city. Then she works into her story the petition the parents had presented to the city council. Her finding that the evening hours were particularly dangerous for youngsters had not been discovered by the parents, who had asked for daytime restrictions on traffic. Before writing, the reporter calls the head of the parents' group and tells her about the evening accident rate. The reporter is told that the group probably will renew its petitioning, this time with the request that in the summer some streets be permanently blocked off to traffic. This new material—the concept of 24-hour play streets—goes into the story also.

The reporter not only turns out a meaningful story by linking certain facts but performs a public service for her community as well.

Summing Up

Journalists use their intuition and feelings to provide new insights into events and situations. Hunches and emotions are valuable but must be checked to see whether they are legitimate—verifiable and not injurious to individuals or groups. Particularly sensitive are the sentiments we carry with us from childhood—some positive, some negative. Some of these stereotypes stigmatize people.

The reporters who constantly replenish their storehouses with relevant material are able to make creative breakthroughs. They can match the deviations from the norm that they encounter in their reporting with material in their storehouse to come up with worthwhile insights.

Further Reading

Hayakawa, S. I. *Language in Thought and Action.* New York: Harcourt Brace Jovanovich, 1978.
Lippmann, Walter. *Public Opinion.* New York: Free Press, 1965.
Ochse, R. A. *Before the Gates of Excellence: The Determinants of Creative Genius.* New York: Cambridge University Press, 1990.

Part Five: Introduction

The preceding chapters have described the processes that underlie reporting and writing. Now we are ready to move to specific areas of coverage, beats. To help the new reporter handle these, we can devise a checklist of the necessary elements for any type of story.

For example: An obituary requires the name and identification of the deceased; the cause, time, place and location of death; the survivors; funeral and burial plans and some background about the deceased. We can make similar lists of necessities for other story types.

Using the Checklist

When a reporter goes out on an assignment, the aim should be to gather information on the checklist, the essentials of the story. The checklist is a starting point, a takeoff point for imagination and enterprise. No rote learning of what to look for and how to structure a particular kind of story can substitute for creative journalism, just as no memorization of writing techniques can transmute slaglike prose into soaring sentences.

The elements on the checklist are not in the order they should appear in the story. Any one of the elements could be made into a lead, depending upon the circumstances. Reporters must use their judgment to determine what constitutes the news angle or theme of the event. Also, not all of the elements will appear in every story, but most will.

Students should not regard the checklist as a cook approaches a recipe for flapjacks—a cup of pancake mix, one large egg, a cup of milk, a tablespoon of liquid shortening; stir until fairly smooth and then pour on a preheated, lightly greased griddle. That may make for a satisfying short stack, but this is a textbook, not a cookbook. Creative cooks always depart from recipes anyway. The reporter's task is to put his or her personal stamp on copy. The checklist is designed to help point the reporter in the right direction.

Types of Beats

There are two kinds of beats—topical and geographical. Some of the topical beats are education, politics, business—beats that take reporters over a wide physical area in pursuit of stories. Some of the geographical beats are the courthouse, city hall, police—beats that require the reporter to report from a specific location.

In recent years, new types of beats have emerged in the belief that the media have to reach out to the "citizen consumer." Thus, beats have been built around investing and saving, personal relationships, parents and children, health and medicine.

The beats listed in the next seven chapters cover areas of reporting to which beginning reporters are most likely to be assigned.

Covering a Beat

The reporter starting on a beat tries to meet everyone—clerks, secretaries, typists, assistants as well as those in charge of the offices and agencies on the beat. A sound idea is to give sources a business card or a note with your name, address and phone number.

"Shoot the breeze," says an experienced beat reporter. "That's the way to develop sources and how you find good stories. People usually are happy to chat with a reporter.

"You need to establish a relationship of trust with sources. But you make no promises you cannot fulfill or that interfere with your responsibilities as a reporter."

The editor of *The Charlotte* (N.C.) *Observer,* Rich Oppel, distributed to his staff eight tips for managing a beat. Here, in summarized form, are his suggestions:

1. **Get started fast** and get out of the office. Don't waste time. Not many stories are found in newsrooms.
2. **Set daily goals.**
3. **Build sources.** There is no substitute for regular, perhaps daily, contact.
4. **Do favors.** Where appropriate, do a favor for a source. The council member's daughter needs a copy of a month-old edition for a class project. Why not?
5. **Ask the sweeping questions;** ask the dumb questions. What's taking most of your time these days? What's the biggest problem you face in your job?
6. **Listen carefully, watch carefully.**
7. **Look at the record.** In managing a beat, go for original source material.
8. **Set up calls.** Make phone checks. Phone calls are a supplement, not a substitute, for direct contact.

Know the Beat

We can add a No. 9 to this list: **Know the beat.** A survey of editors found that they rated their reporters' knowledge of their beats mediocre at best. They said their staffers were poorly prepared to cover education, police and the courts, budgets, business and other subjects.

Jack Cox, president of the Foundation for American Communications, which co-sponsored the survey, said action is essential "to improve the depth and quality of coverage. These stories are at the heart of local news."

The following chapters are presented as a means of helping you master these and other beats.

18 Accidents and Disasters

Craig Lee,
San Francisco Examiner

Rescued . . . and interviewed.

Preview

Local stories about accidents and disasters must include:

- Names and addresses of dead and injured.
- Extent and cost of property damage.
- Time, location and cause of accident.
- Comments from eyewitnesses and authorities when possible.

Because these stories tend to read alike, an attempt is made to find an aspect of the event that sets it apart from others like it. Eyewitness accounts can provide a unique perspective of the event.

For natural disasters, rescue and relief operations are highlighted along with casualties and property damage.

Motor Vehicle Accidents

Motor vehicles kill, injure and maim an enormous number of people each year. News of collisions, of trucks and cars careening into trees and smashing into each other on fog-bound freeways is given good play in newspapers and on local radio and television news programs. Only the routine "fender benders," as reporters describe minor accidents, are ignored or summarized. Rare is the reporter who has never written a *fatal,* a story about an accident in which at least one person died. Newsrooms frequently check so that they have the latest accident reports right up to deadline.

One accident story tends to read like another. But the enterprising reporter finds an aspect of the event that sets his or her story apart. In this story from *The News-Gazette* in Champaign-Urbana, Ill., the location of the fatality was newsworthy:

DANVILLE — A 55-year-old Martinsville, Ind., man was killed Wednesday night as he was walking across the highway in the 2500 block of Georgetown Road.

Harold Owens was killed when he was struck by a car and a pickup truck while walking across Illinois 1 in the Hegler area south of Danville at 9:40 p.m.

That dark stretch of the road has been the scene of numerous fatal pedestrian accidents, according to Vermilion County Coroner Lyle Irvin.

Mr. Owens was with a logging crew that is working in the county. He was staying at a motel in the area and was walking across the road to a tavern, Irvin said.

The "dark stretch of road" has an ominous sound to it. We all know dangerous places like that. The story would have been more effective had those words in the third paragraph been worked into the lead.

Quotes Useful

We look for good quotes that set this particular accident apart from other accident stories:

CADIZ, Ky., Dec. 16 (AP) — Seven teen-age boys who had squeezed into a compact car were killed in a head-on collision on Wednesday, plunging this small town into mourning.

None of the boys was wearing a seatbelt when their car crossed the center line and collided with a four-wheel-drive vehicle outside this town of 1,600 in southwest Kentucky.

"No community this size can take seven at one time," David Goodcase, administrator of Trigg County Hospital, said as the hospital filled with friends and relatives. Boys and girls sat in clusters and wept.

Sometimes the remarks of the coroner or an official can provide material for the lead, as in this story from the *Herald-Dispatch* in Huntington, W. Va.:

ELK CREEK, W. Va. — Two brothers died early yesterday when their car went off W. Va. 65 and struck a tree, a county official said.

The deaths were the second and third traffic fatalities in Mingo County in two days, said interim County Coroner Larry Wood.

He identified the victims as Jimmy Nichols, 16, of Varney, and Clyde R. Nichols, 18, of Columbus.

He said their car left the highway about 12:15 a.m., wrapped around a tree and "practically disintegrated."

Although wreckage was scattered over a wide area, evidence at the scene indicated that Jimmy Nichols was driving, the coroner said.

"From the appearance of the car and where it left the road, excessive speed probably caused the accident," said Deputy Bill Webb of the Mingo County Sheriff's Department.

There were no witnesses to the crash, he said. . . .

That partial quote in the fourth paragraph is too good to be buried. Try your hand at including it in the lead.

Ricardo Ferro,
St. Petersburg Times

Daring Rescue

Eyewitness accounts of accidents can provide detail and drama. Here, motorists extricate a driver as a vehicle burns dangerously close.

Checklist: Motor Vehicle Accidents

—Victims: names, identification of dead and injured.

— Type of vehicles involved.

— Location.

— Time.

— Cause (from official source).

Caution: Pedestrians

Walking is the most dangerous way to get from one place to another, 20 times more dangerous than traveling by car and a thousand times more dangerous than air travel. But few reporters pay attention to the dangers to foot travelers, more than 5,000 of whom are killed annually.

The most dangerous places to take a walk, according to the surface Transportation Policy Project, are:

1. Orlando, Fla.
2. Tampa–St. Petersburg, Fla.
3. Miami–Fort Lauderdale, Fla.
4. Providence–Pawtucket, R.I.; Fall River, Mass.
5. Phoenix
6. Houston–Galveston–Brazoria, Tex.
7. Atlanta
8. Los Angeles–Anaheim–Riverside
9. Buffalo–Niagra Falls, N.Y.
10. Charlotte–Gastonia, N.C.; Rock Hill, S.C.

In this the age of the car, most streets are built for vehicles, not pedestrians, says the author of the study, Barbara McCann. "Some subdivisions don't even have sidewalks, let alone crosswalks," she says. Although 12 percent of all motor vehicle fatalities are pedestrians, only 1 percent of federal highway safety funds go to pedestrian safety.

— Names and identification of other drivers and passengers.

— Cause of death, injuries.

— Where dead taken.

— Where injured taken and how.

— Extent of injuries.

— Heroism, rescues.

— Latest condition of critically injured.

— Funeral arrangements if available.

— Damage to vehicles.

— Arrests or citations by police.

— Unusual weather or highway conditions.

— Accounts by eyewitnesses and investigating officers.

— Speed, origin and destination of vehicles.

Sources

State highway patrol; local, suburban police; sheriff's office; hospital; ambulance service; mortuary; coroner.

Cautions

Art Carey of *The Philadelphia Inquirer* says that one of the first warnings he received about covering accidents was to be careful of inadvertently attributing blame when writing about the cause. Unless one of the drivers has been cited or arrested, it is best to avoid a detailed description of the cause. The reporter must be especially careful about saying which vehicle struck the other because such statements may imply responsibility. Also, be wary of eyewitness accounts and verify addresses and the spelling of names in police reports.

Airplane Accidents

Airplane accidents make headlines. A motor vehicle collision in which two are killed will not receive the attention given the crash of an airplane with the same number of fatalities. Airline crashes are big news. Local newspapers and stations will scan the casualty list carried on the wires for the names of local residents.

Checklist: Airplane Accidents

— Number of dead and injured.

— Time, location and official cause of crash.

— Origin and destination of plane.

— Airline and flight number.

— Type of plane: manufacturer, number of engines.

— Victims: names and identification (including hometown).

— Survivors by name.

— Condition of injured.

— Where dead and injured taken.

— Cause of death: impact, fire, exposure.

— Altitude at time of trouble.

— Weather and flying conditions.

— Last words of pilot.

— Police, fire, rescue units at scene.

— Unusual incidents; heroism.

— Eyewitness accounts of survivors.

— Eyewitness accounts of people on ground.

Careful. Resist the temptation to write that airplanes collided in midair, a word that has no meaning. Just write that they collided, says the AP. If they collide on the ground, say so in the lead.

Resist pressure to give the cause. The National Transportation Safety Board usually takes a year or more to find the reason. The Aviation/Space Writers Association advises, "Don't jump to conclusions. Avoid oversimplifications. Attribute statements and conclusions."

- Comments by air controllers, officials, airline company.
- Cost of aircraft.
- Prominent people aboard.
- Fire and other destruction as result of crash.
- Direction aircraft heading before crash.
- Flight recorder recovered?
- If aircraft was missing, who found wreckage and how.
- Funeral arrangements, if available.
- Survivors of deceased, if available.
- Official inquiry.
- Previous crashes in area.
- Previous crashes of same type of plane or same airline.

Sources

Airline; police, fire, and other rescue units; Federal Aviation Administration (which in many large cities has a special telephone number for accident information); air traffic controllers; airport officials; National Transportation Safety Board; hospital; mortuary; coroner; morgue.

Cautions

Eyewitnesses on the ground are notoriously inaccurate about aircraft crashes. Early reports of casualties tend to be exaggerated. Passenger flight lists can be erroneous; verify if possible.

Disasters

For journalists, the line between accidents and disasters is difficult to draw. If the difference is the number of lives lost, the amount of property destroyed or damaged, then who would set down the numbers that distinguish the two? The fatal plunge of a school bus into a river that takes the lives of six children is a tragic accident in a metropolis, but to the residents of a town of 25,000 it is a disaster and much of the news staff will be mobilized.

Some define a disaster as massive, widespread destruction of the kind usually associated with the vagaries of nature—floods, earthquakes, hurricanes, storms and drought. It might be a famine in Ethiopia, an earthquake in Mexico, a volcanic eruption in Colombia that takes 22,000 lives in one hellish night. Generally, journalists use the word *disaster* to cover large loss of life:

OKLAHOMA CITY (AP) — A car bomb ripped deep into America's heartland Wednesday, killing at least 31 people and leaving 200 missing in a blast that gouged a nine-story hole in a federal office building.

This was one of the early bulletins from the bombing that took 168 lives and made Americans wonder what could have provoked those responsible to commit such a depraved act.

The National Guard is sometimes mobilized for disasters, and the Red Cross may dispatch units to help. Civil defense agencies may be present. State and federal agencies are often called upon to arrange access to the scene or to engage in rescue operations:

OKLAHOMA CITY (AP) — Choking through dusty smoke and the overpowering stench of the decaying dead buried around them, they push on. At times forced to inch along on their backs through foot-high crawl spaces, they push on.

Haunted by creaks, groans and cracks, they eye small chunks of rubble that shower them sporadically and stay alert for the scream of "Get out!," the signal that the collapse of tons of debris may be imminent.

Checklist: Disasters

As in the accident story, the human toll is more important than the loss of property.

— Dead.
— Injured.
— Total affected or in danger.
— Cause of death.
— Estimated death and injury toll.
— Eyewitness accounts.
— Property loss:
   — Homes.
   — Land.
   — Public utilities.
   — Permanent damage.
— Rescue and relief operations:
   — Evacuations.
   — Heroism.
   — Unusual equipment used or unique rescue techniques.
   — Number of official personnel and volunteers.
— Warnings: health department, public utility commission, police and highway department statements.
— Looting.
— Number of spectators.
— Insurance.
— Suits.
— Arrests.
— Investigations.
— Cleanup activities.

AP photo

KWTV-9 Live

About a third . . . about a third of the building has been blown away and you can see this smoke and debris and fire on the ground downtown on the ground. This is just devastating as we are uncertain what caused this explosion at this time. It happened around nine o'clock.

It was felt as far away as Channel 9. That's a good, at least five miles from downtown and there's heavy damage downtown to office buildings, as emergency crews try to assist the injured.

We have no report yet on the number of injured people, just that there are numerous injuries. . . .

(The Murrah Federal Building blew up at 9:02 a.m. At 9:04, KWTV-9 began broadcasting; 168 lives were lost.)

Lloyd B. Cunningham,
Argus Leader

Tornado Cleanup

Sources

In disaster coverage, statements may be issued by presidents and prime ministers, local police and priests. The destruction may be so vast no single source is adequate for coverage. Usually, the first place the reporter turns is to the experts—meteorologists for the weather picture, the Federal Aviation Administration for plane crashes, the Red Cross for disaster assistance.

Experts sometimes speak in technical language and the reporter should know some of these terms. In a flood situation, for example:

Flood stage—The height of the river above which damage begins to occur, usually because the river overflows its banks.

Crest—The highest level that a river reaches.

Human Interest

Many accident and disaster stories lack human interest because they focus on numbers of dead and injured, causes and property damage. When a cold wave swept through the East over Christmas, it left seven dead in New Jersey. For his story of the disaster, Jim Dwyer chose five of the dead and began his story with vignettes: One man had in his pocket a 16-year-old newspaper clipping about his son's death; another was found dead in the front seat of a truck in which he had sought shelter.

A homeless man had dozed off under the Atlantic City boardwalk. "The temperature was basically warm when John went to sleep," said a friend, "but then it dropped rather drastically. In that drastic drop was when he died."

Caution: Eyewitness accounts should be treated with care, especially if they are of events that unfold rapidly and particularly if the witness to the event is emotionally involved.

R. Edward Geiselman of the psychology department at the University of California at Los Angeles and Ronald P. Fisher of the psychology department at Florida International University make recommendations useful to reporters:

1. Ask the eyewitness to reconstruct the incident "in general." Ask the witness to describe the scene. This will stimulate recall.
2. Tell the witness not to hold back just because he or she thinks the detail isn't important. Report everything.
3. Tell the eyewitness to recall the event in different order. "Now that you have told it from the beginning, start with the most impressive incident, or start at the end."
4. Have the witness change perspectives. "Think about the event from the view of others who were there."

Restructuring the event in these ways aids recall, the authors say.

Writing the Disaster Story

With stories of the dimension of a disaster, the reporter is tempted to pull out every writing device he or she knows. Resist. If resisting is difficult, pause and reflect on the story—part fact, part fiction—told of the reporter from a Philadelphia newspaper sent to cover a mine disaster in Donora, Pa., where hundreds of miners were entombed dead or facing imminent death from mine gas. The mine was surrounded by weeping relatives, and when it was opened 200 bodies were taken out.

The reporter looked at this scene of death and grief and wired his newspaper the lead: "God sits tonight on a little hill overlooking the scene of disaster. . . ."

As these words came over the telegraph machine in the newsroom in Philadelphia, an editor shouted out, "Stop," and he handed the telegraph editor a message to send back to the reporter in Donora: "Never mind disaster—interview God."

Dave Kline,
Eagle-Gazette, Lancaster, Pa.

A story lies behind every death.

Preview

Obituaries are among the most frequently read stories in the newspaper. The obituary sums up the activities and outstanding qualities of the individual and includes:

• Name, age, occupation and address of deceased.
  • Time, place and cause of death.
  • Survivors.
  • Funeral and burial plans.

The obituary usually centers on the person's most noteworthy accomplishment or activity. Useful information can be obtained from the news library and from reference material and the friends and relatives of the deceased. The obituary can be enlivened with anecdotes about the person.

Here are two views of the obituary:

1. "The obituary is a routine story that no reporter enjoys writing."
2. "On the obituary page may be found the summing up of the glories, the achievements, the mediocrities, and the failures of a life which the rest of the paper chronicled day by day."

The first description is taken from a journalism textbook, the second from a veteran journalist's article about writing obituaries. Strangely, both summaries are accurate. Most obituaries are indeed routine, written by writers who rigorously follow a formula so that only names, addresses, ages and the other vital statistics differentiate one obituary from another. However, the writers who use their reportorial and writing skills on obituaries develop interesting stories and devoted subscribers. Obituaries are among the best-read staples in the newspaper.

No reporter should approach any story with the intention of writing routinely. Of course, some stories are difficult to make interesting, but the obituary hardly falls into this category, for the reporter has a wide panorama from which to select material—a person's entire life. No life lacks drama, if the reporter has the intelligence and the time and the desire to look for it.

William Buchanan of *The Boston Globe* was guided in writing obituaries by the thought "that what I wrote would probably be the last words ever printed about the person. That's why I always worked hard to include something in that person's life of which he or she would have been most proud."

I recall one woman who worked for years in the office of a candy factory. The part of her life she loved most was playing the violin at special Masses at St. Peter's and St. Paul's Churches in Dorchester. Or, for another example, there was a man who started as a busboy in a restaurant and later became the owner; after he became the owner, no job was too menial for him to handle. That clearly showed his character.

Even when the life is brief, the obituary can be interesting or moving. Here is an obituary of a 12-year-old boy written by a young reporter, James Eggensperger, for the *Sanders County Ledger* in Thompson Falls, Mont.

Goodbye, Ron

Ronald Laws, a rising star in Thompson Falls athletic competition, died Friday night doing one of the things he liked best, playing baseball. He was 12 years old.

Ron, as his friends and teachers and coaches called him, was batting in a Little League baseball game when he was hit in the chest by a pitched ball.

Then, according to one witness, he started running. After about 20 feet, he turned to the call of his coach, fell to the ground and never rose.

Spectators at the game rushed Ron to the Clark Fork Valley Hospital at Plains where the game was being played, but efforts there to start his heart failed.

His funeral was Monday in Thompson Falls. The Rev. Bruce Kline performed the service with special feeling because he had known Ron through Sunday school and liked him greatly. The Rev. Kline also performed graveside services at the Whitepine cemetery.

In fact, everyone who knew Ronnie liked him, teachers, classmates and teammates. He was a good sportsman and student and took pleasure in anything he undertook.

He left behind his parents, Mr. and Mrs. Larry Laws, and two brothers, Larry Lee and Timothy, and a sister, Lori.

Fittingly, the Thompson Falls and Plains All Star baseball teams are planning a two-game fund-raising baseball marathon for the 8th and 9th of July. Proceeds from the games will go to a memorial fund in Ron's name, a fund which will be used to support sports activities in both towns.

Other memorials for the fund may be sent to his parents.

Eggensperger recalls the day he took the call about the accident:

I remember feeling sick that such a thing should happen to such a good kid. But even more, that he had not had a chance to bloom into his potential and to enjoy all the things in life there are to enjoy. I put myself in his shoes and thought of all the memories, good and bad times, people and places I would have missed if I had not lived past 12, and the impact was overwhelming.

And in the back of my head was something I had been taught, which ran something like this: "An obit may be the only time a guy gets into the paper, and it's his last chance."

So I talked to some people and wrote what I felt.

Obituaries Can Enlighten Us

The obituary can tell us something about our past along with details of the life of the deceased. In the obituary of S. I. Hayakawa, a noted scholar on language usage who also served as a U.S. senator from California, it was reported that in 1937, while teaching at the University of Wisconsin, he married one of his students. "At the time, marriages between whites and Asians were not recognized in some states, including California, and the couple lived for nearly two decades in Chicago," the obituary reported.

Emma Bugbee was a pioneer woman reporter in New York. When she died, her obituary stressed the unique niche she had filled in the days when women were a rarity on newspaper reporting staffs:

> A founder of the Newspaper Women's
> Club of New York, Miss Bugbee was one of
> a handful of prominent female reporters who
> sought to expand the role of the women in
> what was the largely all-male world of jour-
> nalism when she entered it in 1911.

Bugbee worked for *The New York Herald Tribune* for 56 years. For many of those years, she was one of only two women reporters at the newspaper. They were not allowed to sit in the city room, the obituary recalled, "but had to work down the hall."

In the obituary of Louis Loss, a professor of law at Harvard, the writer noted that after Loss' graduation from Yale Law School "he was attracted to Washington by the excitement of the New Deal, and because he knew he could not go to the big Wall Street law firms because he was Jewish." And then the writer, no doubt with a smile on his face, writes: "He would eventually become the William Nelson Cromwell Professor of Law at Harvard, a chair financed by one of those firms, Sullivan & Cromwell, in the name of one of its founders."

Causes Informative　　The causes of death inform us of some of our personal and social problems:

• The obituary of Eddie Kendricks, the former lead singer of the Temptations, who died of lung cancer at the age of 52, stated, "He said the disease was caused by 30 years of smoking."

• The deadly combination of cold weather and alcohol—a too-frequent cause of death among Native Americans—was Jerry Reynolds' theme for this obituary in the newspaper *Indian Country Today:*

MARTIN S.D. — The icy claw of winter claimed another young life in Indian Country last week.

Twenty-year-old Sidney Brown Bear of Allen was found dead in the back seat of a car in Martin the morning of March 5. Companions said he had been drinking at a bar in nearby Swett, S.D., the night before and fell down twice before leaving.

A preliminary autopsy report placed his blood alcohol content at almost four times the legal limit. . . .

The preliminary report indicated that exposure appeared to be the cause of death. . . .

The Druggist and the Laborer

Deborah Howell, managing editor of the *St. Paul Pioneer Press,* says that "too many big-city dailies report just the deaths of important people—captains of industry and political leaders. That's a mistake. These newspapers ignore the woman who always feeds the ducks in the late afternoon at the city lake, the tireless youth worker at the neighborhood park, the druggist dispensing sage advice along with medicine for 50 years."

Howell recalled the obituary of a woman who died of cancer and who had asked for a party after her funeral. She was memorialized this way in the *Pioneer Press:*

> The ladies sat in a circle of lawn chairs
> in the neatly clipped backyard, between
> the pea patch on the right and the tomatoes
> and cucumbers on the left, sipping their
> gentle scotches and bourbons and beers,
> while the mosquitoes buzzed around their
> ears, and the evening slowly faded without
> pain into the night.

Of Tom Flaherty, Howell said, "To most folks, Tom might have seemed quite ordinary. He worked his whole life as a laborer on the Great Northern Railroad, as did many of the Irish immigrants in St. Paul. At first, I worried how I was going to make an obit on Tom interesting. Then I decided that his life represented so much that is so Irish, so Catholic, so railroad, so St. Paul. When any Irish railroadman died, Tom was at the wake. At the St. Patrick's Day parade, Tom led the Flaherty section.

"I explained the kind of obit I wanted to one of our better writers. His obit began:

> Tom Flaherty was an Irishman's Irish-
> man, a John Henry of a man who for 50
> years matched his mighty muscle against
> the hardest work the railroad had to offer.

"The trick is to make the dead person come alive again in an obituary, to remind family and friends and co-workers why someone was important," Howell said.

"Too often reporters come away with just the basic facts about birth, education, marriage, vocation and perhaps a few war medals. Obituaries can be examples of the paper's best writing, meaning reporters must search for the kind of detail—the unusual facts—that makes any news story interesting to read."

Richard G. West, whose comments on the obituary are quoted as No. 2 at the start of this chapter, says of the obituary, "Preparing an obituary is a delicate and exacting task, demanding the utmost diligence, insight and imagination. His obituary should be, as far as human judgment and ability may create it in the limits of a newspaper's space, a man's monument."

Monuments take time to carve, and the newspapers that attempt to carry obituaries for most of those who die within their circulation area cannot possibly devote much time or space to each. Still, some should be thoroughly reported and carefully written.

Beginning reporters often are broken in by a stint of obituary writing, because it tests the journalist's accuracy in reporting names and dates and his or her ability to work under pressure—people are always dying on deadline.

Most reporters consider obituary writing a dull assignment of little importance. "What nonsense. What an opportunity," says Joseph L. Galloway, senior writer for *U.S. News & World Report,* who wrote his share of obituaries when he broke into newspaper work on a small Texas daily:

> The obits are probably read by more people with greater attention to detail than any other section of a newspaper. Nowhere else is error or omission more likely to be noticed.
>
> A good reporter gives each obit careful and accurate handling. He or she searches in the stack for the one or two that can be brought to life.
>
> Veteran of World War II, the funeral home sheet says. Did he make the D-Day landing on the beaches of Normandy? Taught junior high school English for 43 years? Find some former pupils who can still quote entire pages of Longfellow because somehow she made it live and sing for them.

Checklist: Obituaries

The following items are required in all obituaries:

— Name, age, occupation and address of deceased.

— Time, place and cause of death.

— Birthdate, birthplace.

— Survivors (only immediate family).

— Memberships, military service.

— Funeral and burial arrangements.

Many obituaries also will include:

— Outstanding or interesting activities and achievements.

— Memberships in fraternal, religious or civic organizations.

— Anecdotes and recollections of friends and relatives.

Sources

First news of deaths can come from different sources. Many newspapers rely on the death notices mortuaries send newspapers to be placed in the classified advertising section. The news department is given a copy. Some mortuaries will call in the death of a prominent person, and on some newspapers and stations reporters regularly make the rounds of mortuaries by telephone.

The police and the coroner's offices will have news of deaths caused by accidents. Reporters scan wire service stories for the names of local people who may have been involved in disasters or accidents out of town.

Background material for the obituary is gathered from many sources. The starting point is the newspaper or station library. Friends and relatives can provide information, some of it human interest material that makes an obituary interesting, and they can clarify questionable or vague information. Here are the various sources:

- Mortuary.
- Relatives, friends.
- Newspaper clippings.
- References such as *Who's Who.*
- Police, coroner and other officials.
- Hospital.
- Attending physician.

Digging Pays Off

By checking the files and by talking to different people—his boss, her college classmates, a co-worker, the teacher's students, the merchant's customers—the writer can turn up the nuggets that make an obituary glitter. In the obituary of Saul Pett, the AP's gifted feature writer, *Los Angeles Times* writer Mathis Chazanov wrote that Pett wrote scores of profiles, including one of the writer Dorothy Parker that began with Parker asking Pett for assistance:

> "Are you married, my dear?"
> "Yes, I am."
> "Then you won't mind zipping me up."

The following incident was recalled by Robert D. McFadden in his obituary of *New York Times* reporter Peter Kihss:

> On the night of Nov. 9, 1965, moments after a huge power failure plunged the Northeast into darkness, an assistant metropolitan editor of *The New York Times* — candle in hand — groped his way through the newspaper's darkened newsroom.
>
> "Peter," he called. "Peter."
>
> In the face of crisis, it seemed only right for the editor to call on Peter Kihss, his best reporter, to do the story.

For the obituary of James B. Reston, long-time Washington correspondent and bureau chief of *The New York Times,* the publisher of the newspaper, Arthur Sulzberger Jr., said: "His impact on The Times was profound and lasting. He was a star at The New York Times, and like a star, he may twinkle, but his light will never fade."

A colleague, Tom Wicker, said of Reston, "he had far and away the best sense of where to look for a story and whom to question. Scotty was lucky, too, and nobody who isn't lucky will ever be a good reporter."

Much is available about well-known people. In the AP's obituary of Frank Sinatra, material was included that had appeared in a magazine 18 years before the singer's death. Sinatra, Pete Hamill had written, "was the original working class hero. Mick Jagger's fans bought records with their allowances; Sinatra's people bought them out of wages."

In checking the files for an obituary of A. Leon Higginbotham Jr., one of the country's most prominent black judges, the writer came across a talk Higginbotham had given to the graduating seniors at Wesleyan University in 1966. He ended the obituary with Higginbotham's words:

> "I will make two requests of you. They are that you always attempt to see those human beings who become invisible to most people, and that you always try to hear the pleas of those persons who, despite their pain and suffering, have become voiceless and forgotten."

Writing the Obit

The circumstances of the death determine how the obituary is written. When the death is sudden, unexpected—as in a traffic accident, a disaster, an air crash—the lead highlights the circumstances of the death. When the death is anticipated, as it is for the elderly and those who are seriously ill, the obituary concentrates on the individual's background and accomplishments.

In both cases, the obituary includes the vital facts from the checklist. Here are some examples of the two types:

FDR Dies at Age 63

Unexpected

MISSION VIEJO, Calif. (AP) — Florence Griffith-Joyner, the glamorous Olympic speed sensation who won three gold medals at the 1988 Games, was found dead Monday at 38 after a history of heart trouble.

FloJo, as she was known, apparently died at home during the night. Her husband and coach, Al Joyner, called 911 to report she was not breathing. An autopsy was scheduled.

Track champion Greg Foster said he was told by Griffith-Joyner's sister-in-law, Olympic track-and-field medalist Jackie Joyner-Kersee, that Griffith-Joyner apparently died of a heart problem. She had also suffered a seizure in 1996. . . .

CHICAGO (AP) — Chris Farley, the blubbery "Saturday Night Live" comic whose specialty was sweaty, tightly wound characters who erupted in vein-popping frenzies, was found dead Thursday in his apartment. He was 33.

The cause of death was not immediately known.

Farley died young like his comic idol, John Belushi. Both had a hearty appetite for food, drink and drugs.

Police said Farley's brother John called 911 after finding his brother in his 60th floor apartment in the 100-story John Hancock Building on a stretch of Michigan Avenue known as the Magnificent Mile. There was no sign of foul play.

The Cook County Medical Examiner's Office said Farley's body, clad in pajama bottoms, was found on the floor. . . .

Anticipated

LOS ANGELES (AP) — Frank Sinatra, the dashing teen idol who matured into the premier romantic balladeer of American popular music and the "Chairman of the Board" to his millions of fans, died Thursday night of a heart attack. He was 82.

> Walter Lippmann, the retired columnist and author and the elder statesman of American journalism, died today in New York City at the age of 85.

Deaths of the Famous

With the speedup in news delivery, the death of a well-known person is widely known quickly, and for stories that appear hours later on stations and in newspapers a different approach is required.

Some radio and TV stations began these later stories of Sinatra's death this way:

> They called him the Chairman of the Board.
> Or Old Blue Eyes.
> He was probably the most widely known singer in the world—Frank Sinatra. Dead at 82 in California. . . .

Princess Diana   The news of the death of Princess Diana flashed quickly and was the number one story on newscasts. By the time newspapers reached newsstands and doorsteps her death was not news. Here is how the AP wrote its 4th Lead-Wrtitethru, its obituary for morning newspapers:

^By AUDREY WOODS=

^Associated Press Writer=

^With AP Photos PAR101-106, NY154-159, 175, 177-178, 188-189<

^Eds: LEADS throughout to add background. Edits to conform. No pickup.<

¶ LONDON (AP) — Princess +Diana+, beautiful, famous and wealthy, won the admiration of millions but found simple happiness elusive.

¶ A year after her supposedly fairy tale marriage to Prince Charles ended in divorce, 36-year-old +Diana+ seemed finally to have found, in Dodi Fayed, a kind of uncomplicated joy.

¶ But the pressures of an insatiable press and public had not abated at the time of her death from injuries suffered in a car accident early Sunday in Paris.

¶ In an interview published last week, she told the French newspaper Le Monde she would like to move to another country, but couldn't because of her sons, who are in line for the British throne.

¶ "Any sane person would have left long ago. But I cannot. I have my sons," 36-year-old +Diana+ said.

¶ She had often pleaded with the press — particularly the pack of photographers who followed her every move — to leave her alone.

¶ A steady stream of photographs in the tabloids over the past month showed +Diana+ and Dodi Fayed, the son of Egyptian billionaire Mohamed Al Fayed, embracing, laughing and relaxing in the Mediterranean.

Find the Theme

As with any story, the obituary should concentrate on a major theme. The reporter must find the aspect of the person's life that is most noteworthy.

A Crusader   When William H. Jones, managing editor of the *Chicago Tribune,* died at the age of 43 of leukemia, his professional accomplishments as an investigative reporter and an eminent editor were emphasized. The obituary noted his "tireless work, creative thinking and total integrity."

The obituary writer found in the newspaper files a story about a talk Jones gave to a graduating class at the Medill School of Journalism at Northwestern University. The reporter quoted from that talk in order to show Jones' philosophy of journalism. Jones had spoken about journalism as a career:

> It's a commitment to use your skills to improve your community, to speak loudly for the victims of injustice and to speak out against those who perpetuate it. Some of the best reporting begins with a single, voiceless citizen who seeks help from a newspaper that is willing to listen, and to dig out the facts.

The obituary quoted an investigator with the city's Better Government Association who worked with Jones on a series of stories that exposed widespread corruption in Chicago's private ambulance companies, which won Jones a Pulitzer Prize when he was 31. The investigator said, "Bill hated to see people abused, especially the helpless."

A Humorist   Henry Morgan was a radio and television performer years before the days of talk shows. Admired for his quick wit—he usually worked without a script—he was derisive about the media and his sponsors. It was natural, then, for his obituary to dwell on some of Morgan's caustic comments and their consequences.

Richard Severo's obituary in *The New York Times* recalled that one of Morgan's sponsors was the candy bar Oh! Henry. The sponsors thought that the similarity of names would incline Morgan to sheathe his rapier wit. Hardly.

"Yes, Oh! Henry is a meal in itself," the obituary quoted a Morgan monologue, "but you eat three meals of Oh! Henrys and your teeth will fall out."

"On another broadcast," the obituary continued, "Mr. Morgan said that if children were fed enough of such candy bars they would 'get sick and die.' The makers of Oh! Henry withdrew."

When he was working for WCAU in Philadelphia as an announcer, Morgan broadcast a list of missing persons, and he included in the list the names of station executives. "It was days before they discovered it," Morgan recalled. WCAU let him go.

Then a serious note that recalled the Communist scare of the 1950s when self-appointed Communist hunters snared entertainers as well as politicians and foreign service personnel in their nets:

> His mordant humor did not sit well with certain people, and some of them concluded that he must be either a Communist or friendly to Communists. Mr. Morgan was amazed to find himself named in the book "Red Channels," which was issued in the 1950s and listed television entertainers thought to be either Communists or friendly to Communists.

He was blacklisted and "despite a proven ability to attract audiences, had a hard time finding work."

Serious stuff. But the obituary ended on a humorous note: Morgan said little about his origin, contending that he was of "mixed parentage"—one parent was a man, the other a woman.

Use Human Interest

Too many obituaries read like the label on a bottle. The major ingredients are listed, but the reader has no idea of the actual flavor. Details, human details, help the obituary writer move readers close to the person being written about. Few lives lack interest, even drama, if the reporter digs deeply enough to find it.

In an obituary of Helen Childs Boyden, who taught science and mathematics at Deerfield Academy, the reporter used several incidents from her life. When Mrs. Boyden had applied for work, the obituary reported, the principal was "not at all enthusiastic about the young applicant. But the school was too poor to insist on someone more experienced. He hired her on a temporary basis." She taught there for 63 years. The obituary continues:

> . . . In a highly personal style she cajoled thousands of students through the intricacies of mathematics and chemistry.
>
> Even in a large class she taught the individual, not the group. Her tongue was quick but never cutting. One boy, later a college president, recalls her telling him:
>
> "Victor! When will you stop trying to remember and start trying to think?"

The Boy Is a Man. Some alert students at Syracuse University point out that the writer of the Boyden obituary has a "boy" doing the recalling in the second paragraph when obviously it is a man recalling something. Boyden told him when he was a boy.

Writing with a Flair

Here are some paragraphs from obituaries of the well-known and the not-so-well-known:

Hyman G. Rickover, — Washington (AP) — Adm. Hyman G. Rickover, the salty engineer who refused to go by the book and goaded the Navy into the nuclear era, died today. He was 86. . . . Rickover was a tiny, tidy man who was as demanding of himself as he was of others, suffering neither fools nor superiors—indeed, he often pronounced them one and the same.

Bill Stern, a radio and television sports announcer — While some radio and television critics and sportswriters contended that Mr. Stern's stories were sometimes taller than the highest infield fly, millions of listeners looked forward to his Sports Newsreel commentaries and anecdotes.

Martin Gershen, a journeyman reporter — An intense, tenacious man, he made his search for news a personal quest and treated any withholding of information as a personal affront. As a result, his life and the news often ran together.

A wealthy retired business executive who lived on an estate — He knew the butcher, the baker, the news dealer and it was significant that he died in a moving-picture theater surrounded by a fireman, a policeman and the head usherette.

Duke Ellington, composer and musician — "Duke, he went all over the world after that, but nobody ever loved him better than we did," said an old-time tap dancer who goes by the name of Kid Chocolate.

Homer Bigart, much-honored reporter — His articles remained taut, witty and astringently understated, even when created under deadline pressure and the appalling working conditions imposed by war and famine; even when they concerned mundane events that lesser reporters regarded as routine, Mr. Bigart knew that what counted was not the place but the poetry and that a reporter could create memorable prose from even the most unremarkable happening.

Paul Santangelo, Norristown, Pa., politician — The funeral drew about 100 people, which struck many as not enough of a turnout for a man said to have devoted his life to helping his constituents in every aspect of life — getting them jobs, helping them vote, performing political favors. "I guess when you live that long (94), many people are already gone," said Borough Manager Anthony Biondi, a longtime family friend.

Jerry Garcia, lead guitarist, Grateful Dead — His gentle voice and gleaming, chiming guitar lines embodied the psychedelic optimism of the Grateful Dead for three decades.

Marguerite Higgins, Pulitzer Prize reporter — Marguerite Higgins got stories other reporters didn't get. . . . Miss Higgins won her job at The Herald Tribune in a characteristic way. . . . She heard that Mrs. Chiang Kai-Shek was a patient at the Columbia-Presbyterian Hospital and had refused to grant interviews. Miss Higgins got to Mrs. Chiang's room, got her story — and her job.

The widow of a politician — She avoided the spotlight that focused on her husband through his long political career, but among teachers in local schools she was well-known as a tireless and cheerful volunteer who could be counted on to dry the tears of a newcomer to the first grade or to hand out graham crackers and milk at recess.

Richard F. Shepard, *New York Times* reporter — Although he had been undergoing radiation therapy and other treatment for cancer, Mr. Shepard died of a heart attack while eating a bowl of chicken soup, said his wife, Gertrude, known as Trudy. A few days earlier he had said wryly that he didn't want to be one of those people who died on a tennis court — he had never played tennis in his life — but would prefer to go over a good meal.

John McCormally, editor and publisher of *The Hawk Eye,* Burlington, Iowa — McCormally was born Oct. 8, 1922, in Chapman, Kan. His parents, Patrick H. and Anna Nicholson McCormally, were farmers who were broken by the Great Depression. He was 13 in 1936 when he watched his family's friends and neighbors bid on his father's last team of mules. He watched his father cry over his lost independence. The experience helped shape McCormally's belief in fighting for the underdog, a characteristic he would carry throughout his life.

Ralph Abernathy, one of the co-founders of the civil rights movement— The flower-laden coffin was taken away on a wagon drawn by mules. Mr. Abernathy, who died Tuesday, had once requested the arrangements. He also asked, as an epitaph, two words — "I tried."

Andrew Guanche, an infant who died after a hurricane struck Miami — Baby Andrew was 9 days old when he died. He slipped away, not in a home surrounded by toys and pets, but in the coldness and loneliness of a Red Cross shelter, in a donated crib that suffocated him. (AP)

Milton Bracker, a reporter for *The New York Times* — A restless, high-strung, energetic man whose unceasing productivity carried his work into just about every editorial corner of the Times, Mr. Bracker had a compulsion to write and his typewriter raced to appease his appetite for words.

> **Forgotten.** "When a good newspaperman dies, a lot of people are sorry, and some of them remember him for several days."
> —*Stanley Walker*

Frank Sinatra — Above everything, there was The Voice.

Say what you will about the style and swagger, the women, money, fame, power, mob ties, the tastes and habits that long ago fell out of favor.

There was, and always will be, the light baritone, seasoned by age, flavored by whiskey and cigarettes, romantic, vulnerable, tough and completely original. It was the source of all of Frank Sinatra's power and greatness.

Who Is Chosen

Most small newspapers run at least a short item on every death in town. In large cities, where 50 or more people die daily, newspapers will run an obituary on a handful. Alden Whitman, for years the chief obituary writer for *The New York Times,* said for a person to rate an obituary in a metropolitan newspaper, a person has to be "either unassailably famous or utterly infamous."

Most of those selected are men. This is the consequence of the emphasis society places on certain kinds of occupations and achievements. Traditionally, women have been housewives, clerks, school teachers, typists and secretaries, not considered newsworthy occupations. But the perceptive reporter knows how important such tasks can be. There is as much drama—perhaps more—in the life of a woman who has reared three children or struggled to educate herself as there is in a man whose obituary is justified by the fact that he headed a local concern for 25 years.

Here is the beginning of an obituary in a Maine newspaper:

> Mrs. Verena C. Hornberger, 92, died Tuesday at a Waldoboro nursing home. She was the widow of Hiester Hornberger.
>
> She was born at Bremen, daughter of Franklin and Emma (Hilton) Chaney. . . .

No Reporting Not only is the obituary routinely written, it finds Mrs. Hornberger's prominence to be in her relationship to her husband, which might be newsworthy if he is shown to be prominent. He is not. But the obituary does contain some clues that, if followed up, might have made a fascinating story:

> . . . She graduated in 1910 from Colby College where she was a member of Chi Omega sorority.
>
> She was a teacher, first working in local schools. She also taught in Essex, Conn., and Verona, N.J., following graduate work in Germany at the University of Jena and Columbia's Teachers College.

Paid Obits. Many newspapers publish paid-for obituaries that friends or relatives submit. These allow a record for those of the deceased who do not make the news columns of the obit page. In a few instances, obituaries are used as a moneymaker. The Rockford, Ill., *Register Star* runs free a "six- to nine-line obituary that lists the basic information," says Linda Grist Cunningham, executive editor. "Families who desire longer, more detailed obituaries pay for them."

Was she the last surviving member of the class of 1910? Does the college have any information about her? Do some of her students recall her? It was unusual for women in those days to finish high school, much less to graduate from college, and graduate work abroad was rare. Can someone cast light on this? Obviously, the writer simply took the mortuary form and rewrote the data. No one was interviewed. Contrast this obituary with the work of Nicolaas Van Rijn of *The Toronto Star:*

Ann Shilton didn't become the first woman principal of an academic secondary school by being a pussycat.

The principal of Jarvis Collegiate Institute from 1975 to 1983, Miss Shilton "was a very strong single woman, with strong opinions and the will to make them known," her brother Paul said yesterday.

Miss Shilton, 69, died Thursday of abdominal cancer in Princess Margaret Hospital. . . .

Accuracy Essential

Obituaries go into family albums, are clipped and sent to friends and relatives. They have a life of their own. A mistake in an obituary is as lasting, and as embarrassing, as an error on the deceased's tombstone.

One of the most common causes of mistakes is the unchecked assumption. In the obituary of an atomic physicist who provided much of the theoretical work for the development of the atomic bomb he was described as having worked in "the research center taking shape in the sands of Los Alamos."

Los Alamos is high in the mountains of northern New Mexico.

Another cause of error is not checking every line carefully. How else could have the reporter allowed this to go into print in the physicist's obituary: "But on the way, he stopped at the University of Wisconsin at Ann Arbor . . ."?

Frequently Asked Questions

Here are answers to some questions about writing obituaries.

Q. Does it make sense to prepare advance obituaries?

A. Yes, even before a prominent person is ill. The AP keeps some 700 "biographical sketches" on hand, frequently brought up-to-date. A newspaper, depending on its size, may have a score or a handful. When a well-known person dies, the background, or B Matter, is ready so that all the reporter need write is a lead and the funeral arrangements.

Second-Day Leads

Q. Must all second-day leads begin with the funeral or burial arrangements?

A. Not necessarily. An enterprising reporter can turn up interesting and significant material. Although many newspapers do require the standard second-day lead, nothing is as likely to discourage a reader from a story as the lead that begins: Services for (name) of (address) will be held at (time) tomorrow at the (church or funeral home). (She/he) died at (her/his) home (date).

Late Reports

Q. If we are days late with our obituary, do we try to bury the old time element?

A. This is an old wire service practice:

NAJA, Mexico, Jan. 1 (AP) — Chan K'in Viejo, the spiritual leader of the Lacadone Indians in southeastern Mexico, has died. A son said he was 104.

The son, Kayum Garcia, said his father died at his home on Dec. 23 and was buried the following day. . . .

This practice deserves interment. Be straightforward with the reader and state the date of death in the lead.

Verification

Q. Do I verify reports of deaths?

A. Always. Do so by telephoning relatives, the funeral home or mortuary, the police or hospital.

KING D. ROME

AGE: 1 1/2 • HIGHLAND PARK

King Demarest Rome died yesterday. He was 1 1/2 years old.

He was born in New Brunswick and lived with his family in Highland Park.

Surviving are his mother, Debra; four brothers, Billy, Thorndyke, Kate, and Alex Demarest, and a sister, Sarah Meredith.

Cremation will be private.

A few days later, the following appeared in the New Jersey newspaper:

Correction

Due to a reporter's error, The Home News & Tribune mistakenly published an obituary for a family pet in Sunday's editions. The obituary was published under the name King D. Rome. The error occurred because the newspaper's procedure of verifying all obituaries was not followed.

Embarrassing Material

Q. Should I omit material from a person's life that might offend some readers or embarrass survivors or friends?

A. Follow the policy of the newspaper or station. Generally, newspapers have become more frank since the 1930s when a new reporter for *The New York Herald Tribune* would be told by City Editor Stanley Walker that there were two rules for writing obits: "First, make sure he's dead. Second, if he's a rich drunk, call him a clubman and philanthropist."

We follow Walker's first rule by verifying reports of deaths. The second rule may be applied to a local businessman everyone in town knows was a heavy and habitual drinker in the last years of his life and lost most of his business because of his drinking. But when the novelist Jack Kerouac died in 1970, *The New York Times* said he had "increasingly eased his loneliness in drink." And a former member of the Federal Communications Commission who died in a rooming house in Miami was described by physicians in an obituary as a "chronic alcoholic." We are also frank about the subject's legal entanglements, personal beliefs and his or her sexual preference.

Unsavory activities from the person's past may be used. In the obituary of the FCC member, the lead described him as having been charged with plotting to fix the award of a television license. One obituary of Joseph P. Kennedy, the father of President Kennedy, reported that during the elder Kennedy's life there had been "whispers that Mr. Kennedy was anti-Semitic."

In its obituary of D. Tennant Bryan, founder of the communications giant Media General Inc., *The New York Times* made a point of Bryan's opposition to the desegregation of public schools despite a Supreme Court ruling. In the second paragraph of the *Times* obituary that Edward Wyatt wrote, Bryan "was a leading voice against school desegregation in Virginia in the mid-1950's," and later in the story Wyatt said Bryan's newspapers "were leading supporters of the campaign of 'massive resistance' to racial integration in public schools. . . ."

Jerry Garcia's obituaries all stated that he died in a California residential drug treatment center, and *The New York Times* said in the third paragraph of its page 1 obituary, "In the 1960s, he was known as Captain Trips, referring to his frequent use of LSD, and he struggled through the years with a heroin addiction."

On smaller newspapers, the tendency is to look at the brighter side. However, incidents well known to the public cannot be disregarded. On the other hand, when a man or woman had led a useful life after making a mistake years past, no harm to truth is done by passing over the incident. The obituary of the former city treasurer who was sentenced to the penitentiary for graft 30 years before his death will be handled differently by different newspapers. Some will include his crime; others will not, on the ground that he paid for his mistakes and thereafter led a blameless life.

Please Omit Flowers

Q. When people request no flowers, what do I write?

A. Ask the caller if the family prefers that donations be made to an organization, scholarship or charity and name it: The family requests that remembrances be sent to the Douglas County Heart Association.

Interviewing Survivors

Q. Do I press grieving survivors to speak to me even though they may not want to?

A. Editors usually want background about the deceased that only people close to the person can provide. An obituary celebrates the person's life, and an interview with relatives can help capture that life. Few subjects have ample material in the clip file.

Still, reporters must be sensitive to grief. If the source is unwilling to talk, do not press. But give reasons for needing the information, and try to conduct a personal interview if there is no deadline problem.

Cause of Death

Q. Do I always use the cause of death?

A. The cause is given, unless policy is otherwise. For years, cancer—the country's second leading cause of death—was replaced in many obituaries by the euphemisms "long illness" or "lingering illness." For some reason, many people regarded cancer as a disease too horrible to name. Under the educational program of the American Cancer Society, newspapers were encouraged to mention the disease. The cause of death should be reported whenever possible so that the public becomes aware of the major causes of death.

When lung cancer is the cause of death, reporters ask whether the deceased was a heavy smoker. For a time, newspapers ignored the deceased's smoking habit. But in recent years—after considerable criticism of this reluctance to list this possible cause of death—smoking is included, if not played up, as in this AP story:

COSTA MESA, Calif. (AP) — Wayne McLaren, who portrayed the rugged "Marlboro Man" in cigarette ads but became an anti-smoking crusader after developing lung cancer, has died. He was 51.

McLaren, who smoked for about 25 years and was diagnosed with the disease about two years ago, died Wednesday.

"He fought a hard battle," his mother, Louise McLaren, said. "Some of his last words were: 'Take care of the children. Tobacco will kill you, and I am living proof of it.' "

On the other hand, when Sammy Davis Jr. died, the cover story in *People* did not mention that he died of cancer presumably caused by his two-pack-a-day cigarette habit.

AIDS

Q. What about AIDS? Do I include it as a cause of death?

A. Yes, if it is newspaper policy to do so. Most of the media report AIDS as the cause of death. The taboo has lessened with the growing acceptance of the illness as a major killer. "Reporting AIDS deaths reflects the world as it is," *The Washington Post* reported in an article that said the newspaper would include AIDS as "the cause of death in its news obituaries whenever possible."

Here is how *The New York Times* reported the death of Arthur Ashe:

> Arthur Ashe, the only black man to win Wimbledon, the United States and Australian Opens and a longtime human-rights activist, died yesterday. He was 49.
>
> A New York Hospital administrator, Judith Lilavois, said Ashe died at 3:13 P.M. of pneumonia, a complication of AIDS.

Some newspapers will honor family requests if they insist cause of death be left out of the obituary, but fewer and fewer are making such requests.

Toby Gardner

AIDS Memorial

Suicide

Q. How do I handle suicides?

A. Follow the newspaper's policy. Most are frank; some avoid the word. The *Bangor* (Maine) *Daily News* uses the term "died unexpectedly," and the *Eagle-Tribune* in Lawrence, Mass., uses the words "short illness" for suicides. *The Morning Record and Journal* in Meriden, Conn., describes the cause of death in the final paragraph of the obituary, which allows the family to cut off the paragraph before preserving the story or sending it to others. Be careful to attribute suicide to an authority, the medical examiner or the coroner. Without such attribution, do not state suicide was the cause of death. Avoid details about the method of death.

Localizing Obituaries

Q. Should I try to localize obituaries whenever possible?

A. Yes, if the person is a resident of your community and died elsewhere or was a former well-known resident. For example:

> John A. Nylic, 68, a retired mainte-
> nance worker at General Electric Co., died
> Friday night after suffering an apparent
> heart attack while visiting in Lebanon
> Springs, N.Y.
>
> Mr. Nylic, who lived at 78 W.
> Housatonic St. . . .
>
> —*The Berkshire Eagle* (Pittsfield, Mass.)

Humorous Obituaries

Q. Must the obituary always be solemn?

A. Most are and should be. Now and then the subject lends himself or herself to lighter treatment. When the screenwriter Al Boasberg died, the lead to his obituary shocked some readers. Others found it appropriate. Boasberg had written many of the gags that were used in the Marx Brothers' movies. Some of his most famous sequences involved death, such as the one of Groucho Marx posing as a doctor taking a patient's pulse and intoning: "Either this man is dead or my watch has stopped." For the lead on Boasberg's obituary, Douglas Gilbert wrote:

> The joke's on Al Boasberg. He's dead.

But humor can backfire, even when unintended. When Jorge Mas Canosa, a leader in Miami of the anti-Castro Cuban-American National Foundation, died, the weekly *Tropic* magazine of *The Miami Herald* had a cover photo of his funeral procession. The headline over the photo read "No Mas." (In Spanish, *no mas* means *no more* or *enough.*) The edition was withheld and the following week the headline read "Farewell."

The Specialist

A few newspapers assign specialists to write obituaries. Alden Whitman, for years the master obituary writer for *The New York Times,* was allowed to comment on the personal habits and the accomplishments of his subjects. When he wrote the obituary of Mies van der Rohe, the prophet of an austere modern architectural style, Whitman noted that the architect chose to live on the third floor of an old-fashioned apartment house on Chicago's north side.

In his obituary of André Malraux, the French writer, Whitman wrote that he was "a chain smoker of cheap cigarettes." In his lengthy obituary of the American socialist, Norman Thomas, Whitman said Thomas' socialism "was to Marxism what Musak is to Mozart."

Further Reading

Mitford, Jessica. *The American Way of Death.* New York: Fawcett Crest, 1978.
Whitman, Alden. *The Obituary Book.* New York: Stein and Day, 1971.
Whitman, Alden. *Come to Judgment.* New York: Viking Press, 1980.

Rodolfo Gonzales,
San Antonio Light

Juvenile crime is increasing.

Preview

Police reporters cover a vast array of news. Their beat calls upon them to handle:

• **Breaking stories:** Accidents, crimes, arrests, fires.
• **Features:** Profiles of police personnel, criminals; stories about police investigations.
• **Interpretative articles:** Law enforcement policies, changes in personnel and procedures.
• **Investigative reporting:** Examination of false arrests, corruption, lax enforcement.

Police news is given prominent play in most newspapers because of its dramatic nature and the fact that so many people are affected. Almost 35 million Americans are victims of crimes each year, only a third of which are reported.

The Beat with Everything. "The police beat is about people and what makes them tick, what turns them into homicidal maniacs, what brings out the best in them, what drives them berserk. It has it all: greed, sex, violence, comedy and tragedy. You learn more about people than you would on any other newspaper job."
—*Edna Buchanan,*
The Miami Herald
police reporter.

Few beats produce as much news as the police beat, and few reporters are called upon to do as much as quickly as the police reporter. Each day, a dozen or more potential stories develop on the beat. The police reporter covers:

• **Crime:** reports of crime, investigation, arrest, booking, arraignment.
• **Accidents:** traffic, airplane, drowning, rescue.
• **Fires:** reports and on-the-scene coverage.
• **Departmental activity:** coverage of police department personnel, policies, efficiency and accountability.
• **Departmental integrity:** standards, policies and procedures for dealing with internal and external allegations, assumptions and attitudes about corruption that is systemic or sporadic.
• **Other law enforcement agencies:** sheriff's office, state highway patrol, suburban police departments, federal marshals.

The Range and Cost of Crime

Crime affects everyone, and news of crime interests most of us. One of four households is hit by crime every year, mostly by burglary and theft. One in 20 households is struck by a violent crime—murder, rape, robbery, assault. A rape is committed every 5 minutes, a murder every 21 minutes. We all know someone who has been the victim of some kind of crime.

The number of crime victims approaches 35 million. Of these, a fourth are the victims of violent crimes. The U.S. Department of Justice reports that almost 9 million people were the victims of murder, rape, robbery or assault last year.

Prison officials report that the prison population grew from 300,000 in the mid-1970s to more than 1.7 million 20 years later. Another 570,000 are held in local jails, and 3.5 million are on probation or parole.

The crowded jails and prisons are the result of several converging forces—the public demand for longer sentences, the elimination of parole in some states, the belief that taking criminals off the streets will lower violent crime rates and the imprisonment of increasing numbers of men and women convicted of crimes involving drugs. In 25 years, the number of inmates in prisons for drug offenses went from 1 in 16 inmates to 1 in 5.

The incarceration rate in the United States is 445 per 100,000 population. The rates for other countries—South Africa, 311; England, 97; France, 81, Japan, 45. The prison population in the past decade grew by 168 percent despite a gradual decline in the number of violent crimes.

Juvenile Crime   Arrests of juveniles increased at a rapid rate during the 1990s. In a recent year, female juvenile arrests increased 23 percent over the previous year, whereas the increase in male arrests was 11 percent. The states with the largest percentage of increases in juvenile commitments to a holding facility are Oklahoma, Rhode Island, Idaho and Kentucky.

Juvenile detention has also increased, at considerable cost. More than 750,000 juveniles are sent to juvenile facilities each year. The arrest rate among juveniles ages 10 to 17 jumped 100 percent from 1983 to the mid-1990s. The number of homicides among juveniles that involved handguns increased fivefold. More juveniles are being locked up, fewer placed on probation.

Vulnerable Areas   As would be expected, large cities are hardest hit by violent crime, less populated areas by property crime. In Milwaukee, in 1965 there were 27 murders, 33 rapes and 214 robberies. Thirty years later, with a smaller population, there were 170 murders, 700 rapes and 4,500 robberies. The number of murders in the Los Angeles area is so great that only half lead to arrests and charges, and only a third result in conviction of murder or manslaughter.

Los Angeles Times reporters found that the law enforcement system was overwhelmed by the number of crimes and that structural changes were needed to improve police work.

The Philadelphia Inquirer reported that residents of the suburbs were increasingly being threatened by property crime. The newspaper's computer-assisted reporting project found that the newer suburbs with their through highways that provide escape routes and the big malls and construction sites that provide prime targets for theft were attracting large numbers of criminals.

Causes. Studies show that 75 percent of violent juvenile offenders have suffered abuse by a family member and more than 60 percent of juveniles in custody have parents who abused alcohol or drugs. Says John J. Dilulio, Jr., of Princeton, "Very bad boys come disproportionately from very bad homes in very bad neighborhoods."

Table 20.1 Crime Rate

	Metropolitan Areas	Other Cities	Rural	National Average
Murder	7.4	4.2	4.6	6.8
Forcible rape	37.6	36.0	24.7	35.9
Robbery	223.3	71.8	18.1	186.1
Aggravated assault	416.1	343.3	183.2	382.0
Burglary	963.3	931.7	621.7	919.6
Larceny-theft	3,086.6	3,586.2	1,082.0	2,886.5
Motor vehicle theft	590.8	234.0	129.4	505.8

Rates per 100,000 residents. From *Crime in the United States.*

High Costs   The cost of crime to the public is high. More than $75 billion is spent each year on the police, courts, prisons and jails and the parole and probation systems by cities, states and the federal government. This amounts to $300 a person a year.

It costs $16,000 to $25,000 a year to confine an inmate, much more in large cities; New York's cost is $58,000 a year. Costs spiral upward with the public's demand for fewer releases and longer prison and jail terms.

High Interest in Crime News

You might think that over the years of intense crime coverage the public's appetite would reach the saturation point. Not so. Crime news remains high on the media agenda.

Perhaps it is the increasingly bizarre nature of crimes:

- The perfect neighbor who stabbed his next-door neighbor 13 times after she resisted his sexual advances.
- The Mormon church leader who had an entire family executed to protect his standing in the church.
- The teen-ager who persuaded his college classmates to kill his stepfather.
- The lawyer who had his buddies on the police force shoot his wife and dump her and her car into a Chicago canal.
- The widow who rid herself of a series of husbands by feeding them arsenic.

Senseless Murders

Perhaps it is our sympathy for the victims. Daily, we read about and watch coverage in evening newscasts of the deaths of innocent people caught in drive-by shootings, children shot as they cowered in their apartments during drug wars. We read of seemingly senseless stabbings and shootings during holdups:

When the two men demanded his leather jacket and her shearling coat, the couple did not resist.

Alexander Ortiz, 22, took off his jacket. Arlyn Gonzales, 23, terrified, fumbled over a buckle at the collar of her coat. One of the men roughly tugged at her coat.

"Don't do it," Ortiz said. "Don't hurt her. She's pregnant."

In response, one of the men shot Ortiz, once in the throat and once in the left chest.

"C'mon, c'mon, Get her jacket," Ms. Gonzales said the gunman told his associate.

Though fatally wounded, Ortiz spoke to his girlfriend. "I don't want to die. I'm afraid. Take care of the baby for me. Take care of my baby, please." He died two hours later at Jamaica Hospital.

School Fears

Perhaps it is the fear parents live with when they send their children to school. The Bureau of Justice reports 9 percent of students aged 12 to 19 were crime victims in or near their schools over a six-month period; 15 percent said their schools had gangs; 16 percent said a student had attacked or threatened a teacher; 30 percent said marijuana was easy to obtain at school; 9 percent said crack and 11 percent said cocaine were easy to obtain in school; 31 percent said alcohol was easy to obtain.

Among black students in the central cities, 24 percent said they were afraid of being attacked while going to and from school. Three percent of students in central cities reported taking some kind of weapon to school to protect themselves.

Parental fear for the safety of their children at school is understandable in the wake of several fatal school shootings like the Jonesboro, Ark., shooting we examined in Chapter 1, and the high school shooting in Littleton, Colo., that took the lives of 14 students and a teacher.

Gangs. Law enforcement agencies report more than 665,000 youths are members of gangs, that almost 60 percent of gang members are in California, Illinois and Texas. A fourth are in Los Angeles County and Chicago.

Juvenile justice materials are available by e-mail at askncjrs@ncjrs.org.

At Century's End: Crime Declining

Violent crime began to decline in large cities in the mid-1990s. In New York, for example, murders went from more than 2,000 a year to less than half that, and shootings from 5,860 to 2,930 as the century ended. In Los Angeles, the number of murders went down 33 percent. The national murder rate was the lowest since 1967.

Why? No one is certain. One theory is that through tougher enforcement of the law and longer prison sentences criminals were no longer on the streets. Another is that there were fewer people in the high-crime age group—men in their 20s—in the last part of the 1990s.

Background. Profiles of those arrested show that most had a history of crime—65 percent had served time or had been sentenced to probation. Two-thirds were regular drug users, and almost half said they had been in substance abuse programs. Almost half said they were under the influence of alcohol at the time of the offense.

Disorder Theory   Another theory suggests that the neighborhood police presence had been absent. The police had been concentrating on serious crime and had ignored and all but decriminalized minor offenses such as spraying graffiti, public drunkenness, pot smoking, playing loud music, committing public nuisances. The result was that people turned inward, shunning public places. People were no longer actively engaged in monitoring their neighborhoods. Also, a climate was created that tolerated crime. Criminologists of this school say there is a link between community disorder and crime.

When the police began making disorder arrests, as they did in New York, they found the people they arrested were carrying guns and many were wanted on felony warrants.

The Police

To cope with crime there are almost 600,000 state and local police officers, and efforts are constantly being made to add to police power.

One response to the threat of crime has been the growth of private police, who number about 1.5 million. They guard office buildings, apartment complexes, shopping malls, gated communities and even the streets of some residential communities. Most universities use their own police to monitor campuses.

Those who can afford private protection do so. The commercial and residential areas that cannot afford to do so rely on police forces usually spread thin.

Police Department Organization

The police department is organized around the three police functions—(1) enforcement of laws, (2) prevention of crime and (3) finding and arresting criminals.

The department is headed by a chief or commissioner who is responsible to the mayor, director of public safety or city manager. The chief or commissioner is appointed and although he or she makes departmental policy, broad policy decisions affecting law enforcement come from a superior and are often made in a political context. The chief's second in command may be an assistant chief or inspector. Commissioners have deputy commissioners under them.

The rest of the organizational chart depends upon the size of the city. In large cities, deputy inspectors are put in charge of various divisions or bureaus—homicide, detective, robbery, juvenile, rape, arson, traffic. The larger the city, the more bureaus. As the patterns of criminal activity change, organizational changes are made. These changes make good stories.

The next in command in large cities are captains, who are assigned to run precincts and are assisted by lieutenants. Sergeants are placed in charge of shifts or squads at the precinct house. The private in the organization is the police officer.

The beat reporter's day-to-day contacts are for the most part with sergeants and lieutenants. Reporters, trained to be suspicious of authority, are sometimes irritated by the paramilitary structure, secretiveness and implicit authoritarianism of the police department.

Diana K. Sugg, a police reporter for *The Sacramento Bee,* circulation 250,000, is blunt: "In most cities around the country, big or small, the cops don't like reporters." Often the reporter and the police work at cross purposes. "We want the information they can't or won't release."

The Police Reporter

As these incidents and these data indicate, crime is a looming presence in our lives. What we know about it is the result of the work of reporters assigned to the police beat.

Some of these reporters are new to journalism and are assigned to cover the police as a way of introducing young journalists quickly to the community. Covering the police gives the reporter a sense of the city's geography and its demographics, its places and its people. As editors know, it helps toughen those fresh from campus life.

Let's accompany Sugg as she works her beat.

Making Her Rounds

It's 9 a.m. and Sugg is in the police station with her portable police scanner, pager, map and notepad. Some days she takes the sheriff's office first and then the police station.

She flips through the watch summaries of the significant events of the previous day and night. With her scanner buzzing in the background, she carefully reads every page, every notation. "I'm looking for anything strange, anything particularly cruel.

"Once a woman managed to catch a rapist by running into her bathroom with a portable telephone and calling 911. Another time a man tied up three children and then raped their mother in front of them. Or you may find material for a short feature story—like the man named the 'inept robber' by the police because he made four robbery attempts at markets—and made off with only one beer."

Diana K. Sugg

She also reads the arrest reports, sometimes as many as 200 a day. For the detailed reports and the watch summaries, her eyes go automatically to the name, age and, she says, "particularly the occupation. A 45-year-old unemployed man arrested for theft isn't much of a story. But a 45-year-old teacher? Why would he need to steal? When you contact him, will he tell you the arrest was a mistake?"

She looks at the section marked "Comments" at the bottom of the arrest sheets for unusual circumstances the officers may note. "Once a man threw a rock through a window and waited for the police to come because he wanted to be arrested—he was homeless and he had AIDS. He figured the jail officers would at least take care of him."

Consulting the Penal Code   Sugg occasionally consults a small handbook, the penal code, as crimes sometimes are listed only by the code number. "That's done to keep reporters from noticing certain arrests," she says.

She makes a point of looking in on the sergeant in charge that day. "Even if things are slow and I don't have anything to ask the sergeant, I always make a point to talk with him, sometimes sharing the hard parts of my job so he could understand why some stories were shorter, or why we weren't interested in covering some.

"During all this checking, the scanner is babbling and my pager is ringing as I am talking with a secretary. It can get nerve-wracking, because I am afraid I might miss something." Her ear is tuned to the code numbers for kidnappings, shootings, homicides, and she knows the police codes, too, those they use when they report they are going to eat, taking a bathroom break or going off duty.

To the Newsroom   Her morning checks completed, Sugg drives to the newsroom with a couple of items to run by her editor to see whether they are worth pursuing. She has to return a phone call to someone who read one of her stories and had something to add to it.

It's noon and she takes a break, her second Mounds bar, a diet Coke, maybe a giant chocolate chip cookie. The *Bee* is a morning paper, and Sugg has the afternoon to continue to gather information, to look deeper into some items, to call people on continuing stories.

Then she's off in the paper's Ford Bronco with her pager, scanner, portable radio, map and notebook. On the way to the scene, she's listening to officers talk to their supervisors. She moves fast. One day while working the night police shift—the newspaper covers the beat 'round the clock—she heard on her scanner a report of a shooting. She was off. On the way to the crime scene she heard officers report that one shooting was fatal, and then a second . . . and then a third. "Within half an hour I was dictating the story of a triple shooting over the portable radio," Sugg says. She made the deadline.

On the Scene   "Neighbors are incredible sources," Sugg says. "Especially if you find the one busybody who watches the street like a hawk and knows everything about the neighbors. People like this know where someone works, the hours he or she keeps, the age of his children, when he was divorced. All this information has to be checked out, but it's a starting point."

Many crimes do not have eyewitnesses, but Sugg looks for the neighbor who heard a shot, a scream. "Once I interviewed a 7-year-old boy who watched a shooting through his apartment window."

She always tries to interview the victims. "Often, when they discover your sincerity they open up and give you unbelievable details." She makes sure to absorb the scene—the ambulance door slamming shut, the smell of the burned house, the cold fog over the scene of the triple shooting.

Smaller-City Coverage

The Sacramento area, like many fast-growing regions, has more than its share of crime, and so crime receives considerable coverage. But even in smaller cities, crime is thoroughly covered. Although these newspapers and stations may not have a regular reporter covering the environment or business, education or county government, all assign a staffer to cover the police on a daily basis.

The items may include "juveniles throwing snowballs in front of the City Center, hindering pedestrians" and "moose on the highway" (*The Times Argus* in Barre-Montpelier, Vt.) and the kidnapping of a scarecrow "value $15" (*The Quincy Herald-Whig* in western Illinois). In larger cities they will include the following items from a daily listing in the *Argus Leader* in Sioux Falls, S.D.:

POLICE LOG

VANDALISM: Vandals spray-painted a pentagon, a pitchfork and assorted other graffiti on the Knights of Columbus hall at 315 N. Summit Ave. on Monday, police said. The graffiti, which was found on the back wall of the hall, caused $50 damage.

VANDALISM: Vandals uprooted a fence post and threw display items such as wooden geese into the Laurel Oaks Pool at 3401 E. 49th St. on Saturday or Sunday, police said. The damage amounted to $100.

VANDALISM: A 57-year-old Sioux Falls man told police someone broke the windshield on his 1970 Ford Galaxy with rocks while it was parked at 1021 W. Bailey Ave. on Saturday, police said. Jerome K. Salwei, 521 S. Ebenezer Ave., said the damage amounted to $250, police said.

VANDALISM: Someone broke the left headlight, removed the hood ornament and scratched and dented the driver's side of a 1984 Cadillac El Dorado, causing $725 damage, on Friday or Saturday, police said. The car's owner, Alvin R. Clausen, 69, 816 W. 15th St., said he wasn't sure where the vandalism occurred.

AGGRAVATED ASSAULT: A 15-year-old boy and his 14-year-old friend told police three boys pulled what resembled a black automatic handgun on them as they rode their bikes on Westview Road from their homes to a convenience store and back Friday, police said. The "handgun" turned out to be a squirt gun.

AGGRAVATED ASSAULT: A 16-year-old Sioux Falls girl told police that her ex-boyfriend slapped and punched her on the back of her head and then struck her with a green garden hose May 31, police said. The girl said the assault occurred at her ex-boyfriend's residence in the 3300 block of South Holly Avenue and was not the first time he had struck her, police said. No arrest was made.

Table 20.2 The Most Dangerous Cities in the United States

Violent Crime Rate		Property Crime Rate	
1. Washington, D.C.	2,024.2	1. Myrtle Beach, S.C.	9,968.8
2. Pine Bluff, Ark.	1,904.5	2. Miami	9,100.5
3. Miami	1,691.8	3. Tuscaloosa, Fla.	8,934.2
4. Springfield, Mass.	1,424.6	4. Monroe, La.	8,234.6
5. Memphis	1,306.2	5. Gainesville, Fla.	7,928.1
6. Gainesville, Fla.	1,211.4	6. Washington, D.C.	7,814.9
7. Tallahassee, Fla.	1,183.1	7. Albuquerque, N.M.	7,787.1
8. Myrtle Beach, S.C.	1,180.6	8. Lakeland-Winter Haven, Fla.	7,739.1
9. Baltimore	1,140.9	9. Baton Rouge, La.	7,659.1
10. Gary-Hammond, Ind.	1,135.8	10. Corpus Christi, Tex.	7,517.1
National Average	**684.4**	**National Average**	**4,640.7**

Rates per 100,000 residents. From *Crime in the United States.*

New on the Beat

Editors like to assign their younger reporters to the police beat in the belief there is no faster way to test a reporter's ability and to teach him or her about the city. The new police reporter immediately becomes acquainted with the organization of the police department and sets about making contacts with key officers. Survival depends on establishing a routine and developing good sources. Otherwise the police beat can become an impenetrable maze, and the reporter may be given only the information that the department deigns to hand out.

The new police reporter quickly learns the difference between a minor crime, which can be a violation or misdemeanor, and a major crime, a felony. Stealing a scarecrow may violate a city regulation, but stealing $10,000 from the local A&P is a felony as defined in state law. Misdemeanors are punishable by less than a year in jail and/or a fine, whereas felonies send the convicted perpetrator to the state prison, or a federal prison, for more than a year.

Types of Felonies

There are seven types of felonies, which fall into two general categories, not including the so-called possessory felonies involving weapons and drugs.

- **Violent crime:** murder, rape, robbery, aggravated assault.
- **Property crime:** burglary, larceny-theft, motor-vehicle theft.

The FBI keeps crime data in these categories, as do local police. Ten percent of all felonies are violent and 90 percent are crimes against property.

Sources Are Essential

Police reporters depend on inside sources. Without them—given the guarded nature of the police—the reporter has a hard time covering the beat. This is why big-city media keep at least one reporter on the police beat for years. It takes time to cultivate the police.

With the Police: Drugs, Teens, Death

Randy Piland, *The Macon* (Ga.) *Telegraph*

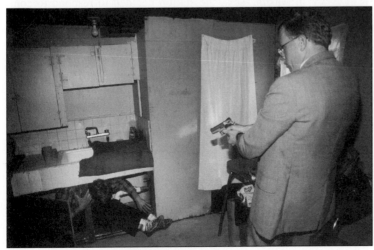

Other photos: Rodger Mallison,
Fort Worth Star-Telegram

Edna Buchanan of *The Miami Herald* is a veteran of the beat. "I talk to cops a lot," she says. "Talking to cops is the only way to get a lot of the stories I do. Of course, a lot of policemen don't recognize a good story, so you just have to keep talking to them so it'll come up in conversation."

Many police departments have gone to computerized reports which, Buchanan says, require that the officers only fill in blanks. The old reports, handwritten by arresting officers, had color and the officers' comments. What this means, Buchanan says, is that reporters have to go to "hands-on, person-to-person human contacts." She recalls learning about a robbery where "a guy got robbed and knocked down. No big deal." But she learned from a contact that the victim had artificial legs and was pushed off his legs "for something like a dollar and forty cents."

Crime Coverage Changes

"If it bleeds, it leads" is an old newsroom guide to handling crime stories. But in recent years the media's hot pursuit of tabloid crime has resulted in reassessments of crime coverage. Instead of concentrating on headline-type crimes, the suggestions center on examining crime prevention policies and the effectiveness of the criminal justice system.

David Simon, crime reporter for *The Baltimore Sun,* wants crime reporting to cover substantive issues—the effectiveness of drug legislation, the crime bills introduced in Congress and state legislatures, the effect of crime in the minority community.

Simon was critical of the media for making crime reporting an entry-level beat. "Once you get good at it you're promoted to something more dignified." The result: "You never learn anything particularly useful about crime because by the time anybody's mastered the beat, they're gone."

One Station's Response

At KVUE-TV in Austin, Tex., the station decided to respond to complaints of viewers about crime coverage. Viewers told management they were tired of "seeing violent crimes that didn't affect them." Michelle Kemkes, a news producer at the station, said viewers called such coverage "sensation crime reporting." They asked for "responsible and balanced reporting," she said.

Guidelines   The station responded by setting up the following guidelines. "If we can't answer yes to one of these questions, we don't report the story," she said:

1. Is there an immediate threat to the public?
2. Is there a threat to children?
3. Does someone need to take action?
4. Does the crime have a significant impact on the community?
5. Is there a crime prevention element?

Kemkes said that the approach differed from what she was taught in journalism school about covering crime. "We didn't learn to put our stories in perspective, but that's what everyone in the newsroom is learning now."

Application   She describes a crime story the station covered:

A husband shoots his wife, child and then himself at the University of Texas. We send a crew, and they call back with all the facts. We go through the guidelines and none of them seem to fit. The suspect is dead, so there's no threat to children or the public. Viewers don't need to take any kind of action, and it's definitely not about crime prevention. We try "significant community impact." None of the neighbors knew the family because they had just moved into their apartment. So, on the 5:30 p.m. news we didn't report the story. Other stations led with the story, which made me think twice about what I'd done.

Then our crew dug deeper. That night the apartment complex held a community meeting to talk about what happened and if they could have stopped it. Obviously this crime did have an impact on the neighbors, and that was the story we went with at 10.

Another story that generated heated discussion in the newsroom—the man who opened fire on a schoolyard of kindergartners in Scotland, killing 17 and then killing himself. How could I not run this heartbreaking story? Once again we applied the guidelines. I found out that this was a huge crime for Great Britain: only one percent of their crimes are committed with guns, compared with the U.S., in which about 32 percent of crimes involve guns. This was the bigger story.

The Arrest Process

The police reporter knows arrest procedures, and because on some smaller newspapers and on many radio and television stations the same reporter who covers an arrest might stay with the case through the trial, a knowledge of the criminal court process is necessary, too. Here, we will discuss the arrest process. In the next chapter, criminal court procedures are outlined.

A person may be arrested on sight or upon issuance of a warrant. Let us follow a case in which a merchant spots in his store a man he believes robbed him the previous week.

The store owner calls a police officer who arrests the man. The suspect is searched on the scene and taken to the station house. The suspect is then searched again in front of the booking desk. His property is recorded and placed in a "property" envelope. The suspect's name and other identification and the alleged crime are recorded in a book known to old-time reporters as a *blotter*. (The blotter supposedly takes its name from the work of turn-of-the-century police sergeants who spilled considerable ink in their laborious efforts to transcribe information and then had to sop up the splotches with a blotter.)

Miranda Warning   The police are required to tell a suspect at the time of arrest that he has the right to remain silent and to refuse to answer questions. (This is called the Miranda warning.) He also has the right to consult an attorney at any time and is told that if he cannot afford a lawyer one will be provided.

> **Jails, Prisons.** Jails are locally administered and hold persons who are awaiting trial or sentence or are serving sentences of a year or less. Prisons, state and federal, hold inmates with sentences of more than a year.

The Arrest Process

The police reporter covers all aspects of the arrest process, from the report of the arrest through the arraignment of the suspect. Most arrests receive bare mention, but the high-profile crimes are covered fully. Reporters rely for information on the police, the district attorney and the suspect's lawyer. The reporter is aware that the original charge often is reduced by the prosecutor because either the original charge cannot be sustained or the prosecutor believes the suspect is more likely to plead guilty to a lessened charge than he or she would to the original charge.

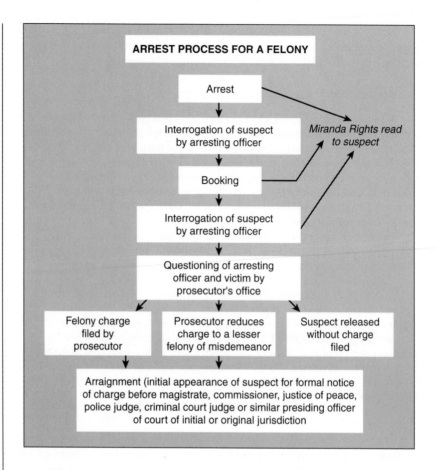

ARREST PROCESS FOR A FELONY

Arrest

Interrogation of suspect by arresting officer

Booking

Interrogation of suspect by arresting officer

Questioning of arresting officer and victim by prosecutor's office

Miranda Rights read to suspect

Felony charge filed by prosecutor

Prosecutor reduces charge to a lesser felony of misdemeanor

Suspect released without charge filed

Arraignment (initial appearance of suspect for formal notice of charge before magistrate, commissioner, justice of peace, police judge, criminal court judge or similar presiding officer of court of initial or original jurisdiction)

Unless the suspect waives these rights, his statements cannot be used against him at his trial.

The signed waiver permits the police immediately to interrogate the suspect about his actions, background and whereabouts in connection with the crime. If it is a homicide case, the practice is to call in an assistant prosecutor to ensure the admissibility of any admission or confession.

The officer then prepares an arrest report, which is written in the presence of the suspect who also supplies "pedigree information"—age, height, weight, date and place of birth and other details.

The Complaint   The suspect may then be photographed and fingerprinted and he'll be permitted to make a telephone call. A record is made of the number and person called and the suspect is returned to a detention cell to await arraignment. The arresting officer goes to the complaint room to confer with the victim and an assistant district attorney so that a complaint can be drawn up. The police officer may ask the complainant to identify the suspect again in a lineup.

The assistant district attorney has to decide whether the case is strong enough, the witness reliable, the offense worth prosecuting before a complaint is drawn. The prosecutor must also decide whether to reduce a felony charge to a lesser felony or to a misdemeanor. She may reduce the charge if she feels the reduction would lead to a guilty plea.

The police officer may have to file additional reports. If he fired his weapon, he must file an "unusual incident report," as it is described in some jurisdictions, and if he shot someone, he files an "inspector's report."

The fingerprints are checked in a central state agency to determine whether the suspect has a record, and the suspect's file is sent to the courts, which require the information before arraignment. The presiding judge decides whether bail should be set and the amount. A suspect with no record who is arrested for a minor crime may be released on his own recognizance—that is, without putting up bail.

Most large cities have overcrowded detention facilities and a backlog of untried cases. To cope, they may release suspects on low bail or none at all. Later, plea bargaining may be arranged in which the defendant agrees to plead guilty to a lesser charge so that the case can be disposed of at arraignment (see Chapter 21).

Elvis' Autopsy. The official report said Elvis Presley died of "Hypertensive Heart Disease with Coronary Artery Heart Disease as a contributing factor." And that's what the obituaries said on his death. But investigative reporters heard stories about Presley's reliance on prescription drugs in his later years, and they found a secret autopsy report that attributed death to "multiple drug ingestion." His private physician was prescribing "immense quantities of drugs to Elvis," the reporters wrote, including codeine, quaaludes, Placidyl, Valium and Valmid.

Arrest Stories

Most crimes are committed by young men, and a growing number involve teen-agers. Juveniles who are arrested are turned over to the juvenile court and their names are not released. In some states, in response to the rise in violent crime by youngsters, serious offenses by youths, particularly murder, are handled by the regular court system and their names can be used, as an upstate New York newspaper did in the following crime.

Murder   The battered body of a 77-year-old man was discovered in his home at 11 p.m. by a neighbor who called the police. The neighbor said she saw two youths running from the scene. Police conducted an investigation and within five hours arrested a 16-year-old and a 14-year-old. The two were charged with second-degree murder and at their arraignment entered pleas of not guilty.

The reporter for the local afternoon newspaper learns all this on his 7 a.m. check. He calls the coroner to obtain information about the cause of death, and he questions the police about the murder weapon and the motivation. He also asks where the youths are being held and the time they were arrested. With the information on hand, he calls his desk to report what he has and the city editor tells him to give the story 200 words. The dead man was not prominent.

The editor asks about the neighbor: Did she identify the youngsters, and if not, how did the police learn their identities? The reporter says the police will not comment about the neighbor. Nor will the neighbor talk. The story will have to be a straight murder-and-arrest piece. Here is how the reporter wrote it:

Two Saratoga youths were arrested early today and charged with the murder of 77-year-old Anthony Hay, a local fuel oil and coal dealer, whose battered body was found last night in his home.

Police identified the youths as Arthur Traynor, 16, of 61 Joshua Ave., and John Martinez, 14, of 15 Doten Ave. Police said a neighbor saw two youths fleeing from Hay's residence at 342 Nelson Ave. The

Not Me, Officer

Photographer O. Gordon Williamson Jr. of *The Orlando Sentinel* chanced to see a bearded man make a getaway from a bank he had just robbed. Williamson followed the man to a barber shop, and while the identifying beard was being removed, Williamson called the police . . . and then took this picture.

arrests were made within five hours of the slaying.

The youths entered pleas of not guilty at their arraignment this morning on charges of second-degree murder and were being held in the county jail pending a preliminary hearing.

Hay's body was found at 11 p.m. in the business office of his home. He was "badly beaten about the head and face and had a fractured skull," Coroner Clark Donaldson reported. Police said they recovered the death weapon, a three-foot wooden club. They declined to give any motive for the slaying.

Caution: Be careful about identifying the arrested. A libel suit resulted when a newspaper identified a crime suspect who had stolen a wallet from which police took the name. "Use special care in reporting the arrest of a public figure," advises the AP. "It is not uncommon for crime suspects to give police false names, and frequently those they provide are from sports figures, politicians, etc." Press authorities for authentication of the identification.

Be especially careful about identifying anyone as a suspect before the person has been formally charged. This had been common practice until a suspect in a bombing at the 1996 summer Olympics in Atlanta won large awards against the media that used his name in their accounts. *The Atlanta Journal-Constitution* reported the man had become a suspect and NBC and CNN picked up the story. Three months later, he was cleared. Rather than have to fight a libel suit, the networks settled out of court for large sums, but the newspaper claimed it accurately quoted authorities.

In Dallas, a woman who named two football players on the Dallas Cowboys team as having raped her was later charged with perjury. But the police department had released the names of the players to the media and they were the subject of massive coverage. The police later announced a policy of not identifying suspects until they are arrested or charged.

Next, let's look at a high-profile arrest story that was in the headlines and on network television for some time. It begins with the discovery of two bodies.

O. J. Simpson

After the bodies of O. J. Simpson's ex-wife and her friend were discovered, police went about the investigation without releasing much information. Police sources told the *Los Angeles Times* the name of their suspect and the newspaper decided to use the information:

> Mounting evidence links former football star O. J. Simpson to the brutal slayings of his former wife and a man she knew, and the famous athlete could be arrested within days, Los Angeles police sources said Tuesday.

Blood Samples   As the murder investigation continued, more tips found their way into the *Times:*

> The blood type of samples recovered at the scene of a brutal double slaying matches that of O. J. Simpson's blood, a potentially important piece of evidence in the investigation of the killings of his exwife and a man she knew, Los Angeles police sources said Wednesday.

Manhunt   The police issued a warrant for Simpson's arrest and a manhunt was on:

> O. J. Simpson, the football great who rose from the mean streets of San Francisco to international celebrity, became the subject of a massive police manhunt Friday, after a warrant was issued for his arrest in connection with the murders of his ex-wife and a male friend.

Arrest   And then the arrest:

> O. J. Simpson was arrested Friday for the murders of his ex-wife and a male friend after leading police on a gripping, two-hour chase through the rush-hour freeways of Southern California.

In Jail   The police reporter stays with the story as the suspect is jailed and writes:

> A day after being captured outside his 5,700-square-foot Brentwood estate, football legend O. J. Simpson spent Saturday

under suicide watch in a 7-by-9 foot jail
cell, where he is being held without bail as
prosecutors prepare to seek murder indictments from the county grand jury.

Notice the wordplay on the size of Simpson's accommodations.

Once the grand jury issued the indictment, Simpson was arraigned and the story went to the court reporters. We will pick up the Simpson saga in the next chapter where we cover the courts. Here, we will move on to reporting specific crimes.

Murder

In some areas, murder is rare—Vermont may have two homicides a year. When one is reported, coverage is intense. In metropolitan areas, where one to four murders are reported each day, only the prominence of the victim or the suspect merit full-scale coverage. There are exceptions, of course, such as the senseless shooting of the young man in a holdup that we described a few pages back.

Prominence clearly was the news value that motivated the minute cover-age of the death of O. J. Simpson's ex-wife—not hers, of course, but his. Look at how the AP wrote the first lead on the discovery of the bodies:

LOS ANGELES, (AP) — Hall of Fame football player O. J. Simpson's ex-wife and
a man were found dead early Monday outside the woman's condominium, and
Simpson was being interviewed by police.

This began what some critics described as a "media circus" or a "media feeding frenzy." Journalists countered by pointing to the near-insatiable public appetite for the story.

Table 20.3 Murder and Nonnegligent Manslaughter Rates

Metropolitan Areas		States	
1. Washington, D.C.	56.9	1. Louisiana	15.7
2. New Orleans	25.1	2. Mississippi	13.1
3. Pine Bluff, Ark.	23.1	3. Nevada	11.2
4. Richmond, Va.	20.1	4. Alabama	9.9
5. Jackson, Miss.	18.7	5. Arkansas	9.9
6. Gary-Hammond, Ind.	17.9	6. Maryland	9.9
7. Memphis	15.9	7. Tennessee	9.5
8. Mobile, Ala.	15.1	8. Illinois	9.2
9. Miami	14.7	9. Alaska	8.9
10. Little Rock, Ark.	14.1	10. South Carolina	8.4
National Average	**7.4**	**National Average**	**6.8**

Rates per 100,000 residents. From *Crime in the United States.*

Checklist: Homicide

Crime

— Victim, identification.

— Time, date, place of death.

— Weapon used.

— Official cause of death or authoritative comment.

— Who discovered body.

— Clues; any identification of slayer.

— Police comments; motivation for crime.

— Comments from neighbors, friends.

— Any police record for victim; any connection with criminal activity.

— Consequences to victim's family, others.

Arrest

— Name, identification of person arrested.

— Victim's name; time, date, place of crime.

— Exact charge.

— Circumstances of arrest.

— Motive.

— Result of tip, investigation.

— Officers involved in investigation, arrest.

— Booking.

— Arraignment; bail, if any.

— Suspect's police record (in states where it is not illegal to publish such information).

Mug Shot

After a suspect is arrested, booked and interrogated, he or she is photographed. The pictures, called *mug shots,* go into the suspect's file, which also contains his or her criminal record, known as a *rap sheet.* This is a photo of Joseph (Crazy Joe) Gallo, whose rap sheet showed an extensive record. Gallo was gunned down by rival mob hit men as he celebrated his 43d birthday in Umberto's Clam House a block away from New York City police headquarters.

Burglary, Robbery

Burglary (B) is a crime against property, usually involving a home, office, or store break-in. Robbery (R) is a crime against a person, involving the removal of the person's goods or money with force or threat of force and is categorized as a violent crime.

Checklist: Burglary, Robbery

Crime

— Victim, identification.

— Goods or money taken; value of goods.

— Date, time, location of crime.

— (R) Weapon used.

— (B) How entry made.

— (R) Injuries and how caused.

— Clues.

— Unusual circumstances (overlooked valuables, frequency of crime in area or to victim, etc.).

— Statements from victim, witness.

Arrest

— Name, identification of person arrested.

— Details of crime.

— Circumstances of arrest.

Additional Elements   Some newspapers and stations have added these essentials to their stories about violent crime:

— Where was the weapon obtained?

— Were alcohol or drugs involved?

— Did the victim and the perpetrator know each other?

Note: Half or more of those arrested are not formally charged with the crime for which they were arrested. The names of those arrested but not charged can be used without worrying about legal action. The question is one of fairness.

Targeting Blacks

Her story began with a hunch, says Carolyn Tuft. For years, Tuft says, blacks had been going to the *Belleville* (Ill.) *News-Democrat* newsroom to complain that they had been abused by local police and wrongly arrested. "We noticed lots of blacks were being pulled over in west Belleville, taken out of their cars and handcuffed for what appeared to be routine traffic stops."

Tuft thought there was a pattern to what seemed to be harassment of black motorists in the small city of 42,000 near St. Louis. Belleville's west end is affluent and white. Its neighbor, East St. Louis, is poor and 98 percent black.

The year before, Tuft had written a series of stories about conflict of interest by the Belleville police chief and low morale in the department. Officers liked Tuft's reporting, and one of them provided the tip that cemented Tuft's hunch that the police department was engaged in an attempt to keep blacks out of Belleville.

Carolyn Tuft

Special Unit

A former officer said that the department had set up a special unit to discourage blacks from driving into west Belleville by ticketing them whenever possible.

"I then met several officers at odd hours of the night in dark bars to get the inside story on the unit," Tuft says. "Everyone backed up the account. But they worried about a story. One officer met me in a greasy spoon and tried to convince me that this story could begin a race riot in the town."

Tuft's major problem was that there was nothing in writing about the unit, no physical evidence of what it had been doing, nothing to prove what she had been told: A unit of four officers—the blue team—had been set up with the express purpose of harassing black motorists.

Seeking Documentation

"I was determined to get the story, and determined is what you have to be," Tuft says. She knew that the proof would be in the traffic tickets. And that is where she looked.

"I spent three months in a stuffy old parking garage storage room sorting through dusty, musty old traffic tickets in banana boxes almost too heavy for me to pick up. They weighed 50 pounds each, and I weigh about 100."

Tuft looked through more than 175,000 tickets. And she interviewed many of those who were ticketed for their personal experiences. She organized her ledger entries by computer.

Finally, she was ready to write. When she finished, the story went to her city editor, Gary Dotson, who had encouraged her despite the possibility of a strong reader reaction. Then it went to the newspaper's attorneys for a libel check. Here is how the first piece begins:

Blacks receive a disproportionately higher percentage of traffic tickets in west Belleville than elsewhere in the city, an investigation by the Belleville News-Democrat shows, and former and current officers say police operated a special unit to target blacks.

The four-month investigation into 18,681 traffic tickets written by Belleville police for two years found that blacks received 42 percent of the tickets issued in west Belleville, compared with 8 percent in the rest of the city.

And a separate survey of 390 traffic tickets written this year shows the trend continues, with blacks six times more likely to be ticketed in west Belleville than in other parts of the city.

Police Chief Robert Hurst formed the special patrol shortly after he became chief in 1985, and it operated . . .

The Reaction   Readers and advertisers reacted, most with anger at Tuft and the *News-Democrat*. A dozen businesses pulled their advertising, and almost 1,200 readers canceled subscriptions.

"I received about 300 angry calls, many telling me and the newspaper to leave town," Tuft says. Some callers accused her of sleeping with a black man, and most of the those furious with the newspaper for the stories used the word *nigger* in their calls.

"I received at least half a dozen death threats. One hoped I'd be raped by a 'group of AIDS-infected wilding niggers.' "

One of Tuft's stories disclosed the city's hiring practices: Not one of the city's 384 employees was black, and in the city's 175-year history it had never hired a black, although the city has a 7 percent black population.

This revelation, she says, "caused the most hatred against me."

The Results   After her series, the city hired a black sanitation worker and a black fireman and initiated an affirmative action program to hire minorities and to promote women in a manner that reflects the makeup of Belleville. Programs were set up to educate the public in racial and ethnic diversity.

Tuft's work was recognized. She won 13 local, regional and national awards, and her stories were used on the television program "60 Minutes." The *St. Louis Post-Dispatch* offered her a job, which she accepted.

Tuft would have been spared her arduous examination of tickets had the department put its records into a computer system. Most agencies do that, making it easier for reporters to analyze data and to make correlations.

Database Reporting

It's not difficult, for example, to take the list that the state provides of the names of all school bus drivers and compare it with court and prison databases. Reporters regularly do this to see whether child molesters, drunk drivers or frequent offenders are driving children to and from school.

Drunk Drivers   You know drunk drivers are involved in traffic accidents. But how many of them are responsible for highway fatalities in your state? Easy. Ask the U.S. Department of Transportation, www.dot.gov, for the percentage of fatalities in the state in accidents involving alcohol. The DOT's National Highway Traffic Safety Administration keeps the data.

You'll find Texas, Louisiana, Alaska, North Dakota, Nevada, New Mexico and Washington are high in the rankings, usually with more than half the fatal accidents involving drivers with a blood alcohol content of .10 or higher.

And that takes you to another story. If many fatal traffic accidents involve drunk drivers, perhaps the state should clamp down on those drivers. Some states have lowered the acceptable blood alcohol content from .10 to .08 and have increased the penalties. What is your state doing? You can find out by using another website, www.hwysafety.org, the Insurance Institute for Highway Safety.

Police Efficiency

Police reporters use databases to check on the effectiveness of their police forces. The questions: How many reported crimes are solved, especially felonies? Are low-level property crimes such as burglaries and auto theft investigated or in effect decriminalized?

What percentage of the arrests result in a complaint? Prosecutors will not take a case to court unless they have sufficient evidence and good witness support, which is the work of the police. In some cities, prosecutors drop as many as half the cases because of inadequate police work.

Another question: Which police officers are the most efficient? In Washington, D.C., a tenth of the force accounted for half the convictions. Some officers reveal a special skill in finding witnesses, obtaining evidence and making arrests that will stand up in court.

A follow-through question: How are officers on the force evaluated for promotion? Does their arrest and conviction rate figure in the decision making?

Another check of departmental efficiency can be made by examining the response to calls made to the police. A study of 2,000 calls to the St. Louis Police Department found that 25 percent of the calls were ignored. Of the 75 percent to which the police responded, arrests were made 50 percent of the time. Ten percent of those arrested went to trial, and 4 percent of those arrested were convicted.

Data Available

Along with their monitoring of individual crimes, police reporters keep track of crime patterns. Are certain types of crimes increasing, others decreasing? How does the city's crime rate compare with cities of the same size? Is there a relationship between drug and alcohol use and crime?

Data of this sort is available from several sources. The National Criminal Justice Reference Service e-mail: askncjrs@ncjrs.org, fields questions of all kinds. Its files contain extensive information on criminal justice.

The FBI issues an annual report, Crime in the United States, Uniform Crime Reports, www.fbi.gov/ucr.CIUS/99CRIME/99CRIME2.PDF. (Insert the year for which you want the data.) The material includes total number of crimes and crime rates by state and city.

The Bureau of Justice Statistics makes available free copies of its reports that cover a wide range: national crime surveys, domestic violence, parole and probation, ages of rape victims, sentencing patterns, juvenile crime.

To be placed on the Bureau's mailing list, call toll-free 1-800-732-3277 or write: Justice Statistics Clearinghouse, P.O. Box 179, Dept. BJS-236, Annapolis Junction, MD 20701-0179. The website is www.ojp.usdoj.gov/bjs/.

Single copies are free. Public-use tapes of Bureau data sets are available from the Criminal Justice Archive and Information Network, P.O. Box 1248, Ann Arbor, MI 48106, telephone (313) 763-5010.

The Bureau also makes crime and justice data and a wide range of its publications available on CD-ROM, which can be purchased for $15 a CD. Order through the Maryland address.

Solved

The U.S. Department of Justice released these figures:

Crime	Cleared by Arrest
Murder	72%
Aggravated assault	58
Forcible rape	48
Robbery	24
Larceny-theft	19
Burglary	14
Motor vehicle theft	14

Prison Data

The highest incarceration rates:

Texas	717
Louisiana	672
Oklahoma	617
South Carolina	536
Mississippi	531
Nevada	518

Largest prison population:

California	153,000
Texas	137,000
New York	70,000
Florida	65,000
Ohio	47,000

Demographics:

White	35.7 percent
Black	44.2 percent
Hispanic	17.6 percent

Of every 100,000 population, those in prison:

White	370
Black	3,096
Hispanic	1,276

Departmental Integrity

Because of highly publicized inquiries into endemic police corruption in such cities as Albany, Boston, New York, Indianapolis and Miami, police reporters know that their editors and their readers expect them to dig into departmental integrity.

A reporter may be required to learn a new vocabulary to understand the underworld of deals, bribes and corruption. Some police officers have an "organized pad," by which they mean a secret list of underworld figures who pay them for protection. Most often, a pad contains the names of drug dealers and suppliers, vice operators and gambling operators.

The "grass eaters" are police officers who take small gratuities in connection with minor infractions, such as traffic violations, or who coerce merchants into giving them gifts and free meals. The "meat eaters" are the corrupt police who take payoffs to release suspects or who deal in drugs or perjure themselves on the witness stand.

Let's pause for a bit and look at those affected by crime, the victims.

The Victims

Crime falls heaviest on the poor, the young and members of minority groups. Half the victims of violent crimes are aged 12 to 24 although they represent only a fourth of the population. Blacks and Hispanics across all age groups are more at risk from violence than whites of comparable age: 1 in 30 blacks, 1 in 35 Hispanics, 1 in 58 whites.

Murder rates for blacks are 8 times higher than that for whites—1 in every 894 blacks, 1 in every 7,334 whites. The lifetime chance of being a murder victim is 1 in 131 for white males, 1 in 21 for black males. Blacks and Hispanics have robbery rates twice those for whites.

Reporters have studied victimization rates in their communities. In St. Louis, they found 1 in 13 black males will be murdered by age 45. In Philadelphia, the *Daily News* examined 433 murders committed in one year and found 340 of the victims were black. The city's black population amounted to 39 percent of the total population but 78.5 percent of the murder victims were black. Half the victims were 16 to 31, and 84 of the 89 victims under 20 years of age were black.

The *News* found the murder rate in a white working-class neighborhood was 2, but in the predominantly poor, black north Philadelphia area it was 66. In the heart of the black area known as the Badlands the rate was more than 100 per 100,000 residents.

Two-thirds of murder victims are killed by firearms, most by handguns.

Violence against Women

About 2.5 million women are the victims of violent crime each year. The most frequent crime committed against them is assault, often domestic assault. Studies by the Bureau of Justice found that the women "most vulnerable as the victims of violence are black, Hispanic, in younger age groups, never married, with lower family income and lower education levels and in central cities."

More than two-thirds of the women victims knew their attackers. Almost one-third of the attackers were husbands, boyfriends, or relatives; a third were acquaintances. Women victimized by strangers were six times more likely to report their attack to police as were those women attacked by relatives or friends. These women said they feared reprisals from their attackers.

Although the violent crime victimization rate for males has declined, the rate for females has not.

"In general," states the Bureau, "violent crime against women was primarily intra-racial. Eight of 10 violent crimes against white women were perpetrated by white offenders. Similarly, nine of 10 violent victimizations sustained by black women were committed by black offenders."

Rape

More than 140,000 rapes are reported a year. Nine of 10 rape victims are women, but only about half the women report their victimizations to the police. The Bureau of Justice found about half of all rapes were perpetrated by someone known to the victim and that, in one-fifth of the cases, the offender was armed.

"Of female rape victims who took some self-protective action such as fighting back and yelling and screaming, most reported that it helped the situation rather than made it worse," the Bureau reported.

The Bureau estimates that one in six rape victims is under the age of 12. Of the 14 states that reported the age of the victim, Florida reported a total of 7,280 rapes, 14 percent of them of girls under age 11; Michigan, 4,731 rapes, 28 percent under age 11; Pennsylvania, 2,996 rapes, 14 percent under age 13; North Carolina, 2,397 rapes, 20 percent under age 16; South Carolina, 2,193 rapes, 16 percent under age 13. (States reported differently on age data.)

Of the states reporting, one in three rape victims was under age 13 in Delaware, Michigan and North Dakota; under 16 in Nebraska, Pennsylvania and Wisconsin; under 17 in Alabama; under 18 in Idaho and Washington, D.C.

Arrests. The states with the highest rates of arrests for rape were Delaware, Michigan, Alaska, Missouri and Mississippi.

The states with the highest arrest rates for offenses against the family and children were Ohio, New Jersey, New Mexico, Hawaii and Mississippi.

Table 20.4 Forcible Rape Rate

Metropolitan Areas		States	
1. Memphis	107.4	1. Alaska	66.2
2. Pine Bluff, Ark.	100.7	2. Delaware	65.0
3. Gainesville, Fla.	87.3	3. Nevada	58.9
4. Beaumont, Tex.	86.0	4. Tennessee	56.9
5. Rapid City, S.D.	85.8	5. Minnesota	52.2
6. Bremerton, Wash.	80.8	6. Florida	51.9
7. Dover, Del.	80.6	7. Michigan	51.9
8. Jacksonville, Fla.	76.4	8. New Mexico	50.4
9. Bryan-College Station, Tex.	76.1	9. South Carolina	48.9
10. Tallahassee, Fla.	72.5	10. South Dakota	48.4
National Average	**37.6**	**National Average**	**36.8**

Rates per 100,000 residents. From *Crime in the United States.*

Behind Closed Doors

Domestic abuse is the silent plague of American households. Half the occurrences are not reported to police, and journalists rarely cover the crime. Yet it affects about a quarter of households and is the single greatest cause of injury to women.

Donna Ferrato,
Domestic Abuse Awareness Project

Child Abuse. The Justice Department reported child abuse and neglect reports tripled over the past decade, rising from one million to three million. The department said studies link the victims of child abuse and neglect to future delinquency and adult criminality.

Idaho, Alaska and Washington have the highest rates of physical and sexual child abuse.

Domestic Violence

The home, figures tell us, is more dangerous for women than the streets. Domestic violence is the single greatest cause of injury to American women. The American Medical Association considers family violence a public health menace and estimates it affects one-fourth of all families in the United States. The AMA reports domestic violence is responsible for a third of all murders of women.

Yet, coverage of the subject is minimal, lost in the reporting of murders, gang wars and drug busts. Also, the actual dimension of the crime is not reflected in the police reports. Close to half of all incidents of domestic violence against women are not reported to police. Of married women not reporting their husbands, 41 percent were subsequently assaulted by them within six months. Of those who did report their husbands, 15 percent were reassaulted.

A Reporter's Perspective

Edna Buchanan, the prizewinning police reporter for *The Miami Herald,* says:

Sometimes, we are all the victim has got.

Sometimes you feel like Wonder Woman, or Superman, going to the rescue. Reporters can find missing kids, lost grandmothers, and misplaced corpses. We fish out people who fall through the cracks. Publicity rescues people tangled in the hopeless mazes of government and bureaucracy. We recover stolen cars and priceless family heirlooms. A story in the newspaper can secure donations of blood, money, and public support—and occasionally that rarest gift of all: justice.

Cynicism   Police reporters say cynicism comes with the job. Things are seldom what they seem. A heartbroken father tells police a hitchhiker he picked up forced him out of his car at gunpoint and drove off with his 2-year-old daughter in the back seat. A distraught mother reports her 4-year-old daughter and 2-year-old son disappeared in a department store on Christmas Eve. Newspapers and television carry the woman's prayer for the safe return of her children.

Two days after the hitchhiker story is played up by Canadian newspapers and television, the child's body is found in a garbage bin in an Ontario city. The father is charged with second-degree murder; authorities say he left the child in the car on a hot day and she was asphyxiated.

Two days after a mother's tearful prayer on TV, this lead appears on a story in a New York newspaper:

> Two small Queens children whose mother had reported losing them in a crowded Flushing department store on Christmas Eve were found dead in a rubblestrewn lot in East Harlem last night, and the mother and a man with whom she lives were charged with the murders.

Hardened   Reporters say it is difficult not to become calloused by the endless array of tragedy and senseless, vicious crimes. Elinor J. Brecher of *The Courier-Journal* in Louisville, Ky., moved to features after five years on the police beat. She decided to move after she covered the murder of an elderly shopkeeper. The behavior of onlookers bothered her.

"If the senseless death of an innocent human being means no more to people than the fantasy television deaths they gorge on daily, I wanted no further part of it."

Buchanan has covered 5,000 murders, and many affect her: A young father had spent six months at the bedside of his 2-year-old, who had gone into a coma after strangling herself in a recliner chair. He finally could endure no more and shot the child to death as he rocked her in his arms. The man was sent to prison with a mandatory 25-year sentence. Buchanan remains on the beat.

Cautions

Garish details of rapes, homicides, suicides and assaults are considered unnecessary. Details essential to an investigation are not used, although there is no legal prohibition against using information obtained legally. Usually, police will not give reporters confessions, statements, admissions, or alibis by suspects; names of suspects or witnesses; details of sex crimes against women. (Publication of a confession or statement can jeopardize a defendant's rights.)

Double Checks   All names, addresses, occupations should be double-checked against the city directory, telephone book and any other available source.

Contacts Above All. When a *New York Times* reporter was handcuffed and arrested during her coverage of the funeral of rapper Biggie Smalls she was charged with disorderly conduct. But when the *Times* apologized, the charges were dropped. Apologized for what? asked the president of the New York Press Club. For doing her job? The reason may lie in a statement a *Times* lawyer made later: "We have to look beyond the individual incident to the continuum of dealing with the police department. To be antagonistic would not serve us in the long run."

Beware of sudden cleanup drives for vice, gambling. Usually, they are designed for public consumption.

When the police arrest a suspect, reporters ask for his or her arrest record or rap sheet. In many cities and states, the record may be denied or only a portion of it released. Sometimes the refusal is the result of state law. There has been a growing sensitivity among officials concerning the need to guarantee the accused a fair trial. Revelations about past crimes might compromise the defendant's rights.

Using Prior Convictions   Conviction data—information about a guilty plea, a conviction, or a plea of *nolo contendere*—usually can be used. Half the states make it illegal to use nonconviction data. Nonconviction material covers:

- Acquittals and dismissals.
- Information that a matter was not referred for prosecution or that proceedings have been indefinitely postponed.
- Records of arrests unaccompanied by dispositions that are more than a year old and in which no prosecution is actively pending.

State laws that seal arrest records take precedence over sunshine laws. Where there are no explicit prohibitions against the use of such records, it is permissible to use them, whatever the disposition of the arrests. Reporters can use nonconviction information that they find in public documents that are traditionally open to the press: court records of judicial proceedings, police blotters, published court opinions, wanted announcements, traffic records.

Juvenile Records   Juvenile records usually are sealed, and family court rules almost always prohibit press coverage. But there are few state laws that make it illegal to identify a juvenile as a suspect or that prohibit stories about a juvenile's conviction. Generally, the press has gone along with the contention that such publicity could make rehabilitation of the young offender more difficult.

When a 9-year-old boy turned himself in to the FBI as a bank robbery suspect, newspapers and television stations gave the story huge play. The youngster, who took $118 from a teller, held what looked like a pistol.

The newspapers and stations were unhappy about using the story but said they had no recourse. It was "pointless" not to publish a picture of the youngster, said the metropolitan editor of *The New York Times,* that was already "on television all over town."

Remember: An arrest is just that. It does not mean that the person has been charged with a crime. Charges are brought by the district attorney and indictments are made by a grand jury. When a person is arrested, the reporter can write that Jones was "arrested in connection with the robbery of a drugstore at 165 Massachusetts Ave." Or: "Jones was arrested in an investigation of the embezzlement of $45,000 from the First National Bank of Freeport."

The U.S. Department of Justice has found that half the arrests are disposed of prior to indictment.

Meaningless. ". . . the media have done an increasingly poor job of developing a balance between what is interesting and what is important. This is the difference between a crime story and crime coverage, between a story about yet another anecdotal crime and one that identifies the anecdote as either representative of a trend or representative of absolutely nothing."
—David J. Krajicek, (*"Scooped! Media Miss Real Story on Crime While Chasing Sex, Sleaze, and Celebrities,"* Columbia University Press, 1998.)

Covering Campus Crime

Table 20.5 Violent Crimes and Rape on Campus

Violent Crimes		Forcible Rape	
1. Ohio State Univ.	37	1. Univ. Minnesota, Twin Cities	11
2. Florida A&M Univ.	34	2. Northern Arizona Univ.	8
2. Louisiana State Univ., Baton Rouge	34	2. Colorado State Univ.	8
2. Univ. Michigan	34	2. Indiana Univ., Bloomington	8
5. Univ. Calif., Berkeley	33	5. Rutgers Univ., New Brunswick	7
6. Univ. Calif., Los Angeles	32	6. Univ. Massachusetts, Amherst	6
7. University of Florida	29	6. Ohio State Univ.	6
8. Morgan State Univ.	28	6. Utah State Univ.	6
9. Calif. State Univ., Monterey Bay	26	9. Oklahoma State Univ.	5
10. Univ. Maryland, College Park	25	9. Univ. Alabama, Tuscaloosa	5
10. Savannah State College	25		
10. Southern Univ. and A&M College, Baton Rouge	25		

Number of offenses reported to police and campus authorities. From *Crime in the United States.*

College journalists on many campuses have been engaged in a running dispute with campus authorities over the availability of disciplinary records. Crime handled by local police has always been a matter of public record. But criminal matters handled by campus security officers were said to be covered by the Family Educational Rights and Privacy Act—the so-called Buckley Amendment—which defined campus criminal activity as "education records," which are closed to the public.

Congress and the court have tried to unfreeze these records. In 1992, the Crime Awareness and Campus Security Act was passed that requires schools as a condition of participating in the federal loan program to report the number of murders, sex offenses, robberies, aggravated assaults, burglaries and motor vehicle thefts on campus.

But unless the details were available from local law enforcement agencies, they were not released to the public. Students in states with open-meeting laws sought to have the files opened, some successfully, and a few state courts ruled that Congress meant to open disciplinary records.

Key Ruling, Key Act

In 1997, the U.S. Supreme Court let stand a ruling by the Ohio Supreme Court that Miami University could not withhold disciplinary records from the student newspaper *The Miami Student,* which had protested the closure. The Ohio court stated in its ruling, "Crime and other student misconduct are escalating at campuses across the nation." Reporting such incidents is clearly justified, the court stated.

The following year, as part of the Higher Education Act, the law requires that all schools, public and private, that receive federal funds must:

1. Maintain daily logs of criminal incidents reported to their police or security offices. The nature, date, time, location and disposition of each complaint must be added to the log within two business days of the initial report, and any further information learned after the initial report also must be disclosed within two days of its availability. The logs must be available to the public.

Exemptions: Information that would jeopardize ongoing investigations and material that would reveal the identity of victims of sexual assault.

2. Not use the Federal Educational Rights and Privacy Act, also known as the Buckley Amendment, to avoid disclosing the outcome of disciplinary proceedings against students found to have committed a violent crime or non-forcible sex offense.

3. Make annual reports on the crimes of manslaughter and arson. Murder, sex offenses, robbery, aggravated assault, burglary and motor vehicle theft had already been required for annual reports. Statistics are also required from schools for those arrested or referred to campus courts for violations of the laws regarding liquor use and possession, drug and weapon possession.

Colleges and universities must also report crimes that occur near the campus—on property and in buildings owned by the college, at a student organization recognized by the college and on public property adjacent to a facility owned by the college.

Colleges also are required to keep statistics on violent crimes directed against individuals because of their race, gender, religion, ethnicity, sexual orientation or disability.

A college that deliberately misrepresents any crime data is subject to a fine.

Table 20.6 Car Thefts and Property Crimes on Campus

Car Thefts		Property Crimes	
1. Univ. New Mexico	123	1. Ohio State Univ.	1,525
2. Univ. Calif., Los Angeles	104	2. Univ. Michigan	1,518
3. San Diego State Univ.	78	3. Arizona State Univ.	1,383
3. Florida International Univ.	78	4. Univ. Calif., Riverside	1,323
5. Univ. Tennessee, Knoxville	75	5. Univ. Calif., Berkeley	1,179
6. Georgia Inst. Technology	67	6. Univ. Arizona	1,143
7. Univ. Calif., Fresno	52	7. Univ. Florida	1,110
8. San Francisco State Univ.	45	8. Univ. Minnesota	1,072
9. Arizona State Univ.	44	9. Duke Univ.	952
9. Univ. Arizona	44	10. Purdue Univ.	859
9. Univ. Florida	44		

Number of offenses reported to police and campus authorities. From *Crime in the United States.*

Source

The Student Press Law Center has booklets on campus crime for guidance of student journalists and offers advice to students needing information. It can be reached at Student Press Law Center, 1101 Wilson Blvd., Suite 1910, Arlington, VA 22209; e-mail, splc@splc.org.

Fire Coverage

The police reporter monitors the police radio for reports of fires. If a fire is serious or involves a well-known building or downtown area, the reporter will go to the scene. Importance can be determined by the number of units dispatched, usually expressed in terms of the number of alarms.

When a fire broke out in a downtown tire store at noon, it was too late for the staff of *The Anniston* (Ala.) *Star* to cover it for that day's newspaper. The presses had already started to roll. Because of the intensive radio coverage of the fire, the reporter assigned to the story knew that her piece for the next day's newspaper would have to feature some aspect other than the basic facts. Pam Newell Sohn found a feature angle and put a delayed lead on her story.

On the jump page, Sohn wrapped up the details of the fire under this lead:

> Virgil Coker Tire Service officials said today they are considering whether to rebuild a downtown Anniston warehouse blitzed by a spectacular fire Thursday.

Ask for Information   At fires, as with any emergency situation, reporters seem to be in the way, and some hesitate to grab a police officer or firefighter to ask for details. Ask. Wayne Dawkins recalls covering a fire for his New Jersey newspaper:

> Firefighters were coming out of the building gasping for oxygen, and there I was, trying to ask questions about what it was like inside. I expected to hear, "Get the hell away from me. I don't want to talk to you." But they made an effort, once they caught their breath.

Here are the beginnings of two fire stories that appeared in *The Tennessean* of Nashville:

A resident of an East Nashville rooming house suffered massive burns early today before fellow residents braved flames and yanked him to safety through a second-floor window.

The house at 256 Strouse Ave. was gutted by the blaze, which Metro fire officials have labeled "suspicious."

A 3-month-old Nashville girl asleep on a sofa-bed perished last night as her house went up in flames and relatives clawed in vain at an outside wall to rescue her.

The victim is the daughter of Janice Holt, who shares her 1925 16th Ave. N. home with several relatives, police said.

Firefighters arrived at the one-story dwelling off Clay Street shortly after the 6:45 p.m. call, and found the house consumed by flames, said Metro District Fire Chief Jordan Beasley.

Entire block endangered by disabled

butane truck too near flaming building

Heroes

By PAM NEWELL SOHN
Star Staff Writer

They talked like it was all in a day's work.

. . . like anyone would work on a disabled, half-filled butane truck a few feet from a building burning out of control.

. . . like the expectation the truck might explode and level the entire block was of no more consequence than answering a ringing phone.

Their apparent attitude: It had to be done. And the handful of men did it.

WHILE POLICE were evacuating about 100 spectators from the scene of a savage fire Thursday at Virgil Coker Tire Service on Noble Street, and while firemen were trying to tame the flames, four men ignored warnings and made fast, makeshift repairs on the tank truck. Then they half-drove, half-dragged it out of immediate danger.

The four men were Anniston Police Sgt. Mike Fincher, wrecker driver Kenneth Garrett and brothers Lamar Crosson and Buford Crosson, both employees of Virgil Coker Tire Service.

The Southern Butane Co. truck, carrying about 400 gallons of highly flammable gas, was parked for repairs near the rear of the building when a fire broke out there at about 11:20 a.m.

The front-end of the truck was near a telephone pole and could not be moved forward. Two rear wheels and the drive axle

had been removed from the truck. The empty wheel space was on the side of the burning building. Coker employees said work on the truck had reached a standstill waiting for the delivery of a new wheel hub.

WHEN IT BECAME apparent that the fire could not be extinguished quickly, some firemen and the four men began contemplating how to move the disabled truck.

Lamar Crosson said he heard mention of pulling the truck away from the blaze just as it stood. "But the (gas) valve was right there on the bottom and it could have broke and burned," said Crosson.

Crosson said that at about that time, the new hub was delivered and he and his brother began to reassemble the wheel hub and mount the tire, working between the truck and the burning building. They were assisted by fireman Jimmy Crossley, fincher and Garrett.

The men said they had to work "on and off" because of the intense smoke from the fire. And at times, according to Garrett, flames were as close as 10 feet away. When the smoke wasn't blinding and choking them, they were being doused with water from a fire pumper truck spraying cooling water on the butane tank, they said.

FINALLY, the men were able to secure one

(See **Truck**, Page 12A)

Checklist: Fires

— Deaths, injuries.

— Location.

— Cause.

— When, where started.

— How spread.

— When brought under control.

— Property loss: how much of structure damaged.

— Estimated cost of damage.

— Type of structure.

— Measures taken to protect public safety.

— If rescue involved, how carried out.

— Who discovered fire.

— Number of fire companies, firefighters assigned. (How much water used.)

— Exact cause of deaths, injuries.

— Where dead, injured taken.

— Quotes from those burned out; effect on their lives.

— Comments of neighbors, eyewitnesses.

— Insurance coverage.

— Arson suspected?

— Any arrests.

— Unusual aspects.

Sources

- Fire chief, marshal, inspector.
- Police department.
- Hospital.
- Morgue, mortuary.
- Welfare agencies, rescue groups (Red Cross).
- City building, fire inspection reports.

If a fire is serious enough to merit a follow-up story, possible themes are the progress of the investigation into the cause of the fire and the conditions of the injured. Another may be the cost of replacing the destroyed structure.

Cautions

A newspaper sent a young reporter to cover a fire in the business section. The fire had started in a hardware store, and the reporter asked one of the firefighters about the cause. "Looks like he had naphtha in the place," he replied, and the reporter wrote that. After the newspaper appeared, the store owner called the editor to complain that he never kept naphtha in the store. Statements about causes should be carefully handled. Only the chief, a marshal, or the fire inspector should be quoted about the cause.

Further Reading

Benedict, Helen. *Virgin or Vamp, How the Press Covers Sex Crimes.* New York: Oxford University Press, 1992.

Buchanan, Edna. *Never Let Them See You Cry: More from Miami, America's Heart Beat.* New York: Random House, 1992.

Capote, Truman. *In Cold Blood.* New York: Signet, 1967.

Krajicek, David J. *Scooped! Media Miss Real Story on Crime While Chasing Sex, Sleaze, and Celebrities.* New York: Columbia University Press, 1998.

Reiss, Albert. *The Police and the Public.* New Haven, Conn.: Yale University Press, 1971.

Reuss-Ianni, Elizabeth. *Street Cops and Management Cops.* New Brunswick, N.J.: Transaction Publishers, 1993.

21 The Courts

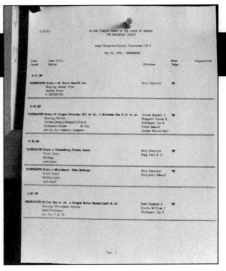

Circuit court docket posted for the day's trials.

Preview

Coverage of state and federal courts involves:

- **Civil law**—actions initiated by an individual, usually a person suing another individual or an organization for damages. Many actions are settled out of court.
- **Criminal law**—actions initiated by the government for violation of criminal statutes. The process begins with the arraignment of the accused and concludes with dismissal or a not-guilty verdict or sentencing after a conviction.

Stories about aspects of the legal system interest readers:

- Plea bargaining.
- Sentencing patterns.
- Pretrial detention, probation, judges' efficiency.
- Politics and the courts.

For every one of the 2.2 million men and women behind the bars of jails and prisons, five others are being processed in the criminal justice system. At the same time, increasing numbers of lawsuits flood the civil courts. People are turning to civil courts to claim damages for impaired health from toxic waste dumps, for what survivors claimed were cigarette-induced deaths and for injuries from automobile accidents.

The courts over the land have become overwhelmed. They are at the confluence of a swollen tide of lawmaking, arrests and litigation. Watching over all this, pencil poised, is the reporter.

What a dramatic image. The truth is that the courthouse reporter constantly struggles to keep from being engulfed. The only way the reporter maintains stability in this swelling tide of words—most of which are dense and arcane—is through knowledge of the judicial system, good sources and the ability to pick out the significant and interesting cases.

The Basics

There are two judicial systems, state and federal. State systems differ in detail but are similar in essentials. There are two kinds of law, criminal and civil. In criminal law, the government is the accuser. In civil law, an individual or group usually initiates the action; the government also can bring an action in the civil courts. Because crime stories make dramatic reading, the criminal courts receive the most media attention. Reporters cover the civil courts for damage suits, restraining orders and court decisions on such issues as taxes, business operations and labor conflicts.

These criminal and civil proceedings take place in state courts with a variety of titles—district, circuit, superior, supreme. The lower-level courts of original jurisdiction at the city and county levels—criminal, police, county, magistrate and the justice of the peace courts—handle misdemeanors, traffic violations and arraignments. The federal court system includes the federal district courts, the circuit courts of appeals and the Supreme Court.

The county courthouse or court reporter covers state and local courts and the office of the district attorney. The federal courthouse reporter covers the U.S. attorney, the federal magistrate and the federal courts. The magistrate arraigns those arrested and sets bail.

There are special state and local courts, such as the domestic relations or family court, sometimes called juvenile or children's court; small claims; surrogate's court (where wills are probated) and landlord-tenant court.

The court reporter's major emphasis is on the civil and criminal proceedings in the state courts of superior jurisdiction—district, superior, circuit or supreme courts—and in the federal system.

Before we go into our examination of court coverage, a note of caution: Reporting the courts has been the subject of considerable legal action. Some areas are off-limits—grand jury deliberations, certain activities of jurors—and some have been hemmed in by judicial decree. Chapter 25 surveys the continuing push-and-pull between journalists, who seek freedom to cover all aspects of the judicial system, and the courts, which have sought to limit coverage on the ground that it can compromise the defendant's right to a fair trial. Many states have press-bar guidelines.

> **Terminology.** A list of officers of the court and court terms is included at the end of this chapter. When you come across a word you don't know, consult the list of Court Terms.

Civil Law

Civil law consists of two major divisions: actions at law and equity proceedings.

Actions at Law

These suits are brought for recovery of property, damages for personal injury and breach of contract. The reporter who thumbs through the daily flow of suits filed in the county courthouse singles out those in which large amounts in damages are sought and those with unusual, important or timely elements.

The federal judicial system has three tiers:

District courts: Trial courts located throughout the nation.

Circuit courts: Intermediate regional appeals courts that review appeals from the district courts.

Supreme Court: Takes appeals on a discretionary basis from circuit courts.

The federal courts have power only over those matters the Constitution establishes: "controversies to which the United States shall be a party; controversies between two or more states; between a State and a citizen of another State; between citizens of different states. . . ."

The following story is about a lawsuit involving unusual circumstances:

OREGON CITY — A 13-year-old who broke both arms during a Little League baseball game has filed a $500,000 suit in Clackamas County Circuit Court through his guardian. It charges the Lake Oswego School District and Nordin-Schmitz, Inc., a private corporation, with negligence.

According to the suit, plaintiff Martin K. McCurdy was injured when he fell into a ditch on the boundary between the school district and Nordin-Schmitz property as he was chasing a ball during a Little League game May 16.

The O. J. Civil Trial Perhaps the most famous lawsuit in recent years was brought by the families of the man and woman whose murders were charged to O. J. Simpson. In Simpson's criminal trial, the unanimous verdict was not guilty. But in the civil trial, where the burden of proof is much lower, a jury found Simpson "liable" and awarded a total of $33.5 million in damages to one of the families.

Although there is a constitutional prohibition against double jeopardy, private civil suits have not been considered a violation of the prohibition. This has led to an increase in wrongful death actions after murder acquittals in criminal cases.

Caution: Lawyers often file damage suits seeking large sums. A $1 million lawsuit is commonplace. Most damage suits are settled for far less or tossed out of court. Relatively few go to trial. The reporter examines the suit to see whether it has newsworthy elements in addition to the amount sought.

When a 26-year-old New York woman brought a $4.5 million punitive damage suit, it was news only because of the name of the defendant—Mike

Tyson, former heavyweight champion of the world—and the circumstances: The woman claimed he grabbed her breasts and buttocks and threatened her when she refused his advances in a disco. The case went to trial and the jury awarded the woman $100 in compensatory damages for his actions but declined to award any punitive damages.

Fortunate in this civil suit, Tyson had no luck later in a criminal case, as we shall soon see.

Explain, Explain

The language of the courts can be difficult, and when the reporter has mastered it, he or she must remember to define for readers all technical terms and to explain actions that appear unusual.

Here is an example of how a reporter anticipated and then clarified a situation readers could find mystifying:

> The wife of a Dallas minister was found near death from what appeared to be an attempt to strangle her. Her husband was suspected, but police said they had no evidence to charge him. The woman is in a coma.
>
> The woman's mother sued her son-in-law in civil court and won a $16 million judgment, the money to be used for the lifetime care of the minister's wife.

Whoa, the reader says. How can a man be ordered to pay for a crime the police say they cannot charge him with? The reporter answered the question with this sentence:

> Unlike the criminal system, which requires proof beyond a reasonable doubt to convict a defendant, a civil suit requires only a preponderance of credible evidence.

The Key Differences   In a criminal trial, the issue is the guilt beyond a reasonable doubt of the accused. In a civil trial, in which damages, contracts and the like are involved, the issue is the likelihood of the defendant's liability.

In a criminal trial, the verdict must be unanimous. In a civil trial, 9 of the 12 jurors constitutes a verdict.

Equity Proceedings

The courts have the power to compel individuals and organizations to do something or to refrain from action. When such an order is requested, the complainant is said to seek equitable relief. Reporters come across these legal actions in the form of injunctions and restraining orders. Here is a story about a restraining order from the radio news wire of the UPI:

PROVIDENCE, R.I. — A federal judge has issued a temporary order stopping efforts to put a reservist on active army duty because he refused to shave off his beard.

District Judge Edward Day in Providence, R.I., yesterday gave the army 10 days to answer a suit filed Friday by the American Civil Liberties Union. . . .

Temporary injunctions, also known as preliminary injunctions, are issued to freeze the status quo until a court hearing can be scheduled. Thus, it makes no sense to write that the petitioner has "won" an injunction in such a preliminary proceeding (which is also called an "*ex parte* proceeding") because a permanent injunction cannot be issued until an adversary hearing is held in which both sides are heard. The respondent is ordered to show cause at the hearing—usually set for a week or two later—for why the temporary injunction should not be made final or permanent.

In this equity proceeding, a party asked the court to compel another party to take an action:

> The developers of a proposed shopping
> center and office complex at the intersec-
> tion of Route 13 and West Trenton Avenue
> have asked Bucks County Court to order
> Falls Township to issue a building permit.
> —*Bucks County Courier Times*

Court Documents Privileged Documents filed in the clerk's office usually are privileged as soon as the clerk stamps the material received. The reporter is free to use privileged material without fear of libel because it has been given official status. Statements in court also are privileged.

Pretrial and Trial

A complaint lists the cause of action, the parties to the action, and the relief sought. The defendant has several alternatives. He or she may file a motion seeking to delay, alter or halt the action. He or she can ask for a change of venue or a bill of particulars or can file other motions. When the defendant is ready to contest the action, or if motions to stop the action have not been granted, the defendant files an answer.

The case may then move to trial. Although there are more civil trials than criminal trials, few civil trials are covered. Reporters rely on records, lawyers and court personnel for information. Civil court stories are written on filing of the action and at the completion of the trial or at settlement.

Checklist: Civil Actions

— Identification of person or organization filing action.

— Background of plaintiff or petitioner.

— Defendant; respondent.

— Type of damage alleged.

— Remedy sought.

— Date of filing; court of jurisdiction.

— Special motivation behind action, if any.

— History of the conflict, disagreement.

— Similar cases decided by courts.

— Could suit lead to landmark decision? Is it a precedent?

— Possibility of an out-of-court settlement.

— Significance of action; effect on others.

— Lawyers for both sides; types of firms they are associated with.

— Date and presiding judge for trial, hearing.

— Judge's reputation with similar cases.

Should the reporter cover the trial, key points for reporting are selection of the jury; relevant evidence; identification and expertise of witnesses; demeanor of witnesses on the stand; judge's rulings; pertinent material from opening and closing statements of attorneys; the damages, if any are assessed; whether the losing party intends to appeal.

Checklist: Verdict Stories

Here are the essentials of verdict stories for civil actions:

— Verdict; damages, if awarded (same, less, greater than those sought).

— Parties involved.

— Judge's statement, if any; deviations by judge from jury's findings.

— Summary of allegations by plaintiff.

— Key testimony and attorneys' points.

— Length of jury deliberations.

— Comment by jurors on deliberations, verdict.

— Any appeals or motions.

Sources

Private attorneys representing plaintiff and defendant; judges and their law clerks and clerks of the court; court stenographers; county courthouse clerk or assistant who is in charge of filing such actions. The clerk is usually the best source for tips on important cases.

Cautions

Negotiations between the sides often will continue even after a trial begins, and the reporter should be aware of the possibility of a sudden settlement. In many damage suits, the plaintiff threatens to go to court to support his or her demand for a certain sum or other remedy. In turn, the defendant appears to be unconcerned about the possibility of a court battle. In reality, neither side welcomes the inconvenience, cost and unpredictability of a trial. The judge, too, wants a settlement. The civil courts are overwhelmed.

Attorneys for the losing side usually indicate an appeal will be filed. Do not overplay these assertions, but when an appeal is filed it can be a good story.

In civil cases, the defendant may ask the judge to dismiss the plaintiff's complaint or cause of action. Make sure to use the word *dismiss,* not *acquit,* which is a criminal term and refers to a verdict, after a full trial, by either a judge or a jury. In either a civil or criminal case, after the matter is finally decided, the judge usually orders a *judgment* to be entered in favor of the party prevailing in the action.

Criminal Law

Whether it is night court where the sweepings of the city streets are gathered for misdemeanor charges, or a high-paneled district courtroom where a woman is on trial for the murder-for-hire of her wealthy husband, the criminal courts offer endless opportunities for coverage.

The assumption that underlies the criminal justice system is that an injury to the individual affects the general public. Crimes are therefore prosecuted in the name of the state as the representative of the people.

The public prosecutor, an elected official, is usually known as the district attorney, state's attorney, county attorney or people's attorney. In the federal system, the prosecutor, a presidential appointee, is called the United States attorney.

Criminal Court Process

The criminal court system goes into operation shortly after the arrest and consists of pretrial and trial periods.

The pretrial period can be divided into four phases: arraignment, preliminary hearing, grand jury action and jury selection. Usually, these are accomplished in line with the constitutional provision: "In all criminal prosecutions, the accused shall enjoy the right to a speedy and public trial. . . ."

Arraignment

At arraignment, the defendant is told of the charges and of his or her right to an attorney and can enter a plea to the charge. If the defendant cannot afford a

City and State Courts

Justice of the Peace, Police Courts	District, County Courts	Municipal Courts

Handle violations of city ordinances

These courts are called the courts of original or least jurisdiction. They handle violations, misdemeanors and conduct arraignments.

Superior Court
(Also known in some states as the Circuit Court, Court of Common Pleas; in New York, the Supreme Court.)

The basic trial court to try civil cases and felonies. These courts are often divided into specialty areas: probate, juvenile, domestic relations. They handle violations of state laws.

By appeal

Intermediate Appellate Courts

Half the states have these courts.

By appeal

State Supreme Court
(Also known in some states as the Supreme Court of Errors, Court of Appeals, Supreme Judicial Court, or Supreme Court of Appeals.) (Federal matters can be appealed to the U.S. Supreme Court.)

Highest state appellate court.

O. J. Arraigned

LOS ANGELES — O. J. Simpson, looking dazed and haggard, pleaded not guilty at his arraignment Monday to charges that he murdered his ex-wife and a friend of hers.

For most of the brief session, Simpson — who was dressed in a dark suit but without tie, belt or shoelaces — stood with his head cocked to one side. He sighed deeply several times as he looked around the courtroom.

lawyer, the court assigns one. Arraignments are held in courts of original or least jurisdiction. These courts are empowered to try only misdemeanors and violations, such as gambling, prostitution, loitering and minor traffic offenses. In a felony case, the court will determine bail. The prosecutor is present at arraignment, and he or she may decide to dismiss or lower the charge. If a felony charge is lowered to a misdemeanor, the case can be disposed of then and there.

The arraignment court, often called the criminal or city police court, acts like a fine-necked funnel, allowing only those felonies to pass through that the district attorney considers serious. Others are reduced to violations and misdemeanors and handled forthwith.

If the defendant pleads guilty to a misdemeanor, the court can sentence immediately. If the defendant pleads guilty to a felony charge, the case is referred to a higher court.

If a plea of not guilty is entered to a misdemeanor, the judge can then conduct a trial or preliminary hearing. For felony not-guilty pleas, the case is referred to the appropriate court for a preliminary hearing. If the preliminary hearing is waived, the defendant is then bound over to the grand jury for action. Felonies are handled by courts which are variously called district, superior or circuit courts, depending on the state.

Checklist: Arraignments

— Formal charge.

— Plea.

— Bail (higher, lower than requested; conditional release).

— Behavior, statements of defendant.

— Presentation, remarks of prosecutor, defense lawyer, judge.

— Summary of crime.

Preliminary Hearing

At a preliminary hearing, determination is made whether there are reasonable grounds, or probable cause, to believe the accused committed the offense and whether there is sufficient evidence for the case to be bound over to the grand jury. If the presiding judge considers the evidence insufficient, he or she can dismiss the charge. Also, bail can be increased, eliminated or reduced at the hearing.

The defendant has another opportunity to seek to have the charge lowered through plea bargaining at this point in the process. Some attorneys handling criminal cases prefer to have their clients plead guilty and receive probation or a light sentence rather than risk a trial and a lengthy sentence.

The prosecutor usually goes along with plea bargaining, but if the crime is serious, the defendant has a long record or the presiding judge is convinced there is reason to believe a serious crime was committed, the case will be sent to a grand jury to decide whether the defendant should be indicted.

Here is the beginning of a story of a preliminary hearing in the federal system:

BOSTON, Dec. 24 — A Harvard Law School student, who allegedly enrolled under separate identities twice in the last seven years, was ordered yesterday bound over to a United States grand jury on charges that he had falsified a federal student loan application. . . .

United States Magistrate Peter Princi found probable cause yesterday that the student falsified applications for $6,000 in federally insured loans, which helped to see him through 2 1/2 years of law school. . . .

Grand Jury Action

Criminal defendants can be brought to trial in three ways, depending on the state. In half the states, a grand jury indicts. A jury of citizens, usually 23 (of which 16 make a quorum), decides whether the evidence is sufficient for a trial on the charges brought. If 12 jurors so decide, an indictment, known as a *true*

| **Preliminary Verdict** |

LOS ANGELES — Judge Kathleen Kennedy-Powell ruled today that O. J. Simpson must stand trial on murder charges.

The six-day preliminary hearing featured the presentation of blood samples from the crime scene by the district attorney's office. Simpson's lawyers, who did little to tip their defense at the hearing, are expected to file a motion asking for dismissal of the charges because of lack of evidence.

What Happens to the Defendant After Indictment

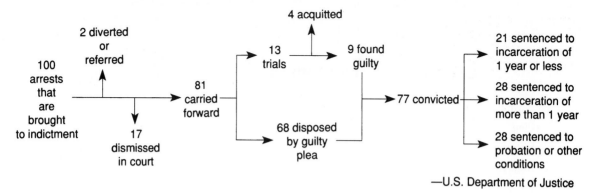

—U.S. Department of Justice

bill, is voted. If not, dismissal, known as a *no bill,* is voted. Only the state's evidence is presented to the jury.

In 20 states, the prosecutor files a charge called an *information* and a judge decides at a preliminary hearing at which witnesses testify whether there is cause for a trial. In a few states, the prosecutor files affidavits to support the charge and the judge decides whether to move to trial.

Here are leads to grand jury indictments, the first by an Indiana state grand jury, the other by a federal grand jury:

INDIANAPOLIS — Former heavyweight champion Mike Tyson was indicted here today on a charge of raping an 18-year-old Miss Black America beauty pageant contestant and on three other criminal counts.

OKLAHOMA CITY — Timothy J. McVeigh and Terry L. Nichols, former army buddies who shared a hatred for the government, were indicted by a federal grand jury today on charges of blowing up a federal building here in April with a rented truck packed with 4,800 pounds of homemade explosives.

Rearraignment

After the indictment, the defendant is again arraigned, this time before a judge empowered to try felony cases. If the defendant pleads not guilty, a date for trial is set and bail is set. For example:

INDIANAPOLIS — Mike Tyson pleaded not guilty to charges he raped a beauty pageant contestant and was released on $30,000 bail.

In a 10-minute court appearance, Marion Superior Court Judge Patricia Gifford read Tyson the rape, criminal deviate conduct and confinement charges against him. If found guilty on all those charges, Tyson could face up to 63 years in prison. A trial date of Jan. 27 was set.

Plea bargaining continues at the rearraignment following grand jury indictment. Felonies, which usually are classified by degree—Class A, B, C, D

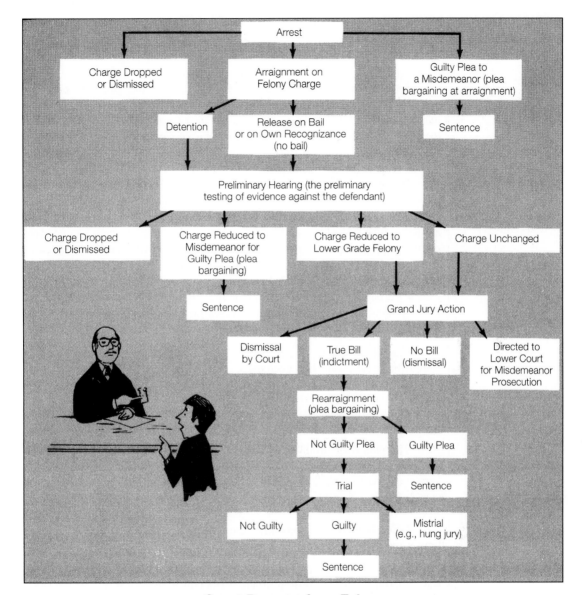

Court Process for a Felony

and E—can be adjusted downward, a Class A felony moving down to a C or D, a Class C or D being negotiated down to a Class E felony or a misdemeanor.

Plea Bargaining

If every arrest were to be followed by a plea of not guilty and the accused granted the speedy trial promised by the Bill of Rights, the court system in every large city would collapse. The only way the courts can cope with the crush is to permit or to encourage arrangements whereby the defendant and the prosecutor agree that, in return for a lowered charge, the defendant will plead guilty. The nature of the sentence is often explicitly promised by the judge as a condition to the defendant's agreement to plead guilty.

Even serious crimes such as murder and rape are the subject of plea bargaining. In New York City, three-fourths of all murder arrests are plea bargained, and in Philadelphia three-fifths are plea bargained. Prosecutors defend the practice by saying that plea bargaining is necessary to cut down the backlog of cases in the courts. In Philadelphia, the backlog was cut from 20,000 to 13,000 through plea bargaining.

When the Bronx district attorney announced he would no longer allow plea bargaining in felony cases, legal experts said the move "could cripple the borough's criminal-justice system by overburdening judges, crowding jails and allowing some suspects to go free," *The New York Times* reported. The newspaper described the system as "a necessary evil in an overwhelmed court system," and said it is the "leading way criminal cases are decided in New York City and around the nation." Almost 85 percent of all city cases are plea bargained.

Plea bargaining continues even as the criminal trial is underway. Here is the beginning of a court story that involves plea bargaining. It was written by Joseph P. Fried of *The New York Times:*

The last defendant in the St. John's University sexual-assault case interrupted his trial yesterday to plead guilty to sharply reduced charges, then admitted he had done virtually everything he had originally been accused of.

The wrenching case came to an end in an emotional scene in a Queens courtroom in which a female spectator yelled out that the 22-year-old defendant was a "rapist" and his mother responded with screaming vituperation.

The plea bargain allowed the defendant, a student at the largest Roman Catholic university in the country who was accused with five others of what is known as acquaintance rape, to be given three years' probation. They were accused of sodomizing the victim and sexually abusing her in other ways.

Offer Spurned   Sometimes the bargaining is unsuccessful. Here is the beginning of a story from *The Humboldt Beacon* by Nancy Brands Ward:

EUREKA — The case of three Headwaters activists arrested in Rep. Frank Riggs' Eureka office on Oct. 16 moved one step closer to trial this week as attorneys failed to reach a deal on a plea bargain.

After Judge Marilyn Miles asked during a pretrial hearing Monday if the case could be settled short of going to court, Deputy District Attorney Andrew Isaac offered to let the three women plead guilty to

trespass and resisting arrest. In exchange, vandalism charges would be dropped, though the prosecution would reserve the right to bring them to the court's attention during sentencing.

"It was no offer," said Mark Harris, who represents Terri Slanetz, Jennifer Schneider and Lisa Sanderson-Fox, who'd locked themselves in Riggs' office in an October protest.

Pretrial Motions

After the defendant has been formally accused, several kinds of motions can be filed:

- **Motion to quash the indictment:** The defendant can challenge the legality of the indictment. If the motion to dismiss is granted, the indictment is quashed. The prosecutor can appeal the quashing. He or she also can draw up another indictment if the grand jury again hands up a true bill, even if the first has been quashed, because the constitutional protection against double jeopardy does not apply.
- **Motion for a bill of particulars:** When the defense attorney wants more details about the allegations against the accused, such a motion is filed.
- **Motion to suppress the evidence:** Evidence shown to be seized or obtained illegally may not be used in the trial if the court grants such a motion.
- **Motion for a change of venue:** A defendant who believes he or she cannot receive a fair trial in the city or judicial area where the crime took place may ask that it be transferred elsewhere. Such motions also are filed to avoid trials presided over by particular judges.

During the pretrial stage of the Tyson case, the boxer's defense team made a motion to exclude a videotape on which Tyson was supposed to have made a disparaging remark about his accuser at a news conference following his arraignment. The defense motion was upheld when the judge later ruled the tape inadmissible at the trial.

Jury Selection

When a case emerges from the pretrial process and has been set for trial, a jury is usually empaneled. (The accused may waive the right to jury trial, in which case the judge hears the evidence in what is called a *bench trial*.)

Jurors' names are drawn from a wheel or jury box in which the names of all jurors on a jury list were placed. The list is made up of names drawn from the tax rolls, voting lists, driver's license files and so on.

Twelve jurors and several alternates are selected in a procedure during which the defense attorney and prosecutor are permitted to challenge the seating of jurors. There are two types of challenges: *peremptory,* when no reason need be given for wanting a person off the jury, and *for cause,* when a specific disqualification must be demonstrated. The number of peremptory challenges allotted each side is usually set by statute, usually 10 per side. A judge can set any number of challenges for cause.

In the Tyson case, prosecutors tried to exclude a potential juror for cause because he supposedly was biased against Tyson's accuser. The judge refused. Then the prosecution switched to a peremptory challenge, and the defense countered by contending that the challenge was based solely on the defendant's race.

Motions Prepared

LOS ANGELES — Attorneys for O. J. Simpson are laying out a battery of motions to try to undermine the case against the former football star, Simpson's lead attorney said in an interview today.

Motion Denied

LOS ANGELES — The judge in the O. J. Simpson murder trial today denied the football great's attorneys the right to review a police detective's military records.

Simpson's lawyers are seeking to show that the detective, who found key evidence, is a racist. Judge Lance A. Ito said he found nothing in the records relevant to the case.

Alternates Chosen

LOS ANGELES — Nine women and three men were selected yesterday as alternate jurors for the O. J. Simpson murder trial.

Immediately after the alternate panel of seven blacks, four whites and one Hispanic was sworn in, Superior Court Judge Lance Ito went into closed session with the lawyers to discuss allegations of misconduct by two members of the regular jury that was selected last month.

(The U.S. Supreme Court has ruled that peremptory challenges cannot be used to exclude people from juries on the basis of sex or race.)

The Right to Say No   The Tyson prosecution asked potential jurors whether they believed a woman had the right to say no: "No means no. Do you agree with that proposition?" The prosecutor then added, "If a woman says no and a man forces her against her will, that means rape."

One of those on the jury panel, a 42-year-old radio repairman, said he had trouble with that assertion because, he countered, it depended on "when did she say no and how did she say it." Suppose, he continued, a woman waited "until they're right down into doing it, that would be a little too late, wouldn't it?" The lead prosecutor used the man's question to drive home his point that a woman is in control of her body and has the right to say no at any time. The man did not serve on the jury.

Potential jurors in the Tyson case were asked by defense attorneys whether they would hold a celebrity to a higher standard of conduct than they would apply to others.

Selection a Key   "Most trials are won or lost in jury selection," says Larry Scalise, a trial lawyer. In the trial of a woman accused of murdering her abusive husband, her lawyer said he concentrated on selecting a jury that was well-educated and sensitive to the victims of domestic violence. His client was acquitted.

Jury selection was a key factor in O. J. Simpson's acquittal at his criminal trial, court observers say. Through the use of surveys and focus groups, Simpson's lawyers learned that black men were three times more likely than black women to believe Simpson was guilty and that the more educated black men and women also considered him guilty.

In focus groups, Simpson's lawyers found, "Virtually every middle-aged African-American woman supported Simpson and resented the murder victim (Nicole Simpson)," says Jeffrey Toobin, the author of *The Run of His Life: The People v. O. J. Simpson.*

Toobin adds that the lead prosecutor Marcia Clark seriously compromised her chance of winning a conviction by not following the advice of jury consultants who told her that black women were hostile to the prosecution.

The criminal trial jury in the Simpson case included eight black women. The only whites were two women.

In the civil trial that found Simpson liable for the deaths, there was not a single black juror.

"No one wanted to tell what I regard as the truth about the Simpson case— that race was always at the heart of it," says Toobin.

Jury selection is so important it has spawned an industry—jury consultancy. Behavioral consultants advise attorneys how to select sympathetic jurors and how to use psychological techniques to persuade juries.

Jury Consultants   Jo-Ellan Dimitrius, one of about 250 jury consultants in the country, says that, in assessing prospective jurors, she seeks clues from what they take to court—their reading matter, their body language and their responses to the questions lawyers ask.

Robert B. Hirschhorn, a consultant, advised lawyers defending a young man accused of murdering a 16-year-old girl to ask potential jurors, "Can you look Kevin in the eye and say, 'Kevin, I can give you a fair trial'?"

Those who replied, "I think I can" were dismissed by the defense. Those who said yes and then "looked at their shoes, we got rid of," Hirschhorn said. Those who gave an unequivocal "yes" were accepted by the defense.

The jury acquitted Kevin.

Consultants advise their clients on everything from the clothing to wear at a trial to whether men should wear their hairpieces. San Antonio attorney and trial consultant Harry Munsinger says that if he had been advising Mike Tyson at Tyson's rape trial he would have played down the boxer's size and strength by dressing him in pastels and looser-fitting suits.

Reporter's Fare

All of this is fair game for the court reporter. A careful eye to jury selection will indicate the strategy of prosecutor and defense attorney. Does the defense attorney want women on the jury because he believes they will be sympathetic to the abused wife who shot her husband? Is the prosecutor asking questions about the television shows and movies the jury panelists watch? Does she prefer those who like westerns and police dramas? If so, what does that tell you?

Are jury consultants in the courtroom? On whose side? What can they tell you?

We are ready to examine the procedure for trials, which the court reporter must master to do his or her job properly. But first a suggestion from the dean of court reporters, Theo Wilson of the New York *Daily News:* "Take the reader into the courtroom with you."

The Trial

A reporter cannot attend all the trials conducted in the courthouse that he or she covers. A reporter may sit through opening and closing statements and key testimony, but only the most celebrated cases are covered from opening statement to verdict and sentence. Reporters cover most trials by checking with the court clerk, the prosecutor and the defense attorney.

Because the reporter is dependent on sources who often have a stake in the trial, court transcripts are used in important trials if they can be obtained in time for broadcast or publication. A friendly court stenographer can quickly run off key testimony in an emergency.

Trial Process

The trial procedure follows this pattern:

Opening Statements

1. Opening statements by prosecuting attorney and the defense attorney outline the state's case and the defense or alibi of the defendant and give a general preview of the evidence.

"The opening statement is the single most important part of the trial," says Joseph W. Cotchett, a Burlingame, Calif., lawyer. "This is the time you win your case. It's the rule of primacy; the jurors hear the details of the case for the first time. You give them the critical facts you're going to prove."

Direct Examination

2. The prosecution presents its case through testimony of witnesses and evidence. At the end of the presentation, a judge can direct a verdict of acquittal if he or she finds that the state has not established what is called a *prima facie* case, failing to present sufficient proof of the crime that is charged. The questioning by the prosecutor of his or her witness is called *direct examination.*

In direct examination of the woman who accused Tyson of raping her, the prosecutor led her to describe the event after her introductory statement: "If I was a quitter I wouldn't be here. I start what I finish," she told the jury. Then she described in three and a half hours of testimony what had happened. She said, "I was terrified. I was begging him, trying anything that would work. It just felt like someone was ripping me apart."

The story in the *Daily News* began:

INDIANAPOLIS—Mike Tyson's 18-year-old accuser testified yesterday that the former champ laughed while she wept in agony as he raped her in his hotel suite here last July.

"Don't fight me," Tyson growled menacingly during the attack as he grabbed her, pulled her clothing off and pinned her while she feebly pushed his heavyweight arms and back, she testified.

"I was telling him, 'Get off me, please stop.' I didn't know what to do," the woman said, her almost childlike voice captivating the hushed courtroom as she recounted the incident.

The prosecution calls other witnesses to support the contention of its major witnesses. In the Tyson case, the prosecutor drew from Tyson's chauffeur the statement that, when the woman left the hotel and returned to the limousine, "she looked like she may have been in a state of shock. Dazed. Disoriented. She seemed scared."

Cross-Examination by Defense

3. The defense attorney may cross-examine the state's witnesses.

In a criminal defense trial, says Cornelius Pitts, a defense lawyer in Detroit, "relentless cross-examination is necessary. The objective is to prevent the prosecution from winning and to do what you have to do to

Cross-Examination

LOS ANGELES — A population geneticist acknowledged today that he made mistakes when he compiled statistics that linked O. J. Simpson to the killings of his former wife and her friend.

Under cross-examination, the geneticist said he was "sincerely sorry" and "embarrassed" by his errors.

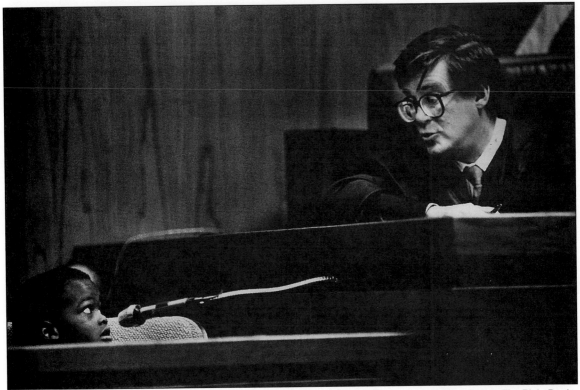

Nancy Stone, *The Plain Dealer*

Witness to His Mother's Murder

Here is the beginning of the story by Katherine L. Siemon and Eric Stringfellow of *The Plain Dealer* that accompanied this dramatic photograph by Nancy Stone:

Five-year-old DeVon Stapleton vividly remembers the night last spring when a stranger bludgeoned his mother to death while he watched from the back of a van.

Yesterday he spent about an hour trying to recount for a three-judge panel in Common Pleas Court what happened that night in April, how he and his mother tried to escape, and how he was left standing alone on a dark street corner after his mother was killed.

Barely tall enough to see over the witness stand and with a voice barely loud enough to be heard without a micro-phone, DeVon pointed to the man who is on trial for the death of Ruby Stapleton.

"There, he's right there," DeVon said, shaking his finger at Reginald Jells when Assistant County Prosecutor Carmen Marino asked the boy if he saw the stranger in the court-room.

Jells, 21, faces the death penalty for Stapleton's killing last April 18. He also is charged with kidnapping and aggra-vated robbery. During opening arguments yesterday, Marino said Stapleton's blood was found inside Jells' van and a foot-print matching Jells' was found near the body.

Jells has denied the killing.

(*Jells was convicted and sentenced to death.*)

attack the complainant and the complainant's witnesses to the extent their testimony is no longer credible to the jury."

Tyson's attorney spent three hours cross-examining the boxer's accuser: "Do you recall telling Tanya St. Clair that (Tyson) has the money and the build that you like? . . . Do you recall saying you like men with 'something you can hold on to'?"

In cross-examining the chauffeur, the defense attorney's questions sought to suggest that the driver was exhausted from overwork and could not have seen the woman clearly.

INDIANAPOLIS — The attorney defending Mike Tyson failed to shake his accuser from her story in more than three hours of cross-examination yesterday, but he did set the stage for other witnesses to discredit her account of what happened that night in Tyson's hotel suite.

In a rapid-fire series of questions, attorney Vincent Fuller questioned the accuser about statements she allegedly made to other contestants in the Miss Black America Pageant and to pageant participants in the days immediately preceding and following the July 19 incident in which she says she was raped by the former heavyweight boxing champion.

—*New York Post*

Redirect Examination

4. Redirect examination is permitted the prosecutor should he or she want to re-establish the credibility of evidence or testimony that the defense's cross-examination has threatened.

Motions

5. The defense may make a motion for a directed verdict of acquittal or of dismissal based on its contention the state did not prove its case.

Rebuttal

6. The defense may call witnesses to rebut the state's case. The defendant may or may not be called, depending on the defense attorney's strategy. The prosecutor is not permitted to comment on the defendant's failure to take the stand.

Tyson's attorneys called beauty pageant contestants to testify that his accuser had flirted with him and repeatedly talked about his money. Tyson did take the stand and under questioning by his attorney said he and his accuser had engaged in consensual sex. "No, she never told me to stop. She never said I was hurting her. She never said no. Nothing."

Cross-Examination by Prosecutor

7. The prosecutor may cross-examine the defense witnesses.

In cross-examination of the contestants, the prosecution elicited testimony that the plaintiff was naive and "not streetwise" about a date with Tyson. Tyson also was cross-examined:

INDIANAPOLIS — A visibly rattled and slightly peevish Mike Tyson, after an hour of intense cross-examination, left the stand yesterday having had some inconsistencies in his testimony high-lighted but with his basic story intact.

Attacking less with a sledgehammer than with a chisel, special prosecutor J. Gregory Garrison chipped away at Tyson's testimony but refrained from grilling Tyson about precisely what went on in Room 606 of the Canterbury Hotel on the morning of July 19, when an 18-year-old beauty pageant contestant says she was raped.

—*New York Post*

In the Simpson trial, the defense introduced an expert witness who said that the killings took too long for Simpson to have committed them. On cross-examination by the prosecutor, the witness stood fast:

> LOS ANGELES — The prosecution today attacked the theory of an expert witness for O. J. Simpson that the two victims fought long and hard for their lives. But the expert, the former chief medical examiner for New York, fended off the attack and cited his long experience with murder cases.

Redirect Examination by Defense

8. Should the state seem to weaken the defense's case through its cross-examination, the defense may engage in redirect examination of its witnesses.

Rebuttals

9. Rebuttals are offered on both sides. Witnesses may be recalled. New rebuttal witnesses may be called, but new witnesses ordinarily cannot be presented without the judge's permission after a side has rested its case.

Note: At any time during the trial, the defense may move for a *mistrial,* usually on the basis that some irregularity has made a fair verdict by the jury impossible. If the judge grants the motion, the jury is discharged and the trial is stopped. Because double jeopardy does not apply in such situations, the defendant can be tried again.

Summations

10. The defense and the state offer closing arguments in which they summarize the case for the jurors. These presentations, known as *summations,* provide reporters with considerable news. Attorneys sometimes make dramatic summations before the jury.

Charge to Jury

11. The judge charges or instructs jurors before they retire for deliberations. The judge may review the evidence, explain the law that should be applied to the facts of the case and explain the verdicts that can be reached. The jury must accept the judge's explanation of the law but is the sole judge of the facts in the case.

Jury Deliberation

12. Jury deliberations may be short or extended. In important trials, the reporter may want to stay with the jury until deadline because verdicts make headlines. A jury may ask for further instructions on the law, or it may wish to review certain material from the trial. Stories can be written speculating on the meaning of lengthy deliberations or the questions the jury asks the judge.

Verdict

13. The verdict in criminal trials must be unanimous. After being discharged, jurors may report their discussions in the jury room to the press unless the judge gags the jurors. (In most states, the judge does not have the right to gag jurors, and the First Amendment would seem to forbid such power anywhere.) A jury may return a verdict of guilty or not guilty.

If the jury reports it is hopelessly deadlocked, the judge declares a mistrial because of the *hung jury.* After a verdict of guilty, the defense may file to set aside the verdict, or it may make a motion for a new trial. The motion usually is denied but the decision can be appealed.

Verdict Essentials The time the jury deliberated, the counts on which the jury convicted and the possible length of the sentence(s) must be included in the verdict story.

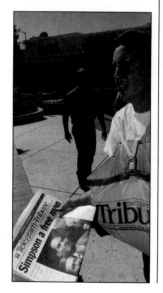

INDIANAPOLIS, Feb. 10 — Mike Tyson, the former heavyweight champion and one of the world's most recognized figures in and out of boxing, was found guilty tonight of raping an 18-year-old beauty pageant contestant last July.

In a verdict handed down almost 10 hours after it went to the jury, Mr. Tyson was found guilty on one count of rape and two counts of criminal deviate conduct.

Sentencing is set for March 6. Each of the counts carries a maximum sentence of six to 20 years. Under Indiana law, Mr. Tyson will likely receive an eight to 12 year sentence as a first-time offender with a juvenile record, Reuters reported.

In the case of an acquittal, the time of deliberation, the charge and the length of the trial usually go into the lead. In some cases, the makeup of the jury is considered relevant, as in this lead:

> LOS ANGELES — O. J. Simpson was found not guilty of the murders of his ex-wife and her friend after a year-long trial that attracted worldwide attention.

> The jury of eight blacks, two whites
> and one Hispanic reached their verdict yes-
> terday after less than four hours of deliber-
> ation. The verdict was announced today in
> Superior Court by Judge Lance Ito.

The AP blended several elements in its lead when Timothy McVeigh was convicted of the Oklahoma City courthouse bombing:

> DENVER (AP) — Timothy McVeigh was convicted Monday of the deadliest act of terror on U.S. soil, a verdict that brought jubilation and bitter tears to relatives of the 168 people killed in the Oklahoma City bombing. The jury will now decide whether he should pay with his life.

In major trials, there will be more than the major verdict story. *The New York Times* ran a sidebar by Rick Bragg alongside its verdict story that began:

> OKLAHOMA CITY, June 2 — After
> the explosion, people learned to write left-
> handed, to tie just one shoe. They learned to
> endure the pieces of metal and glass embed-
> ded in their flesh, to smile with faces that
> made them want to cry, to cry with glass
> eyes. They learned in homes where children
> had played, to stand the quiet. They learned
> to sleep with pills, to sleep alone.

Sentence

14. The sentence may be pronounced immediately after the verdict or later, pending a probation report. State laws usually set ranges—minimum and maximum sentences—that may be imposed. Always include the probable time the defendant will serve.

> INDIANAPOLIS, March 26 — Mike Tyson, the former heavyweight champion who was convicted of rape last month, was sentenced to 10 years in prison today. But the judge suspended the last four years, meaning he will spend no more than six years behind bars.
>
> In a rape case that has attracted world-wide attention and prompted debate about sexual roles and racial attitudes in the criminal justice system, Mr. Tyson is likely to be freed in three years with time off for good behavior.
>
> —*The New York Times*

The AP lead to the sentencing of Timothy McVeigh centered on McVeigh's cryptic brief statement to the court. Here is how the story begins. Notice the inclusion of the reaction of the spectators:

> DENVER (AP) — Making no apologies and no plea for mercy, Timothy McVeigh was formally sentenced to death Thursday after borrowing the words of a Supreme Court justice to suggest the blame for the Oklahoma City bombing rests with the government itself.

"Our government is the potent, the omnipresent teacher. For good or for ill, it teaches the whole people by its example," McVeigh said, quoting from a 1928 opinion written by Justice Louis Brandeis in a wiretapping case.

McVeigh, standing before the judge in khakis, a tan shirt and orange prison shoes, spoke for less than a minute in clipped, rapid-fire tones, ending: "That's all I have, Your Honor."

It was the first time he had spoken at any length in court.

Across the courtroom, some of his living victims and relatives of the 168 people killed in the April 19, 1995, blast at the Oklahoma City federal building sat stone-faced. Others stared angrily. They heard no admission of wrongdoing, no remorse.

The Full Story. It's not enough to give the sentence in the story. Tell the reader when the convicted person could be paroled. Except for sentences that specify no parole is possible, most criminals are let out of jail long before their full sentences, even for murder. For example:

He will be sentenced Feb. 6 to a mandatory life term with a possibility of parole after 9 1/2 years.

Convictions on more than one count can lead to concurrent or consecutive sentences. A judge also may issue a suspended sentence, place the defendant on probation or levy a fine.

A majority of offenders in all states are placed under community supervision of some kind rather than incarcerated.

In some states, in trials involving the possibility of a death sentence, the jury decides the sentence following conviction, or a new jury is empaneled to decide.

Tougher Sentences   An increasing number of states are turning from the indefinite sentence to definite or determinate sentences which are fixed by law with no judicial latitude and no parole. This is a response to the public demand that the justice system be tougher with those committing violent crimes.

Studies indicate that only 15 percent of those arrested are first-time offenders, that 60 percent are recidivists—criminals who already have served prison terms—and 25 percent have been convicted but were given probation. These findings have led to the "three strikes and you're out" laws—life sentences for three-time offenders.

Checklist: Criminal Trials

A story written at any one of the 14 stages outlined here should include the current developments and the following basic information:

— Formal charge.

— Full identification of defendant.

— Circumstances surrounding criminal act.

— Summary of preceding developments.

— Likely next stage.

Sources

Private attorneys; prosecutor's office, which includes assistant prosecutors, investigators and bureau heads; legal aid attorneys; law clerks of the judges; clerks of the court; court stenographers; bailiffs and security guards; police officers; probation department; state parole office; trial judges, many of whom like to chat with reporters. Clerks also can tip off reporters to important motions, hearings and trial dates.

Look for Color, Strategy, Tactics

Material that gives the trial individuality may include the behavior of the defendant or of the defense attorney, unusual testimony. Drama is enhanced by describing the setting, the reactions of spectators and the reactions of jurors.

Stories about testimony can be dramatized by using the question-and-answer technique for crucial testimony:

Q. Can you identify the man you say attacked you?

A. Yes, I can. He is sitting there, to your right at the other table where I'm pointing.

Material for the Q and A usually is taken from the court transcript to ensure accuracy.

Reporters understand the necessity of finding patterns of strategy and tactics during a trial. Every prosecutor has a plan, and every defense attorney keys his or her presentation to a theme. Each witness, every bit of evidence is presented with a purpose. The reporter's job is to discover the design of each side in this adversary proceeding. Strategy and tactics shift with the evidence, requiring the reporter to be alert during each day's testimony. The reporter asks himself or herself: What is the purpose of this line of questioning, this witness, this piece of evidence?

This kind of coverage gives the reader, listener or viewer a sense of the movement and direction of the trial. All other coverage is episodic.

Appeals

Convictions may be appealed to a higher court. In criminal cases, the appeal usually concerns errors or improper actions by the presiding judge. Sometimes, jury selection is appealed. Here is how the *Chicago Tribune* handled the disposition of Mike Tyson's appeal:

Boxer Mike Tyson's rape conviction and six-year sentence was upheld Friday by a state appeals court, which rejected arguments that a judge improperly limited defense testimony.

In a 2–1 decision, the Indiana Court of Appeals ruled that the trial court acted within its authority in blocking the testimony of three witnesses who would have contradicted the woman who accused the former world heavyweight boxing champion of raping her in a hotel room in 1991.

Danger: Reporter in the Courtroom

When I sat on the bench I always wondered about any reporter I saw in my courtroom. Often I knew that the reporter had no idea what I was doing, what the judicial system was about, what the language being used in the courtroom meant, and what rights were being protected and advanced through the legal system. Rarely do reporters have any expertise in the law; the vast majority come from journalism or liberal arts schools, not law schools. Covering "cops and courts" is usually an entry-level position at newspapers and is subject to general-assignment reporting at television stations. Trained court reporters are a dying breed. Turnover is high.

As a result of this ignorance of the system, the public usually gets superficial and inaccurate reporting on the judicial process. Reporters often portray the judiciary merely as an extension of the prosecutors and police, and commonly overemphasize the day-to-day proceedings of the court without looking at the entirety of the judicial system. Court reporting is therefore often inaccurate, sensational, oversimplified, distorted, and routine.

—Thomas S. Hodson

USA Today interviewed a friend of Tyson for his reaction to the appeals court decision and began its story this way:

> Ex-heavyweight champion Mike Tyson was not shocked, but was upset when an Indiana appeals court KO'd his request for a new rape trial.
>
> "He wasn't expecting too much from these people" longtime friend Jay Bright said Sunday. "But the day it happened he was disappointed. There was some tension in his voice. He was edgy."

The magazine *Sports Illustrated,* which came out a week after the appeals court decision, used Tyson's reaction and his lawyer's performance at his trial for its lead that combined straight reporting with interpretation:

> Mike Tyson was reportedly "angry and disappointed" last Friday after an Indiana court of appeals ruled 2–1 to uphold his March 1992 rape conviction. Tyson, who has served 17 months of a six-year prison sentence, would do well to consider his lawyer's role in last week's decision.

Stories about the System

Courthouse reporters are increasingly being asked to take an overview of their beats. Editors want stories about trends in the handling of criminal cases, how Supreme Court decisions affect the local judicial system, plea bargaining, new investigative techniques by the prosecutor's office, politics and the courts. Some editors want their reporters to do accountability pieces: Does the system work; are some judges giving unusually light sentences to mobsters or drug pushers; are judges efficient in clearing caseloads; are white-collar criminals being treated leniently?

One of the most sensitive issues in setting crime control policy is pretrial detention. Denial of bail resulting in detention deprives the defendant, presumed not guilty, of freedom, limits his or her participation in preparing a defense and deprives the person of earnings. Pretrial release, however, makes it possible for the defendant to commit crimes or to flee.

Court Records. With the docket number, records may be obtained, such as the police complaint, the affidavit filed by the complainant, the felony complaint, the disposition if a plea was made at the arraignment or preliminary hearing, the amount of bail. If a trial has been held, the trial record may be kept in another file, again by docket number.

Profiles   The court reporter can write profiles of prosecutors and defense attorneys to show how the prosecutor's office works. Diane M. Goldie began her portrait of a 41-year-old prosecutor this way in the *Sun-Sentinel* of Ft. Lauderdale, Fla.:

> Before the sun has even considered rousing itself and before most of us get our motors running each morning, Palm Beach County Assistant State Attorney Michael Gersten is setting the wheels of justice in motion.
>
> At 5 a.m., on many weekday mornings, Gersten can be found telephoning police officers to alert them that the deadline for filing a case is that day.

Getting Tough   How tough are the courts on those convicted of violent crimes? A national survey found these results when it asked whether the court system dealt too harshly or not harshly enough with defendants:

Too harshly	3%
Not harshly enough	79
About right	12
Don't know	6

A computer check of sentences by crime committed has turned up sentencing stories for a number of newspapers and stations.

Capital Punishment   Many stations and newspapers have examined their state's death penalty. Although more than 3,200 prisoners are under sentence of death, executions average 40 to 50 a year with an average wait of almost 11 years from sentence to execution. California, Texas and Florida alone

Behave or Face the Consequences

Aware of the public dissatisfaction with the treatment of prison inmates, authorities have adopted measures to make the time behind bars hard time. In some jurisdictions, there are no-smoking rules. Also, cells no longer contain TV sets.

A technique used with the increasing number of young prisoners is the adoption of army training procedures. Youthful offenders are given the equivalent of a basic training course. Those who refuse to abide by the rules and regulations pay the consequences.

John Davenport, *The Houston Chronicle*

have 40 percent of those awaiting execution. Twelve states do not have a death penalty.

The disproportionate number of black men on death row has spurred an examination of the judicial process. Although blacks make up about 12 percent of the population they constitute 42 percent of those sentenced to death.

A recent study has shown that people convicted of killing whites were 11 times more likely to be given the death penalty than were those convicted of killing blacks.

Sentencing Blacks   The state prison population is mostly male, young and minority. Data show that almost half (48 percent) of all prison inmates are black. The Sentencing Project in Washington, D.C., reports that "on any given day one in four black men between the ages of 20 and 29 is in prison or on probation or parole."

In some cities, the figures are staggering: 42 percent of the black men in Washington, D.C., aged 18 to 35 are in prison; for Baltimore, the figure is 57 percent.

Does this mean that the law enforcement and judicial systems have a bias that makes for these statistics?

Donna Wasiczko of the *Contra Costa Times* tried to answer this question. She looked at the local situation, and although she found no definitive answers she did find some troubling indicators.

She quotes lawyers for minority defendants who do say there is bias. For example, there is a greater tendency to deny bail to black defendants, who are therefore confined while awaiting trial. All but one of the local judges (the exception is a Hispanic woman judge) are white. Most of the juries are all white.

In the county, 9 percent of the population is black. Of inmates in the state prison from Contra Costa County, 51 percent are black.

Underage Drinkers Tom Puleo of *The Hartford Courant* examined the practice of arresting and trying the owners of bars for serving underage drinkers but not prosecuting the customers who had used forged and faked drivers' licenses. He found 95 percent of the underage drinkers were not arrested. After two months of stories, the state liquor control division issued a new set of guidelines calling for the arrest of the underage customers.

Deadbeat Dads Bonnie Britt of the *Asbury* (N.J.) *Park Press* found that some parents—most of them fathers—were avoiding child support ordered by the courts. More than $650 million was owed in the state, but law enforcement officers did nothing to require a penny in collections. Some mothers who were owed child support, she wrote, were evicted from their homes when they could not pay rent.

Aggressive Dads Monica Rohr of the *Sun-Sentinel's* Miami bureau described a new factor in child-custody cases. Fathers are becoming more aggressive:

In the child custody war, the stakes are high, the strategies sometimes ruthless. Everything can become a weapon—child support, visitation, accusations of child molestation.

Now, something new is happening: Dads are fighting back. They're forming support groups and lobbying for legal reform.

They say child custody procedures often push fathers out of the family picture, leaving them to pay excessive child support while being isolated from their children.

These dads say the family court system is skewed against non-custodial parents — who in 90 percent of cases are men, legal experts say.

Inequities in family court do exist, with many older judges unwilling to give fathers the same rights as mothers, says Nancy Palmer, an Orlando lawyer who is chairman of The Florida Bar's legislative committee on family law. . . .

Doing Time Few reporters bother with life behind bars. Once the man or woman is sentenced, coverage concludes. The work of David Ward, professor of sociology at the University of Minnesota and a four-decade student of prisoners and prisons, points the way to a trove of stories about prison life. From his research in maximum security prisons he has concluded:

- Most prisoners advocate harsh measures to deter crime. "They are as concerned about what's happening in our society as everybody else. They are disgusted by child molesters and rapists and drive-by shooters. If anything, their remedies for crime are harsher than the general public's."

• Maximum security prisons, which some civil libertarians condemn, provide protection for inmates who, Ward says, told him that they "are concerned about personal safety. They're willing to give up some of the freedoms of a more open environment to feel safer."

• The general prison population is treated too leniently. "As far as I'm concerned inmates are living in hotels with amenities and people to wait on them. The staff takes care of their every need. There is not enough time for reflection."

Ward supports mandatory sentences and has little confidence in psychological counseling. He finds "not a shred of evidence that psychological treatments work."

Juvenile Defendants   State law closes the doors of juvenile hearings to the public. The theory is that rehabilitation is enhanced without publicity. But changes are being made in the system:

• More juveniles are being tried as adults, and the hearings and trials are open.

• Because of the heinous nature of some crimes, the media are using names of juveniles.

• In states where laws are stringent, the media are seeking access to the judicial process.

When a teen-ager was accused of murder in Sioux Falls, S.D., the *Argus Leader* asked for public hearings for the defendant. By law, juvenile proceedings are closed in South Dakota unless a judge decides there are compelling reasons to open them. In response to the paper's request, the judge proposed a contract with the newspaper in which the newspaper would agree not to publish certain material such as names, photographs and addresses of witnesses or those involved in the slaying. The newspaper's story of the judge's suggestion begins:

A circuit judge wants to know if the *Argus Leader* is ready to compromise before he decides whether to allow reporters into juvenile hearings for a teen-ager accused of killing a 16-year-old Sioux Falls boy.

Circuit Judge Gene Paul Kean told the *Argus Leader* on Monday to compose a contract by which it would abide if the judge allows reporters to watch hearings for Michael Christopherson. Christopherson faces a juvenile petition for delinquency for first-degree murder in the Sept. 1 shooting of 16-year-old Vernon Estenson.

The *Argus Leader* filed a motion Nov. 10 asking Kean to allow the public to observe juvenile proceedings for Christopherson, which by law are closed unless a judge decides compelling reasons exist to open them. Kean decided Oct. 28 in a closed hearing not to transfer Christopherson to adult court. . . .

The *Argus Leader* declined to compromise. The newspaper and other newspapers and broadcast stations had used the juvenile's name and address and run photos of him, which the teen-ager's lawyer said violated state law.

Note: The prohibition against disclosing the names of juvenile offenders usually applies to officials, not the media, which means that if a reporter obtains a name, he or she is not prohibited from using it.

In reply to the judge's request that the newspaper limit coverage, Jack Marsh, executive editor of the *Argus Leader,* said, "Our request is that this court case be conducted in the public's full view. It would not be appropriate, nor practical, for us to be admitted to the courtroom and then be restricted in the information we publish. As the public's eyes and ears, the *Argus Leader* needs to be free to report fully what we observe." The news story stated:

> The *Argus Leader* declined a judge's offer Tuesday, saying it won't compromise its efforts to fully report juvenile hearings for a teen-ager accused of killing a 16-year-old Sioux Falls boy.
>
> One day after Circuit Judge Gene Paul Kean asked the newspaper to propose a contract by which it would abide if allowed to view hearings for Michael Christopherson, the *Argus Leader* told the judge it wouldn't agree to restrictions on the information it publishes.
>
> "Our request is that this court case be conducted in the public's full view," said *Argus Leader* Editor Jack Marsh. . . .

In response, the judge said the teen-ager's right to privacy outweighs the public's right to know.

> Saying he heard no evidence to change his mind, a circuit judge on Wednesday denied a request by the *Argus Leader* to open juvenile proceedings against Michael Christopherson, a teen-ager accused of fatally shooting a 16-year-old Sioux Falls boy.
>
> In a written opinion that didn't mention Christopherson by name, Circuit Judge Gene Paul Kean said the accused boy's right to privacy outweighs the public's right to know what happens in the case.

Politics and the Courts

Elected or appointed, the judiciary has a deep involvement in politics. Mayors, governors, senators and the president reward party members and campaign supporters, despite their campaign promises of appointments to the bench on the basis of merit.

In many areas, the path to the bench begins with a political apprenticeship, either in a campaign or in a party post. Or it may be paved with contributions to a campaign. A vacancy on the Sixth Circuit, which includes Kentucky, Ohio,

Michigan and Tennessee, was considered a Tennessee seat and priority was given to Sen. James Sasser of that state. He favored Gilbert Merritt, a contributor to Sasser's campaigns. (Three contributions of $1,000 each were made to Sasser by three of Merritt's children, the oldest 12 years of age.) Merritt was given the appointment as a federal judge.

When President John Kennedy wanted congressional action on key legislation he found it bogged down in the Senate, blocked by Sen. Robert Kerr. A Kennedy aide called Kerr and asked why, and Kerr answered, "Tell him to get his dumb (expletive) brother to quit opposing my friend Ross Bohannon for a federal judgeship in Oklahoma." (Kennedy's brother, Robert, was attorney general.) Kennedy thereupon called up his brother, Bohannon was confirmed as a federal judge and Kennedy soon had Senate action on his bill.

Appointees Screened   During the Reagan and Bush administrations, federal court appointees were screened for their attitudes toward abortion, affirmative federal action and First Amendment rights.

The approach that the Reagan-Bush presidencies took to the Supreme Court could be seen in George Bush's appointment of Clarence Thomas to the so-called black seat on the Court, which had been held by Thurgood Marshall. Thomas passed Bush's tests on abortion rights (against) and affirmative action (against). Marshall supported both in cases before the Court.

One of the results of the Reagan and Bush screening was nominees who were male, white and rich:

- **Reagan:** 93 percent Republican, 93 percent white, 91 percent male, more than 20 percent millionaires.
- **Bush:** 89 percent white, 80 percent male, 64 percent reporting a net worth of more than $500,000.

Clinton's appointments were consistent with his campaign promise to diversify the judiciary. Thirty percent were women, 25 percent black, 10 percent Hispanic. His first appointment to the U.S. Supreme Court was a Jewish woman, Ruth Bader Ginsburg. Politically, he favored his party but selected as judges men and women with a centrist position on legal issues.

Elected Judges   In 21 states, candidates for the judiciary run for office in elections. Those wanting to seek a second term must run for retention in 38 states.

Judicial campaigns can be so costly that some candidates have to seek campaign contributions from lawyers and others who may appear before them in the courts. Some qualified candidates refuse to consider running because of the costs of a campaign. The Fund for Modern Courts has found that among elected—as opposed to appointed—judges there are fewer women and minorities.

Good judges have come out of the political system. Some of the great justices on the Supreme Court of the United States owed their appointments to political considerations. The reporter who examines the system of election and appointment to the bench must be careful not to predict performance.

The Grand Jury

The grand jury may initiate investigations as well as act on charges brought by a prosecutor. It can look into the administration of public institutions and the conduct of local and state officials and investigate crime. In some states, grand juries must be empaneled to make periodic examinations of specific state institutions and official bodies.

Special grand juries can be appointed to look into matters such as mistreatment of patients in a state hospital or a tie-in between the police vice squad and organized crime. The district attorney or the attorney general's office directs the inquiry, although the governor may appoint a special prosecutor to direct the investigation.

When a grand jury initiates action on its own and hands up a report on offenses, the report is known as a *presentment.* A presentment may be a statement of the jury's findings or it can charge a person with a crime.

Grand jury deliberations are secret and any publication of the discussions is treated severely by the courts. However, reporters are free to write about the area of investigation, and witnesses can talk to the press about their testimony in most states. Reporters often will try to learn who is testifying by stationing themselves near the jury room. Knowing the identity of witnesses, reporters are free to speculate. But the morality of publishing the names of witnesses is questionable because the grand jury may question witnesses not directly involved in wrongdoing, and even those under suspicion are not to be considered guilty.

One way reporters have learned about witnesses is by watching for motions to dismiss subpoenas issued to require witnesses to appear before the grand jury. Such motions are usually part of the public record and thereby provide the reporter with a document that can be reported.

In covering grand jury matters, as any pretrial proceeding, the danger is that publicity may harm innocent people or impair a defendant's right to a fair trial. Several verdicts have been reversed because of newspaper and broadcast coverage. The reporter must balance the right of the individual with the public's need to know what its official bodies are doing. Once the grand jury takes formal action, the report can be publicized.

Trouble Areas   Some reporters knowingly violate or skirt the laws to obtain information about grand jury investigations. They act in the belief that there will be no prosecution of their deeds. Sometimes they are mistaken, as the managing editor, city editor and two reporters for *The Fresno Bee* learned after their newspaper published material from a sealed grand jury transcript. They refused to reveal their source and were charged with contempt of court.

The reporter should check local and state laws, particularly when assigned to the police or court beats. Here are some actions that violate the laws of many states:

- Publishing confidential grand jury information leaked by someone in the prosecutor's office. (It is legal to use information provided by a witness about what he or she told the grand jury.)

- Using documents or property stolen from the police or an individual.
- Using confidential records transmitted or sold by the police.

In these instances, the reporter becomes an accomplice to a criminal act and can be prosecuted.

Time Out for a Good Laugh

Court coverage is usually serious, sometimes high tension. But courtrooms sometimes ring with laughter. Attorneys do crack jokes, judges deign to comment sarcastically on cases and witnesses unwittingly provide laughs:

- A reporter heard this aside in a South Dakota federal district court from a man charged with theft of livestock when the jury returned a not-guilty verdict: "Does this mean I get to keep the cows?"
- In his summation before a state district court in the Midwest, the lawyer for a man charged with armed robbery pleaded, "I ask you, ladies and gentlemen of the jury, to give the defendant your best shot."
- When a Minnesota county court judge was asked to perform a marriage for two men, the judge turned to one of them and asked, "Which one of you has the menstrual cycle?"

"Not me," said one of the men. "I got a Harley-Davidson."

- The judge in a New York case looked at the divorcing couple and announced, "I am going to give Mrs. Sheldon $3,000 a month."

"Great," her husband said. "And I'll toss in a few bucks myself."

Court Language

The judicial system has a language of its own that lawyers, judges and clerks use with exactitude. The beginning reporter should learn these terms and add to them through reading and experience.

Officers of the Court

attorneys Prosecutors and defense lawyers whose duties are to represent their clients; the attorney's role is partisan; he or she is an advocate; it is not unusual, therefore, for an attorney to try to sell his or her case to the press. The press should be skeptical of statements outside the courtroom.

bailiff Keeps order in courtroom; takes charge of the jury; sees to it no one talks to the jury.

court clerk Calls the court to order before each stage of the proceedings and administers the oath to witnesses. The clerk's office contains records of all judicial proceedings. This office is an excellent source of news.

court reporter Records the courtroom proceedings. Unless records are sealed, transcripts can be purchased; the price varies from court to court and state to state.

judge Presides over a trial, rules on points of law dealing with trial procedure, evidence and law. The jury determines the facts.

Court Terms

acquit A verdict of not guilty; the legal and formal certification of innocence of a person charged with a crime.

adjudicate To make a final determination through legal action.

adversary proceeding An action that is contested by opposing parties.

alibi Used in criminal law: to be elsewhere, in another place.

allegation The assertion, declaration or statement of a party to an action; an assertion of what is expected to be proved.

amicus curiae A friend of the court; one who interposes and volunteers information about some matter of law.

answer A pleading by which the defendant tries to dispute the plaintiff's right to recover by disproving the facts alleged by the plaintiff or the principle of law relied on by him or her, or both.

appearance The formal proceeding by which a defendant submits himself or herself to the jurisdiction of the court.

appellant The party appealing a decision or judgment to a higher court.

appellate court A court that hears appeals and reviews lower-court decisions, generally on the lower-court record only.

appellee The successful party in the lower court against whom an appeal is taken.

arraign In criminal practice, the formal calling of a prisoner to the bar of the court to answer charges in the indictment or to give information as to whether he or she is guilty or not guilty. The suspect is acquainted with the charge against him or her following arrest; bail is set at arraignment.

arrest The deprivation of a person's liberty by authority of the law.

autopsy The inspection and dissection of a body to learn the cause of death.

bail The security given for the release of a prisoner. Cash or a bond is placed in the court to guarantee that the person held in legal custody will appear at the time and the place the court sets. Defendants are usually entitled to be set at liberty on bail unless charged with an offense punishable by death and even sometimes in these instances. The judge or magistrate sets bail. The Constitution prohibits excessive bail.

bench warrant An order issued by the court ("from the bench") for the attachment or arrest of a person.

beneficiary One for whose benefit a trust is created.

bind over To hold on bail for trial.

booking The process whereby a suspect's name, address and purported crime are entered into a book in the police precinct or police headquarters.

bribery The receiving, offering or soliciting by or to any person whose profession or business involves the administration of public justice or who has other official status in order to influence behavior. Giving or taking a reward in connection with voting also constitutes bribery.

brief A written document prepared by counsel to serve as the basis for argument. It embodies the points of law that the counsel desires to establish.

burglary Breaking and entering the house or other property of another with intention of committing a felony, whether the felony is committed or not. Burglary does not involve a crime against a person, which is **robbery.**

certiorari An order commanding judges or officers of a lower court to certify the record of a case for judicial review by an appellate court.

challenge for cause An objection to the qualifications of a juror for which a reason is given; usually on the grounds of personal acquaintance with one of the parties or the existence of a bias that may affect the verdict.

chambers The private room or office of a judge.

change of venue The removal for trial of a suit begun in one county or district to another or from one court to another in the same county or district.

charge In criminal law, an accusation.

circumstantial evidence All evidence of indirect nature; the process of decision by which the court or jury may reason from circumstances known or proved to establish by inference the principal fact.

code A collection, compendium or revision of laws.

common law Law that derives its authority solely from usages and customs of immemorial antiquity or from the judgment and decrees of courts.

commutation The change of a punishment from a greater degree to a lesser degree, as from death to life imprisonment.

complainant A person who brings a criminal or civil action.

complaint The first or initiatory pleading on the part of the complainant, or plaintiff, in a civil action.

concurrent In a prison sentence, terms that are to be served together (not in succession). In the judge's action or opinion, an agreement.

conspiracy In criminal law, an agreement between two or more people for the purpose of committing some unlawful act.

contempt of court Any act calculated to embarrass, hinder or obstruct a court in the administration of justice or calculated to lessen its authority or dignity. Contempts are of two kinds: direct or indirect. Direct contempts are those committed in the immediate presence of the court; indirect is the term chiefly used with reference to the failure or refusal to obey a lawful order.

contract A promissory agreement between two or more persons that creates, modifies or destroys a legal relation.

cross-examination The practice whereby an opposing lawyer questions a witness at a hearing or trial.

cumulative sentence Sentences for two or more crimes to run successively rather than concurrently.

declaratory judgment One that declares the rights of the parties or expresses the opinion of the court on a question of law, without necessarily ordering anything to be done.

decree A decision or order of the court. A final decree is one that fully and finally disposes of the litigation; an interlocutory decree is a provisional or preliminary decree that is not final.

de facto In fact or actually. Usually refers to a situation or an action that has the appearance of legality and is generally accepted as such but is actually illegal.

default In an action of law, occurs when a defendant fails to plead within the time allowed or fails to appear at the trial.

defendant A person in a criminal or civil action who defends or denies the allegations.

de jure Rightful, legitimate, legal.

deposition The testimony of a witness not taken in open court in pursuance of authority given by statute or rule of court to take testimony elsewhere.

discovery A proceeding whereby one party to an action may be informed about facts known by other parties or witnesses.

dissent The explicit disagreement of one or more judges with the decision passed by the majority in a case before them.

docket The list of cases set for trial in a court.

eminent domain The power to take private property for public use by paying for it.

entrapment The act of officers or agents of a government in inducing a person to commit a crime not contemplated by him or her, for the purpose of instituting a criminal prosecution against him or her.

evidence Concrete objects presented at trial through witnesses, records and documents for the purpose of inducing belief in the minds of the trial judge or jury.

exculpatory Clearing or tending to clear from alleged guilt.

ex parte By or for one party; done for in behalf of or on the application of one party only, without notice to the other.

extradition When one state (or nation) surrenders to another state an individual accused or convicted of a crime outside its territory.

felony A crime of a graver or more atrocious nature than one designated as a misdemeanor. Usually punishable by more than one year in a penitentiary.

grand jury A jury of inquiry whose duty is to receive complaints and accusations in criminal cases, to hear the evidence presented by the state and to find bills of indictment when the jury is satisfied a trial ought to be held.

habeas corpus "You have the body." The name given a variety of writs whose object is to bring a person before a court or judge. In most common usage, it commands the official or person detaining another to produce the prisoner or person detained so the court may determine if such person has been denied liberty under due process of the law.

hearsay Evidence not proceeding from the personal knowledge of the witness.

homicide The killing of a human being.

in camera In chambers; in private.

indeterminate sentence An indefinite sentence of "not less than" and "not more than" so many years, the exact term to be served being afterward determined by parole authorities within the minimum and maximum limits set by the court or by statute.

indictment An accusation handed up to the court by a grand jury.

indigent A poor person. In court, an indigent is usually defended by legal aid or an attorney in the public defender's office.

information A formal accusation of crime by the appropriate public official such as the prosecuting attorney. In some states, accused persons may be brought to trial by an information—a sworn, written accusation that leads to an indictment without a grand jury investigation.

injunction A mandatory or prohibitive writ issued by a court.

instruction A direction given by the judge to the jury concerning the law of the case.

jury The court-approved individuals—12 for criminal cases and 6 or 8 for civil cases depending on the attorneys' stipulations—who decide the guilt or innocence of defendant(s) in a trial; their verdict in a criminal case must be unanimous. (Referred to as petit juries in criminal and civil cases.)

manslaughter The unlawful killing without malice of another human being.

misdemeanor Offenses lower than felonies and generally punishable by fine or imprisonment in other than a penitentiary.

mistrial An erroneous or invalid trial; a trial that cannot stand in law because of lack of jurisdiction, wrong drawing of jurors or disregard of some other fundamental requisite.

no bill This phrase, endorsed by a grand jury on the indictment, is equivalent to "not found" or "not a true bill." It means that, in the opinion of the jury, evidence was insufficient to warrant the return of a formal charge.

nolo contendere "I will not contest it." The defendant's announcement that he or she does not contest the facts. The plea has the same legal effect as a plea of guilty, but it cannot be used as an admission of guilt elsewhere, as in a civil suit.

parole The conditional release of a prisoner from confinement. The condition usually is that if the prisoner meets the terms of the parole, he or she will be given an absolute discharge from the remainder of the sentence. If not, the prisoner is returned to serve the unexpired term.

peremptory challenge The right of parties in criminal and civil cases to dismiss a prospective juror without giving any reason. The number of such challenges is limited by statute.

plea A response to the court made by the defendant or a representative either answering the charges or showing why the defendant should not be required to answer.

plea bargaining The arrangement between prosecutor and defendant whereby the state offers to reduce the charges against the defendant in return for a guilty plea.

pleading The process by which the parties in a suit or action alternately present written statements, each responding to the other and each narrowing the controversy until one or a few points—called "the issue"—become the basis of the trial.

preliminary hearing Follows arraignment; evidence is heard to determine if a crime has been committed and whether the matter should proceed to trial. The judge may dismiss the case if he or she feels the evidence against the suspect is insufficient or was illegally obtained. If the evidence is sufficient, he or she will bind the case over to the grand jury for possible indictment. If an indictment ensues, the case is transferred to a higher court.

presentment The written action by a grand jury without an indictment; a presentment usually seeks to change the nature or operation of a particular institution that permitted offenses against the public.

probation A suspension of sentence allowing a person convicted of a criminal offense to stay out of jail during good behavior and generally under the supervision or guardianship of a probation officer.

search warrant A court order authorizing an officer or a citizen to search a specified house or other premises for evidence, stolen property or unlawful goods.

stay An action that stops or arrests a judicial proceeding by order of the court.

subpoena A process to cause a witness to appear and give testimony before a court or magistrate.

summons A notification to the named person that an action has been commenced against him or her in court and that he or she is required to appear, on the day named, and answer the complaint in such action.

suspended sentence A sentence withheld or postponed by the judge. In most cases, the suspension is indefinite and depends upon satisfactory probation reports.

term Used in some jurisdictions to denote the ordinary session of court.

tort An injury or wrong committed, either with or without force, to another person or the property of another.

unconstitutional An action or law that is contrary to the Constitution or to state constitutions. (Do not confuse with **illegal.**)

venire Technically, a writ summoning people to court to act as jurors; popularly used for the body of names thus summoned.

venue The place or county in which an injury or crime is said to have been committed.

voir dire The preliminary examination that the court or lawyers may make of a prospective juror to determine whether he or she is acceptable to decide a case as a juror.

waiver of immunity A means authorized by statutes by which a witness, in advance of giving testimony or producing evidence, may renounce the fundamental right guaranteed by the Constitution that no person shall be compelled to be a witness against him- or herself.

warrant of arrest A writ issued by a magistrate, justice or other competent authority to a sheriff or other officer requiring him or her to arrest a person therein named and bring him or her before the magistrate or court to answer to a specified charge.

writ An order issuing from a court of justice and requiring the performance of a specified act or giving authority and commission to have it done.

Further Reading

Chiason, Lloyd Jr., ed. *The Press on Trial: Crimes and Trials as Media Events.* Westport, Conn.: Greenwood Press, 1997.
(A study of 16 major criminal trials from the 1735 trial of colonial printer Peter Zenger through the trials of John Brown, Lizzie Borden and Bruno Hauptmann to the O. J. Simpson murder trial and how they reflected the concept of justice at the time of the trials.)
Thaler, Paul. *The Spectacle Media and the Making of the O. J. Simpson Story.* Westport, Conn.: Praeger Publishers, 1997.
Toobin, Jeffrey. *The Run of His Life: The People v. O. J. Simpson.* New York: Random House, 1996.

Two issues of the *Media Studies Journal* published by The Freedom Forum Media Studies Center are useful:

"Crime Story," a selection of articles about the police and courts by a variety of authors that include judges and reporters: Winter 1992 issue.

"Covering the Courts," articles about cameras in the courtroom, the Simpson and McVeigh trials and legal aspects of court coverage: Winter 1998 issue.

The *Journal* is available from the Center at 580 Madison Avenue, New York, NY 10022.

Mike Roemer

**Excitement is the name
of the game**

Preview

The most heavily read section of the newspaper after local news is sports news. Television coverage draws millions of viewers. The nation is made up of fans, many of them experts on the sports they follow.

The sports reporter handles:

• **Game stories:** Coverage requires the score, key plays and players, effect of the game on standings, turning point of the game and post-game interviews.

• **Profiles:** Personality stories on new players, athletes having outstanding seasons, game stars, coaches. Profiles require background, plenty of quotations, the individual in action.

• **Illegal and improper activities:** Payoffs to college players, drug use, racism, academic violations by coaches and schools, penalties to colleges.

• **Also:** Recruiting, salaries, personal lives of athletes, recollections.

When Susan V. Hands went to her first job to cover sports for *The Charlotte Observer,* she was anxious to investigate the growth of participant sports and to promote the development of women's athletics. Hands, the *Observer*'s first woman sportswriter, quickly shifted gears.

"I learned that people buy the morning paper to find out what happened in last night's football or basketball game. And our readers would be angry if, instead of finding the highlights and statistics of yesterday's North Carolina State basketball game, there was an investigative piece on the lack of athletic training available to girls in Charlotte high schools," she says.

Readers want to read about the game. They want to savor the important plays again, despite having seen them twice—once as they unfolded and once again, courtesy of instant replay. But the assumption that readers have seen the game on television may no longer be valid, says Frank Barrows, managing editor of the *Observer.* With so many games available to television viewers, the reporter cannot presume that the reader saw any particular game.

"Game results sell newspapers," says Hands.

Fans also want to know what goes on off the court and the field. "We take you behind the scenes," says Mark Mulvoy, the publisher of *Sports Illustrated,* whose circulation of 3 million is said to reach 16 million men and 5 million women for each issue. And that is with a subscription cost of $70 a year, one of the highest among magazines.

Insatiable Demand

The appetite for sports is voracious. The Super Bowl draws 150 million viewers, and advertisers line up to spend more than a million dollars for a brief commercial. The Associated Press assigns 100 writers to cover sports, and these writers send out more than 150,000 words a day plus statistics—enough to fill 20 pages of an eight-column newspaper. And that doesn't include the outpouring of the local sports staffs.

Then there are the sports briefs every 15 minutes on all-news radio stations. And the all-sports radio stations and television channels that broadcast everything from midget car racing to table tennis tournaments.

It wasn't always this way, of course, although the interest in sports is longstanding. Hearst and Pulitzer recognized the appeal of sports news as they waged their battle for the pennies of the emerging working class. But the plunge into sports mania, some historians say, came with a boxing match in 1926.

The Fight that Did It

When the Manassa Mauler, Jack Dempsey, met the erudite Gene Tunney for the heavyweight championship, the nation—and parts of the world—stood still. Publishers who had paid sports scant attention now found that "it is impossible to print too much," reported Will Owen Jones, the editor of the *Nebraska State Journal.* Jones had been asked by the American Society of Newspaper Editors to look into the "national obsession for sporting intelligence" because the serious editors were alarmed by the interest in what they considered entertainment.

Seven hundred reporters covered the fight. They dispatched two million words to an enthralled public, says Bruce J. Evensen of DePaul University in his article in the *Journalism Quarterly.* " 'Cave Man' Meets 'Student Champion': Sports Page Storytelling for a Nervous Generation During America's Jazz Age." Evensen writes, "Press coverage of the Dempsey-Tunney 1926 title fight signaled the arrival of the modern sports page as a major player in the struggle for circulation."

Tunney won that match, dethroning the mighty Dempsey who had reigned as champion for seven years. The rematch the following year generated even more print, and it is still discussed on the sports pages. In the seventh round, Dempsey knocked Tunney down. But the referee did not begin to count over the downed new champ because, so it's said, Dempsey failed to go to his corner. Tunney went on to win the rematch.

To test prospective hires, some sports editors ask the applicants, "What's the 'long count'?" Those who answer, "Dempsey-Tunney, 1927," get the job.

Expanded Coverage

Quiz. Which sports events require the largest sportswriting team the AP sends out? The Olympics. But for annual events, it is the Indianapolis 500. The wire service stations men and women in the infield hospital, garages, the crow's nest, the pits and in the stands.

Today's sports reporters do much more than offer an account of athletic events. New areas of coverage have opened up: labor negotiations, increasing women's competition, the use of drugs by athletes, the commercialization and sometimes the corruption of college sports, high school recruiting.

Considerable man- and woman-power is devoted to sports coverage. A fifth of the country's reporters are assigned to sports, more than to any other beat. And sports makes up about 20 percent of the editorial content of a metropolitan newspaper.

Participant sports have grown enormously. Hunting and fishing columns are regular features in many newspapers. Local tennis and golf tournaments attract coverage. A young journalist who fancies a sportswriting career would be wise to learn about all sports.

Savvy Fans   Sports reporters write for a discerning audience. There may be no more knowledgeable reader and viewer than the sports fan. The fan knows why Roger Maris had an asterisk next to his name in the record books before his 61 home runs were eclipsed. They know what "in the paint" means, and they know who Vince Lombardi was.

Fans want more than the scores. They turn to the sports pages to find out why the UCLA coach pulled his quarterback in the second half, the strategy by which Missouri managed to hold Kansas State to three baskets in the last six minutes of play. Game stories must tell the fan what happened and also how and why.

Fans also want to know something about the athletes they watch on television and read about in game stories. There is an interest in the personal lives of athletes.

Personal Lives

At one time, what athletes did off the field was their business, even if it affected their play. No one tried to find out why Hank Thompson played third base so strangely for the New York Giants. "I had always supposed it was simply Thompson's way to scoop up a grounder along with the bag and whatever bits of grass and gravel were in the area and hurl the entire package across the diamond, leaving the first baseman to sort it out as best he could," said Peter Andrews of the days he covered the team.

Today, he would find out and probably report that Thompson often played third base drunk.

Alan Robinson, an AP sportswriter, says, "We're people writing about people instead of people writing about heroes. That's healthy."

Athletes as Models

When Charles Barkley threw a man through a plate glass window in a bar, he received a call from Michael Jordan.

"Charles, I love you like a brother," Jordan said he told Barkley, "but you can't do that kind of thing. It's stupid. And you have to stay out of bars. They're only trouble."

Jordan, who had seen an HBO documentary about Joe DiMaggio was impressed. DiMaggio, who played baseball for the New York Yankees in the 1930s, saw himself as a symbol to Italian-American immigrants and their sons and daughters trying to overcome prejudice. DiMaggio, Jordan said, behaved like a gentleman on and off the field.

Jordan remarked to a sportswriter that he is no DiMaggio. Nor, he continued, is he Muhammad Ali, Joe Louis or Jackie Robinson. "They carried the burden of a whole race. I've never had to do that," Jordan said. But he added: "I can only do what I'm comfortable doing, and working with kids in the inner city is one of them."

Truth-Telling   On Jordan's retirement, sports writers lauded him as the best basketball player of his time, probably of all time. But they were less laudatory about his off-the-court activities. When it was revealed that Nike exploited its workers abroad, Jordan said little and did nothing to deplore the activities of the company that had paid him tens of millions of dollars to sell its athletic shoes. And when he refused to endorse a Democratic black candidate for the U.S. Senate in Jordan's home state of North Carolina who was running against a candidate with a deep conservative stance on race relations, Jordan replied, "Republicans buy shoes, too."

Ira Berkow of *The New York Times* wrote that now Jordan "might be able to make a contribution of the kind he has consistently avoided. . . . What he can do is take a stand when the situation requires."

Pluses and Minuses   In another column, Berkow wrote that "aberrant acts by high-profile athletes occur regularly. . . . The times have produced a remarkable chemical reaction in some players; it has fattened their wallets and bankrupted their wits."

Some sportswriters look deeply at the professional athletes they cover. What are they doing for the communities that reward them so richly? The answers make for good stories.

"Most of what Americans know about the humanistic traditions—about excellence in act, about discipline, about community, about unity of body and will and spirit—they learn first-hand from their experience in sport," says Michael Novak, a writer and theologian.

Off-Court Activities

Sports Illustrated checked on the extracurricular activities of players in the National Basketball Association and came up with the report that many NBA players have fathered illegitimate children, one with seven by six different women. Another player has five illegitimate children to add to the two by his wife.

Andrew D. Bernstein,
NBA photo

Michael Jordan

"High in the air, his legs splayed, his tongue flopping out of his mouth, he seems weirdly relaxed, calm, as if there were no one special around and plenty of time to think through his next move, floating all the while. Faced with double coverage, as he almost always is, Jordan finds a way to wedge between defenders, elevate as if on an invisible forklift, his legs dangling, and then drop the ball through the hoop. The ease of his game makes the rest of the players, all of them stars in college, look rough, somehow—clumsy, a step slow."— David Remnick

The detailed disclosure named several players on its "NBA All-Paternity Team." They include Patrick Ewing, Juwan Howard, Shawn Kemp, Jason Kidd, Stephon Marbury, Hakeem Olajuwon, Gary Payton and Scottie Pippen. Kemp pays an average of $6,000 a month for each of his seven children. Not to worry. He has a seven-year contract for $107 million.

One of the major basketball agents told the magazine, "I'd say there might be more kids out of wedlock than there are players in the NBA." He said he spends more time "dealing with paternity claims than negotiating contracts," *Sports Illustrated* reported.

Sports reporters prefer the brighter side of sports, and there are plenty of stories about athletes' overcoming adversity.

A Tragic Childhood   When Terry Glenn of the New England Patriots set an NFL record of 90 catches as a rookie, Thomas George of *The New York Times* interviewed him and told of Glenn's childhood:

> Glenn's mother was murdered in his hometown, Columbus, Ohio, when he was 13. His father lives somewhere in Columbus and Glenn has never met or seen him. Glenn grew up in his earliest years on welfare and wearing goodwill clothes. There were days when there was no electricity in his home.

A Dream Realized   Jerry Tipton of the *Herald-Leader* in Lexington, Ky., wrote a moving profile of George Adams, a University of Kentucky tailback, from interviews with the football player and his friends and family. Tipton begins:

> When Ruth Adams, mother of nine, sits in the living room of her Lexington home, she can look at nine photographs of her children. Five of them are of her younger son, George.
>
> "The others get on me for having so much about George," she said. "I love them all, the grandchildren, too. But George has a special place."

Tipton develops his story slowly, and the picture that emerges is of a family with many difficulties. Adams' father drank. A brother and a sister have served time in jail. Another son, the mother said, is "in trouble."

"George never gave me no kind of trouble," she said, breaking a long pause. "He always brought good things home from school. He made me happy."

When others caused so much trouble, why didn't George?

"He saw so much pain in his mother's eyes," said Donnie Harville, who coached Adams in basketball at Lafayette High. "And he decided he wouldn't make his mother suffer more."

Tipton delves into the family's problems:

> Adams can remember seeing his father walking unsteadily down a street. The son would cross to the other side to avoid a face-to-face meeting. . . .
>
> "When I was young, it hurt a lot," Adams said. "I mean a whole lot. I told myself I'm not going to be like that."

Adams had a dream. "If I can play pro football, the first thing I want to do with my first contract is buy my mother a house," he told Tipton.

Adams was selected in the first round of the professional football draft. He signed a four-year contract for $1.5 million, and he did buy a house for his mother.

Little Leaguers　　A stroll over to the local fields some weekend to watch the youngsters playing Little League baseball can pay off with fascinating features. So can recollections of adult athletes.

"I still remember it like it was yesterday," Paul O'Neill, a New York Yankee outfielder, told a reporter about his Little League days in Columbus, Ohio. "I pitched the championship game and struck out a kid named Darren Waugh to end it. I remember every detail. The games then meant as much to you as these games do now. And you got to go to Dairy Queen afterward."

Four of five of the major leaguers played Little League baseball. Ten-year-old Mark McGwire in his first at-bat in Southern California hit a home run, he recalls.

Looking back on a career with more strikeouts than any pitcher and more no-hit games, Nolan Ryan told Alan Schwarz of *The New York Times* his happiest memories of baseball were playing Little League in Alvin, Tex. "We played for the love of the game and the camaraderie. Little League was the first opportunity for children in Alvin to get involved in any organized activity. It was one of the biggest events in our lives," Ryan said.

Tomorrow's Major Leaguers

The Beat

In addition to covering games, the sports reporter attends sports banquets, drops by the pro shops at the golf and tennis courts, chats with the unsung athletes on the high school swimming, soccer, wrestling and track teams. The high school and college athletes who may go through a season never playing before more than a handful of spectators make for good stories. Not many readers understand why a youngster will run 10 to 20 miles a day to prepare for a cross-country meet, what it is like to engage in a noncontact sport in which the only adversary is the athlete's own mind and body. The runners, the javelin throwers, the swimmers, the gymnasts, the fencers and the wrestlers should not be overwhelmed by the glut of basketball and football coverage.

Tough Beat. Professional basketball writers say theirs is the most grueling of all sports beats. Covering games in so many cities requires frequent travel, sometimes coast-to-coast twice in a week. "I take care of my body as if I were a player," says David DuPree of *USA Today.* "I don't drink or smoke." Jackie MacMullan of *The Boston Globe* says she works out daily on road trips.

On most newspapers, a reporter will cover several sports and has a list of key contacts who can supply background quickly and accurately. Usually, the first name on the reporter's list is the athletic director or the publicity director. For high school sports, the coach is the major source.

Fans, especially the armchair expert who has made a vocation of following one of the local teams, can be excellent sources. The "sports nut," as some reporters call this person, has at his or her fingertips records, statistics and standings going back years.

Enterprise

Editors count on their sports reporters to enterprise stories. In such a competitive field, the reporters who go far are those with imagination as well as talent.

When Columbia University's new football coach arrived at a New York airport, he spotted a man holding a sign with the new coach's name, "Ray Teller." Presuming the sign holder was a driver who would take him to the university, the coach walked over. "Yes, I'm Ray Teller."

But the sign holder was a reporter who was after, and was given, an exclusive interview with the new coach.

Good Writing

The Greatest. Some sportswriters consider Ted Williams the best hitter in baseball's long history, but Williams disagrees. "I can't say I was a better hitter than Lou Gehrig." As for the best players he ever saw, "without question, Joe DiMaggio and Mickey Mantle."

Sportswriting, which used to be considered hyperactive and cliché ridden, now is seen as one of the newspaper's brightest showcases. Truth is that sports has always brought out some of the best in writers. Consider this gem by John Updike about the last at-bat of the great Boston Red Sox outfielder Ted Williams. Williams had done the unbelievable—he hit a home run.

Though we thumped, wept, and chanted "We want Ted" for minutes after he hid in the dugout, he did not come back. Our noise for some seconds passed beyond excitement into a kind of immense open anguish, a wailing, a cry to be saved. But immortality is not transferable. The papers said that other players, and even the umpires on the field, begged him to come out and acknowledge us in some way, but he never had and did not now. God does not answer letters.

When the New York Yankees were winning pennant after pennant and Mickey Mantle was the home run king, Jim Murray of the *Los Angeles Times* wrote, "Rooting for the New York Yankees is like rooting for U.S. Steel."

Good writing means retaining the colorful language of sports, not falling into the homogeneous prose that infects too much of newspaper and television writing. Russell Baker, a columnist on *The New York Times* editorial page and a die-hard sports fan, bemoaned the decline of baseball talk that, he wrote, once "crackled with terseness, vibrancy and metaphor."

Baker had heard a television sportscaster say, "Ryan has good velocity and excellent location." He meant, Baker wrote, that "Ryan is throwing very fast and putting the ball where he wants to."

Dizzy and Yogi

The stilted writing of some reporters makes a sports fan long for Dizzy Dean, the St. Louis Cardinals pitcher and later a sports announcer who was known for his picturesque language. Once he was struck on the toe while pitching and a doctor examined him on the mound. "This toe is fractured," the doctor said. To which Dean replied, "Fractured hell. The damn thing's broken."

Sportswriters carry stories such as the Dizzy Dean incident in their hip pockets. They also have a collection of Yogi Berra's comments handy for use when appropriate:

- It's not over 'til it's over.
- It gets late early at Yankee Stadium.
- That place is too crowded; nobody goes there anymore.
- Ninety percent of baseball is half-mental.
- It's déjà vu all over again.
- When you come to a fork in the road, take it.
- If people don't want to come out to the ballpark, nobody's going to stop them.
- Slump? I ain't in no slump. I just ain't hitting.

Did Berra, former catcher for the New York Yankees and manager of a couple of major league teams, really say that, or are they creations of baseball writers who needed to brighten their copy? No one is talking.

Great Lines   Sportswriters have written some memorable lines, such as this one about a midwestern quarterback who was a wizard on the field, a dunce in the classroom: "He could do anything with a football but autograph it." (The line came back to some sportswriters when they wrote about a football player at UCLA who was arrested for killing his drug dealer. The player, it turned out, could not read—the product of the win-at-any-price philosophy of big-time sports.)

Red Smith was a master writer. Of a notorious spitball pitcher, he wrote that "papers needed three columns for his pitching record: won, lost and relative humidity." Look at this lead he wrote about Buck Leonard, a black first baseman whose career ended before baseball was integrated:

> Wearing a store suit, horn-rimmed glasses, and a smile that could light up Yankee Stadium, a sunny gentleman of 64 revisited his past yesterday and recalled what it was like to be the black Lou Gehrig on a food allowance of 60 cents a day.

The last few words chill an otherwise warm recollection. They sum up a period of American life in a phrase.

Read and Learn

Sports writing has a glorious past. Some of the finest writers in journalism toiled in the sports department. Their work is worth reading. Jimmy Cannon was one of the best.

Cannon, who worked for New York newspapers, spent a lot of time with athletes. They felt at ease talking to him, and they liked his respect for them and their sports.

Cannon knew the tedium of their lives on the road, and he occasionally wrote about it. When the Boston Celtics were in New York for a game with the Knicks, Cannon spent the day with Bob Cousy, regarded then as the best basketball player on the court.

The piece begins with the arrival of the Celtics:

> The Celtics arrived here Monday at 1:30 in the afternoon and checked into the Paramount Hotel where Cousy roomed with Tommy Heinsohn. He took a shower and put on fresh clothes and talked a while with Heinsohn. The topics were unimportant but occasionally basketball intruded and they recalled fragments of games they had played.

They go to lunch, and Cannon writes: "Cousy ate pea soup, roast beef, potatoes, salad, ice cream and milk. He is a few pounds underweight and his face is lined."

Notice the details in Cannon's account. He accompanies Cousy on a visit to an agent. "He took the subway back to the hotel. He didn't feel tense or nervous but what would happen in the game was always on the rim of his consciousness. It seemed his body was tired in a heavy way."

They chat in the hotel, and Cousy talks about an opposing player he respects who is not given much credit for his playing, Cousy says.

The piece ends with two sentences about the game that night: "Cousy made 35 points, but the Celtics lost 110–99. They caught a late plane to Boston."

Know Them All

People in sports are always looking around the next corner. Branch Rickey, owner of the baseball Dodgers remarked, "Hope springs eternal in April." Baseball fans are looking for the next Willie Mays or Jackie Robinson. Basketball fans wonder whether the new center will be another Kareem Abdul-Jabbar. When Red Smith became nervous about covering so many mediocre baseball players he would cheer himself up by saying, "Some day there will be another Joe DiMaggio."

Century's Best. *GO* magazine called Muhammad Ali the sportsman of the century. David Remnick, editor of *The New Yorker,* who wrote the book *King of the World: The Creation of Muhammad Ali,* says, "I think he is the most electric sporting figure of the century. I can't imagine who else it would be. I'm talking out of my childhood. Maybe for someone twenty-five years older than me, Joe Louis, Joe DiMaggio or Willie Mays would be."

Mays? Kareem? DiMaggio? Wilt Chamberlain, Joe Louis, Wilma Rudolph, A. J. Foyt, Althea Gibson, Jesse Owens, Martina Navratilova, Ben Hogan, Joe Namath, Willie Shoemaker?

The sportswriter should be able to identify most of these important figures in sports. Red Smith said the best, most likable athlete he'd known was a 96-pound jockey named Willie Shoemaker.

And you should be able to tell what these terms have in common: Elk Hair Caddis, Adams, Royal Wulff, Prince Nymph, Hare's Ear Nymph and Wolly Bugger. If you know these are flies favored by those who fish for the wily trout, go to the head of the class.

Who He?   The sports information director at Syracuse University said he had received a call from a local TV reporter one day and was startled by the request.

"He said he wanted to get in touch with Ernie Davis, our only Heisman trophy winner," the information director said.

One of football's greatest college running backs, Davis was named All-American three times and won the Heisman Trophy in 1961. His career ended abruptly and tragically. He died of leukemia in 1963.

Predictions

Sportswriters cannot resist telling fans how the coming season or series will turn out. Most of the time they only prove that their insights are no better than those of 10-year-old followers of the games. One well-known baseball writer picked the San Francisco Giants to finish last in the National League west division. They finished first that year. A television hockey analyst predicted that the Philadelphia Flyers would win the Stanley Cup four games out of five. Sorry. They were swept four straight games by their opponents.

The Green Bay Packers were the year's dream team, and the Denver Broncos had no chance at all in the Super Bowl. Oops. Evander Holyfield was such an underdog in his heavyweight match with Mike Tyson you could buy a Porsche with the winnings from a small bet on Holyfield. Tyson was KO'd in the 11th round.

The moral: Don't make forecasts if you want to keep fans believing you know something about the sports you cover.

Anecdotes

Sportswriters are insatiable collectors of anecdotes they tuck away for use at the appropriate moment.

When an imaginative boxing promoter was trying to schedule a match between Muhammad Ali, who had made a friendly visit to Arab countries, and Mike Rossman, who carried the nicknames the Jewish Bomber and the Kosher Butcher, James Tuite of *The New York Times* recalled in his story a similar

Go Ahead. Some coaches warn their players not to talk to the press. Not basketball coach Gary Williams, who says, "College basketball players are going to meet a lot of weirdos in the real world, so why not let them talk to the press?"

ethnic promotion. Years before, Irish Eddy Kelly and Benny Leonard, a Jewish fighter, were in the ring. Leonard was battering Kelly. Finally, in a clinch, Kelly whispered to Leonard, "Hub rachmones. [Yiddish for "take pity."] I'm really Bernie Schwartz."

Rossman, Tuite pointed out, was born Mike DePuano and took to wearing the Star of David on his trunks along with his new name to help sell tickets. The Ali-Rossman match was laughed out of the ring by pieces such as Tuite's.

When Reggie Jackson was elected to the Baseball Hall of Fame, sportswriters trundled out a battery of anecdotes about Jackson, who once referred to "the magnitude of me."

Jackson, who played with the Oakland Athletics, California Angels and New York Yankees, was a massive presence on the field: He hit 563 home runs in his 12 seasons, the sixth highest total in the history of the game, and led his teams to 11 division championships. He struck out more often (2,597) than any other player. And he was as large a force off the field as on, bragging, "I'm the straw that stirs the drink," to one reporter and to another, "I help intimidate the opposition just because I'm here."

He bragged to fellow players that he had an IQ of 160, to which Mickey Rivers, a Yankee teammate, replied, "You don't even know how to spell IQ."

Rivers was a man of plain talk and said to Jackson one day as Jackson—whose full name is Reginald Martinez Jackson—was rattling on about his greatness: "You got a white man's first name, a Puerto Rican's middle name and a black man's last name. No wonder you're so screwed up."

Let 'em Talk

The reporter's technique of letting the source talk works well for sports coverage. In a piece about Billy Williams, a Chicago Cubs outfielder for many years and later its batting coach, Frederick C. Klein of *The Wall Street Journal* quotes him on hitting:

> "You hear fans saying that this star or that one was a 'natural,' but 99 percent of the time they're wrong. Sure, you gotta have ability, but you also gotta work, and every good hitter I knew worked hard to get that way. You have to practice your swing all the time, just like a golf pro. And if you think golf's hard, try it sometime with a guy throwing the ball at you."

One of the best places to listen to athletes, and to ask talk-inducing questions, is the locker room.

"Right after a game when you're talking with athletes . . . that's when they're at their most vulnerable, and that's when you get the most out of a player," says Suzyn Waldman of radio station WFAN in New York, whose beat includes the New York Yankees and the Knicks. She says, "Sports is flesh and blood, people and stories, and so much humanity."

Reporting Is the Key

As Yogi Berra put it, "You can see a lot just by observing." And that's the basis of good sportswriting, of all journalism, for that matter.

The game trophy may seem to go to the writers of the trade. But that's a superficial assessment. Roger Angell, who covers baseball for *The New Yorker* and is called the laureate of the sport because of the high quality of his writing, calls himself a journalist, a working reporter.

He says that his reporting, his insistence on using carefully observed details in his writing, gives his work authenticity. He also knows his trade. He knows, for example, whom to interview.

Pick the wrong player, Angell says, and you get clichés.

The reporters who spend time on their beats know who the right players are, and they realize that, no matter how much they think they know about the sports they cover, there is always an insightful athlete who can add to their understanding. They seek out these players.

They also know the way games are won and lost. How, for example, pulling the starting pitcher one batter too late led to the winning run. Why calling a run instead of a pass in the last minute of the game crossed up the opposition and led to a victory. They know why players fouled the star center at the end of a close basketball game, and not the guard who carried the ball downcourt.

They can examine data for a story on the disparity in salaries for men and women coaches, and they can track the graduation records of white and black athletes. They realize that there is as much going on off the field as on, and in the long run it may well be more important than this game or that one.

Starting Out

Many sports reporters learn the basics covering high school sports. Cathy Henkel, sports editor of *The Seattle Times,* began her career covering high school football games for *The Register-Guard* in Eugene, Ore.

"It was the best start I could have gotten," she says.

Some aspiring sportswriters begin in high school as stringers for local and regional newspapers and stations. Then they go on to cover college sports. Sam Smith, who covers the Chicago Bulls for the *Chicago Tribune,* was an accounting major at Pace College in New York. He liked sports and decided to cover it for the college weekly newspaper, the *Pace Press.*

The newspaper adviser spotted Smith's talent and suggested he add journalism to his studies. He did, found it a close fit with his interests and abilities and sold his accounting textbooks.

To the young reporter who can quote the pass completion records of the quarterbacks in the National Football League, being assigned to cover a high school football game may seem a letdown, if not a putdown. Not so.

Who Won? When keen observation and a knowledge of the sport join writing ability the result can be memorable, as is this lead by boxing writer Jack Cuddy who sent this bulletin from ringside to the United Press:

NEW YORK (UP)— Jersey Joe Walcott, the ancient dancing master from Camden, N.J., gave Joe Louis a 15-round boxing lesson tonight but the officials gave the fight and the title to Joe Louis.

Joel Sartore,
The Wichita Eagle-Beacon

Turning Point

The end-zone catch, the successful goal-line stand, the last-second missed three-point attempt, the ninth-inning double play—these turning points in the game usually are the ingredients of the game story lead.

High School Sports

Richard H. Growald, the UPI's national reporter, noted that "despite the growth in popularity of such attractions as professional football, local high school sports remains a dominant civic factor. An American may not be too familiar with the workings of his city hall, but he knows his high school football team lineup."

High school sports are the major sports entertainment in most towns and cities because they are the only local spectator sports available to these fans. For every Ohio State enthusiast, there are a dozen high school fans in the state.

"It's not uncommon in North and South Carolina for 10,000 people to watch a regular season high school football game," says *The Charlotte Observer*'s Susan Hands. "And every one of those 10,000 is a potential reader of the sports page, if his or her hometown high school hero's name is in the paper."

In fact, Hands says, the most widely read stories in the *Observer* are high school sports. Hands was responsible for covering 116 high school teams in the Carolinas. She handled most of the coverage by telephone and covered one game a week.

In Danville, Ill., the *Commercial-News* covers two local high schools and 30 area high schools as well as a local junior college and Big Ten sports at the University of Illinois and Purdue. Fowler Connell, the sports editor, says that during the school year, "football and basketball on the local scene are king, although the other sports are covered also.

"We feel we are obligated to do more for our readers than any big-city paper can possibly do. Danville and our area towns belong to 'us' and, conversely, we like to think they want us in their homes," he says.

The paper covers all home and away games of the local teams and each of the other 30 high schools at least once. If an area team is in contention for the state playoffs, the newspaper will cover it several times.

Don't Push

Young sportswriters sometimes try too hard. They push the language, reach too hard for words and phrases. When this happens, the result is sawdust and shavings.

Direct, slender, purposive prose flows naturally from the event. Sports has the built-in essentials of drama—conflict, leading characters, dramatic resolution. There are enough incidents and examples to highlight the event, anecdotes that illustrate the situation; high-quality quotations that reveal the nature of the individual and the event.

Good sportswriting is not confined to the big newspapers covering major teams. Jack Schlottman of *The Globe-Times* of Bethlehem, Pa., learned just before game time that the coach of a high school football team had benched 22 of his players for the season-ending traditional game with an intracity rival. The players had been told to go directly to their homeroom, not to stop for breakfast the morning of the game. Instead, they stopped off at a restaurant and started a food fight that led to a disturbance.

After the game that night, which the team with the benched players lost 43–0, Schlottman interviewed the coach, whose comment ended the piece:

"I'm still in the boy business and I hurt some boys tonight," the coach said. "Hopefully, I made some men."

Checklist: Games

— Result: final score, names of teams, type of sport (if necessary, explain that it is high school, college, professional); league (NFL, AFC, Big Eight, Ivy League, Western Conference).

— Where and when game took place.

— Turning point of game; winning play; key strategy.

— Outstanding players.

— Effect on standings, rankings, individual records.

— Scoring; details of important baskets, goals, runs, etc.; summaries of others.

—Streaks, records involved, by team or player.

—Postgame comments.

—External factors: weather, spectators.

—Size of crowd.

—Injuries and subsequent condition of athletes.

—Statistics.

—Duration of game when relevant.

Leads

The game story can begin with a key play or player and the score:

By The Associated Press

Instead of spiking the ball to stop the clock and set up a field goal in the final seconds, Neil O'Donnell saw the Pittsburgh Steelers lagging, and threw deep. His 25-yard touchdown pass to Carl Pickens with 20 seconds left gave the Bengals a stunning 25–20 victory yesterday in Cincinnati.

If the game involves a record, this goes into the lead. In this case, the record is a negative one:

> Thanks to Randall Cunningham and his high-flying receivers, the Green Bay Packers' three-year home winning streak is over and so is their control of the NFC Central.

Notice that the lead does not have to include the score. With radio and television broadcasts the night before presenting the score, the print journalist can put the score in the second, sometimes even the third, paragraph:

EAST RUTHERFORD, N.J. — The Kentucky Wildcats, favored by as many as 14 points, were supposed to breeze past the Syracuse Orangemen tonight in the NCAA championship final.

But Syracuse kept coming back, once moving to within two points of the much deeper Kentucky team.

Finally, the Orangemen ran out of steam with four minutes to play and Kentucky took a hard-earned 76–67 victory.

Quick Learning

Because many fans are experts in the sports they follow, the sports reporter has to know as much and probably more than his or her readers or viewers. When Andrea Sachs, a journalism student, was assigned to interview a

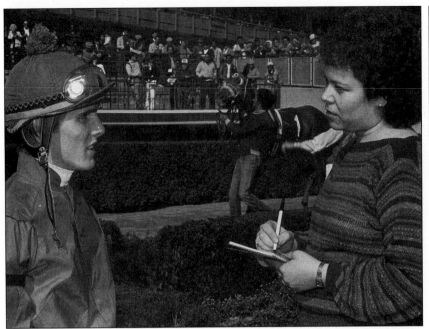

New York Racing Authority

jockey at a horse track, she was worried. Sachs had never been to a track and, as she put it, "I did not know the difference between a horse and a goat."

That night, I bought a copy of *The Daily Racing Form* and two track magazines at a newsstand. I asked the man behind the counter if he knew anything about racing. He suggested that I talk to the customer standing next to me.

The customer was able to give me the names of the top jockeys at the track, and he explained a little about racing.

Before I went to the track, I read the racing section of the newspaper. I discovered that a race was being televised that Saturday and bought another *Racing Form* and watched the race. That provided me with background knowledge and some conversation openers for my interviews.

Sachs left early for the track to watch the horses being exercised. She wandered around the track, chatting with jockeys and trainers. At the coffee stand, she asked a man to explain the betting system. Finally, it was time to interview her jockey, Robbie Davis, a youngster from Pocatello, Idaho, who had just won his first race at the track.

"He was amazingly open and willing to answer any questions. I spoke to him several times during the afternoon."

Her article for her class assignment began:

Robbie Davis' first race at Belmont was a young jockey's dream.

The shy 21-year-old apprentice jockey from Pocatello, Idaho, had driven to New York a week earlier from Louisiana Downs, where he had been riding since May. After exercising horses for a few days at Aqueduct, Davis went to Belmont in early September for the first time.

He was to ride Comanche Brave in a mile-and-an-eighth claiming race with experienced jockeys such as Angel Cordero and George Martens.

Davis recalls his feelings: "I didn't know the track at all . . . it was the biggest track I'd ever seen."

Comanche Brave went off at 20–1 odds, on a muddy track. Davis, who was used to shorter tracks, said that he watched "real close, trying to save as much horse as I could, because I knew it was a long straightaway."

The strategy worked. The next thing he knew, Davis was sitting in the winner's circle. "I couldn't believe it."

Encouraged by her instructor, Sachs sold the article to Davis' hometown newspaper, *The Idaho Journal.*

Coverage Preparation

Game stories can be difficult to handle because of the pressure to meet a deadline and because of the essential similarity of the stories—one team wins, the other loses. The reporter copes with deadlines with careful preparations. This may mean arriving at a high school gym well ahead of the game to find a telephone that will be available late in the evening so that the story can be called in to the sports desk.

"With starting times constantly being pushed back—all World Series games are now played at night, for example—and deadlines always being moved forward, you simply can't have too much in your notebook too soon," says Ron Rapoport, deputy sports editor of the *Chicago Sun–Times.*

"As for post-game interviews in the locker room," says Rapoport, "the two worst things a reporter can do are (a) not have a line of inquiry or some questions prepared, and (b) not deviate from this preplanning when circumstances dictate. This may sound easy but sometimes the hardest thing to do is to abandon the idea you worked so hard to formulate when something better suddenly comes along."

When she covered high school games out of town, Hands would trade information with local reporters. The exchange turned up nicknames, personal information about the players and the detail that gives a game story an individual touch.

Keeping Statistics

One way to avoid trouble about game facts is to keep statistics of the event. Let us watch Hands cover a high school football game.

When she arrives at the field, she checks the program to make sure the numbers on the players' jerseys are the same as those on the program. Then she sets up her scoring sheet.

"Every sportswriter has developed his or her own method of keeping a play-by-play and statistics, and of course, each sport lends itself to a different method," she says. "It's a good idea for a beginner to check with his or her editors or other sportswriters and to try a few out on radio or TV games before trying the first one at a game. It's necessary because you can't count on being able to remember the sequence of plays, and you'd better not count on anybody else keeping statistics.

"You have to keep all the statistics you can because you can never tell what's going to be important. The game may be decided by punting. It may be decided by return yardage (which is not included in total offense). The key to the game may be one player's ability to set up tackles.

"If you can bring along a friend to spot tackles while you keep offense, that's great. Sometimes you can trade off with another sportswriter in the press box. I've never seen anybody who can keep offense and defense at the same time, but I'm told there are a couple.

"Use halftime to tally up. Sometimes it is surprising to see what the statistics reveal. They don't always match the appearances."

From the Players' Perspective

To see the game the right way, look at it the way the players do. The advice is given by Thomas Boswell, a sportswriter for *The Washington Post,* in his book *Why Time Begins on Opening Day* (New York: Doubleday, 1984). Boswell writes about baseball, but his suggestions apply to most sports that reporters cover:

Judge slowly. "Never judge a player over a unit of time shorter than a month . . . you must see a player hot, cold, and in between before you can put the whole package together."

Assume everybody is trying reasonably hard. ". . . giving 110 percent . . . would be counterproductive for most players. . . . Usually something on the order of 80 percent effort is about right."

Forgive even the most grotesque physical errors. "It's assumed that every player is physically capable of performing every task asked of him. If he doesn't it's never his fault. His mistake is simply regarded as part of a professional's natural margin of error."

Judge mental errors harshly. "The distinction as to whether a mistake has been made 'from the neck up or the neck down' is always drawn."

Pay more attention to the mundane than to the spectacular. "The necessity for consistency usually outweighs the need for the inspired."

Pay more attention to the theory of the game than to the outcome of the game. Don't let your evaluations be swayed too greatly by the final score. "If a team loses a game but has used its resources properly . . . then that team is often able to ignore defeat utterly. Players say, 'We did everything right but win.' "

Keep in mind that players always know best how they're playing. "At the technical level, they seldom fool themselves—the stakes are too high."

Stay ahead of the action, not behind it or even neck and neck with it. "Remember that the immediate past is almost always prelude."

Hands says she does not mind doing most press box chores herself. "That way, I'm never at the mercy of PR men. I'm glad to have them help me, but I don't have to count on it," she says.

Reporters hang on to these statistics, their recollections and their score cards. Nothing beats having that one vital encounter, that one vital number close at hand. When Ben Johnson's use of steroids cost him the Olympic gold medal in the 100-meter dash at the 1988 Olympics in Seoul, it was important to remember that Johnson's chief rival, Carl Lewis, had implied Johnson used the illicit drug after losing to him a year earlier at a race in Rome. Johnson had set the world record at that meet and Lewis' remarks had been widely ridiculed as sour grapes. Johnson's time, his victory over Lewis and Lewis' vindication were all important parts of the Johnson-steroid story.

Game Details

Unless a game is exciting or important, Rapoport says he tends not to include much detail.

"Usually a couple of paragraphs are enough to sum up the key plays. I prefer to use the space to concentrate on one or two or three of the most interesting things that happened and to tell what the players involved or the manager thought about them.

"Often, a game story will be built around somebody who had a large effect—positive or negative—on the outcome," Rapoport says. "It is almost mandatory that we hear from this key player and, though there are some spontaneous talkers who begin at the sight of a notebook, it is almost always better to have a question in mind. This sounds simple enough, but often takes some thought. The right question will often do wonders.

"I also like to listen to what's being said by the players—not to reporters—but to each other. They often have funny conversations when they've won, sympathetic ones when they've lost. Good dialogue can dress up a story."

Listen to Edd Roush, who played for the Cincinnati Reds from 1916 to 1931 and had a lifetime .323 average. He is talking about today's ballplayers: "Don't ask me about these modern players. If they had come out to the park when I was playing we'd have run them out of town. These fellers bat .265 and think they're hitters. Their gloves are as big as two of ours and they still can't catch the ball. And they're millionaires." (From "A Visit to Edd Roush," by William Zinsser, *The American Scholar,* Winter 1989.)

Actions sometimes are as revealing as words. The small moves, the slight shift in the linebacker's position, a change in the way a guard plays his man—these details that the observant reporter picks up often mean the difference between victory and defeat. Watch a center fielder play each batter differently. Keep an eye on the way a forward moves to the basket in the second period after all his shots were missed or were blocked in the first period.

Specifics. "Always look for something to make your story more colorful. Don't just say someone made a diving catch. Describe the dive. Describe the winning hit. Did it hit the wall? Did it roll into the left-field corner? Did that line drive knock off the shortstop's glove?"
—*AP*

Two Developments

As sports attracted more and more fans, two aspects emerged that concern the sportswriter. One is the tug of partisanship, the pressure by fans on the journalist to become a rooter as well as a reporter. The other is the role of money in sports and its pervasive and sometimes corrupting influence.

Partisanship

Sports reporters by and large are closer to the teams and the players that they cover than other beat reporters are to their sources. Out of this relationship there are positive and negative consequences, says Rapoport.

"If you are around a group of people a lot you are going to learn a great deal about them and this can only help your reporting," he says. "The flip side of this, of course, is that familiarity breeds both admiration and contempt. Some sports personalities are delightful human beings; others are selfish creeps. Yet you cannot—must not—play favorites in your coverage even while you are expressing your opinion. Likewise, the team must not become 'we.' You must guard against letting your prejudices show."

Bob Thayer,
The Journal Bulletin

Fans Cheer, Reporters Observe

Ahmad and Michael   On the other side of the equation is the cozy relationship some sportswriters cultivate with athletes. Ahmad Rashad, an NBC sports reporter, began an account of a Chicago-Orlando basketball game this way: "Here in Chicago, Michael Jordan and I have a ritual. We ride to the game together."

This angered Richard Sandomir, who reports on media sports coverage for *The New York Times.* Sandomir wrote in his column, "Isn't Rashad labeled a *reporter?* Or is he just a celebrity pal, whose friendship with Jordan can flout journalism's rules?"

In response, the executive producer of NBC sports said he was happy with their "great relationship. It accentuates his (Ahmad's) believability that they're friends. They often have dinner together. They drive to the games. Ahmad stays at Michael's house when he's in Chicago."

Distance Best   "Reporters and players should not have a game day 'ritual.' If they do, the journalist is compromised, his reporting rendered suspect for what is not revealed from their private rituals," says Sandomir.

The sportswriter Jimmy Cannon wrote, "Sportswriting has survived because of the guys who don't cheer." He was friendly with some of the players whose teams he covered but never a cheerleader.

Stanley Woodward, the legendary city editor of *The New York Herald Tribune,* remarked when he was its sports editor and read stories in which his reporters idolized athletes, "Will you please stop godding up these ball players."

Red Barber, radio's great baseball announcer, described the Brooklyn Dodgers in his warm southern drawl with affection, but it was no greater than his feeling for the Giants or Cubs. His love was for the game, not the team.

His calling the game impartially probably cost Barber his job when baseball coverage on television came under the control of team owners.

Team Control

"Every radio and television broadcaster for the 30 major league baseball teams is either paid by the club he or she covers or is hired with that club's approval," writes Ted Rose in the media review *Brill's Content.*

"As a practical matter, these broadcasters are not independent journalists but conduits to the public for the team that directly or indirectly employs them."

Costs of Independence

Many athletes are accustomed to being idolized, but when "the media want to show some perspective about sports or get behind something more important than who won or lost, the athletes generally dislike them," says former pitcher Jim Bouton. "Generally speaking, athletes dislike the media in direct proportion to the extent that reporters exercise their journalistic responsibilities."

Albert Belle of the Cleveland Indians may be the classic angry athlete. He doesn't like reporters and demonstrates his animosity. He was fined $50,000 for swearing at TV reporter Hannah Storm, and after he threw a baseball at *Sports Illustrated* photographer Tony Tomsic the American League ordered him to undergo counseling.

Some sportswriters have been such "homers"—rooters for the home teams—that they have ignored or downplayed NCAA violations, criminal acts by athletes and the mockery of sportsmanship.

A former basketball coach at Clemson says sports reporters must have known of the corruption and sleaziness in collegiate sports. "When I say, 'What's going on?' and you reply, 'I don't know. I didn't seen anything,' that's a lie. You see what kind of clothes he wears, you see his car, you've been to his room. And he comes from the Pulpwood city limits—you gotta be kidding."

Money

Sports is big business. The 100 major sports universities have revenues of more than $1 billion. The professional leagues continue to expand to tap new markets. Teams that were bought for a few million dollars 30 years ago sell for more than $100 million today.

Multimillion dollar signings are no longer news unless they approach $100 million. The top basketball and baseball players make $5 to $10 million a year in salaries, and endorsements can double that.

Fans like a winner, and so the bidding for top athletes goes higher and higher, and the star player who at one time spent his career playing with one team—a Ted Williams, Joe DiMaggio, Bob Cousy—now is available to the highest bidder. Teams, too, shift locations, moving from market to market.

Honesty's Reward. After 16 years as a TV analyst for the New York Mets baseball team, Tim McCarver was fired and a former Mets pitcher, Tom Seaver, was hired as McCarver's replacement. Sandomir described McCarver as "one of baseball's best and most outspoken analysts," which, baseball insiders said, was what cost McCarver his job. "I always tried to give fans the honest truth," McCarver said. Seaver will also be the Mets' pitching adviser and serve as a marketer and in promotion activities, hardly roles that indicate a middle-of-the-road approach to calling games. Sandomir wrote, "It's hard to see how a person would not find conflict in these multiple roles."

Big Contracts. Thirty years ago, the average salary of a major league baseball player was $35,000 a year. Today it is around $1 million. More than 60 players are paid more than $5 million a year. Mike Piazza of the New York Mets makes $13 million a year, about $20,000 for every time he goes to bat.

Kevin Brown signed with the Los Angeles Dodgers for $15 million a year, which amounts to $60,000 for every inning he pitches in a season.

Other sports: Basketball, Michael Jordon, Chicago Bulls, $33 million; hockey, Eric Lindros, Philadelphia Flyers, $8.5 million; football, Steve Young, San Franscisco 49ers, $8.2 million.

Cash Conscious

The historian Henry Steele Commager commented about the consequence of player and team mobility, "We have nothing to be loyal to."

Hank Aaron, the Hall of Fame baseball player and baseball executive, says money has corroded sports. "Today's players have lost all concept of history. Their collective mission is greed. Nothing means much of anything to them. As a group, there's no discernible social conscience among them; certainly no sense of self-sacrifice, which is what Jackie Robinson's legacy is based on. Where there is no conscience, there are no heroes."

Money is the name of the game in collegiate sports as well. Despite the crowded college stadiums and field houses, few universities make money from their teams. Only 10 to 20 schools take in more than they spend. Deficits can hit a million dollars a year. But a winning team can break even or make money, and so the impetus is to lure star athletes to campuses. The price can be high.

The Goal: Win at Any Cost

The drive to build winning teams has led to lying, cheating and hypocrisy, some of which sports reporters have documented. They have shown that teams have recruited semiliterate athletes and that some schools have gone out of their way to keep the players eligible.

Black athletes have been recruited for basketball who have little chance of graduating. A study by the NCAA shows low graduation rates of black basketball players at Arizona University (14 percent); University of Georgia (20 percent); Georgia Tech (33 percent); University of Kentucky (22 percent); Louisville University (8 percent); University of Minnesota (20 percent); Seton Hall (13 percent). The figures for Syracuse University for black athletes who enrolled from 1987–91 show none graduated.

Among the institutions that regularly graduate more than half their black basketball players are Duke, Georgetown, North Carolina, Providence, Stanford, Villanova and Virginia. Stanford graduated 100 percent in a recent period, Providence 92 percent.

A Miscellany

Some other news items:

• At the Nike Camps where 120 of the best high school basketball players in the country demonstrate their athletic ability for college coaches, a test showed that one-fourth read below a sixth grade level and 10 were functionally illiterate. The chancellor of Louisiana State University said that the competition for high school athletes is so intense that some of those recruited "read at the fourth-, fifth- or sixth-grade level." A few years ago, a North Carolina State basketball recruit was admitted with a total SAT score of 470. For signing your name and answering a single question, you can achieve a score of 400.

Baseball Hall of Fame Library

Record Home Run

As Hank Aaron approached Babe Ruth's record 714 home runs, fans hurled insults at him. "Vitriolic racial prejudice," wrote *The New York Times.* Atlanta police gave him a bodyguard. Here he is shown hitting the record 715th homer. He went on to hit 755 home runs.

• *The Albuquerque Tribune* revealed that despite promises to trim its debts, the University of New Mexico athletic department had tripled them in two years. Among the hidden costs: The University paid $2.6 million for a weight-training complex. Athletes complained of being told to take courses that did not count toward a degree. Several athletes had to pay for additional credit hours in order to graduate after their eligibility ran out.

• The University of Pennsylvania football team had to forfeit five victories after a university panel ruled that a star player who dropped a course and was enrolled in only two classes was a part-time student and thus ineligible. The day before the final game of the season the athletic department arranged an independent study course for the player, but the panel said the course had no bearing on the player's eligibility. The issue was brought up by two faculty members who said the athletic department had engaged in a "sleazy" maneuver to keep the player eligible.

• Over a 10-year period, the University of Louisville, a basketball power, graduated 16 percent of its scholarship players.

• Indiana University, another basketball power, graduated 75 percent of its white players and no blacks from the freshman classes of 1983–87.

• When an SMU head football coach spotted a bulletin board in a Texas high school with cards from other recruiters, he took a $100 bill and tacked it over the rival recruiters' cards and announced to prospects nearby, "That is our business card."

• Steve Courson, an offensive lineman with the Pittsburgh Steelers and the Tampa Bay Bucaneers, said he was told to take steroids as a 19-year-old sophomore on the University of South Carolina team. The team physician wrote out a prescription. In his book *False Glory,* he says steroid use was widespread among linemen, and amphetamines were pushed by coaches to get players "up" for games.

• From 1985 through 1991, not one North Carolina State basketball player earned a degree.

• An Australian basketball player enrolled at Seton Hall University in New Jersey in October, stayed long enough to help the team make the NCAA finals and left the following April. While he was at the university, his courses included First Aid, Youth Activities, Creative Movement and Ethics.

• At Texas Christian University, a high school prospect was taken to a motel and entertained with meals and prostitutes. He signed a letter of intent. During his four seasons with TCU, he was paid $27,100 to play.

• An SMU football player told Dallas TV station WFAA, "I received $25,000 to attend SMU."

• A community college instructor in Nevada said she was going to give a star basketball player an incomplete in a summer English correspondence course, but the grade form handed her by a college official had a C already written in. The incomplete would have made him ineligible to play for the University of Nevada at Las Vegas. The student, the nation's second highest scorer, ran into trouble at UNLV anyway when it was revealed that his tutor had written a paper for him after the player had "verbalized" his thoughts to the instructor. He was suspended from post-season play.

• Dexter Manley, a professional football player, testified before Congress that he was illiterate during the four years he played football at Oklahoma State.

• Notes O. J. Simpson wrote that turned up in his trial coverage reveal what one writer called his "low level of literacy." His suicide note stated: "My momma tought me to do un to other." A letter to Nicole Brown Simpson, his former wife, includes: "I love you and losing you is the only thing that madder to me. So lets not forget the past. Let's work together (for the first time) to improve the futurr live together. Know manner what I love you." Simpson played football for the University of Southern California.

• A former football player at Texas Tech University sued the institution charging it had engaged in fraud, forgery and racketeering to keep him eligible. He said he was given grades he did not earn, was enrolled in a summer course in Florida without his knowledge and was wired money by the university when he was a junior college student. The suit was filed a week after the *Houston Chronicle* reported that the school's All-American running back and another player had earned a 0.00 grade-point average for the fall semester but were allowed to play in the Alamo Bowl. Texas Tech acknowledged that 76 athletes in eight sports had been ineligible to compete over a six-year period.

• At Northwestern University, two former basketball players were sent to prison for trying to fix games against Wisconsin, Penn State and Michigan, and four of the university's football players were indicted for lying to a grand jury about betting against their team. One admitted fumbling intentionally to protect a bet he had made against his team.

Press Relations. On many campuses, the student newspaper is prohibited from interviewing athletes. All such material has to be filtered through the school's sports information office. Officials say they are protecting the athletes' privacy. Ted Gup, a journalism lecturer at Georgetown University, says the probable reason is the coaches "fear that some of their athletes might not be able to avoid saying things that would expose recruiting scandals, academic chicanery and other abuses by the institutions."

Information Available

Because of the exposure of the win-at-all-costs philosophy of many institutions, rules have been tightened and more information made available.

The NCAA maintains on its website www.ncaa.org a Major Infractions Database in the Membership Services section where journalists can obtain details on NCAA actions regarding violations.

Graduation Rates

The NCAA also issues an informative annual report that lists graduation rates and academic data for Divisions I, II and III teams. The report is titled "NCAA Division I (II and III are in a second volume) Graduation Rates Report." Let's look at some sections of the page for the University of Kentucky, a basketball powerhouse.

First, an explanation. The figures head "90–91" refer to full-time, degree-seeking students who entered the university in 1990–91 and had graduated by 1997. The figures headed "4-CLASS" refer to students who had entered in the four years beginning in 1987–88 and had graduated by 1997.

University of Kentucky

Freshman-Cohort Graduation Rates	All Students	Student-Athletes
1990–91 Graduation Rate	50%	48%
4-Class Average	50%	48%

1. Graduation-Rates Data

a. ALL Students

	MEN FRESHMAN RATE 90–91 N	%	MEN 4-CLASS N	%	WOMEN FRESHMAN RATE 90–91 N	%	WOMEN 4-CLASS N	%	TOTAL FRESHMAN RATE 90–91 N	%	TOTAL 4-CLASS N	%
Am. Indian/AN	1	100	11	36	0		13	62	1	100	24	50
Asian/PI	19	42	71	34	22	55	73	52	41	49	144	43
Black	65	31	217	33	87	43	287	41	152	38	504	38
Hispanic	9	33	29	24	11	55	31	52	20	45	60	38
White	1,119	47	4,831	48	1,144	55	5,140	54	2,263	51	9,971	51
Other	34	53	61	46	18	67	35	57	52	58	96	50
Total	1,247	46	5,220	47	1,282	54	5,579	53	2,529	50	10,799	50

b. Student-Athletes #

	MEN FRESHMAN RATE 90–91 N	%	MEN 4-CLASS N	%	MEN TRANSFER 4-CLASS N	%	WOMEN FRESHMAN RATE 90–91 N	%	WOMEN 4-CLASS N	%	WOMEN TRANSFER 4-CLASS N	%	TOTAL FRESHMAN RATE 90–91 N	%	TOTAL 4-CLASS N	%	TOTAL TRANSFER 4-CLASS N	%
Am. Indian/AN	0		0		0		0		0		1	0	0		0		1	0
Asian/PI	0		0		0		0		0		0		0		0		0	
Black	16	31	55	40	11	18	5	60	17	71	0		21	38	72	47	11	18
Hispanic	1	0	1	0	2	0	0		0		0		1	0	1	0	2	0
White	20	55	115	50	15	73	14	50	65	48	9	67	34	53	180	49	24	71
Other	2	0	5	20	3	33	4	100	6	67	1	100	6	67	11	45	4	50
Total	39	41	176	45	31	45	23	61	88	53	11	64	62	48	264	48	42	50

MEN'S BASKETBALL

	FRESHMAN RATE 90–91 % N	4-CLASS % N	TRANSFER 4-CLASS % N
Indian/AN	-	-	-
Asian/PI	-	-	-
Black	0-a	22-b	-
Hispanic	0-a	0-a	-
White	-	40-a	100-a
Other	-	-	-
Total	0-a	27-c	100-a

Values for N (a. 1–5, b. 6–10, c. 11–15, d. 16–20, e. greater than 20)
Only student-athletes receiving athletics aid are included in this report.

Academic Records

The NCAA report also carries the grade-point average, SAT and ACT scores of athletes by sport. At most of the Division I schools in big-time intercollegiate athletics, the basketball and football recruits have the lowest scores. The report also lists the majors of student-athletes. Communications is usually number one or two at the Division I schools.

On the next page are some academic scores for a football powerhouse, the University of Florida.

STUDENT-ATHLETE * ADMISSIONS DATA (four-year average, entering Freshmen 1993–94 through 1996–97)

a. High School

Preparation Data		– AVERAGE – CGPA		– AVERAGE – SAT		– AVERAGE – SUM ACT	
MEN'S		N	GPA	N	SAT	N	ACT
	Baseball	36	3.10	24	1,041	12	88
	Basketball	12	2.76	8	919	4	86
	CC/Track	37	3.07	23	1,077	15	82
	Football	76	2.64	29	883	47	73
	Other	39	3.30	34	1,065	8	90
WOMEN'S							
	Basketball	14	3.01	6	890	8	76
	CC/Track	21	3.12	16	1,004	6	92
	Other	84	3.33	64	1,065	27	91

*If two or fewer individuals appear in a cell, scores are not reported.

Coaches' Salaries

In 26 states, the football coach at the largest state university is paid more than the governor of the state, and in 17 states the basketball coach makes more than the governor. But their salaries are only a part of their income. When broadcast and other contracts are added in, salaries are doubled and tripled. Steve Spurrier, the football coach at the University of Florida, makes $2 million a year.

When Auburn University hired a football coach—salary $750,000 to $900,000 a year, depending on the team's performance—it contained a clause giving him a $50,000 bonus if the football program stays in the good graces of the NCAA for five years, and $100,000 if he takes the team to the national championship.

Men's basketball coaches are the highest paid individuals in college sports. Their median compensation is $290,000 a year; football coaches, $268,000; baseball, $79,750; soccer, $42,000; track, $52,268. In all the categories, women coaches were paid less: basketball, $98,400; baseball, $44,725; soccer, $38,592; track, $44,784. Included in the compensation for the football, basketball and baseball coaches' salaries are benefits such as automobiles and radio and television contracts. Some coaches of basketball and football teams have contracts that give them a percentage of the money the teams receive for going to tournaments and bowl games.

Hidden Income   Newspapers and stations look into these salaries, often using the Freedom of Information Act to obtain the figures. The *Union-News* in Springfield, Mass., used the Act to learn that although the University of Massachusetts had listed the salary of the basketball coach at $132,000, he was actually making $600,000 a year. The newspaper learned the coach's contract includes 35 percent of any money the team receives for going to the NCAA tournament.

The Commercial Appeal in Memphis examined the contract a new basketball coach received and found it included: $135,000, salary; $135,000 for "public relations" work for the university; the use of two cars and the opportunity for unlimited income for a summer camp he will run at the university in exchange

Hidden Costs. Many expense items are removed from athletic department books: Interest and debt payments on new fields and stadiums are often paid by student activity fees; personnel—costing as much as $5 million a year at big-sports schools—are placed on staff and faculty payrolls; athletic scholarships are funded out of regular student scholarship money; legal and medical costs are placed on the regular university bill, as are utility and telephone charges. In some states, money is appropriated directly to athletic programs, shortchanging general education.

The Texas State Auditor found that Stephen F. Austin State University was spending $2 million a year in discretionary funds to cover budget shortfalls in the athletic department. The auditor said the university neglected "significant academic needs" and told the university to change its priorities.

for $100 a week in rent. The newspaper also published the salaries of the president of the university—$142,285 plus use of a house, a car and a university-paid club membership—and faculty members and other coaches whose salaries exceed $100,000 a year.

Equity   The salaries of the coaches of women's teams in Division I average 70 percent of the salaries of coaches of men's teams. The disparity is greatest in basketball, where the coaches of the women's teams make 37 percent of the salaries of men's teams.

As a result, the U.S. Equal Employment Opportunity Commission made a study and found "such extreme pay differentials" that it now requires similar salaries if the jobs require similar "skill, effort and responsibility."

Enterprising reporters make interesting stories about the disparities at local colleges and universities and the efforts made to comply with the Commission's guidelines when the salaries are out of line.

Recruiting Stories

The lengths to which coaches will go to lure promising athletes to their schools provide the makings of fascinating sports stories. Lenn Robbins of the *New York Post* talked to a New Jersey high school basketball player eagerly sought by scores of colleges and universities. Robbins also met with his family.

The athlete, Al Harrington, told Robbins he has 16 Nike shoe boxes filled with letters, and more than 300 FedEx overnight envelopes. "His parents had to have a separate phone line installed in Big Al's room," Robbins writes.

Enthusiasm   Villanova's coach was enthusiastic, during his visit to the Harrington home, ending every sentence with, "Al! You the man." The Kentucky coach was armed with 16 cards with facts about the university. "He read every word on front and back. That's 32 cards. Then he said. 'Would you like to see the highlight tape?' We all said, No!'"

Sincerity   The Seton Hall coach's hour-long presentation was a hit with Harrington's mother. "He was real sincere. To me, it was heartfelt, the things he feels he can get accomplished for Al. He just talked to you like, 'I know this is your baby and it's his first time going away and you want the best for him. Believe me, we can be the best for him.'"

The North Carolina State coach had a 6-foot-high cardboard "with a picture of the student body and the words, 'We want Harrington' emblazoned across the top," Robbins wrote.

Georgetown coach John Thompson was also a visitor and awed Harrington with talk of the NBA players who had played for Georgetown.

Tattooed   The St. John's coach removed his jacket, shirt and tie to reveal on his left shoulder a tattoo of a basketball and above the ball were the words, "Big Al. S. J. U."

10,000 to 1. "You have a better chance of being a brain surgeon than you do of being an NBA player. Only one of every 10,000 high school players will make the pros."

—Bob Minnix,
NCAA director of
enforcement

The story ends with Harrington saying:

> "It's amazing how they're all No. 1 in something. Whether it's this part of their education or that part of their education. All of them are No. 1, so I don't really know who No. 1 in the country in anything is."

Spurned. Against the advice of his mother and his high school coach, Big Al decided not to go to college. He was drafted 25th by the Indiana Pacers.

Recruiting Youngsters

The demand for winning teams by boosters, fans and television is intense, so much so that many colleges accept high school athletes with grade-school-level academic scores. They even take criminals.

Seton Hall University in New Jersey grabbed one of the country's leading high school basketball players although he did not earn more than a combined score of 700 on his SAT test. The university kept its offer open to the youth even after he pleaded guilty to sexual abuse in a plea bargain. He had sodomized a young woman on the high school stairway.

When journalists wrote about the incident, the university grudgingly rescinded its scholarship offer. Two weeks later, a major basketball power in Utah made the student an offer but he accepted a full basketball scholarship to a Long Island university.

A leading schoolboy basketball player in Hampton, Va., was convicted on three felony counts of malicious wounding by a mob. Would that affect his chances to play college ball? "Every school in the country wants him," Bob Gibbons, a top scout of high school basketball players, told *USA Today*. "If he was John Dillinger, they'd take him."

Why stop with recruiting high school players for college? High school sports is, as we've seen, a major attraction in hundreds of cities. High schools are recruiting. "Now the college fan is wanting to follow the kids," says Mike Lardner of Sports Channel. "Teen-agers are part of a $10 billion market."

A Case Study

In a two-part series, Sam Roe of *The Blade* described how some Toledo high schools were violating state high school athletic association rules by recruiting athletes from other high schools and from junior high schools. More than half the players on one nationally ranked basketball team were transfers. Roe quoted the mother of one transfer as saying that the coach had pressured her to lie about her residence. At another basketball powerhouse, a player's mother said the coach and his aides found an apartment for her family within the school district and paid the security deposit and two months' rent.

Some parents transferred "legal custody of their children to relatives in other school districts so the students can be eligible to play for the best teams," Roe wrote.

The reaction to the series was immediate. The state high school athletic association announced an inquiry, and a coalition of ministers held a rally at which Roe was denounced. More than 500 people at the rally condemned Roe, chanting, "In the South, they had Jim Crow. In Toledo, we have Sam Roe."

The group demanded a front-page retraction of the series and Roe's dismissal.

Six months later, the high school athletic association completed its investigation and placed the two high schools Roe wrote about on probation for two years and fined them $1,000 each for recruiting violations for their basketball teams.

Roe's experience with fans is hardly unusual.

Outraged Fans

Sportswriters learn early that when they depart from straight game coverage and upbeat profiles of the home team's players, there can be trouble. Fans want to admire their heroes.

Kentucky: Bomb Threats   The *Lexington Herald-Leader* described cash payments by boosters to basketball players at the University of Kentucky. The reaction was swift and angry. Michael York, who wrote the articles with Jeffrey Marx, said "basketball has been called the most widely practiced religion in the Bluegrass state."

Fans canceled subscriptions. The newspaper received bomb threats. York was offered a bulletproof vest by a member of the police department. What was especially galling was the reaction of some radio and television journalists, most of whom lined up behind the university. An ABC affiliate said the stories were evidence of the newspaper's "self-serving sensationalism."

The reporters were awarded the Pulitzer Prize for investigative reporting.

Oklahoma: Angry Calls   After editorials in Oklahoma newspapers called for the resignation of the football coach, fans reacted with letters and phone calls berating the newspapers. Never mind that five players were arrested

Chris Dawson, *The Press Democrat*

Sore Losers

To some fans, games are serious matters, life and death struggles between powerful adversaries. And when the calls go against their team, they voice disapproval of the offici-ating. Some go further and stalk their prey. After a game between Drake and Petaluma high schools in California, angry Petaluma fans and players attacked a referee.

within two months of the NCAA putting the school on three years' probation. What counted was that Barry Switzer was a winning coach.

Phil Dessauer, former managing editor of *The Tulsa World* who teaches journalism at the University of Tulsa, says winning "created a Sooner subculture, if not a religion, and the more than 70,000 seats in the stadium only begin to tell the extent of the fervor."

A president of the university years ago noted the football team's prowess and remarked sardonically that he hoped the state would "have a university the football team can be proud of."

Arizona: Boycotts　When William J. Woestendiek was running *The Arizona Daily Star* in Phoenix, he suggested his reporters check the university football program. Clark Hallas and Bob Lowe discovered some unusual hotel bills and learned they were not for the stays of football recruits but for women. "We ran the story and the roof fell in," Woestendiek recalls. "As our reporters began an intensive investigation of every aspect of the football program, I became the target of a vicious campaign by the community.

"In more than 35 years in the business, I have never been vilified or threatened more." The threats, he said, were from "business leaders, wealthy alumni, the president of the university and other prominent citizens." Automobile dealers boycotted the newspaper. Letters threatened his family. Woestendiek bent backwards. After the first story, he held off additional pieces so that the school could respond and the team could play in the Fiesta Bowl untarnished.

When the coach failed to meet with the newspaper to answer the charges, the pieces were printed and the *Star* won a Pulitzer Prize for the investigation.

Iowa: Racism When Tom Witosky and a fellow reporter on the staff of *The Des Moines Register* revealed that three members of the University of Iowa basketball team had undergone substance abuse treatment during the summer at a cost to the university of $16,000, a colleague in the newsroom told him, "You have destroyed my son's faith in his hero (one of the players)." Witosky received letters and calls telling him he was a troublemaker and a racist (the players are black). A month later, two Iowa State athletes attempted an armed robbery of a Burger King and engaged in a shootout with police while trying to escape. Iowa State fans complained that the *Register*'s coverage was too thorough.

And More After *The Montgomery Advertiser* published secretly taped conversations between a former Auburn football player and his coaches about payoffs, the football coach suggested that Auburn fans begin a subscription and advertiser boycott.

A story about ticket scalping by football players led to death threats to Oklahoma City reporters, and when Texas A&M football players were shown to be receiving secret payments, bricks were thrown through a Dallas editor's windows.

Breaking Baseball's Barriers

Sports has not been in the forefront of social change. Slow to admit minorities on the playing field and women in the press box and locker room, sports can look back only in sorrow at its behavior. This history is part of the sportswriter's background knowledge.

When Jackie Robinson took the field for the Brooklyn Dodgers on April 15, 1947, and 11 weeks later when Larry Doby began playing for the Cleveland Indians, the color line in both major leagues was breached.

Robinson and Doby had to endure race baiting, not only from fellow players but from fans as well. Pitchers threw at them, teammates would not talk to them. On the road they had to eat separately in some cities, room in different hotels. Fans shouted insults at them, and some threatened to shoot them.

Jimmy Cannon wrote of Robinson, "He is the loneliest man in sports."

Robinson

The St. Louis Cardinals were especially vituperative. In one game with the Dodgers, Enos Slaughter was an easy out but went out of his way to spike Robinson across the calf.

Robinson quietly endured the taunts and the spikings and the beanballs. But as he settled in, he became more aggressive. In 1949, as Slaughter was coming into second on what would have been a routine double play, Robinson took the throw from the shortstop and instead of relaying it to first, he planted the ball in the mouth of the sliding Slaughter. Slaughter got to his feet slowly, his mouth bloodied, teeth broken. He turned and slowly walked to the Cardinal dugout.

Doby

In the American League, Doby had it no easier. As it was for Robinson, Doby's introduction to major league baseball was troubled. When the manager of his team, the Cleveland Indians, introduced Doby to his teammates, some refused to shake his hand.

On the field, it was more of the same, sometimes worse. The taunts from opposing players when Doby was at bat were especially nasty. A pitcher for the Philadelphia A's recalls: "I was on the bench and heard some of my teammates shouting things at Larry like, 'Porter, carry my bags,' or, 'Shoeshine boy, shine my shoes,' and, well, the N-word, too. It was terrible."

Doby said he was called "coon" and "jigaboo," and when he would slide into second base the opposing infielders would sometimes spit in his face.

The end of a game was especially hard for Doby. "It's then you'd really like to be with your teammates, win or lose, and go over the game," he said. "But I'd go to my hotel in the black part of town and they'd go to their hotel."

Bill Veeck, the owner of the Indians, said he received 20,000 letters after signing Doby, "most of them in violent and sometimes obscene protest."

Unlike Robinson, Doby had little experience with prejudice until he became a major leaguer. Veeck said that the bigotry Doby faced made him unable "to realize his full potential. If Larry had come up just a little later when things were better, he might have become one of the greatest players of all time."

A friend who later pitched for the Dodgers said Doby played under "so much pressure—from slurs to death threats—that he had to suppress some of his flair." But, like Robinson, Doby triumphed. He spent 13 years in the majors, hit 253 home runs and had a .283 career batting average. He played in six All Star games.

Robinson and Doby are in the Baseball Hall of Fame.

Breaking the Basketball Barrier

In 1966, the basketball team from Texas Western at El Paso played the University of Kentucky for the national championship. The Kentucky team was all-white, the El Paso team all-black. In those days, basketball teams started one,

Jackie Robinson

Baseball Hall of Fame Library

Larry Doby

Slow to Integrate

David Halberstam recalls in his book *October 1964* that the Cardinals owner Gussie Busch visited spring training one year and noticed no black players.

"Where are our black players?" he asked a coach. He was told there were none. "How can it be the great American game if blacks can't play? Hell, we sell beer to everyone." (Busch owned the St. Louis brewery Budweiser.)

The 1964 season ended with the Cardinals, heavily dependent on black players, defeating the white New York Yankees in the World Series.

two and occasionally three black players. Never all five. The coach at El Paso, Don Haskins, told other coaches who questioned him that he had never heard of the then tacit agreement on a quota for black players.

Adolph Rupp, the Kentucky coach, had never played a black player. After the underdog El Paso team beat Kentucky 72–65, Rupp did not congratulate the team and, Haskins recalls, was cool to him.

When interviewed, Rupp was asked about the El Paso guard voted the all-tournament best player, all Rupp could say was, "He's a good little boy, but there's a lot of good little boys around this year."

Ten of the 12 El Paso players, who were recruited from Chicago, New York and Detroit, graduated. And a few years after the tournament, Rupp began to recruit black players.

Haskins was admitted to the basketball Hall of Fame in 1997.

Major Impact

Since Robinson's day, blacks have been the dominant figures in many sports. In baseball, over a recent dozen years, 22 of the 24 National and American League stolen-base leaders were black, as were most of the batting champions. Every rushing leader in the National Football League since 1963 has been black, and in the National Basketball Association only a few white players have led the league in scoring since 1960 and only two in rebounding since 1957.

Today, blacks make up 25 percent of baseball rosters, 40 percent of the players in the National Football League and 80 percent of the players in the National Basketball Association.

Although they make up only 6 percent of the college population, they account for more than 20 percent of all college athletes, more than 40 percent of the football players and about 60 percent of the basketball players.

At some colleges, a survey by *The Chronicle of Higher Education* found, more than half the black men on campus were athletic scholarship students.

Women: Players, Reporters

Long relegated to the sidelines of playing fields, women athletes have come into their own. Not that colleges and universities initiated the change. It took federal action requiring schools to equalize expenditures on male and female athletic programs.

Today, women engage in many intercollegiate sports, and women's basketball is a big TV draw, both the collegiate and the professional varieties.

Women make up 37 percent of the athletes who compete in major college sports programs. Of the more than $500 million in athletic scholarships awarded by Division I teams, women athletes received 38 percent.

Title IX, which prohibits sex discrimination at schools and colleges that receive federal funds, requires the institutions to meet a "substantial proportionality test," one of three criteria that determine compliance with Title IX. The test requires institutions to match the percentage of female athletes with the percentage of female undergraduates. In practice, a school is complying if the percentage of female athletes is not more than 5 percentage points less than the percentage of female undergraduates.

Since October 1996 institutions have been required under the Equity in Athletics Disclosure Act to provide the percentage information. The data indicate that less than a tenth of Division I members have met the proportionality test. Among the high-rate programs are the service academies, the University of Kansas, Dartmouth College and the University of Massachusetts at Amherst. Among the low-rated are the University of Southern Mississippi, Arkansas State University, University of Southwestern Louisiana, Texas Southern, Alcorn State, Drake, Howard and McNeese State.

In the Press Box

The distance women reporters have traveled is revealed by an incident Rapoport describes involving Lesley Visser, a television sports reporter. When Visser graduated from Boston College in 1976, the *Boston Globe* assigned her to cover the New England Patriots professional football team. She was the first female beat writer in the National Football League.

After a Patriots game with the Pittsburgh Steelers, Visser waited outside the Steelers locker room to interview quarterback Terry Bradshaw. When Bradshaw spotted her with her notebook, he automatically took it from her and signed his name.

Today, the editors of half a dozen major newspaper sports departments are women, and they are seen on all the major TV sports shows. Women are assigned to cover all the major sports on a regular basis.

But the transition for women from the sidelines was not easy. Owners and players resisted.

"I think women belong in the kitchen," said the owner of the San Francisco 49ers football team, Edward DeBartolo Jr. He was commenting after a federal judge ruled that the National Football League team had to grant equal access to its locker room to a female sports reporter for *The Sacramento Bee*. Many athletes wanted no women in locker rooms either.

Two incidents symbolize the change. One occurred in the locker room of the New England Patriots after a football game, the other in a Chicago White Sox lounge, again after a game.

With the Patriots   Linda Olson is covering the Patriots for the first time and after the game she asks a player to go to the media room for an interview. "No," he says, "come over here to my locker and we'll talk."

"As we sat on the bench in front of his locker, the prank began," Olson recalls. She said players "approached me, flashed their genitals and tried to get me to look while other players egged them on." They dared her to touch their genitals and made lewd comments. "Is this what you want?" one player yelled repeatedly.

Olson's newspaper did not report the incident, but the *Boston Globe* did, and a firestorm erupted. Sports reporters, women's groups and others were outraged.

Blaming the Victim   But the Patriots owner Victor Kiam called Olson a "classic bitch," and during home games Patriots fans threw trash at her. When she went on to cover Celtics basketball games, the anger continued. She said she came home after covering a practice "to find the words 'Leave Boston or die' written in red spray paint on my living room walls."

She had to change her telephone number many times because of calls "threatening to mutilate me for what I had done," she recalls. *Hustler* magazine ran a cartoon showing Olson being gang-raped by football players.

She was attacked on the road by a man who punched her in the face.

Olson decided to accept an offer to cover sports in Australia to get away from the anger and harassment. In an article six years after the 1990 incident, she recalls, "Lives were changed irrevocably because of those few minutes in the locker room. The general manager lost his job, the coach lost his job, all but one of the players involved is out of the NFL. Kiam had to sell the team and I moved to Australia, the point on the map that was farthest away."

And Today?   So much for history. Almost. There are still minor skirmishes. But the women give back as much, or more, as they are given.

Suzyn Waldman, who covers sports for WFAN, says baseball players are among the worst, basketball players the best.

After a baseball game, Waldman was bothered by a baseball player. "I told him, 'Brad, if you spent less time hassling women and more on baseball you wouldn't have done eight years in the minors.'"

Tracy Dodds, assistant sports editor of *The Orange County Register* and national president of the Association of Women in Sports Media, was confronted in a locker room interview by a naked athlete who, she said, "presented his pride and joy" to her and asked, "Do you know what this is?" Her reply: "It looks like a penis, only smaller."

Most athletes no longer care whether they are interviewed by a male or a female sportswriter. The story is told about a female sportswriter in a San Diego team's locker room following a game. As Randy Smith started to pull off his uniform, a teammate cautioned him, "Randy, there's a lady in the room." Smith replied, "That's no lady. That's only a writer."

An Overview

Kahn—who wrote a fine book about baseball, *The Boys of Summer*—has a basic approach to his reporting. Most good sportswriters do. Here, from one of Kahn's columns in *Esquire,* is how he describes his approach to his beat:

Sports tells anyone who watches intelligently about the times in which we live: about managed news and corporate policies, about race and terror and what the process of aging does to strong men. If that sounds grim, there is courage and high humor, too. . . .

. . . I find sport a better area than most to look for truth. A great hockey goalie, describing his life on ice, once said, "That puck comes so hard, it could take an eye.

I've had 250 stitches and I don't like pain. I get so nervous before every game, I lose my lunch."

"Some football players," I said to the goalie, whose name is Glenn Hall, "say that when they're badly scared, they pray."

Hall looked disgusted, "If there is a God," he said, "let's hope he's doing something more important than watching hockey games." Offhand I can't recall a better sermon.

Red Smith, who was writing his sports column for *The New York Times* until a few days before he died in 1982, said of sports:

> Sports is not really a play world. I think it's the real world. The people we're writing about in professional sports, they're suffering and living and dying and loving and trying to make their way through life just as the bricklayers and politicians are.
>
> This may sound defensive—I don't think it is—but I'm aware that games are a part of every culture we know anything about. And often taken seriously. It's no accident that of all the monuments left of the Greco-Roman culture, the biggest is the ball park, the Colosseum, the Yankee Stadium of ancient times. The man who reports on these games contributes his small bit to the history of his times.

Rapoport takes what he calls a practical view of sports coverage. "If you can't find something light or something that will make the reader smile or laugh, at least remember and try to show, in style or substance, that these are games these people are involved in, not foreign policy discussions," he says.

However, says Rapoport, "intensely dramatic and emotional things do happen, and when they do the reporter should not be afraid to haul out the heavy artillery.

"Just remember that in such cases the facts are usually enough."

They were for Rapoport on a November day when he received a phone call telling him to be at the Los Angeles Forum in two hours for an important announcement by Magic Johnson. Rapoport described the event in a column:

> Earvin Johnson is the only man I know who could smile while announcing he had contracted the virus that causes AIDS.
>
> Perhaps I shouldn't have been surprised at this, because over the years Johnson has done so many things no one else could ever do. But on Thursday afternoon, he outdid even himself.
>
> Wearing his sharpest suit and smiling his nice smile, Johnson strode into the Forum Club as if he were about to be handed another Most Valuable Player Award, or announce one more lucrative commercial endorsement.
>
> Instead, he said he had contracted HIV, the human immunodeficiency virus, and was quitting basketball as part of the treatment doctors hope will keep him from dying.

Further Reading

Anderson, David, ed. *The Red Smith Reader.* New York: Random House, 1983.

Berkow, Ira. *Red: A Biography of Red Smith.* New York: Times Books, 1986.

Halberstam, David. *October 1964.* New York: Villard Books, 1994.

Kahn, Roger. *The Boys of Summer.* New York: New American Library, 1973.

Klatell, David A., and Norman Marcus. *Sports for Sale: Television, Money, and the Fans.* New York: Oxford University Press, 1988.

Mantle, Mickey, and Phil Pepe. *My Favorite Summer 1956.* New York: Doubleday, 1991.

Miller, Marvin. *A Whole Different Ball Game: The Sport and Business of Baseball.* Secaucus, N.J.: Birch Lane Press, 1991.

Chapter 22

Rapoport, Ron. *A Kind of Grace.* Berkeley, Calif.: Zenobia Press, 1994. (A collection of 73 articles by women sportswriters.)

Remnick, David. *King of the World: Muhammad Ali and the Rise of an American Hero.* New York; Random House, 1998.

Robinson, Ray. *The Home Run Heard 'Round the World: The Dramatic Story of the 1951 Giants-Dodgers Pennant Race.* New York: HarperCollins, 1991.

Smith, Red. *Strawberries in the Wintertime.* New York: Quadrangle Times Books, 1974.

Whittingham, Richard. *The Meat Market: The Inside Story of the N.F.L. Draft.* New York: Macmillan, 1992. (Whittingham says that every year of the 4,500 college players, 336 are drafted, 130 survive their team's final cuts and 30 become starters.)

23 Business Reporting

Josh Estey,
The Register-Guard
(Eugene, Ore.)

Local businesses are covered.

Preview

Business and economic activity affects the cost and quality of the goods we buy; whether people buy or rent a home; the kind of car a person buys; even the college a high school graduate attends.

The business reporter handles:

• **Local spot news stories:** Store openings and closings, company personnel changes, new construction, changes in the business climate, annual reports of local companies.

• **Features:** New products developed by local enterprises, profiles of company officials and workers.

• **Interpretative stories:** Effects of national and international economic activity on local business, the influence of local business leaders on municipal policies and the budget.

Good Writing. Business stories need not be dull:

BURBANK, Calif. — After a year and a half of courtship, Mickey Mouse left Miss Piggy at the altar.

This *Wall Street Journal* lead began a story of the breakdown in plans by Walt Disney Co. to acquire the Muppet characters.

News about business and economics has become everybody's personal business. People want to know about the cost of living, job possibilities, how high or low interest rates may go, whether layoffs are imminent in local industries and the value of a bond or stock that they own.

Our food, clothing and shelter are produced by business enterprises, and their quality and the prices we pay for them are largely a result of business decisions. Even the quality of the air we breathe and the water we drink is affected by decisions made by the business community. We have a large stake in those decisions, and we want to be informed of them and to know how they are made.

News about commerce is as old as the newspaper itself. The gazettes and newsletters of the 17th century were established in the business centers of Europe for the emerging commercial class. Though it seems obvious that everyone would have a great interest in pocketbook news—news of the economy—editors came late to the realization and, until recently, business news was a minor part of the newspaper.

One cause of the awakening was the consumer movement in the 1970s that resulted in a new kind of coverage for television and for many newspapers—consumer journalism. Reacting to what appeared to be an attitude of *caveat emptor* (let the buyer beware) among U.S. businesses, newspapers and broadcast stations went into the marketplace to find out why the quality of goods and services was declining while prices were steadily rising.

Curiosity, if not skepticism, about business was strong. Consumers were irritated by products that fell apart too soon and too often, and they were infuriated by the indifference of manufacturers, sellers, repair people and mechanics.

The environmental movement also turned public attention, and then media attention, to the boardrooms of corporations. Journalists decided that their job was to make corporate power accountable. Tom Johnson, publisher of the *Los Angeles Times,* said, "Business news has become page one news because of the emergence of highly controversial issues in which there is an obvious potential for conflict between the corporate and the public interest." In 1968, the *Times* business staff had eight reporters. Today, there are 10 times as many.

Ample Opportunities

Business and economic reporting has exploded, making a wide range of opportunities for those who master the basics of the field. Newspapers publish business sections and have large reporting and editing staffs devoted to the subject. Television has grown from the nightly reading of the Dow Jones closing averages to full-scale coverage with several reporters assigned to the half-hour programs on the subject. Cable offers 24-hour business news.

Specialized business publications from *NursingLife* magazine and *Computer Design* to *Food Management* and *Construction Equipment* examine their fields in depth. Sal F. Marino, president of Penton Publishing, Inc., which publishes 30 business magazines says, "The business press is one of the best-kept secrets." He says there are "tremendous opportunities and rewards for the average journalist in the business press." There are more than 4,000 magazines, newsletters and newspapers of the business press.

Online information providers also have business journalists on their staffs. In Silicon Valley—the heart of the computer industry south of San Francisco—business reporters prowl the companies looking for news for news servers like CNET's NEWS.COM (www.news.com).

The Scope of Business News

On Friday night, Tom and Ann Ryan sit down after dinner to make a decision. The birth of their second child means they will need another bedroom. They must decide whether to rent a larger apartment or buy a house.

Tom Ryan spreads out a page of the local newspaper on the dining room table. He points to an article with a headline, "Mortgage Shopping." It begins:

> New York (AP)—Attention mortgage shoppers: Today's specials are 30-year conventional loans—just a 7.5 percent rate and no points if you buy your home now.

The story says that "at no time have there been so many loan options available for those looking to buy or refinance a home. Not since nearly 20 years ago have rates been so low and home prices so stable."

That clinches it for the Ryans. They decide to buy a new home.

Interest rates also are a concern of the Goldensohn family. Robert, a high school senior, wants to attend a private college. The tuition is high and he must have a student loan. The family income meets the necessities and little more. Robert may have to borrow at least $10,000 a year.

If they cannot handle the loan, Robert will have to attend a community college. Their newspaper carries a story on the latest information about student loans and interest rates. The Goldensohns decide they can afford a loan. Robert will go to a private college.

From Cattle Prices to Exchange Rates

In homes in every part of the city, people look to business stories for information. Workers whose contracts are tied to the cost of living watch the papers and television to see how their paychecks will be affected by the latest figures from Washington. Farmers follow the livestock and commodity markets. Vacationers search through the list of foreign exchange rates to see what the dollar is worth abroad before deciding where to spend their vacations. Residents north of the city hear that a new shopping center will be built there; they look through the business pages to find out more about it.

When the interest rates on savings accounts and certificates of deposit sank below 3 percent in the early 1990s, people began to look for higher-interest investments and were lured by advertisements: "Good News for C.D. Holders." What the ads did not point out is that unlike the certificates of deposit, whose principal is guaranteed by the Federal Deposit Insurance Corporation, the touted new investments had high risk.

Business reporters warned their readers of the risk, as they did when investment firms pushed closed-end government bond funds. Investing in such funds, wrote a *Wall Street Journal* reporter, was like paying $1.10 for a roll of 100 pennies.

And More The Associated Press reports that the giant Merrill Lynch & Co. agreed to pay Orange County $400 million for giving the county "bad investment advice that led to the county's bankruptcy." The county had sought $2 billion.

The Gannett News Service in Washington reports a panel of experts recommends that people should be allowed to put their Social Security payments into private investments.

The *Los Angeles Times* reports that House and Senate committees want to make it harder for people with family incomes of more than $50,000 to wipe out their debts by filing for bankruptcy.

NEWS.COM reveals that some telephone companies are planning to include e-mail addresses in the white pages of their directories.

Two of *Commercial Carrier Journal*'s editors pose as businessmen and travel thousands of miles from Chinatowns in the United States to Hong Kong, Singapore and Taiwan to expose "the flood of counterfeit merchandise pouring into the United States from the Far East."

The *Argus Leader* in Sioux Falls, S.D., reports that a new pizza place, Papa Murphy's Take-N-Bake, will sell "fresh-made pizzas that can be baked at home." A pepperoni pizza sells for $6.

A business reporter for *The New York Times* watched a recruiter lecturing potential insurance sales personnel for Primerica Financial Services and heard what he later wrote was "a mix of fact and half-truths." Then the reporter, Michael Quint, widened his scope to describe "a companywide pattern of exaggerations in the recruitment of agents and the selling of policies to hundreds of thousands of Americans."

He pointed out that the company has 110,000 agents, "more than 90 percent of them part-timers with little training but a need for extra income." The sales tactics, Quint found by firsthand reporting, "are often misleading and sometimes dangerous to a customer's financial security."

The Human Element

Because business stories can be complicated, writers try to introduce human interest whenever possible in their copy. Vivian Marino—the AP business writer whose story on mortgage rates influenced the Ryans to buy a home rather than rent—says, "I try to keep my stories as interesting and memorable as possible, often by using anecdotal examples to which readers can relate."

In a story about the financial problems of some retirees, she began with a retired worker trying to get by on his pension:

NEW YORK (AP) — After three decades laboring in the grimy steel mills around Pittsburgh, Richard L. Walters thought he earned a clean retirement.

But since taking early leave from LTV Corp., Walters, 60, and his wife Audrey, 54, have been barely getting by. His $922 monthly pension check isn't enough for the loan payments on the couple's New Brighton, Pa., Victorian, along with food bills and other escalating expenses.

So he's trying to go back to work. "Right now, it's pretty hard to get a job around here. I've been tinkering around on people's cars, making a couple of dollars here and there. I would like to just stay retired, but the way things are now I can't."

Marino ranges widely. She has written pieces about compulsive credit card spenders, growing numbers of auto repossessions, how to obtain a credit file and how to challenge inaccurate information. For her New Frugality series, she described what happened to Yuppies, the free-spending generation of professionals. Some have now become Grumpies, she writes—grown-up mature professionals—who skimp along on reduced incomes.

For a piece on college scholarships, her reporting turned up the availability of thousands of scholarships offering billions of dollars. In fact, she writes,

Business Writer

When Vivian Marino joined the Miami bureau of the AP, she was assigned to do a series on the labor problems of Eastern Airlines. When she had done that, she was given more business assignments.

"I decided to carve out my own niche by concentrating on business and finance." Soon she was appointed regional business writer.

Then she was transferred to New York. "I had to learn about the markets and more complicated business and financial issues. I learned from my colleagues and from many of my sources. I also read a lot. "

Marino writes a column on consumer affairs and personal finance for the AP.

nearly "$7 billion in college money goes unclaimed each year, or about $600 for every student in the United States." Her piece begins:

NEW YORK (AP)—Short of cash for college? Billions of dollars are waiting for the right students to come along.

The Two-Ten International Footwear Foundation, for instance, provides up to $2,000 for undergrads with parents in the shoe business. Post-graduate students can get $12,500 from the International Union for Vacuum Science, provided they study—you guessed it—vacuum science.

Even comedian David Letterman has gotten into the act, offering scholarships for telecommunications majors at alma mater Ball State University in Muncie, Ind. Grades aren't important.

Personal Finance

The Ryan and Goldensohn examples and Marino's story about Walters' retirement are called personal finance stories. A survey of readers found that personal finance is the most sought-after material on the business page. Readers—and listeners, too, stations have learned—seek information about solving credit problems, making decisions on investments, deciding whether to buy or lease.

The Atlanta Journal-Constitution carries a page weekly on personal finance. For the page, individuals open their checkbooks and bank books to reporters. The *Journal*'s business page feature "Money Makeover" deals with subjects such as planning for retirement and recovery from bankruptcy.

The Beat

The business reporter ranges widely. In the morning, she interviews local service station dealers about their price war, and that afternoon she localizes a story about the new prime rate and the failure of the coffee crop in Brazil.

Local stories she has covered include:

- Store openings, expansions and closings.
- Real estate transactions. New products from local enterprises. Construction projects planned.
- Plants opened, expanded, closed. Personnel changes, awards, retirements. Layoffs, bankruptcies.
- Annual and quarterly business reports. Annual meetings.
- Bond offerings by local government units.

If the newspaper or station has no labor reporter, the business reporter covers labor-management relations and the activities of labor unions.

In addition to these spot news stories, the business reporter is aware of trends and developments in the community and area. The business reporter knows the relationship between the prime rate and the local housing market and understands how the city's parking policies affect downtown merchants.

Local Stories

Here is how Bob Freund of *The Times-News* in Twin Falls, Idaho, began a roundup that blended local and national business and economic activity with area trends:

TWIN FALLS—As spring turned into summer, the brightest news for the Magic Valley economy was coming from consumers.

They climbed into new cars at an accelerated pace, and sought credit both to pay for the new wheels and for improvements at home.

They benefited from a vicious war of price cutting and couponing among area grocery stores.

Indicators compiled by The Times-News for the second quarter ending June 30 show some momentum in the Magic Valley economy, but also some significant drags.

Despite lower mortgage rates and a national surge in homebuying, the biggest consumer of all, the home buyer, still is not pounding down the doors at Magic Valley real estate agencies.

Agriculture, the underlying financial pump for the valley economy, remains grounded by low commodity prices.

Of course, the Magic Valley is not alone in these problems. Idaho's economy generally is weak, and with trade imbalances pressing more and more on manufacturing, the U.S. is wavering in a twilight zone between recession and growth.

Nationally, economists are calling the situation a growth recession. The economy is growing, but it is not gaining enough strength to cut unemployment substantially.

A Drugstore Opening

The more the newspaper or station stresses local news, the more detailed business stories will be, and in small communities the line between news and free advertising is so narrow it approaches invisibility. A large department store opening will be reported by the biggest newspapers. But a drugstore opening will not. The smaller newspaper or station will carry the drugstore opening and might cover the enlargement of a hardware store.

Here is the beginning of an 11-paragraph story that appeared in a newspaper in Massachusetts:

For 10 years, tailor Frank Saporito plied his trade with Davis & Norton Inc. on North Street here, where he was in charge of all alterations. When that business closed last month, Saporito was out of work—but not for long.

Saporito landed on his feet and decided to go into business for himself at 251 Fenn St., just across the street from the post office. He's been open there a little more than a week.

"I wanted to try it by myself," Saporito said. "I think it's a good move. I sure hope so."

Chain Store Alert

Business reporters keep an eye open for any moves into town by the major chain stores. Such moves can have a major impact on local business.

When Wal-Mart started building a store two miles outside Hudson, N.Y., local store owners took notice. The massive chain, the nation's largest retailer, has in other areas driven out local businesses because of its pricing policies. In Hudson, which marked a move into the northeast for the chain, local businesses spruced up their stores and decided that they will profit from the new shoppers who will be attracted to the area.

In other areas, the mood has been pessimistic. In Greenfield, Mass., local residents voted to bar Wal-Mart from moving into town.

Among the story possibilities: Sale of land for the new store; new employment; new tax revenues; impact on local business now, a year later, five years later.

Coffee Beans and Burritos

The photo that opens this chapter accompanied an article by Sherri Buri in the Sunday business section of *The Register-Guard* in Eugene, Ore., that begins:

Before Sony opened its compact disc factory in Springfield, it held a coffee tasting to decide which brand would flow through the company cafeteria's espresso machine.

One morning about two years ago, several local vendors set up shop at Sony's temporary offices in the Delta Oaks shopping center in Eugene. Nearly two hours and three gallons of coffee later, Eugene-based Full City Coffee walked away the winner.

"Money was never a question," recalled Michael Phinney, who owns Full City with his wife, Terril. "In fact, they never asked me how much we charge."

Josh Estey,
The Register-Guard

Ready to Go

The 6-year-old coffee roasting company is just one of a huge network of local businesses that supply everything from coffee to custom steel work to the 375-employee high-tech company. These local suppliers demonstrate how high-tech giants, such as Sony and Hyundai, send out economic ripples far beyond the factory's payroll when they enter Lane County. . . .

In another article in the section, Jim Boyd profiles a local woman who decided to expand her weekend business:

It wasn't getting the financing. It wasn't finding a location. It wasn't recruiting good workers. The biggest obstacle that Ritta Dreier had to overcome when she recently expanded her business was simply deciding to do it.

For 19 years, Dreier has operated the 10-by-10-foot Ritta's Burritos booth at Saturday Market and other regional events. Despite its nomadic nature, the booth has been a money-maker.

"I can say there's some booths down at Saturday Market—food booths—that are probably happy to make $400 on a Saturday, and I would say there's several Saturday Market vendors that can—on a really, really busy day—can reach probably $1,800 dollars on a Saturday," she said. "And I'm one of the top-grossing vendors at Saturday Market and always have been."

On April 1, Dreier expanded her food service operation by opening Ritta's Burritos Home Cafe, a 29-seat restaurant at 755 Monroe St. that will serve as a permanent home for her business. It's in the same Blair Boulevard neighborhood as the Bagel Bakery, Taco Loco, Pacific Winds Music and Fisherman's Market.

She chose Home Cafe as the name because she has a great affection for her homes—her family home in Cedar Falls, Iowa; her own home on Polk Street; and now the Home Cafe.

Dreier, 41, was born in Cedar Falls and earned a degree in theater and speech in 1977 from Morningside College in Sioux City, Iowa. After graduation, she wanted to get out on her own so she joined her brother, Dan Dreier, and his first wife, Roberta, who were living in rural Eugene. . . .

Josh Estey,
The Register-Guard

New Business

Puff Pieces

Advertising salespeople sometimes promise an advertiser a story about a store expansion or about the cashier who has spent 25 years behind the Hamburger Heaven checkout counter. When the publisher orders a story, the piece is known as a BOM (business office must).

These stories are considered free advertising. Still, it could be argued that some of these events can make good stories. The perceptive business reporter sent to interview the hardware merchant who is enlarging his store might find that the store owner is staking his last dime on this gamble to keep from losing business to the Kmart outside town. And the Hamburger Heaven cashier could become a human interest story.

The Reporter's Requirements

The business reporter is a specialist who feels at home with numbers and is not frightened by lengthy reports and press releases, many of which contain rates, percentages, business and consumer indexes and the jargon of the business world.

Among the skills and attitudes the business reporter takes to the job is the recognition of the power business exerts. Along with this, the reporter has a healthy skepticism that keeps him or her from being awed by the muscle and money that business power generates.

The business reporter approaches the money managers and manipulators with the same objectivity and distance that any reporter takes on an assignment. In his profile of a corporate raider, Michael A. Hiltzik of the *Los Angeles Times* was able to find sources and anecdotes to get to the heart of his subject, Irwin L. Jacobs of Minneapolis. Jacobs acquires and merges companies, usually at great profit.

Jacobs usually would pledge to operate rather than to dismantle the firms "on the insight that Americans lionize industrialists and not liquidators," Hiltzik says. For his piece, Hiltzik was able to show that Jacobs dismantled one firm in 17 days, despite his promise to operate Mid American Bancorporation of Minnesota "for his children and his children's children," the story said. Jacobs' profit: an estimated $4 million.

Specialist though he or she may be, the business reporter must know much more than the world of finance. When Hiltzik was assigned to cover the tribulations of a precious metals investment firm, he had to look through court documents with the same scrupulous and knowledgeable attention a courthouse reporter gives the records. In fact, Hiltzik found in one of the documents a human interest lead to his story about the complicated activities of the firm.

He began his lengthy account of Monex International Ltd. with the story of Kathleen Ann Mahoney, a professional singer who was living in Newport Beach, Calif., when she bought $10,000 worth of silver through Monex. The price of silver went up, and Hiltzik reports, she "invested another $12,000, then another $10,000, and then her last $13,000, relying on what she says was a Monex salesman's pitch that silver prices were rising so fast they might earn $100,000 for her over a year's time." The price of silver reached $50 an ounce.

"Four days later, Mahoney was wiped out. Silver had plunged to $28, and the crash had taken most of her investment with it," Hiltzik wrote.

Two Types of Companies

Publicly held: Company owned by investors who bought its stock. Stock is traded on exchange or market where its price or market value is determined by what investors pay to own it. Must file documents with SEC and publish annual reports, which are sources of information for reporter.

Privately or closely held: Company is usually controlled by a small group or a family. Stock is not publicly traded on an exchange. Value is set by owners. Information is difficult to obtain. Company may be regulated by state or federal agency, which will have some information about it.

Sources of Information

The business reporter has a harder job digging for information than most journalists do. Most reporters deal with public officials who live in goldfish bowls. Laws and a long tradition have made the public sector public.

The business world, however, is generally private, secretive and authoritarian. The head of a company can order his or her employees not to talk to reporters. Because businesspeople usually are in competition, secrecy is a natural part of business life. True, businesses are required to file many kinds of reports with various governmental agencies, and these are excellent sources of information. But in the day-to-day coverage of the beat, the business reporter must rely on human sources. Good sources can break the code of silence and secrecy.

Human Sources

Good contacts and sources can be made among the following:

- Bank officers, tellers.
- Savings and loan officials.
- Chamber of Commerce secretaries.
- Union leaders and working people.
- Securities dealers.
- Financial analysts.
- Real estate brokers.
- Trade organization officials.
- Teachers of business, economics.
- Transportation company officials.
- Federal and state officials in agencies such as the Small Business Administration, Commerce Department, various regulatory agencies.

Sources Are Everywhere

Brenda Schmidt, business editor of the *Argus Leader* in Sioux Falls, S.D., writes the "Eye on Business" column. Usually, she has four or five items about the local business scene. On the next page is a typical column with Schmidt's comments about her sources alongside.

Schmidt's co-workers pass along information. An *Argus Leader* employee saw a sign that The Keg on East 10th Street was moving. Schmidt called the owner of the neighborhood bar known for its deep-fried chicken, and he told her, "We've just kind of outgrown the place."

Friends pass along tips. One said a piece of ground in The Empire mall parking lot would be used by Burger King, making it the city's ninth outlet for the fast-food chain.

Mike Kuehl called Schmidt to tell her his Powerhouse Gym, Fitness and Rehabilitation Center would open in three weeks. Sharon Busch called to say her Toys & Treasures store would be honored at the national toy fair in New York "for sponsoring a Goetz doll signing in October."

Grocery Will Feature Ethnic Twist

■ When Matt Sapari was deciding on a name for his new specialty grocery store, he chose something that reminds him of a popular Middle Eastern dish — stuffed grape leaves.

The Grape Vine, at 1921 S. Minnesota Ave., will sell Mediterranean sweets, cheese, olives, coffees, spices, Middle Eastern breads and groceries. Sapari said the store will be similar to the Olive Branch, which opened a few years ago on East 10th Street.

He hopes to be open by the end of March. The fresh baked products, such as baklava, will be shipped in from Detroit.

"There was a demand for something like that in South Dakota," Sapari said.

Sapari, who moved here from Kuwait seven years ago, has been in the construction business the last two years. His wife and a brother will operate the store.

■ Walt and Nancy Landry open Mind Games at noon today at 2012 S. Minnesota Ave.

The store will sell board games that have been tough to find in Sioux Falls and will rent game rooms to players who want to gather a group to play at the store. Popcorn is free.

"We think we'll appeal to a crowd that goes from 10-year-olds all the way up to kids of 60," he said.

The Landrys decided to start their business after they noticed friends going to Omaha, Neb., and Minneapolis to shop for games. With a little research, they found out Sioux City, Iowa, has three game businesses.

"If Sioux City can support three stores at 75,000, surely Sioux Falls at 120,000 could support one store," he said.

BRENDA SCHMIDT
EYE ON BUSINESS

Mind Games will sell strategic and tactical games such as Dungeons and Dragons, Wild West and Micro Armor, a game that uses mini tanks and recreates famous wars.

"You actually play against other people vs. playing against a computer," he said.

■ Dan Winkler of Sioux Falls has opened The Next Dimension, stand-up virtual reality games in the Dayton's wing at The Empire mall. A game is $5 for about five minutes.

Players also can join forces with other players to meet the computer challenges. Participants wear headsets, see texture mapped 3-D color graphics and hear stereo sound.

"You don't just play the game, you are the game," Winkler said.

■ Gateway 2000 opened its factory outlet this week at 3109 W. 41st St., Suite 4. The outlet is open from 9 a.m. to 9 p.m. Monday through Friday, 9 a.m. to 5 p.m. Saturday and noon to 4 p.m. Sunday.

The personal computer manufacturer's previous outlet was at 700 E. 54th St. N.

Brenda Wade Schmidt is business editor of the *Argus Leader.* You can write her at P.O. Box 5034, Sioux Falls, S.D. 57117-5034, or call 331-2321.

Even her husband pitches in. He told her about a longtime downtown fixture, 3 & Co. Antiques, leaving for a nearby town. Schmidt checked and a co-owner told her parking was the problem. Customers, he said, "are not going to concentrate on a $1,000 piece of furniture if they're worried about a $3 parking ticket."

Cultivating Sources

On first contact with a reporter, the business source is likely to be wary, says James L. Rowe Jr., New York financial correspondent of *The Washington Post.* "As a result, it is often difficult to gain the source's trust.

"But if the reporter does his or her homework, learns what motivates business people, is not afraid to ask the intelligent questions but doesn't have to ask the dumb one, more than enough sources will break down."

In developing these sources, the reporter will want to find people who can put events into perspective and who can clarify some of the complexities the reporter cannot. Caution is important. Not only must the sources be dependable, they must be independent of compromising connections and affiliations. Obviously, such sources are hard to find. The traditional independent source was the academician, the cloistered professor who had no financial stake in the matters he would comment about. But no more. Academicians now serve on the boards of banks, chemical companies and pesticide manufacturers. The alert reporter makes certain that background information from such sources is neither biased nor self-serving.

When quoting a source, note all of the person's business affiliations relevant to the story. In a banking story, it's not enough to say that Professor Thomas Graham teaches economics at the state university. His membership on the board of directors of the First National Bank should also be included.

Background Source The background source is rarely quoted, and so readers and viewers cannot assess the information in terms of the source's affiliations. Because background sources influence reporters by providing perspective, the independence of these sources is essential. Good background sources can be found without leaving the office. The accountants, marketing people and the legal adviser to the newspaper or station can figure out some of the complexities of reports and documents. They also are close to the business community.

The business office has access to the local credit bureau and the facilities of Dun and Bradstreet, which can provide confidential information. These are helpful in running a check on a local business.

Chris Welles, a veteran business writer, says, "By far the most important sources on company stories are former executives. Unconstrained by the fear of being fired if word gets out that they talked to you, they can be extremely forthcoming about their former employer." Competitors are another good source, as are suppliers, the managers of investment portfolios, bankers and others who are likely to know the company's financial situation, such as the financial analysts who prepare reports on public corporations.

In interviews, Welles will share his problems in obtaining material. "Most people are predisposed to respond favorably to someone who, in a non-threatening way, asks for a little help." Welles says he listens "with great interest and sympathy." He says that "sources have a great deal of trouble terminating a conversation with someone who seems to be hanging on their every word."

Physical Sources

At the local level, reporters know how to use city and county tax records. The city and county keep excellent records of real estate transfers, and the assessor's office has the valuation of real property and of the physical plant and equipment—whatever is taxed. The sales tax shows how much business a firm is doing. Many local governments issue business licenses on which the principals involved are named and other information is given.

State governments also issue business licenses. There are scores of state boards; they license barbers, engineers, cosmetologists, doctors, morticians, lawyers, accountants and others. These agencies usually keep basic information about the businesses they oversee.

The state corporation commission or the secretary of state will have the names, addresses and sometimes the stock held by directors of corporations incorporated in the state and of firms that do a large amount of business in the state. The company's articles of incorporation and bylaws are also on file.

Bankruptcy filings are an overlooked source of local stories. Journalists are content to report the total number filed every so often, but behind each one is a story. All the figures are public records. The reporter interviews the filers for the human story.

Bankruptcies

The commercial on the all-news radio station is friendly, helpful. "Deep in debt? Let us help you with your bankruptcy filing." The commercial goes on to tell the listener that bankruptcy is benign, no headaches afterward. The soothing voice of the announcer indicates everyone is doing it. Well, not exactly. But a lot of people in debt are: In 20 years, bankruptcy filings went from 200,000 to more than 1.3 million a year.

It's true that people seemingly with plenty of money are filing. Toni Braxton filed for bankruptcy under federal law, and news reports said she owned a Porsche, Lexus and baby grand piano. "I'm gonna go out and enjoy myself," she told a reporter as she left the federal building. Also filing: M. C. Hammer, Burt Reynolds and Kim Basinger.

But most people who file are really in trouble, and this is where there are stories. A local merchant opens a jewelry store with high hopes, and within a year he files. Why? Was it a poor location? Did he fail to have sufficient funds for a varied stock? Did a chain store open and undercut his prices?

Credit Card Debts   There are personal bankruptcies as well, many of them the result of credit card debt that finally overwhelms the cardholders. It's estimated that almost 60 million households carry a credit card debt of more than $7,000 from month to month. Interest on credit cards can average 18 percent.

College students are big on credit cards, and there are stories there, too. Many students carry three, four, five cards so that when they reach the maximum credit allowance on one they use another, and then another.

Many credit card issuers make no check of applicants' ability to pay. A fourth of households with less than $10,000 annual income have credit card debt, as do more than 40 percent of those with income from $10,000 to $25,000.

Ideas for stories like those on bankruptcies do not spring up out of the blue. Some come from tips from sources, but many come from wide reading in the field.

Reading

Daily reading of *The Wall Street Journal* is necessary for the business reporter. Written for businesspeople and those with some involvement in financial matters, the stories nevertheless are written in everyday language. The newspaper is both record keeper for the business community and its watchdog. Its investigative reporting is among the best in the country.

Business Week, a weekly business newsmagazine, is staffed by journalists with a good command of business, finance and economics. The magazine con-

---

Covering the Business Beat Better

Here are some suggestions from Henry Dubroff, editor of *The Denver Business Journal* and vice president of the American Business Editors and Writers:

• Become a financial news junkie. Pay attention to developments on your beats even if there is no obvious local angle.

• Look for hidden hooks in releases and routine earnings announcements. You may find something the competition has overlooked. Hint: Read the last line first.

• Use your sources for insight, not necessarily quotes. It's called building relationships.

• Be comfortable with basic financial terms.

• Never be afraid to go back to a company or a source two or three times to get the whole story.

• As deadline approaches, it's time for that extra special push. The best stories often are the ones that break late on your beat.

• Learn from reading and rereading major publications like *The Wall Street Journal, Forbes* and *Barron's*. Not just for content but for how they approach a big research project or for how they tell a story.

• It's always better to get off the phone and get on the streets to actually see what a company looks like up close and personal.

• You've got to prepare if you want to win.

---

centrates on the major industries and companies. Its long articles are aimed at the men and women who are in executive posts in business.

Forbes is addressed to investors, people who own stock in companies. The *Journal, Business Week,* and *Forbes* are pro-business. Although they do go after the bad apples in the barrel, they never question the barrel, the system itself, as former *Journal* staffer Kent MacDougall puts it. The most pro-business publication is *Nation's Business,* which is published by the U.S. Chamber of Commerce and the National Association of Manufacturers.

Many publications have online versions of their newspapers and magazines. (See **Appendix E, Sources Online.**)

References

A good local library or any business school library at a college or university will have the following references that business reporters find useful:

- **Dun and Bradstreet directories:** One covers companies with capital under $1 million; another is for those whose capital exceeds $1 million. (Provides address, corporate officers, sales, number of employees.)
- **Who Owns Whom:** To find the parent company of a firm you are checking.
- **Standard & Poor's Register of Corporations, Directors and Executives.**
- **Moody's Manuals.**
- **Standard & Poor's Corporation Record:** Seven volumes of basic information on almost every publicly traded stock.

Most of these references are available online.

Regulatory Agencies

All levels of government regulate business. Local laws prescribe health, fire and safety regulations to which businesses must adhere. The city grants franchises and checks to see that the provisions are followed, such as those requiring public access to the local cable television company. Regional and county governments set standards for factory emissions.

The state regulates some banks, savings and loan institutions, insurance companies and public utilities. State agencies handle rate applications and oversee operational procedures of utilities. Basic information about these businesses is available to the journalist.

State licensing boards also regulate the trades and professions they license. Usually, they have the power to investigate complaints and to hold hearings. Although most of these boards are creatures of the businesses and professions they regulate, occasionally a board will act decisively. Failure to take action is an even better story, as one reporter learned when the board regulating veterinarians failed to hold a hearing for a veterinarian who was the subject of a number of complaints by pet owners whose dogs and cats had died in his care.

Although most federal regulatory agencies are in Washington and too distant for personal checking, a local business reporter can ask the newspaper's Washington bureau or the AP to run something down. Federal agencies compile considerable material about companies and individuals seeking permission to operate interstate. Some agencies:

- **Federal Communications Commission (FCC):** Regulates radio and television stations. Ownership and stock information are available.
- **National Labor Relations Board (NLRB):** Concerned with labor disputes.

Developing sources on the beat, wide reading and a knowledge of how business works and is regulated allow the journalist to develop stories, to enterprise interesting and significant articles for readers and viewers and listeners.

Enterprise

Don Moffitt, a *Wall Street Journal* editor, says that business reporters "should consider that they have a license to inquire into the nuts and bolts of how people make a living and secure their well-being.

"For a local paper, the fortunes of the community's barbers, auto mechanics, bankers and public servants are business stories. Business is how people survive.

"If people are falling behind in their mortgage payments, show how and why they are falling behind, how they feel about it and what they're trying to do about it," he says.

"Local government financing and spending is, in part, a business story. Who's making money off the local bond issues, and why? Is the bank keeping the county's low-interest deposits and using the cash to buy the county's high-yielding paper? Who suffers when the township cuts the budget, or can't increase it? Show how they suffer."

Always go beyond the press release, business reporters say. When a $69 million reconstruction job at a shopping center was announced, the developers sent out stacks of press releases. By asking why so much money was being spent on releases, a reporter learned that sales at the center had sharply declined recently—a fact not mentioned in any of the releases.

Steve Lipson, business news writer for *The Times-News,* develops ideas for stories by a simple technique—keeping his eyes open. "I read ads, I notice changes in the businesses where I shop. I count the number of cars in a car dealer's lot, and I look at what people wear, eat and drink," Lipson says.

"I look for unique stories," he says. He did one on the growing popularity of potato-skin appetizers. "This big boost to potato consumption would land someone in the Idaho Hall of Fame if anyone knew who was responsible. Alas, my story found no one really knows."

Ideas can turn up anywhere, even in the small print in the back of the business section under "Foreign Exchange." The figures show how much the U.S. dollar is worth abroad. The exchange rates affect business. Let's see why.

Mike Roemer

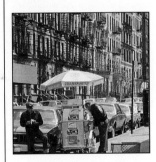

Entrepreneurs

The enterprising reporter will pull up alongside the two girls and will stop on a lunchtime stroll when the street vendor is spotted. The perennial question: How's business?

The Dollar's Value Abroad

When the dollar is worth a lot—the sound dollar—you would think everyone would be happy. Not so. A rise in the dollar makes U.S.-made goods more expensive abroad, and this makes it harder for U.S. products to compete with foreign goods. So growers, manufacturers—everyone who sells goods and services overseas—have to cut prices, thus lessening profits.

But the sound dollar has its plus side as well. It helps hold down inflation because the dollar buys more, and for those traveling abroad lodging and merchandise are less expensive.

Gloom in Florida   When the Canadian dollar went into steep decline, the tourist industry in Florida went into deep gloom. Many Canadians travel to Florida to escape the harsh Canadian winter. But when the Canadian dollar buys little, people stay home. Also, communities along the U.S.-Canada border that do business with Canadians out on the town or on a shopping spree are badly hurt.

Helen Huntley of the *St. Petersburg Times* in Florida looked at what might happen to the billion-dollar tourist industry if the Canadian dollar kept sinking:

> If the Canadian dollar continues its slide, thousands of Canadians could cancel their annual winter pilgrimages to Florida.
>
> "There's definitely going to be an impact," predicted Jeff Fraser, vice president of sales and marketing for the Canadian Snowbird Association in North York, Ontario. He expects as many as 10 percent of those who ordinarily head south each winter will decide to stay home, at least partly because of their currency's decline.
>
> The problem is that the Canadian dollar is currently trading at only 68 cents to the U.S. dollar, just above its all-time low of 67.85 cents recorded last week. Last year at this time, the Canadian dollar was worth about 72 cents and as recently as March it was 71 cents.

The slide continued. At one point, a Canadian dollar was worth only 64 cents U.S. If you have a calculator, divide one U.S. dollar by 64 cents. You get $1.5625. In other words, it would take about $1.56 Canadian to buy $1 U.S. Hold on. That's the bank rate, given only to big operators. The average tourist would have to dig up at least $1.60 Canadian to buy one U.S. dollar.

Smiles in Regina   On the other hand, an exporter of farm machinery in Regina, Saskatchewan, was delighted. Farmers with American dollars found his rock pickers a bargain as the U.S. dollar went a long way in terms of Canadian prices.

This led to another story:

> REGINA, Saskatchewan—Some businesses here are happy about the steep decline of the Canadian dollar. They report foreign buyers, not only those from the U.S., are buying at a record clip.

Speaking of the small print at the back of the business section—let's look at the bond prices. There are stories there as well. Not so much in the fluctuating bond market, but in the subject of bonds.

Municipal Bonds

The school system and the city, county and state often decide on major construction projects. To finance them, large amounts of money have to be raised by selling bonds.

The bond story involves interest rates, the financial standing or rating of the local government and related matters that may seem complex for readers but that can be simplified with good reporting. First, check the rating of the governmental unit.

If the local government is not rated financially healthy, the bonds might not be seen as a good investment. To attract buyers of the bonds, the interest rate then might have to be set high, and just half of 1 percent more in interest could mean millions of dollars more that the taxpayers will have to pay in interest over the life of the bonds.

Reporters can learn about the health of the local government by examining two kinds of documents, the bond prospectus and the analysis by the rating agencies:

Prospectus: This document is required by law for the information of potential investors. It contains considerable information about the government entity offering the bonds.

Rating: The government entity's debt (which is what a bond is) is rated by organizations such as Moody's and Standard & Poor's. The lower the rating, the higher the interest rate on the bonds and the greater the cost to taxpayers. Reporters can obtain these ratings.

University Bonds

Almost all governments issue bonds and so do many private entities. Your university probably has issued bonds for a dormitory or classroom construction, possibly for building a stadium or field house. Just as governments that issue bonds are rated, so are colleges and universities. Some are given high ratings, others less than the best. Here is a story about a rating one university was given:

Standard & Poor's today announced it has upgraded Columbia University's debt rating from AA+ to AAA.

Only eight other universities are in the rating agency's top bracket: California Institute of Technology, Grinnell, Harvard,

MIT, Princeton, Rockefeller University, Stanford and Yale.

Standard & Poor's upgraded Columbia's rating on the basis of a successful fund-raising campaign, effective financial strategies and the selectivity of the undergraduate and graduate programs.

Georgetown University was given a rating in the middle range by Moody's, A-1. An official with the agency said the institution has "not historically been strong at raising funds. Plus they run a teaching hospital, and they are in an urban area, and the hospital is in the District of Columbia. Those things are all weak credit factors."

Standard & Poor's rated Seton Hall College in Pennsylvania "below investment grade." Moody's below-investment-grade list includes Odessa, Bennington College in Vermont, Colby-Sawyer College in New Hampshire, the University of Hartford in Connecticut, Dowling College in New York, Franklin Pierce College and New England College in New Hampshire. Moody's gave its lowest rating to Bridgewater College in Virginia.

Skepticism and Doubt

"The business page is singularly marked by credulity," says Bernard Nossiter, a veteran business reporter. "Corporate and even Treasury pronouncements are treated as holy writ. Corporate officials are likely to be regarded with awe, at least until they are indicted."

One reason, he says, is that "reporters are literate rather than numerate," more at home with words than with figures.

One of the stories business interests find reporters eager to write is the new business or development piece. Anything that promises new jobs or an expanding economy in town is snapped up, even when the venture is speculative. In Alexandria, Va., a developer put up a huge sign announcing an 800,000-square-foot office building, and *The Washington Post* ran a picture and story. No tenant was ever signed up. Reporters need to dig deeper:

- **Questions for new ventures:** What evidence is there of secure financing? Who are the lenders?
- **Questions for developers:** What tenants have signed leases? Are they being given free rent? Have building permits been issued?

Morton Mintz, for many years a digging reporter at *The Washington Post* who exposed corporate greed that resulted in danger and death to the public, says that the press has failed to audit "impersonal crime committed by the large corporation." He recalls the response of Alfred P. Sloan Jr., head of General Motors, when GM was urged to use safety glass for windshields, as Ford had been doing for years.

GM was using ordinary flat glass, which, Mintz says, "breaks into shards, disfiguring, slashing, killing." Sloan's response:

Accidents or no accidents, my concern on this matter is a matter of profit and loss. . . . I am trying to protect the stockholders of General Motors and the

Corporation's operating position—it is not my responsibility to sell safety glass. . . . You can say, perhaps, that I am selfish, but business is selfish. We are not a charitable institution—we are trying to make a profit for our stockholders.

Checking the Ladies   The women were fantastic investors. The feature stories about their investment group said they were getting better than 23 percent for their stock market purchases. Their books became best sellers. Their first book, in which they claimed their investment club had an annual return of 23.4 percent from 1984 through 1993, sold 800,000 copies. They were popular speakers, these Beardstown Ladies.

Assigned to do a piece on the Ladies by *Chicago* magazine, Shane Tritsch was hardly moved by the prospect. "I wasn't all that excited about doing the 500th fawning story on the Beardstown Ladies," he told *Brill's Content* writer Elizabeth Lesly Stevens. "What in the world was left to say?"

He started to browse through the Ladies' famous *Investment Guide*. A small note on the copyright page said the Ladies included monthly dues when adding up their returns. Another glitch caught his eye, and this time he dug into the book. He came up with a return of 12.2 percent, a bit over half the Ladies' claim.

The Wall Street Journal picked up Tritsch's story and it became headline news. This story sparked a Price Waterhouse audit that found the actual return to be 9.1 percent annualized return over the decade.

The story of Tritsch's investigation is told in the July/August 1998 *Brill's Content.*

Checking the Banks   Banks spend lots of money trying to cultivate an image of friendliness, no doubt to counter their reputation as cold hearted. "For some time," says Michael Selz of *The Wall Street Journal,* "the nation's largest commercial banks claimed in advertisements and corporate promotions that they were lending aggressively to small businesses." He and Edward R. Foldessey, the *Journal*'s computer-assisted reporting expert decided to test the claims.

They had access to 12,000 bank reports filed with federal regulators. Banks are required to disclose the amount and number of commercial and industrial loans of less than $1 million as well as mortgage loans. The *Journal* examined the loans of the big banks.

"The study contradicted many of the big banks' claims about serving the small business market," Selz says, despite claims such as that of one bank that it is the "market leader" in such loans. The big banks, the figures showed, were lending less to small businesses than much smaller banks were. Here is the beginning of Selz's story:

To prove its commitment to small-business lending, New York's Chemical Banking Corp. annually stages what it calls the "biggest blitz in banking history."

In each of the past three years, more than 1,000 officers of the nation's third largest bank holding company—including its chairman and chief executive, Walter V. Shipley—go "knocking on the doors" of prospective small-business borrowers in five states to make clear that Chemical wants to lend them money.

When it comes to small-business lending in the New York area, "we're the market leader," says Frank Lourenso, an executive vice president for Chemical's New York bank.

There's one problem with that claim: Federal banking reports show it isn't true.

Numbers Count

Many students are attracted to journalism because they like to write and because journalism is concerned with how people get along with each other. These students are interested in the qualitative aspect of life. Journalism, with its feature stories and its emphasis on human interest, can use the talents these students take to the job. But much of what we know about the world—and people—is derived from quantitative studies.

The student who is thinking about a career in business journalism—and this is one area of journalism that never seems to have enough reporters and editors—cannot manage without an ability to deal with numbers. If business is the bottom line on a balance sheet, then the student thinking of becoming a business reporter has to know what to make of the numbers on the line.

Checking on Numbers

Pauline Tai, former director of the Knight-Bagehot Fellowship Program in business journalism at Columbia University, says business reporters must be able to "analyze numbers. You can't just accept what a CEO tells you. You should be able to calculate. You have to know how the CEO came to a figure and what it means. You just don't take what you are being told as the truth. You have to look into it, and sometimes you have to stick your neck out and make judgments."

Note: More than a third of business executives polled by the Freedom Forum First Amendment Center said they regularly lie to the media. See *The Headline vs. The Bottom Line* by Mike Haggerty and Wallace Rasmussen, available from the Center at Vanderbilt University, 1207 18th Avenue, Nashville, TN 37212, (615) 321-9588.

The ability to blend the qualitative and the quantitative is essential to the business journalist. Numbers alone do say a lot, but when these barometers are matched with human beings, they take on dramatic significance. When home loan applications increase (quantitative), the reporter finds a family like the Ryans we met a while back and shows why this family decided to buy rather than to rent (qualitative).

Let's look at an example of a story the business reporter handles that is concerned primarily with figures. In our list of stories the business reporter deals with, we mentioned annual reports, the yearly accounting of publicly owned companies.

Annual Reports

Newspapers usually run a summary of the annual reports of industries and businesses in their readership area. Readers want to know the economic health of the companies that employ local people, and some may own stock in these firms. Many readers also want to know about the status of the firms that have large numbers of shares of stock distributed nationwide—IBM, Kodak, General Motors, Polaroid, AT&T, Ford, General Electric. These readers may be shareholders—more than half the adult population owns stock—or they may be planning to invest in stocks. Or a part or all of their retirement benefits may be tied to stocks. The business reporter must be able to swim through a sea of figures toward the few pieces of essential information in the report.

What to Look For

First, read the auditor's report, which is usually at the back. "Generally, if the Auditor's Report is two paragraphs long, the financial statements have been given a clean bill of health," says the American Institute of Certified Public Accountants. "Anything longer—an extra paragraph or so—and normally that's a red flag alerting you to look further."

Jane Bryant Quinn, CBS business commentator, says the words "subject to" in the auditor's report are a warning signal.

"They mean the financial report is clean *only* if you take the company's word about a particular piece of business, and the accountant isn't sure you should," she says.

Reader Friendly. Some companies are making their annual reports easy on the eye. Reebok, McDonald's and Wal-Mart have adopted a magazine format. They are also putting their reports on the World Wide Web, and they are adding material online that does not appear in their reports. For example, McDonald's put a reply online to charges about its environmental and employment practices. Wal-Mart rebuts a charge it is planning a store on the site of George Washington's boyhood home. GTE offers a "Forum" feature to Web users that allows them to ask questions or register complaints.

The CPA Institute has a general caution about the auditor's report: "All it means is that the financial statements are fairly presented in conformity with generally accepted accounting principles." It doesn't mean that the company is in great financial shape, or even in adequate condition. All it means is that the books are kept properly.

A number of suits have been filed against major auditing firms for failing to catch slippery entries in the books. The SEC has tightened up its requirements for auditors as a result of a number of businesses failing despite approval from the auditors.

Next, skim through the footnotes, says Quinn. Sometimes they explain the figures that seem surprising, even alarming. Earnings might be down. But the footnote may explain that the company has applied a policy of accelerated depreciation on plants and other equipment. "This," says the CPA Institute, "could reduce earnings, while a slower depreciation rate could boost earnings."

Next, look at the letter from the chairman or the president's report in front of the annual report. It usually is frank—if it adheres to the standards set by the CPA Institute. Usually, the statement is a candid summary of the past year and of prospects.

The Figures

The figure in which most people are interested is *earnings per share,* also called *net income per common share.* (See Table 23.1.) This is the bottom line, a sign of the company's health. It is, in effect, the profit the company has made. It is computed by dividing the total earnings by the number of shares outstanding. The CPA Institute says that slight year-to-year changes can be ignored. Look for the trend in the 5- and 10-year summaries. "If the EPS either remains unchanged or drops off, this may pinpoint trouble ahead," it says.

Look at the record of dividends as well as the current dividend. Is there a trend? Here is a five-year period of dividends of NRW Enterprises:

Dividends per	1998	1997	1996	1995	1994
common share	$1.14	$1.03	$0.93	$0.90	$0.85

This firm shows a steady climb in dividends over the past five years. However, the business reporter will note that although the 1998 dividend is larger than the previous year's dividend, the company's net income per share on continuing operations is down—from $3.27 to $3.01. (See Table 23.1.) In other words, the company plowed less of its earnings back into the firm in 1998 than it did in 1997 in order to keep the dividends on an upward course.

Be careful about earnings per share. A sudden increase can come from selling a plant or cutting advertising or research, says Quinn. The footnotes will explain unusual increases if they have unusual causes. A sudden decrease can come from an increase in the number of shares, a stock split or a new issue— which is also noted in the report.

Next, look for the figures on working capital. "This is regarded as an important index of a company's condition because it reports whether operations

Table 23.1 Net Income per Common Share: NRW Enterprises

	1998	1997	% Change
Net sales from continuing operations	$671,227,000	$601,960,000	+11.5
Income from continuing operations	$36,031,000	$43,685,000	−17.5
Income from discontinued operations	—	$1,112,000	—
Gain on sale of discontinued operations	$5,300,000	—	—
Net income	$41,331,000	$44,797,000	−7.7
Discontinued operations	—	$.08	—
Gain on sale of discontinued operations	$.39	—	—
Net income per common share	$3.01	$3.27	−7.7
Dividends per common share	$1.14	$1.03	+10.7
Cash dividends paid	$15,251,225	$13,736,454	+11.0
Capital expenditures	$27,535,000	$20,722,000	+32.9
Stockholders' equity	$259,668,000	$233,529,000	+11.2
Equity per common share at year end	$18.91	$17.02	+11.1
Outstanding common shares at year end	13,730,288	13,720,186	—

Key Figure. Net income per common share, the eighth item from the top in Table 23.1, is an indicator of the company's health. Also called *earnings per share,* it can be tracked over several years to determine how the company is doing.

generate enough cash to meet payroll, buy raw materials and conduct all the other essential day-to-day operations of the company," says the CPA Institute.

After all the expenses have been met, the company uses part of its net income to pay dividends. These are paid from net working capital, and if this figure (net working capital) shrinks consistently from year to year, even quarter to quarter, it is a sign the company may "not be able to keep dividends growing rapidly," says Quinn.

For further information about how to read an annual report, write the CPA Institute, 1211 Avenue of the Americas, New York City, NY 10036, and ask for the booklet "What Else Can Financial Statements Tell You?"

Stories about Earnings

Companies issue quarterly earnings reports as well as their annual reports, and reporters also write up these quarterly reports. The AP says that the most widely written business news story is the earnings report. And the most important part of the earnings story, says *The Wall Street Journal,* is "net income because that gives us a consistent gauge from company to company and quarter to quarter."

Here is a quarterly report from McDonald's Corp. for the period July 1 to Sept. 31 of this year compared with the same period of the preceding year.

	Current	Preceding Year	% Change
Sales	$6,964,000,000	$6,145,700,000	+13.3
Revenue	2,270,100,000	1,931,900,000	+17.5
Net. inc.	308,900,000	264,500,000	+16.9
Sh. earn	.43	.36	

Here is a story based on these figures:

> The McDonald's Corporation said yesterday that earnings rose 17 percent in the third quarter on continued robust sales from the company's expansion abroad.
>
> The company earned $308.9 million, or 43 cents a share, up from $264.5 million, or 36 cents a share, in the corresponding quarter a year ago.

Note: The word *revenue* sometimes is mistaken for the key figure. Revenue includes several cost items. *Net income* is what people want to know about, how much profit the company is making.

Checklist: Quarterly Earnings

Here is a checklist that the AP provides its reporters for quarterly earnings stories:

— Percentage of increase or decrease in earnings for quarter.

— Reasons for increase or decrease.

— Net income for quarter and income per share, compared with net income and income per share for same quarter previous year.

— Brief description of company's business, products, etc.

— Total revenue for quarter and total revenue for quarter previous year.

— Net income for year to date, net income per share and total revenue for year to date compared with same figures for previous year.

— If quarterly dividend is increased or decreased, amount of the increase or decrease, when the new dividend will be paid and shareholders eligible.

This checklist is also appropriate for stories based on annual reports.

Local Folos

If you work in Topeka or Birmingham, chances are you will not be handling the McDonald's quarterly report data. But what about checking the local McDonald's outlets? How did they fare in the same period?

When Annheuser-Busch reports a 2.2 percent gain in total sales, you might find that the local distributor contributed a significant increase—or decrease—to the total sales picture. This, in turn, could lead to another story about the changing habits of local beer and soft drink imbibers. Beer and soft drinks are among the most hotly contested retail commodities.

By following the annual and quarterly reports of the parent firms, the reporter can initiate local stories of considerable reader interest.

Business reporters also can check the reports of local companies in federal records for stories.

Federal Records

For companies with $1 million in assets and at least 500 stockholders, the Securities and Exchange Commission requires regular reports. Some 10,000 companies file such reports, listed in the annual Directory of Companies Required to File Annual Reports. To obtain the directory and other reports write: Public Reference Section, Securities and Exchange Commission, 450 Fifth St. N.W., Washington, D.C. 20549. For general information, call (202) 272-2650.

10K

Among the SEC reports available is the 10K, an annual report that many reporters use because it includes the company's finances, ownership, major contracts, management history, salaries and other compensation paid the major officers.

Welles, who has been writing about business and economics for 30 years, says that when he is to write about a company, the first step he takes is to obtain three basic documents: the 10K, the annual report and the proxy statement. Like the 10K, the other two are available from the SEC. Welles describes the annual report as "a kind of public relations version of the 10K."

He says that "no single body of information is more crucial to the understanding of a corporation than its financial statements." We will be looking at the annual report in detail later in this chapter.

The proxy statement, an SEC-mandated document, is sent to all stockholders before an annual meeting. It contains the salaries and bonuses of the five top company officers and stockholdings of most senior executives. The statement also lists any deals between the firm and its management or directors. Proxy statements also include biographies of the directors. Some of these directors are from outside the company and are good sources.

Other useful documents are the 8K, which is filed monthly for important company activities such as mergers, and the 10Q, a quarterly report with information like that in the annual 10K.

Form 990

Nonprofit organizations must file Form 990 with the Internal Revenue Service. The report includes information on the income and expenses of officials of the organizations. The expenses can be illuminating. Often, a small part of the money raised by the organization is used for the purpose the organization says it is seeking donations.

SEC material can be obtained from regional SEC offices. Companies will send on request their 10Ks, proxy statements and annual reports.

SEC Online

Many documents are available free from the SEC's Edgar system. Allan Sloan of *The Wall Street Journal* says that the database uses reference numbers for finding information. You have to know, for example, that a 14D is a proxy statement, an 8K is a document describing an extraordinary event.

Here are some of the useful documents Sloan uses and his comments:

- Quarterly 10Q financial reports, issued for the first three quarters of a company's fiscal year.
- Annual reports, which cover an entire year.
- 10K annual reports, which sometimes have details the regular annual reports don't.
- Proxy statements, which include information on how much a company's five top executives were paid, stock options, relationships between members of the board of directors and the company and other fun stuff.
- Proxy-prospectuses, which describe details of one company taking over another.
- 8K special events reports.
- 13D filings, in which stockholders owning 5 percent or more of a company disclose details of what they own, what they paid, and what they intend to do.
- 13G filings, which cover institutional shareholders, like mutual funds, which are supposed to be passive investors.
- 13D and 13G amendments.
- Initial public offering prospectuses describing securities, usually stock, being issued to public investors for the first time, and a source of terrific stuff, usually including information on how much existing stockholders paid for their shares.
- Regular prospectuses, describing new issues of stock and bonds being floated by companies whose securities are already publicly traded.

Cautions   Sloan has the following caution signals for the use of these documents:

> These documents are guides, not smoking guns. The point of a prospectus usually is to show everything that can possibly go wrong, so that people who buy these securities can't successfully sue after the company tanks. Don't misinterpret warning language as the company saying it's about to go belly-up. Documents provide a base on which you can build a story.
>
> You have to do enough reporting to make sure stuff means what it seems to mean. The best thing to do, especially when the company isn't talking because it's in the process of selling securities, is to tell the company your conclusions, and ask it to refute them. This not only allows the company to talk to you—it's not supposed to promote itself, but it's allowed to answer questions—but can save you from making ghastly mistakes.

Databases

To obtain company information online from the SEC such as 10Ks and 10Qs—www.sec.gov/edgarhp.htm.

For business news information and links to many free information sources—Moneynet (Reuters)—www.moneynet.com/

USA Today's "Money" section online includes most of the articles in each weekday's paper and breaking business and financial news stories as well as updated market data during the day—www.usatoday.com/money/mfront.htm.

Depth Reporting

The Founding Fathers were concerned about the dangers of a strong central government. They could not have imagined the power that business would acquire. International banks and the conglomerates exercise enormous influence over the lives of people everywhere, and this power is worthy of scrutiny by the press in its role as watchdog.

Such examination starts at the local level. How much power do local realtors have over planning and zoning decisions? What role does money play in elections? Does local government really have to give businesses and developers tax write-offs and abatements as an incentive? Is the tax structure equitable or does it fall too heavily on families, working people, home owners? In states with natural resources, is the severance tax properly balanced with other taxes, or are the extractive industries penalized or given preferential treatment?

Business reporters who dig deeply can come up with answers to some of these questions. Their articles are called public service journalism, journalism that gives people insights into the deep currents that swirl about us and are, to most of us, impenetrable.

Stock Tables

The business reporter sometimes needs to check the current price or the dividend of a stock listed on one of the exchanges. Here are a few stocks listed on the New York Stock Exchange and a guide to understanding the symbols:

High	Low	Stock	Div.	Yld %	P-E Ratio	Sales 100s	High	Low	Close	Net Chg.
68½[1]	**43¼**	[2]**ATT**	[3]**1.32**	**2.3**	19	10740	57⅜	56⅝	57⅜	+⅜
75¼	49	Gannett	.80	[4]**1.5**	[5]**16**	1833	52⅛	51¼	52	−⅝
28	25½	GMot **pf**[6]	2.17	8.3	—	[7]**35**	26½	26	26¼	−⅛
76½	45⅛	Goodyr	1.20	2.3	14	632	[8]**51**	49½	51	+½
74	42⅞	McDonalds	.36	0.6	26	2997	58¼	56½	[9]**57½**	−¾

1. The highest and the lowest price the stock has sold for in the past 52 weeks.

2. Abbreviated name of the corporation that lists the stock. Stocks are common stocks unless an entry after the name indicates otherwise.

3. The annual dividend. When a letter follows the dividend, consult a box at the bottom of the stock table for reference.

4. Yield, the dividend paid by the company expressed as a percentage of the current price of the stock. A stock that sells for $50 at the current market value and that is paying a dividend at the rate of $2 a year is said to return or to have a yield of 4 percent. In the example of Gannett, the dividend of $.80 divided by the price of 52 results in the yield percentage of 1.5.

The New York Stock Exchange

Trading Center

Behind the pillars of the New York Stock Exchange hundreds of millions of shares of stocks and bonds are sold and bought daily. These transactions between bulls (those betting on an upturn in prices) and bears (those who think prices will go down) affect and reflect finance.

5. The price-earnings ratio. The price of a share of stock is divided by the earnings per share over a 12-month period. A stock selling for $50 a share with annual earnings of $5 a share is selling at the price-earnings ratio of 10 to 1. The P-E ratio is 10. In the table, Gannett's P-E ratio of 16 is calculated by dividing the closing price of 52 by Gannett's annual earnings of $3.25: $52 \div 3.25 = 16$.

6. A preferred stock. Usually, preferred stock entitles stockholders to a specified rate of dividends, here $2.17 a year. Holders of preferred stock are entitled to a claim on the company's earnings before dividends may be paid to holders of common stock.

7. The number of shares traded this day for the stock, listed in 100s. Here, 3,500 shares of General Motors preferred stock were sold.

8. The highest price paid for this stock during the day's trading (51). (The lowest price paid was 49 1/2.)

9. The closing price, or the price of the stock on the last sale of the trading day. Here, the closing price was 57 1/2, or $57.50 a share. The closing price was down $.75 from the closing price of the previous day.

Further Reading

Daniells, Lorna. *Business Information Sources,* 2d ed. Berkeley, Calif.: University of California Press, 1985.

Galbraith, J. Kenneth. *The Affluent Society.* Boston: Houghton Mifflin, 1958.

Kluge, Pamela Hollie. *Guide to Business and Economics Journalism.* New York: Columbia University Press, 1991.

Mintz, Morton. *At Any Cost.* New York: Pantheon Books, 1985.

Moffitt, Donald, ed. *Swindled: Classic Business Frauds of the Seventies.* Princeton, N.J.: Dow Jones Books, 1976.

Silk, Leonard. *Economics in the Real World.* New York: Simon & Schuster, 1985.

Smith, Adam. *The Money Game.* New York: Random House, 1976.

Business Terms

assets These are anything of value the company owns or has an interest in. Assets usually are expressed in dollar value.

balance sheet A financial statement that lists the company's assets, liabilities and stockholders' equity. It usually includes an *Earnings* or *Income Statement* that details the company's source of income and its expenses.

calendar or **fiscal year** Some companies report their income or do business on the regular calendar year. Others do it on a fiscal year that could run from any one month to the same month a year later. Always ask if the companies do business on a fiscal or calendar year. If the answer is fiscal, ask the dates and why. You might find out something unusual about the company.

capital expenditures This is the amount of money a company spends on major projects, such as plant expansions or capacity additions. It is important to the company and the community as well. If the company is expanding, include it in the story. Frequently, such plans are disclosed in stock prospectuses and other SEC reports long before the local paper gets its press release.

earnings Used synonymously with *profit.* Earnings can be expressed in dollar terms (XYZ earned $40) or on a per-share basis (XYZ earned $1 per share for each of its 40 shares of stock). When used as an earnings figure, always compare it to the earnings for the same period in the prior year. For example, if you want to say XYZ earned $1 a share during the first quarter, half or nine months of 1993, compare that with the 50 cents per share the company earned in the first quarter, half or nine months of 1992. That would be a 100 percent increase in profit.

liabilities These are any debts of any kind. There are two types of liabilities: short term and long term. Companies consider anything that has to be paid off within a year a short-term liability and anything over a year a long-term liability.

sales or **revenues** These terms are used synonymously in many companies. A bank, for example, doesn't have sales. It has revenues. A manufacturer's sales and revenues frequently are the same thing, unless the company has some income from investments it made. Always include the company's sales in a story with its earnings. If you say a company earned $40 in 1993 compared to $30 in 1992, you also should tell the reader that the profit was the result of a 100 percent increase in the company's sales, from $100 in 1992 to $200 in 1993. Use both sales and earnings figures. Don't use one and not the other.

stockholders' equity This is the financial interest the stockholders have in the company once all of its debts are paid. For example, say XYZ company has assets of $1,000 and total debts of $600. The company's stockholders' equity is $400. If that figure is expressed on a per-share basis, it is called *book value.* (If XYZ had issued 40 shares of stock, each share would have a book value of $10.)

This material was prepared by Jim O'Shea for *The Des Moines Register*.

Deficit: The difference between expenditures and revenues.

Debt: The total of all deficits. It is covered by debt obligations such as Treasury bonds and bills.

24 Local Government and Education

Debbie Noda,
The Modesto Bee

Homelessness, a growing urban problem

Preview

Local government reporters cover the actions of municipal agencies and departments and the interplay of interest groups and local government in making policy. Some areas of coverage are:

- Budgets, taxes, bond issues.
- Politics.
- Zoning and planning.
- Education.

Reporters check on whether city agencies and departments are carrying out their responsibilities efficiently, effectively and economically.

Newspaper readers, television viewers and radio listeners are more interested in local events than in any other kind of news. They want to know what the city council did about the proposal for free downtown parking, why the principal of the Walt Whitman High School was dismissed and how the new city manager feels about lowering the property tax.

Newspapers and stations respond to this interest by assigning their best reporters to key local beats, and usually the best of the best is assigned to city hall, the nerve center of local government. From city hall, elected and appointed officials direct the affairs of the community—from the preparation of absentee ballots to the adoption of zoning regulations. They supervise street maintenance and construction, issue birth and death certificates, conduct restaurant inspections, collect waste and dispose of it and collect parking meter coins.

The city hall reporter is expected to cover all these activities. To do this, the reporter must know how local government works—the processes and procedures of agencies and departments, the relationship of the mayor's office to the city council, how the city auditor or comptroller checks on the financial activities of city offices.

City Government Activities

The city government engages in many essential activities that the reporter scrutinizes:

1. Authorization of public improvements such as streets, new buildings, bridges, viaducts.
2. Submission to the public of bond issues to finance these improvements.
3. Adoption of various codes, such as building, sanitation, zoning.
4. Issuance of regulations affecting public health, welfare and safety. Traffic regulations come under this category.
5. Consideration of appeals from planning and zoning bodies.
6. Appointment and removal of city officials.
7. Authorization of land purchases and sales.
8. Awarding of franchises.
9. Adoption of the expense and capital budgets.

The city is a major buyer of goods and services and usually one of the city's largest employers. Its decisions can enrich some businesses, as indicated in the beginning of this story by Josh Getlin of the *Los Angeles Times:*

During the last year, Los Angeles Councilman Howard Finn and his wife enjoyed a free weekend in Newport Beach and Councilwoman Peggy Stevenson was wined and dined at some of New York's finer restaurants.

In both cases, Group W Cable TV officials were wooing council members to round up votes for the East San Fernando Valley franchise that could be worth $75 million.

Lavish entertaining is just part of a multimillion dollar campaign by six firms to win the city's last major cable franchise. . . .

The city is the creature of the state. The state assigns certain of its powers to the city, enabling the city to govern itself. The city has the three traditional branches of government—a judicial system and executive and legislative arms. In some cities, the executive is a powerful mayor who has control over much of the municipal machinery. In others, the mayor's job is largely ceremonial and the mayor may not even have a vote on the city council.

Legislative branches differ, too. But for the most part, the city council or commission has the power to act in the nine areas outlined. The council or commission takes action in the form of ordinances and resolutions. An *ordinance* is a law. A *resolution* is a declaration or an advisory that indicates the intention or opinion of the legislative branch.

An ordinance is *enacted:* The city council last night enacted an ordinance requiring dog owners to have their pets innoculated against rabies. A resolution is *adopted:* City commission members last night adopted a resolution to make June 18 Frances Osmond Day in honor of the longtime city clerk who died last Tuesday.

Forms of Local Government

The city council–mayor system is the most common form of local government. In large cities, the mayor is usually a powerful figure in city government, the centerpiece of what is called the strong mayor system. In this system, the mayor appoints the heads of departments and all other officials not directly elected. This system enables the mayor to select the people he or she wants to carry out executive policies.

One way to classify local government is by the strength of the office of the mayor, the power the chief executive has to initiate and carry out programs and policies. The two systems have variations:

Weak Mayor	Strong Mayor
Commission	Council-mayor
Commission-manager	Mayor-manager
Council-manager	

Strong to Weak, Back to Strong

The weak mayor systems and the creation of the post of city manager were reactions to the misuse of power by strong mayors and their inability to manage the bureaucracy. To be elected and to hold office, the mayor had to be an astute politician, not necessarily an able administrator. The wheelings and dealings of the strong mayors—exposed by such muckrakers as Lincoln Steffens—led people to reject a system that some critics said encouraged corruption. A movement toward less-politicized and more efficient local government developed early in the 20th century. It took the form of the council-manager system.

The manager, who is hired by the council, is a professionally trained public administrator who attends to the technical tasks of running the city government—preparing the budget, hiring, administering departments and agencies. Although the manager does increase the managerial efficiency of local government, the system has been criticized as insulating government from the electorate by dispersing responsibility and accountability. Several cities have returned to the strong mayor system in an effort to place responsibility in the hands of an identifiable, elected official.

An offshoot of the council-manager system is the mayor-manager plan, the most prevalent system today. This combines the strong mayor, politically responsive to the electorate, with the trained technician who carries out executive policies and handles day-to-day governmental activities.

In weak mayor systems, elected commissioners serve as the legislative branch and the executive branch. The commissioners are legislators and also head various municipal departments—finance, public works, public safety, planning, personnel. Often, the commissioner of public safety also serves as mayor, a largely ceremonial post in this system. The commission form has been criticized for blurring the separation of powers between the legislative and executive branches. In the commission system, there is no single official that the electorate can hold responsible for the conduct of local affairs.

Governing the City

Mayor-Manager Form

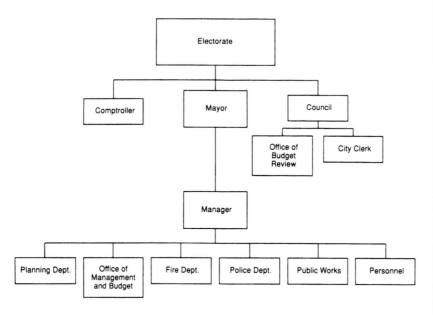

Strong Mayor System

The mayor appoints most department and agency heads and the city manager, who is responsible for day-to-day operations.

Council-Manager Form

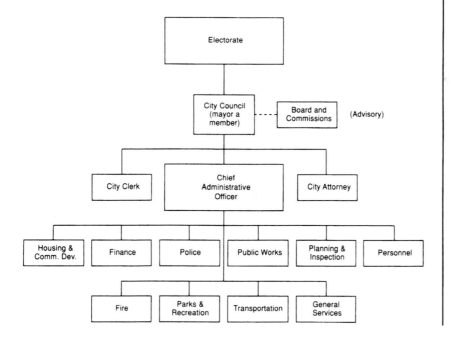

Weak Mayor System

The mayor serves as a member of the city council, which makes most of the major appointments of agency and department heads. The mayor's powers are mostly ceremonial.

The Public Interest

Political Axiom. Government reacts to the interplay of pressure groups in setting policy rather than constructing policy from an agenda.

As we saw, the city manager plan was initiated during a period of reform as a means of taking politics out of local government. Other means have been advanced: the nonpartisan ballot, extension of the merit system and career services to protect city jobs from being used for patronage, the payment of low salaries to mayors and council or commission members to take the profit out of public service. Many cities have been the battlegrounds between the good government groups and their opponents, who contend that the result of taking power from party leaders and elected officials is its transfer to nongovernmental groups and bureaucracies that are not answerable to the public.

There are few identifiable public interests that most people agree upon. There can be a public consensus on such matters as public safety and good roads. But the majority of issues resolve into a contest among differing special interests. The political process involves much more than the nomination and election of candidates. We can define the political process as the daily interaction of government, interest groups and the citizenry.

Participants in the Political Process

Professors Wallace S. Sayre of Columbia University and Herbert Kaufman of Yale put the political process in terms useful to the government reporter. They describe the participants as actors in a contest for a variety of goals, stakes, rewards and prizes. The police officer on the beat whose union is seeking to fend off reductions in the police force is an actor in the contest, as is the mother of three who is urging her school's Parents Association to speak out for more crossing guards at the elementary school. They are as much a part of the political process as the mayor who journeys to the state capital to seek a larger slice of state funds for welfare and health or who decides to seek re-election and lines up backing from unions and ethnic groups.

We can group the participants in the city's political process as follows:

- **The political party leaders:** The leaders and their organizations have a strong hand in the nominating process, but the other participants have increased their power and influence as the political party has declined in importance. Insurgents sometimes capture nominations, and the leaders must compromise their choices for the highest offices in the interest of finding candidates who can win.
- **Elected and appointed officials:** The mayor, members of the city council or commission and their administrators occupy key roles in governing the city. As the party's power has waned, the mayor and the visible elected and appointed officials have become independent decision makers.
- **Interest (pressure) groups:** Every aspect of city policy making is monitored by one or more of the political interest groups. Business groups are especially interested in the school system and the tax structure. When a

school district reported that 66 percent of third-graders were reading at grade level compared to 88 percent in other districts, parents were concerned. So were real estate agents. Their reason: Poor schools would make it harder to sell homes in the district.

As for the city's tax structure, real estate interests will want a low property tax so that the cost of homes will be as low as possible. They will also want large and efficient police and fire departments because these keep insurance premiums low.

The banks are interested in policies about the city's indebtedness because they are the buyers of the bonds and notes the city issues to pay for large-scale construction projects such as roads and schools. Contractors push for public improvements. The bar association checks on law enforcement and the judiciary.

Religious groups and educational organizations keep track of school policies. Medical and health professions examine the activities of the health department. The nominating process and the election campaigns attract ethnic and labor groups as well as the good government groups.

Interest groups compete with each other to influence the city leadership and its bureaucracy, and this limits their influence. Sometimes, however, an interest group may control the decision making of a department or agency, as when, for example, the real estate interests take over the planning and zoning department or the banks and bond market control decisions about the sale of bonds.

• **Organized and professional bureaucracies:** City employees became independent of the party organization with the merit system, unionization and the professionalization of city services. Police, firefighters and teachers have been among the most active in influencing the political process.

• **Other governments:** The city government is in daily contact with a variety of other governmental units: the county, the state, the federal government, public authorities and special assessment districts. These governments are linked by a complex web of legal and financial involvements. State approval is often necessary for certain actions by the city. State and federal governments appropriate funds for such city services as education, health and welfare. City officials are almost always bargaining with other governmental units.

• **The press:** "The communication media provide the larger stage upon which the other participants in the city's political contest play their parts with the general public as an audience," says Kaufman. But, he continues, the media "do more than merely provide the public stage." They also take a direct part in the process. Having its own values, emphasis, stereotypes and preoccupations, the press is not an exact mirror or reporter, he says. The media highlight personalities, are fond of exposés, are prone to fall for stories about new public works, are too zealous in looking for stories about patronage crumbs—and are too skeptical of officials and party leaders, he says.

Lewis W. Wolfson, a professor of journalism at American University, says that the press too often depicts government "not as a process, but as a succession of events, many of them in fact staged for the media." He suggests that the press "tell people more about how government works, how it affects them, and how they can influence it."

Auditing the Community

Along with covering the nine governmental activities listed at the beginning of this chapter, the local government reporter keeps tabs on the city's economic and social conditions.

The Economy

Much of the community's health depends on its economy—the availability of jobs, the ability of the city to meet its bonded indebtedness and to support first-rate schools and services. Reporters use several measuring sticks to gauge the local economy:

- Employment and unemployment rates.
- Housing construction and sales.
- Telephone and utility connections.
- Automobile sales.
- Hotel and motel occupancy rates.
- Sales tax revenues.

These factors also are considered by the agencies that rate the city's credit. A high rating means the city will be able to sell bonds at a low interest rate. A low rating means the city is in poor financial condition and will have to offer high interest rates as an inducement to buy its bonds, which furthers the city's tight financial condition. The local reporter regularly checks the city's credit rating.

Job Search   The Bureau of Labor Statistics makes monthly checks on employment in every state and for large metropolitan areas. It calls people at their homes and asks if they are working; if not, whether they are looking for work. The BLS also questions employers about their payrolls. Are they growing, shrinking? It asks about wages. The results of these surveys provide reporters with what *Baltimore Sun* business reporter Jay Hancock says is "the single best piece of current, state-based economic information you can get."

The data for states and large cities are available from the BLS home page: www.stats.bls.gov. Click *Data* on the main menu. Then click *Most Requested Series,* which gives you another menu. Go down to the *Employment and Unemployment* heading and click *State and Area Employment, Hours and Earnings* under the category *Nonfarm Payroll Statistics from the Current Employment Statistics.*

Click in your state and zero in on *Total Nonfarm Employment.* Hancock says not to base stories on a single month but to look for trends. Or take several months and strike an average. Then compare this current average with the same months from a year and five years ago.

The Schools

Good schools help make the city financially secure because industry and business are attracted to communities with an educated work force. Telemarketing has created new business centers around the country to handle catalog orders, to make hotel reservations, to plan vacations, even to help computer owners get back on track. These businesses look for pockets of hard-working, well-educated people to do their work.

The "toll-free capital of the U.S." is located in Omaha where tens of thousands of people work in telemarketing. South Dakota's major industry is processing credit card transactions. North Dakota workers handle half the reservations of the big Rosenbluth International travel company of Philadelphia. These areas are marked by above-average national test scores and high graduation rates for their high school students.

Dismal Showing The national picture is, however, far from bright. Tests of high school seniors show that one-fourth are in effect functionally illiterate. A third of the others are barely proficient.

Education is not keeping pace with the skill requirements for a good job. Half the nation's 17-year-olds cannot read or do math well enough to do production work in an automobile plant.

Employers hire college graduates because they know that a high school diploma does not guarantee literacy or mathematical competence.

Some measures of the quality of education include dropout rate; high school graduation rate; percentage of graduates going on to college; SAT and ACT scores; pupil-teacher ratio; average teacher salary.

We will look in greater detail at education later in this chapter.

Additional Checkpoints

Journalists also keep track of other facets of community life that are indicators of how the city is meeting its obligations to all its residents, how the people get along with each other, whether problems are being solved.

These other measures of a community's well-being include:

Health: Reporters look at the children's immunization rate; infant and maternal death rates; suicide rate; availability of child health and prenatal clinics; health-information programs.

Social conditions: Percentage of children in single-parent homes living in poverty; teen-age motherhood rates; divorce rate; racial harmony; crime rates.

One of the most important indicators of a community's health is its social harmony. Is diversity a community goal? Here, the reporter relies on sources among the community's religious, political and economic leaders; teachers and students; working people.

The larger the city, the more pressing the problems of race. But race is entwined with class—that is, minority groups are poor: 46 percent of black and

40 percent of Hispanic children live in poverty. Despite a steady rise in the economic condition of many, the poor have become poorer.

Another indicator of social conditions is teen-age motherhood. The United States has the highest rate of unwed teen-age childbearing. More than 1 million adolescent girls become pregnant every year, and half give birth. The likelihood of these young women finishing high school diminishes by 50 percent. More than 70 percent of the men in prisons and jails were born to teen-age mothers. A third of the children in the United States are born to unmarried women.

In most communities, these indicators point to pockets where the problems are magnified, areas that one writer describes as "dreadful enclosures." These areas are marked by drugs, crime, poverty, poor health, high infant mortality rates, low educational attainment and unemployment.

Inner-City Problems

In some areas, these pockets or enclosures exist on the outskirts of the city, but in most cases they are usually inside the city, often in the oldest sections where deteriorating housing has led the middle-class residents to leave and the poor to move in. Most of these pockets are occupied by minorities.

For a long time, any examination of these areas and their problems was ignored by the media. One reason was self-interest. Few inner-city residents bought the goods the media advertised, few read the city daily. Another reason was that any revelation of the economic and social conditions could lead to charges of racism, the response that befell a study in 1965 by Daniel Patrick Moynihan who warned that the growing numbers of children being born to single black mothers was likely to result in serious social problems.

At the time Moynihan published his study, the illegitimacy rate among blacks was 26 percent. Today it is 68 percent. The white rate of out-of-wedlock births, 23 percent, is growing at an even more accelerated rate.

The consequence can be seen in some data sociologists find disturbing: More than two-thirds of juveniles confined for violent offenses grew up in single-parent homes. Violent crime is being committed by younger and younger men, most the product of fatherless homes.

Today, the Moynihan analysis is accepted, as is the media's attention to the problems of the inner city. The charge of racism became hollow when the figures were openly discussed, for what emerged was a pattern of joblessness, early death and debilitating illness, high crime rates.

The murder victimization rate for white males is 9.0, for white females 2.8. For black males, it is 69.2, and for black females 13.5. The Department of Justice estimates that one of every 21 black men can expect to be murdered.

Speaking Out   The situation led many in minority communities to call for attention to the situation. Rep. John Lewis, a Georgia Democrat, said:

> All across the nation black communities are under an assault of crime and
> violence that is without precedent in our history. Under the savage assault, it is not
> too much to say that the low-income black community is disintegrating and
> violence and crime are the order of the day.

City Tensions

From Idyllic Village
to Urban Nightmare

". . . Not only are the streets dominated by the criminal element, but the schools and the housing projects as well. One's life is up for grabs, one's children will either be victimized by the criminal element or recruited into criminal enterprise. Almost nothing can be done to help the law-abiding majority of the ghetto unless and until crime and the drug trade are brought under control. . . ."

—Irving Kristol, *The Wall Street Journal.*
Right, Mel Finkelstein,
© *New York Daily News,* Inc.
Above right, Larry C. Price,
The Philadelphia Inquirer Magazine.
Above left, The Plumas County Museum.

He went on to cite homicide data and illegitimacy rates, and he said that when "schools dare to record the truth, the dropout rates are a continuing disaster."

Black children, he said, "are the principal victims of child abuse and neglect. The leading cause of death for black children aged one to four is fire."

He said, "Increasingly over the past 30 years, crime and violence have been allowed to run virtually unchecked through poor black communities . . . more and more the most conspicuous models of success were the racketeer, the pimp and the insidious drug dealer. . . . It is not only poverty that has caused crime. In a very real sense it is crime that has caused poverty, and is the most powerful cause of poverty today."

By the mid-1990s, the conspiracy of silence was broken. The media were describing the tragedies and triumphs of daily life in the ghetto.

The New York Times ran a series, called "Children of the Shadows." One story tells of Ladeeta, an 18-year-old high school senior, who has "survived almost every plague of adolescence in neighborhoods defined by hopeless girls with babies and angry boys with guns." Her father drank himself to death. Her mother, a crack addict, died of AIDS. Ladeeta ran with a gang of girls that beat and robbed other girls. "Her first job was holding drugs and cash for a major neighborhood crack dealer," the story states.

Her grandmother plucked Ladeeta from the street life and sent her to a school where teachers took an interest in her. They are struggling to convince her she can have a future. She wonders: "Sometimes I think, how far am I going to be able to go being female and black—two things against me."

The Demographics

Who lives in the city? What's the average age of the population, the male-female ratio, the income brackets, the educational attainment, the racial and ethnic makeup? What's the birthrate, the deathrate? Is the infant mortality rate higher than the state or national average? What is killing people in the community, heart attacks, cancer, AIDS, accidents?

Reporters who know the answers find significant stories in the community, not only in the way things are now, but also in the changes in demographics.

Hispanic Population   The experts are predicting that the increasing numbers of Spanish-speaking people will soon outnumber the black population, which is now about 12 percent of the total population.

The two groups have conflicting as well as converging interests. Hispanics and blacks support affirmative action and tend to vote Democratic. But Hispanics are less vocal on racial issues and are said to be more conscious of class than of race. These tendencies have significant consequences in the life of a community.

The dynamic between the majority white group and the two minorities may change as Hispanics intermarry with whites. The Census reports that almost a third of Hispanic women were married to non-Hispanics, an intermarriage rate three times that of the rate for blacks marrying whites. Demographers say that the children of Hispanic intermarriages may identify with whites and thus lessen the influence of Hispanics.

What should a reporter be looking at in his or her community so that its residents are aware of whether it is meeting people's needs?

The Good Community

An African proverb states, "It takes a whole village to raise a child." Here may be the answer to our question. The journalists who examine the multiple facets of community life may want to adopt as a guideline how well the community protects, nurtures, educates and cares for its children. In short, we need a children's quality of life index.

One guideline is offered by the organization Zero Population Growth which every two years examines dozens of studies and reports for its "Children's Environmental Index."

How well, ZPG asks, do the cities it studies provide the means by which all the children can grow into healthy, happy adults? ZPG studies 219 cities for its report. Let's look at the measures it uses to reach its conclusions:

Health: infant mortality rate, percentage of low-birth-weight infants, percentage of births to teens, number of physicians per 10,000 population.

Economics: unemployment rate, percentage of children in poverty, median family income.

Crime: violent crimes per 1,000 population, property crimes per 1,000, juvenile arrests.

Education: student-teacher ratio, dropout rate.

Physical environment: number of bad air days, pounds of toxic releases per 1,000 population, hazard ranking (toxic wastes).

All of these figures are available to the journalist, many of them from online sources.

The Good and the Not So Good

Let's look at how cities fared in these categories. We'll take the top five and the bottom five in each category:

Health: Top—Santa Rosa, Calif.; Sioux Falls, S.D.; Overland Park, Kan.; Irvine, Calif.; Thousand Oaks, Calif.

Bottom—Detroit, Mich,; Hartford, Conn.; Washington, D.C.; Newark, N.J.; Memphis, Tenn.;

Economics: Top—Naperville, Ill.; Irvine, Calif.; Plano, Tex.; Livonia, Mich.; Santa Clarita, Calif.

Bottom—Brownsville, Tex.; Laredo, Tex.; Gary, Ind.; Miami, Fla.; Flint, Mich.

Crime: Top—Naperville, Ill; Sterling Heights, Mich.; Fargo, N.D.; Simi Valley, Calif.; Sunnyvale, Calif.

Bottom—Gary, Ind.; Newark, N.J.; St. Louis, Mo.; Atlanta, Ga.; Tampa, Fla.

Education: Top—Arlington, Va.; Stamford, Conn.; Madison, Wis.; Overland Park, Kan.; Hampton, Va.

Bottom—Santa Ana, Calif.; El Monte, Calif.; Ontario, Calif.; Pomona, Calif.; Lancaster, Calif.

Environment: Top—Honolulu, Hawaii; Albany, N.Y.; Lafayette, La.; Charleston, W. Va.; Durham, N.C.

Bottom—Pasadena, Tex.; Los Angeles, Calif.; San Bernardino, Calif.; Houston, Tex.; Glendale, Calif.

The Top and Bottom 10 Taking the individual ratings the organization made these overall rankings:

Top 10

Naperville, Ill.	Madison, Wis.
Overland Park, Kan.	Sterling Heights, Mich.
Irvine, Calif.	Ann Arbor, Mich.
Plano, Tex.	Livonia, Mich.
Fargo, N.D.	Sioux Falls, S.D.

Bottom 10

Gary, Ind.	San Bernardino, Calif.
Detroit, Mich.	Flint, Mich.
Newark, N.J.	Baltimore, Md.
St. Louis, Mo.	Atlanta, Ga.
Hartford, Conn.	Tampa, Fla.

If you would like to see where your city ranks in the five categories and its total on the Index, ZPG is at

1400 16th St., NW (Suite 320)
Washington, DC 20036
1-800-767-1956
e-mail: development@zpg.org

Politics

Many issues that face communities are settled by elections. Parties and candidates differ in the solutions they offer for problems, and it is the task of the reporter covering politics to make clear the positions that define and differentiate the candidates so that an informed choice may be made.

Campaigns are carefully planned. Ralph Whitehead at the University of Massachusetts says, "It is possible to read a campaign. Assume that every decision is made for a reason. A reporter's job is to do the decoding."

As David Broder, who covers politics for *The Washington Post,* puts it, the reporter's job is to cull from the campaign rhetoric "those few words incidents and impressions that carry the mood and the significance of what occurred."

Reportorial Agenda

But suppose the campaign skirts issues of importance. Suppose, and this is hardly theoretical, the candidates play it safe and avoid taking a stand on issues that could cost them votes. The journalist has no choice. He or she is obligated to push candidates to declare themselves on issues the journalist considers important.

The journalist no longer plays stenographer to candidates.

John Herbers, a veteran political reporter, says that "news organizations have been too willing to let the candidates and the parties define the issues." He suggests reporters and editors draw up "a list of issues they believe are important to the coverage."

Then if the candidates ignore these issues, Herbers says he sees "nothing wrong with writing that 'Candidate X opened his campaign with a long speech that detailed a list of problems he sees facing the nation. But he did not mention racial divisions, which many see as a growing threat to the country.' "

Although Herbers was addressing campaigns for national office, his advice applies to all elections—mayor, city council, school board. Issues, important issues, need to be addressed in all campaigns.

Selling Candidates

Candidates for public office usually hire political consultants. A study of consultants by the Pew Research Center for the People and the Press found that consultants have a narrow view of the public and the media and that they impose this on the candidates they advise.

Consultants think the media are more responsive to negative campaigning than to an issue-oriented campaign, that the public is poorly informed and lacks sound judgment about issues. Seven of ten of the consultants said it is easy to sell a "mediocre candidate" to voters, and many said they had come to regret having helped to elect some of their clients.

Some Tips on Campaign Coverage

Candidates go where the votes are. This is a useful guide for covering candidates for local and state offices, less so for candidates for the major national offices because television takes their campaigns into homes everywhere. The reporter covering a mayoral or gubernatorial campaign who watches the candidates' schedules for the week can draw some informed conclusions, says Whitehead.

Key Elements. David Yepsen of *The Des Moines Register* says there are four elements to a political campaign—the candidate, the money, the issues and the organization. Coverage of each involves:

Candidate: profile, interviews with friends, associates.

Money: political fundraisers, campaign disclosure reports, advertising program.

Issues: candidate's platform, public's input.

Organization: key figures, campaign plans.

Voter Preferences. A Roper poll shows voters want more coverage of issues, less on the personal lives of candidates, more on how elections affect their lives, less emphasis on the front-runners.

The Electorate. "Half of the American people never read a newspaper. Half never vote for president. One hopes it is the same half."

—*Gore Vidal*

Where does the candidate go, how often and on what terms? When a Jewish candidate spends most of his time in the Catholic areas of town, one conclusion may be drawn. If he gives a large part of his time to appearances at synagogues and Jewish organizations, another conclusion may be drawn.

Another tip: Watch the media purchases. If the candidate is buying television spots near daytime soap operas, he or she is looking for the homemaker's vote.

Follow the Buck   Whose money fuels the candidates' campaigns? It's easy to find out because all states require financial disclosure in state and federal races. Some states demand reports as often as every two weeks before the election. Political action committees are large donors. PACs favor incumbents. A study showed they donate 10 times as much to House incumbents as to their challengers.

"Money follows power" is a political axiom. When the Democrats controlled Congress, military contractors donated 60 percent of their funds to that party. When the Republicans took over, the contractors shifted, donating 70 percent of their political funds to the GOP.

PACs and other large donors are not giving from the goodness of their hearts. They want favorable legislation. In the Nebraska legislature, for example, the PAC of the state's 4,000 liquor retailers wanted a no vote on a bill that would require bars to post signs warning that drinking during pregnancy could cause birth defects. On the legislative committee considering the bill, legislators who opposed it had received an average of 53 percent more in PAC contributions than did the legislators who voted for the bill.

Thomas Winship, former editor of the *Boston Globe,* suggests that it should be a matter "of routine coverage for all newspapers to print an updated financial profile of each member of their congressional delegation before they go to Washington for an upcoming session." He says such an accounting can be had from the Federal Elections Commission and the Center for Responsive Politics, both in Washington, D.C. The Center publishes a handbook, *Follow the Money,* by Larry Makinson that is designed to help reporters set up databases to relate campaign donations to a politician's votes.

ALL IN THE INTEREST OF GOOD GOVERNMENT...

Vern Herschberger,
Waco Tribune-Herald

Tax Cuts   One of the favored political pledges is to cut taxes. Fair enough. Nobody likes taxes. But the candidate has to be asked what will happen when these revenues are not going into government. What services will be cut? Spending, the candidate replies. The journalist seeks specifics: Spending on what? On the police department? On education? On the child immunization program?

No, we won't have to cut, says the candidate, because we have a plan to attract new industry and business. Better ask for the specifics of the candidate's plan.

Several of these plans, much heralded at their inceptions, turned out to be less than advertised. One such was the idea of lowering taxes or cutting them altogether to attract new industry and business.

School Impact   Industries were attracted, and they hired workers. Fine, so far. But the workers have children who crowded into already stretched schools.

The result: In Texas, a state senate committee estimated the loss in tax revenues of half a billion dollars to the schools over a decade. In Cleveland, the teachers union said abatements had cost the hard-pressed school system $21 million.

In Rio Rancho, N.M., the city and state gave Intel Corp. $114 million in tax breaks and incentives to attract the microchip maker. Intel moved in, as did workers and their children, who had to be bused to Albuquerque schools. After the situation got out of hand, Intel agreed to pay for a new high school in Rio Rancho.

New Power Centers

Time was when it was legal for a man to beat his wife, as long as the stick he used was no wider that the width of his thumb. Times have changed. Women are no longer voiceless, voteless, powerless. But progress has been slow for women in politics. In the United States, they gained the right to vote in 1920, but by the end of the 1990s, they held only about one-tenth of the 535 seats in the Senate and the House. They have fared better in cities and in state legislatures. They hold the mayor's office in 150 large cities and have one-fifth of the seats in state legislatures. Several women have been elected governor.

Women have become a powerful voting bloc. Studies show they tend to vote on issues more than men do. In recent elections, they have made decisions on the basis of the candidates' positions on abortion, day care, education, care for the poor and the elderly and health care.

Women steadily have turned to the Democratic Party in national elections. Their votes helped elect Bill Clinton president twice.

Another growing issue-oriented bloc emerged as a political force in the 1990s, this one on the conservative side of the political fence.

To the Point. "I think it's about time we voted for senators with breasts. After all, we've been voting for boobs long enough."
—*Claire Sargent, Arizona senatorial candidate, 1992 (She lost.)*

Religious Right   "We want you to deliver. This is what we want and we're going to demand it. We want to be team players. But it's time for us to start leading the team."

The words were addressed to 100 Christian Coalition members by Pat Robertson, the head of the Coalition. He told them to take the message to their members of Congress.

The Coalition and about a dozen other groups that constitute the Religious Right have become more outspoken, more organized, more influential. They claim to have helped the Republican Party capture Congress in 1994 and retain it thereafter. They issue magazines and newspapers, sponsor radio and television shows.

Focus on the Family has 3.5 million members, a $110 million annual budget, prints 10 monthly magazines, has a vast radio network with an estimated five million weekly listeners. The Christian Coalition, founded by Pat Robertson, has 1.9 million members and a $27 million budget. Other conservative religious groups include the Family Research Council, Eagle Forum, American Family Association, Concerned Women for America and the Traditional Values Coalition, the American Center for Law and Justice and the Rutherford Institute.

They have in common an agenda that is anti-abortion, anti-gay, anti-sex education not abstinence-based. Some favor vouchers for religious education, a school prayer constitutional amendment, censorship of school books.

Here are some website addresses for these organizations:

American Center for Law and Justice	www.aclj.org
American Family Association	www.afa.net
Christian Coalition	www.cc.org
Concerned Women for America	www.cwfa.org
Family Research Council	www.frc.org
Focus on the Family	www.fotf.org
Rutherford Institute	www.rutherford.org

For material on positions opposite those of the religious right, here are the names of several organizations and their websites:

American Civil Liberties Union	www.aclu.org
Americans United for Separation of Church and State	www.au.org
The Interfaith Alliance	www.tialliance.org
People for the American Way	www.pfaw.org

Issues once decided upon become policies and for policies to be put into motion money must be allocated to grease the machinery. How this money is to be spent and where it is to come from is determined by the budget. Budgets are made in a give-and-take process by school boards, city and county governments, the state and the federal governments. Reporters cover each of these units as they wrestle with insufficient revenues and overwhelming requests.

The Budget

Covering local government—indeed, covering all levels of government—requires a knowledge of how money is raised and how it is spent. Money fuels the system. The relationship between money and the workings of government can be seen in the budget process.

"I've had to learn how to cover five governmental units, and I find the single best way to learn what they are doing is to attend budget hearings," says David Yepsen, political reporter for *The Des Moines Register*. "They let you know the current situation, what the problems are, the proposed solutions and where government is headed."

"Follow the buck," says the experienced reporter. The city hall reporter follows the path of the parking meter dime and the property tax dollar as they make their way through government. The path of these dimes and dollars is set by the budget.

Income

General Revenues

Property Tax
 & Spec. Asses.
Returned State Funds
License & Privilege
Fines & Fees
Sales & Charges
Federal Aid
Transfer from Utilities
Other

Utility Revenue

Revenue
from
Water & Electric & Gas
Utilities
(Where City-Owned)

New Borrowing

New Bond Issues

&

Temporary Notes

City
Treasurer

Expenses

Current Operations

General Admin.
Police & Fire
Parks & Recreation
Garbage & Trash
Band & Music
Cemetery
Trust Funds
Airport
Library
Public Health
Streets, Alleys,
 & Sewers
Other

Debt Service

Retirement of
 Bonds, Temporary
 Notes & No
 Fund Warrants
Principal &
 Interest Pay-
 ments

Utility Expenses

The Cost of
 Operating Electric,
 Water & Gas
 Utilities

Capital Outlay

New City Bldgs.
Street Paving
New Sewers
Utility Expansion
Flood Control
Airports
Hospitals
Sewage Disposal
 & Sanitation
 Plants
Parking Meters
Other

City's Money Flow

This chart shows the major sources of revenues and the major outlets for expenditures of a city.

By following the lines, you can see that general revenues are used for general purposes, except for utility expenses in cities in which the utilities are municipally owned. Utility revenue is used for all types of expenditures, but new borrowing is used for capital outlays for the most part.

Occasionally, temporary notes are issued in the form of anticipation notes sold to banks to pay for bills due immediately. These are short-term loans.

The anticipation notes take the following forms:

RANS—Revenue Anticipation Notes. Paid off when anticipated revenues develop.

TANS—Tax Anticipation Notes. Paid back when taxes are collected.

BANS—Bond Anticipation Notes. Paid off when bonds are sold.

The budget is a forecast or estimate of expenditures that a government will make during the year and the revenues needed to meet those expenses. It is, in short, a balance sheet. Budgets are made for the fiscal year, which may be the calendar year or may run from July 1 through June 30 or other dates. The budget is made by the executive branch (mayor, governor, president, school superintendent) and then submitted to the legislative body (city council, state legislature, Congress, board of education) for adoption.

A Compromise The budget is the final resolution of the conflicting claims of individuals and groups to public monies. This means that the conscientious reporter watches the budgeting process as carefully as he or she examines the finished document. Aaron Wildavsky of the University of California at Berkeley describes the budget as "a series of goals with price tags attached." If it is followed, he says, things happen, certain policy objectives are accomplished.

The budget is a sociological and political document. As Prime Minister William Ewart Gladstone of Britain remarked more than 100 years ago, the budget "in a thousand ways goes to the root of the prosperity of the individuals and relation of classes and the strength of kingdoms."

The budget can determine how long a pregnant woman waits to see a doctor in a well-baby clinic, how many children are in a grade school class, whether city workers will seek to defeat the mayor in the next election.

Here is the beginning of a budget story by Paul Rilling of *The Anniston* (Ala.) *Star:*

A city budget may look like a gray mass of dull and incomprehensible statistics, but it is the best guide there is to the plans and priorities of city government.

Rhetoric and promises aside, the budget says what the city council really sees as the city's top priorities.

Tuesday, the Anniston City Council will consider for formal adoption the proposed city budget for fiscal . . .

Cover the Whole Process

City hall, education, county and state legislative reporters handle budget stories on a regular basis. Reporters on these beats begin to write stories several months before the budget is adopted so that the public can be informed of the give-and-take of the process and participate early in the decision making. In a six-week span, Bill Mertens, city hall reporter for *The Hawk Eye,* wrote more than a dozen stories. Here are the beginning paragraphs of two of them:

School crossing guards may be one of the programs lost if Burlington city councilmen intend to hold the new budget close to the existing one.

The city council has asked Burlington fire department heads to cut $30,000 from their budget request.

Most of the dozen-plus stories were enterprised by Mertens. Knowing the budget process and having good sources, Mertens was able to keep a steady flow of interesting and important copy moving to the city desk. In his stories, Mertens was always conscious of the human consequences of the belt tightening. By writing about possible cuts in such areas as school crossing guards and the fire department, Mertens alerted the public. Residents could, if they wished, inform their council members of their opposition to the cuts.

Types of Budgets

Two types of governmental expenditures are budgeted—funds for daily expenses and funds for long-range projects. At the local governmental level, these spending decisions are included in two kinds of budgets: expense budgets and capital budgets.

Expense Budgets　The expense or executive budget covers costs of daily expenses, which include salaries, debt service and the purchase of goods and services. Expense budget revenues are gathered from three major sources:

- Taxes on real estate—the property tax—usually the single largest source of income.
- General fund receipts, which include revenues from fines, permits, licenses, and taxes such as income, corporation, sales and luxury taxes. (States must give cities permission to levy taxes.)
- Grants-in-aid from the federal and state governments.

Capital Budgets　The capital or construction budget lists the costs of capital projects to be built, such as roads and schools, and major equipment and products to be purchased. Capital budget funds are raised by borrowing, usually through the sale of bonds pledged against the assessed valuation of real estate in the governmental unit. Bonds are approved by the voters and then sold to security firms through bidding. The firms then offer them for public sale. The loan is paid back much like a home owner's payments on a mortgage over an extended period, 10, 20 or 30 years. Principal and interest are paid out of current revenues and are listed in the expenditures column of the expense budget as "debt service," which should run under 10 percent of the total budget for the city to be on safe economic footing.

Making the Budget

Most budgets are adopted in this series of steps:

1. Budget request forms go out to all department heads, who must decide on priorities for the coming year and submit them to the budget officer, mayor or school superintendent.

2. Meetings are held between the budget officer and department heads to adjust requests and formulate a single balanced program.

3. The budget is submitted to the city council or commission, the board of education or other legislative arm of the governmental unit. The budget is sometimes accompanied by a narrative explaining the requests.

4. The legislative body examines budget items for each department and agrees on allocations for each.
5. Public hearings are held.
6. The budget is adopted.

The reporter can cover each stage of this process, the behind-the-scenes bickering, dickering and politicking as well as the formal activities of the various department heads, executives and legislators. All sorts of pressures are brought to bear on the budget makers. Property owners and real estate interests want the budget held down, for increased expenditures usually mean higher property taxes. The businessmen and -women who rely on selling goods and services to the city seek hefty budgets for the departments and agencies they serve. Employees want salary increases, generous fringe benefits and more lines in the budget for promotions. Politicians seek to reward constituencies and to fulfill campaign promises.

The Aftermath   After the budget is adopted, the reporter watches the consequences. Few, if any, agencies and departments are given what they request, which usually does no harm as most units purposely hike up their requests. But, sometimes, damage is done. In Ohio, the *Akron Beacon Journal* investigated school finances and found that "legislators and governors have siphoned hundreds of millions of dollars from education for other purposes." The result: "High school seniors in tears when their football season and marching band are canceled . . . elementary school children have to wait after school because there are not enough buses in working condition to take them home."

Checklist: Budgets

Adoption

— Amount to be spent.

— New or increased taxes, higher license and permit fees and other income that will be necessary to meet expenditures.

— Cuts, if any, to be made in such taxes, fees or fines.

— Comparison with preceding year(s) in dollars and in percentage increase or decrease. How much will an increase cost the typical home owner?

— Justification for increases sought, cuts made.

— Rate of current spending, under or over budget of previous year.

— Patterns behind submission and subsequent adjustments, such as political motives, pressure groups, history.

— Consequences of budget for agencies, departments, businesses, public.

— Per-person comparison of costs for specific services with other cities
or school districts of same size.

— Check of one or more departments to see how funds are used,
whether all funds were necessary.

Sources

There are five major interest groups that seek to influence budget making
and constitute the reporter's sources:

1. **Government:** chief executive, who submits the budget; mayor,
governor, school superintendent, president; city manager; head of budget
bureau or budget director; department heads; finance and taxation
committees of the city council or commission; council members. (Party
leaders outside government are sometimes helpful.)

2. **Money-providing constituencies:** local real estate association;
property owners' association; chamber of commerce; taxpayer
organizations; merchant and business groups; banks; savings and loan
associations.

3. **Service-demanding groups:** lobbyists for education, health,
welfare and other services.

4. **Organized bureaucracies:** public employees; municipal unions;
civil service associations; the public employees' retirement fund manager.

5. **Independent groups:** League of Women Voters; National
Municipal League; National League of Cities; U.S. Conference of Mayors;
Advisory Commission on Intergovernmental Relations.

Concrete Costs

Promises to cut spending and therefore lower taxes make for political rhetoric that entices voters, but the truth is that many items in the budget are mandated costs that cannot be shifted or eliminated without massive political
changes. The mandated funds include salaries, debt service, pensions and matching funds that localities must produce to meet state and federal grants, particularly for such services as health, welfare and education. When the city accepts
grants from the state or federal government, it must abide by rules and regulations that often require local expenditures.

The actual maneuvering room in most budgets is not great, especially because salaries, which represent the largest single expense item, are set by contract in many cities. Because of mandated costs, less than 10 percent of the
budgets for most large cities is discretionary.

Costs can be reduced if commitments to the poor, the elderly and the ill
are cut back. This, however, would antagonize the service-demanding constituencies. Maneuvering room could be created by changing earmarked funds,
such as those for education, to general funds. Again, groups that benefit from the

status quo would object. In tight times, city employees are pressed to forego wage increases.

Trade-Offs and Rewards   The competition for free-floating general funds is always intense, and the perceptive reporter will examine this contest during the budgetary process. In this competition, the administrator finds it necessary to trade off the demands of various groups. The trade-offs make good stories.

Some aspects of the process are hidden from view. The reporter must dig them out and learn which constituencies are involved, the motives of the participants. Are political debts being paid by building a school in one section of the city or by increasing salaries in a particular agency? Have cuts been made in the department of a critical or independent administrator?

Budget Politics

During a legislative session, the Republican governor of New York proposed a new formula for the distribution of state aid to local school districts that reflected the demands of big-city school officials. A few days later, a group of Republican state senators and assembly members from Long Island met with the governor, who was facing re-election. Following the meeting, the governor's aid formula was changed to give more aid to suburban school districts.

"What happened at the gathering," reported *The New York Times,* "was summed up later by Joseph M. Margiotta of Uniondale, the powerful Nassau County Republican leader, who related that the Long Island delegation had simply delivered to the governor the stern message that without more state education aid, Long Island property taxes would skyrocket in September and the governor's campaign would sink in October."

When Mayor John Lindsay of New York "dropped the broom and picked up the nightstick"—the graphic phrase the *Daily News* used to describe the shift in budget priorities from clean streets to public safety—it was widely interpreted as Lindsay's recognition that law and order would make a more attractive national issue than sanitation. Lindsay had presidential ambitions.

The 1990s were marked at the state and local levels by budget cuts, and the consequences were often dramatic: student protests against tuition increases at tax-supported colleges and universities, homeless people sleeping in welfare offices, oversized classes and school closings leading to parent protests.

> **Suburban Growth.** Almost half the country's population lives in suburbs; 14 states have a majority suburban population. Some effects: political strength (majority Republican) shifting to the suburbs; a hostility to central-city government; greater concern for security and privacy; less concern for inner-city problems of race and class.

Property Tax

The property tax is the largest single source of income for municipalities, counties, special districts and school systems. It affects more people than any other local tax but the sales tax. Considerable local, county and school coverage centers on the action of the council, commission or board in setting the property tax.

The tax is formally known as the *mill levy.* A mill is .1 cent (1/10¢), and the property tax technically is expressed in terms of mills levied for each dollar of assessed valuation of property. One-tenth of a mill per dollar works out to 10 cents per $100 in assessed valuation, or $1 per $1,000 in valuation.

Here is the formula for figuring the property tax or mill levy:

Mill levy = taxes to be collected ÷ assessed valuation

Let us assume budget officials estimate that $1 million will have to be collected from the property tax and that the assessed valuation of real estate in the city or school district is $80 million. Here is how the tax is figured:

Mill levy = $1 million ÷ $80 million

Mill levy = $1 ÷ $80 = $.0125

Mill levy = 1.25 cents on each $1 of assessed valuation

Because mill levies are usually expressed against $100 or $1,000 in assessed valuation, the levy in this community would be $1.25 for each $100 in valuation, or $12.50 for each $1,000 in valuation.

Note that the mill levy is applied to assessed valuations, not to actual value as determined in the marketplace. Assessed value is usually a percentage of market value.

Here is the beginning of a story about the adoption of the city budget:

The Mt. Pleasant City Council adopted a $217 million budget last night and set a tax rate of $108.50 for each $1,000 in assessed valuation.

The rate represents a $6 increase in the tax rate for property owners for next year.

Those owning homes assessed at $50,000, which is the average Mt. Pleasant assessment, will pay $5,425 a year in city property taxes. The current bill for a $50,000 home is $5,125.

Remember that the property tax is a major source of revenue for several governmental units—city, county, school, special assessment districts, each of which sets its own tax levy on property. When covering the action of one unit in setting a tax rate, it is necessary to inform the reader that this particular property tax is not the only one the property owner will pay.

Property taxes levied by special assessment districts can add a large chunk to the tax bill. The special districts construct and maintain services such as power and water lines, hospitals, sewage systems and community development projects. Each district has the power to levy taxes on property within the district.

Property valuations are made by the tax assessor and are public record. The tax rate is set each year, but valuations on individual pieces of property are not changed often. Total assessed valuation does change each year because of new construction and shutdowns that add to or subtract from the tax rolls. The taxing district must establish the total assessed valuation each year before a new tax rate can be set.

Reassessments

When the assessor does make new valuations, the intensity of feeling is considerable, as revealed in this story:

SPRING VALLEY, N.Y., Dec. 12 — Listening to people here, a visitor would almost think that someone was stalking the streets, sowing horror and destruction.

But it is only the tax assessor, equipped with a collapsible 10-foot measuring stick, a set of appraisal cards, a practiced eye that can tell the difference between a toilet and a water closet and experience that tells him which adds more value to a house.

This village of 22,450 persons, 2,219 dwellings and 109 commercial properties is nearing the end of a year-long reappraisal. . . .

The purpose of reassessments is not to increase the city's property tax income but to redistribute the tax burden. With reassessment, some pay less, and some pay more. People on fixed incomes whose property is valued higher than it was in previous years often have trouble, especially the elderly. Some states have what is known as "circuit breaker" regulations that limit tax hikes for certain groups.

When their assessments were increased, 2,000 Greenwich, Conn., property owners complained, including a multimillionaire developer and the singer Diana Ross. In his story, Christopher Keating of *The Hartford Courant* quoted the chairman of the Board of Tax Review: "If we knock down everybody, the mill rate will have to go up."

Keating was pointing out that when a community decides to increase revenues through the property tax, it has two choices: raise assessed valuations or raise the property tax rate. A reassessment generally is more equitable.

The assessor sometimes is politically motivated in establishing assessments. In some cities, residential properties are consistently underassessed in order to placate home owners. In Philadelphia, tax officials assessed residences at 40 percent of market value, whereas commercial property was assessed at 54 percent and industrial property at 59 percent. In Chicago, the political machine of Mayor Richard J. Daley underassessed large corporations and industries. At election time, these beneficiaries of the assessor could be counted on for large campaign contributions.

Borrowing

Most cities need seasonal funds to tide them over while waiting for income from taxes or grants to arrive. They also need money to finance major construction projects.

Anticipation Notes

For seasonal borrowing or for emergencies when small amounts are needed, the city may issue and sell to banks anticipation notes. Future tax collections and anticipated grants-in-aid are pledged as security. Usually, the state must approve.

Short-term low-interest borrowing consists of three types of anticipation notes—revenue, tax and bond. All notes must be repaid in a year.

Bonds

The idea behind the sale of bonds is that the costs of such long-range projects as schools, hospitals, streets, sewage plants and mass transit should be borne by those who use them over the anticipated lives of the projects.

There are three major types of bonds. They differ as to the type of security pledged to repay them:

- **General obligation:** Most frequently issued. Security is the general taxing power of the city. Bonds are retired by taxes on all property in the city.
- **Special improvement:** For construction of sidewalks, sewers and similar public works. Taxes are levied on the property owners who will benefit from the construction. Charges levied on the property are called *special assessments.* Special assessment districts are set up to levy and collect the taxes.
- **Revenue bonds:** To pay for the acquisition, construction and improvement of such properties as college dormitories and public utilities. The pledge is a lien on earnings, which are used to redeem the bonds. These earnings come from room charges in dormitories; water, gas and electric collections from utility customers; toll charges on bridges and highways.

Bonds are paid off in two ways:

- **Term bonds:** The securities are retired at the end of the specified term, 10, 15, 20 years. Meanwhile, money is set aside regularly in a sinking fund and invested to be used to retire the bonds at the end of the term.
- **Serial bonds:** Most common. A portion is retired each year.

Give Total Cost   In writing bond stories, the reporter should make sure to include the cost of the bonds to taxpayers. Some readers will be astonished to learn how much a seemingly small rate of interest can add to the principal.

When Nassau County in New York sold $103 million in bonds for roads, land purchases and new sewers, officials estimated that interest would cost about $50 million over the life of the bonds. One reason for the high cost of debt was the downgrading of the county by bond-rating agencies as a result of the county's financial problems. The downgrading resulted in the county having to offer higher interest rates to attract investors worried about the lowered rating of the bonds.

Ratings. Bond rating agencies assess the financial standing of cities and states that issue bonds. The higher the rating, the lower the interest rate. Here is Standard & Poor's rating schedule:

AAA: Highest.

AA: High-grade, slightly riskier than AAA.

A: Upper-medium-grade. Secure finances, but if problems arise, paybacks could suffer.

BBB: Medium-grade. Finances precarious. Lowest level of investment-quality bonds.

BB, C, CCC: Speculative. Uncertain whether long-term bonds can be repaid.

Here is the beginning of a story about a credit downgrading:

> TROY, N.Y. (AP)—The City of Troy, which continues to struggle with a four-year-old financial crisis, had its credit rating reduced below investment grade Friday by Moody's Investors Service.
>
> Moody's said it had cut Troy's credit rating from B-aa to B-a, one step below investment grade. . . .

Checking Up

Wherever public money is involved, audits are made to see that the money is spent properly. Most governmental units undergo internal checks made by their own auditors, and these make good stories. Here is the beginning of a story by Jayne Garrison of the *San Francisco Examiner:*

> OAKLAND—A Social Services Department audit says mismanagement and internal squabbling are so severe that clients would be better off if the agency were dismantled.

In addition, checks are made by an independent government agency or office. Cities, states and the federal government have a department or office independent of the executive that checks the financial activities of all agencies within government. At the federal level, the Government Accounting Office does this work. At the state level, the state auditor or comptroller is the watchdog, and at the city level an elected official, also known as the auditor or comptroller, examines the financial records of city offices.

A regular or preaudit examination determines whether there is money to pay for the goods, whether there are certified receipts for the delivered goods, whether there has been competitive bidding when required by law and whether the prices are reasonable.

Increasingly, auditors and comptrollers are conducting performance audits, which check the efficiency of the services, the quality of the goods and the necessity for purchasing them.

Preaudit example: A state official claims travel reimbursement for an official trip between Boulder and Denver. The auditor will determine whether the 39 miles claimed on the official's expense account attached to a pay order is the actual distance and will see whether the 29 cents a mile claimed is the standard state payment.

Performance audit example: The comptroller has decided to make a check of welfare rolls to see whether money is going out to ineligible people. The office makes a computer check of the welfare rolls against (a) death lists; (b) marriage certificates (if a person receiving aid to dependent children has married, the working spouse is obligated to support the children); (c) children in foster care homes still listed as at the residence; (d) city and state payrolls to determine if any employed people are receiving welfare.

Looking at the Files

Journalists make their own checks. They regularly look through vouchers and pay orders in the auditor's office, and they look at the canceled checks in the treasurer's office.

When a governmental unit wants to buy something, it sends a purchase order to the comptroller's or auditor's office, which makes a preaudit. Records are kept by the number of the purchase order, by the agency involved and often by the name of the vendor.

On delivery of the goods or services, a voucher is made up with the accompanying bill, and this starts the payment to the vendor. The payment is made in the form of a check, a warrant.

Dining Out　When Christopher Scanlan of *The Providence Journal* was examining vouchers of the Providence Housing Authority, he came upon payments of $3,319.59 made to restaurants in Providence and Warwick for "authority meetings." On checking, he learned that members of the authority had been meeting over meals for years. "The restaurant tabs were paid from authority funds, the majority of which are derived from rents paid by low income tenants at the city's 14 public housing projects and from federal subsidies," Scanlan wrote. After the story ran, the authority members agreed to hold meetings in the housing projects it manages.

High-Level Thievery　An examination of vouchers and warrants enabled George Thiem, a reporter for *The Chicago Daily News,* to expose a multimillion-dollar corruption scheme by the Illinois state treasurer. Thiem could see that a number of checks were endorsed by typewriter. Interviewing some of those who supposedly were paid by these checks for work done for the state, he learned that the people listed on the checks had never done state work; nor had they received the checks. The treasurer went to prison as a result of Thiem's investigation.

Investigating Government

Official misconduct is the subject of most investigative projects. Reporters have a keen sense of their obligation to check on public officials who are entrusted by their constituents to spend money wisely and to make policy decisions with the public welfare in mind. It doesn't always work that way, and often someone who knows what is going on tips a reporter.

Reporters describe such sources as being "inside the factory." Not all tips are useful and some are extremely difficult to verify. All must be handled with caution. Bill Marimow of *The Philadelphia Inquirer* says he does the following after receiving allegations of misconduct from a source:

1. Asks the source whether he or she knows of anything in writing: an audit by an official agency or a report by a private accounting firm; a deposition in a civil suit or any other documents that support the allegations.

2. Finds out whether anyone else knows about the misconduct and is willing to talk about it—"preferably, on-the-record, but, if not, on a not-for-attribution basis." Would this person know of anything on the public record?

"At all times, in the initial phase of research, the emphasis should be on finding out if there is anything whatsoever—however small—on the public record to document the allegations," Marimow says.

3. Tries to assure the source that although the allegations sound plausible, they need to be proved "through documentable and attributable information" to write a story. "If you were me," Marimow suggests telling the source, "how would you go about documenting these allegations?" Does the source know of any official inquiry—by the FBI, district attorney, auditor, comptroller?

The Shoebox Papers

While she was gathering material for an article about the effects of federal budget cuts on the poor, Carol Matlack of the *Arkansas Gazette* spoke to a church worker who told her about an elderly man and his wife who had lost their home through foreclosure.

"She told me there was something suspicious about it," Matlack says.

"She gave me a bundle of the man's papers—he had recently died—that had been stored in a shoebox in his house.

"The documents proved the key to the story."

With the papers and from records in the county courthouse and through interviews, Matlack was able to piece together the story of an interlocking relationship between a private investment firm and a special assessment district in a poor neighborhood that cost residents their homes through foreclosures.

Her series begins this way:

> Hosie and Clover Mae Willis were stunned when they got a letter ordering them to move out of their home. It was their first notice that their modest frame house on College Station's Frazier Pike had been sold for nonpayment of $62 in special improvement taxes several years earlier.

After describing the couple's improvements to the property, in which they had reared three children, Matlack disclosed that Southern Investment Co. of Little Rock had purchased the property from Water Improvement District 74 for $124.71 in taxes and penalties. The story continues:

Had the Willises inquired further, they would have learned that the commissioners of Water Improvement District 74 who sold their property—W. J. White, Jack Barger and Marcelite Cook—all were affiliated with Southern Investment.

They would also have learned that at least two dozen College Station residents have lost their property in similar fashion because of a failure to pay taxes—sometimes as little as $20—to one of five water improvement districts in the predominantly poor, black community south of Little Rock Airport.

Never Notified   Residents said they had never been told their taxes were delinquent. Nor were they notified their land was being sold.

Why all the activity in a poor, black neighborhood? Matlack answers the question in her third article that begins:

"Little nuggets of gold." That's how Pratt Remmel Sr., a Little Rock businessman, describes a string of weedchoked lots he owns along a potholed road in College Station.

Matlack points out that a highway would soon go by the area, carrying "one of the heaviest traffic volumes in Arkansas." An interchange was to be built north of College Station, and the area would have hotels, restaurants, motels and an industrial park.

Follow the buck. The paper trail Matlack followed led from the simple homes of poor folk to the offices of wheelers and dealers.

Postscript: In its next session, the General Assembly of Arkansas reformed procedures for delinquent tax notification.

Assessment Districts

Most states allow for the creation of independent taxing districts, sometimes called special assessment districts. These districts are put together for particular purposes such as the installation of sidewalks or street lights, building a sewage treatment plant or creating a fire department. These districts often are outside cities that provide these services. Property owners within the districts are assessed taxes to pay for the particular service.

Few reporters bother to look at these districts, but when Tom Puleo of *The Hartford Courant* examined one of the 260 districts in Connecticut, the Thompsonville Fire Department District, he found the chairman had steered contracts to his family. The districts, it turns out, are not subject to state laws because they raise their own taxes. The paper's investigation led to a re-examination of state laws.

Zoning and Planning

For centuries, the mentally ill were locked up. The reasons seemed logical: Isolated, the mentally ill could be healed more rapidly; free in society, their conditions worsened; they were a danger to others and to themselves. Gradually, the truth seeped out. Journalists showed that institutions for the mentally ill were snake pits where the patients were treated inhumanely. Few were cured, and many were made worse. With the development of tranquilizing drugs and other treatment, it became possible to offer outpatient care. But there had to be a transition, a halfway house to help the patient adjust after institutionalization.

In New Jersey, the Catholic Diocese of Trenton decided to administer several such houses. The state intended to deinstitutionalize its mental patients, and the diocese sought to help. The diocese found a structure in Willingboro that fit its needs. But permission was required from the zoning board because the building was in a residential area.

The Willingboro zoning board, like thousands of other such boards, carries out the community's planning goals, which are usually set by the planning commission. The zoning boards divide an area into zones or districts and designate them residential, commercial or industrial. The boards then grant building and construction permits consistent with these designations.

The boards also regulate the height of buildings, lot size, yard dimensions and other aspects of construction. City councils enact the ordinances that the zoning boards enforce.

Zoning can be restrictive, a way of keeping certain people out of an area. By requiring that new construction be of single-residence homes on one-acre lots, a zoning regulation will effectively keep out of the area all but the well-to-do. When Laura King, who covered Willingboro on her suburban beat, attended the zoning board meeting at which the diocese requested a variance for its halfway house, she was struck by the hostility of the spectators. King decided that the opposition to the house was the story.

Neighborhood Stories

City hall reporters spend too much of their time in city hall, says a veteran municipal government reporter. He recommends that they make regular trips out of the protected environs of the municipal building and into the neighborhoods of the community to see what is on the minds of people, to check how city programs and policies have been carried out. Here is the beginning of a neighborhood story by Jayne Garrison of the *San Francisco Examiner:*

OAKLAND—In the heart of the Oakland flatlands, the moms and pops of small business are plotting to sweep out the rubble: dope, litter and boarded buildings.

About 35 merchants meeting in churches and stores the last few weeks have organized a voice they hope will boom across town to City Hall—the Central East Oakland Merchants Association.

This is the first time in more than a decade that merchants along central East 14th Street have tried to wield clout together. The odds against them are steep.

They have little political pull and even less money. They face absentee landlords who own some boarded storefronts, and youths who have no work outside the drug trade.

But they do have determination.

"You see that red church down there?" said Al Parham, nodding toward a tall brick steeple half a block past Seminary Avenue on East 14th Street. "They just built that. So people are coming back into the community. And they're going to church. They care."

Computer-Assisted Reporting

Local government reporters no longer have to dig through dusty files in their search for records. Almost everything—from payrolls to response time for medical emergency calls—is in a database, available quickly and easily.

Jeff South of Virginia Commonwealth University, who worked on many computer-assisted reporting projects, says the first step is to find out what kinds of data local agencies collect. "If necessary, submit an open-records request for the list of databases," he says.

"Look at the reports produced by the bureaucracy and see if there is underlying data: Do they contain such specific numbers that it's clear somebody distilled them from a computerized file? Reports frequently contain computer printer printouts, like a list of new hires with their names, titles and salary."

State agencies also collect and store local data that can be used to make city-to-city comparisons.

CAR Story Ideas

South lists the following CAR story ideas for coverage of local government:

Building permits: Get the database of permits issued and look for trends. Has there been an increase in permits for commercial buildings or single-family homes? Which areas of town are seeing the most construction?

Restaurant inspections: The typical American eats out 213 times a year, according to the National Restaurant Association. So there probably will be high interest in a story about restaurant inspections conducted by your city or county Health Department.

Traffic tickets: Who are the biggest parking violators in your city, and what spots are ticketed most often? From your state auditor, get budget data on each municipality and see which ones depend most on traffic violators. Maybe they're running a speed trap on out-of-towners. (If you get a good lead, check the Web site http://www.speedtraps.com)

Zoning variances: Get a list of all variances requested, along with actions taken by the board that handles such matters. What percentage of applications is granted? Does the percentage vary from neighborhood to neighborhood?

Salaries: See who the highest-paid employees are. In many cities, they're police officers, thanks to generous overtime. Look at salaries for different demographic groups. Is overtime a perk mostly for good ol' boys?

Employee residency: Payroll or other databases should say where local public employees live. This could be a concern if a city is losing its residents and tax base to the suburbs. What percentage of the city employees live in the city? Does living in the suburbs diminish their effectiveness working for the city?

Nepotism: How many employees are related—and do they work in the same department? You may find that many summer youth employees are the children or relatives of city administrators.

Sick leave and absenteeism: For privacy reasons, you probably can't get how many times each employee has been absent. But you should be able to find out the number of people who've called in sick each day (especially if an agency, like a school, must hire substitutes). What's the absentee rate on Mondays and Fridays?

Cellular phone usage: Get the records for each cellular phone your local officials have. Find out how many calls they make, and to whom. Do they make a lot of calls unrelated to government business?

Property assessments: Compare assessments to sales prices. You may find that expensive homes are being assessed at a lower percentage of their actual value than are modestly priced homes. Or that homes in certain neighborhoods, or homes owned by government officials, are getting a break.

Exemptions: Look at property that doesn't get taxed: property owned by churches, nonprofits and governments. Identify properties that get agricultural tax exemptions: How did they qualify, and who owns them? In Texas, the biggest beneficiaries of agricultural exemptions often are developers, contractors and high-tech companies.

Distribution of city facilities: Use mapping software to plot the location of parks, swimming pools, libraries and other public facilities. Does one side of town have one swimming pool for every 20,000 residents—and the other side one pool for every 100,000?

Code enforcement: Analyze complaints and citations involving housing code violations, junk cars, trashy yards and other signs of blight. How many of the violators are absentee landlords? How often are they punished?

Program evaluation: The *Star Tribune* recently analyzed Minneapolis' Neighborhood Revitalization Program, which has provided millions of dollars to fix up residential areas. City officials said the program had raised property values. But the *Star Tribune* found "no link between NRP investments and rising single-family home prices. The analysis shows home prices dropping in some neighborhoods that received a lot of NRP money and home prices rising in some areas where little or no NRP money has been spent."

Sources The U.S. Census Bureau, www.census.gov, keeps extensive data on city and county finances and demographics. The Center for Urban Policy at Rutgers University, http://policy.rutgers.edu/cupr/soNC.htm, has a database on 77 cities and their suburbs that covers demographics, employment, income and poverty and other material.

Covering the Schools

Communities spend more money on public education than on any other single tax-supported activity. Free public education has a long history in the United States. In 1642, the Massachusetts Bay Colony made education compulsory in the primary grades and required towns to establish public schools. The cost is borne by all in the community, whether the individual has children in the public school or not. The reason was given succinctly by Thaddeus Stevens to the Pennsylvania state legislature in 1835 when some legislators objected to the general financing of the schools.

"Many complain of the school tax," Stevens said, "not so much on account of its amount, as because it is for the benefit of others and not themselves. This is a mistake. It is for their own benefit, inasmuch as it perpetuates the government and ensures the due administration of the laws under which they live, and by which their lives and property are protected."

The faith in education as the underpinning of democracy is a constant theme in American life, along with the belief that it paves the way to a good job, if not to the good life. Education pervades the life of most families because they have children in school.

The interest in schools—which really means a concern for the community's children—led *The Fincastle Herald* in Virginia to run a banner across page 1 when the Scholastic Aptitude Test (SAT) scores for the county were made public. "Low SAT scores surprise school officials," read the headline. The story was accompanied by a large box comparing county scores with those in Virginia, southern states and the nation. The story by Edwin McCoy begins:

> Botetourt County students scored at least 20 points below the state and national averages on both parts of the Scholastic Aptitude Test (SAT), according to figures provided by the county school system this week.

McCoy described education as the "focal point in the community" in an editorial accompanying the news story. "The quality of education is important to industrial or commercial development because developers are interested in the quality of life in any area they choose to expand in or move to."

Structure of the System

The school system is based in school districts. The schools are independent of municipal government and are subject to state regulations through a state

The Process. The school budget is drafted by the city school superintendent and presented to the school board for approval. In many cities, the voters then must approve the budget.

Usually, the schools seek as much as possible and the board attempts to cut back in order to lower the mill levy. The board members have mixed motives: Although sensitive to the needs of schoolchildren, members reflect property owners' desires to keep taxes down.

Student Performance. Tests given in mathematics and science to students in the seventh and eighth grades in 41 countries showed that U.S. students finished 28th in math, 17th in science, the result, some said, of the failure of the United States to make education a national priority and a less than rigorous teacher-training program.

board of education. School boards, usually with five to seven members, are elected in nonpartisan elections, although in some cities board members are appointed by the mayor. The board hires a superintendent of schools who is responsible to the board.

Stories from the board and the superintendent's office involve such subjects as changes in the curriculum and personnel, teacher contracts, the purchase of new equipment, aid to education, teacher certification, school dates for opening, closing and holidays and the vast area of school financing that includes budgeting and the issuance of bonds.

The school administration can provide material for assessing the performance of the system and its schools. Dropout and truancy records are kept, as are the results of standardized tests. Reporters can compare the scores in their communities with those of other cities. Comparisons also can be made of schools within the system. Do the students in the low-scoring schools come from economically depressed areas with serious social and economic problems? Is there a correlation between income and achievement?

A check of high school graduates would indicate what percentage is going to college from each school. Interviews with the students may uncover information just as revealing as the students' test scores.

Financing Schools

Schools are financed by several sources. The averages work out to 48 percent from the state, 45 percent from local taxes and 7 percent from the federal government. In the Northeast, most states rely on 55 percent or more of their support from local taxes, which favors students in well-to-do areas. In an attempt to equalize support for schools, several states have altered their school-financing formulas to make the state the major provider. In New Mexico, for example, 90 percent of school operating funds are provided by the state. Later in this chapter we will look at suggested changes in school financing to equalize support.

In the Classroom   The education reporter's responsibility is to hold the school system accountable to parents and to the community. The United States has committed itself to an educational system that will turn out large numbers of people educated beyond the level that the country demanded only of its educated elite a century ago. How well is it doing this?

The best way to begin to find out is to visit the classroom, to look at what is happening day after day and to check your observations against test scores and the assessments of parents and educators. When Bob Frazier of the *Register-Guard* in Eugene, Ore., covered education, he would scrunch all 6′ 4″ into a grade-schooler's chair and sit in class. The stories he wrote were much more significant than any release from the superintendent's office.

School visits will tell the reporter whether the principal has a sense of mission and exerts strong leadership. They will reveal the professional level of teachers, whether they are given respect and whether they, in turn, give students

To the Rescue. Private industry is making overtures to schools short of money. The most widely used source is Channel One, which provides television sets and audio equipment for the right to broadcast its TV newscast, with advertisers, in classrooms. Coca-Cola and Pepsi are signing up school districts for exclusive rights to sell their products. A school district in New York received $1.53 million for a 10-year deal from Coca-Cola, and in Colorado Springs a school official urged administrators to push Coca-Cola sales, even in classrooms.

Most of these deals are negotiated without public notice or meetings.

respect and attention. The school environment is checked: Is the school safe? Is there a strong code of behavior, and are violators punished? Is truancy increasing or declining? Records can be examined for the frequency, number and type of discipline problems and vandalism.

Does the high school have various tracks for its students, such as academic, vocational and general, and, if so, what percentage of students is in each? In the early 1960s, one of 10 students nationally was in the general track; by 1990, almost half were. (The general track usually gives credit for physical and health education, work experience outside school, remedial English and mathematics and developmental courses such as training for adulthood and marriage.)

How much homework is given? A national survey of eighth-graders found youngsters spent 5 1/2 hours a week on homework, 21 hours a week watching television. *The Raleigh Times* put at the top of page 1 its education reporter's story that half the state's students in the sixth and ninth grades do less than three hours of homework a week.

Hanging Out

Student life outside the classroom is worth covering, too. Thomas French of the *St. Petersburg Times* spent a year at Largo High School, listening to students talk about music, their sexual activity, their studies. He watched them sport chunks of gold jewelry, beepers and speed by the school in their late-model cars, "monster stereos with up to 1,000 watts" blaring.

The student culture is, some educators say, more important than the influence of the schools and of parents. Reporters have found a culture that pressures students to do the minimum work or be called "nerds." Students say they purposely do not do well because they want to avoid being ostracized. Many don't bother to do the homework, with no punishment by their instructors.

Asked what their parents think of their schoolwork, the little time they spend on homework, their C or worse grades, students say their parents are indifferent.

Widening Scope

Some education reporters consider themselves consumer reporters whose job it is to check on the quality of the product. They also understand that the schools have become the focus of an intense political battle that ranges from what students should be allowed to read to how the schools should be financed. Every week seems to see battle lines forming in the community over a school issue. Let's start with one of the most contentious—textbooks.

What Can Jane and John Read?

For many years the answer in Texas was that they could read only the textbooks approved by a conservative religious majority on the state textbook adoption agency. The result was that Darwin was a nonperson in biology textbooks, evolution barely mentioned, creation science a plausible explanation of the origin of the universe and its species.

Depressing Data. Studies have shown:

- Fewer than a fifth of 11th graders can write a note applying for a summer job at a swimming pool.
- Of 21- to 25-year-olds, only 38 percent could figure their change from $3 if they had a 60-cent cup of soup and a $1.95 sandwich. One of five young adults can read a schedule well enough to tell when a bus will reach a terminal.
- Among college seniors, 58 percent could not identify Plato as the author of *The Republic;* 60 percent could not recognize the definition of Reconstruction; 58 percent knew that the Civil War was fought between 1850 and 1900; 25 percent did not know that Columbus landed in the New World before 1500.

Maurice Rivenbank, *St. Petersburg Times*

Inside Largo High

"I wore my Nikes and stayed away from ties," says Thomas French. Students talked openly with him.

Because the state adopted few textbooks in each subject, it ordered vast quantities of the few approved books. Textbook publishers, like any business, played to the market. So the Texas approach to science, for example, became the norm for books used everywhere.

The Texas board would not use certain dictionaries because they contained profane and obscene words, and textbooks on health were especially vulnerable if they discussed sexuality, AIDS and breast self-examination techniques.

Reaction　　As journalists called attention to the board's actions, voters sent less zealous guardians to serve on it and publishers stiffened. When anti-abortion and other groups demanded scores of changes in the health textbook, one publisher pulled out of the bidding.

"We simply cannot produce a product that does not provide children with adequate instruction on life-threatening issues," the publisher stated. An official of the Association of American Publishers said the requested changes were made "for political reasons. This was another case in which factions of the religious right are getting more involved in boards of education all over the country."

But the protectors of student morality have resources to thwart publishers—scissors, gluepots and volunteers to wield them.

The Franklin County, N.C., school board tore out three chapters from text-books on student health. The chapters concerned the transmission of sexual diseases, contraception, pairing, marriage and parenting. The board said the chapters do not conform to its policy of abstinence. "Shades of 1936 Germany," Wayne Wilbourne, principal of Bunn High School, told *The News & Observer* of Raleigh.

Creation Science　　Although the courts have ruled that creation science is a religious tenet and has no place in the public school curriculum, the battle to include it rages on. Creation science is the belief that a divine being created life about 10,000 years ago, a literal reading of the Bible. Close to 50 percent of Americans agree: "God created humankind in its present form about 10,000 years ago."

In Kentucky, a public school superintendent was so offended by a science textbook's discussion of the Big Bang theory of the origin of the universe that he glued together the pages of hundreds of books. He was angry that the creationist theory was not in the textbook. "We're in a conservative area and a conservative county, and we want to maintain the relationship with our local churches and community," he said. "It has nothing to do with censorship or anything like that."

In New Mexico, the Board of Education removed from science guidelines any mention of evolution.

The Fairfax County, Va., school board voted 6–4 against putting a disclaimer in a biology textbook that discussed the scientific basis for the formation of the universe. The American Family Association had requested the insertion because, the association said, the language would offend students who believe in creationism.

Creationism in Classrooms

"Creationism—which includes any theory that the universe was created by a divine being—may be included in a class on comparative religion as an example of how some religious groups believe human life began. However, it may not be taught as scientific fact in public schools. The theory of evolution is the result of scientific inquiry and is subject to ongoing academic scrutiny and review. Creationism is a religious doctrine which has no place in a science class.

"Virtually every religion deals with creation, and their doctrines are by no means the same. To guard against religious coercion, the law prohibits any religious belief about creation—be it Christian, Hindu, Buddhist, Jewish or other—from being taught as scientific truth in public schools."

—Anti-Defamation League

Dumbed Down Textbooks   A study of textbooks by the U.S. Department of Education found that many have decreased in difficulty by two grade levels since the mid-1970s. Few, if any, publishers aim their books at above-average students, the federal study found.

In one Massachusetts school district, the board dropped books by Mark Twain, John Steinbeck, Charles Dickens and others because they feared the authors' books might bore students. Among the books tossed out: *Tom Sawyer* and *A Tale of Two Cities.*

In *The New York Review of Books,* Alexander Stille writes, "The most recent textbooks appear to be designed on the debatable premise that they must compete with Nintendo games and MTV." Such books, he continues, "appeal to the lazier teachers who want both to keep the class busy and to avoid working with longer and more detailed texts."

Library Books   Periodic attempts are made to purge books from school libraries, especially the books that deal with sex, race and sensitive contemporary subjects. Sometimes even the librarian is purged. The West Valley School Board of Kalispell, Mont., fired its grade school librarian after she had helped two seventh-grade students with their research for a class report on witchcraft in the middle ages.

In Ouachita Parish, La., more than 200 books were removed from a high school library after the principal ordered the librarians to get rid of anything having to do with sex.

In Georgia, a minister asked for the removal of art books from an elementary school library because they contained nudity. He was especially offended by reproductions of Michelangelo's Sistine Chapel and the statue of David.

Subjects for Coverage

Here are some suggestions for an education reporter's beat checklist.

Crumbling Buildings   Less than $3.5 billion is being spent a year to repair and replace school buildings. The General Accounting Office estimates the total needs at $112 billion. Children are being taught in trailers and are bused to nearby communities as the population increases and voters turn down bond issues to build new school buildings or repair old ones. The school-age population, now about 52 million, is expected to reach 56 million in 2004.

In Ohio, the *Akron Beacon Journal* found school buildings in serious disrepair. Instead of fixing them, the state legislature exempted schools from parts of the building code.

Packed Classes   Overcrowding has become commonplace as money-starved schools find it difficult to hire additional teachers and school construction bond issues have been rejected by voters. Journalists have shown the tension in communities between retired homeowners living on limited incomes and young newcomer families with school-age children. The older people vote against the bonds that young families favor.

Hard. "Mathematics cannot be made easy. Nor, equally, can any school subjects which stretch the mind. That is because the life of the mind is not easy."
—*John Casey, Fellow, Gonville and Caius College, Cambridge University*

Most Often Banned. *Of Mice and Men,* John Steinbeck; *The Catcher in the Rye,* J. D. Salinger; *The Adventures of Huckleberry Finn,* Mark Twain; *I Know Why the Caged Bird Sings,* Maya Angelou; *The Color Purple,* Alice Walker.

James Woodcock,
The Billings Gazette

Crowded

Bonnie Olson tries to cope with the 26 children in her Billings, Mont., classroom. The state sets 20 as the classroom limit, but the school district did not have money to hire enough teachers.

By showing the crowded conditions in classrooms and the consequences—overwhelmed teachers, low test scores—newspapers and stations have helped alleviate some of the worst problems in many communities.

Vouchers

Increasing pressure is being put on state legislatures to direct tax money to parents who could then use the funds for schools of their selection. Advocates say that this would give parents choice and result in better education for all children.

Opponents of the voucher system say that the result would be the destruction of the public school system. Also, they say, the voucher system would allow tax monies to be used for religious schools, a breach of the First Amendment.

Among the states in which the voucher plan has considerable support: Arizona, Connecticut, Florida, Indiana, New Jersey, New York, North Carolina, Ohio, Pennsylvania, Texas, Wisconsin.

Newspapers have conducted polls to see about community support for using tax money to support nonpublic schools, and their results and those of polling organizations indicate a majority oppose vouchers.

Required Courses

Just what coursework is required for a high school diploma? Colleges and universities required to admit high school graduates found that they were admitting high school graduates who were semiliterate and had no idea of how to do basic arithmetic. They put pressure on the high schools to tighten their requirements for graduation. Reporters have dug into the high school curriculum to see what is being taught.

At the elementary school level, the battle has been between the whole language approach to teaching reading and the traditional phonics approach. *The Baltimore Sun* devoted several staff members and several months to an examination of the area school system and among its conclusions found that a return to phonics would lead to higher student language competence.

Religious Values

As the religious right strengthened in the 1990s, its influence was felt in the nation's public schools. In a special report, the Anti-Defamation League stated, "Religion is currently entering the public school system through a variety of means, including school prayer, graduation prayer, religious clubs, religion in the curriculum, creationism, censorship, distribution of religious materials and voucher plans."

The so-called wall of separation between church and state in effect keeps government out of religion and religion out of government. The Supreme Court ruled unconstitutional such practices as ceremonial readings from the Bible in the classroom and organized prayer at student assemblies, athletic activities and special events.

Yet such practices exist and are stoutly defended in a number of communities. They continue until someone goes to court to challenge the breach in the wall of separation.

Conservative Christian candidates have been winning school board elections in many states. "Right now the religious right movement has a lot of mus-

Lawsuit. Disturbed by the strongly religious repretoire and the frequent church appearances of her Salt Lake City public school choir, a 16-year-old West High School choir member and her parents filed suit. The student was called a "dirty Jew" and a "Jew bitch," and when she ran for school office, swastikas were drawn on her campaign posters.

A federal appellate court dismissed the suit but ordered the choir to refrain from performing two religious songs at the school graduation. At the next graduation ceremony a student leaped on the stage and urged people to sing one of the songs. They did so, with enthusiasm.

The suit, *Bauchman v. West High School,* was appealed to the Supreme Court.

cle," reports People for the American Way. On its agenda are the removal of certain books from school libraries, the introduction of school prayer, an emphasis on abstinence in sex education classes and the teaching of creationism.

Segregation   Because of housing patterns, black and Hispanic students make up the majorities of students in many urban schools. In Hartford, for example, more than 90 percent of the students were in these two groups, whereas in the nearby community of Farmington, the schools had a 90 percent white student body. The differences in achievement were marked:

	Percentage above remedial level	
	Hartford	Farmington
Reading	39.3	93.4
Writing	71.5	96.8
Math	58.9	97.0

Thirty-one percent of the Hartford high school students went on to four-year colleges, compared with 76.4 percent of the Farmington students.

Some African-American groups have pressed for Afrocentric academies, given the seemingly impenetrable segregation of schools. Private academies supported with tax funds for black children have been developed in some cities.

Single-sex schools are also a matter of controversy. There are many such private schools, but the issue is being fought in the public school realm. Some parents want their daughters to be in all-girl middle schools. But the American Civil Liberties Union has gone to court to oppose what it says is illegal segregation by sex.

Standards   U.S. school systems are decentralized, locally controlled. But is there some need to have these local schools meet national academic standards in subject matter? One side is anti-Washington. The other side maintains that without standards of some sort students will continue to be mediocre at best compared to students in other countries. Bruce Alberts, president of the National Academy of Sciences said, "Everyone is afraid of saying the truth: that we'll get nowhere as a nation until we make use of all our resources and that there are some things all students should know regardless of what state they live in."

The compromise: Some states are volunteering to adopt standards on their own so that California, Alabama and Kansas students learn the same math, English, science and geography.

Teacher Misconduct   School administrators report an increasing number of charges against teachers, some of whom have records of making sexual advances to students, and of theft and child abuse. The computer makes it possible for journalists to check to see how carefully schools are screening applicants for teaching, coaching and administrative jobs in the schools.

The *Arkansas Democrat-Gazette* in Little Rock compared a statewide database of misdemeanor and felony charges kept by the state court system with the names and birth dates of 38,000 licensed teachers. The newspaper found 103 cases ranging from negligent homicide to embezzlement, from child rape to delivery of cocaine.

Although state law mandates state and FBI background checks for those seeking teaching licenses, the law does not allow for revocations of licenses. Reporters traveled the state to check police departments, court documents and schools. Administrators blocked access in many schools, and reporters had to make 333 Freedom of Information Act requests.

The five-part series by Mary Hargrove and Susan Roth detailed failures to revoke licenses of a teacher who took off with a 14-year-old girl and pled no contest to "handling/fondling a child under 16 years old," a principal who pleaded guilty to contributing to the delinquency of a minor and several similar incidents. The series led to remedial action by the state legislature.

Academic Performance   Twenty states give public warnings to schools that are in academic trouble. In one of them, Alabama, 24 schools were placed on "academic alert," meaning that a majority of students in the schools scored under the 23rd percentile on the Stanford Achievement Test. In Baker Hill, Ala., the two weekly newspapers put the local schools' low scores on page 1, which galvanized the system. Fred Cooper, the principal of the elementary and middle school, told a reporter, "This school is like my child. You always want people to talk nice about your child. And it upsets you when something bad is said. You want to correct whatever is being said that is giving people such a bad impression."

Cooper talked to parents, screened students who needed extra help, and a year later Baker Hill was taken off the "academic alert" list.

Tests   How do you test a school's performance? The reporter usually looks to test results. But some administrators say the standardized tests really don't measure a school's effectiveness.

Albert Shanker, who was president of the American Federation of Teachers, said administrators would tell him, "they had a new plan or policy or initiative that was making a tremendous difference.

"You couldn't see any difference in the test scores, they'd say. But that was not the whole story. If I would only go into the schools, I'd see kids smiling, and I'd feel the warmth in the classroom. That would tell me a whole lot more than test scores."

Shanker did not buy the reassurances. "The whole point of school reform," Shanker said, "is to have students learn more. If this doesn't happen, the experiment is a failure, no matter how happy the children, the parents and teachers— and the reformers—are."

Assessing High Schools   *The Seattle Times* spent eight months examining the performance of high schools in the area. Reporters looked into everything from attendance to the grades that graduates received at the University of Washington. A total of 91 schools were examined, 66 of them public schools. The newspaper found some schools whose students excelled in academic performance, some whose students did not do well in their college freshman year.

The *San Jose Mercury News* found that many California high school graduates are unprepared for college work. Half those admitted to the California State University system were required to take remedial English. Many of these remedial students had good grades in their high school English classes, the newspaper found.

The *Atlanta Journal-Constitution* found that nearly a third of all college freshmen drop out of college within a year, 40 percent of high school graduates need remedial work in their first year and fewer than half the freshmen graduate within a six-year period.

The *Daily News* in the Virgin Islands found that although the Islands spend more money per pupil than most states, their high school graduates finish last on every standardized test they take. Their honor roll students in high school find themselves in remedial English and math classes as college freshmen. The newspaper found students often have no textbooks, teachers fail to show up for work, parents are indifferent, the Education Department has lowered standards so that "even valedictorians and salutatorians must take remedial classes in college." Seventy-eight percent of high school seniors read below grade.

Equal Funding　The disparity in tax support for the schools has led to court battles in more than 30 states. State courts have split almost evenly on the question of whether schools should be supported from local property taxes or should be supported equally from state funds. Only Kansas and Vermont have passed statewide property taxes to support their schools. The Vermont action was in response to situations like this: Richford spent $3,743 per pupil, whereas Peru spent $6,476 per pupil because of differences in the valuation of property in the two communities.

These wide differences are not unique to Vermont. A school district in Texas spent $56,791 for each student, whereas the poorest school district in the state spent $2,337 per student. In Montana, spending per pupil ranged from $2,650 to $9,750. Some states are experimenting with a state sales tax mandated for school expenditures.

The differences in funding make for dramatic comparisons. Ramon Renteria in Texas and Sam Roe in Ohio compared the schools two girls attend to illustrate the consequences of unequal school financing.

Renteria's story begins:

Veronica Marin and Kelli Freeman—two bright and vibrant 8-year-olds—share the same dream. They want to go to college and become teachers.

But these two laughing little Texas girls live 600 miles and a world apart. And that

could make all the difference. One's dream is endangered.

In Texas, poor school districts like Veronica's have far less to spend on education than rich district's like Kelli's. And that, according to a lawsuit moving through Texas courts, means the quality of education often depends on the wealth of the districts.

"Bienvenido a Nuestra Escuela Welcome to Our School" reads the sign at the door of San Elizario Elementary School.

Her dark hair swaying, her backpack heavy with books, Veronica Marin walks down a dusty caliche road to school. Like a gentle princess in blue jeans, she hardly notices the harshness along the way: the outhouses and open irrigation ditches; the neighbors living in rusty school buses, cardboard-covered shacks and feeble homes of tar paper, railroad ties and cinder blocks. . . .

Across most of Texas, just north of Dallas, cheerful, red-headed Kelli Freeman, with her freckles and ponytail and hot pink jogging suit, hops into the family car in suburban Richardson.

Her dad drives her one block to school. And like Veronica, she hardly notices the familiar neighborhood: the crewcut lawns and neat brick homes of doctors, professors, engineers.

Roe's story begins:

Joanna Hammer and Anne Marie Meiers both live on 288th Street in Toledo. Joanna lives on the east side, Anne Marie on the west. Joanna is in the fifth grade. So is Anne Marie.

Each weekday, they walk down their street to go to school. For Joanna, that means Toledo Public Schools, a district beset by mounting deficits, violent crime, and an uncertain future.

But Anne Marie doesn't go to Joanna's school. Because she lives on the opposite side of the street, she boards a bus that takes her to an entirely different public school system: Washington Local. It is richer, safer, and, according to many key statistics, simply better than Toledo Public Schools.

This scenario is nothing new. It has been common in Toledo for years.

But it bewilders and outrages people today the same way it has for a quarter-century.

"I've never understood this," says Fred Hammer, Joanna's father. "What is the ra-tionale for Toledo having two separate school districts? I'd much rather have my daughter go to Washington Local, but she can't. I see that as a form of discrimination."

One city. Two districts. Scores of split neighborhoods.

Nowhere else in Ohio is there a situation like it: two large, independent school systems almost wholly within the same city boundaries.

It is an arrangement that few local officials like to talk about but one that affects tens of thousands of students and parents each year.

It is also an arrangement that didn't happen by chance.

Since the 1950s, some of the area's most powerful leaders, men like the late Ned Skeldon, struck deals and maneuvered around laws to keep the districts separate.

The result: a school boundary line splitting the city in two, much like it splits Anne Marie's and Joanna's street right down the middle.

Politics and Education

The conventional wisdom is that education is "above politics." The proof: The administration of the schools is separated from city government and placed in an independent board whose members are chosen without regard to party affiliation, usually in elections set apart from the partisan campaigning of the regular local election.

The truth is that education is inextricably bound up with politics. Politics enters the scene because, to put it simply, people differ in their notions of how youth should be trained, who should pay for it, who should control it. These differences are resolved in a political context. The conflict and its resolution should be at the heart of much of the reporter's coverage. The political debate runs from the White House to the local school board that meets in the little red schoolhouse.

Pleased Parents, Disturbing Data

Surveys have shown that a majority of parents are pleased with their children's education. Yet every measure of school achievement contains alarming material about students in many states.

The education reporter who consults the National Assessment of Educational Progress conducted by the U.S. Department of Education has available an unbiased insight into his or her state's schools. A recent NAEP survey found that fourth-graders in 13 states could not read at the "basic" level, defined as "partial mastery" of the knowledge and skills in reading that are expected of a fourth-grader.

These states are Alabama, Arizona, Arkansas, California, Delaware, Florida, Georgia, Hawaii, Louisiana, Maryland, Mississippi, New Mexico and South Carolina.

Nationally, 42 percent of fourth-graders score below the basic level. If we divide this overall figure into ethnic and racial groups, we find these percentages of low-scoring students:

White	32 percent
Black	72
Hispanic	67
Asian	23

The 10 states with the highest scoring fourth-graders in the NAEP test were Connecticut, Indiana, Iowa, Maine, Massachusetts, Montana, Nebraska, New Hampshire, North Dakota and Wisconsin.

The enterprising reporter will try to find causes for these figures. Among the factors that educators consider to affect academic performance are class size and pupil-teacher ratio. The better performing states showed a much higher overall percentage of classes with fewer than 25 students than did the states with poorly performing students. Also, the highest pupil-teacher ratio in the better states was 15.8 whereas the lowest ratio in the poor-performing states was 16.6. The median class size for the high-scoring states was 15.3; the median class size for the low-scoring states was 17.3.

Maine's class size averaged 14.1, California's 24.1.

The NAEP describes itself as "the only nationally representative and continuous assessment of what America's students know and can do in various subject areas." It issues "Report Cards" frequently. They are available to the public at this address: National Library of Education, Office of Educational Research

Not Mine. Asked to rate the schools their children attend on a scale of A to F by the Gallup poll, 66 percent of parents rated the schools A or B. But when asked about grade schools in general, only 21 percent gave an A or B grade.

Parents Matter. "If every parent in America made it their patriotic duty to find an extra 30 minutes to help their children learn more each and every day, it would literally revolutionize American education."
—Richard Riley, Secretary of Education

and Improvement, U.S. Department of Education, 555 New Jersey Avenue, NW, Washington, DC 20208-5641, (202) 219-1651.

Covering a School Board Election

Increasingly, school board elections have become the focus of community tensions. As special-interest groups with a conservative agenda put candidates on the ballot, the lines dividing residents grow sharper.

In Sioux Falls, S.D., in a recent school board election, two conservative candidates challenged two incumbents seeking re-election. The incumbents were part of a 3–2 liberal majority, and the local newspaper made it clear that much was at stake in the election: What values shall the community's children be taught, and how would the school board respond to property tax concerns?

Early in the campaign, the *Argus Leader* asked the candidates about these two issues, and it ran their replies along with biographical information about the four candidates. The newspaper was stating what it believed were key issues the candidates should speak about so that voters would have relevant material on which to base their votes.

One of the candidates said that to save money he would eliminate sex education and "social agenda items not academic." As for teaching of values, this

'Control Spending, Emphasize Values'

A candidate in a school board election in Sioux Falls, S.D., outlines her program for the local schools. She wants administrative cutbacks to protect teaching positions and calls for a return to "basics" in instruction, along with an emphasis on "values."

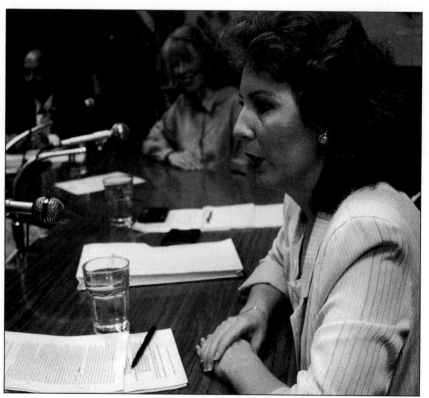

Mike Roemer, *Argus Leader*

candidate stated, "We need Bible reading back in the school, not interpretation, but reading."

In her coverage of the election campaign, Corrine Olson, explored the candidates' approaches to the teaching of "values." The challengers were quoted as emphasizing "values in the instruction and discipline of children." The incumbents contended that the schools in Sioux Falls have been teaching values and stressed the importance of "tolerance" as "one of the values that should be embraced." One challenger said that Christian teachers should be able to practice their faith in their instruction in the schools.

Paralleling the news coverage, the editorial page set the issues out early. Rob Swenson, the editorial page editor, wrote a month before the election, "Voters will determine whether the board stays the present course or turns further to the right." In a final editorial before the vote, Swenson wrote that voters faced a choice between "ideologues of the radical, religious-tinged right" and the incumbents, described as "moderates" who would join with a liberal member to form a majority of three on the five-member board. The other two incumbents were described as having "reactionary views on issues such as patriotism and sex."

Olson's story of the election results begins:

> Sioux Falls voters decided Tuesday to stick with incumbents just one year after they supported a new direction for the school board.
>
> The incumbents won by a vote of almost two to one.

Board of Education Meetings

School board meetings are often political battlegrounds on which important issues are fought out. The well-prepared reporter is able to provide depth coverage of these issues. The reporter is aware of the positions of the key players on some of the important matters that have come before the board and has kept track of developing issues. Here is a guide to covering board meetings.

Meetings Checklist

— Actions taken.

— How each member voted. If no formal vote but an informal consensus, get nods of heads or any other signs of approval or disapproval. Ask if uncertain.

— Size and makeup of audience.

— Reaction of audience to proposal(s).

— Position of groups or organizations with a position on issue. (Obtain beforehand, if possible.)

— Arguments on all sides.

— Statements from those for and against proposal on what decision of board means.

New Educational Programs

Many meetings of school boards are concerned with new programs. Here is a checklist of items for the reporter:

Checklist

— Source of idea.

— Superiority to present program as claimed by sponsors.

— Cost and source of funding program.

— Basic philosophy or idea of program.

— Other places it has been tried and results there. (Make independent check of this, if possible. How well is it working there? What is cost?)

— Whether it has been tried before and discarded.

— How does it fit in with what system is doing now? How it fits with trends in area, state, nation.

— If someone is suggested to head it, who?

— Arguments pro and con, naming those involved.

Knowing the Community

In this chapter, we have looked at how local government works, the role of money in the community, politics and education. There's much more to covering a community, of course, and the following 20 questions touch on some of these areas of community life the reporter should know about. The list was compiled by Gloria Brown Anderson, executive editor of *The New York Times* news service:

1. How is your community different from others in your state? How did it come to be established where it is?

2. Who are the major employers? What's the unemployment rate?

3. What are the most popular entertainment activities? What single event in the past year drew the biggest crowd?

4. What are the major institutional assets (museums, colleges, tourist attractions, sports teams, etc)?

5. Who are the town characters? Who's the most powerful person in town (politics, business, sports, education, etc)?

6. Who are your experts and what are their fields of expertise?

7. What's the dominant religion/philosophy? How are people treated who are not part of it?

8. What's driving the economy? (May not be the same as dominant employers.)

9. What are the major social problems?

10. Who are the most creative people in town (business, the arts, education, social scene, etc.)?

11. How many people move into your community every week? How many people leave? Why are they coming and going?

12. What's been the biggest change in the nature of the community in the past 10 years?

13. What's the high school dropout rate? Do most high school students go to college?

14. What legends or true stories do old-timers tell and retell?

15. How old is the oldest business and what is it?

16. What famous/accomplished people have roots in the community?

17. What kinds of books have been your community's best-sellers over the past five years?

18. What are the most popular TV shows? How many people have cable?

19. What happens in your community that has a significant impact on people elsewhere?

20. What's the demographic profile of your town? How does it compare with nearby communities?

Further Reading

Adrian, C. R., and C. Press. *Governing Urban America,* 5th ed. New York: McGraw-Hill, 1977.

Cremin, Lawrence A. *Transformation of the School: Progressivism in American Education.* New York: Random House, 1964.

French, Thomas. *South of Heaven: Welcome to High School at the End of the Twentieth Century.* New York: Doubleday, 1993.

Hewlett, Sylvia Ann. *When the Bough Breaks: The Cost of Neglecting Our Children.* New York: Basic Books, 1991.

Kidder, Tracy. *Among Schoolchildren.* Boston: Houghton Mifflin, 1989.

Rathbone, Cristina. *On the Outside Looking In.* Boston: Atlantic Monthly Press, 1998. (The author spent a year in a high school for rejects.)

Sayre, Wallace S., and Herbert Kaufman. *Governing New York City.* New York: Norton, 1965.

Shefter, Martin. *Political Crisis/Fiscal Crisis: The Collapse and Revival of New York City.* New York: Basic Books, 1985.

Wildavsky, Aaron. *The Politics of the Budgetary Process,* 2nd ed. Boston: Little, Brown, 1974.

Part Six: Introduction

The final three chapters concern general guidelines for the journalist. As in most of journalism, there are few absolutes in these areas, and even those we tend to think of as unchanging do shift in time. Take libel law: Before 1964, libel was state law and wire service journalists had to exercise special care, for what was acceptable in one state could be the basis of a lawsuit in another. But with the Supreme Court decision in *The New York Times v. Sullivan* everything changed. In Chapter 25, we will examine the wide latitude this decision has given journalists.

Perhaps the greatest changes have occurred in the area of taste, where once journalists were hemmed in by a long list of taboos and agreed-upon prohibitions. In this Age of Candor, little seems off-limits, as we shall see in Chapter 26.

The last chapter, 27, takes us to the area of ethics, and here, too, journalism has changed. Once-acceptable practices are now considered unethical, such as racial and religious identifications.

The areas overlap, as the photo of a family's grief on page 685 illustrates. It was legal for the photographer to snap this public scene at a California beach. But is it so wrenching that it approaches bad taste to spread the photo across the page of a newspaper? Another question: Is it an invasion of this family's privacy to show them grieving moments after the child's body was recovered? This is a matter of ethics, the morality of journalism. The newspaper apologized later, but the photographer said use of the photo was a public service in that it shows what can happen when water safety rules are not observed.

25 Reporters and the Law

Stuart Noble,
The Stuart (Fla.) *News*

**Embarrassing, humiliating? Yes.
Libelous? No.**

Preview

The laws of libel and privacy limit what reporters may write. Stories that damage a person's reputation can be libelous, unless the material is privileged or can be proved to be true. Stories about an individual's personal life can invade the person's right to privacy.

• **Libel:** Most libelous stories are the result of careless reporting. Material that might injure someone is double-checked. The courts have made it more difficult for public figures or public officials to prove libel; but recent court decisions have limited these exceptions.

• **Privacy:** The right to privacy is protected by law. The personal activities of an individual can be reported if the material is about a newsworthy person and is not highly offensive.

One of the most dangerous areas for the journalist is libel. To the beginner, the region of libel is a land of mystery in which all the guideposts read, "Don't." To the experienced reporter, danger of libel is a cautionary presence in the newsroom.

Libel is published defamation of character. It is writing or pictures that:

• Expose a person to hatred, shame, disgrace, contempt or ridicule.
• Injure a person's reputation or cause the person to be shunned or avoided.
• Injure the person in his or her occupation.

Of course, many articles and pictures do libel individuals. In most cases, the defamatory material may be safe for publication if it is *privileged*. By privileged, we mean that the article is a fair and accurate report of a judicial, legislative or other public official proceeding or of anything said in the course of such sessions, trials or proceedings. The contents of most public records are privileged. Those who made our laws recognized that open debate of serious issues would be impeded unless the public had full access to official actions.

Another defense against libel is *truth*. No matter how serious the defamation may be, if the statement can be proved to be true and to have been made without malice, the defamed individual cannot successfully bring legal action.

A third defense, *fair comment and criticism,* most often involves editorial writers and reviewers. As long as the comment or criticism is directed at the work and not at the individual, the writing is safe.

In summary, the libel laws hold that a reporter is not in danger if the material is from a privileged proceeding (public *and* official) or if the material is substantially accurate or constitutes fair comment.

For broadcast journalists, defamatory statements made from a prepared script fall under libel, whereas extemporaneous defamatory remarks are treated as *slander,* which can be defined as oral or uttered defamation.

Grounds for Libel Suits

Matter that might be held libelous by a court would have to:

1. Imply commission of a crime.
2. Tend to injure a person in his or her profession or job.
3. Imply a person has a disease, usually a loathsome disease that might lead to the individual's ostracism.
4. Damage a person's credit.
5. Imply unchaste behavior.
6. Indicate a lack of mental capacity.
7. Incite public ridicule or contempt.

For years, libel was a great weight on the shoulders of the press, particularly for newspapers that handled controversy and emphasized investigative reporting. The press associations had special concerns, for libel law was state law and was beyond the protection of the Constitution. What was legal in one state might have been libelous in another.

In effect, libel laws restrained the press, as the Supreme Court recognized in an epochal decision in 1964 that was to lighten the burden on the press. The court ruled that defamatory statements could have First Amendment protection. Our seven danger points are still to be watched, but the press now has much stronger defenses, thanks to the Supreme Court. To understand that decision—and to understand the organic nature of the law—we must travel back in time to Montgomery, Ala.

An Incident on a Bus

When Rosa Parks boarded the Cleveland Avenue bus in December 1955, she spotted an empty seat just behind the section reserved for whites. Tired from a day's work in a downtown department store, she eased into the space, only to be ordered to move. Seats were for white passengers only.

Mrs. Parks, a quiet, reserved woman, refused to give up her seat. She was taken off the bus and arrested. That weekend, plans were made by the black community to boycott Montgomery's buses.

Martin Luther King Jr., a black minister who helped plan the boycott, recalled how he awoke early Monday morning to see whether Montgomery's black residents would heed the word that it was better to walk in dignity than to ride in shame. The bus line that passed by the King home carried more blacks than any other line in the city. The first bus went by at 6 a.m. It was empty. Another, 15 minutes later, was empty, too.

That was the beginning of the boycott. Some 42,000 Montgomery blacks said they would walk to and from work or use volunteer vehicles and black-owned taxis until the bus system altered its seating arrangements and hired black drivers for buses along the predominantly black routes.

For 381 days, they stayed off the buses rather than be told to move to the back. Many people went to jail for violating the state's anti-boycott laws, including Mrs. Parks asnd Dr. King. Finally, the Supreme Court ruled bus segregation illegal.

Tension Mounts

Tensions mounted. In 1963, Medgar Evers, a black civil rights worker, was murdered in the doorway of his home in Jackson, Miss. The following year, three young civil rights workers were murdered in Philadelphia, Miss.

Newspapers and television stations sent waves of reporters to the South to report the conflict. Viewers saw fire hoses, police dogs and cattle prods used on blacks in Birmingham, and they saw the clubs of state troopers in Selma. The press reported the cry of blacks for an end to humiliation, economic exploitation, segregation in schools and discrimination at the polls.

It was also obvious the South was hardly budging. The border areas, portions of Tennessee and Kentucky and metropolitan communities such as Atlanta and Richmond accommodated. But not the towns and parishes of the Black Belt—Selma, Plaquemines, Yazoo City. Here, nonviolence met intractable resistance. Blacks might wait patiently outside the courthouse in Selma to register to vote. But the doors would stay closed to them, unless they were broken down by the federal government and the courts.

Press Coverage Increases

Because of the intensive coverage in the press, a consensus was developing outside the Black Belt. Most of the nation saw the anguish of the blacks who were hurling themselves against the wall of segregation, and some believed the nation was heading toward a race war.

In 1963, President Kennedy, aware of the developing conflict, declared that the struggle of blacks for civil rights was a "moral issue." Then four girls attending Sunday school in the black Sixteenth Street Baptist Church in Birmingham died in a bomb blast at the church.

The press stepped up its coverage. In some northern newspapers and on network television, the South was presented as a forbidding region of racism, its law officers openly defiant of the law, its white citizens unwilling to adjust to the changing times. Southerners were dismayed by the coverage, and some whites assaulted reporters covering civil rights demonstrations. The retaliation also took the form of suits against the press and television.

A Legal Club

Millions of dollars in damages were claimed by officials, who asserted they had been defamed by press and television. By 1964, libel suits seeking $300 million were pending against news organizations covering the racial story. One of the largest suits was brought against *The New York Times* by five officials in Alabama who contended that they had been inferentially damaged in an advertisement in the *Times* in 1960 that sought to raise funds for the civil rights movement. The advertisement, headlined "Heed Their Rising Voices," described the treatment of black schoolchildren by the Alabama police. The five officials brought suit for a total of $3 million.

The first case to be tried involved L. B. Sullivan, a Montgomery city commissioner responsible for the police department. The judge in the case ordered segregated seating in the courtroom, and after he praised the "white man's justice" that had been brought to the country by the "Anglo-Saxon race," the all-white jury heard testimony. The jurors, whose names and photographs were printed in the local press, were told that although Sullivan's name had not been mentioned in the advertisement, his reputation had been damaged by the erroneous statements about the police.

During the trial, it was evident that the advertisement contained errors. It stated that Montgomery students had been expelled from school after singing "My Country 'Tis of Thee" on the steps of the state capitol. Actually, they were expelled for a sit-in in the courthouse grill. The advertisement also said students had been locked out of their lunchroom to "starve them into submission," which was false.

The jury agreed that Sullivan had been libeled and awarded him $500,000 in compensatory and punitive damages from the *Times*.

In a headline over the story about the suits against the *Times,* a Montgomery newspaper seemed to reveal the motives behind the libel suits: "State Finds Formidable Legal Club to Swing at Out-of-State Press."

The Court Acts

It was in this atmosphere that the Supreme Court considered the appeal of the *Times* from the state court decision. The case of *The New York Times v. Sullivan* (376 US 254) in 1964 was to mark a major change in the libel laws. But more important, by granting the press wider latitude in covering and commenting on the actions of public officials, the decision gave the press greater freedom to present issues of public concern, like the racial conflict that was tearing the country apart.

The Supreme Court understood the unique nature of the appeal. The Court commented, "We are required for the first time in this case to determine the extent to which the Constitutional protections for speech and press limit a state's power to award damages in a libel action brought by a public official against the critics of his official conduct."

In its decision, the Supreme Court took from the states their power to award damages for libel "in actions brought by public officials against critics of their official conduct." The Constitutional protections for free speech and free press would be seriously limited by state actions of the kind the Alabama court took, the Court said.

Brennan's Opinion

Justice William J. Brennan wrote, "The Constitutional guarantees require, we think, a federal rule that prohibits a public official from recovering damages for a defamatory falsehood relating to his official conduct unless he proves that the statement was made with 'actual malice'—that is, with knowledge that it was false or with reckless disregard to whether it was false or not."

The Court apparently agreed with the argument of Herbert F. Wechsler, who wrote in a brief for the *Times,* "This is not a time—there never was a time—when it would serve the values enshrined in the Constitution to force the press to curtail its attention to the tensest issues that confront the country or to forgo the dissemination of its publications in the areas where tension is extreme."

Justice Brennan noted in his opinion that the Supreme Court had seen in the use of such legal concepts as "insurrection," "contempt," "breach of the peace," "obscenity" and "solicitation of legal business" attempts to suppress the open discussion of public issues. Now it was libel.

In the Sullivan libel case, the Court extended the First Amendment in order to accomplish a social-political purpose—the protection of dissident voices in a repressive atmosphere. The right to criticize government, Brennan wrote, is "the central meaning of the First Amendment."

The decision, establishing what became known as the Times Doctrine, noted that the "Constitutional safeguard was fashioned to assure unfettered interchange of ideas for the bringing about of political and social changes desired by the people." To accomplish this, there must be "maintenance of the opportunity for free political discussion to the end that government may be responsive to the will of the people and that changes may be obtained by lawful means, an opportunity essential to the security of the Republic. . . ."

"Erroneous statement is inevitable in free debate," Brennan said. Running through the decision is the belief that free discussion will lead to a peaceful settlement of issues. Free expression, he was saying, has social utility. The Court seemed to be addressing itself to the millions of Americans in trauma because of the racial conflict.

"Actual Malice"   In summary, the decision in the case makes it clear that, under the Constitution, no public official can recover damages for defamation in a newspaper article or "editorial advertisement" concerning his or her official conduct unless he or she can prove the article is defamatory and false and also show that:

1. The publication was made with the knowledge that it was false; or
2. The statement was made with reckless disregard of whether or not it was false.

Politic Action. The Sullivan case, like the school desegregation case 10 years before and the Nixon tapes decision 10 years later, reflected the need for a unanimous court decision in order to show the nation that certain issues were beyond debate.

The Sullivan decision supported a searching, vigorous and free press. *Brown v. Board of Education, Topeka,* said the 14th Amendment guaranteeing equal protection under the laws made school segregation unconstitutional.

The Watergate tape decision came at a time the president was under grave suspicion and a crisis of leadership threatened the nation.

"Throughout history," said an editorial writer for *The New York Times,* "the Court has been a vital factor on the political scene, even when trying to float majestically above it."

Items 1 and 2 constitute the Court's concept of "actual malice."

The decision is the law in every state and takes precedence over federal and state laws, state constitutions and all previous state and federal court decisions.

Extension and Contraction of Times Doctrine

In the decade following the enunciation of the Times Doctrine, the Court went beyond applying it to public officials and included public figures and then private individuals involved in matters of public concern.

In a significant case, a businessman lost a libel suit that involved a clear case of error by a radio station. A distributor of nudist magazines was arrested while delivering magazines to a newsstand. The Philadelphia, Pa., police reported the incident to a local radio station, which broadcast an item about the distributor's arrest on a charge of selling obscene materials. Further, the station stated that the magazines were obscene. In a subsequent trial, the distributor was acquitted. The distributor said he had been defamed by the radio station and sued. A jury awarded him general and punitive damages.

The radio newsman had violated one of the first rules a beginner learns: Never state as fact what is only charged and therefore subject to determination in the courts.

The reporter and his station were fortunate, however. The Court of Appeals reversed the lower court verdict, and in 1971 the Supreme Court upheld the reversal on the distributor's appeal (*Rosenbloom v. Metromedia, Inc.,* 403 US 29). The Court ruled:

> We thus hold that a libel action, as here by a private individual against a licensed radio station for a defamatory falsehood in a newscast relating to his involvement in an event of public or general concern may be sustained only upon clear and convincing proof that the defamatory falsehood was published with knowledge that it was false or with reckless disregard of whether it was false or not.
>
> Calculated falsehood, of course, falls outside the "fruitful exercise of the right of free speech."

Rosenbloom was neither a public official nor a public figure. But he was involved in an event of "public or general concern," and ordinary citizens so involved can successfully bring a libel action only by a showing of actual malice, the Court stated.

Rosenbloom might have been luckier had his troubles occurred later, for the Supreme Court in 1974 reversed directions and did so again in 1976 and 1979. These rulings made it possible for many more libel plaintiffs to collect damages for defamatory falsehoods because for private citizens the proof of defamation may be negligence or carelessness, not the more difficult actual malice public figures are required to prove.

Brennan on Rosenbloom

"We are aware that the press has, on occasion, grossly abused the freedom it is given by the Constitution. All must deplore such excesses. In an ideal world, the responsibility of the press would match the freedom and public trust given it. But from the earliest days of our history, this free society, dependent as it is for its survival on a vigorous free press, has tolerated some abuse."

Public or Private Figure?

In the 1974 case of *Gertz v. Robert Welch, Inc.* (418 US 323), the Supreme Court suddenly ceased the steady expansion of First Amendment protection to publications in libel actions. Elmer Gertz, a civil rights lawyer in Chicago, had been defamed by *American Opinion,* a monthly magazine published by the John Birch Society. The magazine described Gertz, who was representing a client in a case, as a "Communist-fronter" and said he had designed a national campaign to discredit the police. Although the trial judge had found no evidence the magazine had published recklessly, a jury awarded Gertz $50,000. The magazine appealed.

The Supreme Court ruled that as a private citizen "who had achieved no general fame or notoriety in the community" Gertz did not have to show "actual malice" but was entitled to damages if he could prove the material was false and defamatory and that it had been the result of negligence or carelessness by the publication. The Court returned to an emphasis on the plaintiff's status rather than the subject matter.

Courts Differ

Just where is the line that divides a public figure from a private figure? The Supreme Court has not clarified the point. Lower courts have differed.

The Washington Post escaped a libel judgment when a federal district court ruled a police informant was a public figure and had to prove actual malice. The *Post* had incorrectly stated the informant was a drug user. But three months later, a federal judge in Maryland ruled that a police informant was a private individual and thus need only prove that a Baltimore newspaper was careless in mistakenly stating he had broken into a lawyer's office to steal documents for the police.

Public Officials and Public Figures

Public officials: Government employees who have responsibility for governmental activities—elected officials, candidates for political office, appointed officials such as judges, police officers and some others engaged in the criminal justice system. The Supreme Court has said that not all public employees are public officials.

Public figures: People who have considerable power and influence and those who "voluntarily thrust" themselves into public controversy. Newspaper columnists, television personalities and some celebrities who seek to influence the public are included. But not all prominent people are covered.

In state courts, a Kansas judge ruled that a lawyer appointed to defend a penniless criminal defendant was a public official. Two months later, a Michigan judge said that an attorney appointed to represent an impoverished defendant was neither public figure nor public official.

In Virginia, a circuit court ruled that a high school English teacher was a public figure. The teacher had sued the *Richmond Times-Dispatch* for a story that criticized her teaching. She appealed and the state Supreme Court concluded she was not a public figure because she was in no position to influence or control "any public affairs or school policy." The newspaper appealed to the U.S. Supreme Court and lost. The teacher was awarded $100,000.

The Supreme Court may have clarified the status of police officers. In 1989, it ruled that an officer *The Danville* (Ill.) *Commercial News* had linked to a suspected burglary ring was a public official and would have to prove actual malice. A student newspaper at Cleveland State University profited from this decision when a suit in which a campus police officer sought $300,000 in damages was dismissed. The newspaper had stated in an editorial that the officer had a reputation for "excessive force, brutality and discrimination."

Caution: Events that are the subject of gossip or public curiosity and have no significant relation to public affairs usually do not confer on the persons involved in them the status of public figures. This means that no matter how public a person's marriage rift may be, that person is not necessarily a public figure.

If the reporter can prove that an event relates to public affairs or an important social issue, then the persons involved may be classified as public figures. For example, if a physician or a lawyer injects himself or herself into a controversy over a local bond issue, then the person has become a public figure for news about the bonds but not about his or her personal life.

Attributing a Libel Is No Defense

In a story about a development scheme in an area adjacent to the university, a student newspaper said that a member of the local planning board had received a "kickback" from the developer. (A kickback is an under-the-table payment for special treatment.) Asked whether he knew that such a charge is clearly libelous, the student replied, "But I attributed it."

His instructor could only shrug in exasperation. A reporter can be held liable if he or she repeats a libelous statement or quotes someone making such a statement unless the original material is privileged.

If the assertion had been made in court or at an official meeting, the statement—even if untrue—would be privileged and the privilege would be a defense against claims for damages, provided the report was fair and accurate.

Costly Attribution When the FBI zeroed in on a suspect in a deadly bombing at the Summer Olympics in Atlanta, the media identified the supposed bomber. Tom Brokaw on NBC said the investigators were close to "making the case" and that they "probably have enough to arrest him right now, probably enough to prosecute him, but you always want to have enough to convict him as well. There are still holes in the case."

Yes, there were holes in the case, holes so wide the FBI finally admitted it had spent two months investigating the wrong man, a security guard who had seen a suspicious backpack just before the explosion.

The *Atlanta Journal-Constitution* also used the FBI's identification: "Richard Jewell . . . fits the profile of the lone bomber."

When the media hunt was over, Jewell clearly had grounds for a libel suit. Rather than contest it, NBC settled for what was reported to be $500,000. The New York *Daily News* headlined the settlement story: BROKAW GOOFED AND NBC PAID.

The Atlanta newspaper said it will not settle, having acted in good faith by quoting official sources.

The moral of this tale: Make sure in criminal matters that charges have been filed or arrests made. What officials say they plan to do or will do or are doing—these are not libel proof.

Conditional and Absolute Privilege

The privilege to those participating in court cases and legislative sessions is an "absolute privilege," meaning the participants—the judge, lawyers, witnesses—cannot be held legally accountable even for malicious and deliberately false statements that are made within the scope of their participation in the proceedings. A newspaper or station, however, cannot use absolute privilege as a defense in libel suits. Their protection is known as "conditional" or "qualified privilege." The newspaper must present full, fair and accurate reports that are free of actual malice in order to be granted privilege.

A candidate for re-election to Congress who says of his opponent, "That man is a swindler" on the floor of the House of Representatives can make the statement with impunity, and a reporter can publish the accusation. (Obviously, the reporter would also carry the accused's reply.) But should the congressman make the charge in a political rally and the reporter's newspaper print the allegation, both are in trouble, unless the reporter can prove the man is indeed a swindler, and this would require proof of the man's conviction on that charge.

Warning: These protections do not cover proceedings, meetings, or activities that are private in nature. They also do not cover records that are sealed by law or court order.

Time Copy

The Supreme Court has been generous to reporters who make mistakes under pressure of deadline. But reporters who have time to check material may not fare so well under the Court's distinction between "hot news" and "time copy." The differences were spelled out in two companion cases decided in 1967, *Curtis Publishing Co. v. Butts* and *Associated Press v. Walker* (both 388 US 130), involving public figures.

Edwin Walker was a former Army general who had become involved in the civil rights disputes in the South and had taken a position against desegregation. He was on the campus of the University of Mississippi in September 1962 when it erupted over the enrollment of James Meredith, a black student.

The AP moved a story that Walker had taken command of a violent crowd and had personally led a charge against federal marshals on the campus. The AP said Walker had encouraged rioters to use violence and had instructed white students how to combat the effects of tear gas. He sued for $800,000 in damages. Walker testified that he had counseled restraint and peaceful protest and had not charged the marshals. The jury believed his account and awarded him the sum he sought. The trial judge cut out the $300,000 in punitive damages because he found no actual malice in the AP account.

Wally Butts was the athletic director of the University of Georgia in 1962. He was employed by the Georgia Athletic Association, a private corporation, and so, like Walker, he was a private citizen when, according to *The Saturday Evening Post,* he conspired to fix a football game between Georgia and Alabama in 1962. An article in the magazine said an Atlanta insurance salesman had overheard a conversation between Butts and Bear Bryant, coach of the Alabama football team, in which Butts outlined Georgia's offensive strategy in the coming game and advised Bryant about defending against the plays.

Butts sued for $5 million in compensatory damages and $5 million in punitive damages. The jury awarded him $60,000 on the first charge and $3 million on the second, which was subsequently reduced to $460,000.

The Curtis Publishing Co., publishers of *The Saturday Evening Post,* and the AP appealed to the Supreme Court. Butts won his appeal, but Walker lost. The Court ruled that the evidence showed that the Butts story was not "hot news," but that the Walker story was. The *Post*'s editors, the Court stated, "recognized the need for a thorough investigation of the serious charges" but failed to make the investigation.

In the Walker case, the Court noted, "In contrast to the Butts article, the dispatch which concerns us in *Walker* was news which required immediate dissemination. . . . Considering the necessity for rapid dissemination, nothing in this series of events gives the slightest hint of a severe departure from publishing standards. We therefore conclude that Walker should not be entitled to damages from the Associated Press."

All Speech Not Equal

In a decision that worried some journalists, the Supreme Court in 1985 ruled that punitive damages can be awarded without the plaintiff's proving actual malice if the libelous material is not a matter of "public concern." The case, decided in 1985 by a vote of five to four, arose from an erroneous credit report by Dun & Bradstreet about a firm, Greenmoss Builders. The court let stand a $300,000 award for punitive damages.

"We have long recognized that not all speech is of equal First Amendment importance," wrote Justice Lewis E. Powell in his opinion. "It is speech on 'mat-

Punitive Damages. "Money a court awards to an individual who has been harmed in a malicious or willful way. The amount is not related to the actual cost of the injury or harm suffered. Its purpose is to keep that sort of act from happening again. Punitive damages serve as a deterrent."

ters of public concern' that is 'at the heart of the First Amendment's protection.' . . . Speech on matters of purely private concern is of less First Amendment concern."

The court did not define "public concern," and this worried journalists and their lawyers, who were also concerned by the Court's decision not to apply what is known as the Gertz rule, which prohibits the award of punitive damages when there is no showing of actual malice. The court said the Gertz rule does not apply on matters of nonpublic concern.

Accuracy the Best Route

Most libel cases originate in a reporter's error. The lesson is clear: Follow Joseph Pulitzer's three rules for journalism, "Accuracy, accuracy, accuracy," or risk trouble.

Well, you might say, look at how many cases were won despite the mistakes. True, but in most of these cases the legal costs were ferocious. It can cost up to a million dollars for the average case, and *Time* estimated that had it not won its case against the Scientology organization, its legal fees might have amounted to $10 to $15 million.

When ABC decided to settle a libel suit brought by Philip Morris, *The Washington Post* media critic described the settlement as a "clear black eye" for ABC because its material about the tobacco company probably would have stood up in the ensuing legal battle. But a member of *The New York Times* legal staff said, "ABC's legal costs were approaching $1 million a month. Even if it had won the case, the cost of defending itself would have been ruinous."

Journalists who cost their employers libel-suit money—either in the huge awards juries are now making or in legal fees—are not popular people. On the other hand, the better media organizations will defend their reporters with a reputation for accuracy, even at considerable cost.

Libel Online

The U.S. Supreme Court has given the Internet the same First Amendment protection as the print media, but the laws are being written about where responsibility lies for libel.

Matt Drudge, the Internet tipster-gossip who puts out The Drudge Report, carried an item that the communications adviser to President Clinton had beaten his wife. His sources were identified as "top GOP operatives" who told Drudge "there are court records" to prove their charge. Drudge did not produce the records, and the adviser sued.

Drudge retracted, saying he had been used "to broadcast dirty laundry. I think I've been had."

Who is liable? Not the carrier, AOL. Online service providers were immunized from libel suits in the Internet Decency statute. But Drudge is not exempt.

Expensive. The threat of a libel suit can be intimidating because of the cost involved in fighting such a suit. The *St. Petersburg Times* spent $500,000 defending itself against a suit by a former sheriff and his deputy. The jury took less than three hours to find the articles were true and thus not libelous.

Jury awards for libel in the 1980s averaged $500,000. In the 1990s, they averaged $3 million. Much of the increase resulted from large punitive awards to plaintiffs.

Next, to another cautionary area, that of privacy, an area that is increasingly troublesome to journalists because of the public's anger at the media for what it considers media intrusiveness.

Privacy

Whereas truth is the strongest defense against libel, it is the basis of invasion of privacy suits. Invasion of privacy is said to occur when an individual is exposed to public view and suffers mental distress as a consequence of the publicity. Unlike defamation, which has deep roots in the common law, the right to privacy is a fairly new legal development and one in which there is less certainty for the reporter than in the area of libel.

A balance must be struck by the courts between the public's right to know—a right commonly accepted though not in the Constitution—and the individual's right to privacy.

Three categories of privacy concern the reporter:

1. Publicity that places a person in a false light in the public eye. The Times Doctrine applies, provided the matter is of public interest.
2. Public disclosure of embarrassing private facts about an individual. If the facts are in an official document, they can be published, but not if they are private acts of no legitimate concern to the public.
3. Intrusion by the journalist into a private area for a story or a picture without permission—eavesdropping or trespassing. The use of electronic devices to invade a home or office is illegal. Newsworthiness is not a defense.

The Test: Newsworthiness

Except for intrusion, the newsworthiness of the event is a defense against invasion of privacy suits. A public event cannot have privacy grafted on it at the behest of the participants. However, the reporter cannot invade a person's home or office to seek out news and make public what is private. Nor can he or she misrepresent the purpose of reporting to gain access to home or office. There is no prohibition against following and watching a person in a public place, but the reporter cannot harass an individual.

Although the law of libel and the right of privacy are closely related, they involve distinctive legal principles and are fundamentally different. Libel law is designed to protect a person's character and reputation. The right of privacy protects a person's peace of mind, feelings, spirits and sensibilities. Generally, privacy guarantees an individual freedom from the unwarranted and unauthorized public exposure of the person or his or her affairs in which the public has no legitimate interest.

The right of privacy is the right of a person to be let alone unless he or she waives or relinquishes that right. Certain people, defined by the federal courts as "newsworthy," lose their right to privacy, but the material published about them cannot be "highly offensive."

In making rulings on the claim of invasion of privacy, the Supreme Court has applied the Times Doctrine. That is, even if the claimant could prove that the report was false, if it were a matter of public interest, the person bringing the action would have to show the error was made "with knowledge of its falsity or in reckless disregard of the truth."

"Calculated Falsehoods"

In one case, decided in 1974 by the Supreme Court, such disregard of the truth was proved by a claimant. The Court in *Cantrell v. Forest City Publishing Co.* (419 US 245) upheld an award against *The Plain Dealer* in Cleveland on the ground that a reporter's story about a visit to the home of the claimant "contained significant misrepresentations." Although the woman was not at home when the reporter visited, the article said she "will talk neither about what happened nor about how they were doing. . . ." He wrote that the widow "wears the same mask of nonexpression she wore at the funeral." A lower court jury awarded her $60,000 to compensate for the mental distress and shame the article caused. An appeals court reversed the verdict, and the woman appealed to the Supreme Court, which found the reporter's statements implying that the woman had been interviewed were "calculated falsehoods."

Rape Victims The decision was eight to one. Some months later in another eight to one decision, the Supreme Court ruled on the second category involving privacy—the rights of private individuals to keep their personal affairs from public disclosure. In this case, the Court nullified a Georgia law that made it a misdemeanor to print or broadcast the name of a rape victim. The case involved the father of a young woman who had been raped and killed by a gang of teen-age boys. An Atlanta television station had used the victim's name, and the state court had ruled in favor of the father under the state law. The station appealed.

In setting aside the Georgia law, the Supreme Court stated that "once true information is disclosed in public court documents open to public inspection, the press cannot be sanctioned for publishing it." The Court stated (in *Cox Broadcasting Corp. v. Martin Cohn,* 420 US 469):

> The commission of crimes, prosecutions resulting therefrom, and judicial proceedings arising from the prosecutions are events of legitimate concern to the public and consequently fall within the press' responsibility to report the operations of government.

In both cases, the Supreme Court cautioned against broad interpretations of its rulings. Nevertheless, the first case clearly indicates that the press must take care in publishing material about individuals that is false, and the second indicates the Court will not extend the right of privacy to private persons involved in actions described in official documents.

Pictures. The picture was stark and it led to a suit for invasion of privacy. The photo in *Today* of Cocoa, Fla., showed a woman covered only by a towel as she fled from a house where her estranged husband had kept her hostage. A lower court jury awarded her $10,000 in damages, but the state Supreme Court upheld an appeals court decision that overturned the verdict. The appeals court said the law is clear "that when one becomes an actor in an occurrence of public interest, it is not an invasion of privacy to publish her photograph with an account of such occurrence. . . . The published photograph is more a depiction of grief, fright, emotional tension and flight than it is an appeal to other sensual appetites."

Privacy Guideline   Here is a useful guide from a federal appeals court ruling:

> A reporter or publication that gives publicity to the private life of a person is not subject to liability for unreasonable invasion of privacy if the material (1) is about a newsworthy person—who need not be an elected official or a celebrity— and (2) is not "highly offensive to a reasonable person, one of ordinary sensibilities and is of legitimate public concern."

Secret Taping

The courts are not sympathetic to the use of hidden electronic devices for newsgathering. When used, the courts have ruled, they can intrude on a person's right to privacy. In a 1998 decision, the California Supreme Court ruled that newspapers and television stations can be sued for intrusion if reporters or photographers are "unlawfully spying on them in the name of news gathering."

But the court pointed out that private individuals involved in a newsworthy event do not have the protection.

When *Life* had a reporter pose as someone needing help in the magazine's exposé of a man who claimed to heal people with herbs, clay and minerals, he sued. The reporter had a radio transmitter hidden in her pocketbook. Also, a photo was taken with a hidden camera.

In its defense, *Life* said investigative reporting would be difficult without such tactics. But the federal appeals court disagreed:

> We agree that newsgathering is an integral part of news dissemination. We strongly disagree, however, that the hidden mechanical contrivances are "indispensable tools" of newsgathering. Investigative reporting is an ancient art; its successful practice long antecedes the invention of miniature cameras and electronic devices. The First Amendment has never been construed to accord newsmen immunity from torts or crimes committed during the course of newsgathering. The First Amendment is not a license to trespass, to steal, or to intrude by electronic means into the precincts of another's home or office. . . .

Telephone Taping   Reporters routinely tape their telephone conversations with sources who are sensitive about being quoted accurately, and they tape when reporting sensitive issues. In most states, one-party consent (the reporter's) is all that is necessary. But in 10 states all parties involved must agree to the taping—California, Connecticut, Illinois, Maryland, Massachusetts, Montana, New Hampshire, Pennsylvania, South Dakota and Washington.

Monica Lewinsky's telephone conversations about her relationship with President Clinton were taped by her friend Linda Tripp, who lived in Maryland. Tripp did not inform Lewinsky she was being taped. A grand jury decided to look into the taping.

Food Lion   The ABC news magazine show "Primetime Live" infiltrated a supermarket with hidden cameras used by people the market chain had hired. The program charged that the store was selling old and tainted meat disguised to look fresh. Food Lion sued, and in his charge to the jury the judge told it to assume the story was correct but to consider Food Lion's allegation of fraud, trespass and breach of loyalty. The jury awarded Food Lion $5.5 million in punitive damages.

Public Angry   People, polls show, are not happy with such intrusions. A poll conducted by the Scripps Howard News Service and the E. W. Scripps School of Journalism at Ohio University asked: How often do you think newspapers and television news programs violate the privacy rights of private citizens who are not celebrities?

The responses:

Often—33 percent

Sometimes—45 percent

Rarely—13 percent

Never—4 percent

Don't Know—5 percent

Another question: Should journalists be subject to criminal prosecution and even prison if they violate a person's privacy?

The responses are startling:

Yes—56 percent

No—27 percent

The Ethical Factor   There is an ethical as well as a legal aspect to privacy, which the polls hint at in reflecting the aversion the public has to the media's probing into the personal.

This repulsion was evident in the reaction to the lengthy videotape of President Clinton's grand jury testimony about his affair with Monica Lewinsky. In a CNN poll, 55 percent said they would not watch, and 15 percent said they would look only at what the news programs considered the important segments.

Clearly, many people see the media's interest in private lives as prying, feasting on the distasteful, even immoral.

Avoiding the Dangers

The guide in libel and invasion of privacy suits seems fairly clear. Caution is necessary when the following are *not* involved—public officials, public figures, public events. When a private individual is drawn into the news, the news report must be full, fair and accurate. Of course, no journalist relies on the law for loopholes. He or she is always fair and accurate in coverage.

Libel suits usually result from:

- Carelessness.
- Exaggerated or enthusiastic writing.
- Opinions not based on facts.
- Statements of officials or informants made outside a privileged situation.
  - Inadequate verification.
  - Failure to check with the subject of the defamation.

When a libel has been committed, a retraction should be published. Although a retraction is not a defense, it serves to lessen damages and may deprive the plaintiff of punitive damages.

Rush + Inference = Libel Troubles

Most libel suits result from a reporter's rush to publish or broadcast the story. The usual care is not exercised in the speed-up. When the *New York Post* reported that Whitney Houston had been hospitalized in Miami after overdosing on diet pills, a $60 million libel suit was filed. The reporters handling the story would have learned it was a hoax had they called the hospital, which had no record of the singer's admission or treatment. The newspaper retracted the story the next day.

Libel suits also result from one of our old enemies—the inference, or jumping from the known to the unknown. A copy editor for an Indiana newspaper wrote this headline over the story of the closing of a restaurant: "Health board shuts doors at Bandido's; Investigators find rats, bugs at north-side eatery." The restaurant owner sued, contending the investigators did not find rats in his eatery. The copy editor testified in the trial: "When I saw the word 'rodent' or 'rodent droppings,' that said rats to me."

The jury awarded the restaurant owner $985,000.

The Reporter's Rights

The press carries a heavy burden. It has taken on the task of gathering and publishing the news, interpreting and commenting on the news and acting as watchdog in the public interest over wide areas of public concern. The burden of the press has been lightened by the foresight of the Founding Fathers through the guarantee in the First Amendment of the Constitution that Congress shall make no law abridging freedom of speech or of the press. This means that the press has the right to publish what it finds without prior restraint.

To journalists, it also means that they have the freedom to gather and prepare news and that the processes involved in these activities are shielded from a prying government and others. Also, journalists understood that their sources, their notes, their thoughts and their discussions with sources and their editors were protected.

Wide Protection

They had good reason to believe all this. State legislatures and the courts interpreted the concept of press freedom to cover these wide areas of newsgathering and publication. In 1896, for example, the state of Maryland passed a law allowing reporters to conceal their sources from the courts and from other officials. The concern of the public traditionally has been that the press be free and strong enough to counterpose a powerful executive. This sensitivity to central government began with the revolution against the British Crown. It was reinforced by the generations of immigrants who fled czars, kings, dictators and tyrants.

Old as the story of the abuse of power may be, and as frequent as the exposures of its ruinous consequences have been by the press, the dangers implicit in centralized government are always present. This tendency of government to excessive use of its power was foreseen by the American revolutionaries who sought to make in the press a Fourth Estate outside government control and free to check on government.

But Not Absolute

There is, however, no clear-cut constitutional statement giving the press the privileges it came to consider immutable. Absolute freedom of the press has never been endorsed by a majority of the Supreme Court, but the federal courts usually have been sympathetic to the rights of the press. However, in the 1970s following Watergate, as the press started to dig and check with growing tenacity, a former ally in its battles with governmental power—the judiciary—began to render decisions the press found to be increasingly restricting. Many of these decisions—particularly those of the Supreme Court—convinced the press that its assumptions about its privileges were false. The press, the courts ruled, has no greater rights than any citizen of the land.

In its balancing of the public right to know against individual rights to privacy and the accused's rights to a fair trial, the courts denied the confidentiality of sources, the protection of unpublished material and the privacy of the editorial process. The courts gradually limited the press' access to information, and some newsgathering was specifically prohibited.

Newsgathering

There are, of course, still wide areas of newsgathering open to the press. Generally, the actions of official bodies are accessible to journalists. Judicial, legislative and executive activities can be freely covered—with some exceptions. A reporter has the right to cover a city council meeting, except for executive sessions. But the reporter has no legal right to sit in on a meeting of the board of the American Telephone & Telegraph Co., a private company.

Journalists have rights—along with all citizens—to vast areas of official activities. The Supreme Court has ruled (*Branzburg v. Hayes*) that the press has protection in some of its newsgathering activities. The Court stated that "without some protection for seeking out the news, freedom of the press would be eviscerated."

But the Court also ruled in *Branzburg* that a reporter cannot protect information a grand jury seeks, and that grand jury proceedings are closed to the press. When *The Fresno Bee* published material from a grand jury inquiry and its staff members refused to tell the court how they had obtained the information, they were sent to jail for contempt of court.

Executive sessions of public bodies may be closed to the press, but the reason for holding closed-door sessions must not be trivial. Usually, state laws define what constitutes an executive session. Reporters are free to dig up material discussed at these closed meetings.

Material of a confidential and personal nature held by such agencies as health and welfare departments is not available to the press. A reporter has no legal right to learn whether a certain high school student was treated for gonorrhea by a public health clinic. But the reporter is entitled to data on how many were treated last month or last year and at what cost, how many people the clinic has on its staff and so on. Nor are there prohibitions against a reporter interviewing a clinic user who is willing to talk about his or her treatment, just as a person who appears before a grand jury may tell reporters about the testimony he or she gave to the jury.

Free Press—Fair Trial

Judges contend that some news can prejudice jurors and thus compromise a defendant's Sixth Amendment "right to an impartial jury," making a fair trial impossible. Criminal convictions have been set aside because of such publicity.

Judges do have ways to protect the defendant from damaging publicity that would compromise the defendant's right to a fair trial. In *Nebraska Press Association v. Stuart* (427 US 539), the Supreme Court discussed changing the location of the trial, adjourning the trial until pretrial publicity that may be prejudicial has dissipated, careful questioning of jurors during the voir dire (jury impaneling), sequestering the jury and other strategies.

Confidentiality Requires Protection

Many attacks on the press in the courts have concerned confidentiality. The courts have been determined to seek out the sources of information to assist law enforcement officers and defendants. The press has been equally determined to honor its promise of confidentiality to sources.

A Boston television reporter was sentenced to three months in jail for contempt of court for refusing to identify a source who told her he saw police officers loot a pharmacy. A grand jury was looking into the matter and a prosecutor told the judge his office was stymied without the testimony of the witness.

Journalists traditionally have honored the request for confidentiality, sometimes at a heavy price. In 17th-century England, a printer, John Twyn, refused to give the Star Chamber the name of the author of a pamphlet about justice that Twyn had published. The Chamber called the pamphlet treasonous, and when Twyn would not speak, it passed the following sentence:

> (You will be) . . . drawn upon an hurdle to the place of execution; and there you shall be hanged by the neck, and being alive, shall be cut down, and your privy members shall be cut off, your entrails shall be taken out of your body, the same to be burnt before your eyes; your head to be cut off, your body to be divided into four quarters, and your head and quarters to be disposed of at the pleasure of the King's Majesty.

Shield Laws

One effect of the attack on confidentiality was the enactment of state shield laws, in effect in most states. These laws provide varying degrees of confidentiality for sources and materials.

Reporters contend that their notes—which may include the names of confidential sources as well as the reporters' own investigative work—should be treated as confidential. State shield laws grant the reporter this protection unless in a criminal case the defense can prove that the notes are relevant and that alternative sources of information have been exhausted.

Shield laws are important. When the highest state court rules on matters covered by the state constitution, the issue cannot be reviewed by the U.S. Supreme Court because the state court is the final authority on the meaning of the state's constitutional guarantees. Some state constitutions have even broader protections than the U.S. Constitution.

The shield law is a helpful successor to the sunshine law, which requires public bodies to meet in public unless there is a compelling reason for privacy.

Newspapers and broadcast stations contend that confidentiality is essential to freedom of the press. The press points out that the power of the government to punish people involved in unpopular causes led the courts to safeguard anonymity in many areas. The courts recognize the doctor-patient and lawyer-client relationship as generally beyond legal inquiry. Journalists have sought the same protection for their sources.

If the press is to be the watchdog of government, as the press believes the framers of the Constitution intended, then the press must be free to discover what public officials are doing, not limited to publishing what officials say they are doing. In order to ferret out the activities of public officials, insiders and informants are necessary. These informants usually must be promised anonymity. The courts, however, have not been sympathetic to reporters who seek to honor confidentiality in the face of court demands for disclosure.

Keep the Promise Once a reporter promises confidentiality, he or she must honor that pledge, the Supreme Court ruled in *Cohen v. Cowles Media* in a 1991 decision. St. Paul and Minneapolis newspapers promised a source that damaging information he gave them about a candidate would not carry his name.

After the newspapers decided to use the source's name, he was fired from his job. The source sued, and the court ruled that First Amendment protections do not prevent a newspaper from being held liable for violating a promise of confidentiality. The state law on an implied contract was violated, the court ruled.

Tips and Tidbits

Here is some useful advice taken from court decisions, laws and the experience of journalists:

Interviewing Jurors   Jurors are free to talk about their experiences once a trial ends. But contact with jurors while they are deliberating can lead to contempt-of-court charges.

The same general rule applies to those serving on grand juries. The laws affecting witnesses appearing before grand juries vary from state to state. Some allow witnesses to talk about their testimony, but others forbid it until the grand jury inquiry is over.

Taping   The courts have ruled that it is illegal to use a tape recorder secretly while posing as someone else. This is invasion of privacy through *intrusion*.

Don R. Pember of the University of Washington, author of a mass media law textbook, advises his students to turn on the tape recorder and to ask permission. Then the consent is recorded. Generally, he says, be "up-front with recorders."

Wire Service Defense   Newspapers that publish wire service stories with libelous material have been protected by the "wire service defense." This legal concept holds that if the newspaper was not aware of the defamatory material in the story, could not reasonably have been expected to detect such material and reprinted the material without substantial changes, then the publication will not be held liable, whether private or public figures are defamed by the article.

Altering Quotes   The U.S. Supreme Court has ruled that changing a quote does not necessarily constitute libel unless the change gives a different meaning than the source intended. The Court stated:

> If every alteration constituted the falsity required to prove actual malice, the practice of journalism, which the First Amendment standard is designed to protect, would require a radical change, one inconsistent with our precedents and First Amendment principles.

Press Disclosures Affect Freedoms

The press considers itself a critic not only of sacred cows, but also of sacred institutions. This disturbs those who want and need ideals and heroes, men and women to look up to, to be loyal to. Few individuals or institutions can stand up under the scrutiny to which the press subjects them.

The public reaction has been to resort to the ancient technique of blaming the messenger.

Tyrone Brown, a law clerk to Chief Justice Earl Warren in the 1960s, then general counsel for Post-Newsweek Broadcasting and later a member of the Federal Communications Commission, said the Court's rulings reflect attitudes toward the press.

"All those so-called absolute principles like the First Amendment are functions of the time when they're decided," Brown says. "The Justices' role is a process role—making accommodations between various power groups in the country at various times."

In several decisions affecting the press, some justices have suggested that the Times Doctrine be re-examined. They have asserted that subsequent rulings favorable to the press have permitted the press to abuse privacy and to be held exempt from responsibility for its coverage.

The courts have been more willing to close judicial proceedings and to gag those involved in civil and criminal trials. And countless officials are more reluctant to allow reporters access to public records and entrance to meetings.

"There is an attitude of too many public officials that the material they are caretakers for belongs to them and not to the public," said Paul K. McMasters, the deputy editorial director of *USA Today.*

Although every state and the District of Columbia have open records and open meetings laws, "many newspapers ranging in size from the smallest to the largest national dailies find themselves almost continually snarled in disputes over one of our most basic democratic rights: To find out what branches of the government and its agencies are doing," reported the American Society of Newspaper Editors.

Summing Up

- The police cannot arbitrarily deny a press pass to a reporter.
- Except for placing reasonable restrictions on access to events behind police lines, the police cannot interfere with a reporter engaged in newsgathering activities in public places.
- Reporters cannot be denied access to open meetings of legislative or executive bodies.
- The reporter can try to use state law to open certain hearings of public bodies that have been closed as "executive sessions." But there is no constitutional right to attend. Several states have adopted "sunshine laws" that require public agencies to have open meetings and open records.

- Reporters do not have a constitutional right to documents and reports not available to the general public. (The Supreme Court has equated the press' right to access with the right of access of the public.)
- Reporters cannot guarantee a source confidentiality, should be careful about what they print about the criminal past of defendants, may be required to surrender documents to a grand jury or testify before it, should be careful about assuring sources they are protected by a state shield law.

Further Reading

Cater, Douglass. *The Fourth Branch of Government.* New York: Vintage, 1959.

Chaffee, Zechariah Jr. *Free Speech in the United States.* Cambridge, Mass.: Harvard, 1948.

Denniston, Lyle. *The Reporter and the Law.* New York: Hastings House, 1980.

Hand, Learned. *Liberty.* Stamford, Conn.: Overbrook Press, 1941.

Lewis, Anthony. *Make No Law: The Sullivan Case and the First Amendment.* New York: Random House, 1992.

Oran, Daniel. *Law Dictionary for Non-Lawyers.* St. Paul, Minn.: West, 1975.

Pember, Don R. *Mass Media Law,* 11th ed. New York: McGraw Hill Companies, 1999.

Sanford, Bruce W. *Synopsis of the Law of Libel and the Right of Privacy.* New York: World Almanac Publications, 1984.

26 Taste—Defining the Appropriate

Tim Lovette,
Foster's Daily Democrat

Photos cause most complaints.

Preview

Material that is obscene, vulgar or profane can offend readers and listeners. But it also can be informative, and sometimes the reporter risks offending to move closer to the truth.

Decisions to use such material depend on:

• **Context:** If the event is significant and the material is essential to describing the event, offensive material may be used.

• **Nature of the audience:** A publication for adults or a special-interest group will contain material that a mass medium might not.

• **Prominence of those involved:** Public officials and public figures lead public lives. What would constitute prying into the life of a private individual may be necessary reporting of the activities of those in public life.

Two Cornell University astronomers had an idea for the Pioneer 10 spacecraft flight. For its journey beyond our solar system it would carry a drawing of a man and a woman as well as information about the planet Earth. Should the spacecraft then nuzzle down on some distant civilization the inhabitants could visualize what Earth man and woman look like.

The National Aeronautics and Space Administration accepted the suggestion, and when Pioneer 10 was launched, a gold-plated aluminum plaque engraved with a sketch of the Earth and its solar system and a drawing of a naked man and woman standing next to each other was aboard. NASA released the drawing to newspapers, thereupon confronting many editors with a dilemma. The picture was newsworthy, but would its publication be in bad taste?

The *Chicago Sun-Times* published the drawing in an early edition after an artist had removed the man's testicles. In a later edition, the rest of the genitals were erased. *The Philadelphia Inquirer* did even more brushwork: The male had no genitals and the nipples had been removed from the woman's breasts. The *Los Angeles Times* ran the drawing untouched. "Filth," a reader wrote in protest.

Now, less than 30 years later, the assertions of bad taste and the editors' anxieties seem as obsolete as the embarrassment that pregnant women once were made to feel in male-oriented society. (The word *confinement* to describe

Changing Times

When this drawing, which was carried on the first human-made object to leave the solar system, was reproduced in the *Los Angeles Times,* a reader complained that it was "filth," and many newspapers removed various parts of the bodies of the man and woman before running it. Twenty years later, newspapers were carrying stories about AIDS and condoms and running advertisements about birth control by the Planned Parenthood Federation of America.

Too Considerate. "If all printers were determined not to print anything till they were sure it would offend nobody, there would be very little printed."
—*Benjamin Franklin*

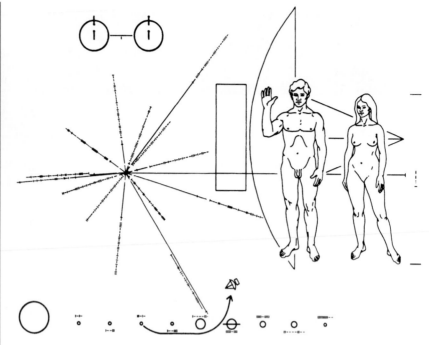

the term of pregnancy goes back to this period because pregnant women were kept at home to hide their supposed shame.) But no matter how liberated we may think ourselves, matters of taste still concern the reporter. The question is, where do we draw the lines?

Changing Guidelines

Clearly, the guidelines for avoiding the indecent and tasteless are changing. R.W. Apple, the Washington bureau chief of *The New York Times* recalls being told to stake out President Kennedy's hotel room during his overnight stay in New York. He said he watched "a well-known actress take the back elevator to his suite." Apple eagerly reported his find to the paper. "I was told to forget my 'scoop.' The *Times* was interested in visitors with affairs of state on their mind, not the other kind."

Today, the *Times* carries material like the following in a wedding story quoting the new bride:

> "We went to dinner and it was like
> we'd never been apart. He put me in a cab
> and kissed me good night, and I went
> home and told my boyfriend to move out."

From Falwell to Clinton   In 1981, when Sandra Day O'Connor was nominated to the Supreme Court, some conservative leaders questioned her conservative credentials. They thought she might be liberal on abortion and other social issues. Jerry Falwell, founder of the Moral Majority, told reporters that "every good Christian should be concerned" about the nomination.

To which Barry Goldwater, whose conservative credentials landed him the Republican Party's 1964 presidential nomination, replied, "Every good Christian should line up and kick Jerry Falwell's ass." A few newspapers printed Goldwater's remark. Most paraphrased it, and broadcast stations took a pass on the Arizona senator's remark.

But few media outlets avoided the explicit details that emerged in 1998 from the grand jury investigation of President Clinton's affair with Monica Lewinsky. There were references to oral sex and to Clinton's kissing Lewinsky's breasts. Newspapers printed explicit sexual details and four-letter words from the Starr report.

No one wants to offend readers or viewers. Nor—in the case of broadcast journalists—is there sense in offending the Federal Communications Commission, which has rules about obscenity, indecency and profanity. But how does a reporter or an editor decide when to risk giving offense in order to provide essential information? Just what is the "good taste" that journalists are supposed to exercise?

Freud on Language. "Anyone who considers sex as something mortifying and humiliating to human nature is at liberty to make use of the more genteel expressions 'Eros' and 'erotic.' I might have done so myself from the first and spared myself much opposition. But I did not want to, for I like to avoid concessions to faintheartedness. One can never tell where that road may lead; one gives way first in words, and then little by little in substance too. I cannot see any merit in being ashamed of sex. . . ."

—Sigmund Freud, Group Psychology and the Analysis of the Ego (1921)

Taste Is Relative

Taste is usually defined as a set of value judgments in behavior, manners, or the arts held in common by a group or class of people. Generally, these values help keep society stable and insulate it from sudden and possibly destructive change. Those who advocate strict controls on pornography, for example, argue that such material stimulates anti-social behavior.

The values that determine decisions about taste are not absolute. They change with time, place and context.

Time

The Washington Post tells its reporters that "society's concepts of taste and decency are constantly changing. A word offensive to the last generation can be part of the next generation's common vocabulary."

In 1939, people were scandalized when in the movie *Gone with the Wind*, Rhett Butler turned to Scarlett O'Hara and said, "Frankly, my dear, I don't give a damn." The word *rape* was taboo in many newspapers until the 1950s.

By the 1990s, movies, theater, books and magazines left little to the imagination. For those with exotic tastes, a $7 billion a year pornography industry catered to every conceivable fantasy, with not much legal interference. In time, journalism dropped many of its taboos, too.

Offensive Words The story that appeared in the April 18, 1966, issue of *The New York Times* about the Masters-Johnson study used sexually explicit words such as *vagina, vaginal lubrication, intravaginal diaphragms* and *orgasm*. As the story was being edited, a problem came up on the copy desk.

As the event is recounted by a *Times* copy editor, the desk noticed the frequent and explicit references to the female sex organ (six) and only euphemistic references (two) to the male organ—"genital organ" and "the organ." The question was referred to an assistant managing editor who served as the arbiter of language and taste at the *Times*. He decreed *vagina* for the woman and *organ* for the man as proper.

Two years later, the *Times* was more forthcoming in its use of explicit language. Reporting the changes *The Washington Post* and *Chicago Tribune* had made in a review appearing in their Sunday book review supplement, "Book World," the *Times* reported that the newspapers had called back a press run of the supplement to delete a section that "consisted of a paragraph containing reference to the penis in a discussion of the sexual behavior of primates."

Here is the paragraph that so offended the sensibilities of decision makers at the *Post* and *Tribune* that they called back a million copies of the press run at a cost of $100,000:

> Many a cocktail party this winter will
> be kept in motion by this provocative chit
> chat; man is the sexiest primate alive; the
> human male and not the gorilla possesses
> the largest penis of all primates. . . .

The *Post* and *Tribune* were clinging to the concept of the newspaper as family reading, although *Life* and *Newsweek* had used the word in their stories about the book, *The Naked Ape* by Desmond Morris, and although it was commonplace among millions of nursery school children who had been told to call a penis a penis.

Integration Battles In 1960, during a school integration demonstration in New Orleans, the AP quoted some of the women who were shouting at the leader of the school sit-ins: "Jew bastard, nigger lover." In answer to many protests that the use of such words was in bad taste, the AP said it "judged them essential to establishing the temper and the mood of the demonstrators."

Gradually, pertinence or significance was becoming the guideline in determining whether an obscenity or profanity should be included in news accounts.

Watergate Tapes A major turning point was reached during Watergate when the tapes of the White House conversations revealed a profusion of vulgarities and profanities. As the West Coast journalism review *feed/back* put it, the "Nixon administration made inoperative the detente that existed in the daily press against words once excised by editors."

The words *shit* and *fuck,* used in the White House, appeared in such papers as *The Washington Post,* the *St. Paul Pioneer Press,* the *Atlanta Journal,* the *Kansas City Star* and *The Seattle Times.*

It would have been impossible, many editors felt, to have changed the emphatic language of a statement by President Nixon from the key tape of March 22, 1973:

> I don't give a shit what happens. I want you all to stonewall it, let them plead
> the Fifth Amendment, cover up or anything else if it'll save the plan. That's the
> whole point.

The AP made a survey of newspapers using the Watergate material and found nearly a third of them printed all or nearly all of the obscenities without alteration. Slightly more than half sanitized the word *shit* or other words, and 15 percent of the papers completely edited out the vulgarities and profanities by paraphrase or deletion.

One of the newspapers that did not use Nixon's language was the Huntington (W. Va.) *Herald-Dispatch* and *Advertiser,* whose executive editor said, "In this very Fundamentalist market, we came to the conclusion that there was no reason to offend unnecessarily."

Hypocrisy Turning away from some kinds of reality while daily parading humanity's most obscene acts—murder, torture, terrorism—seems an act of hypocrisy to some editors. Another kind of hypocrisy—the discrepancy between private and public morality—is revealed by an incident involving television station WGBH in Boston. The station decided to do a program a few days after the 1968 student demonstrations on the Harvard campus. It invited people from the community to have their say. One of those who showed up took the microphone at the beginning of the program and shouted, "What I have to say is fuck Harvard and fuck Pusey [Harvard's president] and fuck everybody." David Ives, the president of the public TV station recalled, "I was upstairs, and you have never seen so many telephone calls. The most interesting thing about them was the quality of what they said.

"One woman said, 'I just want you to know that no language like that has ever been permitted in this house.' And in the background you could hear a man saying, 'You know God damn well it has.' Another protest came from a man who called and said, 'I'm just not going to have any of that kind of shit in my living room' "

Profanity-Obscenity In a story about the decline of classroom decorum, *The Chronicle of Higher Education* quoted a student's *goddamned* but used hyphens for another student's *shit* and *fuck.* The senior editor for copy explains:

> We try to keep all tasteless and offensive language out of the paper. However,
> we see the need for flexibility when specificity seems called for, as it did . . . we
> felt that there was no way around quoting at least a couple of examples of the
> offensive language of some students in the classroom.

Public Outrage, Private Delight. When it was discovered that Miss America was being displayed in the nude in *Penthouse* magazine (the photos had been taken before she won the title), the public was outraged and the pageant took away her crown. The issue with the photos sold 6 million copies, twice the magazine's normal circulation.

So we made a series of judgment calls, which are certainly subjective decisions. "Shit" is a word we are simply unwilling to publish, and so it got the hyphens. So is "fuck," in a subsequent passage. By comparison, "goddamned" seemed like a milder imprecation, and so we spelled it out.

The editor cites *The New York Times Manual of Style and Usage,* which advises "obscenity and offensive vulgarity . . . should not appear in the paper . . . but profanity in its milder forms can on some occasions be justified." (In its new stylebook, the *Times* warns that use of profanity "will enrage some readers.")

Disease and Disability

For reasons now difficult to understand, mentioning certain diseases and disabilities was considered poor taste in days past. It was considered improper to call attention to the fact that President Franklin D. Roosevelt used a wheelchair and that he could not stand unaided. No one wrote about his physical condition—the result of polio—and no one photographed FDR in ways that would reveal his disability.

When President Eisenhower had a heart attack in 1955, the press did follow that closely. But two years later when his wife underwent a hysterectomy reporters were satisfied with the explanation that she had undergone a "two-hour operation . . . similar to those many women undergo in middle age."

Gradually, good sense took over. When Betty Ford, wife of President Ford, underwent a mastectomy in 1977, the press reports were explicit.

But some frank language remained taboo longer.

AIDS

At first reluctant to use direct language and graphic descriptions, television, radio and newspapers finally faced the reality of AIDS reporting. They dropped the euphemism *safe sex* and spoke and wrote about *condoms.* They replaced vague allusions to *sexual practices* and used *anal* and *oral intercourse* in describing how the disease can be transmitted.

The New York Times, hardly an innovator among newspapers, ran a story in 1987 headlined, "Among Women, the Talk Is of Condoms." Here is an excerpt from the piece:

"I keep them with me," said Rebecca Pailes, a 25-year-old fashion designer. "I have them in my house. I won't have sex without them."

She uses a diaphragm also for birth control. "I use condoms," she said, "just to prevent disease."

"I don't trust anybody," said Judith, the 37-year-old owner of a small employment agency, who asked that her last name not be used. "I'm cynical about men. Nobody's worth the risk. Who knows who the people they've been with have been with? But I'm not going to give up sex."

Judith, who described herself as alternating between celibacy and promiscuity, keeps a drawerful of condoms in her kitchen.

"I give them to my friends who are celibate and say 'Here, now you can have sex,' " she said.

This was quite a change from the guarded coverage of the death from AIDS of the movie star Rock Hudson in 1985. Although many publications used the death to illustrate the danger of unsafe sex, only *Time* used the word *condom.*

Sexuality   The taboos against explicit reference to intercourse and other sexual activities were broken by news events that made it impossible to avoid the specifics. We've seen how the AIDS epidemic was one of these events. President Clinton's sexual liaisons were another. If journalism is the mirror held to life, then a journalism prohibited from chronicling important events in our lives offers a distorted image.

With the understanding that the media lagged in informing the public on such issues as sex education, venereal disease and how sex influences our behavior, journalists have come to report more fully the area of sex. Although cable TV, fiction, the movies and magazines flung off the fig leaf and discarded the asterisk and dash years ago, the networks and newspapers are slowly moving toward being more candid about sexuality.

The early breakthroughs came as the result of two studies of human sexual behavior. Alfred C. Kinsey's *Sexual Behavior in the Human Male,* was treated gingerly by the mass media when it was published in 1948. In 1966, another important work on sexual activity, *Human Sexual Response,* by Dr. William H. Masters and Virginia E. Johnson, was published. The result of a detailed 11-year study of sexual physiology, the work was too important to be ignored.

A related subject, homosexuality, was taboo for years until AIDS came on the scene and required frank discussion of one of its transmission routes. Given this opening and the increased activity of gay and lesbian groups, the opening was widened.

Gay Activities   Movies, even a TV sitcom, openly discussed single-sex relationships. Slowly, and despite complaints from some religious groups, newspapers are acknowledging gay and lesbian activities, public and personal. In 1993, *The Salina Journal* published the first gay or lesbian wedding announcement ever printed in a Kansas daily newspaper. The announcement was carried in a full-page story in the Lifestyles section under the headline "Out of the Closet."

The reaction: A handful wrote to support the newspaper. Most wrote that they were shocked and appalled, and 116 readers canceled subscriptions. But for the first time in anyone's recollection at the paper, the Sunday issue sold out.

The *Journal*'s editor, George Pyle, said, "Our editorial policy has always been in favor of equal rights. It would be kind of hypocritical to say that on the editorial page and then to say on the lifestyle pages that 'We're not going to include you.' "

In an editorial follow-up, Pyle recommended that Kansas legalize gay and lesbian marriages: "It's time for America to get out of this massive state of denial. They're queer. They're here. Get used to it."

Rape   Almost as incendiary in the area of taste is the subject of rape. Is it offensive to name the victim? Generally, newspapers do not print the names of

STD. The incidence of sexually transmitted diseases—chlamydia, gonorrhea and syphilis—is highest in Baltimore, Newark, St. Louis, New Orleans and Washington, D.C. STD, which is described as the pathway for infertility among women and AIDS among both sexes and children, receives little or no attention in the media, according to those in the health field.

women who allege that they have been raped, even when they testify at trials. Some reasons:

- The victim risks being blamed. Some people believe the victims want to be raped.
- Publication would stigmatize the woman.

When she was editor of *The Des Moines Register,* Geneva Overholser said that although her newspaper did not run the names of rape victims she favored their publication because it would help erase the stigma and focus attention on the crime which is one of "brutal violence" rather than a "crime of sex."

Rape, she said, is "an American shame. Our society needs to see that and to attend to it, not hide it or hush it up. As long as rape is deemed unspeakable—and is therefore not fully and honestly spoken of—the public outrage will be muted as well."

As we see, our guidelines for the line between the acceptable and the unacceptable have changed with the passage of time. As events of considerable magnitude affected society, journalists had to describe them, and to do so fully they had to loosen the bindings that the arbiters of good taste had placed on language and subject matter.

But the changes are not, have not been, absolute. Taste varies with place and context, our next subject.

Place and Context

We know that communities differ. Some are more easy-going, cosmopolitan, more accepting of the different, the unique, the unusual. Language inoffensive in a newspaper or on a station in San Francisco would be tasteless to many residents of Salt Lake City.

Taste also is a function of the context in which the material is used. A story in *Rolling Stone* would contain language and references abhorrent to a reader of *The Christian Science Monitor.* Here is a sidebar to an article by Karen Rothmyer in the *Columbia Journalism Review:*

Meeting Mr. Scaife

Richard Scaife rarely speaks to the press. After several unsuccessful efforts to obtain an interview, this reporter decided to make one last attempt in Boston, where Scaife was scheduled to attend the annual meeting of the First Boston Corporation.

Scaife, a company director, did not show up while the meeting was in progress. Reached eventually by telephone as he dined with the other directors at the exclusive Union Club, he hung up the moment he heard the caller's name. A few minutes later he appeared at the top of the Club steps. At the bottom of the stairs, the following exchange occurred:

"Mr. Scaife, could you explain why you give so much money to the New Right?"

"You fucking Communist cunt, get out of here."

Well. The rest of the five-minute interview was conducted at a rapid trot down

Park Street, during which Scaife tried to hail a taxi. Scaife volunteered two statements of opinion regarding his questioner's personal appearance—he said she was ugly and that her teeth were "terrible"—and also the comment that she was engaged in "hatchet journalism." His questioner thanked Scaife for his time.

"Don't look behind you." Scaife offered by way of a goodbye.

Not quite sure what this remark meant, the reporter suggested that if someone were approaching it was probably her mother, whom she had arranged to meet nearby. "She's ugly, too," Scaife said, and strode off.

The *Review*'s editors wanted to show its readers the full dimension of Scaife's personality. Because most of the readers are journalists, the editors knew this brief exchange would enlighten rather than offend them.

Reactions

The steady lifting of taboos has not gone unnoticed by those in society who describe themselves as having traditional values. They are convinced that a liberal approach to matters of taste is really a corruption of our value system, and their organizations pepper broadcast stations and publications with complaints.

Ignored at first as the grousing of a small segment of the public, the protests found widening support in the 1990s. So much support, that politicians—whose sensitivities to public sentiment are finely tuned—made "values" a political issue. They could tell a mood change was in the air. Violence in films, mayhem on television, rap lyrics that glorified killing the police and described women as whores . . . many people were beginning to wonder whether the media were going too far.

The Religious Right has led some of these counterstruggles on the battleground of decorum and taste, sometimes with the weapon of censorship, and this has alerted organizations like the American Civil Libertries Union. The ACLU has defended the publication of pornography as a First Amendment issue.

Obscenity and the Law

On matters of obscenity, indecency and profanity, *Miller v. California* in 1973 (413 US 15) is the standard for determining whether a printed work is obscene. The Court set state rather than national standards. It asserted, "Diversity is not to be strangled by the absolutism of imposed uniformity."

The test is whether the work, taken as a whole, (a) appeals to the prurient interest as decided by "an average person applying contemporary community standards," (b) depicts or describes in a patently offensive way sexual conduct specifically defined by the applicable state law, and (c) lacks to a reasonable person any serious literary, artistic, political or scientific value.

For the work to be ruled obscene, all three elements must be present.

The Four-Letter Word. In a case before the Supreme Court over a "particular four-letter word," Justice John Marshall Harlan wrote that although the word is "perhaps more distasteful than most others of its genre, it is nevertheless true that one man's vulgarity is another's lyric."

Although the courts have ruled that obscenity is not constitutionally protected, they have been reluctant to rule against printed material, even the pornographic publications that are sold at newsstands.

Limits on Broadcasting

The FCC is empowered to enforce federal statutes and the decisions of the courts in the areas of obscenity, indecency and profanity. The FCC can fine a station or revoke its license if it finds that it violated section 1464 of the federal Criminal Code, which provides for penalties for uttering "any obscene, indecent or profane language by means of radio communication." ("Radio" includes television.)

But even broadcasters and the FCC have changed with the times. In 1960, NBC censored the use of the initials *W.C.* on a nightly televised network talk program. *W.C.* stands for *water closet*, which in Britain means *toilet.* A dozen years later, the Public Broadcasting Service showed an "education entertainment" called the "V.D. Blues." There were no protests about the initials, and there were surprisingly few objections to some of the language in such songs as "Don't Give a Dose to the One You Love Most" and "Even Dr. Pepper Won't Help You," which was about the futility of douching as a contraceptive practice.

Although some stations made cuts, and stations in Arkansas and Mississippi did not carry the program, the majority of public broadcast stations decided that the program was a public service. When "V.D. Blues" was followed by a 2-1/2 hour hotline on a New York City station, 15,000 people called with questions about venereal disease. One of the city's V.D. clinics reported the next day that the number of persons seeking blood tests went up by a third.

The program obviously was aimed at teen-agers, whose venereal disease rate is epidemic. But stations must be aware of children in the audience, as the FCC and Congress have indicated.

The Case of the "Filthy Words"

In 1973, in a broadcast in the early afternoon over station WBAI (FM) in New York City, George Carlin gave a comedy monologue entitled "The Seven Words You Can't Say on Radio and Television." Carlin said his intent was to show that the language of ordinary people is not threatening or obscene. The station later said in its defense that the broadcast was in the tradition of satire. In the broadcasts Carlin had said:

> I was thinking one night about the words you couldn't say on the public
> airwaves . . . and it came down to seven but the list is open to amendment and in
> fact has been changed. . . . The original seven words were shit, piss, fuck, cunt,
> cocksucker, motherfucker and tits. . . .

He repeated the tabooed words several times in what he said later was a purposeful "verbal shock treatment."

FCC Rules. The FCC has stated that no words as such are indecent, but case studies show that the Commission has acted when there are *expletives,* as in the Carlin case, when *sexual innuendo* is clear and when sexual or excretory activities are described.

There was one complaint, and the FCC investigated. In 1975, it issued a declaratory order finding that the words were "patently offensive by contemporary community standards for the broadcast medium and are accordingly 'indecent' when broadcast by radio or television. These words were broadcast at a time when children were undoubtedly in the audience."

The station was not prosecuted. The finding, however, was made part of the station's file. In effect, the station was put on probation.

Limited Protection   The station appealed to the federal courts, and many stations and civil rights advocates joined the appeal against what was seen as a threat to freedom of expression. The case—which became known as the "Filthy Words Case"—reached the United States Supreme Court, and in 1978 in *FCC v. Pacifica,* the Court ruled five to four that radio and television stations do not have the constitutional right to broadcast indecent words. It said that the government has the right to forbid such words because of the broadcast medium's "uniquely pervasive presence in the lives of all Americans." The Court stated that "of all forms of communication, it is broadcasting that has received the most limited First Amendment protection."

The Supreme Court emphasized the limits of its ruling:

> It is appropriate, in conclusion, to emphasize the narrowness of our ruling. . . . The Commission's (FCC) decision rested entirely on a nuisance rationale under which context is all important. . . . The time of day was emphasized by the Commission. . . .

Since the court ruling, the FCC and Congress have tried to find the fine line between First Amendment freedom for broadcasters and regulation of what it considers indecent material. In 1987 it established a "safe harbor," the six hours between midnight and 6 a.m. when children ostensibly would be asleep and stations could broadcast so-called indecent programming.

Two years later, Congress imposed a 'round-the-clock ban on such material, but a federal Court of Appeals found the law unconstitutionally broad. In 1992, as a warning to commercial broadcasters, the FCC fined shock-jock Howard Stern $600,000 for broadcasting indecent material. But that did not stop him, nor his imitators. At last count, Infinity Broadcasting, Stern's boss, had paid $1.7 million. Much of the material broadcast today that is not considered indecent would have shocked the FCC a few years ago. The boundaries of taste are elastic.

Political Pressure

Fines and other pressures on broadcasters do not arise spontaneously. Like much else involving the government, FCC actions are touched by politics. During the 1980s and into the 1990s, pressures from the American Family Association, the Religious Roundtable and other religious and so-called family-values organizations led Congress to confirm FCC nominees who took a hard line in enforcing the rules against indecency.

Over the Line. "I think we've gone too damned far." —Chris Marrou, anchor for KENS-TV in San Antonio after the station's local newscast showed footage taken by a hidden camera of two men having oral sex in a park restroom. The segment from "Perverts in the Park" aired during the ratings sweep when viewership is measured.

Toward the end of the decade, with a less strict agenda, the FCC issued far fewer fines. Milagros Rivera-Sanchez and Michelle Ballard of the University of Florida tell the story of FCC enforcement in the Spring 1998 issue of *Journalism and Mass Communication Quarterly.*

Pictures

The page 1 color photograph of the dying racing bicyclist infuriated many readers of *The Sacramento Bee* as did the equally graphic photo on page 1 in *The Press-Enterprise* of Riverside, Calif., of a woman who had hanged herself in Bosnia.

The *Bee*'s ombudsman, Art Nauman, said, "Only a few times in my 15-year tenure as an ombudsman have I had as an intense outpouring of negative reader comments as I had on this picture."

Readers, says the Reader Representative of *The Hartford Courant,* may be appalled at a news story, but they are shocked and outraged at a news photo."

The Defense

In response, editors are equally vehement. Managing Editor Mel Optowsky of *The Press-Enterprise,* responded: "The story that picture tells is a horror. What is going on in Bosnia is a horror. It is a holocaust, the destruction of a people's body, mind, spirit and their worldly goods.

"The picture tells the story of the holocaust in a way that tens of thousands of words cannot."

Optowsky said the staff had a long discussion about using the photo.

"We discussed, for instance, the failure of much of the American press 60 years ago to adequately describe another holocaust and the consequent failure of a good people, the American people, to do something about it."

The Flint (Mich.) *Journal* published a photo of a Somali mother mourning the death of her young son whose emaciated body is clearly visible in the photo. Readers complained and in an editorial, the newspaper responded:

> Good. It should.
>
> It should offend all of us.
>
> We should be outraged and incensed— not that newspapers would publish such a graphic and tragic image, but that the world would allow such suffering, such violence to continue.
>
> Yes, the picture was horrifying. It made people uncomfortable. That was the point in publishing it. It was to open people's eyes to the catastrophe that continues to unfold there.

'Too Horrible'

Graphic photos arouse greater anger than printed or spoken words. These stark photos of a cyclist dying and a despondent Bosnian woman's suicide provoked heavy reader response critical of their use.

The cyclist, bleeding from the head and curled in a fetal position, had just hit a rock wall at 55 miles an hour.

The woman apparently hanged herself in fear of Serbian atrocities during the civil strife in the former Yugoslavia.

Top: AP photo by Pascal Pavani
Bottom: AP photo by Darko Bandic

Photo Guidelines

Claude Cookman, who worked as a picture editor for newspapers, says that these questions must be resolved:

1. What do the pictures really show?
2. What are the readers likely to add to or read into their interpretation of the photos' content?
3. What are the circumstances under which the photographs were obtained?
4. How compelling is the news situation out of which the photos arose?
5. How compelling or significant are the photos in terms of what they teach us about the human experience?
6. Do the positive reasons for publishing the photos outweigh the almost certain negative reaction they will elicit from a sizable portion of the readership?

Application

The photo of a family crying over the body of the drowned child on the facing page became one of the most disputed photographs of the 1980s. Many readers protested its use in *The Bakersfield Californian* as an invasion of the family's privacy. The managing editor apologized: "We make mistakes—and this clearly was a big one."

The photographer, John Harte, did not apologize for taking it or for his newspaper's using it:

> Our area is plagued by an unusually high number of drownings annually. During the week this photo was taken, there were four drownings, two that day, in our area's public waters. . . . We hoped that by running this one our readers would have gotten the message that we felt it was important they witness the horror that can result when water safety is taken lightly.

Harte was applying No. 6 in Cookman's list. Is this sufficient to defend the use of the photograph?

Christopher Meyers, a member of the philosophy department at the California State University at Bakersfield, wrote that the basic defense for use of the photograph was its journalistic merit: "It was timely; the 'story' was relevant to *Californian* readers; the photograph is both artistically compelling and emotionally gripping. . . ."

But he finds its use morally indefensible. It was an invasion of the family's privacy and it reduced the family to objects of our interest, denying them their status as "part of the human family." As for the argument the photographer presents, Meyers says that it would be impossible to determine that the photograph did indeed save any lives. This use of utilitarian ethics as a defense might "justify some use of the photo," he said, but not the way it was used.

There was in this case, he says, "too much emphasis on journalistic values and not enough on moral values."

John Harte, *The Bakersfield Californian*

Death

Nora Ephron, a media critic, says of pictures of death: "I recognize that printing pictures of corpses raises all sorts of problems about taste and titillation and sensationalism; the fact is, however, that people die. Death happens to be one of life's main events. And it is irresponsible—and more than that, inaccurate—for newspapers to fail to show it."

A sensitivity to personal feelings is essential to the journalist, not because invasions of privacy are illegal but because compassion is a compelling moral demand on the journalist. The photograph can be as callously intrusive as the television crew at the scene of a disaster poking camera and microphone in the faces of the bereaved. Yet death is part of reality, and it is possible to be overly sensitive to it.

Death has provided the press with almost as many problems as has sexual material. We cringe at confrontation with our mortality. Morticians try to make death resemble life. Wakes are no longer fashionable. Black for the bereaved is a past practice. Children are kept from funerals by solicitous relatives. Death is said to be our last taboo.

Young reporters sometimes go to the other extreme. Carried away by the drama of violence, they may chronicle the details of death—the conditions of bodies strewn alongside the airliner, the mutilated homicide victim, the precise plans of the youngster who committed suicide in the family's garage.

This enthusiasm is as tasteless as prurient sexual interest, for it uses the tabooed subject as the means to shock readers, to call attention to the reporting rather than to the subject. Death can be terrible and horrifying. But its terror and horror are best made known through understatement. In sensitive areas, the whisper speaks louder than the shout.

Summing Up

Standards of taste traditionally were set by the upper class and the elders of the community. This held on, more or less, until the Depression of the 1930s, World War II and the postwar social upheavals.

With the economic collapse of the Depression came a questioning of the old ways, an unwillingness to accept edicts from authorities and a willingness to experiment with new, daring and different ideas. The old ways had given the country malnourished children, had uprooted families and had forced poor but proud men and women to seek welfare.

Social Ferment   World War II thrust an isolationist nation into a maelstrom. Not only did the shrinking of the protective oceans force the country to change its geopolitical assumptions, the war caused massive social disruption: Millions of young men were uprooted, hundreds of thousands of women were enlisted in the work force, blacks migrated from the agrarian south to the industrialized Midwest and Northeast. Classes, sexes and races mixed and mingled.

At the same time, unspeakable atrocities occurred over Europe and Asia. The Nazi brutalities, at first disbelieved as too vile, too incomprehensible to be true, were verified. Murder of the children, the disabled and the different had become German state policy. A nation that had given the world Beethoven and Goethe had acquiesced in the state's policy of slaughter.

The pictures of stacks of dead, Edward R. Murrow's broadcast from Buchenwald, the testimony of the killers at their trials could not be overlooked.

Nor could the changes at home.

Old Balances Upset   The civil rights struggles of the 1950s and the liberation movements of the 1960s involved actions and language the old rules of taste would have deemed improper. But journalists knew that they had to be reported. The profanities and obscene acts that accompanied the country's crises were symbols of the collapse of the old order. The battles and the new balances—the young, for example, were exerting greater social and political power—had to be reported.

Although some of the more conservative members of the community considered the young to be the modern counterparts of the barbarians at the gates, the young unquestionably were causing significant changes in society. But to report the full dimensions of these activities—the language and slogans—the press would risk censure by the upholders of order in the community, the very people upon whom the newspaper depends for its survival. Radio and television station managers had less leeway. The FCC, they said, required them to conform to contemporary community standards.

But new technology widened the gap between those who tried to uphold the old rules and those who were offering words and pictures. Cable TV moved a wide variety of experiences, including explicit sexual material, into the home.

But taste is not a free-for-all for journalists. Those who work for the standard media need guidelines.

General Guidelines

First, some personal rules of the road. Although journalists are told that decisions on matters of taste are made by their editors, individual criteria are helpful.

Obviously, what and how a reporter sees are influenced by his or her attitudes and values. A censurious reporter may block out relevant material. A prurient reporter may overindulge his or her fantasies. An open attitude toward these issues is a corrective to the natural propensity to be guided, and consequently victimized, by impulse and sentiment.

By their nature, editors are conservative. Like libel lawyers, when they are in doubt they tend to throw out questionable material. Reporters learn early in their careers to fight for stories. The reporter who has a set of standards from which to argue his or her story past the desk will be better able to do a good job of presenting to readers and listeners the world of reality.

The self-appointed guardians of good taste no longer have the power to issue dicta. Now, it's the journalist who decides what is essential and what is offensive and unnecessary. Guidelines are essential for responsible use of this power. Here are some:

1. Is the questionable material essential to a story of significance? If so, there is compelling reason to use it.

2. Use depends on the nature of the publication's readers and the station's listeners. But care should be taken to see to it that all are considered, not just those who are most vociferous.

3. The tradition of the publication or station is a consideration.

4. The private as well as the public actions of public officials and public figures are the subject of journalism if they bear on matters of public concern.

SOCIETY OF PROFESSIONAL JOURNALISTS.
Code of Ethics

Preamble
Members of the Society of Professional Journalists believe that public enlightenment is the forerunner of justice and the foundation of democracy. The duty of the journalist is to further those ends by seeking truth and providing a fair and comprehensive account of events and issues. Conscientious journalists from all media and specialties strive to serve the public with thoroughness and honesty. Professional integrity is the cornerstone of a journalist's credibility.
Members of the Society share a dedication to ethical behavior and adopt this code to declare the Society's principles and standards of practice.

Seek Truth and Report It
Journalists should be honest, fair and courageous in gathering, reporting and interpreting information.

Minimize Harm
Ethical journalists treat sources, subjects and colleagues as human beings deserving of respect.

Act Independently
Journalists should be free of obligation to any interest other than the public's right to know.

Be Accountable
Journalists are accountable to their readers, listeners, viewers and each other.

"... the duty of journalists is to serve the truth."

Preview

Journalism ethics has developed in two directions.

1. News organizations have adopted codes of ethics and guidelines that:

- Prohibit journalists from accepting anything of value from sources.
- Limit activities that may pose conflicts of interest.
- Stress the journalist's responsibility to society and the obligation to be accurate, impartial and independent.

2. Reporters have adopted a personal code that stresses:

- Compassion for the poor, the disabled, the different.
- Moral indignation when the powerless are victimized.
- Willingness to place responsibility for the failures of policies on those who made them.
- Commitment to the improvement of their skills.

"I don't mean to seem unfriendly," the fragile old man said, "but I just don't want people to see any stories about me." He looked down for a moment and then back to his visitor, Kevin Krajick, a reporter for *Corrections* magazine. Krajick was on assignment to interview elderly prisoners, and during his stop at the Fishkill, N.Y., state penitentiary, he had been told about one of the oldest, Paul Geidel, 84 years old and in his 68th year behind bars for murder.

Geidel offered to make toast and tea for Krajick, and he accepted. Geidel had turned away many reporters before, but a guard had suggested Krajick try anyway, and he had led the young reporter to Geidel's 10 × 10 room in the prison infirmary.

With the gentleness of his age, Geidel said he understood that Krajick's job was "to get a story." He respected that calling, he said, but he really didn't want to talk about himself.

"I began slipping in questions about his past, his feelings about his life," Krajick recalled, "He answered several of them, but he said several times, he did not want 'any story.' "

The Dilemma

"He had tried to live in solitude and repentance, he said, and any notoriety upset him. He wanted to die in obscurity," Krajick said. A reporter had visited Geidel a few years before and had promised that no story would come out of their conversation, Geidel told Krajick.

"I thought they would leave me alone, but then one day I pick up the paper, and oh, there's my name and my picture splattered all over the front page."

Geidel, the son of an alcoholic saloon keeper, was put in an orphanage at seven. At 14, he quit school and worked at menial jobs. When he was 17, he broke into a hotel room in New York, stuffed a chloroformed gag in a guest's mouth, grabbed a few dollars and fled in a panic. The victim suffocated. Geidel was sentenced to life in prison for second-degree murder.

It was all in the newspaper, again, 60 years later.

"It was terrible, just terrible," Geidel said.

No Story . . .

"I had decided at that point that I would not put him through the pain of printing a story about him," Krajick said. "I told him that I would not. I figured there were plenty of interesting elderly prisoners who wouldn't mind being written about."

The two chatted about an hour and parted good friends.

"Then I learned that Mr. Geidel had served the longest prison term in U.S. history. I started to waver. I checked the files and found that several magazines and television stations had run stories on him when he refused parole at the age of 81. I then called the state corrections and parole authorities to find out how Geidel had been held for such an incredible term—a point that had not been made clear in the previous articles.

"It turned out that he had been classified as criminally insane on what turned out to be a pretty flimsy basis and then totally forgotten about. He had not stood up for himself during all those years and had no one on the outside to do it for him."

. . . or a Story of Significance?

"This obviously was a story of more significance than I had first thought. It was the most dramatic demonstration possible of the abuse of power under the boundless mental commitment statutes that most states have. What could be more moving than the story of the man who had spent the longest term ever, whom everyone acknowledged as meek and repentant and who, under other circumstances, would have been released before he reached the age of 40?

Critical. Surveys show that among the major complaints against reporters is their supposed lack of concern about whether their stories hurt people. The other major criticisms are sensationalism and invasion of privacy.

"The public clearly had reason to know about this man's life. It would be difficult to justify leaving him out since I was writing what was supposed to be a definitive article on elderly prisoners for the definitive publication on prisons."

Krajick faced a moral dilemma. Were the reasons for publishing his story sufficiently compelling to outweigh his promise to Geidel and the pain that the article would certainly inflict on the old man?

"I was anxious not to hurt a man who had, as prison records and he himself said, spent his life in mental anguish. I was sympathetic with his wish to remain obscure."

In his work, Krajick had faced situations in which people had been imprudently frank with him and had asked to be spared publicity. Those decisions had not been hard to make. He had reasoned that those who are hurt or embarrassed by the truth usually deserve to be. But Geidel deserved neither society's curiosity nor its condemnation. He had paid his debt to society.

Balancing Values

In the balance Krajick was striking—a balance of conflicting values—were two other factors: Articles had already been written about Geidel and he had become a statistic in the *Guinness Book of World Records,* which would soon draw other reporters whose articles, Krajick felt, would be more flamboyant and less accurate than his.

"On this basis, I decided to print the article, though not without misgivings," Krajick said. "I realized that if Mr. Geidel were to see the article he would be distressed, and he would feel betrayed by the young man who was nice to him but ended up lying. I only hope those around him have the sense not to show him the article. That would be the only escape for my conscience."

The piece appeared in the magazine under the title, "The Longest Term Ever Served: 'Forget Me.' " The concluding paragraph of the article reads:

> As his visitor left, he offered to write to Geidel. "Oh, no, please," he said. "Please. I don't mean to seem unfriendly. But please don't write. Forget me. Forget all about me." A distressed look crossed his face and he turned and hobbled down the hall to clean the teapot.

Privacy Invasion or Public Service?

For 20 years, the photographer Donna Ferrato has been documenting domestic violence. On the scene during or shortly after beatings and abuse, her photographs have shown graphically the violence inflicted on victims.

"I think that a photograph of a face that's been through a lot, a face with emotion, tells more than pages of words," she says. "The photograph makes people identify with and often feel something for the person because they can see the person is real. We can never quite tell if the story is real when it's an essay without photographs. The photos give it a reality."

Ferrato is especially concerned with the damage done to children. Abused women, she says, can heal if they break away from their abusive husbands and boyfriends, "but the children I usually come in contact with, they are like time bombs."

Objections

Although Ferrato is careful to obtain permission from those she photographs and to talk to "everybody connected to the child," her work has been criticized as an invasion of privacy. The chief of pediatrics at a New York hospital told journalists that those who use real names and pictures of children should "fry in hell."

In response, Ferrato says that she is "perhaps one of those who will 'fry in hell.'" She describes a story she told with her camera of a 9-year-old girl in South Africa who was raped by a neighbor and infected with syphilis. "I firmly believed people needed to see her face, to understand that this is a real child.

"I hope that children are not exploited by my work, but that through it they have a chance to show what they are going through. They have a right to be able to show that and to say, 'I hurt, I'm angry, this has happened to me. I need help.'

"I believe photographs can point to that rage far better than any words connected to any anonymous child."

Editor's Reluctance   Ferrato says editors are hesitant to publish photos like hers. "Perhaps it has to do with protecting the rights of the child. Perhaps the child isn't really old enough at 9 or 10 to say whether or not they want to be put in the public's eye. I will give them that. But at the same time I think that what's been going on for the last 10 years is the dumbing down of America. There is a great reluctance on the part of editors to tell stories which are too tough or too strong and show the realities of people's lives.

"And when you get into children's lives, editors are extremely squeamish. But they are not afraid to show children after they've done some horrible deeds, after they've killed the kids in the schoolyard. Then they'll show that picture on the cover of every newspaper in the country and on TV every night."

Ferrato said that so long as people do not see the faces of the children who are victims of abuse, "the men who did these kinds of things are able to hide. The kids were anonymous before. By showing their faces, these children gather their own kinds of strength and power from being heard and being understood about what happens to them . . . it makes people care about what is happening. I don't think it sinks into their minds for very long if they can't see it."

A full interview with Ferrato is included in the Winter 1998 issue of *Nieman Reports* from which some of this material has been excerpted.

Your Call Given some of Ferrato's photographs of a local case of domestic abuse, what would you do? What guidelines would you use in making a decision? To help you make a decision, let's examine how a moral consciousness developed in the media.

Self-Examination

Solicitude for people is fairly new to journalism. For many years, outsiders had urged on the press a sense of responsibility, a caution that the First Amendment was not a license for unconscionable moneymaking and sensation mongering. In the 1970s, the press began to heed these criticisms, and the scrutiny included an examination of ethical problems.

This self-examination led to the adoption of codes and standards that call for accuracy, impartiality and avoidance of conflicts of interest and that proscribe certain activities, such as the acceptance of gifts from sources.

Journalists realized that without some kind of moral framework, the practice of journalism is reduced to a repetitive chase after disconnected stories, and this becomes for the journalist a life empty of meaning and dignity.

Causes for Concern

Some journalistic practices became embarrassing to a craft increasingly concerned with becoming a profession. Reporters accepted gifts, free travel and assorted favors. A study showed that four out of five newspapers accepted free travel for staffers. The situation called for changes, and one direction seemed the adoption of rules, codes of acceptable conduct. In 1974, one of 10 newspapers had such codes. Within a decade, three of four had codes.

Codes of Conduct

The codes prohibit the acceptance of gifts, and they warn against conflicts of interest. For example, a political reporter who accepted theater tickets from a source or worked part time as a speechwriter for a candidate would compromise his or her position as a journalist.

These newspaper codes were modeled on general codes of ethics such as the one adopted in 1923 by Sigma Delta Chi, a journalism fraternity. The codes not only prohibited specific practices, they sought to establish ethical norms. They were a reaction to an outlook and to practices that had tainted journalism with a grubbiness inconsistent with the standards of professional conduct.

The renewed interest in establishing journalism as a profession found a base on which to build in the report of the Commission on Freedom of the Press. The study, issued in 1947, was a response to criticism of the U.S. press as insular, often sensational and sometimes irresponsible. The members of the Commission—most of them prestigious faculty members at leading universities—concluded that the press had not been "adequate to the needs of society."

Theory of Responsibility. In its report, the Commission included five requirements for the media:

1. The press must give a truthful, comprehensive and intelligent account of the day's events in a context that gives them some meaning.
2. The press must provide a forum for the exchange of comment and criticism.
3. The press must project a representative picture of the constituent groups in the society.
4. The press must present and clarify the goals and values of the society.
5. The press must provide full access to the day's intelligence.

One finding was particularly pertinent—that the press had failed to give "a representative picture of the constituent groups in the society." Vast segments of society had been ignored by the press, particularly the young and the aged, racial minorities, the poor and women.

Gradually, the press became more responsive to external criticism. Journalists themselves became outspoken, and their criticisms began to appear in the various press reviews that sprang up around the country. Journalists began to take their trade more seriously—possibly because of the steady infusion of college-trained reporters who were questioning some of the assumptions of the craft. The climate was established for journalists to codify good practices, to set lines between the acceptable and the morally indefensible.

Limitations of the Codes

Although the codes establish boundaries and describe acceptable practices, they are only a beginning. They cannot assist the journalist in resolving some of the most difficult problems. These involve dilemmas in which the choice is between conflicting moral or ethical actions.

Krajick had to choose between what he saw as two positive ends. To print the story would reveal some truths about a system that crushed one prisoner and might still be affecting others. It would be morally right to use Geidel to illustrate the inadequacy of the mental competency process, he believed. Not writing about Geidel would also be a moral action because then Geidel would be spared the agony of the exposure. Surely, a man who has spent 68 years behind bars deserves our compassion. Moreover, there was Krajick's promise not to use the material. Can a public need justify the reporter's going back on his or her word?

Looking to codes for guidance, we find in one of them, that of the Society of Professional Journalists, that the journalist should "serve the general welfare." Krajick would serve the general welfare with publication. The same code stresses "respect for the dignity, privacy, rights and well-being of people encountered in the course of gathering and presenting the news." Clearly, respect for Geidel would mean heeding his plea not to write about him. The codes are no help here beyond identifying the clear moral choices.

No code can make a journalist a person of good conscience. Only a personal commitment to a journalistic morality can do so. Also, most codes emphasize prohibitions, actions not to take, practices not to undertake.

But the great failure of the press, as the Commission on Freedom of the Press stressed, is not its sins of commission, but rather its sins of omission, its failure to look into the significant actions of the powerful and the travails and the longings of the powerless.

Sins of Omission

No code led *The Charlotte Observer* to point out that North Carolina's leading income producer, its tobacco crop, is the single greatest cause of lung

Abuse, Neglect

Alison Young went through stacks of nursing home inspection reports and found needless suffering, poor care, bad hygiene, physical abuse, affronts to human dignity. Her five-part series for the *Detroit Free Press* was based on public records. "I got into this business to give voice to the voiceless and to effect change," she says.

A Calling. "At its best, journalism is a calling for people, just like it is for academics. People often sacrifice much larger incomes to pursue this vocation. Journalism is also imbued with this sense of autonomy and independence, along with a spirit of public responsibility. That is the sense of journalism I picked up while working on my father's paper."

—Lee C. Bollinger, president, University of Michigan

cancer, which is responsible, health authorities say, for 1,000 deaths a day. It was the conscience of the *Observer*'s management and editors that led the newspaper to examine the issue in detail in a special section.

Nor did any code stimulate the *Atlanta Journal-Constitution* to investigate racial discrimination practiced by lending institutions in Atlanta. Bill Dedman took on the task of proving that banks and other lenders were systematically denying loans to blacks. His reporting led to significant reforms. (Dedman won the Pulitzer Prize for investigative reporting.)

These newspapers and their staff members understood the necessity to act in the public interest, just as did Donna Halvorsen and Allen Short of the *Star Tribune* in Minneapolis. Their extensive examination of the careers of 767 sex criminals revealed the state's courts and prisons were ineffective in dealing with child molesters and rapists.

Repeat offenses, they found, were far greater than the state had admitted, and those who had been sent to a psychological treatment center were more likely to commit new sex crimes than those who were not treated.

The newspaper allowed the reporters ample time to make the computer-assisted study—it took nine months. And it devoted considerable space to the series, which ran to 30,000 words.

Sins of omission occur when the journalist refuses to act in situations in which revelation is required. The philosopher Jeremy Bentham described this immoral act as "Keeping at rest; that is, forebearing."

Morality Underlies Journalism

Morality is basic to the theory and practice of journalism. The press justifies its freedom in terms of moral imperatives; it rationalizes much of its behavior with moral declarations.

If public consent freely given is essential to the proper functioning of a democracy, then for the consent to be meaningful the public must be adequately informed by a press free of government or any other control. Thomas Jefferson expressed this simply: "Where the press is free and every man able to read, all is safe." The First Amendment makes this consensual system possible. Although neither the Constitution nor any laws require that the press carry out its essential role in the system, the press takes on the responsibility for setting before the public the issues it considers important so that they can be openly discussed. The cultural historian Christopher Lasch says, "The job of the press is to encourage debate."

Recorders and Activists

Journalists differ in their interpretation of their role as suppliers of information. Some contend that it is sufficient for journalism to create a record, to report the deeds and declarations of those in power. Others go further. They would initiate coverage, make searching examinations of power, practice what some of them describe as an activist or watchdog journalism.

The first group believes that journalists are called upon to present matters that readers are interested in, and some of these editors conduct focus groups and have reader-advisory panels to inform them of their readers' concerns.

The second group prefers to lead from its own conception of community needs, its own insight into what constitutes community misdeeds. Thomas Winship, former editor of *The Boston Globe,* was labeled an "activist editor" by colleagues, a label he bore proudly, he says. He learned about this kind of journalism when he was breaking in as a reporter at *The Washington Post.* The publisher, Philip L. Graham, "burned into my young, impressionistic head the idea that the license to print carried with it the obligation to give something back to the community," Winship says.

Activist and watchdog journalism go back to the work of the colonial printers in a tradition that has taken journalism to its most notable achievements in rendering public service.

Past and Present

During the American colonial period, journalists in the 13 colonies vigorously opposed what they termed "onerous taxes" and the lack of representation in decision making. These journalists became a major force in the struggle for independence. The colonial journalist had a point of view and expressed it.

Before the Civil War, an outspoken and active abolitionist press called for the emancipation of the slaves. And after the abolition of slavery, as Jim Crow laws and practices became commonplace in some parts of the country, journalists spoke out. Ida B. Wells, for example, exposed lynch law and mob rule at great personal risk.

As people moved to the cities and the country grew from an agrarian economy to become an industrial behemoth, exploitation and abuses proliferated. Industrialists—some described as "robber barons" because of their ruthless practices—took control of major industries. Workers were exploited and prevented from forming unions, sometimes at the point of a gun. Crooked politicians ran many large cities. In response, a group of journalists began to tell the story as the 20th century opened.

The Muckrakers

At first derisively described as *muckrakers,* this group of brilliant men and women took on the robber barons, the labor exploiters and the political hacks. They became known as the nation's voices of conscience. Some wrote books and others magazine articles, several took photographs and some worked for the daily press.

Overseer. ". . . watchdog journalism should be an integral part of the daily work of the news department."
—Bill Kovach, Curator, Nieman Foundation

SOUTHERN HORRORS.
LYNCH LAW
IN ALL
ITS PHASES

Miss IDA B. WELLS.

Price, · · · Fifteen Cents.

THE NEW YORK AGE PRINT.
1892.

As the century began, four-fifths of the people in the United States were living in poverty. People were commodities. The mines and mills exploited child labor. Blacks were treated as chattel.

Racism

Ray Stannard Baker in 1908 described racism in Southern courts.

> One thing impressed me especially, not only in this court but in all others I have visited: a Negro brought in for drunkenness, for example, was punished much more severely than a white man arrested for the same offense. . . . The white man sometimes escaped with a reprimand, he was sometimes fined three dollars and costs, but the Negro, especially if he had no white man to intercede for him, was usually punished with a ten or fifteen dollar fine, which often meant he had to go to the chain-gang.

Chain Gangs   Baker points out that one reason for the large number of arrests is the profit to the counties and state in hiring out convicts to private contractors. "Last year the net profit to Georgia from chain-gangs, to which the commission refers with pride, reached the great sum of $354,853.55. . . . The natural tendency is to convict as many men as possible—it furnishes steady, cheap labour to the contractors and profit to the state. . . ."

These journalists did not condemn some vague system. They named names and held individuals responsible for their actions. Baker wrote that "some of the large fortunes in Atlanta have come chiefly from the labour of chain-gangs of convicts leased from the state." He described a banker who was also a member of the city police board and the owner of brickyards where many convicts were used on lease from the state at cheap rates.

Like the other muckrakers, Baker was adept at using files and records:

> From the records I find that in 1906, one boy 6-years-old, seven of 7 years, 33 of 8 years, 69 of 9 years, 107 of 10 years, 142 of 11 years, and 219 of 12 years were arrested and brought into court, 578 boys and girls, mostly Negroes, under 12 years of age.

Pulitzer's Journalism

One of the major practitioners of muckraking journalism was Joseph Pulitzer, the owner of the *St. Louis Post-Dispatch* and the New York *World*. Pulitzer's editors conducted crusades, newspaper campaigns to expose and remedy practices they considered wrong, unfair, unjust. They took their cue from Pulitzer's edict that the newspapers should never be content with "merely printing the news."

Instead, he said, his newspapers should be concerned "with the things that ought to happen tomorrow, or the next month, or the next year," and that they "will seek to make what ought to be come to pass." The "highest mission of the press," he said, "is to render public service."

His legacy continued under editors who were committed to using the press as an instrument of justice, reform and change. One Pulitzer reporter, Paul Y. Anderson, doggedly followed a paper trail that led to the exposure of the collusion of two of President Harding's cabinet members with oil interests that corruptly leased federal oil field reserves.

Making Journalism of Injustice

Pulitzer's edict to his editors to seek out issues, to make news of injustice and wrongdoing could be described as an instruction to journalists to establish agendas for their communities. This is an approach to journalism that has no borders.

Deformed Children   Harold Evans, editor of London's *Sunday Times,* said the "real power" of the press consists of its ability "to create an agenda for society."

Fair play was on Evans' mind when he heard that the manufacturers of the drug thalidomide had pressured parents of children deformed by the drug to accept a pittance in damages. Through its coverage of the issue, Evans said, the *Times* forced the crippled children "into the conscience of the country." The stories led to settlements 50 times greater than the original stipend.

Terror in Argentina   When Argentina was in the grip of a murderous dictatorship in the 1970s and 1980s, few protested the arrests, torture and killing of schoolchildren, pregnant women, college students . . . anyone who spoke out against the tyranny. People were snatched from their homes, grabbed on the streets. Tortured, never given a trial, many were drugged, their stomachs slit and then were tossed out of navy planes over the ocean.

Some risked death to speak out despite what an army chief of state later described as an atmosphere of guilt by "commission or omission, by our presence or our absence, by recommending or passively allowing it to happen."

Robert Cox, an American who was editor of the English-language *Buenos Aires Herald,* published lists of the missing on the front page. Death threats flooded his office. He was arrested, taken to a cell past a huge Nazi flag on the wall, briefly imprisoned and then forced to leave the country.

The journalist Rodolfo Walsh could not remain silent. He wrote a public indictment of "the most savage reign of terror Argentina has ever known"; that its rulers had created "virtual concentration camps in all the principal military bases"; that the torturers felt a "need to utterly destroy their victims, depriving them of all human dignity. . . ."

Walsh knew he was signing his own death warrant through his reporting. He closed his indictment by saying that he had to speak out to be "faithful to the commitment I made a long time ago to be a witness in difficult times." The day after his statement was released, he was abducted. His body has never been found.

Democracy's Base. "Representative democracy is inconceivable without forms of mass communication—to create awareness of public issues that face a society whose members are not personally in touch with each other, who lack common geographic reference points, and whose central institutions are remote from the people they serve or exploit."

—Leo Bogart

Racial Justice   In the United States, racial justice has been a theme of activist journalists. Courageous editors and publishers have bucked community traditions—and advertisers—to support equal treatment and to expose racism.

Hazel Brannon Smith, the editor of two weekly newspapers in the Mississippi Delta country, spoke up. In 1946, she was found guilty of contempt of court for interviewing the widow of a black man who was whipped to death.

In an editorial she wrote in 1954, she accused the sheriff who had shot a young black man in the back of "violating every concept of justice, decency and right." The sheriff sued for libel and was awarded $10,000. The state supreme court overturned the ruling.

That year, Smith was invited to join "something called a 'Citizens' Council," she said, by "a local prominent man." The idea was to maintain segregation in the schools. Legal, nonviolent tactics would be used, she was told. "If a Nigra won't go along with our thinking on what's best for the community as a whole," Smith said the man told her, "he'll simply have his credit cut off." The idea was to use fear, he told her. Smith refused to go along. Her refusal cost her dearly.

She said the community became a battleground with intimidation the weapon, not only against blacks but against those who opposed the Council. "It finally got to the point where bank presidents and leading physicians were afraid to speak their honest opinions because of the monster among us," she said. "The idea was that 'we' would present a solid, united stand.

"I dissented by presuming to say that the truth had to be printed."

She was one of the few who dissented, and the pressure grew.

"My newspapers were boycotted, bombed and burned, a new newspaper was organized in Lexington to put me out of business, my life was threatened, and my husband lost his job as county hospital administrator—all because of pressure brought by this professional hate-peddling organization," she said.

She and her husband managed to keep going, but the income was never enough and she had to mortgage her home to pay her bills. Finally, in 1985, she gave up. The bank took her home. Soon thereafter she died, penniless.

No to Black Vets   Another small-town editor, Hodding Carter, took on the bigots and racists in his newspaper, the *Delta Democrat-Times* in Greenville, Miss. When white townspeople objected to listing black veterans on the town's World War II honor roll, he wrote an editorial, "Our Honor Roll Is a Monument to Intolerance and Timidity." It and others he wrote won the 1946 Pulitzer Prize.

When the White Citizens' Councils resisted the Supreme Court's school desegregation decision, Carter spoke out against them. In response to his criticism, the Mississippi House of Representatives formally denounced Carter. Whereupon Carter responded in an editorial:

By a vote of 89 to 19 the Mississippi House of Representatives has resolved the editor of this newspaper into a liar because of an article I wrote. . . . If this charge were true it would make me well qualified to serve with that body. It is not true. So . . . I herewith resolve by a vote of 1 to 0 that there are 89 liars in the State Legisla-ture, beginning with Speaker Silvers and working way on down to Rep. Eck Windham of Prentiss whose name is fittingly made up of the words 'wind' and 'ham.' . . . Meanwhile, those 89 character-mobbers can go to hell collectively or singly and wait there until I back down. They needn't plan on returning.

Closed College Door   Ira Harkey, the editor and publisher of the small Pascagoula daily newspaper, spoke out when Ross Barnett, the governor of Mississippi, vowed to keep blacks out of the University of Mississippi "forever." Harkey condemned Barnett as a demagogue. The result: Gunshots, a cross ignited on his lawn, failing circulation and canceled advertising.

On Christmas 1962, Harkey wrote this in an editorial.

In Mississippi, a person who attempts to carry Christianity out the church door, who dares to practice the Christian virtue of tolerance outside the church, is cursed as a liberal, a leftist, a communist, a nig-gerlover. Christ was the greatest champion of the underdog the world has ever known. If He were to visit us here, now, by whose

Popularity. "You don't go into this business to be popular. . . . When the first Freedom Riders stepped off the bus in Montgomery, Alabama, the assembled Ku Klux Klan mob of 300 people did not first go for them. They went for the 20 or 30 reporters there. As my young black friend Bernard Lafayette, one of the Freedom Riders, said, they wanted to knock our eyes out and our capacity to record first. And in Vietnam, demonstrably, we were not popular."

—*David Halberstam*

side would He stand, beside the brick-throwing, foulmouthed, destroying, profaning, slavering members of the mob and their "nice-folk" eggers-on, or beside the trembling victim of their hate?

A white woman who worked for the local library read the editorial and wrote Harkey: "Instead of a bullet through your door, I hope you get a bullet through your stupid head."

Activist journalists subscribe to Bentham's moral injunction to refuse to stay silent in the face of wrongs and wrongdoing. They must speak up when injustice exists, whatever the majority opinion in the community, however much those in power prefer to keep things as is.

Current Examples   Racial discrimination continues to be a concern of the activist press. Some recent newspaper campaigns include:

- *The Daily Progress,* **Charlottesville, Va.:** A two-year study revealed racial disparity in sentencing local criminal defendants.
- *Leader-Telegram,* **Eau Claire, Wis.:** A staff project exposed racial discrimination in housing rentals.
- *The Dallas Morning News:* Reporters showed how a development plan would crowd thousands more blacks into one of the city's poorest and most dangerous neighborhoods.

Drunks Driving, Wastes Polluting

Here are some other examples of public service journalism:

- *The Philadelphia Inquirer:* Showed that city police dogs had attacked 350 innocent people.
- *The Albuquerque Tribune:* Showed that drunk drivers are allowed to keep driving despite many convictions. Uncovered extensive dumping of dangerous wastes in New Mexico.
- *The Ledger,* **Lakeland, Fla.:** Revealed that a fungicide caused crop and nursery damage and that the manufacturer, DuPont Co., knew that the fungicide had the potential to cause harm but was silent.
- *Star Tribune,* **Minneapolis:** Revealed that the state's foster care system allowed known criminals and sex offenders to become foster parents.
- *The Muskegon* **(Mich.)** *Chronicle:* Showed that the founder of a chemical plant made huge profits while knowingly exposing his workers to a cancer-causing chemical.
- *Fort Worth Star-Telegram:* Reported that 250 U.S. servicemen had lost their lives as a result of a design problem in helicopters.

An activist journalism calls on the community to act: To see that city officials rid the local water supply of carcinogens (*The Washington* (N.C.) *Daily News*); to make the government regulate the American blood industry (*The*

Weaponry. "If your aim is to change the world, journalism is a more immediate short-term weapon."
—Tom Stoppard, British playwright

Philadelphia Inquirer); to force the Federal Aviation Administration to do a better job of the medical screening of airline pilots (*The Pittsburgh Press*); to require the county child-welfare agency to protect neglected and abused children (*The Blade*).

Results   This activist journalism does achieve results. After the *Winston-Salem Journal* series that showed that the county's high infant mortality rate had not changed in 10 years although the state's rate steadily declined during the decade, the county hired an infant-mortality coordinator and community leaders pledged to undertake a forceful program.

Let's watch one of these activist reporters, Sam Roe of *The Blade* in Toledo, Ohio, go about fulfilling the journalist's obligation not to forebear and to go beyond "merely printing the news." We'll follow his reporting, the reaction to it and the results he achieved with his revealing reporting.

'Abused by the System'

For several years, Roe says, he had been hearing complaints about the Lucas County Children Services. Too often, abused youngsters were returned to homes where they were battered, molested or neglected again. Some children were placed with relatives, friends and previously absent fathers, although some of these people were drug users, sex offenders and child abusers. Children Services often waited months, sometimes years, before removing children from such homes.

To do the story properly, Roe needed records, documents that proved—or disproved—the rumors. But children's records are confidential.

Roe was helped by two of the traditional aids of the reporter—a source and Roe's knowledge of the system. The source had in a downtown basement copies of complete files of Children Services' records. But the records were voluminous, and it would take months to pour through them for a representative group.

Roe decided to use only cases of children currently in foster care, most of whom had been in the system many years. But the names of foster children are confidential.

"Then I discovered a useful bit of information," Roe says. "Foster parents receive monthly checks for caring for abused children." He knew that the county auditor issued the checks, which are public. By obtaining names from the list of those issued checks, he was able to find what he needed in the files in the basement.

The Files   Roe said he found a "wealth of information that included police reports, social histories, psychiatrists' reports and school records." Some of the files were a foot thick, and they were all up-to-date.

"At first, I wasn't sure what I would find," Roe said. "But after reading through the first few cases I knew I was on to something.

"One of the first cases involved a mother who had abused and neglected her children for years. Twice officials took them away, and twice they were returned to her.

From the Files

Here are two pages from Roe's notepad. The first describes a mother whose three children were born addicted to cocaine and were returned to the mother and then taken away. The second involves children who were molested and sexually abused and then returned to the abusive home several times. (Last names are blocked out.)

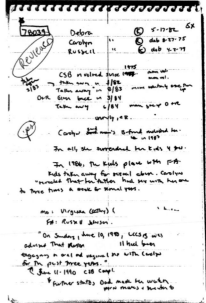

"They even gave the kids back after her infant son died of pneumonia on a night she left him home alone so she could go cruising with friends. Officials never arrested her, though they could have several times."

As he read through the cases, patterns became apparent:

- Abused children were returned home, where they were again battered, molested, neglected.
- Cocaine babies received little or no care.
- Bad parents were sent to counseling classes, not jail.

These groupings became the basis of the organization of Roe's story. "If the file indicated the child was a cocaine baby, I put a circled C on the page. If officials had to remove the child more than once, I wrote down '2X' or '3X.'"

The Writing   By organizing his notes by themes, Roe was able to structure his articles. Then he went back to the files and took detailed notes on the cases that supported these themes. (His source would not allow Roe to make copies of the files.)

"By now, I realized that my story was more than an exposé of Children Services. The entire system, including doctors, lawyers, judges and social workers, was often to blame when kids fell through the cracks."

Roe did not want his story to read like a records-search story. "So I tracked down parents, children and officials in several key cases. Their quotes and anecdotes help bring the stories to life."

His work led to a four-part series, which begins:

Marquell Scott was tired of living this way. Tired of living in a foul, filthy home with no heat, lights, water, and refrigerator.

When he wanted to wash, he had to borrow water from neighbors. When he wanted to see at night, he had to feel around with candles. When his mother's monthly welfare check came in, she blew it on Wild Irish Rose wine.

For six months, the 14-year-old and his four younger brothers and sisters lived like this.

And for six months, child-protection officials did nothing.

So one night, just after midnight, Marquell called the police on his mother himself.

When officers arrived at the Old West End home, they surveyed the squalor. Exposed electrical wires. A toilet that wouldn't flush. An unbearable stench.

The mother was nowhere in sight, and Marquell told the officers the children generally fended for themselves.

Convinced this was no way for children to live, the officers removed them all, including the youngest, who had never been enrolled in school, even though she was 7.

Yet all of this could have been prevented. Lucas County Children Services knew about the conditions but did not act.

Plus, the agency had previously taken custody of the children because of years of neglect, but instead of finding a proper home for them, officials placed them back with their mother.

This case is not unusual. Time and time again, children in the Toledo area have been returned to wretched homes and abusive parents—then battered, molested, or neglected again.

In each case, the children were returned with the blessings of Children Services, the local government agency legally responsible for the welfare of abused children.

Some children have been so severely abused after being reunited with their parents that they had to be hospitalized.

The Reaction

The Lucas county commissioners called for a special meeting with Children Services immediately after the fourth in Roe's series ran. There were a total of 17 front-page follow-up stories, one of which, Roe said, "broke the agency's back. A few days after the series, with pressure mounting, a 5-year-old boy was found bound, beaten and bloodied in his home. Police took him to the hospital, then to Children Services for safekeeping. But officials there returned him home just hours later. Only after the police complained did the agency go back and remove the child."

Two days after Roe wrote about this, the agency announced it would overhaul the system. A month later, Roe wrote:

Lucas County Children Services became involved in more child abuse cases last month than in any month in three years.

It is also removing children from their homes for safekeeping at a skyrocketing rate.

Children Services attributed the increases, in part, to a series of Blade stories that have detailed problems in the child-welfare system.

"There is a heightened awareness in the community," John Hollingsworth, a Children Services program administrator, said yesterday. "There is a heightened awareness even in the agency."

Guiding Values

In their reporting and editing, journalists make choices about what to report, whom to interview, what to put in the story, what to leave out. Selection, the heart of journalistic practice, is guided by values that are established by journalistic practice and the society at large.

These values guide us when the choice is between alternative actions, each of which has some claim to principle. This is no different from the decision making most of us face almost daily. "We are doomed to choose," says the philosopher Isaiah Berlin, "and every choice may entail an irreparable loss. The world we encounter in ordinary experience is one in which we are faced with choices between ends equally ultimate and claims equally absolute, the realization of some of which must inevitably involve the sacrifice of others. . . . If, as I believe, the ends of men are many, and not all of them are in principle compatible with each other, then the possibility of conflict—and of tragedy—can never be wholly eliminated from human life, either personal or social. The necessity of choosing between absolute claims is then an inescapable characteristic of the human condition."

Journalists, then, must choose, just as we watched Kevin Krajick choose at the beginning of this chapter between keeping his word to an aged convict or exposing a system that had unjustly confined him for too many years. Was he wrong? Berlin would say, no, and he would add that yes, Krajick did harm the elderly prisoner.

Life as Referent

Can the journalist refer to some universal values as guides to choice, or is decision subject to particular circumstances—what the philosophers call a *situational ethic?* Traditionally—perhaps instinctively—people have sought absolutes as guides. And as often as the priest or the guru has supplied them, they have been found to be impractical. Or they have been discovered to be a way of keeping a religious, political, economic or social system in power.

Even so, we may find in these searches for an ethic to live by some suggestions for a useful journalistic morality. The concern for the good life, the properly led life, is almost as powerful as the need for sustenance. We may find some guides from religion and philosophy, from the Prophets and Plato, from the guru who traces his ethic to the Bhagavad-Gita and from contemporary philosophers.

"Life is the referent of value," says Allen Wheelis, a psychiatrist, who writes about ethics. "What enlarges and enriches life is good; what diminishes and endangers life is evil." If we start our search for an ethic by first defining life as physical survival and apply Wheelis' referent to one of the immediate problems of industrial societies, we can conclude that what poisons the air, water and earth is bad. To preserve an atmosphere we can breathe is good. Industries that endanger the lives of their workers or nearby residents are bad. Safety procedures—or plant closures if this cannot be accomplished—are good.

But some factory owners and some automobile manufacturers have opposed strict environmental protection standards. To clean up a plant, to make a car that does not emit pollutants, to make a process safe in the factory would increase the price of the car or make operating the plant so expensive it might have to be shut down, owners have said. This means unemployment, a loss of taxes to the local community, a decline in business where the plant or factory is located. No wonder that workers and politicians often join industrialists to oppose proposals for safety, clean air and clean water.

Is it the responsibility of the journalist to continue to point out that the factory is poisoning the air? Or does the reporter turn away? If he or she does, jobs may be saved, the profits of the company assured and taxes kept low, surely good ends.

Timeless Dilemma   The dilemma is not new. The playwright Henrik Ibsen describes it in his play *An Enemy of the People*. Dr. Thomas Stockman, medical officer of the municipal baths, a considerable tourist attraction, discovers that the baths—the source of the town's economic resurgence—are being poisoned by the nearby tanneries. He wants to close them as a menace to public health.

But any revelation about the pollution will lead people to shun the baths, and this will cause economic problems, among them unemployment and higher tax rates for property owners. Dr. Stockman is reviled as an enemy of the people.

The practical concerns of a money-based society have occupied many writers. Dickens' novels cry out against the "cash-nexus" as the "only bond between man and man," as one literary critic put it.

"Breathe the polluted air," Dickens says in *Dombey and Son*. "And then, calling up some ghastly child, with stunted form and wicked face, hold forth on its unnatural sinfulness, and lament its being, so early, far away from Heaven—but think a little of its being conceived, and born, and bred, in Hell!"

No Choice   If "life is the referent of value," what other choice has the professional whose reason for being is service to the public than to see and to speak out so that others may see and understand? In the calculus of values, life means more than the bottom line on a ledger sheet. Joseph Conrad said, "My task which I am trying to achieve is, by the power of the written word, to make you hear, make you feel—it is, before all, to make you see. That—and no more, and it is everything."

Harold Fruchtbaum, a Columbia University social scientist, describes as "one of the intellectual's primary functions" the task of placing "responsibility for the failures of our society on the people and the institutions that control the society." Translated into a moral concern for the journalist, this is the task of holding power accountable, whether the power be held by a nation's president or a school superintendent.

Agenda. ". . . those of us who have been granted the great gift to be journalists, the great gift to perform a public service, must seize the moment. If we don't, we will have failed. . . . We can never stop dealing with the issues that surround us and threaten to overwhelm us. Hunger and housing, health care and elderly care, education for our children and their children, jobs and taxes, our air and land and water and the kind of repressive social environment that doesn't allow every man and woman to live in dignity."
—Gregory Favre, Executive Editor, *The Sacramento Bee*

Peter Brown, *professor of classics and history at the University of California at Berkeley:* "The deep religious anger of the Prophet Muhammad at what he saw around him, wealth squandered, the weak oppressed, the insensitive pride of the well-fed. The Prophet's clear and chilling message: The possible perfection of a human being, living at ease with his fellows."

Abraham Heschel, *an Old Testament historian:* The prophets were "intent on intensifying responsibility." They were "impatient of excuse, contemptuous of pretense and self pity." They "felt fiercely" and were "attuned to a cry imperceptible to others."

Will Campbell, *an activist minister with the Committee of Southern Churchmen:* "Jesus judges us by what we do to the children, the prisoners, the whores, the addicts, the scared and the bewildered—to the 'least of them.' "

Genesis, *Chapter 18:* The Lord tells Abraham that he will destroy Sodom and Gomorrah for their sins. "Wilt thou also destroy the righteous with the wicked?" asks Abraham. No, the Lord replies, "I will not destroy it for ten's sake." But ten righteous men could not be found. (The point is the same one that philosophers have made through the generations: The individual has an inescapable moral obligation to society. On him or her may depend its salvation and survival.)

Communal Life

In holding the powerful accountable to the people, the journalist takes to his or her job a sense of communal life. That is, the reporter has a set of values that reveal when power is being abused to the point that the quality of life in the community suffers. Philosophers through the ages have talked about the "good life," which has its starting point in a communal life whose underpinnings are freedom, tolerance and fairness. In such a society, individuals have basic rights that neither the state nor other individuals may violate, and the individual has, in turn, obligations to the community.

In writing about the American philosopher John Dewey, Sidney Hook said that Dewey believed

> . . . the logic of democracy requires the elimination of economic, ethnic, religious and educational injustices if the freedom of choice presupposed by the ethos of democracy is to be realized.
>
> One man, one vote is not enough—if one man can arbitrarily determine the livelihood of many others, determine where and under what conditions they can live, determine what they can read in the press or hear on the air.

Dewey believed that the community has the responsibility for eliminating hunger and poverty, that political power must be harnessed to solve the problems of group and individual welfare. Economic conditions must be such, he wrote, that the equal right of all to free choice and free action is achieved.

Worthwhile. In addressing the graduating class at Rice University, the novelist Kurt Vonnegut said most of the graduates "will find themselves building or strengthening their communities. Please love such a destiny, if it turns out to be yours, for communities are all that is substantial about what we create or defend or maintain in this world."

"All the rest is hoopla."

Communal life is an unfolding process in which the experienced past and the desired and anticipated future are considered in making the present. The journalist plays a key role in this process. Every day, the reporter describes the immediate and the past while showing the possible future in his or her work.

The Good Life as Guide

When moral philosophers speak of the good life they mean a life in which people can read, speak and choose freely; that they need not live in fear of want; that they can count on shared values such as the desirability of equal opportunity and the undesirability of crime.

Journalists enrich and promote these activities through the values that they take to the job. For example, a journalist is told that at the local university the political science department is promoting socialism, that instructors are doing more than describing the ideology; they are endorsing it. To check on the charge, the reporter disguises herself as a student and attends classes. In her story, she describes her experiences, quoting class lectures and discussions, using the names of students and instructors. The charge is found to be groundless.

We do know that posing and using disguises are generally not acceptable in society. Let us strike a balance in deciding whether the use of a disguise by the reporter was ethical:

- **The benefits:** An irresponsible allegation was proved false. The reporter was able to do firsthand reporting, which is more persuasive and closer to truth than transcribing the instructors' denials.
- **The costs:** Deception was used as a journalistic method. Privacy was violated.

We can say that the costs of some of these actions—no matter how well intended—outweigh the benefits if we keep in mind that the good life is the healthy communal life. What kind of campus community will we have if we cannot speak freely and openly to one another in class because we fear our words may be broadcast or published? What kind of community will we have when we fear peering eyes so much that we must shred our garbage or fear our telephone conversation is being taped?

Actions that hurt people or disrupt the community are immoral, unless justified by powerful moral considerations, we all agree. A story about a convicted rapist will hurt the rapist; but we justify the story because punishment of those who commit crimes shows the community that society does not tolerate and will punish crimes. Crime unpunished can lead to the breakdown of the community.

Survival and the good communal life—are there additional guidelines, more specific guidelines that we can find that are of use to the journalist in helping him or her to make choices? Through an examination of a few of the practical problems reporters face, we may find some.

To Print or Not to Print

The news shocked the people of Missoula. The 21-year-old daughter of a well-known couple had been stabbed to death outside her Washington, D.C., apartment house. She had been a high school honor student and an accomplished musician and had won a scholarship to Radcliffe.

Less than a week later, Rod Deckert, the managing editor of *The Missoulian,* a 32,500 circulation daily in the city, had an even more shocking story on his desk: The young woman had been a streetwalker in Washington, "a $50-a-trick prostitute" who "used to talk freely about her work and bragged about being 'a pro,'" according to a story *The Washington Post* planned to run the next day under the headline, "A Life of Promise That Took a Strange and Fatal Turn." The *Post* had learned she had returned to Missoula after dropping out of Radcliffe and one night in a bar she had been approached by a man who asked her to return with him to the East. He was a pimp who recruited young women around the country.

The Dilemma   Deckert was confronted with a difficult decision. If he ran the story, the family would suffer new anguish. If he did not, he would be suppressing news that was bound to be known because papers distributed in Missoula and nearby might carry the dramatic story of a small-town girl who came to a sordid end in the East. It was, Deckert said, "the most painful day in my 11 years of life in the newsroom."

Deckert reasoned that the young woman's experience could be a warning to other young women in the university community. However, he had to weigh this against the pain it would cause the family and friends.

Deckert decided to run an edited version of *The Washington Post* story with some locally gathered inserts. Deckert played the story on page 12 with no art under an eight-column headline.

You Decide

Seymour Hersh, who won the Pulitzer Prize in 1970 for his disclosures about the My Lai massacre in Vietnam and more than a dozen other major journalism awards, told a gathering of journalists at the Nieman Foundation at Harvard that he found out "some pretty horrible stuff" about a former president. Would you use this information and other material you gather in the following situations?

First incident: "There was a serious empirical basis for believing he was a wife beater, and had done so—at least hospitalized her a number of times. I had access to some records. Okay? I'm talking about trauma, and three different cases," Hersh said.

Second incident: A prominent businessman died and in preparing the obituary it was learned that 30 years before when he was a county official

Public or Private?
A city councilwoman has AIDS. A candidate for governor is known as a womanizer. Newsworthy?

Some guidelines provided by Carl Sessions Stepp of the University of Maryland:

• Does it affect the person's public performance?

• If the fact is well-known, no good is served by keeping it out of print.

• If a competing station or paper uses it, the fact is now public. Use it.

Leonard Downie, managing editor of *The Washington Post,* says to use information "when the private conduct of a public figure is symptomatic of a societal problem."

he was sentenced to prison for embezzling funds from his office. Since then, he had led an exemplary life. Does the conviction go into the obituary?

Third incident: Shortly after a rape charge was filed against a young member of the Kennedy family, a London newspaper and then a U.S. tabloid, NBC and *The New York Times* used her name. Was it right to use the victim's name?

Wife Beater   No, Hersh said, he did not write the story. He decided not to because he said he could not "find any connection between what he did in his private life" with his public life as president.

But today, he continued, he would write the story, name the former president. "It's a different world now," he said. "If I didn't write it, the sources would tell it anyway." In other words, he said, the story could not be kept out of circulation.

Obituary   The newspaper did include the embezzlement conviction, and after readers complained the newspaper apologized in an editor's note.

Rape   NBC and the *Times* defended their breaking the practice of not naming rape victims by pointing out that her name was already in circulation. However, at the *Times,* dozens of staff members protested the decision.

Altering Photos   You can digitally alter these photos. Which, if any, do you change?

- A photo you want to use shows a boy with his fly unzipped.
- The sky is drained of color in otherwise excellent shots.
- You need a super shot for the cover of a photography book but cannot find one.
- An athlete's genital area is slightly visible.

All the photos were digitally doctored:

- *The Orange County Register* zipped up the boy's fly.
- The *Register* also changed the color of the sky, making it bluer.
- The editors of *A Day in the Life of America* took a photo of a cowboy on horseback, put him on a hillside and enlarged the moon. "I don't know if it's right or wrong," said one of the book's editors. "All I know is it sells the book better."
- *The National Geographic* extended a towel around the athlete to cover the genital area.

A Few Conclusions

It is difficult to say with certainty whether the decisions in these situations were moral or immoral. We can, however, make some headway in reaching a defensible decision if we establish some bases from which to launch our assessments.

In balancing a special interest against the general interest, the latter should prevail. Defining the general interest is not easy, for, as some maintain, there is no general public interest but a melange of special interests. Still, access to information is one of the essential underpinnings for the full functioning of a democracy.

The journalist with an overly acute sense of responsibility can be as dangerous to the community as the recklessly irresponsible reporter. When the newspaper published the conviction of the deceased former county official, it did disregard a personal interest (his family's) for the general interest. Yet what general interest was served?

Disclosure of a minor crime committed 30 years before by a person who is dead seems to serve no end but the purpose—often sound enough—of full disclosure. If truth is served by presenting all the facts, then certainly we are on sound moral ground if we include this unsavory but factual detail in the obituary. But the journalist knows that he or she is forced to select for use from a limited stockpile of information the few facts that can be fitted into the restricted time and space allocations. In this selection process, the journalist applies to the material the tests of utility, relevance and significance within a value system.

Had the crime been well-known at the time of the man's death, the journalist could not ignore it. What the public knows the press cannot skip over without risking charges of covering up information.

Missoula   This guideline applies to the Missoula case. There was no way the community would remain ignorant of the death of the young woman. Had the newspaper failed to run some story, accusations could have been made that the newspaper showed partiality to a middle-class family, whereas day after day it chronicles the troubles of others less affluent and influential. The newspaper could have handled the story with an editor's note admitting its dilemma, which might have alleviated the violent reaction to publication—the newspaper's editorial writer condemned the story and scores of people protested with calls and cancellations. (Krajick's dilemma might have been less intense had he considered an editor's note. Although readers usually need not be told the reporter's problems, situations such as these can be less troublesome with full disclosure.)

Suppose the Missoula newspaper alone had learned that the young woman died a prostitute. Should it have included the fact in its story? If her work had been an inextricable part of the crime, there would have been no way to avoid it. But she had been found dead near her apartment house, the victim of an unknown assailant. No newspaper dredges up every aspect of an individual's past, whether for an obituary or a straight news story.

However, as it turned out later, her work was part of her death, for the man charged with her murder was her pimp. The sordid affair would have to have been told when her murderer was arrested and charged.

Postscript: Eight months after the *Missoulian* published the story of the young woman's murder, a late model Chrysler New Yorker rolled into Missoula and the four occupants went to work. Two cruised bars, and two went to the high schools. Within hours, the police were informed by an alerted public. The four men were arrested and convicted of criminal trespass and soliciting for prostitution.

The Author's Problem   The Missoula incident posed an ethical problem for me. In the first draft of this section, I used the young woman's name, following the instinctive reaction of a journalist to supply basic information. Surely, in a book that seeks to examine a subject in detail, the name would seem to be relevant. But is it? What does it add to the information necessary to understand the situation? Nothing. It would appear to be information for the sake of information, which has some merit. Balance this against the damage revelation could cause.

This textbook is used in Montana and it could cause grief to the family. Still, there is a principle no journalist can turn from: What the public knows or will learn, the journalist cannot ignore. Surely, after the newspaper ran the story, most people in town knew the identity of the young woman. But the story is now several years old.

The argument can continue indefinitely. Unlike the philosopher, who may spin out syllogisms for a lifetime, the journalist must act quickly. The decision in this case was against disclosure. What would you have done?

Racial Issues

The reporter who writes straightforward accounts of events may feed the fires of bigotry and violence and occasionally it might seem responsible not to use what some people would consider derogatory material. But such decisions corrode the journalist's moral injunction to be the carrier of information, bad as well as good. In the area of racial news, much has changed since newspapers gingerly approached news about racial and ethnic groups.

In a roundup on the ways the press was handling racial news in the 1970s, *The Wall Street Journal* summarized the journalist's dilemma:

> If the press hews to its ideals and holds a mirror up to society, reflecting all its evils, cankers and tensions as well as its virtues, it runs the risk of stirring dangerous passions. But if it deliberately distorts the image or blots out the parts that might inflame, it casts itself in the dubious role of censor and judge.

Some newspapers and stations, the *Journal* reported, had taken on self-censorship. Some agreed to arrangements whereby news of racial disturbances would be delayed. Most said they strove to be careful in handling sensitive racial news but would not limit coverage. "It is the public, not the press, that must in the end find a way out of racial crisis—and the public can't be expected to do that unless the press gives it an accurate picture of society, warts and all," the *Journal* stated.

The black poet Langston Hughes remarked that he would know television—and society—had matured when TV shows could portray a black as a liar, a cheat or a criminal.

Resolution

Now, 25 years after the *Journal* presented the dilemma and 40 years after Hughes called for honest portrayal, the issue has been resolved. When journalism turned away from reality, society suffered. In fact, the very people who were thought to be protected by this self-censorship were victimized by the journalism of half truth.

By ignoring the fact that minorities are the major victims of violent crime, journalists did little to help society cope with a lawlessness whose victims include children caught in drug-war shootouts. When attention was not paid to the fact that HIV and AIDS strike disproportionately in the black and Hispanic communities, preventive efforts lagged.

Because it has been taboo to examine what some sociologists described as the culture of poverty, fourth- and fifth-generation fatherless families on welfare pose widening problems for these families and for society. The media, usually ahead of the public, learned that the public was concerned when, in a mid-term congressional election, voters sent to Congress legislators who pledged to amend the welfare system drastically.

The accusations that negative racial news is racist have grown fainter, although it is clear that the subject remains sensitive and what the majority journalist may consider racially neutral may appear to the minority journalist as racism. One of the ways journalism has sought to cope with this tension is through the employment of black, Hispanic, Native American and Asian journalists who can provide insights denied whites.

The Pose and the Disguise

Deception has had a long and, until recently, an honorable journalistic history. In 1886, a young and ambitious reporter who called herself Nellie Bly feigned insanity to enter a mental hospital. This enabled her to expose inhuman conditions in the hospital. A century later, a reporter from *The Washington Post* gained admission to St. Elizabeth's, a federal hospital in Washington, D.C., with the same ruse.

Early in this textbook, we saw how a reporter posed as a pregnant woman in order to expose an abortion mill. One of the most revealing and dramatic books about life for blacks in the South, *Black Like Me,* was written by a white man who darkened his skin to pass as a black.

Reporters have disguised themselves as priests and police officers, as doctors and distraught relatives to get stories. Some of the great coups in journalism have come through deception. Although many of the questionable methods are

Doctored. During a shooting spree in New York, a killer murdered a young woman and blinded her boyfriend, who was taken to a hospital. At the hospital, a reporter for a New York TV station prevails on the young man's father to give him a photo of the victim. As the father starts to hand over the photo, a doctor puts his hand over it and says, "That won't be necessary." The reporter leaves the room, and outside the doctor walks over to the reporter and says, "Sorry, mate, that was professional, not personal." The man in a doctor's gown is Steve Dunleavy, a reporter for the *New York Post.*

A Journalist's Moral Framework

• **Loyalty to the facts.** "You inevitably develop an intense sense of revulsion or a mild attachment for one candidate or the other," said Joseph Alsop, Jr., a political writer. "But you have to be loyal to the facts or lose your reputation." John Dewey put it this way: "Devotion to fact, to truth, is a necessary moral demand."

• **An involvement in the affairs of men and women** that requires experiencing or witnessing directly the lives of human beings. Involvement generates compassion, accuracy and fairness, which are the foundations of an ethical journalism.

• **The ability to distance one's self from experience** to generate understanding. Antonio Gramsci, an Italian writer imprisoned by Mussolini for his commitment to freedom, said he had to learn the necessity of being "above the surroundings within which one lives, but without despising them or believing one's self superior to them."

• **A detached curiosity,** an exploratory attitude toward events and ideas. Detachment requires the journalist to be bound by evidence and reasonable deductions. Detachment is not indifference, which develops when, as Northrop Frye puts it, the person "ceases to think of himself as participating in the life of society. . . ."

• **A reverence for shared values, rules, codes, laws and arrangements** that give a sense of community. Such concern causes the journalist to keep careful watch for any action that can divide people by groups, classes or races.

• **Faith in experience** when intelligently used as a means of disclosing some truths.

• **An avoidance of a valueless objectivity.** This kind of objectivity can lead to what philosopher Stuart Hampshire describes as a "ice age of not caring." He writes that such an attitude can mean the end of civilization "not in a flurry of egotism and appetite leading to conflict . . . but in passivity and non-attachment, in a general spreading coldness. . . ."

• **A willingness "to hold belief in suspense,"** to doubt until evidence is obtained, to go where the evidence points instead of putting first a personally preferred conclusion; "to hold ideas in solution and use them as hypotheses instead of dogmas to be asserted: and (possibly the most distinctive of all) enjoyment of new fields for inquiry and of new problems." (John Dewey.)

• **An awareness of our limitations and responsibilities.** The story can never equal the whole truth. A concern for the consequences, the impact of what we write. A firm understanding of the line between fact and fiction.

• **Belief in the methods of journalism**—the conviction that this method will lead to some kind of truth worth sharing.

• **A moral vision of the future.** "If you don't have that vision," says the Indian writer Ved Mehta, "sooner or later the system will collapse." Without a moral vision, the journalist's compulsion may be power, profit and place in society.

• **An understanding that our words have consequences** and that we have some responsibility for the consequences.

• **To be active rather than reactive.** Walter Karp, a contributing editor of *Harper's Magazine,* writes: "The first fact of American journalism is its overwhelming dependence on sources, mostly official, usually powerful." The reporter who develops his or her own agenda for coverage is not source driven. This reporter goes into the community to help define the issues.

The Journalist. "A journalist, in any effort to render truth, has three responsibilities: to his reader, to his conscience and to his human subjects."
—John Hersey, *New Yorker* writer

The reporter's obligation is to "serve the public—not the profession of journalism, not a particular newspaper, not the government, but the public. . . ."
—Clifton Daniel, former managing editor of *The New York Times*

used for laudable ends—usually the exposure of corruption—questions have been raised about their use.

Is there a dividing line we can locate between permissible deception and irresponsible impersonation? Is the line located where an adversary press checks power to serve the legitimate public interest?

If we use life as the referent for testing the moral validity of actions, then posing to gain access to health clinics is morally defensible because lives are involved. But the adoption of poses for routine stories would appear unjustified. The reporter who disguises himself as a health seeker to gain access to the tent of a faith healer may have greater claim to moral justification than does the reporter who poses as a customer to expose a garage that overcharges.

A Philosopher's Guidelines

One of the time-tested guides to behavior is Immanuel Kant's categorical imperative: "Act as if the maxim from which you act were to become through your will a universal law of nature."

Kant had another imperative: "So act as to treat humanity, whether in your own person or that of another, in every case as an end in itself, never as a means." The imperatives of Kant, a major figure in the history of philosophy, may appear old-fashioned at first glance, but his prescriptions can help resolve some of the sticky moral questions journalists face.

In a sense, people are always means to the journalist's end, which is the news story. Even when deception is not used, the reporter maneuvers and manipulates sources to his or her end. The reporter justifies this on the ground that such actions serve useful purposes, even for the source, because the individual is a member of the society that is being served by the reporter.

Dishonesty

Impostors come in different guises. The reporter who poses as a priest to reach a grieving widow is one. The reporter who claims the work of a colleague as his or her own or who invents material is another.

Plagiarism

Incidents of plagiarism are increasing. Some reporters have used the work of syndicated columnists as their own. A reporter for a California newspaper wrote a column that was almost a word-for-word copy of a column by Art Buchwald.

A *Sacramento Bee* television critic was forced to resign when his column was found to contain material from a column in *The Orlando Sentinel* as was the *Chicago Sun-Times* editorial page editor who plagiarized material from *The Washington Post.*

Invention

Sometimes reality isn't enough and reporters fabricate. To attract readers, they invent people, give them phony addresses, devise exciting quotations for them. A reporter for *The Washington Post* invented an 8-year-old heroin addict whose harrowing story won the author a Pulitzer Prize. She lost her job and the prize when she was exposed.

The *Globe*'s Columnists   When she was asked about the newspaper's inability to locate people she quoted in her columns, Patricia Smith of *The Boston Globe* replied, "The type of people I speak to don't have phone numbers or addresses." For a while, the newspaper put its questions aside. But in a story about a cancer victim identified only by a middle name, an assistant managing editor and some reporters found the quotes too good, too perfect. This led to a further check and Smith admitted inventing people in four columns. She was asked to resign.

Further checks showed that more than 50 columns may have included fabricated people and events.

Another *Globe* columnist, Mike Barnacle, was asked to resign when it was revealed that one of his columns contained 10 items from a book he did not cite as his source.

The *New Republic*'s Fabricator   For three years, *The New Republic* published articles by a brilliant young writer the magazine described as having "a flair for keen observation and colorful anecdotes." After reporters on the website of *Forbes Digital Tool* said they could not confirm any of the material in a piece he had written, the magazine checked. After investigating, the magazine concluded, "The whole article was made up out of whole cloth." Further checking determined many of his other pieces were inventions. He was fired as associate editor.

In their defense, some of these inventive reporters contend that their work should be judged like any creative writing—imaginative in detail but true in ultimate meaning. They say they have poetic license. Unfortunately for them, journalism issues no such licenses.

The Seduction of Technique

Everyone who tries to capture meaning—whether on paper, on film, on canvas or in spoken words—inevitably is attracted to the means of conveying ideas. Thus, the writer works on writing skills, the television journalist sharpens techniques of picture taking. Without skill, without a highly honed technique, the reporter may not convey a message with the desired impact.

But style and technique can be fatally attractive. Too often, the means overwhelm the ends. "In television, coverage—the ability to converge on an event and transmit pictures of the scene itself—has largely replaced reporting—the attempt to reconstruct, interpret, and understand what is happening," says Lawrence K. Grossman, former president of NBC News.

Fact and Fiction. A long-time *New Yorker* writer told students at Yale that he fabricated people, sometimes invented scenes and created conversations for some of his pieces. These embellishments, he said, made his articles more accurate, more readable.

John Hersey, another longtime *New Yorker* writer, said there is one sacred rule in journalism: "The writer must not invent. The legend on the license must read: None of this was made up. The ethics of journalism, if we can be allowed such a boon, must be based on the simple truth that every journalist knows the difference between the distortion that comes from subtracting observed data and the distortion that comes from adding invented data."

For print journalists, the message from seminars, institutes and publications over the past few years is clear: Improve your writing.

Writing and related techniques are important, but they are not what journalism is about. Journalism uses style to develop content; substance is the center of our work.

The possible conflict between style and truth was understood by Leo Tolstoy, the Russian writer:

> The aesthetic and the ethical are two arms of one lever; to the extent to which one side becomes longer and heavier, the other side becomes shorter and lighter. As soon as a man loses his moral sense, he becomes particularly responsive to the aesthetic.

When journalists talk about what they do, they call it *reporting;* and when they describe themselves, they use the word *reporters.* The journalist's moral responsibility is to report, and it is in this sphere that his or her major efforts are directed. The journalist cannot see the world clearly without constant replenishment of his or her knowledge of that world, and it is in this area that major work is to be done. Content and substance, not style and technique, are the focus.

Knowledge as a Value

The journalist cannot in conscience be complicitous in any attempt to counter public awareness. "If you are among brigands and you are silent, you are a brigand yourself," a Hungarian poet tells us. The brigands come in all shapes and sizes. Some are treated leniently by the press because they appear innocently misguided, censoring books and TV shows to protect us from wickedness and vice.

The journalist must recognize these people as threats to an immanent value, the necessity of knowing, of having information that will liberate us from ignorance, prejudice and the limitations of time and place. Information becomes memory, and memory, says the Polish writer Czeslaw Milosz, "provides a foundation for values" by which a society lives.

This does not mean that journalists use everything they turn up. All facts are not equal, and other values come into play in the selection of what is to be published and broadcast.

The open society can be perilous. When all the winds of doctrine are set loose, the turbulence can be overwhelming. The journalist hardly contributes to order, for the journalist's task is to broadcast competing ideas and doctrines.

Adversary Journalism

The choice between adversary journalism and compliance with power may seem trivialized by a comment by the Italian journalist Oriana Fallaci, but it does go to the heart of the matter. She said, "Almost every time I have tried to absolve even partially some famous son-of-a-bitch, I have been bitterly sorry."

But journalists also realize that leadership is important, that people need to have faith in their leaders, and they fear feeding the stereotype that politicians are crooked, corrupt or stupid.

And so journalists worry about their traditional role as adversaries to power. But they are more concerned about the uses of power by the state and its functionaries. The powerful state, says Milosz, "like a crab, has eaten up all the substance of society." The society versus the state, he says, "is the basic issue of the twentieth century."

> **Source?** "Only a fool expects the authorities to tell him what the news is."
> —*Russell Baker, columnist*

The Democratic Commitment

The journalist who is committed to the open society, to democratic values, has a moral structure from which to work, an alertness to institutions and their activities that threaten the right of anyone to take part justly, equally and freely in a meaningful community life. Any word or deed that denies this way of life to people because of their sex, age, race, sexual preference, origin, religion or position in society must be revealed by the journalist.

When *Times* columnist Anthony Lewis learned that the Nixon administration had made a deal with Vice President Spiro Agnew for his resignation in return for the promise of a nonprison sentence on his plea of "no contest" to a felony, he wrote that this was the correct action. It was right, Lewis said, on "political grounds: the need to investigate the president's wrongdoing without having as his potential successor someone who was himself under indictment."

But Lewis then had second thoughts following the sentencing to prison of two businessmen who confessed to corrupt payments to Agnew during his governorship of Maryland. "So they go to prison," Lewis wrote, "while the sleazy felon who soiled our politics earns $100,000 in his new career as 'business broker.'" Instead of trusting the democratic institutions of law and politics to work, Lewis wrote, the attorney general had made personal policy.

"That unhappy precedent was carried further in the pardon of Richard Nixon," he wrote. "Of course, Watergate is not alone in examples of law applied unequally. It is commonplace, and terribly damaging to our system of criminal justice, for the powerful to go free while the little wrongdoers go to prison."

Owners' Responsibility

William Dean Singleton, the publisher of newspapers in Houston, Dallas and Denver, has a simple journalistic philosophy: Give readers what they want. After he conducts market research, he orients his newspaper in the direction readers indicate. If it means spending half his editorial budget on sports and entertainment, he says, he will do so.

"The newspaper of tomorrow is going to have to give readers what they want and not what they need," he said. "Who are we to say what they need?"

He described the newspaper as being "like a candy bar. You have to package it to be attractive to the reader. You have to put in the ingredients they want. You have to market it properly."

Compare these remarks with those of Bernard Stein, publisher of *The Riverdale Press,* a weekly newspaper in New York: "We're committed to the idea that people have to band together to shape their own lives and that of their communities. We give them an instrument to do that by telling them about issues."

The *Press* was firebombed in 1989 after it defended an author whose novel had offended Iran's rulers. The newspaper then repeated its contention that Iran's death threat to the author violated civilized behavior.

Political Bias

In the 1948 presidential election, powerful publishers sought to tarnish Harry S. Truman's reputation. Henry Luce, Robert McCormick and William Randolph Hearst demeaned Truman's leadership abilities and ignored the large crowds he was attracting on his cross-country campaign.

Responsibility to Staff   The publisher or station owner who does not carry out his or her obligations to the staff—a decent salary, adequate staffing of reportorial and editing positions, full support for penetrating journalism, intelligent and independent leadership—cannot demand the loyalty of the staff. When he was dean of the School of Journalism at Columbia University, Edward W. Barrett advised students to establish a "go-to-hell fund" on the job, a few dollars squirreled away that would enable them to quit should they find their newspapers or stations irresponsible.

A Personal Credo

Young journalists might consider adopting personal values as guidelines in their work. From a variety of sources—from the Greek philosophers to police reporters—the following emerge as suggestions for consideration:

- A belief in and a commitment to a political culture in which the cornerstone is restraint in the use of power.
- Moderation in life and behavior.
- A secular, scientific attitude toward the work at hand. Knowledge is allowed to speak for itself. The professional does not believe on the basis of hope but of evidence.
- An openmindedness that seeks out and tries to comprehend various points of view, including those in conflict with those the reporter holds.
- Responsibility to one's abilities and talent. To leave them fallow, to fail to labor to develop them through indolence or want of seriousness of purpose demeans the self and punishes the society whose betterment depends on new ideas vigorously pursued. For Homer, the good was the fulfillment of function. For Aristotle, the good was living up to one's potential, and for Kant the development of one's talents was a duty, and adherence to "duties" constituted the moral life. The reporter who fails to report and write to his or her potential is immoral.
- An understanding of and a tolerance for the ambiguities involved in most important issues and the ability to act despite these uncertainties and doubts. The willingness to take responsibility for these actions.
- The willingness to admit errors.
- A capacity to endure solitude and criticism, the price of independence.
- A reluctance to create heroes and villains to the rhythm of the deadline.

Eye of Conscience. During the Depression, a group of photographers set out to show the dire results of poverty. The most noted was Dorothea Lange, who said of herself, "All my life I tried very hard to make a place where what I did would count." Her photos of migrant workers and their children were reproduced in newspapers, magazines and books.

Pare Lorentz, the great producer of film documentaries, said of Lange that she did "more for these tragic nomads than all the politicians of the country." *The New York Times* said, "She functioned as our national eye of conscience. Her constant concerns—the survival of human dignity under impossible conditions, the confrontation of the system by the individual, and the helpless ignorance of children—were perfectly suited to the subject."

A College Education

Charlie Peters, editor of *The Washington Monthly,* said his college education was valuable because of the instructors who taught him "to be skeptical of conventional liberalism while remaining loyal to its basic belief in freedom, fair play and generosity to the down and out . . . skepticism of conventional wisdom of all kinds . . . the importance of trying to strip away the barriers of pride and pretense that keep us from really talking to one another, to be willing to acknowledge instead of concealing one's confusion and anxiety." His education, he said, "was a journey from being lost to finding the guiding principle of my life: No matter how absurd and futile the effort might seem, I had to keep trying to tell the truth as I saw it."

- A knowledge of the pathfinders in fields of knowledge, including journalism.
- A commitment to work.
- A sense of the past. W. H. Auden said, "Let us remember that though great artists of the past could not change the course of history, it is only through their work that we are able to break bread with the dead, and without communion with the dead, a fully human life is impossible."
- Resistance to praise. Humility. "You have to fight against the praise of people who like you," says I. F. Stone, the crusading journalist. "Because you know darn well it wasn't good enough." He tells the story of the great conductor Arturo Toscanini who was engulfed by admirers after a concert. "Maestro, you were wonderful," one said. Toscanini knew the oboe had not come in at the right point and that the violins were off. And Toscanini burst into tears because he knew it had not been good enough.
- Duty. John Dewey said, "If a man is burdened with an idea, he not only desires to express it; he ought to express it. He owes it to his conscience and the common good. The indispensable function of expressing ideas is one of obligation—to the community and also to something beyond the community, let us say to truth."
- Avoidance of the desire to please. Self-censorship is a greater enemy than outside censorship. Pleasing an editor, the publisher or the source is commonplace. Setting one's values to the "pragmatic level of the newsroom group," as Warren Breed puts it, can lead to timid, status-quo journalism.
- A wariness about making words an end in themselves. André Maurois, the French writer and political activist, writes:

Power, Glory and Money are only secondary objects for the writer. No man can be a great writer without having a great philosophy, though it may often be unexpressed. A great writer has respect for *values.* His essential function is to raise life to the dignity of thought, and he does this by giving it a shape. If he refuses to perform this function he can be a clever juggler and play tricks with words such as his fellow writers may admire, but his books will be of little interest to anybody else. If, on the contrary, he fulfills it, he will be happy in his writing. Borne aloft by the world as reflected in himself, and producing a sound echo in his times, he helps to shape it by showing to men an image of themselves which is at once true and disciplined.

Summing Up

Reporters should seek to give voice to all groups in society, not to report solely those who hold power.

The public's need to know is an immanent value.

In determining what shall be reported and what shall be included in a news story, the reporter should consider the relevance of the material to the real needs of the audience.

If the reporter cannot disclose in the story the tactics and techniques used to gather information for the story, such tactics should not be used.

The reporter should:

- Be wary of treating people as a means.
- Believe on the basis of facts, not hope.
- Be committed to a value system but be free from ideologies and commitments that limit thought.
- Be wary of promising to help a source in return for material.

In balancing moral alternatives, the choice can be made on the basis of:

- The importance of the possible actions to life. (Life is the referent of value.)
- The public interest as against the private interest.
- The extent of knowledge of the event. If it is public knowledge or is likely to become so and the material is significant and relevant, the information should be used.
- Serving the needs of society. If the material assists people in participating justly, equally and freely in a meaningful community life, then it should be used.

The code of the Society of Professional Journalists is in Appendix D.

Further Reading

The Adversary Press. St. Petersburg, Fla.: The Poynter Institute for Media Studies, 1983. (A discussion of ethics by 19 editors, publishers and scholars at an Institute seminar.)

Bagdikian, Ben H. *The Effete Conspiracy and Other Crimes by the Press.* New York: Harper & Row, 1972.

Benjamin, Burton. *Fair Play.* New York: Harper & Row, 1988.

Black, Max, ed. *The Morality of Scholarship.* Ithaca, N.Y.: Cornell University Press, 1967.

Commission on Freedom of the Press. *A Free and Responsible Press.* Chicago: University of Chicago Press, 1947.

Fallows, James. *Breaking the News: How the Media Undermine American Democracy.* New York: Pantheon Books, 1996.

Gerald, J. Edward. *The Social Responsibility of the Press.* Minneapolis: University of Minnesota Press, 1963.

Hulteng, John. *Playing It Straight.* Chester, Conn.: The Globe Pequot Press, 1981.

Ibsen, Henrik. *An Enemy of the People.* 1882. (Available in many anthologies and collections.)

McCulloch, Frank, ed. *Drawing the Line.* St. Petersburg, Fla.: The Poynter Institute for Media Studies, 1984.

Pierce, Robert N. *A Sacred Trust. Nelson Poynter and the St. Petersburg Times.* Gainesville, Fla.: University Press of Florida, 1994.

Reston, James. *The Artillery of the Press.* New York: Harper & Row, 1960.

Smith, Z. N., and Pamela Zekman. *The Mirage.* New York: Random House, 1979.

Swados, Harvey. *Years of Conscience: The Muckrakers.* New York:, World Publishing, 1962.

Waldron, Ann. *Hodding Carter: The Reconstruction of a Racist.* Chapel Hill, N.C.: Algonquin Books of Chapel Hill, 1993.

Stylebook

addresses Abbreviate *Avenue, Boulevard, Street* with specific address: *1314 Kentucky St.* Spell out without specific address: *construction on Fifth Avenue.*

Use figures for the address number: *3 Third Ave.; 45 Main St.* Spell out numbers under 10 as street names: *21 Fourth Ave.; 450 11th St.*

age Use figures. To express age as an adjective, use hyphens: *a 3-year-old girl.* Also use hyphens when age is expressed as a noun as in: *a 10-year-old.* Unless otherwise stated, the figure is presumed to indicate years: *a boy, 4, and his sister, 6 months.*

Infant: under one year of age; *child:* someone in the period between infancy and youth, ages 1 to 13; *girl, boy:* under 18; *youth:* 13–18; *man, woman:* over 18; *adult:* over 18, unless used in specific legal context for crimes such as drinking; *middle-aged:* 35–55; *elderly:* over 65. Avoid *elderly* when describing individuals.

a.m., p.m. Lowercase with periods.

amendment Capitalize when referring to specific amendments to the U.S. Constitution. Spell out for the first through ninth; use figures for 10th and above: *First Amendment, 10th Amendment.*

anti- Hyphenate all but words that have their own meanings: *antibiotic, antibody, anticlimax, antidote, antifreeze, antihistamine, antiknock, antimatter, antiparticle, antipasto, antiperspirant, antiseptic, antiserum, antithesis, antitoxin, antitrust.*

bi, semi When used with periods of time, the prefix *bi* means every other; *semi* means twice. A biannual conference meets every other year. A semiweekly newspaper comes out twice a week. No hyphens.

brand name A nonlegal term for a trademark. Do not use them as generic terms or as verbs: *soft drink* instead of *Coke* or *coke; photocopy* instead of *Xerox.*

capitalization Generally, follow a down style.

Proper nouns: Use capitals for names of persons, places, trademarks; titles when used with names; nicknames of people, states, teams; titles of books, plays, movies.

century Lowercase, spelling out numbers less than 10, except when used in proper nouns—*the fifth century, 18th century,* but *20th Century-Fox* and *Nineteenth Century Society*—following the organization's practice.

chairman, chairwoman Use *chairman* or *chairwoman* instead of *chair* or *chairperson; spokesman* or *spokeswoman* instead of *spokesperson* and similar constructions unless the *-person* construction is a formal title.

Use *chairman* or *spokesman* when referring to the office in general. A neutral word such as *representative* often may be the best choice.

co- Use a hyphen when forming nouns, adjectives and verbs that indicate occupation or status: *co-star, co-written.* No hyphen for other constructions: *coeducation, coexist.*

Congress Capitalize when referring to the U.S. Senate and House of Representatives. The term is correctly used only in reference to the two legislative branches together. Capitalize also when referring to foreign governments that use the term or its equivalent.

Do not capitalize *congressional* unless it is part of a proper name.

Constitution, constitutional Capitalize when referring to the U.S. Constitution, with or without the *U.S.* modifier. When referring to other constitutions, capitalize only when preceded by the name of a nation or state. Lowercase *constitutional.*

court names Capitalize the full proper names of courts at all levels. Retain capitalization if *U.S.* or a state name is dropped.

dates *July 6, 1957, was her birth date.* (Use commas.) *She was born in July 1957.* (No comma between the month and year.)

Abbreviate the month with a specific date: *Feb. 19.* Spell out all months when standing alone. With dates, use abbreviations: *Jan., Feb., Aug., Sept., Oct., Nov., Dec.* Spell out *March, April, May, June, July.*

directions and regions Lowercase *north, south, northeast,* etc. when they indicate compass direction: *Police followed the car south on Route 22.*

Capitalize when they refer to regions: *Southern accent; Northeastern industry.*

With names of nations, lowercase except when they are part of a proper name or are used to designate a politically divided nation: *tourism in southern France,* but *South Korea* and *Northern Ireland.*

Lowercase compass points when they describe a section of a state or city except when they are part of a proper name (*South Dakota*) or when they refer to a widely known region (*Southern California; the East Side of New York*).

Capitalize them when combining them with a common noun to form a proper noun: *the Eastern Hemisphere; the North Woods.*

entitled Does not mean *titled. Citizens 18 and older are entitled to vote,* but *the book is titled "News Reporting and Writing."*

ex- No hyphen for words that use *ex* in the sense of *out of: excommunicate, expropriate.* Hyphenate when using in the sense of *former: ex-husband, ex-convict. Former* is preferred with titles: *Former President Gerald R. Ford.*

fireman Use *firefighter* because some women hold this job.

fractions Spell out amounts less than 1, using hyphens: *one-half, two-thirds.* Use figures for amounts larger than 1, converting to decimals whenever possible: *3.5* instead of *three and one-half* or *3 1/2.*

Figures are preferred in tabular material and in stories about stocks.

gay Acceptable as a popular synonym for *homosexual.* May be used as a noun and an adjective.

handicapped, disabled, impaired Avoid describing an individual as *disabled* or *handicapped* unless it is essential to the story. If necessary to use, make clear what the handicap is and how it affects the person's mental or physical activity. *Disabled* refers to a condition that interferes with a person's ability to do something independently. *Handicap* should be avoided in describing a disability. *Blind* means complete loss of sight. For others, use *partially blind. Deaf* means complete loss of hearing. For others, use *partial hearing loss* or *partially deaf. Mute* refers to people who physically cannot speak. For others, use *speech impaired.* Do not use *wheelchair-bound* unless necessary, and then say why.

Do not identify someone as having a disability unless the disability is relevant, and the relevance is clear. People with disabilities should not be described as heroes or victims. Describe the symptoms or difficulties the person encounters and let the reader reach conclusions.

historical periods and events Capitalize widely recognized periods and events in anthropology, archaeology, geology and history: *the Bronze Age, the Ice Age, the Renaissance.*

Capitalize widely recognized popular names for eras and events: *the Glorious Revolution, the Roaring '20s.*

holidays and holy days Capitalize them. In federal law, the legal holidays are New Year's, Martin Luther King's Birthday, President's Day, Memorial Day, Independence Day, Labor Day, Columbus Day, Veterans Day, Thanksgiving and Christmas.

States are not required to follow the federal lead in designating holidays, except that federal employees must receive the day off or must be paid overtime if they work.

Jewish holy days: Hanukkah, Passover, Purim, Rosh Hashana, Shavuot, Sukkot and Yom Kippur.

in- No hyphen when it means *not: invalid; inaccurate.* Mostly used without the hyphen in other combinations, but there are a few exceptions: *in-house; in-depth.* Consult a dictionary when in doubt.

-in Always precede with a hyphen: *break-in; sit-in; write-in.*

initials Use periods and no space: *H.L. Mencken; C.S. Lewis.* This practice has been adopted to ensure that initials will be set on the same line.

like- Follow with a hyphen when used to mean *similar to: like-minded; like-natured.*

-like No hyphen unless the *l* would be tripled: *lifelike,* but *shell-like.*

mailman Use the term *letter carrier* or *mail carrier* because many women work for the Postal Service.

man, mankind *Humanity* is preferred for the plural form. Use *a person* or *an individual* in the singular. A phrase or sentence usually can be reconstructed to eliminate any awkwardness.

National Organization for Women. Not *National Organization of Women.*

nationalities and races Capitalize the proper names of nationalities, peoples, races, tribes, etc. Lowercase *black* and *white.* Lowercase derogatory terms such as *honky* and *nigger.* Use them only in direct quotations.

See **race** for guidelines on when racial identification is pertinent in a story.

nobility Capitalize *king, queen, duke* and other titles when they precede the individual's name. Lowercase when standing alone: *King Juan Carlos,* but *the king of Spain.*

non- In general, do not hyphenate if *not* could be used before the root word. Hyphenate before proper nouns or in awkward combinations: *non-nuclear.*

numerals Spell out *one* through *nine,* except when used to indicate age, votes, building numbers, scores. Use figures for *10* and above.

Spell out a number when it begins a sentence: *Fifteen members voted against the bill.* Use figures when a year begins a sentence: *1999 began auspiciously.*

Use figures for time, temperature, dimensions, percentages, percents and money: *$5,* but *a dollar.*

If a series has mixed numbers, use all numbers: *His table had scattered on it 6 magazines, 13 books and 11 newspapers.*

For amounts of $1 million and more, use the *$* sign and figures up to two decimal places with the *million, billion, trillion* spelled out: *$1.65 million.* Exact amounts are given in figures: *$1,650,398.*

When spelling out large numbers, separate numbers ending in *y* from the next number with a hyphen: *seventy-nine; one hundred seventy-nine.*

people, persons Use *person* when referring to an individual. *People* is preferred to *persons* in all plural uses.

People also is a collective noun that takes a plural verb when used to refer to a single race or nation: *The Philippine people are awaiting the president's decision on the offer of aid.* In this sense, *peoples* is the plural form: *The peoples of Western Europe do not always agree on East-West issues.*

percentages Use figures—decimals, not fractions—and the word *percent.* not the symbol: *2.5 percent; 10 percent.* For amounts less than 1 percent, place a zero before the decimal: *0.6 percent.*

When presenting a range, repeat *percent* after each figure: *2 percent to 5 percent.*

policeman Use *police officer* instead.

political parties and philosophies Capitalize the name of the party and the word *party* when it is used as part of the organization's proper name: *the Democratic Party.*

Capitalize *Communist, Conservative, Democrat, Liberal,* etc., when they refer to the activities of a specific party or to individual members.

Lowercase the name of a philosophy in noun and adjective forms unless it is derived from a proper name: *communism; fascist,* but *Marxism; Nazi.*

In general, avoid the terms *conservative, radical, leftist* and *rightist.* In casual and popular usage, the meanings of these terms vary, depending on the user and the situation being discussed. A more precise description of an individual's or a group's political views is preferred.

post office Should not be capitalized. The agency is the U.S. Postal Service.

prefixes See entries for specific prefixes. Generally, do not hyphenate when using a prefix with a word starting with a consonant.

Except for *cooperate* and *coordinate,* use a hyphen if the prefix ends in the same vowel that begins the following word: *re-elect,* not *reelect.*

Use a hyphen if the word that follows is capitalized: *pan-American; anti-Catholic.*

Use a hyphen to join doubled prefixes: *sub-subclause.*

presidency Always lowercase.

president Capitalized only as a title before an individual's name: *President Bill Clinton,* but *the president said he would spend New Year's in Houston.*

presidential Lowercase unless part of a proper name: *presidential approval,* but *Presidential Medal of Freedom.*

race Race, religion and national origin are sometimes essential to a story but too often are injected when they are not pertinent. When in doubt about relevance, substitute descriptions such as *white, Baptist, French.* If one of these descriptions would be pertinent, use the original term.

religious references
DEITIES: Capitalize the proper names of monotheistic deities, pagan and mythological gods and goddesses: *Allah, the Father, Zeus.* Lowercase pronouns that refer to the deity: *he, him, thee, who,* etc.

Lowercase *gods* when referring to the deities of polytheistic religions. Lowercase such words as *god-awful, godlike, godsend.*

LIFE OF JESUS CHRIST: Capitalize the names of major events in the life of Jesus Christ in references that do not use his name: *the Last Supper; the Resurrection.* Lowercase when the words are used with his name: *the ascension of Christ.* Apply the same principle to events in the life of his mother, Mary.

RITES: Capitalize proper names for rites that commemorate the Last Supper or signify a belief in Jesus Christ's presence: *the Lord's Supper; Holy Eucharist.* Lowercase the names of other sacraments.

HOLY DAYS: Capitalize the names of holy days: *Hanukkah.*

OTHER WORDS: Lowercase *heaven, hell, devil, angel, cherub, apostle, priest,* etc.

rock 'n' roll Not *rock and roll.*

room numbers Use figures and capitalize *room:* The faculty met in Room 516. Capitalize the names of specially designated rooms: *Oval Office; Blue Room.*

saint Abbreviate as *St.* in the names of saints, cities and other places except *Saint John* (New Brunswick), to distinguish it from St. John's, Newfoundland, and *Sault Ste. Marie.*

seasons Lowercase *spring, summer, fall, winter* and their derivatives. Capitalize when part of a formal name: *St. Paul Winter Carnival; Summer Olympics.*

self- Always hyphenate: *self-motivated; self-taught.*

senate, senatorial Capitalize all references to specific legislative bodies, regardless of whether the name of the nation or state is used: *U.S. Senate; the state Senate.*

Lowercase plural uses: *the Iowa and Kansas state senates.* Lowercase references to nongovernmental bodies: *the student-faculty senate.*

Always lowercase *senatorial.*

sexism Avoid stereotyping women or men. Be conscious of equality in treatment of both sexes.

When writing of careers and jobs, avoid presuming that the wage earner is a man and that the woman is a homemaker: *the average family of five* instead of *the average worker with a wife and three children.*

Avoid physical descriptions of women or men when not absolutely relevant to the story.

Use parallel references to both sexes: *the men and the women,* not *the men and the ladies; husband and wife,* not *man and wife.*

Do not use nouns and pronouns to indicate sex unless the sex difference is basic to understanding or there is no suitable substitute. One way to avoid such subtle sexism is to change the noun to the plural, eliminating the masculine pronoun: *Drivers should carry their licenses,* not *Every driver should carry his license.*

Personal appearance and marital and family relationships should be used only when relevant to the story.

state names Spell out names of the 50 U.S. states when they stand alone in textual matter.

The names of eight states are never abbreviated: *Alaska, Hawaii, Idaho, Iowa, Maine, Ohio, Texas, Utah.*

Abbreviate other state names when used with a city, in a dateline or with party affiliation. Do not use Postal Service abbreviations.

Ala.	*Fla.*	*Md.*	*Neb.*	*N.D.*	*Tenn.*
Ariz.	*Ga.*	*Mass.*	*Nev.*	*Okla.*	*Vt.*
Ark.	*Ill.*	*Mich.*	*N.H.*	*Ore.*	*Va.*
Calif.	*Ind.*	*Minn.*	*N.J.*	*Pa.*	*Wash.*
Colo.	*Kan.*	*Miss.*	*N.M.*	*R.I.*	*W.Va.*
Conn.	*Ky.*	*Mo.*	*N.Y.*	*S.C.*	*Wis.*
Del.	*La.*	*Mont.*	*N.C.*	*S.D.*	*Wyo.*

statehouse Capitalize all references to a specific statehouse, with or without the state name. But lowercase in all plural uses: *the New Mexico Statehouse; the Arizona and New Mexico statehouses.*

suspensive hyphenation Use as follows: *The 19- and 20-year-olds were not served alcoholic beverages.* Use in all similar cases.

Although the form looks somewhat awkward, it guides readers, who may otherwise expect a noun to follow the first figure.

syllabus, syllabuses Also: *memorandum, memorandums.*

teen, teen-ager (noun), **teen-age** (adjective) Do not use *teen-aged.*

telecast (noun), **televise** (verb)

temperatures Use figures for all except *zero.* Use the word *minus,* not a minus sign, to indicate temperatures below zero. *The day's high was 9; the day's low was minus 9.*

Temperatures are higher and lower and they rise and fall but they do not become warmer or cooler.

Third World The economically developing nations of Africa, Asia and Latin America.

time Exact times often are unnecessary. *Last night* and *this morning* are acceptable substitutes for *yesterday* and *today.* Use exact time when pertinent but avoid redundancies: *8 a.m. this morning* should be *8 a.m. today* or *8 o'clock this morning.*

Use figures except for *noon* and *midnight: 12 noon* is redundant.

Separate hours from minutes with a colon: *3:15 p.m.*

titles

ACADEMIC TITLES: Capitalize and spell out formal titles such as *professor, dean, president, chancellor and chairman* when they precede a name. Lowercase elsewhere. Do not abbreviate *Professor* as *Prof.*

Lowercase modifiers such as *journalism* in *journalism Professor John Rist* or *department* in *department chairwoman Kim Power,* unless the modifier is a proper name: *French Professor Jeannette Spear.*

COURTESY TITLES: Do not use the courtesy titles *Miss, Mr., Mrs.* or *Ms.* on first reference. Instead, use the person's first and last names. Do not use *Mr.* unless it is combined with *Mrs.: Kyle Scott Hotsenpiller; Mr. and Mrs. Kyle Scott Hotsenpiller.*

Courtesy titles may be used on second reference for women, according to the woman's preference and these guidelines:

• Married women: On first reference, identify a woman by her own first name and her husband's last name, if she uses it: *Betty Phillips.* Use *Mrs.* on first reference only if a woman requests that her husband's first name be used or her own first name cannot be determined: *Mrs. Steven A. Phillips.*

On second reference, use *Mrs.* unless a woman initially identified by her own first name prefers *Ms.: Rachel Finch; Mrs. Finch; Ms. Finch.* Or use no title: *Finch; Rachel Finch.*

If a married woman is known by her maiden name, precede it by *Miss* on second reference unless she prefers *Ms.: Sarah Wilson; Miss Wilson* or *Ms. Wilson.*

• Unmarried women: Use *Miss, Ms.* or no title on second reference, according to the woman's preference.

For divorced and widowed women, the normal practice is to use *Mrs.* or no title on second reference, according to the woman's preference. Use *Miss, Ms.* or no title, according to the woman's preference, if the woman returns to her maiden name.

If a woman prefers *Ms.* or no title, do not include her marital status in a story unless it is pertinent.

GOVERNMENTAL TITLES: Capitalize when used as a formal title in front of a person's name. It is not necessary to use a title on second reference: *Gov. Fred Florence; Florence.* For women who hold official positions, use the courtesy title on second reference, according to the guidelines for courtesy titles: *Gov. Ruth Arnold; Miss Arnold, Mrs. Arnold, Ms. Arnold, Arnold.* (Some newspapers do not use the courtesy title on second reference.)

Abbreviate *Governor* as *Gov., Lieutenant Governor* as *Lt. Gov.* when used as a formal title before a name.

Congressional titles: Before names, abbreviate *Senator* as *Sen.* and *Representative* as *Rep.* Add *U.S.* or *state* if necessary to avoid confusion.

Short form punctuation for party affiliation: Use abbreviations listed under **state names** and set them off from the person's name with commas: *Sen. Bob Graham, D-Fla., and Rep. Barney Frank, D-Mass., attended the ceremony.*

Capitalize and spell out other formal government titles before a person's name. Do not use titles on second reference: *Attorney General Jay Craven spoke. Craven said . . .*

Capitalize and spell out formal titles instead of abbreviating before the person's name in direct quotations only. Lowercase in all uses not mentioned already.

OCCUPATIONAL TITLES: They are always lowercase: *senior vice president Nancy Harden.* Avoid false titles: *bridge champion Helen P. George* should be: *Helen P. George, Sioux Falls bridge tourney winner.*

RELIGIOUS TITLES: The first reference to a clergyman, clergywoman or nun should include a capitalized title before the person's name.

On second reference: for men, use only a last name if he uses a surname. If a man is known only by a religious name, repeat the title: *Pope Paul VI* or *Pope Paul* on first reference; *the pope* or *the pontiff* on second reference. For women, use *Miss, Mrs., Ms.* or no title, according to the woman's preference.

Cardinals, archbishops, bishops: On first reference, use the title before the person's first and last name. On second reference, use the last name only or the title.

Ministers and priests: Use *the Rev.* before a name on first reference. Substitute *Monsignor* before the name of a Roman Catholic priest who has received this honor.

Rabbis: Use *Rabbi* before a name on first reference. On second reference, use only the last name of a man; use *Miss, Mrs., Ms.* or no title before a woman's last name, according to her preference.

Nuns: Always use *Sister* or *Mother: Sister Agnes Mary* in all references if the nun uses only a religious name; *Sister Ann Marie Graham* on first reference if she uses a surname, *Sister Graham* on second.

TITLES OF WORKS: For titles of books, movies, operas, plays, poems, songs, television programs and lectures, speeches and works of art, apply the following guidelines:

Capitalize the principal words, including prepositions and conjunctions of four or more letters.

Capitalize an article or word of fewer than four letters if it is the first or last word in a title.

Place quotation marks around the names of all such works except the Bible and books that are primarily catalogs of reference material, including almanacs, directories, dictionaries, encyclopedias, handbooks and similar publications.

Translate a foreign title into English unless a work is known to the American public by its foreign name.

Do not use quotation marks or italics with the names of newspapers and magazines.

TV Acceptable as an adjective but should not be used as a noun.

upstate, downstate Always lowercase.

venereal disease *VD* is acceptable on second reference.

versus Abbreviate as *vs.* in all uses.

vice Use two words, no hyphen.

vice president Follow the guidelines for **president.**

war Capitalize when part of the name for a particular conflict: *World War II; the Cold War.*

well- Hyphenate as part of a compound modifier: *a well-dressed man.*

wide- Usually hyphenated: *wide-eyed.* Exception: *widespread.*

words as words When italics are available, italicize them. Otherwise, place in quotation marks: *Rep. Ellen Jacobson asked journalists to address her as "congresswoman."*

years Use figures. Use an *s* without the apostrophe to indicate spans of centuries: *the 1800s.* Use an apostrophe to indicate omitted numerals and an *s* to indicate decades: the *'80s.*

Years are the only figures that may be placed at the start of a sentence: *1959 was a year of rapid city growth.*

Punctuation

Keep a good grammar book handy. No stylebook can adequately cover the complexities of the 13 punctuation marks: apostrophe, bracket, colon, comma, dash, ellipsis, exclamation point, hyphen, parenthesis, period, question mark, quotation mark, semicolon. The following is a guide to frequent problems and usages:

Apostrophe Use (1) for possessives, (2) to indicate omitted figures or letters and (3) to form some plurals.

1. **Possessives.** Add apostrophe and *s* (*'s*) to the end of singular and plural nouns or the indefinite pronoun unless it has an *s* or *z* sound.

> *The woman's coat. The women's coats.*
> *The child's toy. The children's toys.*
> *Someone's pistol. One's hopes.*

If the word is plural and ends in an *s* or *z* sound, add an apostrophe only:

> *Boys' books. Joneses' farm.*

For singular common nouns ending in *s,* add an apostrophe and *s* (*'s*) unless the next word begins with s:

> *The witness's testimony. The witness' story.*

For singular proper nouns, add only an apostrophe:

> *Dickens' novels. James' hat.*

2. **Omitted figures or letters.** Use in contractions: *Don't, can't.* Put in place of omitted figures: *Class of '88.*

3. **To form some plurals.** When figures, letters, symbols and words are referred to as words, use the apostrophe and *s*.

    a. Figures: *He skated perfect 8's.*

    b. Letters: *She received all A's in her finals.*

    c. Symbols: *Journalists never use **&**'s to substitute for the* ***and****s in their copy.*

Caution: The pronouns *ours, yours, theirs, his, hers, whose* do not take the apostrophe. *Its* is the possessive pronoun. *It's* is the contraction of *it is.*

Note: Compound words and nouns in joint possession use the possessive in the last word:

- Everybody else's homes.
- His sister-in-law's book.
- Clinton and Gore's party.

If there is separate possession, each noun takes the possessive form: *Clinton's and Gore's opinions differ.*

Brackets Check whether the newspaper can set them. Use to enclose a word or words within a quote that the writer inserts: *"Happiness [his note read] is a state of mind."* Try to avoid the need for such an insertion. Use for paragraphs within a story that refer to an event separate from the datelined material.

Colon The colon is usually used at the end of a sentence to call attention to what follows. It introduces lists, tabulations, texts and quotations of more than one sentence.

It also can be used to mark a full stop before a dramatic word or statement: *She had only one goal in life: work.* The colon is used in the time of day: *7:45 p.m.;* elapsed time of an event: *4:01.1;* in dialogue in question and answer, as from a trial.

Comma The best general guide for the use of the comma is the human voice as it pauses, stops and varies in tone. The comma marks the pause, the short stop:

1. He looked into the hospital room, but he was unable to find the patient.

2. Although he continued his search on the floor for another 20 minutes, he was unable to find anyone to help him.

3. He decided that he would go downstairs, ask at the desk and then telephone the police.

4. If that also failed, he thought to himself, he would have to give up the search.

Note that when reading these sentences aloud, the commas are natural resting points for pauses. The four sentences also illustrate the four principles governing the use of commas:

1. The comma is used to separate main clauses when they are joined by a coordinating conjunction. (The coordinating conjunctions are *for, nor, and, but, or*). The comma can be eliminated if the main clauses are short: *He looked into the room and he froze.*

2. Use the comma after an introductory element: a clause, long phrase, transitional expression or interjection.

3. Use the comma to separate words, phrases or clauses in a series. Also, use it in a series of coordinate adjectives: *He was wearing a long, full cape.*

4. Set off nonessential material in a sentence with comma(s). When the parenthetical or interrupting nonrestrictive clauses and phrases are in the middle of a sentence, two commas are needed: *The country, he was told, needed his assistance.*

Other uses of the comma:

• With full sentence quotes, not with partial quotes: *He asked, "Where are you going?" The man replied that he was "blindly groping" his way home.*
• To separate city and county, city and state. In place of the word *of* between a name and city: *Jimmy Carter, Plains, Ga.*
• To set off a person's age: *Orville Sterb, 19, of Fullerton, Calif.*
• In dates: *March 19, 1940, was the date he entered the army.*
• In party affiliations: *Jim Bunning, R-Ky., spoke.*

Caution: The comma is frequently misused by placing it instead of the period or semicolon between two main clauses. This is called *comma splice:*

WRONG: The computer was jammed, he could not write his assignment.

RIGHT: The computer was jammed. He could not write his assignment.

The computer was jammed; he could not write his assignment.

Dash Use a dash (1) to indicate a sudden or dramatic shift in thought within a sentence, (2) to set off a series of words that contains commas and (3) to introduce sections of a list or a summary.

The dash is a call for a short pause, just as are the comma and the parentheses. The comma is the most often used and is the least dramatic of the separators. The parentheses set off unimportant elements. The dash tends to emphasize material. It has this quality because it is used sparingly.

1. He stared at the picture—and he was startled to find himself thinking of her face. The man stood up—painfully and awkwardly—and extended his hand in greeting.

2. There were three people watching them—an elderly woman, a youth with a crutch at his side and a young woman in jeans holding a paperback—and he pulled her aside out of their view.

3. He gave her his reasons for being there:
    —He wanted to apologize;
    —He needed to give her some material;
    —He was leaving on a long trip.

Note: This third form should be used infrequently, usually when the listing will be followed by an elaboration.

The dash is also used in datelines.

Ellipsis Use the ellipsis to indicate material omitted from a quoted passage from a text, transcript, play, etc.: *The minutes stated that Breen had asked, "How many gallons of paint . . . were used in the project?* Put one space before and one space after each of the three periods. If the omission ends with a period, use four periods, one to mark the end of the sentence (without space, as a regular period), three more for the ellipsis.

The ellipsis is also used by some columnists to separate short items in a paragraph.

Do not use to mark pauses or shifts in thought or for emphasis.

Exclamation point Much overused. There are reporters who have gone through a lifetime of writing and have never used the exclamation point, except when copying material in which it is used. The exclamation point is used to indicate powerful feelings, surprise, wonder. Most good writers prefer to let the material move the reader to provide his or her own exclamation.

When using, do not place a comma or period after the exclamation point. Place inside quotation marks if it is part of the quoted material.

Hyphen The hyphen is used (1) to join words to express a single idea or (2) to avoid confusion or ambiguity.

1. Use the hyphen to join two or more words that serve as a single adjective before a noun: *A well-known movie is on television tonight. He had a know-it-all expression.*

   Caution: Do not use the hyphen when the first word of the compound ends in *-ly* or when the words follow the noun: *She is an easily recognized person. His hair was blond black.*

2. Avoid (a) ambiguity or (b) an awkward joining of letters or syllables by putting a hyphen between prefixes or suffixes and the root word.

   a. He recovered the chair. He re-covered the chair.
   b. Re-enter, macro-economics, shell-like.

Parentheses Generally, avoid. It may be necessary for the insertion of background or to set off supplementary or illustrative material.

Use a period inside a closing parenthesis if the matter begins with a capital letter.

Period Use the period at the end of declarative sentences, indirect questions, most imperative sentences and most abbreviations. Place the period inside quotation marks.

Question mark The question mark is used for direct questions, not indirect questions.

DIRECT: Where are you going?
INDIRECT: He asked where she was going.

The question mark goes inside quotation marks if it applies to the quoted material: *He asked, "Have you seen the movie?"* Put it outside if it applies to the entire sentence: *Have you seen "Guys and Dolls"?*

> **Terse.** "Our composing room has an unlimited supply of periods available to terminate short, simple sentences."
> —*Turner Catledge, managing editor,* The New York Times

Quotation marks Quotation marks set off (1) direct quotations, (2) some titles and nicknames and (3) words used in a special way.

1. Set off the exact words of the speaker: *"He walked like a duck,"* *she said. He replied that he walked* "more like an alley cat on the prowl."

2. Use for titles of books, movies, short stories, poems, songs, articles from magazines and plays. Some nicknames take quotation marks. Do not use for nicknames of sports figures.

3. For words used in a special sense: *"Indian giver" and similar* *phrases are considered to be ethnic slurs.*

Punctuation with quotation marks:

The comma: Use it outside the quotation marks when setting off the speaker at the beginning of a sentence: *He said, "You care too much for* *money."* Use inside the quotation marks when the speaker ends the sentence: *"I* *just want to be careful," he replied.*

The colon and semicolon: Always place outside the quotation marks: *She* *said she wanted no help from him: "I can handle the assignment myself." He* *mentioned her "incredible desire for work"; he meant her "insatiable desire for* *work."*

The dash, question mark and exclamation point: Place them inside when they apply to quoted matter only; outside when they refer to the whole sentence: *She asked, "How do you know so much?" Did she really wonder why he knew* *"so much"?*

For quotes within quotes, use a single quote mark for the inner quotation: *"Have you read 'War and Peace'?" he asked.* Note, no comma is used after the question mark.

Semicolon Usually overused by beginning reporters. Unless there is a special reason to use the semicolon, use the period.

Use the semicolon to separate a series of equal elements when the individual segments contain material that is set off by commas. This makes for clarity in the series: *She suggested that he spend his allowance on the new series at the* *opera, "Operas of the Present"; books of plays by Shaw, Ibsen and Aris-* *tophanes; and novels by Tolstoy, Dickens and F. Scott Fitzgerald.*

Classy. "I think one reason the critics have been slow, even up to this moment, in acknowledging me as a serious writer is that I don't use semi-colons. I never understood them. They don't really stand for anything. I think it's a way of just showing off you've been to college."
—*Kurt Vonnegut*

Grammar

In our grandparents' day, students spent hours diagramming sentences, breaking them down into nouns, verbs, pronouns and the dozens of other segments that describe sentence parts. Today, grammar is not given as much attention in schools, and for journalists, whose living depends on mastery of the language, this is inadequate training.

One way journalists cope with this inadequacy is to invest in a handbook of grammar. It not only solves grammatical problems quickly, but it expands the journalist's writing range.

Think of the humiliation a *New York Times* reporter experienced when he saw in print this sentence he had written:

> While urging parents to remain loving,
> the program, which is controversial in that
> it's techniques are considered questionable
> by a good number of experts, advises them
> to stop being intimidated and manipulated
> by their misbehaving children.

Contorted as this sentence is, the one error that shouts for attention is the misuse of *it's*.

The following guide will help you avoid the grammatical errors that afflict writers.

Agreement

A verb must agree in number with its subject. Writers encounter trouble when they are unsure of the subject or when they cannot decide whether the subject is singular or plural.

Uncertainty often arises when there are words between the subject and the verb:

WRONG: John, as well as several others in the class, were unhappy with the instructor.

RIGHT: John, as well as several others in the class, was unhappy with the instructor.

The subject is *John,* singular.

WRONG: The barrage of traffic noises, telephone calls and similar interruptions make it difficult to study.

RIGHT: The barrage of traffic noises, telephone calls and similar interruptions makes it difficult to study.

The subject is *barrage,* singular.

A collective noun takes a singular verb when the group is considered a unit and a plural verb when the individuals are thought of separately:

RIGHT: The committee usually votes unanimously.

RIGHT: The family lives around the corner.

RIGHT: The family were gathered around the fire, some reading, some napping.

The pronouns *anybody, anyone, each, either, everyone, everybody, neither, no one, nobody, someone* and *somebody* take the singular verb.

A pronoun must agree in number with its antecedent.

WRONG: The team has added two players to their squad.

RIGHT: The team has added two players to its squad.

WRONG: Everyone does their best.

RIGHT: Everyone does his or her best.

WRONG: Each of the companies reported their profits had declined.

RIGHT: Each of the companies reported its profits had declined.

Dangling Modifier

Another trouble spot is the dangling modifier—the word, phrase or clause that does not refer logically or clearly to some word in the sentence. We all know what these look like: *Walking through the woods,* the trees loomed up.

The italicized phrase is a dangling participle, the most common of these errors.

There are also dangling infinitive phrases: *To learn to shoot well,* courses in markmanship were offered.

The way to correct the dangling modifier is to add words that make the meaning clear or to rearrange the words in the sentence to make the modifier refer to the correct word. We can easily fix the two sentences:

- Walking through the woods, *the runaway boy* felt the trees loom up at him.
- To learn to shoot well, *the police* were offered courses in markmanship.

Misplaced Words

Related parts of the sentence should not be separated. When they are separated, the sentence loses clarity.

Adverbs such as *almost, even, hardly, just, merely, scarcely, ever* and *nearly* should be placed immediately before the words they modify:

VAGUE: He only wanted three keys.

CLEAR: He wanted only three keys.

VAGUE: He nearly ate the whole meal.

CLEAR: He ate nearly the whole meal.

Avoid splitting the subject and verb:

AWKWARD: He, to make his point, shouted at the bartender.

BETTER: To make his point, he shouted at the bartender.

Do not separate parts of verb phrases:

AWKWARD: The governor said she had last year seen the document.

BETTER: The governor said she had seen the document last year.

Avoid split infinitives:

AWKWARD: She offered to personally give him the note.

BETTER: She offered to give him the note personally.

Note: Watch long sentences. Misplaced clauses and phrases can muddy the intended meaning. Read the sentence aloud if you are unsure about the placement of certain words. Generally, the problem can be solved by placing the subject and verb of the main clause together.

Parallel Construction

The parts of a sentence that express parallel thoughts should be balanced in grammatical form:

UNBALANCED: The people started to shove and crowding each other.

BALANCED: The people started to shove and crowd each other.

UNBALANCED: The computer can be used for writing and to do finger exercises.

BALANCED: The computer can be used for writing and for doing finger exercises.

Pronouns

A pronoun should agree with its antecedent in number, person and gender. The most common errors are shifts in number and shifts in person.

WRONG: The organization added basketball and hockey to their winter program.

RIGHT: The organization added basketball and hockey to its winter program.

The pronoun *its* agrees in number with its antecedent, *the organization.*

WRONG: When one wants to ski, you have to buy good equipment.

RIGHT: When one wants to ski, he or she has to buy good equipment.

The pronouns *he* and *she* agree in person with the antecedent, *one.*
A common error is to give teams, groups and organizations the plural pronoun:

WRONG: The team played their best shortstop.

RIGHT: The team played its best shortstop.

WRONG: The Police Department wants recruits. They need 1,500 applicants.

RIGHT: The Police Department wants recruits. It needs 1,500 applicants.

Sentence Fragments

A phrase or a subordinate clause should not be used as a complete sentence:

FRAGMENT: The book was long. And dull.

CORRECT: The book was long and dull.

FRAGMENT: The score was tied. With only a minute left to play.

CORRECT: The score was tied with only a minute left to play.

FRAGMENT: He worked all night on the story. And then collapsed in a heap.

CORRECT: He worked all night on the story and then collapsed in a heap.

Note: Sometimes writers use a sentence fragment for a specific writing purpose, usually for emphasis: *When in doubt, always use the dictionary. Always.*

Sequence of Tenses

One of the most troublesome grammatical areas for the beginning journalist is the use of tenses. Improper and inconsistent tense changes are frequent. Because the newspaper story is almost always told in the past tense, this is the anchoring tense from which changes are made.

WRONG: He *looked* into the briefcase and *finds* a small parcel.

RIGHT: He *looked* into the briefcase and *found* a small parcel.

Not all changes from past to present are incorrect. The present tense can be used to describe universal truths and situations that are permanently true:

The Court *said* the Constitution *requires* due process.

When two actions are being described and one was completed before the other occurred, a tense change from the past to the past perfect is best for reader comprehension:

The police officer *testified* that he *had placed* his revolver on the table.

Broadcast writers, who tell most of their stories in the present tense, can handle similar situations with a change from the present tense to the present perfect:

The company *denies* it *has paid* women less than men for comparable work.

In the course of the story, the tense should not make needless shifts from sentence to sentence. The reader is directed by the verb, and if the verb is incorrect, the reader is likely to be confused:

CONFUSING: Moore said he *shot* the animal in the back. It *escaped* from the pen in which it was kept.

The reader wonders: Did the animal escape after it was shot, or did it escape and then it was shot? If the former, inserting the word *then* at the start of the second sentence or before the verb would help make it clear. If the animal escaped and then was shot, the second sentence should use the past perfect tense to indicate this:

CLEAR: It *had escaped* from the pen in which it was kept.

Spelling

Good spellers use the dictionary. Poor spellers do not. Every editor knows that some writers cannot spell well. Editors accept this, but they do not accept excuses for misspelled words. They expect all their reporters to use the dictionary.

The first step in improving spelling is to diagnose the particular spelling problem. One frequent cause of misspellings is mispronunciation. We usually spell as we pronounce, and if we say *goverment, sophmore, Febuary, athalete* and *hinderance,* this is how we will spell these words—incorrectly.

Sometimes we are fooled by words that sound alike or nearly alike but have different meanings:

accent, ascent, assent	formally, formerly
accept, except	irrelevant, irreverent
advice, advise	later, latter
affect, effect	loose, lose
allusive, elusive, illusive	moral, morale
altar, alter	precede, proceed
capital, capitol	prophecy, prophesy
choose, chose	respectfully, respectively
complement, compliment	stationary, stationery
decent, descent, dissent	who's, whose

One way to overcome a spelling problem is to keep a list of words you often misspell. Poor spellers usually assume they are spelling correctly, which is one reason poor spellers give for not using the dictionary. To start your list, here is a compilation of commonly misspelled words. Look them over. If any surprise you, jot them down.

accommodate	exaggerate	parallel
a lot	exhilarate	possess
already	exorbitant	precede
altogether	February	prejudice
arctic	finally	privilege
athlete	forty	restaurant
calendar	governor	seize
career	grammar	separate
cemetery	harass	siege
commitment	hindrance	sophomore
competent	immediately	strictly
consensus	indispensable	tragedy
dependent	judgment	truly
descendant	lightning	undoubtedly
ecstasy	mathematics	vacuum
eighth	nickel	villain
embarrass	nuclear	weird
environment	occurrence	

Basic Reference

A dictionary is kept at hand on the desk. Many reporters carry pocket dictionaries with them on assignments.

Usage

The dictionary is a guide to meaning as well as to spelling. Use it to distinguish between words of similar sound and spelling. The following words are frequently confused. They are not synonyms.

anticipate, expect	lay, lie
because, since	lighted, lit
boycott, embargo	like as
compose, comprise, constitute	majority, plurality
convince, persuade	misdemeanor, felony
due to, because of	pretense, pretext
fewer, less	rack, wrack
flaunt, flout	ravage, ravish
imply, infer	rebut, refute
last, latest	rifle, riffle

Jargon

Avoid using the specialized terminology of the sciences, arts and academic disciplines. Jargon is unintelligible to laypeople, and when it comes into common usage, as has much computer terminology, it is pretentious.

JARGON: As a caterer, she interfaces with many of the city's most prominent businesspeople.

BETTER: As a caterer, she meets many of the city's most prominent businesspeople.

JARGON: Many people have been losing money in the bear market.

BETTER: Many people have been losing money as prices on the stock market have declined.

Clichés

Many once brilliant metaphors and figures of speech are now so commonplace that they are bankrupt of meaning. Don't rely on clichés such as these to describe a situation or to present an image: *an eye for an eye, a far cry, nose to the grindstone, beast of burden, high time, water under the bridge, when the chickens come home to roost.*

Because these sentences and phrases are heard everywhere, all the time, writers have them imprinted in their memory banks, and in the writer's struggle to find an apt expression they pop out. Shove them back in again.

George Orwell advised writers to be wary of using any phrase they are accustomed to seeing in print.

Wordiness

Good writing is crisp and clear. Each word contributes to the meaning of the sentence. Flabby writing can be improved by trimming useless words. Usually this means letting nouns and verbs do the work.

One way to tighten a sentence is to use the positive form for assertions. The positive form not only shortens the sentence, but also replaces adjectives or verb phrases with active verbs.

WORDY: Ms. Jones said she would not buy the company's products because the company advertises on television programs that portray violence.

BETTER: Ms. Jones said she would boycott the company's products because the company advertises on television programs that portray violence.

WORDY: In a campus poll, 35 percent of freshmen said they do not trust politicians.

BETTER: In a campus poll, 35 percent of freshmen said they distrust politicians.

A change from the negative to the positive form emphasizes the meanings of subject complements:

WEAK: Three of the six council members were not present at last night's meeting.

STRONGER: Three of the six council members were absent from last night's meeting.

WEAK: Professor Smith does not care about her students' complaints about homework.

STRONGER: Professor Smith is indifferent to her students' complaints about homework.

Writers who make each word count avoid the use of qualifying adjectives and adverbs such as *very, rather, quite, kind of, sort of* and *somewhat.* A play that is very good is simply good—unless it is excellent. A man who is rather tall is tall—or he towers. Someone who is rather tired is either tired or exhausted.

The use of modifiers also leads to another symptom of muddy writing: redundancies.

Editor & Publisher carried this cutline:

> The Associated Press staff in Santiago, Chile, goes back to work after armed gunmen from the Manuel Rodriguez Patriotic Front raided the office.

If the raiders were gunmen, obviously they were armed.

The use of adjectives and adverbs leads to these absurdities:

fatally killed	successfully docked
first annual	totally destroyed
serious crisis	

Here is a list of the most common redundancies seen in newspaper copy. It was compiled by the Minnesota Newspaper Association:

absolutely necessary	important essentials
advance planning	necessary requirements
ask the question	open up
assemble together	other alternative
at a later day	patently obvious
at the present time	postpone until later
attached hereto	plain and simple
canceled out	reasonable and fair
carbon copy	redo again
city of Chicago	refer back
close proximity	refuse and decline
consensus of opinion	revert back
continue on	right and proper
cooperate together	rise up
each and every	rules and regulations
enclosed you will find	sent in
exactly identical	small in size
fair and just	still remain
fall down	temporarily suspended
first and foremost	totally unnecessary
friend of mine	true facts
gathered together	various and sundry
honest truth	

Sometimes redundancies and other useless words come in the form of prepositions added to verbs:

call up	pay out
drop off	send off, send over
end up	shout out
go out	start up

WORDY: She immediately called up her doctor.

BETTER: She immediately called her doctor.

WORDY: The couple paid out $30,000 in back taxes.

BETTER: The couple paid $30,000 in back taxes.

WORDY: Doc's Diner's sales have dropped off 15 percent since the campus grill opened up in October.

BETTER: Doc's Diner's sales have dropped 15 percent since the campus grill opened in October.

Another way to tighten your writing is to combine sentences:

WORDY: Mitch Ellington is the youngest player to make a hole-in-one on the course. He is 13.

BETTER: Thirteen-year-old Mitch Ellington is the youngest player to make a hole-in-one on the course.

Public Opinion Polling Checklist

The Necessities

Reporters should satisfy themselves on each of the following points before making extensive use of any poll:

- **Date:** When was the poll taken? Later polls are more accurate than earlier ones in political races as people have less time to change their minds.
- **Interviews:** How many were made? How were they conducted? Face-to-face interviews at home are best; telephone polls are quicker and cheaper. Mail surveys achieve small returns and those answering may be nonrepresentative.
- **Methods:** Does the pollster divulge the methods used and allow reporters to see computer breakdowns that are the basis of the pollster's conclusions? How have those who "don't know" been handled in adding up the final percentages? What was the technique used to estimate those who are eligible to vote and those likely or unlikely to vote? How big is the subsample of groups that is being broken out for specific analysis?
- **Disclosure:** What part of the data is disclosed and what part is not? If the data are released by sources other than the pollster, does the material have the approval of the pollster? Is the material self-serving?
- **Sample:** Who was interviewed and how were interviewees selected? Was a probability sample used? (Did everyone eligible have an equal likelihood of being interviewed?) If a probability sample was used, how was the list compiled from which the sample was drawn? The population sampled should be made clear. Make sure the poll claims no more than the people in the sample are qualified to say.
- **Questions:** Is the exact wording of all questions provided? Questions can be slanted to favor a predetermined result. (A national mail survey asking who voters favored for the Republican nomination for president offered only the names of conservative candidates.) The questions may be unclear. Are the questions of the generally accepted type for the purpose? If not, were they pretested?

Guidelines Most news organizations follow these rules:

1. State who sponsored the survey.
2. Give the dates of interviewing.
3. Define the method of interviewing.
4. Describe the population interviewed.
5. Reveal the size of the sample.
6. Describe and give the size of any subsamples used in the analysis.
7. Release the wording of all questions.
8. Release the full results of the questions on which the conclusions are based.
9. Do not remain silent if a client publicly releases and misrepresents a poll result.
10. Give the margin of error.

- **Interviewers:** Who are they? Survey interviewers are supposed to be trained for the task. Campaign workers and reporters often are not. (Most reputable newspaper and television polls are conducted by professional organizations.)
- **Sponsor:** Is it clear who paid for the poll and who made it? Polls made by businesses, trade groups, candidates and political parties should be scrupulously examined.
- **Accuracy:** Does the information include the error allowance or margin of error that will allow the results to be set within the actual limits of reliability? All polls should include this information, and the reporter should include it in the story. A pollster or a politician cannot claim that a 51 to 49 result is conclusive if the margin of error is the usual 3 percentage points in a national poll. Readers and listeners should know this. (See box, "Margin of Error.")
- **Saliency:** Do opinions reflect subject matters of importance to respondents? Do respondents have enough information to understand the question?
- **Interpretation:** What does the pollster or source distributing the results claim? Has the poll been fragmented in the interpretation so that only favorable results are used? Does the pollster or source claim more

Early Polls

Polls taken some time—a month or more—before an election say more about the state of the campaign at that precise moment than about the possible outcome. The closer to election day, the less time for voters to change their minds. But voters are often undecided even as they enter the voting booth.

The release of early polls by a candidate may be intended to influence the election. The press itself may accomplish the same result with its own early polling, although there is no clear evidence that the "bandwagon influence" is any more real than the "underdog influence." The victory the newspapers and everyone else forecast for Thomas E. Dewey in 1948 turned out to be almost as sour a prediction as the Landon victory in 1936. One newspaper, the *Chicago Tribune,* went so far as to banner Dewey's victory across page 1 in an early edition. One of the most famous political photographs shows a beaming Harry Truman holding the *Tribune* the day after the election.

There is no question that a strong start helps a candidate and that early polls showing strength can affect donations and press coverage. Cash tends to follow success. A potential donor may divert a contribution from what appears to be a losing cause. The press also takes cues from early polls. A third or fourth finisher in a preprimary poll will not be given as much coverage as the leaders. Thus, a self-fulfilling prophecy is brought about: The polls say Bettinger is trailing; we will not spend much time covering his primary campaign, which guarantees the public will know little of Bettinger. Without adequate press coverage, Bettinger cannot compete equally, and he loses.

Margin of Error

If a poll were to be made of everyone in a group that we want to learn something about, our conclusions would be completely reliable. But because of such practical considerations as time and cost, population samples must be used, and they lead to sampling error—the difference between what we would have learned from the entire group (called the *universe* in polling parlance) and what we found out from the sample.

The more people interviewed, the smaller the margin of error. At a 95 percent confidence level—which means that in 95 of 100 surveys the data will be within the limits of the margin of error stated—the error will be:

Number Interviewed	Margin of Error
50	± 14 percent
200	± 7
600	± 4
1,500	± 3
9,600	± 1

If we wanted the maximum confidence (99 percent) and the minimum margin of error (plus or minus 1 percent), we would have to interview 16,590 people. In national polls, a 95 percent confidence level with a 3 percentage point margin of error is usually accepted as meaningful.

By the time a national pollster has conducted a number of polls on the same question, his or her cumulative totals sometimes approach the numbers that give maximum confidence and minimum margin of error.

The margin of error should be applied to all polling results so that they do not seem to be more exact than they are. Here is how the margin of error is applied:

With a 3 percent margin of error, a candidate's percentage can move up or down 3 points, which is a 6 percent range or spread. Thus, polling results that are close cannot be said to favor one or the other of the candidates. With a 3 percent margin of error, any results that are separated by 6 percentage points or fewer are too close to call.

A poll that shows Jackson leading Torrance 53 to 47 could actually be a nip-and-tuck race, 50 to 50 (subtracting 3 percent from Jackson; adding 3 percent to Torrance). Or it could be decisively for Jackson, 56 to 44 (adding 3 percent to Jackson and subtracting 3 percent from Torrance).

If the poll showed Jackson leading Torrance 52 to 48 with a 3 percent margin of error, the actual result might be Torrance ahead 51 to 49 (subtracting 3 percent from Jackson and adding 3 percent to Torrance).

Even these margins do not tell the full story. Five times out of 100 (the confidence level) our poll can be off-target. Also, these are the lower limits of possible error. There are problems that exist beyond the statistical area, such as the human errors made during polling and the mistakes made in interpreting the results.

Stories about polls should include the margin of error. Predictions about the results must be measured against the limits set by these statistical necessities. The reporter should tell the whole story, including what he or she does not know.

Subgroups

Pollsters make groupings on the basis of religion, occupation, sex, region, race and income. The generalized assumption of the pollster is that people with particular characteristics will vote in ways that differ significantly from the voting patterns usually evident among persons with other characteristics.

This has led to such generalities as Jewish areas vote more Democratic than the overall average; Lutherans vote more Republican; factory workers vote more Democratic; farmers vote more Republican. When such groups behave differently, change their normal voting proportions, there is a story in the shift.

However, journalists should be cautious about drawing conclusions from such data. The way a person votes is a reflection of a variety of influences. Also, patterns change as old ethnic neighborhoods break up or as workers become more affluent. As the culture becomes more diverse, it is increasingly difficult to establish a cause-and-effect relationship. Beware of single-cause explanations.

than the results indicate? Sometimes a segment of a poll will be used to assert that a certain part of the population favors a candidate when the actual sample of that part of the population is too small for the claims. The smaller the sample, the larger the margin of error.

Summing Up

Polls and surveys are useful additions to the standard reporting techniques. There is nothing magical, nothing fraudulent about polls. Used within the limits of their capabilities by discerning journalists, they extend the reporter's eyes and ears beyond the traditional interviewing process.

Newspapers should describe how they conduct their polls. One way to do this is to run a short piece next to the main story explaining the polling methods used. Here is a piece that could serve as a model:

This poll is based on telephone interviews November 18 through 23 with 600 adults who live in the city.

The telephone numbers were chosen in such a way that all sections of the city were represented in proportion to population. Numbers were formed by random digits, thus permitting access to unlisted and listed numbers.

The results have been weighted to take account of household size and to adjust for variations in the sample relating to race, sex, age and education.

In theory, it can be said that in 95 cases out of 100 the results based on this sample differ by no more than four percentage points in either direction than from what would have been obtained by interviewing all adults in the city.

The theoretical errors do not take into account a margin of additional error that could result from the several practical difficulties in taking any survey of public opinion.

How to Use the FOIA— Freedom of Information Act

Who Can Make a Request?

The FOIA permits "any person" to request access to agency records.

In practice, this includes U.S. citizens, permanent resident aliens and foreign nationals, as well as corporations, unincorporated associations, universities, state and local governments and members of Congress.

How Quickly Will an Agency Respond?

The FOIA requires an agency to respond to an initial request within 10 working days and to an administrative appeal within 20 working days.

An agency may take an additional 10 days to respond to either the initial request or the administrative appeal in "unusual circumstances" involving the agency's need to obtain records from field facilities, process separate and distinct records or consult with another agency or two or more of its own components having a substantial interest in the request.

If the agency fails to comply with the applicable time limit requirements, the requester is deemed to have exhausted his or her administrative remedies and may seek satisfaction in court. In such a case, however, if the agency can show that "exceptional circumstances" exist and that it is exercising due diligence in responding to the request, the court may retain jurisdiction and allow the agency additional time to complete its review of the records.

Otherwise, upon any determination by an agency to comply with a request, the FOIA requires that the records "shall be made promptly available" to the requester.

Sample Request Letter

Tel. No. (business hours
Return Address
Date

Name of Public Body
Address

To the FOI Officer:

This request is made under the federal Freedom of Information Act, 5 U.S.C. 552.

Please send me copies of [*Clearly describe what you want. Include identifying material, such as names, places and the period of time about which you are inquiring. If you wish, attach news clips, reports and other documents describing the subject of your research.*]

As you know, the FOI Act provides that if portions of a document are exempt from release, the remainder must be segregated and disclosed. Therefore, I will expect you to send me all nonexempt portions of the records that I have requested and ask that you justify any deletions by reference to specific exemptions of the FOI Act. I reserve the right to appeal your decision to withhold any materials.

I promise to pay reasonable search and duplication fees in connection with this request. However, if you estimate that the total fees will exceed $ —————, please notify me so that I may authorize expenditure of a greater amount.

[Optional] I am prepared to pay reasonable search and duplication fees in connection with this request. However, the FOI Act provides for waiver or reduction of fees if disclosure could be considered as "primarily benefiting the general public." I am a journalist employed by [*name of news organization*] and intend to use the information I am requesting as the basis for a planned article [*broadcast*]. [*Add arguments here in support of fee waiver.*] Therefore, I ask that you waive all search and duplication fees. If you deny this request, however, and the fees will exceed $ —————, please notify me of the charges before you fill my request so that I may decide whether to pay the fees or appeal your denial of my request for a waiver.

As I am making this request in the capacity of a journalist and this information is of timely value, I will appreciate your communicating with me by telephone, rather than by mail, if you have any questions regarding this request. Thank you for your assistance, and I will look forward to receiving your reply within 10 business days, as required by law.

Very truly yours,

[Signature]

Where to Write

The first order of business in making an FOIA request is to determine which agency should receive it.

If you are uncertain about which agency may have the information you seek, go to the library and check records you want and find the specific mailing address for its FOIA office.

Describing What You Want

The FOIA simply requires that a request must "reasonably describe" the records being sought. This means that the description must be sufficiently specific so that a government employee who is familiar with an agency's filing system will be able to locate the records within a reasonable amount of time. There is no requirement that you explain why you are seeking the information, but such an explanation might be necessary if you want the agency to waive its fees or comply more fully with your request. The more precise and accurate the request, the more likely you are to get a prompt and complete response, with lower search fees. If you do not give a clear description of the information that is being requested, the agency will contact you for clarification.

Plan Your Request Strategy

- Try to limit your request to what you really want. If you simply ask for "all files relating to" a particular subject (including yourself), you may give the agency an excuse to delay its response and needlessly run up search and copying costs.

- If you know that the request involves a voluminous number of records, try to state both what your request includes and what it does not include.

- Try to be specific about the "search logic" you want the agency to follow. Use *and/or* to describe the different subject matters under request. By using the word *and* between different topics (for example, "mail openings *and* surveillance"), you may receive information that falls into both categories but receive none of the documents that relate *only* to "mail openings" or *only* to "surveillance."

- If you want material released to you in an order of specific priorities, inform the agency of your needs; for example, you might want to have materials reviewed and released to you in chronological or geographical order, or you may simply not want to wait for *all* of the records to be reviewed before any are released.

- Decide whether you want to write a local or regional office of a given agency instead of (or in addition to) the headquarters. Headquarters will ordinarily have policy-making information, plus information of a more general nature than the local officials have chosen to report; the field offices ordinarily have the working files.

Identify What You Want as Clearly as Possible

- If there are published accounts—newspaper clips, articles, congressional reports, etc.—of the material requested, these should be cited specifically. If they are brief, it may also be helpful to enclose copies of relevant sections.
- If you know that portions of the requested records already have been released, point this out. (It may eliminate or reduce search fees.) Give information, if possible, to identify that release (i.e., date, release number, original requester).
- If you know the title or date of a document, who wrote it, the addressee, or the division or field office of the agency in which it originated, such information should be included.

Appendix D

Code of Ethics*

Preamble

Members of the Society of Professional Journalists believe that public enlightenment is the forerunner of justice and the foundation of democracy. The duty of the journalist is to further those ends by seeking truth and providing a fair and comprehensive account of events and issues. Conscientious journalists from all media and specialties strive to serve the public with thoroughness and honesty. Professional integrity is the cornerstone of a journalist's credibility.

Members of the Society share a dedication to ethical behavior and adopt this code to declare the Society's principles and standards of practice.

Seek Truth and Report It

Journalists should be honest, fair and courageous in gathering, reporting and interpreting information. Journalists should:

- Test the accuracy of information from all sources and exercise care to avoid inadvertent error. Deliberate distortion is never permissible.
- Diligently seek out subjects of news stories to give them the opportunity to respond to allegations of wrongdoing.
- Identify sources whenever feasible. The public is entitled to as much information as possible on sources' reliability.
- Always question sources' motives before promising anonymity. Clarify conditions attached to any promise made in exchange for information. Keep promises.
- Make certain that headlines, news teases and promotional material, photos, video, audio, graphics, sound bites and quotations do not

*Adopted by the Society of Professional Journalists, Sigma Delta Chi, 1996.

misrepresent. They should not oversimplify or highlight incidents out of context.

- Never distort the content of news photos or video. Image enhancement for technical clarity is always permissible. Label montages and photo illustrations.
- Avoid misleading re-enactments or staged news events. If re-enactment is necessary to tell a story, label it.
- Avoid undercover or other surreptitious methods of gathering information except when traditional open methods will not yield information vital to the public. Use of such methods should be explained as part of the story.
- Never plagiarize.
- Tell the story of the diversity and magnitude of the human experience boldly, even when it is unpopular to do so.
- Examine their own cultural values and avoid imposing those values on others.
- Avoid stereotyping by race, gender, age, religion, ethnicity, geography, sexual orientation, disability, physical appearance or social status.
- Support the open exchange of views, even views they find repugnant.
- Give voice to the voiceless; official and unofficial sources of information can be equally valid.
- Distinguish between advocacy and news reporting. Analysis and commentary should be labeled and not misrepresent fact or context.
- Distinguish news from advertising and shun hybrids that blur the lines between the two.
- Recognize a special obligation to ensure that the public's business is conducted in the open and that government records are open to inspection.

Minimize Harm

Ethical journalists treat sources, subjects and colleagues as human beings deserving of respect. Journalists should:

- Show compassion for those who may be affected adversely by news coverage. Use special sensitivity when dealing with children and inexperienced sources or subjects.
- Be sensitive when seeking or using interviews or photographs of those affected by tragedy or grief.
- Recognize that gathering and reporting information may cause harm or discomfort. Pursuit of the news is not a license for arrogance.
- Recognize that private people have a greater right to control information about themselves than do public officials and others who seek power, influence or attention. Only an overriding public need can justify intrusion into anyone's privacy.
- Show good taste. Avoid pandering to lurid curiosity.

- Be cautious about identifying juvenile suspects or victims of sex crimes.
- Be judicious about naming criminal suspects before the formal filing of charges.
- Balance a criminal suspect's fair trial rights with the public's right to be informed.

Act Independently

Journalists should be free of obligation to any interest other than the public's right to know. Journalists should:

- Avoid conflicts of interest, real or perceived.
- Remain free of associations and activities that may compromise integrity or damage credibility.
- Refuse gifts, favors, fees, free travel and special treatment, and shun secondary employment, political involvement, public office and service in community organizations if they compromise journalistic integrity.
- Disclose unavoidable conflicts.
- Be vigilant and courageous about holding those with power accountable.
- Deny favored treatment to advertisers and special interests and resist their pressure to influence news coverage.
- Be wary of sources offering information for favors or money; avoid bidding for news.

Be Accountable

Journalists are accountable to their readers, listeners, viewers and each other. Journalists should:

- Clarify and explain news coverage and invite dialogue with the public over journalistic conduct.
- Encourage the public to voice grievances against the news media.
- Admit mistakes and correct them promptly.
- Expose unethical practices of journalists and the news media.
- Abide by the same high standards to which they hold others.

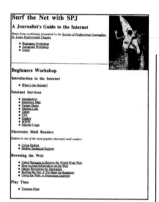

Net Guide

The Society of Professional Journalists offers workshops and guides to using the Internet at the website www.stlouisspj.org/surf/surf. html.

New to the Net? is a guide for those starting out, www.ok.bc.ca/netguide/nubee. html.

Sources Online

More than 2,000 federal, state and local Web sites are available for information. Private organizations also are on the Internet and can provide useful material. Here is a list of some basic sources. There is room for you to add others.

Journalism

Investigative Reporters and Editors—www.ire.org/

National Conference of Editorial Writers—www.insi.net/ncew/

National Institute for Computer-Assisted Reporting—www.ire.org/resources/nicar/

Public Relations Newswire—www.prnewswire.com/

Radio-TV News Directors Association—www.rtnda.org/rtnda/

Reporters Committee for Freedom of the Press—www.rcfp.org/rcfp

Student Press Law Center—www.splc.org/

Provides information on high school and college student press issues, primarily free-press information.

General Information—Background

Encyclopedia Brittanica—www.eb.com/

Foundation for American Communication—www.facsnet.org/

A source for quick access to documents backgrounding current issues and for names of sources.

Lexis®-Nexis®—www.lexis-nexis.com/

Library of Congress—www.loc.gov/

National Archives—www.nara.gov/

The New York Public Library—www.nypl.org/

Poynter Institute for Media Studies—www.poynter.org/home2.htm
    Hot News/Hot Research provides sources for background on breaking stories.

ProfNet—www.vyne.com/profnet
    A collaboration of more than 4,000 public information officers linked by the Internet. Half are at colleges and universities and others are think tanks, laboratories and various associations. Queries are sent to members three times a day for reply at no charge. You can specify that you do or do not want replies from public relations firms.

Sources by Subject

Aircraft

Federal Aviation Administration—www.faa.gov/

Airplane registrations—www.via.net/test.html

Business

Better Business Bureau—www.bbb.org/bbb/

Edgar Database—www.sec.gov/edgarhp.html
    Company information from the Securities and Exchange Commission.

Hoover's Master List Plus Database—www.hoovers.com/
    Information on more than 9,300 companies.

Censorship

American Civil Liberties Union—www.aclu.org/
    Material on FOI, Sunshine laws.

Freedom Forum First Amendment Center—www.freedomforum.org/

National Coalition Against Censorship—www.ncac.org/

People for the American Way—www.pfaw.org/
    School and library censorship, attacks on gay rights, sex education, public schools.

Crime-Law Enforcement

Bureau of Justice Statistics—www.ojp.usdo.gov/bjs/
Data, trend graphics, links.

Federal Bureau of Investigation—www.fbi.gov/

FBI's Uniform Crime Reports—
www.fbi.gov/ucr.CIUS/99CRIME/99CRIME2.PDF.
The annual report of crimes by city and state. Includes violent and property crimes by age, race, sex. Also campus crime.
(Insert year. Here 99 is used for the Reports for 1999.)

Fugitive Alert Service—www.usdoj.gov/criminal/oiafug/fugitives/htm
Photos and criminal history of the most wanted fugitives.

Juvenile justice materials are available by e-mail at askncjrs@ncjrs.org.

National Archive of Criminal Justice Data—
www.icpsr.umich.edu/NACDJ/home.html
For questions about data and documents and other criminal justice material.

National Criminal Justice Reference Service—www.ncjrs.org/

Education

Academe Today—http://chronicle.com.
This is the website of the weekly *Chronicle of Higher Education* and is available to *Chronicle* subscribers. Education reporters find the site indispensable.

National Education Association—www.nea.org/

Elections-Politics

Democratic National Committee—www.democrats.org/

Federal Election Commission Reports—
www.tray.com/FEC/Info/index.html-ssi
For searches by political contributor's name, occupation, employer zip code.

GOP Online—www.gop.org/

Environment

Environmental Protection Agency—www.epa.gov/
Databases, laws and regulations. Contains information on air quality.

National Audubon Society—www.audubon.org/audubon

National Resources Defense Council—www.nrdc.org/

Society of Environmental Journalists—www.sej.org

Government

For general information about the federal government—www.fedworld.gov/
    This is a searchable database.

For a list of federal agencies on the Internet, including links by government branch—www.lib.lsu.edu/gov/fedgov.html

Bureau of the Census—www.census.gov/

Bureau of Labor Statistics—www.bls.gov
    Monthly updates of employment, wages, unemployment regionally.

Bureau of Transportation Statistics—www.bts.gov/

Central Intelligence Agency—www.odci.gov/cia

Commission on Civil Rights—www.usccr.gov

Department of Agriculture—www.usda.gov/

Department of Education—www.ed.gov/

Federal Communications Commission—www.fcc.gov/

General Accounting Office—www.gao.gov/

House of Representatives—www.house.gov/

National Center for Health Statistics—www.cdd.gov/mchswww/default.htm
    Teen births—www.cdc.gov/nchswww/fastats/teenbrth.htm
    Infant mortality—www.cdc.gov/nchswww/fastats/infmort.htm
    STD—www.cdc.gov/nchswww/fastats/stds.htm

Securities & Exchange Commission—/www.sec.gov

Social Security Administration—www.ssa.gov

U.S. Postal Service—www.usps.gov

White House—www.whitehouse.gov/

Guns

Center to Prevent Handgun Violence—www.handguncontrol.org

National Rifle Association—www.nra.org/

Health

Centers for Disease Control and Prevention—www.cdc.gov/

National Center for Health Statistics—www.cdc.gov/nchswww/products/products/htm
    Data tapes and NCHS computer products. Infant mortality, AIDS, drug and other mortality figures.

World Health Organization—www.who.ch/

Medicine

Journal of the American Medical Association—www.ama-ssn.org/

Religion

American Baptist Church—www.abc-em.org/

Buddhanet—www2.hawkesbury.uws.edu.au/BuddhaNet

Evangelical Lutheran Church—www.thelutheran.org/

Interfaith Alliance—www.tialliance.org/

Introduction to Hinduism—www.geocities.com/

Jewish Communications Network—www.jnc18.com/

Institute of Islamic Information and Education—www.iie.net/

Nation of Islam—www.noi.org/

Roman Catholic Church—www.vatican.va/

Southern Baptist Convention—www.sbcnet.org/

Transportation

American Trucking Association—www.trucking.org

Association of American Railroads—-www.arg.org

Department of Transportation—www.dot.gov.
   Provides links to many databases. For state and local statistics, use the Bureau of Transportation Statistics—www.bts.gov.

Insurance Institute for Highway Safety—www.hwysafety.org/

Mothers Against Drunk Driving (MADD)—www.madd.org

National Traffic Safety Board—www.ntsb.gov
   Statistics and press briefings on particular accidents.

National Highway Traffic Safety Administration—www.nhtsa.dot.gov/
   Motor vehicle recalls, consumer complaints, defect investigations, new-car crash test results, crash statistics.

Women

National Organization of Women—www.now.org/

Note: Links sometimes shut down or change. If you cannot connect to a listed source here, use an index site such as Yahoo! or a search engine. You can find the correct link by using the keyword(s) in the listed title(s).

Search Sites on the World Wide Web

Professionals recommend using an index such as Yahoo! before turning to search engines as AltaVista or HotBot. Often, Yahoo! will supply an authoritative list of Web sites to get started. Also, make sure to cross-check to avoid errors.

Yahoo!—www.yahoo.com

A hierarchical index, useful when searching out specific subject areas. (Searches can be made by keyword or concept.)

All-in-One Search—www.albany.net/allinone/

A forms-based list of every major search tool on the Web as well as general Internet search tools.

AltaVista—www.altavista.com

One of the fastest and most complete, although specificity is essential to avoid massive numbers of hits on each word. Also allows for searching of Usenet newsgroups.

Deja News—www.dejanews.com

An archive of Usenet newsgroups. Used to locate experts, resources and to tap into online discussion groups.

HotBot—www.hotbot.com

Calls itself the most complete search engine on the Web.

InfoSeek—www.infoseek.com

Lycos—www.lycos.com

Appendix F

Copy Editing Symbols

Although professionals use the computer to edit copy, some journalists pencil-edit long stories and series after printing them out. Also, some instructors ask to see copy editing on material written early in the semester.

The following page contains the most common editing symbols.

Copy Editing Symbols

Spell out	The (PHA) is pushing for the extension, viewing	The Pittsfield Housing Authority is pushing . . .
Transpose	it as the final link in its urban road renewal	. . . urban renewal road
Begin new paragraph	network. If undertaken, the city is planning	network. / If undertaken, the city . . .
Delete letter	to work in conjunction with a neighbourhood	. . . a neighborhood
Restore marked-out or hard-to-read material	revitalization program for the three-block area that is that is affected.	that is affected.
Change to lower case	The State and federal Governments would pay	The state and federal governments would pay
Separate words	for the road work.	for the road work.
Abbreviate	The (Pittsfield Housing Authority) says that	The PHA says that
Insert	five houses would be taken by the projet with	. . . by the project with
Spell out	a possibility that as many as (8) more would	. . . eight more would
Delete material; close up	have to eventually come down.	have to come down.
Indent for paragraph	The finite takings involve buildings at 90	The finite takings . . .
Capitalize	summer st., 83 and 90 Union St., and 88 and 95	Summer St., 83 and 90. . . .
Run in, or bring copy together	Bradford St. Of the five, only one is a single-family home.	Bradford St. Of the five, only one is a single-family home.
Punctuation	The others are multiple family dwellings.	. . . multiple-family dwellings.

These definitions were provided by the press associations and working reporters and editors. Most of the brief entries are from the *New England Daily Newspaper Study,* an examination of 105 daily newspapers, edited by Loren Ghiglione (Southbridge, Mass.: Southbridge Evening News Inc., 1973).

Print Terms

add An addition to a story already written or in the process of being written.

assignment Instruction to a reporter to cover an event. An editor keeps an assignment book that contains notations for reporters such as the following:

Jacobs—10 a.m.: Health officials tour new sewage treatment plant.

Klaren—11 a.m.: Interview Ben Wastersen, possible Democratic congressional candidate.

Mannen—Noon: Rotary Club luncheon speaker, Horlan, the numerologist. A feature?

attribution Designation of the person being quoted. Also, the source of information in a story. Sometimes, information is given on a not-for-attribution basis.

background Material in a story that gives the circumstances surrounding or preceding the event.

banger An exclamation point. Avoid. Let the reader do the exclaiming.

banner Headline across or near the top of all or most of a newspaper page. Also called a *line, ribbon, streamer, screamer.*

B copy Bottom section of a story written ahead of an event that will occur too close to deadline for the entire story to be processed. The B copy usually consists of background material.

beat Area assigned to a reporter for regular coverage—for example, police or city hall. Also, an exclusive story.

body type Type in which most of a newspaper is set, usually 8- or 9-point type.

boldface Heavy, black typeface; type that is blacker than the text with which it is used. Abbreviated *bf.*

break When a news development becomes known and available. Also, the point of interruption in a story continued from one page to another.

bright Short, amusing story.

bulldog Early edition, usually the first of a newspaper.

byline Name of the reporter who wrote the story, placed atop the published article. An old-timer comments on the current use of bylines: "In the old days, a reporter was given a byline if he or she personally covered an important or unusual story, or the story was an exclusive. Sometimes if the writing was superior, a byline was given. Nowadays, everyone gets a byline, even if the story

Joel Sartore,
Wichita Eagle-Beacon

is a rewrite and the reporter never saw the event described in the story."

caps Capital letters; same as *uppercase.*

caps and lowercase Initial capital in a word followed by small letters. See **lowercase.**

caption See **cutline.**

clip News story clipped from a newspaper, usually for future reference.

cold type In composition, type set photographically or by pasting up letters and pictures on acetate or paper.

column The vertical division of the news page. A standard-size newspaper is divided into five to eight columns. Also, a signed article of opinion or strong personal expression, frequently by an authority or expert—a sports column, a medical column, political or social commentary.

copy Written form in which a news story or other material is prepared.

copy flow After a reporter finishes a story, it moves to the city desk where the city editor reads it for major errors or problems. If it does not need further work, the story is moved to the copy desk for final editing and a headline. It then moves to the mechanical department.

correction Errors that reach publication are retracted or corrected if they are serious or someone demands a correction. Libelous matter is always corrected immediately, often in a separate news story rather than in the standard box assigned to corrections.

correspondent Reporter who sends news from outside a newspaper office. On smaller papers, often not a regular full-time staff member.

crony journalism Reporting that ignores or treats lightly negative news about friends of a reporter. Beat reporters sometimes have a tendency to protect their informants in order to retain them as sources.

crop To cut or mask the unwanted portions, usually of a photograph.

cut Printed picture or illustration. Also, to eliminate material from a story. See **trim.**

cutline Any descriptive or explanatory material under a picture.

dateline Name of the city or town and sometimes the date at the start of a story that is not of local origin.

deadline Time at which the copy for an edition must be ready.

edition One version of a newspaper. Some papers have one edition a day, some several. Not to be confused with *issue,* which usually refers to all editions under a single date.

editorial Article of comment or opinion, usually on the editorial page.

editorial material All material in the newspaper that is not advertising.

enterprise copy Story, often initiated by a reporter, that digs deeper than the usual news story.

exclusive Story a reporter has obtained to the exclusion of the competition. Popularly known as a *scoop,* a term never used in the newsroom.

feature Story emphasizing the human or entertaining aspects of a situation. A news story or other material differentiated from straight news. As a verb, it means to give prominence to a story.

file To send a story to the office, usually by wire or telephone or to put news service stories on the wire.

filler Material used to fill space. Small items used to fill out columns where needed. Also called *column closers* and *shorts.*

flag Printed title of a newspaper on page 1. Also known as *logotype* or *nameplate.*

folo Story that follows up on a theme in a news story. When a fire destroyed a parochial school in Chicago, newspapers followed up the fire coverage with stories about fire safety precautions in the Chicago schools.

free advertising Use of the names of businesses and products not essential to the story. Instead of the brand name, use the broad term *camera* for Leica or Kodak.

futures calendar Date book in which story ideas, meetings and activities scheduled for a later occurrence are listed. Also known as a *futures book.* Kept by city and assignment editors and by careful reporters.

good night An expression meaning there is nothing further for the reporter from the desk for the day. Reporters call in when they take a break. Desks need to know where their reporters are in case of breaking stories.

graf Abbreviation for *paragraph.*

Guild Newspaper Guild, an international union to which reporters and other newspaper workers belong.

Newspapers that have contracts with the Guild are said to be "organized."

handout Term for written publicity or special-interest news sent to a newspaper for publication.

hard news Spot news; live and current news in contrast to **features.**

head or headline The display type over a printed news story.

head shot Picture featuring little more than the head and shoulders of the person shown.

HFR Abbreviation for "hold for release." Material that cannot be used until it is released by the source or at a designated time. Also known as *embargoed material.*

insert Material placed between copy in a story. Usually, a paragraph or more to be placed in material already sent to the desk.

investigative reporting Technique used to unearth information that sources often want hidden. This type of reporting involves examination of documents and records, the cultivation of informants, painstaking and extended research. Investigative reporting usually seeks to expose wrongdoing and has concentrated on public officials and their activities.

In recent years, industry and business have been scrutinized. Some journalists contend that the term is redundant, that all good reporting is investigative, that behind every surface fact is the real story that a resourceful, curious and persistent reporter can dig up.

italics Type in which letters and characters slant to the right.

jump Continuation of a story from one page to another. As a verb, to continue material. Also called *runover.*

kill To delete a section from copy or to discard the entire story; also, to *spike* a story.

lead (pronounced *leed*) First paragraph in a news story. In a direct or straight news lead, it summarizes the main facts. In a delayed lead, usually used on feature stories, it evokes a scene or sets a mood.

Also used to refer to the main idea of a story: An editor will ask a reporter, "What's the lead on the piece?" expecting a quick summary of the main facts.

Also, a tip on a story; an idea for a story. A source will tell a reporter, "I have a lead on a story for you."

localize To emphasize the names of persons from the local community who are involved in events outside the city or region: A local couple rescued in a Paris hotel fire; the city police chief who speaks at a national conference.

lowercase Small letters, as contrasted with capitals.

LTK Designation on copy for "lead to come." Usually placed after the **slug.** Indicates the written material will be given a lead later.

makeup Layout or design. The arrangement of body type, headlines and illustrations into pages.

masthead Formal statement of a newspaper's name, officers, place of publication and other descriptive information, usually on the editorial page. Sometimes confused with *flag* or *nameplate.*

morgue Newspaper library.

mug shot See **head shot.**

new lead See **running story.**

news hole Space in a newspaper allotted to news, illustrations and other nonadvertising material.

obituary Account of a person's death; also called *obit.*

offset Printing process in which an image is transferred from a printing plate to a rubber roller and then set off on paper.

off-the-record Describes material offered the reporter in confidence. If the reporter accepts the material with this understanding, it cannot be used except as general background in a later story. Some reporters never accept off-the-record material. Some reporters will accept the material with the provision that if they can obtain the information elsewhere, they will use it. Reporters who learn of off-the-record material from other than the original source can use it.

No public, official meeting can be off-the-record, and almost all official documents (court records, police information) are public information. Private groups can ask that their meetings be kept off-the-record, but reporters frequently ignore such requests when the meeting is public or large numbers of people are present.

op-ed page Abbreviation for the page opposite the editorial page. The page is frequently devoted to opinion columns and related illustrations.

overnight Story usually written late at night for the afternoon newspapers of the next day. Most often used by the press services. The overnight, or *overnighter,* usually has little new information in it but is cleverly written so that the reader thinks the story is new. Also known as *second-day stories.*

play Emphasis given to a news story or picture—size and place in the newspaper of the story; typeface and size of headline.

P.M. Afternoon or evening newspaper.

pool Arrangement whereby limited numbers of reporters and photographers are selected to represent all those assigned to the story. Pooling is adopted when a large number of people would overwhelm the event or alter its nature. The news and film are shared with the rest of the press corps.

precede Story written prior to an event; also, the section of a story preceding the lead, sometimes set in italic.

press release Publicity handout, or a story given to the news media for publication.

proof Reproduction of type on paper for the purpose of making corrections or alterations.

puff piece or **puffery** Publicity story or a story that contains unwarranted superlatives.

quotes Quotation marks; also a part of a story in which someone is directly quoted.

rewrite To write for a second time to strengthen a story or to condense it.

rewriteman Person who takes the facts of stories over the telephone and then

puts them together into a story and who may rewrite reporters' stories.

roundup A story that joins two or more events with a common theme, such as traffic accidents, weather, police reports. When the events occur in different cities and are wrapped up in one story, the story is known as an *undated roundup.*

rowback A story that attempts to correct a previous story without indicating that the prior story had been in error or without taking responsibility for the error.

running story Event that develops and is covered over a period of time. For an event covered in subsequent editions of a newspaper or on a single cycle of a wire service, additional material is handled as follows:

New lead—important new information; Adds and inserts—less important information; Sub—material that replaces dated material, which is removed.

sell Presentation a reporter makes to impress the editor with the importance of his or her story; also, editors sell stories to their superiors at news conferences.

shirttail Short, related story added to the end of a longer one.

short Filler, generally of some current news value.

sidebar Story that emphasizes and elaborates on one part of another nearby story.

situationer Story that pulls together a continuing event for the reader who may not have kept track as it unfolded. The situationer is helpful with complex or technical developments or on stories with varied datelines and participants.

slant To write a story so as to influence the reader's thinking. To editorialize: to color or misrepresent.

slug Word or words placed on all copy to identify the story.

source Person, record, document or event that provides the information for the story.

sourcebook Alphabetical listing, by name and by title, of the addresses and the office and home telephone numbers of people on the reporter's beat and some general numbers—FBI agent in charge in town, police and fire department spokesperson, hospital information, weather bureau.

split page Front page of an inside section; also known as the *break page, second front page.*

stringer Correspondent, not a regular staff member, who is paid by the story or by the number of words written.

style Rules for capitalization, punctuation and spelling that standardize usage so that the material presented is uniform. Most newspapers and stations have stylebooks. The most frequently used is the common stylebook of the Associated Press. Some newspapers stress the "down" or "lowercase" style in their titles. Some newspapers capitalize (uppercase) frequently. Also, the unique characteristics of a reporter's writing or news delivery.

stylebook Specific listing of the conventions of spelling, abbreviation, punctuation and capitalization used by a particular newspaper or wire service. Broadcast stylebooks include pronunciations.

sub See **running story.**

subhead One-line and sometimes two-line head (usually in boldface body type) inserted in a long story at intervals for emphasis or to break up a long column of type.

text Verbatim report of a speech or public statement.

tight Refers to a paper so crowded with ads that the news space must be reduced. It is the opposite of the *wide open paper.*

tip Information passed to a reporter, often in confidence. The material usually requires further fact gathering. Occasionally, verification is impossible and the reporter must decide whether to go with the tip on the strength of the insider's knowledge.

trim To reduce or condense copy carefully.

update Story that brings the reader up-to-date on a situation or personality previously in the news. If the state legislature appropriated additional funds for five new criminal court judges to meet the increased number of cases in the courts, an update might be written some months later about how many more cases were handled after the judges went to work. An update usually has no hard news angle.

verification Determination of the truth of the material the reporter gathers or is given. The assertions, sometimes even the actual observations, do not necessarily mean the information is accurate or true. Some of the basic tools of verification are the telephone book, for names and addresses; the city directory, for occupations; *Who's Who,* for biographical information. For verification of more complex material, the procedure of Thucydides, the Greek historian and author of the *History of the Peloponnesian War,* is good advice for the journalist:

"As to the deeds done in the war, I have not thought myself at liberty to record them on hearsay from the first informant or on arbitrary conjecture. My account rests either on personal knowledge or on the closest possible scrutiny of each statement made by others. The process of research was laborious, because the conflicting accounts were given by those who had witnessed the several events, as partiality swayed or memory served them."

wire services Synonym for *press associations,* the Associated Press and United Press International. There are foreign-owned press services to which some newspapers subscribe: Reuters, Tass, Agence France-Presse.

Broadcast Terms

actuality An on-the-scene report.

audio Sound.

close-up Shot of the face of the subject that dominates the frame so that little background is visible.

cover shot A long shot usually cut in at the beginning of a sequence to establish place or location.

cue A signal in script or by word or gesture to begin or to stop. Two types: incue and outcue.

cut Quick transition from one type of picture to another. Radio: A portion of an actuality on tape used on broadcast.

cutaway Transition shot—usually short—from one theme to another; used to avoid **jump cut.** Often, a shot of the interviewer listening.

dissolve Smooth fading of one picture for another. As the second shot becomes distinct, the first slowly disappears.

dolly Camera platform. Dolly-in: Move platform toward subject. Dolly-out: Move platform away.

dub The transfer of one videotape to another.

establishing shot Frequently a wide shot; used to give the viewer a sense of the scene of action.

FI or **fade in** A scene that begins without full brilliance and gradually assumes full brightness. **FO** or **fade out** is the opposite.

freeze frame A single frame that is frozen into position.

graphics All visual displays, such as artwork, maps, charts and still photos.

jump cut Transition from one subject to a different subject in an abrupt manner. Avoided with **cutaway** shot between the scenes.

lead-in Introductory statements to film or tape of actual event. The lead-in sets up the actuality by giving the context of the event.

lead-out Copy that comes immediately after tape or film of an actuality. The lead-out identifies the newsmaker again so listeners and viewers will know whom they just heard or saw. Used more often in radio. Also known as *tag lines*.

long shot Framing that takes in the scene of the event.

medium shot Framing of one person from head to waist or of a small group seated at a table. Known as *MS*.

mix Combining two or more sound elements into one.

montage A series of brief shots of various subjects to give a single impression or communicate one idea.

O/C On camera. A reporter delivering copy directly to the camera without covering pictures.

outtakes Scenes that are discarded for the final story.

panning or pan shot Moving the camera from left to right or right to left.

remote A taped or live broadcast from a location outside the studio; also, the unit that originates such a broadcast.

segue An uninterrupted transition from one sound to another; a sound dissolve. (Pronounced *seg-way*.)

SOF Sound on film. Recorded simultaneously with the picture.

SOT Sound on tape. Recorded simultaneously with picture on tape.

trim To eliminate material.

V/O Reporter's voice over pictures.

VTR Videotape recording.

zooming Use of a variable focus lens to take close-ups and wide angle shots from a stationary position. By using a zoom lens, a camera operator can give the impression of moving closer to or farther from the subject.

Internet Terms

chat To talk in real time with others online through a commercial service such as America Online or CompuServe.

content provider Firm or organization that creates content, such as HotWired or CNET.

flaming Hostile chat, commentary or e-mail.

hit Request by a Web user to a server for an image or a file. Hits are used to measure the frequency or popularity of a site. Most sites now use *page views* as the more reliable measure of how many people visit a site.

home page Online site or home for a multitude of information—about movie stars, athletes, pets or commercial messages. Can be in the form of text, graphics, sound, animation.

HTML Abbreviation for Hypertext Markup Language, the language used to create World Wide Web documents.

Hyperlink Location on the Internet that takes the user to another site. Using the mouse, a user *clicks on* the link to be carried to the other document. Hyperlinks are indicated often by highlighting or boldface type.

Hypertext System of coding text to link electronic documents with one another. Elements in a hypertext document are linked to elements in other documents.

Internet Global network of computers communicating in a common language or protocol (TCP/IP, Transmission Control Protocol/Internet Protocol) over telephone lines or microwave links. Home to the World Wide Web, newsgroups and online forums. Always preceded by "the" unless used as a

modifier. The "i" is always capped. Synonymous with the Net.

listserv Mail-handling software that allows people to subscribe to mailing lists. The lists consist of e-mail addresses. Subscribers receive the messages posted to the central mail-handling address.

log on The process of identifying oneself on the computer to gain access to a network.

mailing list Ongoing e-mail discussion devoted to a specific topic. Lists can be public or private, moderated or unmoderated. Also, a group of people (subscribers) with a common interest. The Internet has 15,000 mailing lists.

search engine Way to locate information on the Internet by keyword(s) or concept. With Web access, search engines are free.

snail mail Postal mail.

spam Electronic litter. Unwanted advertisements, junk postings. Similar to junk mail. Spamming is the act of sending spam.

Usenet newsgroups Collection of informal forums, bulletin boards or newsgroups distributed over the Internet and devoted to a variety of interests and topics. More than 16,000 exist.

Web Short for the World Wide Web, part of the Internet that allows users to access text, pictures, charts, documents, graphics, sounds and video.

Web site Collection of pages on the Web that can be accessed through a main title or contents page, which is called a *front door*. A site can be likened to a TV network or a publishing house.

Credits

Literary

Chapter 1

pp. 9-4: Excerpts from news stories by the Associated Press.

Chapter 2

pp. 49-50: News stories from the Associated Press. Used with permission. **pp. 55-56:** Excerpts from news story from *The New York Times:* © *The New York Times.*

Chapter 3

p. 86: Map reproduced with permission of the American Society of Newspaper Editors.

Chapter 5

p. 127: News story from *The Charlotte Observer.* Used with permission **p. 129:** News story from the *Daily News.* Used with permission. **p. 130:** News story from *The New York Times.* Used with permission.

Chapter 6

pp. 147-148: Excerpt from news story used with permission of the *El Paso Herald-Post.* **p. 150:** News story from the *San Francisco Chronicle.* Used with permission **p. 152:** Excerpt from news story used with permission of *The Wall Street Journal.*

Chapter 7

p. 188: News story from *The Miami Herald.* Used with permission. **p. 189:** Front page of the *Daily News.* Used with

permission. **p. 190:** News story from *The State Journal* (Topeka, Kan.). Used with permission. **pp. 190-191:** News story from *The Fresno Bee.* Used with permission.

Chapter 8

p. 204: Excerpts from news story used with permission of the *Lexington* (Ky.) *Herald-Leader.* **p. 206:** Excerpts from news story used with permission of the *Houston Chronicle.* **pp. 208-209:** Excerpts from news story used with permission of *The Evening Sun* (Baltimore). **pp. 213-214:** Excerpts from news story used with permission of the Associated Press. **pp. 225-226, 228, 229-230:** Excerpts from news stories in *The Blade* (Toledo). Used with permission.

Chapter 9

pp. 237-238, 239, 240, 244: Excerpts from Associated Press stories. Used with permission. **pp. 246-247:** Excerpts from ABC "World News Tonight" broadcast. Used with permission. **pp. 251-252:** Excerpts from WSMV-TV script. Used with permission. **pp. 253:** Excerpts from "The CBS Evening News." Used with permission. **p. 256:** Adapted from *Writing Broadcast News* by Mervin Block. Used with permission. (Bonus Books, 1987).

Chapter 10

p. 275: Excerpt from news story in *The Philadelphia Inquirer.* Used with permission.

Chapter 11

p. 309: Excerpt from story in the *Winston-Salem Journal.* Used with

permission **p. 314:** By Charles M. Young. From *Rolling Stone Magazine,* June 1, 1978. By Straight Arrow Publishers, Inc., © 1978. All Rights Reserved. Reprinted by permission.

Chapter 12

p. 325: Excerpt from news story in *The New York Times.* Used with permission. **p. 330:** Excerpt from news story in *The Albuquerque* (N.M.) *Journal.* Used with permission.

Chapter 13

pp. 332-333: Excerpts from news story in *The St. Petersburg Times.* Used with permission. **p. 351:** Portion of front page of *The Wall Street Journal.* Used with permission.

Chapter 14

p. 366: Page excerpt from the *Winston-Salem Journal.* Used with permission. pp. 371-373: Excerpts from news stories in *The Providence Journal-Bulletin.* Used with permission.

Chapter 15

p. 385, pp. 386-387: Excerpts from news stories in *The Sacramento Bee.* Used with permission.

Chapter 16

pp. 406-407: Excerpt from news story in *The Battlesboro* (Vt.) *Reformer.* Used with permission. **pp. 407-408:** Excerpt from news story in The (Louisville) Courier-Journal.

Chapter 18

p. 434: News story from *The News Gazette*, Champaign-Urbana, Ill. Used with permission. News stories from the Associated Press and the *Herald-Dispatch*, Huntington, W. Va. Used with permission.

Chapter 19

p. 443: News story from *Sanders County Ledger*. Used with permission. **p. 444:** Excerpt from *Indian Country Today*. Used with permission.

Chapter 20

p. 469: Police log from *The Argus Leader* (Sioux Falls, S.D.). Used with permission. **p. 451:** Excerpt from news story from *The Anniston* (Ala.) *Star*. Used with permission.

Chapter 21

p. 519: Excerpt from news story from the *Sun-Sentinel*, F. Lauderdale, Fla.

Chapter 22

p. 534: Excerpt from news story from the *Herald-Leader*, Lexington, Ky. Used with permission.

Chapter 23

p. 519: Excerpt from news story by the Associated Press. Used with permission. **p. 579:** Column by Brenda Schmidt reprinted from the *Argus Leader* with permission.

Chapter 24

p. 624: Excerpt from news story by the Associated Press. Used with permission. **pp. 626-627:** Excerpt from news stories in the *Arkansas Gazette*. Used with permission. **p. 628:** Excerpt from news story in the *San Francisco Examiner*. Used with permission. **p. 640:** Excerpt from news story from *The Blade*. Used with permission.

Chapter 26

pp. 678-679: Excerpts from *Columbia Journalism Review*. Used with permission.

Chapter 27

p. 703: Excerpt from news story from *The Blade*. Used with permission.

Photo

Part Openers

1: Kurt Steidle, Pottsville (Pa.) *Republican;* **2:** Val Hoeppner, *Argus Leader;* **3:** Jim Gehrz, *Milwaukee Journal Sentinel;* **4:** Gregg Lovett; **5:** Bob Zellar, *The Billings Gazette;* **6:** Stewart Bowman, *The Louisville Times.*

Chapter 1

p. 7: Ken Klotzbach, *Argus Leader* **p. 11:** Mark Humphrey, Associated Press; **p. 30:** © John Carl D'Annabile, *Times Union.*

Chapter 2

Opener: Ken Klotzbach, *Argus Leader,* **p. 49:** Doug Carroll, *The Norfolk Daily News;* **p. 58:** Edward Reed.

Chapter 3

Opener: Steven Campbell, *The Houston Chronicle;* **p. 70:** The Library of Congress; **p. 75:** Mike Roemer; **p. 76:** Jeff Widener, Associated Press; **p. 78 (left):** James McNulty; **p. 78 (right):** Mike Roemer; **p. 82:** Mark Sluder, *The Charlotte Observer;* **p. 87:** Bob Thayer, *The Providence Journal Bulletin;* **p. 89:** Nancy Pastor.

Chapter 4

p. 103 (left): The Library of Congress; **p. 103 (right):** *Newsday.*

Chapter 5

Opener: Richard Ferro, *St. Petersburg Times;* **p. 137:** Robert Lahser, *The Charlotte Observer.*

Chapter 6

Opener: Al Ransom, *San Antonio Light;* **p. 151:** Jim Hughes, *Daily News.*

Chapter 7

Opener: Jim Peppler, *Newsday;* **p.166:** © Greg Lovett; **p. 181:** Jerome Delay, Associated Press; **p. 185:** Mark Henle, *The Phoenix Gazette.*

Chapter 8

Opener: Anita Henderson, Beloit (Wis.) *Daily News;* **p. 204:** Tom Woods II, *The Lexington Herald-Leader;* **p. 207 (top and bottom):** Steve Campbell, *Houston Chronicle;* **p. 211:** James J. Malloy, *The Providence Journal;* **p. 215:** Steve Ueckert, *Houston Chronicle;* **p. 218:** © Jeffry D. Scott; **p. 219:** © Jeffry D. Scott; **p. 226:** Tom O'Reilly, *The Blade;* **p. 229:** Alan Detrich, *The Blade;* **p. 230:** Alan Detrich, *The Blade;* **p. 232:** Michael Palmer; **p. 233:** Michael Palmer; **p. 234:** American Heritage Center, University of Wyoming.

Chapter 9

Opener: Ken Klotzbach, *Argus Leader,* **p. 255:** KANU-FM.

Chapter 10

Opener: Susan Pollard, *Contra Costa Times;* **p. 279:** © Mark Avery; **p. 280:** Lena H. Sun, *The Washington Post;* **p. 283 (top and bottom):** Vince Heptig, Courtesy of Alicia Patterson Foundation

Chapter 11

Opener: Michael Norcia, *Daily News;* **p. 296:** © Gregg Lovett; **p. 297 (top):** Joel Strasser; **p. 297 (bottom):** Bob Thayer, *The Providence Journal;* **p. 299:** Carlos Antonio Rios, *Houston Chronicle;* **p. 301:** Rodger Mallison, *Fort Worth Star-Telegram;* **p. 309:** Charles Buchanan, *Winston-Salem Journal;* **p. 317:** Charlie Starr, *The San Diego Union-Tribune.*

Chapter 12

Opener: Todd Panagopoulos, *The Star,* Chicago Heights, Ill; **p. 324:** Joe Munson, *The Kentucky Post;* **p. 328 (top):** Plumas County Museum; **p. 328 (bottom):** National Archives in Washington, D.C.

Chapter 13

Opener: Chris Hardy, *San Francisco Examiner;* **p. 334:** Wayne Miller; **p. 338:** James Woodcock, T*he Billings Gazette;* **p. 352:** Ken Elkins, *The Anniston* (Ala.) *Star.*

Chapter 14

Opener: NBC News; **p. 373:** Andy Dickerman, *The Providence Journal-Bulletin;* **p. 377 (top middle):** Bharati

Sadasivam; **p. 377 (top right):** Joseph Noble, *The Stuart* (Fla.) *News;* **p. 377 (bottom):** Mike Roemer.

Chapter 15

p. 384: Rich Turner, *The Stockton Record;* **p. 399:** United Press International.

Chapter 16

Opener: Robert Kollar; **p. 411 (top):** Mike Wintroath, Associated Press; **p. 411 (bottom):** Bob Thayer, *The Providence Journal.*

Chapter 17

Opener: John Walker, *The Fresno Bee;* **p. 417:** The Library of Congress; **p. 418:** The Library of Congress; **p. 419:** John Walker, *The Fresno Bee;* **p. 425:** © Mark Geller.

Chapter 18

Opener: Craig Lee, *San Francisco Examiner;* **p. 435:** Ricardo Ferro, *St. Petersburg Times;* **p. 439 (top):** Lloyd B. Cunningham, *Argus Leader;* **p. 439 (bottom):** Associated Press.

Chapter 19

Opener: Dave Kline, *Eagle-Gazette,* Lancaster, Pa.; **p. 459:** Toby Gardner.

Chapter 20

Opener: Rodolfo Gonzales, *San Antonio Light;* **p. 471 (top left):** Randy Piland, *The Macon* (Ga.) *Telegraph;* **p. 471 (bottom left and right):** Rodger Mallison, *Fort Worth Star-Telegram;* **p. 476:** O. Gordon Williamson Jr., *The Orlando Sentinel;* **p. 486:** Donna Ferrato, *Domestic Abuse Awareness Project;* **p. 492:** Jeff Widener, Evansville Press.

Chapter 21

p. 511: Nancy Stone, *The Plain Dealer;* **p. 520:** John Davenport, *The Houston Chronicle.*

Chapter 22

Opener: Mike Roemer; **p. 533:** Andrew D. Bernstein, NBA; **p. 541:** Joel Sartore, *The Wichita Eagle-Beacon;* **p. 545:** New York Racing Authority; **p. 549:** Bob Thayer, *The Journal Bulletin;* **p. 551:** Baseball Hall of Fame Library; **p. 559:** Chris Dawson, *The Press Democrat;* **p. 561:** Baseball Hall of Fame Library.

Chapter 23

Opener: Josh Estey, *The Register-Guard* (Eugene, Ore); **p. 575:** Josh Estey, *The Register-Guard;* **p. 583:** Mike Roemer; **p. 595:** The New York Stock Exchange.

Chapter 24

Opener: Debbie Noda, *The Modesto Bee;* **p. 607 (top left):** The Plumas County Museum; **p. 607 (top right):** Larry C. Price, *The Philadelphia Inquirer Magazine;* **p. 607 (bottom):** Mel Finkelstein, © *New York Daily News, Inc.;* **p. 633:** Maurice Rivenbank, *St. Petersburg Times;* **p. 635:** James Woodcock, *The Billings Gazette;* **p. 642:** Mike Roemer, *Argus Leader.*

Chapter 25

Opener: Stuart Noble, *The Stuart* (Fla.) *News.*

Chapter 26

Opener: Tim Lovette, *Foster's Daily Democrat;* **p. 683 (top):** Pascal Pavani, Associated Press; **p. 683 (bottom):** Darko Bandic, Associated Press; **p. 685:** John Harte, *The Bakersfield Californian.*

Chapter 27

p. 694: Scripps Howard Awards.

Name Index

Keisling, Phil, 716
Kellogg, Mark, 26
Kelly, Eddie, 540
Kelly, Edna, 208–9
Kelvin, Thomas, 429
Kemkes, Michelle, 472–73
Kemp, Shawn, 534
Kempton, Murray, 193–94, 319, 321
Kendrick, Alexander, 39
Kendricks, Eddie, 444
Kennebec (Maine) *Journal,* 158
Kennedy, Anthony, 396
Kennedy, John F., 76, 78, 270–71, 303, 414, 457, 524, 561, 672
Kennedy, Joseph P., 457
Kennedy-Powell, Kathleen, 503
Kentucky, 354, 463, 523, 558, 634, 651, 656
Kentucky Fried Chicken, 187
The The Kentucky Post, 324
Kenworthy, E. W., xv
Kermode, Frank, 163, 164
Kerouac, Jack, 353, 457
Kerr, Robert, 524
Kerrigan, William, 196
Ketter, William B., 446
KFI (Los Angeles), 448
KGAN-TV (Cedar Rapids, Iowa), xix
KGO-AM (San Francisco), xix
KGO-TV (San Francisco), xix
KGUN-TV (Tucson), xix
Kiam, Victor, 564–65
Kidd, Jason, 534
Kidder, Tracy, 645
Kidnapped, 199
Kihss, Peter, 447
Kimball, Penn, 261
A Kind of Grace, 567
King, Laura, 628
King, Martin Luther, Jr., 651
King, Rodney, 514
King, Stephen, 163
King, Wayne, 155
King Lear, 259
King of the World: Muhammad Ali and the Rise of an American Hero, 567
King of the World: The Creation of Muhammad Ali, 538
The Kingdom and the Power, 39
KING-TV (Seattle), xix
Kinsey, Alfred C., 677
KIRO-TV (Seattle), 552
Kissel, Kelly P., 4, 7–8, 14
Kissinger, Henry, 363
Klatell, David A., 566
Klee, Paul, 85
Klein, Frederick C., 540

Kline, Dave, 442
Klinkenberg, Jeff, xv, 332, 333
Klotzbach, Ken, 5, 7, 42, 236
Kluge, Pamela Hollie, 596
Kluger, Richard, 199
Kmart, 575
KMOX (St. Louis), xix
KNAU-FM (Flagstaff, Ariz.), 255
Kneeland, Carole Kent, 258
Knight-Ridder, 20, 99, 137
Knight-Ridder News Service, 235
KNX-AM (Los Angeles), xix
KNXT-TV (Los Angeles), xix
Koch, Edward, 53
Kodak, 589
Kolata, Gina, 323–24
Kollar, Robert, 402
Koppel, Ted, x
KOTV (Tulsa), xix, 254–55
Kovach, Bill, 23, 85, 104, 695
Kovarik, Bill, xiv
KPIX-TV (San Francisco), xix
KPRC-TV (Houston), xix
Krajicek, David J., 488, 494
Krajick, Kevin, 688–90, 693, 704, 710
Kramer, Joel, 397
Kranz, David, 4, 6, 7
Kress, Mary, 337
Kristol, Irving, 297, 322, 607
Kroeger, Brooke, 39
KRON-TV (San Francisco), xix, 280
KSBW-TV (Salinas, Calif.), xix
KSEE-TV (Fresno, Calif.), xix
KSL-TV (Salt Lake City), xix
KTRH News Radio (Houston), 253
KTRH-AM (Houston), xix
KTUL-TV (Tulsa), xix
KTVS-TV (Detroit), xix
Ku Klux Klan, 2, 119, 328, 384, 699
Kuehl, Mike, 577
Kundera, Milan, 698
Kuralt, Charles, 242, 259
KVUE-TV (Austin, Texas), xviii, 258, 472
KWTV-9 (Oklahoma City), 439
KWWL-TV (Waterloo, Iowa), xix
KWY (Philadelphia), xix
KWY-TV (Philadelphia), xix
KXTV (Sacramento), xix

L

Lack, Andrew, 260
Lafayette, Bernard, 699
Lahser, Robert, 137
Lakota Times, 77
Landauer, Jerry, 415

Landers, Ann, 211
Landi, Joe, 398
Landon, Alf, 119
Lange, Dorothea, 719
Language in Thought and Action, 430
The Language of Prejudice, 421
Lardner, Mike, 557
Lardner, Ring, 174, 417
Larsen, Don, 139
Las Vegas, Nev., 17
Lasch, Christopher, x, 273, 694
Late City Edition, 202
Law Dictionary for Non-Lawyers, 670
Lawlor, Eric, xv, 206–7, 215
Leader-Telegram (Eau Claire, Wis.), 700
League of Women Voters, 619
Leaking: Who Does It? Who Benefits? At What Cost?, 356
Le Carré, John, 344
Lectures in America, 177
The Ledger (Lakeland, Fla.), 700
Lee, Craig, 434
Lee, Irving, 421
Lee, Patrick, 100
Lee, Rosa, 311, 318
Lee, Spike, 181, 188
Lehrer, Jim, 687
Leonard, Benny, 540
Leonard, Buck, 537
Leonard, Elmore, 374
"Leonore No. 3," 62
Lester, Will, 46
Let Us Now Praise Famous Men, 314–15, 318
"Let Us Now Praise Famous Writers," 393
Levi, Primo, 190
Levitt, Leonard, 205
Levy, Howard B., 300
Lewin, Leonard, 156
Lewin, Tamar, 266
Lewinsky, Monica, 47, 78, 79, 398, 429, 662, 663, 673, 687
Lewis, Anthony, 331, 670, 717–18
Lewis, Carl, 548
Lewis, John, 606
Lewis, Oscar, 311, 391
Lewis, Tony, 284
Lexington (Ky.) Herald-Leader, xviii, 204, 534, 558, 656
Lexis®-Nexis®, 33, 98, 114, 115, 359, 758
Liberia, 316
Liberty, 670
Library of Congress, 70, 103, 417, 418, 758

Lieberman, Joseph, 88
Liebling, A.J., 43, 66, 359, 381, 401
Life, 662, 674
Liebling, Joe, 104
Lilienfield, Robert, 66, 273
Lincoln, Abraham, 195, 323
Lindbergh, Charles, 165, 514
Lindros, Eric, 550
Lindsay, John, 620
Lino, Pat, 265
Lippmann, Walter, 270, 306, 331, 337, 421, 430, 449
Lipson, Steve, 583
Lipstadt, Deborah E., 318
Liston, Sonny, 156–57
Literary Digest, 119
Loercher, Diana, 363
Loh, Jules, 202, 212–15, 401
Loizeaux, Jack, 146–47
Lombardi, Vince, 532
Lorentz, Pare, 719
Los Alamos, 43, 455
Los Angeles, viii, 436, 466
The Los Angeles Times, xviii, 24, 98, 463, 477, 570, 599, 671, 672
Los Angeles Times-Washington Post News Service, 95
Loss, Louis, 444
Lott, Trent, 54
Louis, Joe, 533, 538, 539, 541
Louisiana, 111, 354, 478, 482, 610, 641
Louisiana State University, 551
The Louisville Times, xxi
Lovelady, Steve, 233
Lovett, Greg, xxi, 166, 296
Lovette, Tim, 671
Lowe, Bob, 559
Lowry, Lois, 115
Lubow, Arthur, 70, 192
Luce, Henry, 718
Ludlow, Lynn, xv
Lycos, 763
Lyons, Louis, 167

M

Ma Linmei, 280
Mabee, Zell, xiv
MacDougal, Kent, 582
MacLaine, Shirley, 7
MacMullan, Jackie, 536
The Macon (Ga.) *Telegraph,* 471
The Macon (Ga.) *Telegraph and News,* xviii
Madison, James, ix
Magid, Frank, 323
Magna Carta, 323
Mahoney, Kathleen Ann, 576

Mailer, Norman, 174
Maine, 641
Make No Law: The Sullivan Case and the First Amendment, 670
Makinson, Larry, 612
Malcolm X, 188
Malinowski, Zachary, 211
Mallison, Rodger, 301, 471
Malloy, James J., 211
Malraux, André, 461
The Man Without a Country, 123
Manchild in the Promise Land, 31, 35
Manley, Dexter, 553
Mann, Horace, 327
Manning, Bruce, 448
Manson, Charles, 514
Mantle, Mickey, 536, 566
Marbury, Stephon, 534
March, Hal, 427
Marcus, Norman, 566
Marder, Murrey, 414, 415
Marimow, Bill, 625
Marino, Sal R., 569
Marino, Vivian, 571–72
Mariotta, Joseph M., 620
Maris, Roger, 532
Markham, Edwin, 418
Marrou, Chris, 681
Marsh, Jack, xv, 523
Marshall, Thurgood, ix, 157, 298, 524
Marx, Groucho, 460
Marx, Jeffrey, 558
Marx, Paul, 343
Maryland, 354, 478, 641, 655, 662, 665, 717
Mas Canosa, Jorge, 460
Maslin, Paul, 119
Mass Media Law, 670
Massachusetts, 635, 641, 662
Massachusetts Bay Colony, 631
The Massacre of El Mozote: A Parable of the Cold War, 284
Massing, Michael, 284
Masters, William H., 674, 677
Matlack, Carol, 625–26
Mattingly, Terry, 87
Matuschka, 676
Mauro, Tony, xv
Maurois, André, 720
May, Clifford D., 394
Mayer, Louis B., 275, 451
Mays, Willie, 538, 539
Mazzarella, David, 24
McArthur, Charles, 235
McCabe, Carol, 395
McCabe, Charles, 544
McCann, Barbara, 436

McCarthy, Joseph, 59, 60
McCarver, Tim, 550
McCormally, John, xv, 453
McCormick, Mona, 121
McCormick, Robert, 718
McCoy, Edwin, 631
McCoy, Rosemary, 4–5
McCulloch, Frank, xv, 722
McDonald, Dwight, 131
McDonald's, 589, 591–92
McFadden, Robert D., 447
McGill, Ralph, 175–76
McGinniss, Joe, 292
McGrory, Mary, ix
McGuffey's Readers, 389
McGwire, Mark, 535
McKelway, St. Clair, 140
McLaren, Wayne, 458–59
McManus, James, 82
McMasters, Paul K., 669
McMath, Sid, 364–65
McMillan, James, 366–67
McMurry, Christine, 280
McNamara, Joseph, 129
McNeese State University, 563
McNulty, Henry, 164
McNulty, James, 78
McPhee, John, 161, 195, 218, 220
McSorley's Wonderful Saloon, 235
McVeigh, Timothy, 72, 504, 515–16, 529
Mead, Margaret, 309, 311
Mears, Walter R., 66, 141, 142
The Meat Market: The Inside Story of the N.F.L. Draft, 567
The Media Monopoly, 93
Media Studies Journal, 529
Mehta, Ved, 713
Melville, Herman, 196, 205
Memphis Daily Appeal, 139
Mencken, H.L., 197, 320, 698
Mendoza, Martha, 345
Mercer, Lucy, 77
The Merchant of Venice, 32, 321
Meredith, James, 658
Merritt, Gilbert, 524
Mertens, Bill, xv, 616–17
Mexico, 438
Meyer, Philip, 121
Miami, 18, 46, 436, 470, 478, 484
The Miami Herald, xix, 62–63, 144, 153, 188, 209, 460
Miami New Times, 315
Miami Student (Miami University of Ohio), 489
Michelanglo, 321, 635
Michigan, 485, 524, 609, 656
Michigan Chronicle, 44
Mickey Mouse, 568
Miller, Alan, xv

Miller, Ed, 98
Miller, Marvin, 566
Miller, Norman C., 271
Miller, Stephen, 18, 19
Miller, Susan H., 90
Miller, Wayne, 334
Miller v. California, 679
Millikan, Robert, 429
Mills, Kay, 66
Millstein, Gilbert, 196
Milosz, Czeslaw, 717
Milton, John, 105
Milwaukee, 73, 463
The Milwaukee Journal, xix
Milwaukee Journal Sentinel, xxi
Minneapolis Tribune, 426
Minnesota Newspaper Association, 745
Minnix, Bob, 556
Mintz, Morton, 586, 596
Mintz, Phil, 157
Minute by Minute, 261
The Mirage, 722
Miss America, 675
Miss Piggy, 568
Miss Universe, 396–97
Mississippi, 110, 111, 354, 478, 485, 641, 651, 680
Missoulian (Mont.), 710
Missouri, 485, 610
Mitchell, John D., xv
Mitchell, Joseph, 235, 370, 380
Mitford, Jessica, 393, 401, 461
The Mobile (Ala.) *Register,* 232
The Modern Researcher, 121
The Modesto (Calif.) *Bee,* 598
Moffitt, Donald, 235, 583, 596
Molly Ivins Can't Say That, Can She?, 199
Monex International Ltd., 576
The Money Game, 596
The Monitor, 175
Montana, 635, 639, 641, 662
Montandon, Pat, 664
Montano, Louis, 58
Montgomery, Ala., 650–51
The Montgomery (Ala.) *Advertiser,* 560
Moody, Sid, 146, 379
Moody's, 585
Moon, Sun Myung, 146
The Morality of Scholarship, 722
Morgan, Henry, 451
Morgan, Lorrie, 374
Morgenthau, Robert, 408–10
The Morning Record and Journal (Meriden, Conn.), 459
Morris, Desmond, 674
Morris, Richard B., 138
Mosher, Steven, 269
The Most of A. J. Liebling, 359, 401

Mothers Against Drunk Driving, 762
Moyers, Bill, 22, 223
Moynihan, Daniel Patrick, 606
MTV, 132, 635
Muddy Boots and Red Socks, 45
Müller, Johannes, 330
Mulligan, Arthur, 27–29
Mulvoy, Mark, 531
Munsinger, Harry, 509
Munson, Joe, 324
"The Murders in the Rue Morgue," 294
Murdoch, Rupert, 80
Murray, Donald, 161, 193, 198
Murray, Jim, 536
Murrow, Edward R., 38, 39, 60, 61, 242, 258, 261, 303, 686
The Murrow Boys: Pioneers on the Front Lines of Broadcast Journalism, 261
Murrow: His Life and Times, 261
The Muskegon (Mich.) Chronicle, 700
My Brother Sam is Dead, 115
My Favorite Summer 1956, 566
My Lai, 300, 413, 708

N

The Naked Ape, 674
Namath, Joe, 539
Nation of Islam, 102, 281, 762
Nation's Business, 582
National Assessment of Educational Progress, 323, 641
National Association of Manufacturers, 582
National Audubon Society, 760
National Basketball Association (NBA), 327, 533–34, 556
National Coalition Against Censorship, 759
National Collegiate Athletic Association (NCAA), 357, 550, 551, 552, 553–54, 555, 559
National Conference of Editorial Writers, 758
National Criminal Justice Foundation, 465
National Education Association, 760
National Five-Digit Zip Code and Post Office Directory, 96
National Football League (NFL), 53, 541, 543, 564–65, 567
The National Geographic, 709
National Guard, 439

Roosevelt, Franklin D., 77, 119, 257, 272, 449, 676
Roosevelt, Theodore, 420
Roper, 116, 611
Rosa Lee: A Mother and Her Family in Urban America, 318
Rose, Ted, 550
Rosenbaum, David E., 54
Rosenbloom v. Metromedia, Inc., 654
Rosenbluth International, 605
Rosenfeld, Harry M., 397
Rosenfeld, Israel, 427
Rosenthal, A. M., 257–58
Rosenthal, Andrew, 289
Roshco, Bernard, 93
Ross, Brian, 701
Ross, Diana, 622
Ross, Harold, 176, 198, 361
Ross, Lillian, 199, 392, 393
Rossman, Mike, 539–40
Roth, Susan, 638
Rothmyer, Karen, 678
Rothchild, Barbara S., 151
Roush, Edd, 548
Rowe, James L., Jr., 579
RTNDA Communicator, 244
Rudolph, Wilma, 539
The Run of His Life: The People v. O. J. Simpson, 508, 529
Rupp, Adolph, 562
Russell, Betrand, 45
Russell, Bill, 327
Russell, Charles E., 187., 467
Russell, Liz, 327
Ruth, Babe, 551
Rutherford Institute, 613, 614
Ruthland, Robert A., ix
Rwanda, 150
Ryan, Nolan, 535

S

S.S. Monterey, 286
Sachs, Andrea, 544–46
The Sacramento (Calif.) Bee, 385, 682, 714
A Sacred Trust: Nelson Poynter and the St. Petersburg Times, 722
Sadasivam, Bharati, 376, 377
Safer, Morley, 258
Safire, William, 164
St. Clair, Tanya, 511
St. John's University, 556
St. Louis Post-Dispatch, 149, 482
St. Luke, 676
St. Paul Pioneer Press, xviii, xxii, 445, 675

St. Petersburg, Fla., 73, 436
St. Petersburg (Fla.) *Times,* xviii, 122, 332, 435, 584, 633
Salant, Richard, 79
Salina (Kan.) *Journal,* 677
Salinger, J.D., 32, 115, 141, 635
Salon, xix
Saltzman, Mort, xvi
Salvation Army, 297
San Antonio Light, 139, 462
The San Diego Union–Tribune, 317
San Francisco, viii, 18
The San Francisco Chronicle, 83, 117, 150
San Francisco Examiner, 332, 434, 624, 628
San Jose Mercury-News, xviii, 105, 639
Sandburg, Carl, 396
Sande, Mike, xxii
Sanders, Bob, 99
Sanders, Marlene, 318
Sanders, Ralph, 350
Sanders County Ledger (Thompson Falls, Mont.), 443
Sandomir, Richard, 549, 550
Sanford, Bruce W., 670
Santa Claus, 116
Santangelo, Paul, 453
Santyana, George, 303
Sargent, Claire, 613
Singer, John Singer, 698
Sartore, Joel, 541, 766
Sasser, James, 524
The Saturday Evening Post, 658
Saudi Arabia, 399
Sayre, Wallace S., 602, 645
Scahill, Jeremy, 701
Scaife, Richard, 678–79
Scalise, Larry, 508
Scanlan, Christopher, 138, 199, 371–73, 625
Schanberg, Sydney H., xvi, 54–56, 61
Schiller, Dan, 66
Schlottman, Jack, 542
Schmertz, Herbert, 576
Schmickle, Sharon, 64
Schmidt, Brenda, 577–79
Schneider, Andrew, 99
Scholastic Aptitude Test (SAT), 551, 554, 557, 605, 631
Schraeder, Terry, 335
Schroeder, Patricia, 394
Schudson, Michael, 93
Schultz, John, xvi
Schwarz, Alan, 535
Schwartz, Rhoda, 701
Scientology, 659

Scooped! Media Miss Real Story on Crime While Chasing Sex, Sleaze, and Celebrities, 488, 494
Scott, Dred, 322
Scott, Jeffry D., 218, 219
Scripps Howard Awards, 694
The Seattle Times, 638, 675
Seaver, Tom, 550
Selcraig, Bruce, 388–89
The Selling of the President, 292
Selz, Michael, 588
Sentencing Project, 520
Seton Hall University, 352, 551, 552, 556, 557
Seton Hill College, 586
"The Seven Words You Can't Say on Radio and Television," 680
Severo, Richard, 451
Severson, John, xxii
Shakespeare, William 32, 96, 195, 321
Shanker, Albert, 638
Shaw, David, 51
Shaw, George Bernard, 321
Shedden, David, 102
Sheean, Vincent, 38, 39
Shefter, Martin, 645
Shelly, Michael, xix, 327
Shepard, Richard F., 453
Shilton,Wendy, xvi
Shoemaker, Willie, 539
Short, Allen, 99, 694
Shpunt, Loretta M., 176
Siebert, Fred S., 66
Siegal, Allan M., xvi
Siegenthaler, John, 85
Siemon, Katherine L., 511
Sigal, Leon, 356
Sigma Chi Delta, 692, 755
Sigma Chi Delta Awards, xix, 56, 231, 255
Silberman, Laurence, 65
Silk, Leonard, 596
Sill, Melanie, 625
Silvestrini, Elaine, 46
Simon, David, 472
Simpson, Nicole, 508, 553
Simpson, O. J., 73, 420, 477–78, 497, 502, 503, 507, 508, 509, 513, 514, 529, 553
Sims, Calvin, 335
Sinatra, Frank, 44, 169, 448, 449, 453
Singer, Barry, 374
Singer, Eleanor, xvi
Singleton, William Dean, 718
Sinnott, William, 398
Sioux Falls, S.D., 3, 4–5

Sixteenth Street Baptist Church, 651
"60 Minutes," 482
Skaggs, Joe, 339
Skelton, Red, 451
Sketches, 320
Slaughter, Enos, 561
Sloan, Alfred P., Jr., 586
Sloan, Allan, 594
Sluder, Mark, 82
Smith, Adam, 323
Smith, H. Allen, 140
Smith, Hazel Brannon, 698–99
Smith, Howard K., 261
Smith, Merriman, 25
Smith, Patricia, 715
Smith, Randy, 565
Smith, Red, viii, 198, 299, 305, 537, 538, 539, 544, 566, 567
Smith, Sally Bedell, 261
Smith, Sam, 541
Smith, William Kennedy, 709
Smith, Z. N., 722
Smithsonian Institution, 278, 340
The Social Responsibility of the Press, 722
The Social Work Interview, 380
Society of Environmental Journalists, 89, 761
Society of Professional Journalists, xix, 100, 688, 693, 721, 755, 758
Socrates, 420–21
Sohn, Pam Newell, 491–92
Somalia, ii, 92, 258, 682
Sorenson, Erik, 687
Sosin, Milt, 332–33
South Africa, 61, 463, 691
South Carolina, 354, 478, 485, 641
South Dakota, viii, 605, 609, 642, 662
South of Heaven: Welcome to High School at the End of the Twentieth Century, 645
South, Jeff C., xvi, 19, 281, 345, 629
Southern Baptist Convention, 762
Southern Methodist University, 552
Spacek, Sissy, 335
Spargo, John, 418
Speaker, Tris, 429
The Spectacle Media and the Making of the O. J. Simpson Story, 529
"A Speech for the Liberty of Unlicensed Printing," 105
Spell, Debbie, 372–73

Subject Index

Opinion, 54, 124, 664
Ordinances, 599
Outlines, 227
Overwriting, 215
Ownership, 85–87, 718

P

Pack journalism, 294
Panel discussions, 410–12
Parallel structure, 179, 739–40
Paraphrasing, 185, 215, 243, 394, 407, 673
Participant observation, 307–11
Penny papers, 69, 201
Percentages, 109–10, 575, 727
Peremptory challenge, 507
Persistence, 23
Photojournalism, xxii, 671, 682–86, 691, 709
Place, 146, 178
Plagiarism, 714–15, 756
Plea bargaining, 495, 505–6
Polar alternatives, 427
Police reporting, 7–14, 17–18, 258–59, 462–94
  arrest process, 473–78
  burglary and robbery, 480
  campus crime, 489–91
  cautions and warnings, 487–88
  databases, 482–84
  domestic abuse, 484–85, 486
  essentials, 479, 480
  felonies, 470
  juvenile, 253, 463, 488, 757
  leads, 154
  murder, 475–76, 478–79
  police, 466–70
  rape, 485
  rates, 463, 464, 470, 483, 485, 486, 489, 490
  sources, 470, 760
  victims, 484–86
Political action committees, 612
Political stories, 598–631
Polling, 94, 115–20, 273, 611, 663, 747–50
  guidelines, 747
  margin of error, 117, 747, 749
  subgroups, 750
Pornography, 673, 680
Poses, 712, 714, 756
Postal codes, 96, 729
Precede, 768
Predictions, 429, 539
Prepositions, 176
Present tense, 236
Press kit, 268
Press releases, 31, 264, 266, 409, 587, 595, 596, 768
Pressure groups, 602–3

Prima facie case, 510
Privacy, 77–78, 106, 649, 660–63, 668, 689, 690–92
  calculated falsehoods, 661
  difference from libel, 660
  guidelines, 662, 663
  hidden devices, 662–63
  Times Doctrine, 660
Private figures, 655–56
Privilege, 649, 657, 664
Prizes and awards, xii, xvii, xviii, 56, 231, 255, 694, 701
Pulitzer Prizes, xiii, xvii, xviii, 56, 89, 105, 150, 153, 179, 202, 203, 286, 300, 303, 345, 356, 451, 453, 558, 560, 694, 696–97, 708, 715
Presentment, 525
Profanity, 671, 674–76, 679
Profiles, 20, 57, 83, 215, 462, 466, 519, 530
  delayed leads, 147
  interviewing, 357, 365, 369–73
  miniprofile, 371–73
Prominence, 68, 73, 446, 671
Pronouncers, 245
Pronouns, 176, 178, 740
Property taxes, 620–22
Proximity, 68, 74–75, 77
Proxy statements, 594
Pseudo–events, 269–70
Pseudosources, 334
Public officials, 655–56
Public participation, 90–92
Public relations, 273
Public records, 19, 45, 52, 53, 94, 100, 105, 332, 333, 344, 593–94, 669, 756
Public service journalism, xii, 91, 690–92, 696, 700–1, 721
Puff pieces, 575
Punctuation, 96, 176–77, 723, 732–36
Purple prose, 165, 17

Q

Questions, asking, 23, 357, 358, 361–64, 388–89, 433
Quotations, 42, 52, 126, 162, 168–69, 172, 182, 184–86, 208, 215, 221, 334, 360, 364, 370, 374–75, 392, 394–97, 435, 530, 668, 715, 755, 768
  guidelines, 395
  literal, 396–97
Quotation marks, 736
Quote lead, 145

R

Racism, xix, 98–99, 222–25, 328, 420, 422, 520–21, 560–63, 637, 696, 698–99, 711–12
Radio, 72, 192, 246
Random sample, 118
Rap sheet, 326
Rape, 217–18, 485, 506, 661, 677–78, 709, 757
Rapport, 359–61
Rates, 110–11, 551, 575, 606, 710
  crime, 463, 464, 470, 483, 485, 486, 489, 490
  education, 633, 641
  gangs, 465
  infant death, 111–12, 354
  murder, 111, 478, 484
  pedestrian accidents, 436
Re–enactments, 756
"Reader–friendly" news, xii
Readers, 2, 83–84, 217, 293, 337, 598, 715, 757
Readership, xii
Readability, 139, 178
  leads, 157–18, 159–60, 161
Reading, 37, 193, 319, 352, 538
  recommended books, 38–39, 66, 93, 121, 138, 199, 235, 260–61, 292, 318, 331, 356, 380, 401, 430, 461, 494, 529, 566–67, 596, 645, 670, 721–22
  recommended business publications, 581–82
Records, public, 19, 45, 52, 53, 94, 100, 105, 332, 333, 344, 593–94, 669, 756
Redlining, 223–25
Redundancies, 744–45
Reference books, 94, 96, 332, 344, 359, 442, 582, 742
Regulatory agencies, 582–83
Religion reporting, 87–88, 137
Reporter's Equation, 304
Reporters
  appearance and behavior, 382–83
  beats, 62, 78, 319, 323, 340, 432–33, 766
  characteristics, xi–xii, 2, 23–26
  and the law, 649–70
  math skills, 106–14, 321, 327, 588–89
  skills for covering business, 575–76
Reporting, 264–92, 370
  accidents, 434–41
  broadcast, 182, 236–49, 270

computer–assisted, 19, 98–99, 102–3, 265–66, 281–82, 287, 345, 629–31
court, 325, 495–529
crime/police, 7–14, 17–18, 258–59, 462–94
  depth, 20, 595
  in depth, 60
  disaster stories, 4–7, 26, 438–40
  education, 135, 598, 605, 631–45
  environmental, 88–89, 254–55
  fires, 462, 491–94
  government, 598–631
  interpretive, 20, 267, 462, 568
  investigative, 20, 21–22, 24, 264, 284–87, 413, 462, 625–27, 694, 767
  layer I, 266–78, 279, 429
  layer II, 266–67, 269, 271, 278–84
  layer III, 267, 268, 289–90
  live–in, 311–14, 315
  meetings, 402, 405–6
  news conferences, 267, 402, 408–10, 412
  obituaries, 134, 442–62, 708, 709, 768
  obstacles to, 304
  religion, 87–88, 137
  sports, 83, 325, 530–67
  war, 26, 54–55, 69, 193–95
  weather, 89, 140, 154
Reportorial enterprise, 264, 267, 350–52
Resolutions, 599
Responsibility, 64–65, 68, 692
Reverse directory, 96
Rewriting, 196–97
Riots, 46–47
Roundup, 154, 768

S

Said, 173–74
Scandals, 69
Scoops, 25, 70, 72
Scripts, 239–41, 246–47, 251–52, 253–254
Search engines, 20, 100, 102, 332, 762, 763, 770
Secondhand account observation, 47–48, 52
Segregation, 650–52, 674
Selectivity, 62–63
Sentences, 162, 198
  compound, 157
  fragments, 740
  length, 157–58, 161, 177–78, 179, 208

True bill, 503–4
Trust, 368, 381
Truth, 304, 305, 698
  as a defense against libel, 649
Two–element stories, 129

U

University bonds, 585–86
Unobtrusive observation, 306–7
Unusual, 68, 75–76, 293, 296,
  437, 439

V

Verbs, 72, 155, 160, 161, 165,
  176, 189, 198, 248
Verification, 42, 43, 52–56, 68,
  264, 267, 292, 303, 304,
  333, 438, 455, 664
Victims, 217, 348, 386, 437, 464,
  661, 677–78, 757
Video, 236
Viewers, 2, 83–84, 217, 598, 757
Visual direction, 257
Vocabulary, 172, 189, 330
Voice–over videotape, 240, 247,
  400, 770
Voir dire, 666
Voters, 119, 611, 619
Vulgarity, 671, 679

W

War reporting, 26, 54–55, 69,
  193–95

examples of, 55–56, 193
Watergate, xii, 24, 71, 158, 292,
  333, 364, 397, 653, 665,
  674, 675, 718
Weak leads, 154
Weather reporting, 89, 140, 154
Whistle–blowers, 335, 340
Wire services, 12, 14, 44, 85, 94,
  95–96, 237–42, 244,
  532, 668
Witnesses, 48, 332, 341, 365,
  434, 435, 436, 437, 438,
  439, 440
Women, 83, 137, 318, 383,
  563–65, 613, 614,
  726, 762
Words, 44, 160, 174, 198, 208
  misplaced, 739
  offensive, 674
World Wide Web, 98, 101–102,
  589, 770
  addresses, 19, 35, 100, 102,
  107, 108, 115, 354, 482,
  483, 569, 594, 604, 614,
  629, 631
  sites, xix, 19, 89
Writethru, 10, 12–13, 14, 72
Writing, 66, 162–99
  broadcast, 72, 236–61
    attribution, 242, 244
    copy preparation, 256–57
    glossary of terms, 769–70
    guidelines, 237, 248, 256
    language, 236, 242
    long pieces, 250–53
    leads, 245

rewriting wires, 237–42
sentence structure, 242,
  245, 248
cautions and warnings, 171, 221
  accident stories, 437, 438
  arrest stories, 476
  attribution, 51, 52
  business stories, 594, 596
  court stories, 497–98, 501
  crime/police stories, 487–88
Writing, —Cont.
  delayed leads, 152
  disaster stories, 440
  emotions, 420
  fire stories, 494
  Internet, 104, 340
  leads, 152
  libel, 656, 657
  punctuation, 733, 734, 735
  sources, 288–89
  clarity, 63, 65, 68, 139, 164,
    170, 175–81
  clichés, 140, 244, 541, 743
  conviction, 56, 182–86
  copy preparation, 256–57
  documentaries, 22–23, 217–18,
    222–25
  euphemism, 173, 674
  glossaries, 95, 766–70
    broadcast, 769–70
    business, 597
    Internet, 770
    legal, 526–29
    print, 766–69
  grammar, 175, 176, 395,
    737–46

agreement, 737–38
dangling modifiers, 738–39
parallel construction, 179,
  739–40
pronouns, 176, 178, 740
sentence fragments, 740
sequence of tenses, 741
usage, 743
guidelines, 168, 170
humor, 140, 212, 451, 460, 526
jargon, 94, 172, 575, 595, 743
misplaced words, 739
overwriting, 215
rewriting, 196–97
spelling, 65, 96, 150, 174–75,
  268, 292, 348, 352, 723,
  741–42
wordiness, 744–46

XYZ

Yellow Journalism, 201
Youth, 83–84
"zines," 87, 100
Zoning stories, 598, 628, 629